The Integration of the European Community and Third States in Europe

A Legal Analysis

The Integration of the European Community and Third States in Europe

A Legal Analysis

ANDREW EVANS
European Law Centre
University of Umeå, Sweden

CLARENDON PRESS . OXFORD
1996

Oxford University Press, Walton Street, Oxford OX2 6DP
Oxford New York
Athens Auckland Bangkok Bombay
Calcutta Cape Town Dar es Salaam Delhi
Florence Hong Kong Istanbul Karachi
Kuala Lumpur Madras Madrid Melbourne
Mexico City Nairobi Paris Singapore
Taipei Tokyo Toronto
and associated companies in
Berlin Ibadan

Oxford is a trade mark of Oxford University Press

Published in the United States
by Oxford University Press Inc., New York

British Library Cataloguing in Publication Data
Data available

Library of Congress Cataloguing in Publication Data
Evans, Andrew.
The integration of the European Community and third states in Europe: a legal analysis / Andrew Evans.
p. cm.
Includes bibliographical references and index.
1. European Union countries—Foreign relations. 2. Europe—Economic integration. 3. European Union—Europe. 4. European cooperation. 5. Free trade—Europe. I. Title.
KJE5109.E94 1996
341.24'22—dc20 96–261
ISBN 0–19–826229–9

1 3 5 7 9 10 8 6 4 2

Typeset by J&L Composition Ltd, Filey, North Yorkshire.
Printed in Great Britain
on acid-free paper by
Bookcraft Ltd., Midsomer Norton, Avon

Preface

This book examines the legal frameworks for integration provided by the EC Treaty; the Free Trade Agreement concluded between Sweden and the European Community in 1972, which was typical of EC–EFTA Free Trade Agreements; the Europe Agreement between Poland and the Community, which is typical of the Association Agreements concluded with Central and Eastern European States; and the European Economic Area (EEA) Agreement.

The examination is based not solely on traditional legal materials, such as treaties and legislative acts, court decisions, and the academic literature. It also draws on a range of official materials published by national governments and the European Union. On the basis of both kinds of materials, the book not only compares the operation of four types of legal frameworks for integration but also, with the assistance of the comparisons, explores underlying problems in the integration of the European Community and third states in Europe.

Most EFTA States have over the years come to the view that the very status of a third state offers an unsatisfactory basis for their participation in European integration, though Iceland, Liechtenstein, and Norway consider the EEA Agreement satisfactory and Switzerland prefers to rely on a Free Trade Agreement, supplemented by other bilateral agreements, with the Community. The Visegrad countries, i.e., the Czech Republic, Hungary, Poland, and Slovakia, seek replacement of their Europe Agreements by membership of the European Union, though the timing, if not the wisdom, of their admission to membership remains uncertain. In the case of many countries of the former Soviet Union, notably Russia, membership of the Union does not appear to offer a feasible basis for their participation in European integration processes, and so the construction of a mutually acceptable legal framework for close relations between such countries and the Community arguably constitutes one of the most serious and pressing problems to be tackled by European integration law.

The present writer would further argue that construction of such a framework depends on lessons being drawn from the operation of existing or pre-existing frameworks governing relations between the Community and third states. Much the same might be said in respect of plans for the creation of a Euro-Mediterranean Economic Area, involving countries such as Algeria, Morocco, and Tunisia. At the same time, it is felt that a comparison of such frameworks with the EC Treaty may offer insights into problems raised in discussion of the 'internal' development of the Union itself.

The book, therefore, is written for teachers and students of advanced courses in EU law as well as for policy makers, officials, and practitioners in the private sector whose work concerns relations between the Community and third states.

Thanks are due to Tamara Jamil, who assisted with proof-reading and compilation of the Tables and the Index, Märta Nilsson and Anders Rosenhall for research assistance, Susanne Joki of the Umeå University Library for assistance in locating Swedish official publications and to Ulf Färjare, Roger Jacobsson, and Solweig Brand for their computer expertise. Financial support for the research has been provided by the Business School at the University of Umeå, the European University Institute in Florence, the Tercentenary Fund of the Central Bank of Sweden, and the Swedish Council for Research in the Humanities and Social Sciences.

Andrew Evans
Umeå, 1995

Contents

Part Three—Institutional Involvement

Abbreviations

AELE	Association Européenne de Libre Echange
AiH	Aktuellt i Handelspolitiken
All ER (EC)	All England Law Reports (European Community Series)
ANSI	American National Standards Institute
Benelux	Belgium, The Netherlands and Luxembourg
BISD	Basic Instruments and Selected Documents (GATT)
Bull. EC	Bulletin of the European Communities
CCT	Common Customs Tariff
CEAB	Commission Européenne Archives Bruxelles
CECA	Communauté Européenne du Charbon et de l'Acier
CEN	Comité Européen de Normalisation
CENELEC	Comité Européen de Normalisation Electronique
CEPT	Conférence Européenne des Administration des Postes et Télécommunications
CFI	Court of First Instance
CFSP	Common Foreign and Security Policy
CMEA	Council for Mutual Economic Assistance
CMLR	Common Market Law Reports
Cmnd	Command Paper (British Government Publication)
CoCom	Co-ordinating Committee for Multilateral Export Controls
CoCor	Co-ordinating Committee
COM	Communication from the European Commission
Coreper	Comité des Représentants Permanents
CREST	Scientific and Technical Research Committee
Débs PE	Débats du Parlement Européen
DN	Dagens Nyheter
Ds	Departementsserien
EAGGF	European Agricultural Guidance and Guarantee Fund
EC	European Community
ECJ	European Court of Justice
ECR	European Court Reports
ECSC	European Coal and Steel Community
ECU	European Currency Unit
EEC	European Economic Community
EEA	European Economic Area
EFTA	European Free Trade Association
EFTA Bull.	Bulletin of the European Free Trade Association

EG	Europeiska Gemenskaperna
EIB	European Investment Bank
EMU	European Monetary Union
EOTC	European Organization for Testing and Certification
EP Debs	European Parliament Debates
EP Doc.	European Parliament Working Document
EPC	European Political Co-operation
ERDF	European Regional Development Fund
ESA	EFTA Surveillance Authority
ESF	European Social Fund
ETSI	European Telecommunications Standards Institute
ETUC	European Trade Union Confederation
EU	European Union
Euratom	European Atomic Energy Community
Eurostat	Statistical Office of the European Communities
GATT	General Agreement on Tariffs and Trade
GDP	Gross Domestic Product
GNP	Gross National Product
GRUR Int.	Gewerblicher Rechtsschutz und Urheberrecht: Internationaler Teil
HC	House of Commons
HL	House of Lords
JO	Journal Officiel des Communautés Européennes
JOCECA	Journal Officiel de la Communauté Européenne du Charbon et de l'Acier
LO	Landsorganisationen
MEPs	Members of the European Parliament
NATO	North Atlantic Treaty Organisation
NJA	Nytt Juridisk Arkiv
NU	Nordisk utredningsserie
OECD	Organization for Economic Co-operation and Development
OJ	Official Journal of the European Communities
Prop.	Regeringens proposition (Swedish Government Bill)
R & D	Research and Development
Rec.	Recueil de la Cour de Justice des Communautés Européennes
RSDIE	Revue Suisse de Droit International et de Droit Européen
SAF	Svenska Arbetsgivareföreningen
SEC	Internal Document from the Secretariat-General of the European Commission
SFS	Svensk författningssamling

SG	Secretariat-General of the European Commission
SOU	Sveriges offentliga utredningar
SvD	Svenska Dagbladet
SvDN	Svenska Dagbladet, Näringsliv
SÖ	Sveriges överenskommelser med främmande makter
TCO	Tjänstemännens centralorganisation
TEU	Treaty on European Union
UNICE	Union des Industries de la Communauté Européenne
UU	Utrikesutskottets betänkande
VAT	Value Added Tax
VER	Voluntary Export Restraints
WTO	World Trade Organization

Tables

Treaties

Art. 57	232, 274, 381
Art. 58	64–5
Art. 59	20, 24, 54, 381
Art. 60	24–5
Art. 66	18, 20
Art. 73b	31, 44
Art. 73c	44, 273–4
Art. 73d	31
Art. 73f	44, 276
Art. 73g	44, 81, 111–12, 273, 276
Art. 75	273–4
Art. 84	230, 244
Art. 85	13, 21, 32–3, 39, 58–9, 101, 103, 120–3, 137, 143, 153–4, 173, 179, 189, 195–7, 205, 222, 286, 311, 371
Art. 86	20, 39, 41, 58, 120–3, 143, 153–4, 172, 177, 189, 195–7, 206, 286, 311
Art. 87	287
Art. 88	189
Art. 89	286
Art. 90	172–3, 176, 194–5, 214
Art. 91	112
Art. 92	13, 21, 32–3, 59, 121, 124, 154–172, 173–175, 180–194, 196–7, 204, 207, 210, 298
Art. 93	189–195, 224, 275
Art. 94	137, 273–4
Art. 95	21, 32, 34, 41, 62, 67–9, 71, 75, 231
Art. 99	69, 98, 273–4
Art. 100	98–9, 230, 273–4
Art. 100a	140–1, 230–4, 260–1, 276
Art. 100b	32
Art. 100c	50, 91, 273–4, 276
Art. 100d	325
Art. 101	234–5
Art. 102a	79, 355
Art. 103	109, 119, 273–4, 277
Art. 103a	109, 119, 132, 273–4, 276
Art. 104a	274
Art. 104b	274
Art. 104c	273
Art. 105	274
Art. 105a	274
Art. 106	273–4
Art. 107	110–11, 143

Ruling of the GATT Panel

Judgement of the Permanent Court of International Justice

Judgements of National Courts

1
Introduction

From a legal perspective integration between the European Community[1] and third states in Europe may be seen as depending on questions of the adaptability of law originating within the framework of the EC Treaty to the needs of such integration. These are questions 'that . . . hardly can be solved any longer on the basis of traditional distinctions of international, supranational and constitutional law'.[2] For example, they have often been approached by the European Court of Justice on the basis of a constitutional-type definition of the 'external relations' powers of the Community. However, as a recent judgment[3] suggests, consistent application of any such definition in the face of the demands made on Community law by growing international interdependence may be problematic.[4]

In the present book these questions are approached on the basis of an examination of the dynamics of integration law—trade liberalization, harmonization of law and policy and institutional involvement in these processes. For the purposes of the examination, trade is treated as denoting economic activity generally rather than being limited to exchange of goods. For the same purposes, an analytical distinction is made between the terms of the relevant legal provisions and the legal requirements entailed by such provisions. While the former denote the formal meaning of the provisions concerned, the latter denote their operational meaning. It is the latter which determine the effective role of the law in integration.

In particular, it is trade liberalization requirements, as exemplified in the famous '*Cassis de Dijon*' ruling of the European Court of Justice,[5] which lie at the heart of the distinctive contribution made by the EC Treaty to integration between Member States. Hence, the embodiment of such requirements in agreements between the Community and third states may be critical as to

[1] Since there is no legal provision for third states to conclude Association Agreements or Free Trade Agreements with the Union, their relations with the Union depend primarily on agreements concluded with the European Community—the main 'pillar' of the Union—under the EC Treaty.

[2] T. Cottier, 'Constitutional Trade Regulation in National and International Law: Structure-Substance Pairings in the EFTA Experience' in M. Hilf and E.-U. Petersmann (eds.), *National Constitutions and International Economic Law* (Deventer 1993), 409–42, at 440.

[3] Opinion 1/94 (*Competence of the Community to conclude international agreements on services and the protection of international property*) [1994] ECR I–5267.

[4] See, regarding the inconsistencies in this judgment, J. H. J. Bourgeois, 'The EC in the WTO and Advisory Opinion 1/94: An Echternach Procession' (1995) 32 *CMLRev*. 763–87.

[5] Case 120/78 *Rewe-Zentral AG* v. *Bundesmonopolverwaltung für Branntwein* [1979] ECR 649.

the capacity of such agreements to promote integration between the parties thereto. The critical importance of such requirements certainly seems to have been recognized at the Essen Summit in December 1994. Here it was declared that, for the purposes of preparing Parties to the Europe Agreements for future accession to the European Union, 'the key element in the strategy [should be] preparation of the Associated States for integration into the internal market'.[6] In effect, preparation of these States to face the liberalization requirements applicable within the internal market was seen as a precondition for closer relations.

Of course, the internal market and integration more generally do not depend simply on application of liberalization requirements but also on harmonization. Like liberalization requirements, harmonization seeks to reduce obstacles to trade. The former requirements seek to do so through eliminating State measures or practices of undertakings which distort the relative costs of trade. Harmonization, in turn, seeks to do so through eliminating differences in state measures which produce such distortions.

This distinction between liberalization and harmonization might be thought to be a rough legal translation of the distinction between 'negative' and 'positive' integration made in other social sciences.[7] The former kind of integration concerns constraints on national policy-making, while the latter concerns replacement of national policies by common policies of the Community itself.[8] Such thinking tends to concentrate on the outcomes of processes rather than the processes themselves. Legal analysis, to the extent that it concerns processes, may be more enlightening as to the relationship of liberalization and harmonization with each other and with arrangements for institutional involvement therein. Ultimately, insights into what may be described in formal legal terms as relationships between 'economic law' and 'institutional law' may be obtained.

For example, the more developed are trade liberalization and other requirements (requirements relating to public health, environmental protection,

[6] Conclusions of the Presidency (Bull. EU 12–1994, I.13).

[7] J. Tinbergen, *International Economic Integration* (2nd edn. Amsterdam, 1965) defines the former as measures abolishing impediments to the proper operation of an integrated area and the latter as creating new institutions and instruments.

[8] T. Heller and J. Pelkmans, 'The Federal Economy: Law and Economic Integration and the Positive State—The U.S.A. and Europe Compared in an Economic Perspective' in M. Cappelletti *et al.* (eds.), *Integration Through Law* (Berlin 1986), i, 245–412, at 321. See also J. Tinbergen, *International Economic Integration* (Amsterdam, 1954), 95, where integration is defined as 'the creation of the most desirable structure of international economy, removing artificial hindrances to the optimal operation and introducing deliberately all desirable elements of co-ordination or unification'. However, the difficulty of maintaining the distinction is illustrated by the second edition of this work ((Amsterdam, 1965), 78), where 'measures needed to avoid a distortion of the process of free competition' are classified as part of positive integration.

consumer protection, and so on)[9] embodied in an instrument such as the EC Treaty, the more the effects of interactions between the two kinds of requirements will approximate to those of harmonization, i.e., national measures may tend to be brought into closer alignment rather than eliminated. However, the impact of liberalization requirements is essentially dependent on their interpretation and application by the judiciary, whereas harmonization is primarily the responsibility of the legislature. In such circumstances, differences in the operation of the two processes may increasingly reflect and be reflected by differences between judicial and legislative attitudes.[10]

Established and continuing Community practice is such as to allow for use of the comparative method in examination of these complex relationships. In particular, a comparison of the operation of legal frameworks for integration provided by the EC Treaty, Free Trade Agreements, Europe Agreements, and the European Economic Area (EEA) Agreement may be made. The Free Trade Agreements were concluded by the Community with EFTA States in 1972[11] on the basis of Article 113 of the EC Treaty. Attention is focussed on that with Sweden,[12] which is typical of such Agreements. The Europe Agreements have been concluded under Article 238 of the EC Treaty with Bulgaria, the Czech Republic, Hungary, Poland, Romania, and Slovakia.[13] Attention is focussed on the Agreement with Poland,[14] which is typical of this category of Agreements. The EEA Agreement[15] was also concluded under Article 238 of the EC Treaty. It originally covered five EFTA States, i.e., Austria, Finland, Iceland, Norway and Sweden.[16] However, Austria, Finland, and Sweden subsequently acceded to the Union, while Liechtenstein became a Party to the EEA Agreement. For the purposes of this Agreement, therefore, the expression 'EFTA States' now refers to Iceland, Liechtenstein, and Norway.

Comparison of the operation of these legal frameworks may assist identifi-

[9] These 'other requirements' seem to have much in common with what are termed 'diffuse interests' in N. Reich, 'Protection of Diffuse Interests in the EEC and the Perspective of "Progressively Establishing" an Internal Market' (1988) *Journal of Consumer Policy* 395–417, though such interests are apparently treated therein as separate from 'mandatory requirements' (*ibid.* 401).

[10] Subsidiarity considerations (see Art. A of the Treaty on European Union and Art. 3b of the EC Treaty) may also be involved. See J.-M. Sun and J. Pelkmans, 'Regulatory Competition in the Single Market' (1995) *JCMS* 567–89.

[11] See generally A. Evans and P. Falk, *Law and Integration: Sweden and the European Community* (Stockholm, 1991).

[12] [1970] JO L300/96.

[13] Similar agreements are envisaged with the Baltic States and Slovenia (Conclusions of the Presidency, European Council meeting of December 1994, Bull. EU 12–1994, I.13).

[14] [1993] OJ L348/2.

[15] [1994] OJ L1/3.

[16] Following the negative referendum result in Switzerland, the Protocol adjusting the Agreement on the European Economic Area ([1994] OJ L1/572) had to be concluded. This Protocol deletes all provisions of the Agreement regarding Switzerland, while allowing for this state to become a Party to the Agreement in the future. Entry into force of the Agreement in the case of Liechtenstein was postponed pending reorganization of its relations with Switzerland so that these relations would not hinder operation of the Agreement.

cation of specific features of each framework and practice thereunder[17] and may permit speculation at least as to the reasons for such specificities. From a more policy-oriented perspective, examination of the EC Treaty may throw light on questions why, and to what ends, the Community concludes agreements with third states. Examination of the latter agreements may, in turn, indicate the extent to which these ends are achieved or achievable.

Even the most superficial examination would reveal that such agreements may reproduce many trade liberalization provisions—usually those regarding trade in goods—contained in the EC Treaty. Such reproduction has taken place, to varying degrees, in all the above agreements. However, the liberalization required by a particular legal provision may not solely be determined by the language of that provision but may also be affected by characteristics of the legal instrument containing that provision. The result is that the liberalization requirements entailed by provisions of an Agreement between the Community and a third state may be less far-reaching than the requirements of textually equivalent provisions of the EC Treaty. This result demonstrates the extent to which the operation of textually equivalent provisions may vary depending on the legal instrument within which they are contained. In other words, efforts to liberalize trade between the Community and third states face structural legal problems of the kind considered in Part 1 of the book.

The problems are all the greater because the EC Treaty not only embodies the trade liberalization requirements which are the subject of Chapter 2. It also embodies a range of other legally recognized requirements, which are examined in Chapter 3. To the extent that liberalization requirements and other requirements interact, such interactions may determine the trade liberalization secured by the EC Treaty. Hence, the capacity of an agreement between the Community and a third state to secure substantially equivalent liberalization to that secured by the EC Treaty may depend on embodiment of requirements other than those of trade liberalization in the agreement concerned.

Part 2 of the book, which contains Chapters 4 and 5, turns to harmonization questions. In particular, Chapter 4 examines competition policy. Within the EC Treaty framework competition policy plays a central role in trade liberalization, though its elaboration may raise difficult harmonization issues associated with a wide range of policies, not only industrial policy but also regional policy, environmental policy and so on.

Trade liberalization requirements in instruments such as the Free Trade Agreements may prove too limited to allow competition policy to play such a role. The role of this policy in trade between the Parties may be left to depend on administrative harmonization efforts of the Commission and authorities of

[17] As a result, some light may be thrown on the capacity of the integration subsystems created by such agreements to promote pan-European integration rather than to produce new causes of division within the continent. Cf. M. Wijkman, *Patterns of Production and Trade in Western Europe: Looking Forward After Thirty Years* (EFTA Occasional Paper No. 32, Geneva, 1990).

third states,[18] designed to reduce differences in the treatment of anti-competitive conduct by the Community and such states. To the extent that differences remain, the Community may apply its own 'internal' competition policy, though the latter may not be well adapted to tackling obstacles to trade between the Community and the third state concerned.[19]

The Europe Agreements, like the EEA Agreement, seek to ensure that competition policy will not have this dependent role and provide for application of Community competition law requirements to trade between the Parties. Their application may mean that the economies of the third states concerned will be rendered more competitive and that trade liberalization will be promoted. More particularly, to the extent that application of such requirements replaces use of anti-dumping law, companies from those states will be able to compete with Community companies on a more equal basis than in the past. It is questionable, however, whether these requirements are sufficiently adaptable and, at least in the case of the Europe Agreements, whether the enforcement procedures are sufficiently developed to enable their effective application to be reconciled with the need to take account of economic differences between the Parties.

Chapter 5 examines legislative harmonization. This process might be regarded as harmonization proper, though as the 'new approach' of the Commission[20] highlights, the dynamics and effects of harmonization under the EC Treaty may go beyond the formal requirements of legislative procedures and enactments. The dilemma for third states is that the need for harmonization may be in inverse proportion to the degree of liberalization secured by their agreements with the Community. However, the very fact that they are third states implies limits to their opportunities for participation in the Community harmonization process.

The result may be separation of harmonization efforts within the Community from harmonization efforts between the Community and third states, and ultimately the latter efforts may become dependent on the former. This result is closely bound up with questions as to the impact of institutional involvement in liberalization and harmonization processes. These questions are addressed in Part Three, which contains Chapters 6 to 8. These chapters examine in detail the three main forms which such involvement in these processes may take in the context of integration between the Community and third states: joint decision-making, committee work, and judicial control.

[18] In the terminology of S. Woolcock, *Market Access in EC–US Relations: Trading Partners or Trading Blows* (RIIA, London, 1991), p. x, reduction of obstacles to trade has been approached as a 'structural' rather than 'regulatory' matter.

[19] Such considerations may, at least partly, explain why a high degree of interdependence can coincide with limited integration. Cf. P.G. Nell, 'EFTA in the 1990s: The Search for a New Identity' (1990) *JCMS* 327–58.

[20] I.e., an approach which seeks minimum harmonization and places reliance on the work of standards bodies. See sect. 7.2.2 below.

Chapter 6 concerns joint decision-making, i.e., decision-making by bodies representing parties to a legal instrument. The EC Treaty allocates an important role to such decision-making, which takes place in the Council of the Union. However, the role of the Council is tempered by that of an independent institution—the European Commission. No such institution as the latter was created by the Free Trade Agreements or the Europe Agreements. The EEA Agreement provides for the EFTA States to establish a Surveillance Authority (ESA) to ensure respect for EEA law within the EFTA area. It does not, however, provide for the establishment of a body independent of all the Contracting Parties. Hence, this Agreement also seeks to rely more heavily on joint decision-making than the EC Treaty. To the extent of such reliance, decision-making regarding trade within parties is treated as institutionally separable from decision-making regarding trade between parties. Such separation may be consistent with ideas of Community autonomy and national sovereignty. It may not, however, adequately reflect the economic integration taking place between the Community and third states in Europe. In other words, a legal vacuum, inconsistent with the reality of such integration, may be entailed.

Efforts to fill the vacuum may lead to the emergence of arrangements, in which 'comitology' and a variety of linking networks play a central role,[21] for participation by each party in the internal decision-making procedures of the other party or parties.[22] The importance for integration of the committee work entailed by such arrangements is examined in Chapter 7. Within the Community the Merger Treaty of 1965 recognized the Committee of Permanent Representatives of the Member States (Coreper), and a wide range of committees has been established by the Community institutions. Similar, though less formal, arrangements for committee work emerged in connection with the Free Trade Agreements. While the Europe Agreements do little to formalize committee work, a developed legal basis for such work is provided by the EEA Agreement.

Chapter 8 deals, finally, with the role of the judiciary in integration. Judicial development of the liberalization and other requirements contained in the EC Treaty may not simply be an indication of the potential role which the judiciary may play in removing obstacles to trade, at least where, as in the case of the European Court of Justice, there is a formal obligation to promote

[21] Such arrangements may variously be described as 'bureaucratic interpenetration', 'structural coupling' or 'inter-organizational exchange'. See F. Snyder, 'The Effectiveness of European Community Law: Institutions, Processes, Tools and Techniques' (1991) 54 MLRev. 19–55, at 36 and the sources there cited.

[22] To the extent that it is effective, such participation is incompatible with ideas of Community autonomy and national sovereignty. Cf. the concern of the Commission that matters 'internally settled' should not be externally opened in the Explanatory Memorandum to the amended Proposal of 6 Oct. 1993 for a Council Reg. concerning arrangements for implementing the Agreement on the European Economic Area, COM(93)466, 1.

integration. To the extent that the tasks of the other Community institutions are defined by such requirements, the consequence is that the work of these institutions and, hence, their contribution to integration are also affected. While the Free Trade Agreements did nothing, and the Europe Agreements do little, to promote judicial activism in integration processes, the EEA Agreement apparently recognizes the important role which the judiciary may play in such processes, particularly in the reconciliation of institutional separation with application of common trading rules. However, the difficulties of achieving such reconciliation were highlighted by the finding of the European Court of Justice that judicial arrangements in the draft EEA Agreement were incompatible with the EC Treaty.[23]

[23] Opinion 1/91 (*Draft Agreement between the Community, on the one hand, and the countries of the European Free Trade Association, on the other, relating to the creation of the European Economic Area*) [1991] ECR I–6079.

PART 1

Trade Liberalization and Other Requirements

2

Trade Liberalization Requirements

2.1 INTRODUCTION

Agreements between the European Community and third states may reproduce trade liberalization provisions contained in the EC Treaty. Such reproduction has taken place, for example, in the Free Trade Agreements of 1972 between EFTA States and the Community; the Europe Agreements between Central and Eastern European States and the Community; and the European Economic Area (EEA) Agreement between EFTA States and the Community. The Free Trade Agreements were concerned with liberalization of trade in goods,[1] the Europe Agreements concern not only goods[2] but also the movement of persons,[3] services,[4] and capital,[5] while the EEA Agreement reproduces EC Treaty provisions governing the 'four freedoms' generally.[6] However, the operation of EC Treaty provisions has been heavily dependent on their interpretation by the European Court of Justice. Unless provisions of agreements between the Community and third states are interpreted in the same way as corresponding provisions of the EC Treaty, such agreements may not entail the same far-reaching trade liberalization requirements as the Treaty.

The EEA Agreement seeks to take account of this consideration. Article 6 thereof stipulates that provisions of the Agreement which are substantially identical[7] with those of the EC Treaty are to be implemented and applied in accordance with the established case law of the Court of Justice. Arrangements are also made in Article 105 and 111 of the Agreement with a view to ensuring that future developments in such case law are not disregarded in EEA law.[8]

However, the Court of Justice does not determine the requirements of EC Treaty provisions solely by reference to the terms of the individual provision

[1] See, e.g. Art. 1 of the Swedish Free Trade Agreement.

[2] Art. 7 of the Polish Agreement.

[3] *Ibid.*, Art. 37–54.

[4] *Ibid.*, Art. 55–57.

[5] *Ibid.*, Art. 59–62.

[6] Art. 28–45 of the EEA Agreement.

[7] The terminology 'textually identical', which was employed by the Court in Opinion 1/92 *(Draft Agreement between the Community, on the one hand, and the countries of the European Free Trade Association, on the other, relating to the creation of the European Economic Area)* [1992] ECR I–2821, I–2844 may be preferable, in that it does not have the same question-begging character. The French version of the ruling employed the term '*identiques*'. The Title of Prot. 34, on the Possibility for courts and tribunals of EFTA States to request the Court of Justice of the European Communities to decide on the interpretation of EEA rules corresponding to EC rules, refers to 'corresponding rules' but Art. 1 of the Prot. to 'provisions . . . identical in substance'.

[8] See sect. 8.5.3 below.

concerned.[9] Both the limitations of language and social demands may preclude such a simple approach to interpretation. Rather, account may be taken of other Treaty provisions, and conclusions drawn from the general legal framework constituted by the Treaty may be influential. In other words, interpretation may be affected by features of the Treaty structure. To the extent that reproduction of these features is lacking in agreements with third states, Treaty provisions and textually equivalent provisions in such agreements may be interpreted differently.[10] Hence, consideration of the relationship between trade liberalization requirements in the Treaty and the structure of the Treaty is a necessary precondition for discussion of problems involved in embodying such requirements in agreements concluded with third states.

2.2 EC TREATY

Practice under the EC Treaty treats trade as being of three types—domestic, Community and international.[11] Liberalization requirements which are embodied in the Treaty and in the operation of which these types may be identified are by no means static or without overlap. Nevertheless, identification of these types may assist examination of the relationship between the operation of individual Treaty provisions and the framework provided by the Treaty. More fundamentally, interactions between conceptions of trade liberalization requirements and concepts of a free trade area, a common market, and an economic union may be exposed.

2.2.1 Domestic Trade Liberalization

Domestic trade liberalization, i.e., liberalization of trading activity within a single Member State, may be of economic importance for the Community as a whole, though liberalization provisions of the EC Treaty show little specific concern for such trade.

True, Article 96 of the Treaty expressly prohibits the refund of internal taxes on exports at a level higher than that at which taxes have been paid in the

[9] Indeed, in one case Mancini A. G. took the extreme position that the function of common customs tariff headings might be so changed by the practice of national authorities that it would be 'impossible' for the Court to interpret them. See Case 166/84 *Thomasdünger GmbH* v. *Oberfinanzdirektion Frankfurt am Main* [1985] ECR 3001, 3003.

[10] To imagine otherwise would, according to Warner A. G. in Case 51/75 *EMI Records Ltd* v. *CBS United Kingdom Ltd* [1976] ECR 811, 861, be 'heretical'. However, differential interpretation is not inevitable. See, e.g. regarding the concept of social security, Case C–18/90 *Office national de l'emploi (ONEM)* v. *Bahia Kziber* [1991] ECR I–199, I–227. See also Darmon A. G. in Case C–355/93 *Hayriye Eroglu* v. *Land Baden-Würrtemberg* [1994] ECR I–5113, I–5121.

[11] Cf. the two-fold distinction made by the ECJ between 'internal trade' and 'international trade' in Opinion 1/94 *(Competence of the Community to conclude international agreements on services and the protection of international property)* [1994] ECR I–5267, I–5405.

Member State of exportation. Domestic trading activity is thus liberalized, to the extent that Member States are prohibited from employing fiscal measures to disadvantage such trade in comparison with the export trade. Likewise, export aid is treated as being prohibited by Article 92(1) of the Treaty.[12] According to this provision, state aid which distorts or threatens to distort competition by favouring certain undertakings or the production of certain goods shall, in so far as it affects trade between Member States, be incompatible with the common market. Both prohibitions, however, may simply reflect recognition that the state measures concerned may have the effect of distorting competition in trade between Member States. The liberalization of domestic trade which is entailed may be no more than a by-product of such recognition.

In this regard, the interpretation of Article 85(1) of the Treaty by the Court of Justice is particularly instructive. It prohibits restrictive practices between undertakings which may distort competition in trade between Member States. This prohibition is interpreted as extending to restrictive agreements between undertakings within the same Member State relating exclusively to products sold domestically. The prohibition may thus apply to agreements restricting domestic trade, but it only does so where such agreements have the effect of making the domestic market more difficult to penetrate by undertakings from other Member States.[13] Such an effect depends on various factors, including the market position of the parties to such agreements[14] and the actual impact of the agreements on imports,[15] related to the likelihood of the domestic market being partitioned from the markets of other Member States.

Most liberalization provisions of the Treaty, however, have been found by the Court of Justice to entail no requirements concerning domestic trade liberalization.[16] For example, Article 30 prohibits quantitative restrictions and measures having equivalent effect on imports between Member States. This provision was invoked in *Eyssen*,[17] which concerned the prosecution of a Dutch cheese producer by the Dutch authorities for having held in stock for sale for human consumption cheese containing an additive, nisin, banned under Dutch law. Here the Court failed to take the opportunity, despite being

[12] Joined Cases 6 and 11/69 *EC Commission* v. *France* [1969] ECR 523, 540. See, more particularly, Arts. 3 and 4 of Dir. 90/684 ([1990] OJ L380/27) on aid to shipbuilding. Measures may also be taken to prevent Community action from resulting in the provision of such aid. See, e.g. the 'claw-back' arrangement in Art. 9(3) of Reg. 1837/80 of 27 June 1980 ([1980] OJ L183/1) establishing the common organization of the market in sheepmeat and goatmeat.

[13] See, e.g. Case C–234/89 *Stergios Delimitis* v. *Henninger Bräu AG* [1991] ECR I–935. See, earlier, Case 23/67 *SA Brasserie de Haecht* v. *Wilkin and Wilkin* [1967] ECR 407, 415–6.

[14] Case 5/69 *Franz Völk* v. *Etablissements J. Vervaecke* [1969] ECR 295, 302.

[15] Case 247/86 *Société alsacienne et lorraine de télecommunications et d'électronique (Alsatel)* v. *SA Novasam* [1988] ECR 5987, 6008.

[16] Cf., regarding capital, Case 143/86 *John Richard Alan East and Others (Magetts and Addenbrooke)* v. *Thomas and Winnifred Cuddy* [1988] ECR 625.

[17] Case 53/80 *Officier van Justitie* v. *Koninklijke Kaasfabriek Eyssen BV* [1981] ECR 409.

invited to do so by Advocate General Warner,[18] to rule that Article 30 could prohibit application of the Dutch ban on the use of this additive in the case of domestic products marketed in the Netherlands. Such a ban might, it could perhaps be argued, indirectly limit imports of Dutch products containing nisin by other Member States. Such imports would only be available to the extent that Dutch producers were willing to incur the costs of maintaining a production line different from that needed for the domestic market. However, that is not, presumably, the kind of trading obstacle with which Article 30 is treated as being concerned. It is the 'extension' of domestic law to imports which is treated as prohibited by this provision.[19]

'Reverse Discrimination' Issues

The approach adopted by the Court precludes it from following the views of certain Advocates General[20] and subjecting Member States to prohibitions based on the concept of 'reverse discrimination'. Thus less favourable treatment by a Member State of domestic products in comparison with imports or of retailers who sell domestic products in comparison with those who sell imports in a sector not subject to Community rules or the harmonization of national law is held to fall outside the scope of application of Community law and not to be incompatible with Article 30 or the general principle of equality of treatment[21] in Article 6.[22]

Again, the Court has ruled that nationals of a Member State may only invoke rights of entry and residence in their own Member State under provisions such as Article 48 of the Treaty, governing the free movement of workers, where they have already exercised their freedom of movement in order to carry on an economic activity in another Member State.[23] In other circumstances the issues are treated as 'wholly internal'[24] to the Member State concerned or as being without 'any element going beyond a purely national setting'.[25] As a result, a Member State may be permitted by the Treaty to impose restrictions on the entry and residence of its own nationals which would be prohibited in the case of nationals of other Member States.

[18] *Ibid.* 428.
[19] Case 94/82 *De Kikvoorsch Groothandel-Import-Export BV* [1983] ECR 947, 958.
[20] See, e.g. Warner A. G. in Case 175/78 *Regina* v. *Vera Ann Saunders* [1979] ECR 1129, 1142.
[21] See, e.g. Case 355/85 *Driancourt* v. *Michel Cognet* [1986] ECR 3231, 3242.
[22] Art. 6 provides: 'Within the scope of application of this Treaty, and without prejudice to any special provisions contained therein, any discrimination on grounds of nationality is prohibited'.
[23] Joined Cases 35 and 36/82 *Elestina Esselina Christina Morson* v. *State of the Netherlands and Head of the Plaatselijke Politie within the meaning of the Vreemdelingenwet; Sewradjie Jhanjan* v. *State of the Netherlands* [1982] ECR 3723, 3736. The rationale may be that nationals of a Member State might otherwise be deterred from exercising their rights in relation to a Member State other than their own. See Case C–370/90 *Regina* v. *Immigration Appeal Tribunal and Surinder Singh, ex parte Secretary of State for the Home Department* [1992] ECR I–4265, I–4293–4.
[24] Case 175/78 *Regina* v. *Vera Ann Saunders* [1979] ECR 1129, 1135.
[25] Case 20/87 *Ministère Public* v. *André Gauchard* [1987] ECR 4879, 4896.

Even where there has been some prior movement, the liberalization requirements of the Treaty will not necessarily apply. According to the Court, Article 30 does not affect national restrictions on goods which have been exported for the sole purpose of reimportation in order to circumvent national legislation concerning minimum selling prices.[26] In such circumstances there would be no genuine movement between Member States.[27]

Textual Considerations

The terms of particular EC Treaty provisions by no means preclude prohibition of 'reverse discrimination'. Article 48(1) merely provides for freedom of movement for workers to be secured, Article 48(2) for the abolition of discrimination based on nationality between workers of the Member States, and Article 48(3) for such persons to enjoy rights of entry and residence for the purposes of employment. The only reference to national treatment is found in Article 48(3)(c), which requires that beneficiaries of freedom of movement should be subject to the law of the host Member State governing the employment of its own nationals. As regards rights of entry and residence, there is nothing in Article 48 which might seem to justify rulings permitting discrimination by a State against its own nationals.

Article 30, taken in isolation, might be capable of bearing an interpretation such that it leaves a Member State free to restrict the domestic marketing of domestically produced goods and even to engage in reverse discrimination. However, Article 37(1) requires the adjustment of state monopolies of a commercial character so as to ensure that no discrimination exists between nationals of Member States regarding the conditions under which goods are procured and marketed.[28] This provision seems broad enough to prohibit such a restriction to the extent that it discriminates in favour of importers, and in view of the fact that this provision was included in the Treaty to prevent the free movement of goods being undermined by the operation of state monopolies,[29] the implication might be drawn that Article 30 should be understood to entail a corresponding prohibition, even where the operation of such a monopoly is not involved.

At the very least, therefore, it might be said that the refusal of the Court of

[26] Case 229/83 *Association des Centres distributeurs Edouard Leclerc* v. *Sàrl 'Au Blé Vert'* [1985] ECR 1, 35.

[27] This consideration might explain the apparent conflict (see P. Oliver, *Free Movement of Goods in the EEC* (2nd edn. London, 1988), 21) between this ruling and that in Case 78/70 *Deutsche Grammophon Gesellschaft mbH* v. *Metro-SB-Grossmärkte & Co. KG* [1971] ECR 487. The latter ruling did not concern products exported solely for such a purpose, and the Court held that restrictions on reimportation were prohibited by Art. 30.

[28] Cf. Art. XVII(1)(a) of GATT.

[29] Comité Intergouvernemental Créé par la Conférence de Messine, *Rapport des Chefs de Délégation aux Ministres des Affaires Etrangères* (Brussels, 1956), 37. See also Case 59/75 *Pubblico Ministero* v. *Flavia Manghera* [1976] ECR 91, 100–1 and Case 91/78 *Hansen GmbH & Co.* v. *Hauptzollamt Flensburg* [1979] ECR 935, 953.

Justice to apply the concept of 'reverse discrimination' is not unambiguously demanded by the terms of the individual Treaty provisions concerned. However, the Court considers that the scope of the case law regarding Article 30 must be determined in the light of Community objectives and activities as defined in Articles 2 and 3 of the Treaty, which envisage the unification of national markets into a common market having the characteristics of a domestic market.[30] Hence, the approach of the Court apparently reflects its underlying assumptions regarding what is demanded by market unification.[31] According to this approach, not only commerce as such but also private persons engaged in an economic activity across frontiers should benefit from liberalization.[32] On the other hand, the prohibition of disparities in treatment or distortions which may result for persons or undertakings from the application by a Member State of measures that are stricter than those applied in the same sphere by other Member States is not entailed.[33] In short, the concept of the common market is taken to imply limits to the domestic trade liberalization required by individual Treaty provisions.

Economic Considerations

No economic rationale for the approach of the Court is immediately apparent, given that the result is to permit State interference with efficient utilization of resources throughout the Community. In effect, it might be said that market unification requirements are emphasized and possible efficiency losses disregarded.[34] The possibility that discrimination against domestic products might occasionally be a better policy for the national economy of the Member State concerned[35] may not in itself eliminate the losses for the Community as a whole.

The approach of the Court might seem even more questionable when account is taken of dynamic factors apparently affecting the Community economy. It is said that 'in the new social and market environment' standard national solutions are no longer appropriate and should be replaced by policies tailored to improving the productivity and international competitiveness of

[30] Case 270/80 *Polydor Ltd and RSC Records Inc.* v. *Harlequin Record Shops Ltd and Simon Records Ltd* [1982] ECR 329, 348.

[31] See, e.g. Van Gerven A. G. in Case C–145/88 *Torfaen Borough Council* v. *B & Q plc* [1989] ECR I–3851, I–3876–9, regarding the importance of market unification.

[32] Case 15/81 *Gaston Schul Douane Expediteur BV* v. *Inspecteur der Invoerrechten en Accijnen, Roosendaal* [1982] ECR 1409, 1431–2.

[33] Joined Cases C–251/90 and C–252/90 *Procurator Fiscal* v. *Kenneth Gordon Wood and James Cowie* [1992] ECR I–2873, I–2897. See also Joined Cases 185 and 204/78 *Firma J. van Dam en Zonen* [1979] ECR 2345, 2361.

[34] B. Hawk, 'The American (Anti-trust) Revolution: Lessons for the EEC?' (1988) *ECLRev.* 53–87.

[35] D. Greenaway and P. Thakaran, *Imperfect Competition and International Trade* (Sussex, 1986).

specific sectors and individual enterprises.[36] The Court, however, permits such solutions to be applied to domestic trade, irrespective in particular of the possibility that regional diversity may imply the need for differentiated solutions therein.[37]

Political Considerations

It appears that political rather than economic considerations underlie the approach of the Court. For example, Article 95 of the Treaty prohibits a Member State from imposing on products of other Member States any internal taxation in excess of that imposed on similar domestic products and from imposing on the former any internal taxation of such a nature as to afford indirect protection to other products. In holding that this provision does not prohibit the imposition on domestic products of internal taxation in excess of that on imported products, the Court relies on more general considerations than simply its wording. According to the Court, such taxation disparities result from special features of national laws which have not been harmonized in spheres for which Member States are responsible.[38] The implication is that the Court seeks to limit the disruption of national policy making by judicial decisions.

In this connection, the potential interaction that could occur between Community law liberalization of domestic trading activity and requirements of the General Agreement on Tariffs and Trade (GATT) might also be an unexpressed concern of the Court. If Member States could not apply national rules to domestic traders, the application of such rules to traders from other GATT Parties might be difficult to reconcile with the equality of treatment requirements of the GATT Agreement on Technical Barriers to Trade.[39] In other words, to the extent that domestic trade liberalization were secured by the EC Treaty, Member States might be compelled unilaterally to liberalize

[36] W. Streeck and P. C. Schmitter, 'From National Corporatism to Transnational Pluralism: Organised Interests in the Single European Market' (1991) *Politics and Society* 133–64, at 147.

[37] Indeed, the Commission seems to have a preference for such solutions. The very diversity of regional responses to, e.g. environmental problems may be treated by the Commission as entailing trade obstacles contrary to Art. 30 EC. See the Joint Reply by Mr Monti to Written Questions E–327/95 and 387/95 ([1995] OJ C175/33).

[38] Case 86/78 *SA des Grands Distilleries Peureux* v. *Directeur des Services Fiscaux de la Haute-Saône et du Territoire de Belfort* [1979] ECR 897, 913. Similarly, Community law does not detract from the powers of the Member States to organize their social security systems and to adopt, in particular, provisions intended to govern the consumption of pharmaceutical preparations, including those imported from other Member States, in order to promote the financial stability of their health insurance schemes. See Case 238/82 *Duphar BV* v. *The Netherlands State* [1984] ECR 523, 541.

[39] See, in particular, Art. 1(2) of Dec. 80/45 of 15 January 1980 ([1980] OJ L71/299) laying down provisions on the introduction and implementation of technical regulations and standards. According to Art. XXIV(5) of GATT, GATT itself does not prevent establishment of a customs union. However, such a union is defined in Art. XXIV(8) in terms of trade liberalization between the relevant customs territories. It is not clear that obligations relating to liberalization of domestic trade may be implemented irrespective of other GATT rules.

trade with third states to the same extent. A decision so to liberalize such relations may be one which the Court considers can only appropriately be taken by the Member States in the context of development of the common commercial policy.[40]

Apparently, therefore, general conclusions drawn from the framework provided by the Treaty, which limit development of the domestic trade liberalization requirements of individual Treaty provisions, are influenced by State-centred conceptions of limits to judicial decision making at the Community level. If domestic trade liberalization and, hence, the equality of treatment traditionally associated with 'negative' integration[41] are to be fully secured, participation by representatives of the Member States in 'positive' integration through harmonization by the Council of the Union is necessary. In the absence of the necessary participation, domestic trade liberalization will not be secured by liberalization provisions in the Treaty itself. As in 'pure federalism',[42] interference with the most efficient allocation of resources and location of industries within the Community may be the cost of 'political subdivision'.

Legal Instability

The legal position may be somewhat unstable. The case law suggests, for example, that a national of a Member State enjoys a Community law right of residence in his own Member State where he is returning after having exercised his freedom of movement under Articles, 48—66 of the Treaty to carry on an economic activity in another Member State.[43] Apparently, receipt of a service in another Member State or even simply shopping there[44] may constitute exercise of this freedom, and so the former right may only effectively be restricted to the extent that Member States may prevent Community law being employed as a device to evade 'secondary'[45] immigration control.[46]

[40] See, regarding this policy, sect. 2.2.3 below.

[41] See, e.g., J. Pinder, 'Positive Integration and Negative Integration: Some Problems of Economic Union in the EEC' (1968) *The World Today* 88–110.

[42] Cf. R. A. Musgrave, *The Theory of Public Finance* (New York, 1959), 179–80.

[43] Tourists who go to another Member State as recipients of services benefit from freedom of movement. See Case 186/87 *Ian William Cowan* v. *Trésor public* [1989] ECR 195.

[44] The right to go to another Member State to shop is guaranteed by Community law (see Case C–362/88 *GB-Inno-BM* v. *Confédération du Commerce Luxembourgeois Asbl* [1990] ECR I–667), even if the shopper is carrying no means of payment. See Tesauro A. G. in Case 68/89 *EC Commission* v. *Netherlands* [1991] ECR I–2637, I–2647.

[45] See, e.g., A. Evans, 'Secondary Immigration Control and EEC Law' [1984] *New Law Journal* 965–7.

[46] See Slynn A. G. in Joined Cases 35 and 36/82 *Elestina Esselina Christina Morson* v. *State of the Netherlands and Head of the Plaatselijke Politie within the meaning of the Vreemdelingenwet; Sewradjie Jhanjan* v. *State of the Netherlands* [1982] ECR 3723, 3742. Cf., regarding evasion of national legislation regulating vocational training, Case C–61/89 *Marc Gaston Bouchoucha* [1990] ECR I–3551. Cf. also, regarding the need for persons to be genuinely travelling between Member States for purposes of tax exemption for goods contained in their personal luggage, Case 278/82 *Rewe-Handelsgessellschaft Nord mbH and Rewe-Markt Herbert Kureit* v. *Hauptzollamt Flensburg, Itzehoe and Lübeck-West* [1984] ECR 721.

In other words, the practical effect of the limits imposed on trade liberalization provisions may be much less than is suggested by the language of the relevant judgments.

More fundamentally, it would be incompatible with the concept of Union Citizenship, which was 'established' by Article 8(1) of the Treaty,[47] for a Community national wishing to acquire a Community law right to reside in his own Member State to have first to move to another Member State. It might also be argued that it would be inconsistent with the definition of the internal market—an area without internal frontiers in which the free movement of goods, persons, services and capital is ensured—in Article 7a of the Treaty for Community law rights to depend on the prior crossing of frontiers which Community law was supposed to have abolished by the end of 1992. An analogy might be drawn with recognition by the Court that industrial property rights are so likely to affect trade in goods and services and competitive conditions *à l'intérieur de la Communauté*[48] that the prohibition of discrimination in Article 6 is applicable to the exercise of such rights, without it being necessary to establish the applicability of specific rules governing the free movement of goods.

2.2.2 Community Trade Liberalization

At present, the focus of the Court of Justice is on Community trade liberalization, i.e., liberalization of trading activity which takes place within the Community but goes beyond the domestic market of a single Member State. Such liberalization, which is treated as the essence of the common market, or the internal market of Article 7a of the Treaty, covers the importation or exportation of goods, services and capital as well as the migration of persons between Member States.

Formal Discrimination

Member States are prohibited from differentiating between their own products and those of another Member State in such a way that the marketing of the latter becomes more difficult than the marketing of the former. For example, the Court of Justice has ruled that a requirement imposed only on imported souvenirs that they be stamped with the word 'foreign' or their country of origin is prohibited by Article 30 of the Treaty.[49] In the case of exports, any difference in the treatment of products on the basis of their destination

[47] Art. 8a(1) provides that every Union Citizen shall have the right to move and reside freely within the territory of the Member States.

[48] Joined Cases C–92/92 and C–326/92 *Phil Collins* v. *Imtrat Handelsgesellschaft mbH; Patricia Im-und Export Verwaltungsgesellschaft GmbH and Leif Emanuel Kraul* v. *EMI Electrola GmbH* [1993] ECR I–5145, I–5180.

[49] Case 113/80 *EC Commission* v. *Ireland* [1981] ECR 1625.

conflicts with the fundamental unity of the common market and is, in principle, also prohibited.[50]

As regards persons, the prohibition of discrimination against nationals of other Member States is well established, though the full potential of this prohibition may only have begun to be realized in *Cowan*.[51] This case concerned a British Citizen on holiday in France, who suffered injuries during an assault at the exit of a *métro* station but was refused an award under a publicly financed compensation scheme for victims of violent assaults. The Court of Justice ruled that Member States were prohibited from excluding tourists from other Member States, in their capacity as recipients of services under Articles 59—66 of the Treaty, from the benefits of such a scheme.[52]

Discrimination by undertakings may also be prohibited. For example, a refusal by a monopoly to provide services to persons falling outside a certain category defined by nationality or residence is contrary to Article 86 of the Treaty.[53] This provision prohibits undertakings from abusing a dominant position within the common market or a substantial part of it, in so far as trade between Member States is affected. Similarly, discrimination between undertakings or products of a given Member State and those of other Member States as regards access to television advertising is, if practised by a dominant firm, prohibited.[54]

Material Discrimination

It is not only the above kind of discrimination which may be prohibited. According to Article 3 of Directive 70/50,[55] which was enacted with a view to securing the abolition of national measures having an effect equivalent to quantitative restrictions on imports between Member States, measures applicable equally to imports and domestic products are prohibited where their restrictive effects exceed those intrinsic to trade rules. The Preamble to the Directive indicates that this condition will be met where imports are precluded or their disposal is made more difficult or more costly than disposal of domestic products and where the measures are not necessary for attainment of their objective.

[50] Capotorti A. G. in Case 53/76 *Procureur de la République, Besançon* v. *Bouhelier* [1977] ECR 197, 210.

[51] Case 186/87 *Ian William Cowan* v. *Trésor public* [1989] ECR 195. See, generally, F. Schockweiler, 'La Portée du Principe de Non-Discrimination de l'Art. 7 du Traité CEE' (1991) *RTDE* 3–24.

[52] See, most recently, regarding fees for admission to museums, Case C–45/93 *EC Commission* v. *Spain* [1994] ECR I–911.

[53] Case 7/82 *Gesellschaft zur Verwertung von Leistungsschutzrechten mbH* v. *EC Commission* [1983] ECR 483, 509.

[54] Case 155/73 *Giuseppe Sacchi* [1974] ECR 409, 430.

[55] Of 22 Dec. 1969 ([1970] JO L13/29) based on the provisions of Art. 33(7), on the abolition of measures which have an effect equivalent to quantitative restrictions on imports and are not covered by other provisions adopted in pursuance of the EC Treaty.

As regards persons, Article 3(1) of Regulation 1612/68,[56] on the free movement of workers, prohibits national measures where, though being applicable irrespective of nationality, their exclusive or principal aim or effect is to keep nationals of other Member States away from the employment offered. Similarly, Directive 71/304,[57] concerning the abolition of restrictions on freedom to provide services in respect of public works contracts, provides in Article 3(1)(c) that Member States shall abolish restrictions which, though applicable irrespective of nationality, nonetheless hinder exclusively or principally the professional or trade activities of nationals of other Member States.[58]

The conclusion might be drawn that material discrimination as well as formal discrimination against persons, products, or services from other Member States are prohibited, the former kind of discrimination being present, for example, where a measure equally applicable to imports and domestic products has the effect of favouring the latter.

Article 95 of the Treaty may be illustrative of this. The first paragraph prohibits Member States from imposing on products of other Member States any internal taxation in excess of that imposed on similar domestic products. Thus taxation arrangements which apply equally to imported and domestic products are not prohibited by this paragraph. In other words, only formal discrimination is prohibited thereby. However, the second paragraph of the same provision prohibits Member States from imposing on products of other Member States internal taxation of such a nature as to afford indirect protection to other products.[59] Measures having protective effect are envisaged, and it might be deduced that material discrimination is prohibited by this paragraph.

Such concern for effect rather than mere form may underlie the operation of various liberalization provisions in the Treaty. For example, state aid may be prohibited by Article 92 of the Treaty because, despite its formal generality, such aid has the effect of favouring a certain sector of the economy contrary to the terms of this provision.[60] The treatment of the conduct of undertakings may be comparable. For example, an agreement may be prohibited by Article 85 of

[56] Of 15 Oct. 1968 ([1968] JO L257/2) on freedom of movement for workers within the Community.

[57] Of 21 July 1971 ([1971] JO L185/1) concerning the abolition of restrictions on freedom to provide services in respect of public works contracts and on the award of public works contracts to contractors acting through agencies or branches.

[58] See, more particularly, regarding taxation of non-residents, Case C–279/93 *Finanzamt Köln-Alstadt* v. *Roland Schumacker* (not yet reported).

[59] Taxation must have the effect of reducing potential consumption of imports to the advantage of domestic products. See, e.g., Case 356/85 *EC Commission* v. *Belgium* [1987] ECR 3299, 3325.

[60] Case C–169/84 *Société cdF Chimie Azote et Fertilisants SA and Société chimique de la Grande Paroisse SA* v. *EC Commission* [1990] ECR I–3083, I–3116.

the Treaty even though it does not formally relate to trade between Member States at all.[61]

To conclude that Community trade-liberalization requirements embody the concept of material discrimination might be controversial. This concept has been said to be unsuitable in the context of Community law on the ground that Member States would be obliged to differentiate between products so as to level off competitive advantages within the Community in a manner not conducive to rationalization and the optimum utilization of resources.[62] Such an obligation would remove comparative advantage and, hence, the traditional[63] purpose of trade between states. However, the assumption that the prohibition of material discrimination entails such an obligation seems to confuse the prohibition of such discrimination, which merely means that natural disadvantages of traders must not be reinforced through imposition of restrictions on the traders concerned, with a requirement of positive discrimination, which means that action must be taken to reduce the effects of such disadvantages. Liberalization provisions of the Treaty are not apparently interpreted as embodying the latter requirement.[64]

Nevertheless, application of the concept of material discrimination may present serious problems of delimitation. For example, Article 30 of the Treaty may prohibit a Member State from depriving consumers of access to advertising from another Member State.[65] Thus a Member State must not reinforce the obstacles faced by a trader in one Member State who wishes to inform consumers in another Member State of his products or services. On the other hand, the Treaty does not protect persons in one Member State unrelated to a provider of a service in another Member State who advertise in the former State the availability of the service in the latter.[66] Apparently, those who seek to offer consumers special information designed to compensate for natural obstacles to their access to information do not benefit from trade liberalization provisions. However, such distinctions seem too artificial to address the real needs of liberalizing trade between Member States.

[61] See, e.g., Case C–234/89 *Stergios Delimitis* v. *Henninger Bräu AG* [1991] ECR I–935.

[62] A. W. H. Meij and J. A. Winter, 'Measures Having an Equivalent Effect to Quantitative Restrictions' (1976)13 *CMLRev.* 79–104, at 87–8.

[63] Though to the extent that trade between states involves differentiated goods with increasing returns to scale and consumer preferences, gains from trade may arise which have nothing to do with comparative advantage. See E. Helpman and P. Krugman, *Market Structure and Foreign Trade* (Cambridge, Mass., 1985) and R. K. Abrams *et al.*, *The Impact of the European Community's Internal Market on the EFTA* (Washington, 1990), 14.

[64] According to Reischl A. G. in Case 155/73 *Giuseppe Sacchi* [1974] ECR 409, 444, even Art. 7 (now Art. 6) of the Treaty was probably not to be understood as meaning that having regard to the handicap of foreign undertakings, namely their different needs for advertising, provision should be made in their favour to increase publicity by opening up a private television service.

[65] Case C–362/88 *GB-Inno-BM* v. *Confédération du Commerce Luxembourgeois Asbl* [1990] ECR I–667, I–686.

[66] Case C–159/90 *Society for the Protection of the Unborn Child (SPUC)* v. *Grogan* [1991] ECR I–4685, I–4740.

Again, in Article 2(3)(e) of Directive 70/50[67] the Commission included measures fixing the prices of products solely on the basis of the cost price of domestic products at such a level as to create a hindrance to importation in the list of measures 'other than those applicable equally to domestic or imported products'. Similar treatment of such measures seems to be favoured by the Court.[68] Price-fixing measures of such kinds, however, would seem to constitute classic examples of material discrimination.

More generally, to establish the existence of such discrimination, a detailed and complex examination of economic circumstances may be necessary. As such circumstances vary, a measure could oscillate between being discriminatory and thus prohibited, and being non-discriminatory and thus permitted. Even more serious problems would arise where there was no domestic production of the goods concerned in relation to which discrimination against imports could be established.[69]

Discrimination and the State of Origin Principle

In fact, operation of liberalization provisions in the Treaty does not always seem to depend on formal or material discrimination between domestic products or actors and those from other Member States being established.[70]

In *Cinéthèque*[71] the compatibility with Article 30 of French legislation banning the distribution of films by means of videocasettes during the first few months of their release in the cinema was at issue. The Court of Justice noted that if such a system applied without distinction to both domestic and imported videocasettes, it did not have the purpose of regulating trade patterns; its effect was not to favour national production as against the production of other Member States, but to favour cinematographic works as such. Nevertheless, the application of such a system might create barriers to intra-Community trade in videocasettes because of the disparities between the systems operated in the different Member States and between the conditions for the release of cinematographic works in those Member States.[72] Hence, the system was, in principle, contrary to Article 30.

[67] Of 22 Dec. 1969 ([1970] JO L13/29) based on the provisions of Art. 33(7), on the abolition of measures which have an effect equivalent to quantitative restrictions on imports and are not covered by other provisions adopted in pursuance of the EC Treaty.

[68] Case 231/83 *Henri Cullet and Chambre syndicale des réparations automobiles et détaillants de produits pétroliers* v. *Centre Leclerc Toulouse et Centre Leclerc Saint-Orens-de-Gameville* [1985] ECR 305, 324.

[69] P. Oliver, 'Measures of Equivalent Effect: A Reappraisal' (1982) 20 *CMLRev.* 217–44, at 226.

[70] Indeed, the obligation to adapt a product to legal requirements in the Member State of importation may be prohibited by Art. 30, but the obligation may not easily be characterized as involving such discrimination. See A. Mattera, 'De l'arrêt 'Dassonville' à l'arrêt 'Keck': l'obscure clarté d'une jurisprudence riche en principes novateurs et en contradictions' [1994] *Revue du Marché Unique Européen* 117–60, at 149.

[71] Joined Cases 60 and 61/84 *Cinéthèque* v. *Fédération nationale des cinémas français* [1985] ECR 2605.

[72] *Ibid.* 2626.

The position seems to be similar in the case of industrial or commercial property rights. For example, national law may entitle the holder of a trade mark to prevent the marketing by others of any products, domestic or imported, which bear the same or a similar mark. Such law does not entail discrimination against imports. However, application of such law to imports from other Member States will be prohibited by Article 30, unless its application can be justified on grounds of the protection of commercial or industrial property under Article 36.[73] According to the latter provision, the free movement of goods does not preclude trade restrictions on such grounds, provided the restrictions do not constitute a means of arbitrary discrimination or a disguised restriction on trade between Member States.

Such case law apparently reflects conclusions drawn from the Treaty framework. Thus it is said to be because the requirements of the free movement of goods must be interpreted in the light of Treaty objectives that discrimination against imports in comparison with domestic products may not be necessary for a national measure to be prohibited.[74]

The language of certain Treaty provisions governing the free movement of persons may be consistent with such conclusions. For example, Article 59 provides for restrictions on the freedom to provide services to be progressively abolished during the transitional period in respect of nationals of Member States who are established in a Member State other than that of the person for whom the services are intended. No reference is made to the prohibition of discrimination as between nationals of the Member State where the service is provided and providers of services from other Member States. The implication is that restrictions may have to be abolished, even if they do not entail such discrimination.[75] True, Article 60(3) states that the person providing a service may, in order to do so, temporarily pursue his activity in the Member State where the service is provided under the same conditions as are imposed by that state on its own nationals. This provision does not, however, clearly purport exhaustively to define the requirements of the freedom to provide services.

[73] Case 119/75 *Terrapin (Overseas) Ltd* v. *Terranova Industrie C.A. Kapferer & Co* [1976] ECR 1039.

[74] Gand A. G. in Joined Cases 2 and 3/69 *Diamentarbeiders* v. *Brachfeld* [1969] ECR 211, 230. Cf., regarding the equality of treatment demanded for persons by the ECSC Treaty, Joined Cases 24 and 34/58 *Chambre Syndicale de la Sidérurgie de l'Est de la France* v. *ECSC High Authority* [1960] ECR 281. According to Roemer A. G., the international theory that no discrimination occurred when foreigners received no worse treatment than the worst placed nationals of the state concerned was inapplicable, because Community inter-relations differed basically from the usual relations governed by international law (*ibid.* 319).

[75] According to Warner A. G. in Case 52/79 *Procureur du Roi* v. *Debauve* [1980] ECR 833, 871–2, Arts. 59–66 are designed to create a common market in the provision of services, and not merely to abolish discrimination between providers of services.

This freedom is interpreted as entailing the elimination of all restrictions imposed on the person providing the service[76] by reason in particular of his nationality or of the fact that he does not habitually reside in the Member State where the service is provided, which do not apply to persons established within the national territory or which might prevent or otherwise obstruct the activities of the person providing the service. The principal aim of Article 60(3) is to enable the provider of the service to pursue his activities in the Member State where the service is provided without suffering discrimination in favour of nationals of that state. However, it does not follow from this paragraph that all national legislation applicable to nationals of that state and usually applied to undertakings established therein may be applied in its entirety to the temporary activities of undertakings established in other Member States.[77]

Similarly, Community social security rules aim to remove obstacles in the way of full achievement of the free movement of workers, *especially* those arising from inequalities which place migrants at a disadvantage in comparison with nationals of the host Member State.[78] The implication is that such an obstacle may arise and be prohibited by Community law, even in the absence of any such inequality. Certainly, Article 51 of the Treaty provides for the aggregation, for the purpose of acquiring and retaining the right to benefit and of calculating the amount of benefit, of all periods taken into account under the laws of the several countries in which an individual may have worked. This provision thus envisages aggregation of social security benefits in the case of migrant workers, even though it is not clear that non-aggregation would entail discrimination between migrants and nationals of the host Member State.

That Article 51 does not seek simply to prohibit such discrimination has been confirmed by the Court. According to it, this provision seeks to ensure that, as a consequence of exercising their right to free movement, workers do not lose the advantages in the field of social security which are guaranteed to them by the laws of a single Member State.[79] Apparently for this reason, the Court may compare the situation of a worker before migration with his position after migration rather than the respective situations of migrants and nationals of the host Member State who have never migrated.[80]

[76] Case 33/74 *Johannes Henricus Maria Van Binsbergen* v. *Bedrijfsvereniging* [1974] ECR 1299, 1309.

[77] Case 205/84 *EC Commission* v. *Germany* [1986] ECR 3755, 3802. See, earlier, Case 279/80 *Alfred John Webb* [1981] ECR 3305, 3324.

[78] Trabucchi A. G. in Case 66/74 *Alfonso Farrauto* v. *Bau-berufsgenossenschaft* [1975] ECR 157, 168.

[79] Case 254/84 *De Jong* v. *Sociale Verzekeringsbank* [1986] ECR 671, 682.

[80] Case 100/63 *Mrs J. Kalsbeek (née Van der Veen)* v. *Bestuur der Sociale Verzekeringsbank* [1964] ECR 565, 574 and Case 2/67 *Auguste de Moor* v. *Caisse de Pensions des Employés Privés* [1967] ECR 197, 206.

Consistently with such thinking, the free movement of persons is treated as requiring that individuals established in one Member State should have free access to employment in other Member States[81] and as opposing any national measures which might be unfavourable to individuals wishing to extend their activities beyond the territory of a single Member State.[82] For example, the obligation to cancel a policy taken out with an insurer in one Member State in order to take advantage of the tax deductions in respect of contributions available in another, when the person concerned considers continuation of that policy to be in his best interests, constitutes an obstacle to free movement by virtue of the procedures and expenditure involved.[83]

In essence, there seems to be an interaction between the equality principle and the principle that extension of economic activity beyond the confines of the domestic market into the Community market should be free. It is in this sense that Community trade-liberalization requirements might be said to operate on the basis of the 'State of origin' rather than the 'State of destination' principle.[84] What are less clear are the dynamics of the interaction between the origin and the equality principle.

The dynamics might be thought to operate analogously to a prohibition of 'dual taxation'.[85] According to such thinking, in the case of goods traded between Member States, the application of non-discriminatory rules in the Member State of destination may entail compliance costs which cumulate with the costs of complying with rules laid down in the Member State of origin. Such cumulation impedes Community trade because of the dual burden implied for such trade.

In reality, such cumulation seems to entail a sufficient, but not a necessary, condition for operation of trade-liberalization requirements. For example, a trader may not be obliged by the law of the Member State of origin to incur the costs involved in registering a patent in that Member State in order to market his products there. However, provided that he is not prohibited from marketing his products there, he will, in principle, be free under Article 30 to market them in other Member States. Thus the operation of Article 30 is unaffected by the question whether the products concerned are imported from a Member State where they are not patentable.[86] Apparently, therefore, it is not necessary for

[81] Case 298/84 *Iorio* v. *Azienda Autonoma delle Ferrovie dello Stato* [1986] ECR 247, 255.

[82] Case 143/87 *Christopher Stanton and SA belge d'assurances l'Etoile 1905* v. *Inasti (Institute national d'assurances sociales pour travailleurs indépendents)* [1988] ECR 3877, 3894; Joined Cases 154 and 155/87 *Rijksinstituut voor de Sociale Verzekeringen der Zelfstendingen* v. *Heinrich Wolf and Microtherm Europe NV* [1988] ECR 3897, 3912.

[83] Case C–204/90 *Hans-Martin Bachmann* v. *Belgian State* [1992] ECR I–249, I–280.

[84] See, regarding these terms, H. Dicke and R. J. Langhammer, *The Institutional Framework and External Dimension of the EC Internal Market* (Kiel Working Paper No. 453, Kiel 1990).

[85] See, e.g., Verloren van Themaat A. G. in Case 97/83 *CMC Melkunie BV* [1984] ECR 2367, 2390.

[86] Case 434/85 *Allen and Hanburys Ltd* v. *Generics* (UK) Ltd [1988] ECR 1245, 1277.

domestic activity to be burdened but merely that it should be permissible in order for its extension to other Member States to be liberalized by Community law.[87]

Beyond the Equivalence Doctrine

The equivalence doctrine,[88] which is closely associated with the judgment in *Cassis de Dijon*,[89] might be thought to offer elucidation of the relationship between the state of origin and the equality principle. This judgment concerned the applicability to French products of German legislation prescribing a minimum alcohol content of 25 per cent for fruit liqueurs sold in Germany. The Court of Justice ruled that there was no valid reason, provided that they had been lawfully manufactured and marketed in another Member State, to exclude imported liqueurs containing an alcohol content below the minimum level prescribed by domestic legislation.[90] Although the same proviso has been included in subsequent rulings,[91] no explanation for its inclusion is immediately apparent. It is, however, reminiscent of a similarly cryptic reference in *Dassonville*,[92] which concerned a Belgian legal requirement that imports bearing a designation of origin must be accompanied by an official document issued by the government of the exporting country certifying their right to such designation. Here the Court referred to products from a third country having been put into free circulation[93] in another Member State 'in a regular manner', which is presumably the counterpart in the case of such products to lawful manufacturing and marketing in another Member State in the case of products originating within the Community.

The explanation usually offered for the proviso is that the Court was applying an equivalence principle in its determination of whether an exception from Article 30 could be permitted on grounds such as the protection of public health or the defence of the consumer. The conclusion drawn is that domestic legislation protecting such interests cannot be employed as the basis for excluding imports which have been manufactured and marketed in another Member State in accordance with legislation affording equivalent protection to these interests.[94] Indeed, the Commission interpreted the requirement of lawful

[87] See, more generally, Case C–39/90 *Denkavit Futtermittel GmbH* v. *Land Württemberg* [1991] ECR I–3099, I–3106. Cf., regarding freedom of establishment, Case 79/85 *Segers* v. *K. Bedrijfsvereniging voor Bank en Verzekeringwezen, Gothandel en Vrije Beropen* [1986] ECR 2375, 2387–8.

[88] See, e.g., P. Oliver, n. 69 above., 234 *et seq.*

[89] Case 120/78 *Rewe-Zentral AG* v. *Bundesmonopolverwaltung für Branntwein* [1979] ECR 649.

[90] *Ibid.* 664.

[91] See, e.g. Case 788/79 *Herbert Gilli and Paul Andres* [1980] ECR 2071, 2079.

[92] Case 8/74 *Procureur du Roi* v. *Benoît and Gustave Dassonville* [1974] ECR 837, 852.

[93] According to Art. 10 EC, products from third countries shall be considered to be in free circulation in a Member State if the import formalities have been complied with and any customs duties or charges having equivalent effect which are payable have been levied in that Member State, and if they have not benefited from a total or partial drawback of such duties or charges.

[94] See, e.g., P. Oliver, n. 69 above, 234 *et seq.* The proviso is even said to fulfil the same function as that of the 'fair and traditional practices' test employed in cases such as Case 16/83 *Karl Prantl* [1984] ECR 1299, 1328.

production in another Member State as meaning that a product must conform to the rules and processes of manufacture that were customarily and traditionally accepted in the exporting Member State.[95]

However, where no such interests as the protection of public health or the defence of the consumer are at stake, the equivalence or otherwise of national law protecting such interests may be irrelevant. In *Cassis de Dijon* itself the Court took the view that the minimum alcohol level requirement was *per se* unnecessary for the protection of such interests,[96] and so no issue of equivalence of protection arose. Consequently, the usual explanation for the proviso does not account satisfactorily for its inclusion in the grounds, let alone the operative part, of the *Cassis de Dijon* ruling.

Confirmation of the inadequacy of this explanation is provided by *De Kikvoorsch Groothandel*,[97] which concerned Dutch law prohibiting statements as to the strength of the original wort on the labels of beer bottles. Here the Court ruled that requirements relating to the information to be supplied on the labels of beer bottles, which necessitated an alteration of the label under which imported beer was lawfully marketed in the Member State of exportation,[98] were contrary to Article 30.[99] This ruling was not preceded by consideration of the equivalence of information requirements applied to labels of beer bottles in other Member States.[100]

Apparently, the real explanation for the *Cassis de Dijon* proviso is that it reflected the facts put to the Court.[101] Certainly, in the same case Advocate General Capotorti considered that the national restrictions were prohibited simply because they created 'an obstacle to the importation from other Member States of spirits and liqueurs having a lower alcohol content'.[102]

The fact that products may have had to comply with equivalent legal

[95] Communication from the Commission concerning the Consequences of the Judgment given by the Court of Justice on 20 February 1979 in Case 120/78 ([1980] OJ C256/2).

[96] Case 120/78 *Rewe-Zentral AG* v. *Bundesmonopolverwaltung für Branntwein* [1979] ECR 649, 663–4.

[97] Case 94/82 *De Kikvoorsch Groothandel-Import-Export BV* [1983] ECR 947. See, earlier, Case 27/80 *Officier van Justitie* v. *Anton Adriaan Fietje* [1980] ECR 3839, 3853–4.

[98] [1983] ECR 947, 958. Cf., regarding a rule which compelled undertakings to give up certain marketing methods or promotional techniques, Case 382/87 *Regina Buet and Educational Business Services* (EBS) *Sàrl* v. *Ministère Public* [1989] ECR 1235, 1251.

[99] However, it may not only be the costs of altering the packaging which constitute a measure having equivalent effect. See C–317/92 *EC Commission* v. *Germany* [1994] ECR I–2039, I–2060.

[100] There might, perhaps, be said to have been a presumption of equivalence in such cases. However, in Case 53/80 *Officier van Justitie* v. *Koninklijke Kaasfabriek Eyssen BV* [1981] ECR 409, 421 it was enough for the addition of nisin to cheese to be permissible in other Member States for the prohibition of this additive in cheese imported into the Netherlands to be contrary to Art. 30.

[101] Lenz A. G. in Case 94/83 *Albert Heijn BV* [1984] ECR 3263, 3285.

[102] Case 120/78 *Rewe-Zentral AG* v. *Bundesmonopolverwaltung für Branntwein* [1979] ECR 649, 669. In Joined Cases C–401/92 and C–402/92 *Tankstation't Heukske vof and J. B. E. Boermans* [1994] ECR I–2199, I–2233 the Court itself referred simply to products 'from other Member States'.

requirements imposed by the Member State of origin seems not to be a necessary condition to render unlawful their subjection to different requirements in the Member State of importation. In *SMANOR SA*[103] French legislation providing that the designation 'yoghurt' could be used only to denote fresh fermented milk was at issue. The Court drew a simple conclusion from the fact that deep-frozen yoghurts were lawfully manufactured and marketed under that designation in other Member States. The conclusion drawn was that it could not be ruled out that such products might be imported into France and French law applied to them contrary to Article 30.[104]

The Treaty might not, it is true, benefit those who move their production from their Member State of origin to another Member State solely to avoid the national rules of their state of origin, and then only market their products in that state.[105] In general, however, the Treaty seems to benefit traders who produce in one Member State and export their production to another Member State, irrespective of whether they comply with marketing rules in the former. For example, *Schutzverband* concerned German legislation which prohibited the marketing of imported vermouth containing a lower level of alcohol than that prescribed in the state of manufacture for domestic marketing. The Court ruled that the marketing of vermouth lawfully made in another Member State might be prevented by such legislation contrary to Article 30.[106]

Therefore, while the equivalence doctrine and the proviso in *Cassis de Dijou* with which it is associated may exemplify the operation of Community trade liberalization requirements, they do not exhaustively define these requirements. The latter mean that a Member State is not only prohibited from invoking national rules against imported products which satisfy equivalent rules in another Member State. A Member State may also be prohibited from invoking such rules against products which are simply allowed to be manufactured or marketed in another Member State. The mutual recognition of national regulations which is impliedly demanded may go beyond a process conditioned by equivalence.

The formal rationale for the far-reaching liberalization requirements which are entailed is that fundamental freedoms are at stake.[107] This rationale does not, as judgments regarding domestic activity[108] demonstrate, entail that contact with underlying features of the Treaty structure perceived by the Court is lost. On the other hand, as judgments such as that in

[103] Case 298/87 [1988] ECR 4489.

[104] *Ibid.*, 4510. See, similarly, regarding the generic term 'vinegar', Case 193/80 *EC Commission* v. *Italy* [1981] ECR 3019, 3036.

[105] Cf. Case 229/83 *Association des Centres distributeurs Edouard Leclerc* v. *Sàrl* 'Au Blé Vert' [1985] ECR 1, 35.

[106] Case 59/82 *Schutzverband gegen Unwesen in der Wirtschaft* v. *Weinvertriebs-GmbH* [1983] ECR 1217, 1226.

[107] Cf. Case 41/74 *Yvonne van Duyn* v. *Home Office* [1974] ECR 1337, 1350.

[108] Sect. 2.2.1 above.

Cowan[109] show, such requirements, once recognized, are capable of generating prohibitions of state measures which have little real connection with market unification issues. In other words, the distinction between 'structuralist' and 'individualist' thinking in judicial practice[110] may be less clear-cut[111] than such terminology might imply.

The classical concept of equality may, subject to certain modifications, be capable of capturing the liberalization requirements entailed. This concept may prohibit differential treatment of what are alike and like treatment of what are different. Without more, such a concept would be inoperable, not least within the Community law context.[112] Persons or products from the various Member States will usually be alike in some respects and different in other respects.[113] Hence, criteria are necessary to determine which similarities demand like treatment and which differences demand differential treatment.[114] These criteria are provided by market unification demands,[115] which are taken to require that traders should be free to engage in trading activity beyond the confines of a single Member State. Thus differential treatment is prohibited where products or persons are sufficiently similar that such treatment restricts exercise of such freedom, and like treatment is prohibited where products or persons are sufficiently different that such treatment has the same effect. What classical equality theory would describe as comparability problems[116] and present

[109] Case 186/87 *Ian William Cowan* v. *Trésor public* [1989] ECR 195.

[110] D. Chalmers, 'Repackaging the Internal Market—The Ramifications of the *Keck* Judgment' (1994) *ELRev*. 385–403.

[111] While the distinction may be bound up with the '*de minimis* rule', its impact on the operation of the latter may be limited.

[112] According to Lagrange A. G. in Joined Cases 17 and 20/61 *Klöckner-Werke AG and Hoesch AG* v. *ECSC High Authority* [1962] ECR 325, 355, it was necessary to judge a 'complaint of discrimination *in relation to a legislative system*, that is to say, within a general framework'.

[113] As Lagrange A. G. put it in Case 13/63 *EEC Commission* v. *Italy* [1963] ECR 165, 190, the 'concept of relativity . . . permeates' the equality principle.

[114] As the ECJ observed in Joined Cases 3 to 18, 25 and 26/58 *Barbara Erzergebau AG* v. *ECSC High Authority* [1960] ECR 173, 191, the opinion that any comparison between several undertakings must take into account all the circumstances in which they are placed would entail that an undertaking would only be comparable with itself, and thus the equality principle would become devoid of all meaning.

[115] The importance attached to market unification may explain why the ECJ does not, like U.S. courts, as in *Continental T.V. Inc.* v. *G.T.E. Sylvania Inc.*, 433 U.S. 36 (1977), treat restrictive practices affecting intrabrand competition more leniently than those affecting interbrand competition.

[116] Cf. Art. 2(3) of the GATT Agreement on the Application of Sanitary and Phytosanitary Measures, which prohibits measures which 'arbitrarily or unjustifiably discriminate between Members where identical or similar conditions prevail' (Annex Ia to the Agreement establishing the World Trade Organization). However, as the ECJ observed in Joined Cases 7 and 9/54 *Groupement des Industries Sidérurgiques Luxembourgeoises* v. *ECSC High Authority* [1954–56] ECR 175, 195, the comparability test in itself only supplies a relative and transitory criterion for application of provisions prohibiting discrimination, because its effect depends on the scope of its field of application. Hence, recourse must be had to the objectives of the legal framework of such provisions, so as to ensure that the results of the use of that criteria are consistent with those intended by that framework.

themselves as problems of the relationship between the equality principle and the state of origin principle are reducible to problems of establishing the presence or absence of such a restriction.

Anti-competitive Effects

Not all restrictions[117] on imports or exports or on migrants between Member States are prohibited. It is inherent in the idea of liberalizing trading activity in an expanded market that prohibited restrictions are those which affect competition in such activity. Restrictions which do not affect the competitive position of products or actors are not, therefore, prohibited. Were they prohibited, a competitive advantage would be created for traders to whom the restrictions were rendered inapplicable. In other words, distortions of competition incompatible with the requirement in Article 3(g) of the Treaty of undistorted competition in the common market would be created. Such creation would differ from the consequences of the Treaty failure to liberalize domestic trading activity, because a distortion would not simply be replaced by another but would be created where none existed before.

Efforts to identify restrictions which may be prohibited tend to rely on fine analytical distinctions. For example, according to the Commission, application of rules governing the characteristics or presentation of a product is prohibited even in the absence of discrimination, but application of those governing the circumstances in which products may be marketed is prohibited only where discrimination is entailed.[118] A further distinction may be made between 'market circumstances' rules with a territorial element and such rules with no such element, the latter being said to be more objectionable from the perspective of trade liberalization.[119]

Such distinctions are designed to assist national courts called upon to apply preliminary rulings delivered by the Court of Justice under Article 177 of the Treaty.[120] The need for such assistance may seem particularly pressing, given that the questions to be tackled by the courts may often be comparable with those largely reserved for the economic appreciation of the Commission

[117] The prohibition of 'all restrictions' on capital movements between Member States in Art. 73b(1) EC, which was introduced by the TEU, may be problematic, even though comparatively broad derogations are permitted by Art. 73d.

[118] *Management of the mutual recognition of national rules after 1992* ([1993] OJ C353/4), para. 22. See also K. Mortelmans, 'Art. 30 of the EC Treaty and Legislation Relating to Market Circumstances: a Time to Consider a New Definition?' (1991) 28 *CMLRev.* 115–36.

[119] The terms 'static' and 'dynamic' are used to make the same distinction in N. Reich, 'The "November Revolution" of the European Court of Justice: Keck, Meng and Audi Revisited' (1994) 31 *CMLRev.* 459–92, at 471.

[120] Though they may not be readily reconcilable with the case law of the ECJ. Cf. D. T. Keeling, 'The Free Movement of Goods in EEC Law: Basic Principles and Recent Developments in the Case Law of the Court of Justice of the European Communities' (1992) 26 *International Lawyer* 467–83.

under Articles 85 and 92 of the Treaty.[121] However, efforts made to meet this need reflect formalistic conceptions[122] of the relationship between economy and law. According to these conceptions, questions involving economic appreciation should be resolved by the Commission, and courts should be left to determine, pursuant to the preliminary rulings procedure, questions of the interpretation of Community law.[123] As a result, the distinctions which are advanced with a view to providing assistance to national courts may tend to obscure the underlying issues—those of '*accès au marché*'[124]—involved and may be ill-adapted to the real needs of trade liberalization. In practice, for example, 'market circumstances' rules may be more onerous than those regulating the labelling or characteristics of a product,[125] though application of the former kind of rules is said only to be prohibited where their application would entail discrimination.

The underlying issues have been tackled more explicitly in case law under Articles 92 and 95 of the Treaty. In *Italy* v. *EC Commission*[126] it was argued that social charges on Italian textile firms were higher than those of competitors in other Member States and that their reduction by the Italian authorities, which the Commission had found to be aid prohibited by Article 92(1),[127] simply eliminated this disadvantage. The Court, however, ruled that in the application of Article 92(1) the appropriate reference point for deciding

[121] See sect. 4.2 below. Hence, the Commission seeks an expanded role in tackling issues of the former kind, pursuant to the mutual recognition requirements of Art. 100b. See *Management of the mutual recognition of national rules after 1992* ([1993] OJ C353/4). The Commission envisages introducing a requirement that a Member State banning products lawfully produced and/or marketed in another Member State should notify the Commission and other Member States. See the Commission Proposal of 15 Dec. 1993 for a European Parliament and Council Dec. establishing a procedure for the exchange of information on national measures derogating from the principle of the free movement of goods within the Community, COM(93)670.

[122] It is not the formalism *tout court* of these distinctions which is problematic—an element of formalism is inevitable in the process of constructing reality so as to permit application of legal rules—but the degree of formalism involved.

[123] Lenz A. G. in C–44/93 *Namur—Les assurances du crédit SA* v. *Office national du ducroire et Etat belge* [1994] ECR I–3829, I–3855. According to the Commission Notice on co-operation between national courts and the Commission in applying Arts 85 and 86 EEC ([1993] OJ C39/6), para. 4, the Commission has to act in the public interest, whereas national courts have the task of safeguarding the subjective rights of private individuals. See, similarly, EFTA Surveillance Authority Notice on co-operation between national courts and the EFTA Surveillance Authority in applying Arts. 53 and 56 of the EEA Agreement ([1995] OJ C112/7), para. 6. Cf. Case T–24/90 *Automec Sàrl* v. *EC Commission* [1992] ECR 2223, 2277 and Case C–354/90 *Fédération Nationale Extérieur des Produits Alimentaires and Syndicat National des Négociants et Transformateurs de Saumon* v. *French State* [1991] ECR I–5505, I–5528. Jacobs A. G. (*ibid.*, I–5519) distinguished between the role of courts and Commission concern with 'the substance' of competition issues.

[124] Joined Cases C–267 and C–268/91 *B. Keck and D. Mithouard* [1993] ECR I–6097, I–6131. See also Case C–292/92 *Ruth Hunermund* v. *Landesapothekerkamer* [1993] ECR I–6787, I–6823.

[125] A. Mattera, 'De l'arrêt 'Dassonville' à l'arrêt 'Keck': l'obscure clarté d'une jurisprudence riche en principes novateurs et en contradictions' [1984] *Revue du Marché Unique Européen* 117–60, 153-54.

[126] Case 173/73 [1974] ECR 709.

[127] Dec. 73/274 of 25 July 1973 ([1973] L254 OJ/14) on Art. 20 of Italian Act 1101 of 1 Dec. 1971 on the restructuring, reorganization, and conversion of the textile industry.

whether or not trade between Member States was distorted must necessarily be the competitive position existing within the Community before the adoption of the measure in question.[128] In other words, distortions of competition were to be assessed with reference to the pre-aid situation.

The implications of this approach became clearer in *Firma Steinike und Weinlig* v. *Bundesamt für Ernehrung und Forstwirtschaft.*[129] This case concerned a German fund, partly financed by the state, which promoted the agricultural and forestry industries in Germany, in particular by financing market research and advertising. It was argued that such assistance to German industry did not distort competition in trade between Member States, because similar support was provided in other Member States. The Court, however, ruled that a violation of Article 92(1) by one Member State could not be justified by the fact that other Member States were also violating this provision. The effects of more than one distortion of competition on trade between Member States did not cancel one another out but accumulated,[130] and the damaging consequences to the common market were increased.[131]

This approach seems inconsistent with the theory of the 'second best'. According to this theory, distortions of competition entail output restrictions. If there is only one distortion of competition, this theory holds that removing the distortion will increase welfare. If there are distortions in several markets, however, elimination of a distortion in one market may draw resources from some other market in which output is restricted. It may be that output in the market from which resources are withdrawn is worth more, from a social point of view, than output in that in which the restriction is eliminated. In this case, the effect of a partial elimination of distortions will be to reduce overall welfare.[132]

The Court of Justice, however, does not engage in economic analysis of this kind. Rather, Article 92(1) is apparently treated as prohibiting any aid which is capable of affecting the undistorted competition which, as Article 3(g) of the Treaty makes clear, is demanded by establishment of the common market.[133]

[128] [1974] ECR 709, 720.

[129] Case 78/76 [1977] ECR 595.

[130] Indeed, integration in some areas may exaggerate the effects of any remaining distortions. Cf. the British response to French poultry aid, which was condemned in Case 40/82 *EC Commission* v. *United Kingdom* [1982] ECR 2793. According to the Commission, the 'distortive effect of aid is magnified as other government-induced distortions are eliminated and markets become more open and integrated' (Community Guidelines on State Aid for Rescuing and Restructuring Firms in Difficulty ([1994] OJ C368/12), para. 1.1).

[131] [1977] ECR 595, 612. Cf. Joined Cases 6 and 11/69 *EC Commission* v. *France* [1969] ECR 523, 540 and the *Eighth Report on Competition Policy* (EC Commission, Brussels 1979), 155–6. There is an underlying concern to prevent 'an aid war' (*ibid.*, 164).

[132] R. G. Lipsey and K. Lancaster, 'The General Theory of the Second Best' (1956) *Review of Economic Studies* 11–32.

[133] Cf. the argument in W. F. Schwartz and E. W. Harper, 'The Regulation of Subsidies Affecting International Trade' [1972] 70 *Michigan Law Review* 831–58, at 858 that 'international involvement' in dealing with subsidies is desirable but not attempts to uphold 'a free trade ideal deducible from a theory of comparative advantage'.

To expect positive proof that aid was so capable would, according to Advocate General Warner in *Italy* v. *EC Commission*,[134] be unrealistic. Once it was clear that the natural consequence of the grant of an aid to an industry in a Member State—in this case, the Italian textiles industry—must be to increase the competitiveness of that industry *vis-à-vis* its competitors in other Member States, the inference could properly be drawn that the aid would distort competition in trade between Member States.[135] In adopting this position, the Advocate General expressly approved an early characterization[136] of the importance of the state aid prohibition, according to which there would be no real common market in an industry straddling several countries if one of those countries subsidized its own industry.[137]

Likewise, in connection with Article 95 of the Treaty, the Court has made clear that it is the competitive effect of a tax difference which determines whether it is to be treated as amounting to discrimination prohibited by this provision.[138] The mere fact that imports may be restricted by tax measures does not mean that the measures are prohibited. The aim of Article 95, in line with the Treaty objectives outlined in Articles 2 and 3,[139] is to ensure the free movement of goods between Member States in undistorted conditions of competition by the elimination of all forms of protection resulting from the application of internal taxation which discriminates against products from other Member States or is protectionist in its scope.[140]

Conduct, public or private, which differentiates, for example, between domestic and imported goods or which applies only to the latter has an inherent capacity to distort conditions of competition for Community trade. Moreover, such a distortion may usually be inferred where products which may freely be marketed in their Member State of origin (or the Member State in which they are put into free circulation) have to be modified in order to satisfy the (different) legal requirements for their marketing in another Member State. In such cases a distortion of competition may be a necessary consequence of the restriction of trade. In other cases it may have to be positively established[141] that a trade restriction entails a distortion of competition.[142]

[134] Case 173/73 [1974] ECR 709, 729.

[135] [1974] ECR 709, 728.

[136] Lagrange A. G. in Case 30/59 *De Gezamenlijke Steenkolenmijnen in Limburg* v. *ECSC High Authority* [1961] ECR 1, 41.

[137] Case 173/73 [1974] ECR 709, 722.

[138] Case 169/78 *EC Commission* v. *Italy* [1980] ECR 385, 399.

[139] Case 15/81 *Gaston Schul* [1982] ECR 1409. See also Jacobs A. G. in Case C–312/91 *Metalsa Sàrl* [1993] ECR I–3751, I–3763.

[140] Case 142/77 *Statens Kontrol med Ædle Metaller* v. *Preben Larsen; Flemming Kjerulff* v. *Statens Kontrol med Ædle Metaller* [1978] ECR 1543, 1558.

[141] A. Evans, 'Economic Policy and the Free Movement of Goods in EEC Law' [1983] *ICLQ* 577–99. Note, more particularly, the questions put by the ECJ in Joined Cases C–267 and C–268/91 *B. Keck and D. Mithouard* [1993] ECR I–6097, I–6102, regarding the effects of the national legislation at issue.

[142] E.g. a national measure which made access of imported products to the domestic market conditional on the presence of a representative in the importing Member State was prohibited

(i) Price Controls

It cannot be inferred from the fact that a product may freely be marketed in one Member State that its subjection to price controls in another Member State will affect its competitiveness in the latter. This consideration might explain why the Court has found it necessary to illustrate the circumstances in which price controls may distort competition. Such circumstances will be present where maximum price controls take no account of the additional costs associated with importation or prevent increased prices of raw materials or finished products being passed on, so that the products concerned may only be sold at a loss, or where minimum prices prevent imports from competing with domestic products through a lower sale price.[143] In other circumstances national price controls may be permissible. Thus, for example, the imposition on imported bread sold below the minimum price applicable to domestic bread of a compulsory distribution margin applicable also to domestic products is not prohibited by Article 30.[144]

The conclusion drawn from such judgments is that 'discrimination of substance' must be present before price controls may be caught by Article 30.[145] Such a condition may not necessarily be, as is usually imagined, an anomaly in the case law concerning this provision. Rather, it may simply be a consequence of the fact that the likelihood of anti-competitive effects necessary for application of Article 30 cannot be inferred from the imposition of price controls.[146] As the Court puts it, a prohibition which makes no distinction between domestic products and imports, on sales by a retailer at a price below his purchase price, cannot produce detrimental effects on the marketing of imported products alone.[147]

because it was found likely to involve additional costs for importers and, hence, was prohibited. See Case 247/81 *EC Commission* v. *Germany* [1984] ECR 1111, 1119. Similarly, national legislation which reserves the sale of contact lenses and ancillary products to holders of an optician's certificate '*canalise les ventes*' and is contrary to Art. 30. See Case C–271/92 *Laboratoire de prothèses oculaires (LPO)* v. *Union nationale des syndicats d'opticiens de France (UNSOF)* [1993] ECR I–2899, I–2922. See also, regarding auction sales, Case 239/90 *SCP Boscher, Studer and Fromentin* v. *SA British Motors Wright* [1991] ECR I–2023, I–2039; regarding a pharmacists' monopoly for the retail sale of certain drugs, Case C–369/88 *Jean-Marie Delattre* [1991] ECR I–1487, I–1539–40; regarding the prohibition of canvassing in connection with the sale of educational materials, Case 382/87 *Regina Buet and Educational Business Services (EBS) Sàrl* v. *Ministère public* [1989] ECR 1235, 1251.

143 Case 13/77 *NV GB-Inno-BM* v. *Vereniging van de Kleinhandelaars in Tabak (ATAB)* [1977] ECR 2115, 2148.

144 Case 80/85 *Nederlandse Bakkerij Stichting* v. *Edah BV* [1986] ECR 3359, 3381.

145 P. Oliver, n. 69 above, 229, n. 53.

146 See, similarly, regarding national taxation, Case C–132/88 *EC Commission* v. *Greece* [1990] ECR I–1567, I–1593.

147 Case 82/77 *Openbaar Ministerie* v. *Jacobus Philippus van Tiggele* [1978] ECR 25, 39. Such thinking may underlie the more recent and controversial judgment in *Keck*, see n. 164 below.

(ii) Advertising Restrictions

Advertising restrictions in themselves entail a cost reduction for traders, and it cannot be assumed that such restrictions distort competition, in particular, by affecting comparative advantage.[148] In *EC Commission* v. *France*,[149] which concerned French restrictions on the advertising of alcoholic drinks, the Court found it necessary to establish that they had anti-competitive effects before ruling that they were caught by Article 30.[150] It has been argued that in this case the Court was only concerned with establishing the presence of such effects in order to rule on the admissibility of an exception from the prohibition.[151] However, the Court began by noting the agreement between the parties to the effect that a restriction of advertising for certain products could affect marketing prospects for imported products and thus be prohibited. The question to be resolved, ruled the Court, was whether the restrictions to which the Commission objected placed a handicap on the importation of alcoholic products from other Member States.[152] The answer to this question was, therefore, essential for determination of whether the restrictions at issue were, in principle, prohibited by Article 30.

The presence of such a handicap may be more readily established in the case of some advertising restrictions than in the case of others. For example, where a trader seeks to attract consumers to travel from another Member State to purchase his products in his Member State of establishment, advertising may be an effective precondition for the trade sought. Therefore, at least if strategic trade thinking is adopted and problems of market entry are recognized, restrictions on his advertising are likely to be objectionable.[153]

(iii) Measures Governing Consumption or Production

Blesgen[154] concerned Belgian legislation prohibiting the sale in pubs and restaurants of alcoholic drinks exceeding twenty-two degrees in strength.

[148] Cf. Case 286/81 *Oosthoek's Uitgeversmaatschappij BV* [1982] ECR 4575, 4587; Case C–241/89 *SARPP–Société d'application de recherches en pharmacologie et phytothérapie Sàrl* v. *Chambre syndicale des raffineurs et conditionneurs de sucre de France* [1990] ECR I–4675, I–4723–4; Case C–126/91 *Schutzverband gegen Unwesen in der Wirtschaft* v. *Yves Rocher GmbH* [1993] ECR I–2361, I–2388.

[149] Case 152/78 [1980] ECR 2299.

[150] Cf., regarding a prohibition on the advertising of alcoholic drinks of more than 23 degrees, Joined Cases C–1/90 and C–176/90 *Aragonesa de Publicidad Exterior et Publivia* [1991] ECR I–4151, I–4183, and, regarding restrictions on televised advertising, Case C–412/93 *Société d'Importation Edouard Leclerc-Siplec* v. *TF1 Publicité SA and M6 Publicité SA* (not yet reported).

[151] L. Gormley, *Prohibiting Restrictions on Trade Within the EEC* (Amsterdam, 1985), 263.

[152] [1980] ECR 2299, 2314.

[153] Case C–362/88 *GB-Inno-BM* v. *Confédération du commerce Luxembourgeois* [1990] ECR I–667, I–686. See also, regarding a Dutch prohibition of 'cold calling' by suppliers of financial services, Case C–384/93 *Alpine Investments BV* v. *Minister van Financiën* (not yet reported). Cf., however, regarding the possibility that restrictions 'reflect cultural sensitivities to which firms would wish to adapt their marketing strategies to operate effectively in the relevant Member States', Commission Reply by Mr Vanni d'Archirafi to Written Question E–2036/94 ([1995] OJ C81/5) by Bryan Cassidy.

[154] Case 75/81 *Joseph Henri Thomas Blesgen* v. *State of Belgium* [1982] ECR 1211, 1299.

Since this legislation applied to particular forms of consumption rather than marketing generally, a distortion of competition could not be inferred from any need to adapt imported products simply for their marketing in Belgium. Consequently, it had to be established that the legislation put imported spirits at a competitive disadvantage on the Belgian market. Such an effect was not established, and so the Court ruled, noting that the legislation made no distinction based on the origin of the products concerned, that it was not caught by Article 30.[155] Likewise, a prohibition of the distillation of raw materials applying 'without discrimination' to imports and domestic products is not contrary to Article 30.[156]

(iv) Export Restrictions

Article 34 of the Treaty prohibits quantitative restrictions and measures having equivalent effect on exports between Member States. In *Groenveld*,[157] which involved a Dutch ban on the processing or stocking of horsemeat by sausage manufacturers, the Court ruled that such a ban would only be caught by Article 34, where it had as its specific object or effect the restriction of patterns of exports and thereby the establishment of a difference in treatment between the domestic trade of a Member State and its export trade, in such a way as to provide a particular advantage for national production or for the domestic trade of the Member State in question. In other words, it is only measures distorting conditions of competition as between exporters and those marketing products domestically which are caught by this provision.[158]

Fundamentally, this interpretation of Article 34 seems consistent with that of Article 30. Certainly, in *Oebel*[159] the Court ruled that German legislation banning night-time delivery of bakery products to the retailer or ultimate consumer applied equally to domestic products and imports or exports and was not prohibited by either provision. The legislation was clearly capable of restricting imports and exports. However, it was not established that the legislation distorted competition as between importers or exporters and those marketing products domestically, because deliveries to wholesalers were

[155] See, similarly, regarding restrictions on certain kinds of Sunday trading, Joined Cases C–69/93 and C–258/93 *Punto Casa SpA* v. *Sindaco del Commune di Capon and Comune di Capon and Promozioni Polivalenti Venete Soc. coop. arl (PPV)* v. *Sindaco del Comune di Torri di Quartesolo and Commune di Torri di Quartesolo* [1994] ECR I–2355, I–2368.

[156] Case 86/78 *SA des Grandes Distilleries Peureux* v. *Directeur des services fiscaux de la Haute-Saône et du Territoire de Belfort* [1979] ECR 975, 985.

[157] Case 15/79 *Groenveld* v. *Produktschap voor Vee en Vlees* [1979] ECR 3409, 3415.

[158] Consequently, a Member State may impose high quality standards on domestic producers, even if that policy exposes its producers to the risk of price competition from producers of other Member States who are not bound by the same standards. See Case 237/82 *Jongeneel Kaas BV* v. *State of the Netherlands and Stichting Centraal Orgaan Zuivelcontrole* [1984] ECR 483, 505.

[159] Case 155/80 *Sergius Oebel* [1981] ECR 1993.

unaffected.[160] In contrast, pricing rules which operate on the basis of transportation costs from a domestic wholesaler to domestic retailers and do not take account of importation costs, including costs of delivery to the wholesaler, are prohibited.[161]

Against this background, the controversy[162] raised by rulings such as *Forest*[163] and *Keck*[164] seems less justified. The former case involved French legislation imposing quotas on the quantities of wheat which could be milled in France. The Court ruled that, even though the legislation might limit the quantities of wheat purchased by millers, they were free to buy domestic or imported wheat within their quotas. In addition, it was noted that there were no such quotas which could have restricted flour imports. Hence, the competitive position of imports into the French market was taken to be unaffected,[165] and so there was found to be no restrictive effect of the kind prohibited by Article 30.

The *Keck* ruling concerned national legislation which prohibited shops from selling products at a price below that for which they purchased them. The Court ruled that legislation prohibiting 'certain selling arrangements' did not restrict trade between Member States, provided that it applied to all affected traders operating within the national territory and in the same manner in law and in fact the marketing of domestic products and those from other Member States. Where these provisos were met, the legislation did not prevent access to the market of products from other Member States or impede their access any more than it impeded the access of domestic products. In other words, there were no anti-competitive effects. Hence, such legislation was not prohibited by Article 30. The Court prefaced this part of the ruling with the words 'contrary to what has previously been decided.'[166] In reality, the Court seems to have refined previous formulations of what it seeks to reduce to a 'rule' in Article 30 rather than to have redefined the requirements of this provision.[167]

(v) General Restrictions and Measures having Remote Effects

Instead of seeking directly to establish whether a measure has anti-competitive effects, the Court may prefer to draw inferences from the characteristics of the measure concerned. For example, measures characterized as part of 'the

[160] *Ibid.* 2010. Likewise, the legislation at issue in Joined Cases C–267 and C–268/91 *B. Keck and D. Mithouard* [1993] ECR I–6097 did not prevent a producer from another Member State selling to a wholesaler at a loss (Van Gerven A. G., I–6123–4).

[161] Case 188/86 *Ministère public* v. *Régis Lefèvre* [1987] ECR 2963, 2979.

[162] See, e.g., P. Oliver, n. 27 above, 89 and D. Chalmers, n. 110 above, 393.

[163] Case 148/85 *Direction générale des Impôts and Procureur de la République* v. *Marie-Louise Forest, née Sangoy, and Forest SA* [1986] ECR 3449, 3475.

[164] Joined Cases C–267 and C–268/91 *B. Keck and D. Mithouard* [1993] ECR I–6097.

[165] The view of Van Gerven A. G. in Case C–145/88 *Torfaen Borough Council* v. *B & Q plc* [1989] ECR 3851, 3868 that the Court found no actual or potential restriction of imports in *Forest* does not necessarily follow.

[166] [1993] ECR I–6097, I–6131.

[167] According to the Court itself, its aim was to re-examine and clarify its case law (*ibid.* I–6131).

general legislative framework of business activities'[168] may be treated as lacking the requisite anti-competitive effects.[169] Thus national legislation may limit the number of processors of a product, with the consequence that domestic processors need pay only 'minimal prices' for the product concerned, but Article 30 is not infringed, 'since [the legislation] merely concerns the way in which a business is conducted'.[170] The underlying idea is that the competition sought by liberalization provisions of the Treaty does not aim to remove fundamental differences between cost structures of the Member States which contribute to the wider economic and social framework within which firms operate in each Member State.[171]

Such thinking may also be discernible in the treatment of the conduct of undertakings by Community law. For example, a selective distribution agreement is 'an aspect of competition which accords with Article 85(1)' of the Treaty and, hence, is permissible, provided that objective criteria are applied uniformly in the selection of distributors.[172]

Again, Article 86(c) of the Treaty provides that an undertaking which applies dissimilar conditions to equivalent transactions with other trading parties, thereby placing them at a competitive advantage, commits an abuse of a dominant position within the meaning of this provision. However, an undertaking which differentiates generally between trading partners on the basis of legitimate commercial reasons does not offend against Article 86(c).[173]

[168] Darmon A. G. in Case C–69/88 *H. Krantz & Co.* v. *Ontvanger der Directe Belastingen and the State (Netherlands)* [1990] ECR I–583, I–589.

[169] In Case 238/82 *Duphar* v. *The Netherlands* [1984] ECR 523, 541–2 the Court ruled that a Dutch scheme excluding listed pharmaceutical products from reimbursement of a state social security fund was not prohibited by Art. 30, provided that certain conditions were met. Specifically, the lists must be drawn up in accordance with objective criteria without reference to the origin of the products; the lists must be verifiable by any importer; and amendment of the lists must be possible where there was compliance with the requisite criteria.

[170] Case 118/86 *Openbaar Ministerie* v. *Nertsvoderfabriek Nederland BV* [1987] ECR 3883, 3907. The Court also described the legislation at issue in Joined Cases C–267 and C–268/91 *B. Keck and D. Mithouard* [1993] ECR I–6097, I–6132 as applying a general prohibition.

[171] Pursuit of such an aim would undermine the basis for mutually beneficial trade. See the *First Survey on State Aids in the European Community* (EC Commission, Brussels, 1985), 7. Thus a national measure designed to improve the quality of domestic production so as to make it more attractive to consumers 'complies with the requirement of sound and fair competition laid down by the Treaty'. See Case 237/82 *Jongeneel Kaas BV* v. *State of the Netherlands and Stichting Centraal Orgaan Zuivelcontrole* [1984] ECR 483, 504.

[172] Case 26/76 *Metro-SB-Großmärkte GmbH & Co. KG* v. *EC Commission* [1977] ECR 1875, 1904.

[173] Case 322/81 *NV Nederlandsche Banden-Industrie Michelin* v. *EC Commission* [1983] ECR 3461, 3519–20. Price differentiation is permitted, provided it is justified by objectively established distinctions. See Case 27/76 *United Brands Company and United Brands Continental BV* v. *EC Commission* [1978] ECR 207, 301. See, similarly, regarding the ECSC Treaty, Case 8/57 *Groupement des Hauts Fourneaux et Aciéries Belges* v. *ECSC High Authority* [1957–58] ECR 245, 257. Moreover, an undertaking in a dominant position is permitted by the same provision during an international shortage of the product concerned to reduce its supplies to occasional customers more than to contractual or regular customers. See Case 77/77 *Benzine en Petroleum Handelsmaatschappij BV* v. *EC Commission* [1978] ECR 1513, 1527–28.

Apparently, then, the generality of a State measure or the conduct of an undertaking may be such that it may be treated as unobjectionable. However, 'between generality and specificity there is a continuous but blurred range of positions, and placement on this scale is difficult'.[174] Consequently, generality constitutes an imprecise criterion for determining whether or not competition is distorted.

Little may apparently be gained by concentrating not on the generality of a measure, but on the closeness of the relationship[175] between the measure and any possible anti-competitive effects.[176] Application of the latter criterion may mean that a measure may be characterized as having 'insufficiently perceptible, direct or certain effects' to be prohibited.[177]

However, a measure will not escape prohibition merely because its anti-competitive effects are only indirect.[178] For example, a rule requiring a person who places a product on the market for the first time to verify its conformity with the rules in force on that market may be prohibited by Article 30, because it may induce traders who distribute similar domestic and imported products to prefer the domestic products in regard to which verification is the responsibility not of the distributor but of the manufacturer.[179] Likewise, in relation to freedom to provide services, liberalization requirements concern not only specific rules on the pursuit of an occupation but also rules relating to the various general facilities which are of assistance in the pursuit of that occupation.[180] Thus the criterion of remoteness, like that of generality, suffers from imprecision.

Reliance on such imprecise criteria highlights the difficulties involved in the operation of Community trade-liberalization provisions. Their operation

[174] R.H. Snape, 'International Regulation of Subsidies' (1991) 14 *The World Economy* 139–63, at 143.

[175] Cf., regarding the insufficiently close link between means of subsistence and access to vocational training for denial of maintenance grants to constitute discrimination prohibited by Art. 6 EC, Slynn A. G. in Case 197/86 *Steven Malcolm Brown* v. *Secretary of State for Scotland* [1988] ECR 3205, 3230.

[176] It is not the 'quantity' of the effects (see D. Chalmers, n. 110 above, 388), but their reality which is examined. As the Court puts it, Art. 30 is not concerned with 'purely hypothetical effects' (Case C–126/91 *Schutzverband gegen Unwesen in der Wirtschaft* v. *Yves Rocher GmbH* [1993] ECR I–2361, I–2390).

[177] Case C–69/88 *H. Krantz GmbH & Co.* v. *Ontvanger der Directe Belastingen and the State (Netherlands)* [1990] ECR I–583, I–597. See also Case C–93/92 *CMC Motorradcenter GmbH* v. *Pelin Baskiciogullari* [1993] ECR I–5009, I–5021.

[178] Cf., regarding the old 'criterion of operation' theory in Australian law, according to which measures were only treated as unlawfully restricting interstate trade where the measure applied to a fact, event or thing itself forming part of trade, C. Staker, 'Free Movement of Goods in the EEC and Australia: a Comparative Study' [1990] *YEL* 209–42, at 223.

[179] Case 25/88 *Esther Renée Bouchara née Wurmser and Norlaine SA* [1989] ECR 1105, 1127. Where nationals of other Member States, but not nationals of the Member State concerned, are required to pay security for the costs of court proceedings, the requirement is contrary to Arts. 59 and 60 EC. See Case C–20/92 *Anthony Hubbard* v. *Peter Hamburger* [1993] ECR I–3777, I–3794.

[180] See, e.g., Case 305/87 *EC Commission* v. *Greece* [1989] ECR 1641.

depends on whether a State measure or the conduct of an undertaking can be characterized as having anti-competitive effects. The essential concern might be said to be with the impact of such action on the relative prices[181] of those extending their activity beyond the confines of their Member State of origin.

Identification of anti-competitive effects may be difficult in theory,[182] let alone in judicial proceedings.[183] Thus, for example, bananas have been found by the Court to constitute a sufficiently distinct market for an undertaking with a dominant position in that market to be subject to Article 86 of the Treaty,[184] while at the same time competition between bananas and other table fruit has been found to be such that national taxation favouring the former may be prohibited by Article 95 of the Treaty.[185] The difficulties involved cannot be eliminated simply by distinguishing between 'assessing (as a matter of law and policy) the current state of integration, the regulatory objective of a national measure and the Community value of this objective' and 'finding out (as an economic matter) whether a measure raises thresholds between national markets or acts as a deterrent to intra-Community trade',[186] because effective assessment of the former involves findings as to the latter.

It may be an oversimplification to conclude that the approach of the Court is purely 'casuistic', since consistency of underlying principles is discernible. What is apparent is the extent to which formulations of the requirements of a legal provision may vary according to the context in which the provision is applied. This variation may be exaggerated by the nature of preliminary rulings under Article 177 of the Treaty, in which the Court of Justice is not supposed to decide the case before the national court[187] but merely to rule on 'questions' of Community law raised before the latter.[188] However, the fact

[181] It is said that the protective effects of non-tariff barriers can be measured in terms of tariff equivalents. See Y. Bourdet and G. Hansson, 'The Economics of Trade-Policy Harmonization: with Special Reference to the Passenger Car Industry' [1987] *World Competition* 25–41, at 26.

[182] Cf. K. W. Dam, 'The Economics and Law of Price Discrimination: herein of three Regulatory Schemes' [1963] *Univ. of Chicago LRev.* 1–62. Apart from evidential problems, much may apparently depend on the theoretical approach adopted. E.g., in Joined Cases C–267 and C–268/91 *B. Keck and D. Mithouard* [1993] ECR I–6097 the French Government argued that in terms of comparative advantage theory the legislation at issue did not have anti-competitive effects (I–6105), whereas Van Gerven A. G. (I–6119) and the Commission (I–6107) maintained that in terms of strategic trade theory the legislation did have such effects.

[183] Cf., regarding differences in personal property security laws in the various provinces of Canada, M. Boodman, 'The Myth of Harmonization of Laws' (1991) 31 *AJCL* 699–724.

[184] Case 27/76 *United Brands Company and United Brands Continental BV* v. *EC Commission* [1978] ECR 207, 273.

[185] Case 184/85 *EC Commission* v. *Italy* [1987] ECR 2013, 2026.

[186] W. P. J. Wils, 'The Search for the Rule in Art. 30 EEC Much Ado About Nothing?' [1993] *ELRev.* 475–92, at 490.

[187] See, most recently, Lenz A. G. in Case 44/93 *Namur–Les assurances du crédit SA* v. *Office national du ducroire et Etat belge* [1994] ECR I–3829, I–3840–1.

[188] Compare, e.g., Case 8/74 *Procureur du Roi* v. *Benoît and Gustave Dassonville* [1974] ECR 837 with Case 2/78 *EC Commission* v. *Belgium* [1979] ECR 1761.

that adjudication by national courts may, in practice, play a greater role in determining the effective requirements of a provision in some contexts than in others does not in itself justify the conclusion that the provision concerned loses its quality as such and has been transformed into a mere 'standard'.[189]

On the other hand, the quality of the evidence put to the Court of Justice regarding possible anti-competitive effects may often be decisive.[190] Indeed, the decisiveness of such evidence may bring into doubt the proposition that there is a simple trade-off between 'administrative costs' (i.e., the costs of the proceedings) and 'error costs' (i.e., the costs resulting from adoption of a 'wrong' decision).[191] Since administrative costs may be met more easily by the party to a dispute having the greater resources, error costs may increase in direct proportion to administrative costs.

The case law which has resulted may be formally consistent with 'statist' conceptions of supranationalism. Such conceptions treat integration as tending towards the centralization of supreme power and assume that the only constraints on the tendency result from resistance of Member States. In *Cassis de Dijon*, for example, the Court treated the 'first best' solution to the problems raised in this case to be the introduction of common, i.e., centralized, rules by the Community legislature.[192] It was only because such a solution had not been provided by the Community legislature that the Court considered the compatibility of the national rules concerned with trade liberalization provisions in the Treaty.

The implication that the Court is conscious of political constraints on problem-solving through judicial development of liberalization requirements in the Treaty seems to find confirmation in *Schul*.[193] This case concerned the imposition of Dutch VAT on the importation into the Netherlands of a second-hand pleasure boat purchased by a private person resident in the Netherlands from a private person in France. Here the Court ruled that adoption of the country of destination principle for taxation purposes was a political choice for the Community legislature, though importing Member States must reduce the VAT charged on imported goods by the amount levied in the exporting Member State.

However, inadequate performance of supranationalism so conceived has, in practice, led the Court to develop its case law in response to the demands of traders, spurred by technological developments and increasing competitive

[189] W. P. J. Wils, n. 186 above.

[190] More fundamentally, 'the law's traditional taste for concreteness' may impede analysis of underlying economic issues. See A. Winters, 'Goals and Own Goals in European Trade Policy' [1992] *The World Economy* 557–74, at 573.

[191] W. P. J. Wils, n. 186 above.

[192] Case 120/78 *Rewe-Zentral AG* v. *Bundesmonopolverwaltung für Branntwein* [1979] ECR 649, 662.

[193] Case 15/81 *Gaston Schul Douane Expediteur BV* v. *Inspecteur der Invoerrechten en Accijnzen, Rosendaal* [1982] ECR 1409, 1432–3.

pressures to engage in ever more complex transnational relations.[194] As a result, the case law may have substantial consistency with network demands[195] and may facilitate 'market-integration-from-below'.[196] Indeed, the Court may have developed a capacity for learning and self-observation,[197] which self-perceptions, based on statist conceptions of supranationalism, may render more difficult in the case of an institution like the Commission.

On the other hand, it is said that judicial activity is, by its nature, highly discretionary and does not 'match the legal certainty of a truly unified product market'.[198] Whether this feature of judicial activity within the Community is held to be desirable or not is bound up with questions about the relationship between diversity and uniformity[199] and ultimately with assumptions about the proper relationship between state and market.[200] The implications of the case law for this relationship may be fundamental.

To the extent that mutual recognition of national regulations is implicitly demanded by the case law, regulatory autonomy of national institutions may formally be reconciled with reduction of trade obstacles. In substance, however, to the extent that a Member State is prohibited from imposing restrictions on Community trade, the case law entails that the Member State may not employ such restrictions to protect domestic traders against the economic consequences of their subjection to the same restrictions. In other words, the

[194] Cf., regarding the 'paradigm change in the rationality of modern law from materialisation to proceduralisation', N. Reich, 'Protection of Diffuse Interests in the EEC and the Perspective of 'Progressively Establishing' an Internal Market [1988] *Journal of Consumer Policy* 395–417, at 401.

[195] Cf., regarding the emergence of production systems based on economies of scope and the resulting opportunities for networks involving small and medium-sized enterprises, *Europe 2000: Outlook for the Development of the Community's Territory*, COM(91)452, 53.

[196] T. Heller and J. Pelkmans, 'The Federal Economy: Law and Economic Integration and the Positive State—The U.S.A. and Europe Compared in an Economic Perspective' in M. Cappelletti *et al.* (eds.), *Integration Through Law* (Berlin, 1986), vol. i, 245–412, at 320. Cf. CMEA arrangements, which, being based on state trade and obligatory quotas, apparently offered little room for flexibility and the development of ties at the level of firms (B. Kaminski, 'The Framework of Soviet-East-Central European Economic Relations in the 1990s' in R. F. Staar (ed.), *East-Central Europe and the USSR* (New York, 1991) 37–58, at 41).

[197] Cf. K.-H. Ladeur, 'European Community Institutional Reforms: Extra-National Management as an Alternative Model to Federalism' (1990/2) *LIEI* 1–21, 20.

[198] T. Heller and J. Pelkmans, n. 196 above, 359.

[199] Approaches to such questions may be couched in practical terms. E.g., the Commission may oppose such diversity of national rules as to render 'virtually impossible' determination of the equivalence of health protection provided. See the *Explanatory Memorandum to the Commission Proposal for a Directive on in Vitro Diagnostic Medical Devices*, COM(95)130, 7.

[200] The state is said to pursue its economic and social policy, while the undertaking pursues, in the framework defined by this policy, its private interests, notably the realization of profit. See Lenz A. G. in Case C–44/93 *Namur–Les assurances du crédit SA* v. *Office national du ducroire et Etat belge* [1994] ECR I–3829, I–3853 and Darmon A. G. in Case C–185/91 *Bundesanstalt für den Güterfernverkehr* v. *Gebr. Reiff GmbH & Co. KG* [1993] ECR I–5801, I–5827. The limitations of such thinking were admitted in Case C–303/88 *Italy* v. *EC Commission* [1991] ECR I–1433, I–1459. Here Van Gerven A. G. accepted that, the relationship between the public and private sectors being so close, a private holding company could not ignore social and regional considerations.

capacity of a Member State to protect domestic traders against the consequences of its inefficient regulatory activities may be limited. Hence, costs may be incurred by Member States which fail to take into account and respond to regulatory developments in other Member States, and the 'institutional competition'[201] or 'regulatory competition'[202] implied by globalization may be intensified.

The opportunity and the need for Member States to compete in the treatment of traders are implied. The opportunity for Member States derives from the fact that the application of such regulation does not prejudice the possibility for their traders to exercise the 'four freedoms' in Community trade. The opportunity may, indeed, be enhanced by the very fact that regulatory competition may counter a well known source of regulatory failure—lack of information. A 'market-driven' source of information is made available. The need for Member States to compete arises from the mobility of factors of production and increased consumer choice, though traditional consumer preferences[203] and 'friction', such as social and cultural inhibitions on labour migration, applicable to movement of such factors mean that the need should not be exaggerated.[204] States which do not compete effectively may not only face 'exit' responses by their own traders but also increased 'entry' by traders from other Member States.

2.2.3 International Trade Liberalization

Formally at least, the EC Treaty makes a link between Community trade liberalization and international trade liberalization, i.e., liberalization of trading activity between the Community and third states. The Preamble to the Treaty[205] regards the common commercial policy as a means of contributing to the progressive abolition of restrictions on world trade,[206] and Article 110 of the Treaty declares that, by establishing a customs union between themselves, Member States aim to contribute in the common interest to the harmonious development of world trade, the progressive abolition of restrictions on international trade and the lowering of customs barriers.

[201] H. Siebert and M. J. Koop, 'Institutional Competition. A Concept for Europe' [1990] *Aussenwirtschaft* 439–62.

[202] J.-M. Sun and J. Pelkmans, 'Regulatory Competition in the Single Market' [1995] *JCMS* 567.

[203] Note also 'the problem of the installed base' in V. Curzon Price, *1992: Europe's Last Chance? From Common Market to Single Market* (Institute of Economic Affairs, London 1988), 18. [204] *Ibid.* [205] 6th recital. See also Art. 3(g) EC.

[206] Art. 73b EC goes further. It seeks, in principle, the same liberalization of capital movements between Member States and third states as that applying between Member States. Cf. Art. 7 of Dir. 88/361 of 24 June 1988 ([1988] OJ L178/5) for the implementation of Art. 67 EC. To the extent that investment rules are liberal, regional agreements are regarded as more likely to be compatible with a liberal multilateral system. See A. Fishlow and S. Haggard, *The United States and the Regionalisation of the World Economy* (OECD, Paris, 1992). However, other provisions of the EC Treaty permit special restrictions on capital movements between the Community and third states. See Arts. 73c, 73f, and 73g.

The latter provision may be interpreted as opposing State interference with international trade. For example, in *Glaverbel*,[207] which concerned Belgian state aid to a flat-glass producer in Namur, it was argued that the aid at issue served to strengthen the position of the Community on export markets and to ensure its independence with regard to imports. In other words, the aid served an important project of common European interest within the meaning of Article 92(3)(b) of the Treaty, according to which aid to such a project may be considered compatible with the common market. Such thinking was said to have influenced the Community approach to the grant of aid to the coal industry. However, Advocate General Lenz responded by arguing that if, according to Article 3(g) of the Treaty, the principles of the Community included the establishment of a common commercial policy towards third states and, according to Article 110 of the Treaty, the common commercial policy served to contribute to the harmonious development of world trade, the attempt to achieve self-sufficiency and to conquer world markets could not be regarded as an important project of common European interest.[208] Thus Article 110 was treated as opposing measures by individual Member States which distorted competition in trade with third states.

When Community rather than national action is involved, Article 110 may have less impact. Although this provision is said to imply that the Community adheres to the same aims as the GATT,[209] in practice, there is reluctance to treat it as prohibiting Community action which may distort competition in international trade.[210] In other words, there is reluctance to treat Article 110 as requiring the Community unilaterally to liberalize its trade with third states.

Reciprocity

Reciprocity in international trade liberalization is only expressly mentioned in connection with Association Agreements concluded under Article 238 of the Treaty.[211] However, Article 110 refers to the harmonious development of international trade, and Community practice suggests that this reference is treated as implying a general need for reciprocity in liberalization of such trade.[212]

[207] Joined Cases 62 and 72/87 *Executif Régional Wallon and Glaverbel* v. *EC Commission* [1988] ECR 1573.

[208] *Ibid.* 1588.

[209] Joined Cases 21–24/72 *International Fruit Company NV* v. *Produktschap voor Groenten en Fruit* [1972] ECR 1219, 1227. See also Capotorti A. G. in Case 812/79 *Attorney-General* v. *Juan C. Burgoa* [1980] ECR 2787, 2815.

[210] See, e.g., Trabucchi A. G. in Case 154/73 *Firm of Kurt A. Becher* v. *Hauptzollamt Emden* [1974] ECR 19, 30.

[211] This provision describes an Association Agreement as 'involving reciprocal rights and obligations, common action and special procedures'.

[212] Warner A. G. in Case 51/75 *EMI Records Ltd* v. *CBS United Kingdom Ltd* [1976] ECR 811, 860 and 862. See also Warner A. G. in Joined Cases 37 and 38/73 *Sociaal Fonds voor de Diamantarbeiders* v. *NV Indiamex and Association de fait De Belder* [1973] ECR 1609, 1629, regarding questions of negotiating positions. Cf. Commission Press Release 28188 (19 Oct. 1988). See, generally, H. Froment Meurice, *La Dimension Extérieur du Marché Intérieur* (Paris, 1988).

In theory, unilateral liberalization may often increase welfare in the Community,[213] and it is only in 'strategic' sectors that such liberalization might be disadvantageous.[214] However, legislative enactments, such as those relating to merger control,[215] public procurement,[216] and protection of semi-conductors,[217] suggest that such theory has not been readily received by Community institutions. Rather, in the case of subsidiaries within the Community of third country financial institutions,[218] the Commission expressly sought to render their enjoyment of liberalization within the Community dependent on reciprocal treatment of Community institutions in the third country concerned,[219] though this approach was only acceptable to the Council, possibly influenced by GATT negotiations,[220] in a limited form.[221] Most recently, the Council has resolved that 'the use of non-Community resources [by Community air carriers] affords a possibility for access by third countries to the internal market which needs to be looked at in the framework of relations with those countries'.[222]

[213] R. C. Hine, 'Protection in the European Community Before and After 1992' in D. Greenaway *et al.* (eds.), *Global Protectionism* (London, 1991), 69–98, at 79. Some research suggests that a combination of 'internal' and 'external' trade liberalization may be a superior strategy to internal liberalization alone. See A. Sapir, *Regional Integration in Europe* (EC Commission Economic Papers No. 94, Brussels, 1992).

[214] J. Pelkmans, 'Europe—1992 a Handmaiden to GATT' in F. Laursen (ed.), *Europe 1992: World Partner? the International Market and the World Political Economy* (Maastricht, 1991), 125–53, at 151.

[215] Art. 24 of Reg. 4064/89 of 21 Dec. 1989 ([1989] OJ L395/1) on the control of concentration of undertakings.

[216] Art. 29 of Dir. 90/531 of 17 Sept. 1990 ([1990] OJ L297/1) on procurement procedures of entities operating in the water, transport and telecommunications sectors. The latter provision was apparently adopted because the U.S. telecommunications market was 'closed'. See *Financial Times*, 25 Feb. 1992. However, U.S. opposition led to the watering down of reciprocity requirements. See *Financial Times*, 19 June 1992. See now Dec. 93/324 of 10 May 1993 ([1993] OJ L125/54) concerning the extension of the benefit of the provisions of Dir. 90/531 in respect of the United States of America.

[217] Dec. 90/510 of 9 Oct. 1990 ([1990] OJ L285/29) on the extension of the legal protection of topographies of semi-conductor products to persons from certain third states and territories and Dec. 90/511 of 9 Oct. 1990 ([1990] OJ L285/31) on the extension of the legal protection of topographies of semi-conductor products to persons from certain third states and territories.

[218] Prot. 17, concerning Art. 34, to the EEA Agreement envisages EC–EFTA cooperation in relation to the enactment of rules governing such subsidiaries.

[219] [1988] OJ C84/1.

[220] *Agence Europe*, No. 5375 (22 Nov. 1990).

[221] Art. 9 of Dir. 89/646 of 15 Dec. 1989 ([1989] OJ L124/16) on the co-ordination of laws, regulations, and administrative provisions relating to the taking up and pursuit of the business of credit institutions. See also Art. 4 of Dir. 90/618 of 8 Nov. 1990 ([1990] OJ L330/44) amending, particularly as regards motor vehicle insurance, Dirs. 73/239 and 88/357 which concern the co-ordination of the laws, regulations, and administrative provisions relating to direct insurance other than life insurance; Art. 8 of Dir. 90/619 of 8 Nov. 1990 ([1990] OJ L330/50) on the co-ordination of laws, regulations, and administrative provisions relating to life assurance, laying down provisions to facilitate the effective exercise of freedom to provide services and amending Dir. 79/267; and Art. 7(5) of Dir. 93/22 of 10 May 1993 ([1993] OJ L141/27) on investment services in the securities field.

[222] Council Resolution of 19 June 1995 ([1995] OJ C169/3) on relocation in air transport.

More generally, the Community should, according to the Commission, insist that its industrial trading partners match its own contribution to the smooth functioning of the international trading system according to GATT principles. Partly, it is reciprocal liberalization that is demanded.[223] At the same time, managed trade may be sought in certain sectors. Thus the adoption of measures in concert with third states is envisaged along the lines of the Organization for Economic Cooperation and Development (OECD) agreement on steel, which guarantees 'solidarity' between the Community and the other producer countries in restructuring the industry, or the GATT Multifibre Arrangement for textiles.[224]

Therefore, the suitability of Community trade liberalization requirements for application to international trade might be thought to depend on their capacity to secure reciprocity. While ideas of specific reciprocity or reciprocity by reference to outcome may be incompatible with the nature of Community trade liberalization, a highly developed form of generalized[225] or 'diffuse'[226] reciprocity[227] might be taken to be the essence of such liberalization.[228] Certainly, the latter is not treated as being such as entirely to exclude ideas of reciprocity[229] or, as the Court of Justice has put it, an 'equilibrium between advantages and obligations flowing from . . . adherence to the Community'.[230]

On the other hand, Community trade liberalization requirements are also the essence of the 'new legal order' created by the EC Treaty,[231] which, in turn,

[223] In *Completing the Internal Market*, COM(85)310, 8 the Commission maintained that 'the commercial identity of the Community must be consolidated so that our trading partners will not be given the benefit of a wider market without themselves making similar concessions'. Such thinking may be particularly problematic in relation to developing countries. See Club de Bruxelles, *North-South: The EC Development Policy* (Brussels, 1991).

[224] *A Community Strategy to Develop Europe's Industry*, COM(81)639, 9.

[225] Cf., regarding the difference between such reciprocity and specific reciprocity or reciprocity by reference to outcome, W. Sandholtz and J. Zysman, '1992: Recasting the European Bargain' (1989/90) 42 *World Politics* 94–128 and, regarding the 'overall reciprocity' favoured by GATT, A. de la Torre and M. R. Kelly, *Regional Trade Arrangements* (IMF Occasional Paper No. 93, Washington, 1992), 46.

[226] Cf. G. N. Yannopoulos, 'Trade Policy Issues on the Completion of the Internal Market' in G. N. Yannopoulos (ed.), *Europe and America, 1992* (Manchester, 1991), 9–23.

[227] A distinction might be made between reciprocity that is 'qualitative' and that which is 'quantitative', in the sense in which these terms are used by J. Tinbergen, *International Economic Integration* (2nd edn., Amsterdam, 1965), 58.

[228] Cf. G. Wils, 'The Concept of Reciprocity in EEC Law: An Exploration into these Realms' (1991) 28 *CMLRev*. 245–74, at 263. According to the ECJ itself in Case 6/64 *Flaminio Costa* v. *ENEL* [1964] ECR 585, 594, the Community legal system had been accepted by Member States 'on a basis of reciprocity'.

[229] See, e.g., Mancini A. G. in Joined Cases 286/82 and 26/83 *Graziana Luisi and Giuseppe Carbone* v. *Ministero del Tesoro* [1984] ECR 377, 419.

[230] Case 39/72 *EC Commission* v. *Italy* [1973] ECR 101, 116. Such equilibrium was seen by the Court as being closely bound up with the equality principle, though operation of the principle cannot be dependent on the existence of a specific reciprocal agreement between Member States. See Case C–20/92 *Anthony Hubbard* v. *Peter Hamburger* [1993] ECR I–3777, I–3795.

[231] Case 26/62 *NV Algemeine Transport-en expeditie Onderneming Van Gend en Loos* v. *Nederlandse Administratie der Belastingen* [1963] ECR 1, 23.

has an independent capacity to create rights and obligations for economic actors. It is this capacity which enables Community trade-liberalization requirements to go beyond the simple prohibition of discrimination between imports and domestic products or between nationals of the host state and nationals of other states,[232] or between the latter.[233] In these circumstances, a 'public good' analogy, according to which reciprocity depends on processes[234] designed to prevent 'free riding',[235] might seem applicable to Community trade liberalization requirements.

However, such requirements are not only so demanding as to entail serious intrusion into policy making, the implication being that political constraints might set limits to what could be achieved by way of reciprocal liberalization between the Community and third states.[236] Their operational content is also so variable that an essential characteristic lies in their judicial determination in individual cases.

Their resulting potential for dynamism[237] and, at the same time, their failure to secure full uniformity of treatment for traders within the Community mean that they may provide 'no definite yardstick' by reference to which the appropriate treatment for third State traders can be determined.[238] Indeed, legislation may be found necessary to protect Community traders against being disadvantaged in relation to third State traders.[239]

Hence, extension by analogy of Community trade liberalization requirements to trade between the Community as such and third states, i.e., achieve-

[232] Cf. Art. 37(1) of the Polish Agreement. It provides that, in the case of Polish workers legally employed in the territory of a Member State, that state must treat such workers equally with its own nationals, as regards working conditions, remuneration, or dismissal.

[233] Cf. Art. 113 of the Polish Agreement. It provides that, in the fields covered by this Agreement and without prejudice to any special provisions contained therein, Poland must not discriminate between Member States, or their companies or firms, and the arrangements applied by the Community in respect of Poland shall not give rise to discrimination between Polish nationals or companies or firms. Note the problems raised by a Polish plan to divide between Fiat, General Motors, and Volkswagen the quota of duty-free car imports from the Community (*Financial Times*, 26 Feb. 1992).

[234] Cf. L. Tsoukalis, *The New European Economy: The Politics and Economics of Integration* (Oxford, 1991), 272. Emphasis on 'process reciprocity' in the context of international trade is said to reflect the increasing significance of structural rather than regulatory barriers to trade. See, e.g., Y. S. Lanneaux, 'International Trade: Joint Report of the United States–Japan Working Group on the Structural Impediments Initiative' (1991) 32 *Harvard International Law Journal* 245–54.

[235] Cf., regarding opposition of the GATT system to free riding, A. Ahnlid, 'Free or Forced Riders? Small States in the International Political Economy: The Example of Sweden' (1992) 27 *Co-operation and Conflict* 241–76.

[236] Cf., regarding the question of liberalizing the activities of subsidiaries of banks from third states, L. Tsoukalis, n. 234 above, 273.

[237] The concept of *reciprocité pondérée* (see R. Schwok in J. Jamar and H. Wallace (eds.), *EEC–EFTA: More Than Just Good Friends?* (Bruges, 1988), 353) may be an unworkable substitute and may, indeed, be more of a statement of the problem than a solution thereto.

[238] Cf. Warner A. G. in Case 30/79 *Land Berlin* v. *Wigei, Wild-Geflügel-Eier-Import GmbH & Co. KG* [1980] ECR 151, 171.

[239] *Ibid.* 164.

ment of 'mirror' reciprocity,[240] would be problematic.[241] A comparatively liberal regime in a third state would mean that traders therefrom, being entitled to free competition in extending throughout the Community what they were free to do in their own state, might enjoy greater freedom of trade within the Community than traders from Member States. More particularly, they would enjoy greater freedom of trade within any given Member State than nationals of that Member state trading domestically. The result would be distortions of competition radically incompatible with the undistorted competition sought by Community trade liberalization.

Logically, reciprocal extension of Community trade-liberalization requirements to international trade can only be achieved, if it is done in such a way as to cover trade between each and every state involved. Such an extension necessitates adoption of common rules applicable to such trade and establishment of a judicial system capable of maintaining the common quality of those rules and the essence of the trade liberalization requirements embodied therein.[242]

These necessities cannot easily be met in respect of trade between the Community and a single third state. Community liberalization depends on the work of institutions, such as the Commission and the Court of Justice, which are independent of the Member States. Either the extension of such liberalization must apply to a group of third states, so that they can create equivalent bodies, or the jurisdiction of the Commission and Court of Justice must be accepted by third states individually with consequences for sovereignty comparable with some of the most important constitutional consequences of Union membership. As Commission President Delors put it,[243] there must either be a 'two-pillar' framework or simple extension of Community rules[244] to interested third states.[245]

240 See, regarding such reciprocity, V. Curzon Price, *1992: Europe's Last Chance? From Common Market to Single Market* (Institute of Economic Affairs, London, 1988), 40.

241 The problems may have been less apparent when early Association Agreements, such as that with Greece and the Yaoundé Convention, were concluded.

242 EEA arrangements may be regarded as securing 'effective and comparable access' for Community undertakings. See the Explanatory Memorandum to Commission Proposal of 20 Dec. 1993 for a Council Dec. concerning the extension of the benefit of the provisions of Dir. 90/531 in respect of Austria, Finland, Iceland, Liechtenstein, Norway and Sweden, COM(93)667.

243 EP Debs. No. 2-373, 76, 17 Jan. 1989.

244 As in the Agreement on Civil Aviation between Norway, Sweden, and the EC ([1992] OJ L200/21).

245 Such thinking might be thought to have some basis in GATT obligations. Art. XXIV(1) of GATT provides that the General Agreement applies to a customs territory and that 'each customs territory shall, exclusively for the purposes of the territorial application of this agreement, be treated as though it were a contracting party'. This implies that it is only a country or a customs union (i.e. a customs territory) which is capable of entering into an agreement pursuant to Art. XXIV to form a free trade area. See, generally, F. Schoneveld, 'The EEC and Free Trade Agreements: Stretching the Limits of GATT Exceptions to Non-Discriminatory Trade' [1992] *JWT* 59–78, at 76. In practice, however, the Community and many of its trade partners have taken a

Such considerations may explain why the EC Treaty is interpreted as not generally entailing extension of Community trade liberalization requirements to trade with third states.[246] In essence, reciprocity concerns may demand separation of Community trade liberalization from international trade liberalization.[247]

'Separate Development' and the Search for Uniformity

Separation of Community trade liberalization from international trade liberalization[248] means that the latter is left to depend on the requirements of the common customs tariff (CCT)[249] and the common commercial policy.[250] It is in accordance with these requirements that interference with international trading activity by Member States is assessed.[251] The apparent implication is made that a common commercial policy should govern relations between the Community as an independent state-like entity and third states.[252] In practice,

very liberal view of the GATT free trade area exception to the general rule that there should be no discrimination between the treatment of goods originating in any GATT Contracting Party. Most other GATT Contracting Parties have acquiesced in this view. See now the Understanding on the Interpretation of Art. XXIV of GATT, annexed to the Agreement establishing the World Trade Organization.

246 Thus, e.g., Art. 30 only applies to restrictions on imports affecting trade between Member States. See Case 51/75 *EMI Records Ltd* v. *CBS United Kingdom Ltd* [1976] ECR 811, 845. Accordingly, the authorities competent to settle the terms of licences of right may grant or refuse the licensee authorization to import the patented product from a third country without infringing this provision. See Case C–191/90 *Generics (UK) Ltd, Harris Pharmaceuticals Ltd* v. *Smith Kline and French Laboratories Limited* [1992] ECR I–5335, I–5374. Cf., regarding fiscal discrimination, Case 148/77 *H. Hansen jun. & O.C. Balle GmbH & Co.* v. *Hauptzollamt Flensburg* [1978] ECR 1787, 1808–9.

247 According to the Resolution of the European Parliament of 13 June 1985 on consolidating the internal market ([1985] OJ C175/229), para. 6, 'if a Community-wide market is to be established, it must also be capable of defending itself'.

248 See, e.g., Opinion 1/94 *(Competence of the Community to conclude international agreements on services and the protection of international property)* [1994] ECR I–5267.

249 A uniform nomenclature was established by Reg. 950/68 of 28 June 1968 ([1968] JO L172/1) on the common customs tariff, which was replaced by Reg. 2658/87 of 23 July 1987 ([1987] OJ L265/1) on the tariff and statistical nomenclature and on the common customs tariff. There are annual reviews, the results of which are published in the OJ. Uniform rules relating to valuation and origin were introduced respectively by Reg. 803/68 of 27 June 1968 ([1968] JO L148/6) on the valuation of goods for customs purposes, which was replaced by Reg. 1224/80 of 28 May 1980 ([1980] OJ L134/1) on the valuation of goods for customs purposes, and Reg. 802/68 of 27 June 1968 ([1968] JO L148/1) on the common definition of the concept of the origin of goods.

250 Common rules for exports are laid down in Reg. 2603/69 of 20 Dec. 1969 ([1969] JO L326/39), and common rules for imports are laid down by Reg. 3285/94 of 22 Dec. 1994 ([1994] OJ L349/53). In the case of state-trading countries special rules for imports are laid down by Reg. 519/94 of 7 Mar. 1994 ([1994] OJ L67/89).

251 Case 340/87 *EC Commission* v. *Italy* [1989] ECR 1483, 1513. See also Case 70/77 *Simmenthal SpA.* v. *Amministrazione delle Finanze dello stato* [1978] ECR 1453, 1470.

252 Limited steps are also being taken towards development of a common policy regarding immigration from third states. Art. 100c EC, as amended by the TEU, provides for the introduction of a common policy regarding third country nationals who must be in possession of a visa when crossing the external borders of Member States.

this implication is reflected in the way that the Court of Justice treats GATT rules as applying to trade between the Community and third states but not to trade within the Community.[253] It may also be reflected in the 'power-oriented, mercantilist perception of the liberal GATT rules as reciprocal concessions'[254] which the Community is said to exhibit in relation to issues of international trade liberalization.[255] While supranationalism (in the sense of the independence of institutions such as the Commission and Court from Member States[256]) may play a vital role in securing Community trade liberalization, conceptions of supranationalism which favour centralization of decision-making power within the Community may hinder achievement of international trade liberalization.[257]

A formal basis for such practice might be found in the EC Treaty. Article 113(1) provides that, after the transitional period for establishment of the common market has ended, the common commercial policy shall be based on uniform principles, particularly with regard to changes in tariff rates, the conclusion of tariff and trade agreements, and the achievement of uniformity in measures of liberalization, export policy,[258] and measures to protect trade such as those to be taken in case of dumping or subsidies. The Court of Justice

[253] Case 10/61 *EC Commission* v. *Italy* [1962] ECR 1, 10–11. See also Case 266/81 *Società Italiana per l'Oleodotto Transalpino (SIOT)* v. *Ministero delle Finanze* [1983] ECR 731, 780. The greater willingness of the Court to recognize the direct applicability of the Portuguese Free Trade Agreement (Case 104/81 *Hauptzollamt Mainz* v. *C. A. Kupferberg & Cie KG* [1982] ECR 3641, 3665) than of GATT (Joined Cases 21 to 24/72 *International Fruit Company NV* v. *Produktschap voor Groenten en Fruit* [1972] ECR 1219, 1227–8 and Case 280/93 *Germany* v. *EU Council* [1994] ECR I–4908, I–5072–3) is not readily explicable by reference to the terms of each Agreement interpreted by the Court. The explanation may be that the former was concluded by the Community rather than the Member States and thus constituted part of the common commercial policy. Certainly, where Community legislation refers to GATT provisions, the ECJ may be more willing to give effect to these provisions. See Gulmann A. G. (*ibid.*, I–5027–8). Cf. M. Waelbroeck, 'Les effets internes des accords internationaux conclus par la Communauté économique européenne' in *Le Droit des Peuples à Disposer d'eux-mêmes Mélanges Offerts à Charles Chaumont* (Paris, 1984), 579–91.

[254] E.-U. Petersmann, 'Strengthening the Domestic Legal Framework of the GATT Multilateral Trade System: Possibilities and Problems of Making GATT Rules Effective in Domestic Legal Systems' in E.-U. Petersmann and M. Hilf (eds.), *The New GATT Round of Multilateral Trade Negotiations* (Deventer, 1991), 33–113, 68–9.

[255] See, most recently, Gulmann A. G. in Case C–280/93 *Germany* v. *EC Council* [1994] ECR I–4973, I–5020–6.

[256] See, regarding Commission independence, Art. 157(2) EC. See, regarding that of the Court, Art. 167 thereof and Arts. 2 and 3 of the Prot. on the Statute of the ECJ.

[257] Cf., regarding the legal capacity of the Community institutions to prescribe the attitudes to be taken by Member States 'in their external dealings', Opinion 1/94 *Competence of the Community to conclude international agreements on services and the protection of international property* [1994] ECR I–5267, I–5411–2.

[258] Art. 112(1) EC provided that, without prejudice to obligations undertaken by them within the framework of other international organizations, Member States should, before the end of the transitional period, have progressively harmonized the systems whereby they granted aid for exports to third states, to the extent necessary to ensure the elimination of distortions of competition.

deduces from this provision that a single trading system with third states constitutes one of the fundamental objectives of the common market.[259]

For example, where a product is classified under different tariff headings in different Member States, the principle of the uniformity of the CCT is breached and, in accordance with the demands of the customs union, the difference in classifications must be eliminated.[260] Such uniformity is designed not only to counter the risk of trade deflection and distortion of competition within the Community[261] but also to ensure equal tariff treatment[262] for third country importers.[263] This approach appears consistent with Article XXIV(8)(a) of GATT, which entails that barriers eliminated in Community trade must be replaced by substantially identical barriers in relation to international trade.

However, emphasis is placed on aligning conditions of competition between traders in the different Member States.[264] It is not equality between third state traders and Community traders but equality between the former which is entailed.[265] Thus CCT duties are fixed at such a level as to take account of the position of economic sectors in the Community,[266] and the needs of Community user industries may justify suspension of such duties under Article 28 of the EC Treaty.[267] According to this provision, any autonomous

[259] See, e.g., Case 135/79 *Gedelfi Großeinkauf GmbH & Co. KG* v. *Hauptzollamt Hamburg-Jonas* [1980] ECR 1713, 1729.

[260] Case 40/84 *Casteels Pvba* v. *EC Commission* [1985] ECR 667, 672.

[261] See also Joined Cases 37 and 38/73 *Sociaal Fonds voor de Diamantarbeiders* v. *NV Indiamex and Association de fait De Belder* [1973] ECR 1609, 1622 and Case 70/77 *Simmenthal SpA* v. *Amministrazione delle Finanze dello stato* [1978] ECR 1453, 1476–7. See, regarding the need to avoid distortions of competition which favour traders from third states, Case 30/79 *Land Berlin* v. *Wigei, Wild-Geflügel-Eier-Import GmbH & Co. KG* [1980] ECR 151, 164.

[262] Though it may be a formal equality, based on CCT classifications rather than real questions of competition, which is entailed. See, e.g., Case 168/78 *EC Commission* v. *France* [1980] ECR 347, 368.

[263] Trabucchi A. G. in Case 8/73 *Hauptzollamt Bremerhaven* v. *Massey-Ferguson GmbH* [1973] ECR 897, 916.

[264] Joined Cases 267 to 269/81 *Amministrazione delle Finanze dello Stato* v. *Società Petrolifera Italiana SpA (SPI) and SpA Michelin Italiana (SAMI)* [1983] ECR 801, 828. See, generally, J. Bourrinet and M. Torelli, *Les Relations Extérieurs de la CEE* (Paris, 1980).

[265] Cf. Darmon A. G. in Case C–432/92 *Regina* v. *Minister of Agriculture, Fisheries and Food, ex parte S. P. Anastasiou (Pissouri) Ltd* [1994] ECR I–3087, I–3111.

[266] Case 248/80 *KG in Firma Gebrüder Glunz* v. *Hauptzollamt Hamburg-Waltershof* [1982] ECR 197, 213. A completed common commercial policy is said to be necessary to maintain equal chances for Community undertakings within and outside the Community with undertakings or products from third states. See P. VerLoren van Themaat, 'The Contribution to the Establishment of the Internal Market by the Case Law of the Court of Justice of the European Communities' in R. Bieber *et al.* (eds.), *1992: One European Market* (Baden-Baden, 1988), 109–20, at 111.

[267] Case 58/85 *Ethicon* v. *Hauptzollamt Itzehoe* [1986] ECR 1141, 1145. See, e.g., Reg. 3640/92 of 14 Dec. 1992 ([1992] OJ L375/9) temporarily suspending the autonomous common customs tariff duties on a number of products intended for the construction, maintenance, and repair of aircraft. See, most recently, Reg. 1556/95 of 29 June 1995 ([1995] OJ L152/1) temporarily suspending the autonomous Common Customs Tariff duty on certain industrial products (in the microelectronics and related sectors).

alteration or suspension of such duties shall be decided by the Council on the basis of a Commission proposal.

A narrow definition of the commercial policy is not necessarily entailed. For example, introduction of the CCT has been taken to imply a prohibition on the unilateral introduction by Member States of charges having equivalent effect to customs duties and on the raising of existing charges having such an effect.[268] Again, the rules of origin in Regulation 802/68[269] have been found to demand a real and objective distinction between raw materials and processed products. The requirement that virtually all components of a product must be of Community origin, even those of little value which are of no use in themselves unless they are incorporated into a whole, would amount to a repudiation of the very substance of these rules and, hence, would not be permissible.[270]

Moreover, treatment of such issues appears to have evolved along with developments in Community practice and international trade relations generally. Thus in 1973 the Court of Justice found that in the interests of legal certainty, particularly during the transitional period, the Council could lawfully adopt customs valuation legislation[271] on the basis of Article 235 of the Treaty.[272] The latter provides for the Council to adopt measures necessary to attain, in the course of operation of the common market, a Community objective where no other Treaty Article provides for their adoption. However, in 1979 the Court ruled that a restrictive interpretation of the concept of the common commercial policy would risk causing disturbances in intra-Community trade by reason of the disparities which would then exist in certain sectors of trade relations with third states. Hence, the policy could aim at the regulation of markets for certain products rather than mere liberalization.[273] The implications became clearer when the Court subsequently found that legislation implementing the general system of tariff preferences for developing countries[274] was invalid, because it was based on Article 235

[268] Joined Cases 37 and 38/73 *Sociaal Fonds voor de Diamantarbeiders* v. *NV Indiamex and Association de fait De Belder* [1973] ECR 1609, 1623. See also, regarding the importance of allowing speedy checks on customs clearance, Case 317/81 *Howe and Bainbridge BV* v. *Oberfinanzdirektion Frankfurt am Main* [1982] ECR 3257, 3264. On the other hand, application of the CCT is entrusted to Member States, which designate the authorities to undertake tariff classification and decide their training (*ibid.*, 3625). As regards simplifying clearance through customs of goods contained in travellers' personal luggage coming from non-member states, see Case 278/82 *Rewe-Handelsgesellschaft Nord mbH and Rewe-Market Herbert Kureit* v. *Hauptzollamter Flensburg Itzehoe and Lübeck-West* [1984] ECR 721, 756.

[269] Of 27 June 1968 ([1968] JO L148/1) on the common definition of the concept of the origin of goods.

[270] Case 114/78 *Yoshida GmbH* v. *Industrie-und Handelskammer Kassel* [1979] ECR 151, 168.

[271] Reg. 803/68 of 27 June 1968 ([1968] OJ L148/6) on the valuation of goods for customs purposes.

[272] Case 8/73 *Hauptzollamt Bremerhaven* v. *Massey-Ferguson GmbH* [1973] ECR 897, 908.

[273] Opinion 1/78 *(International Agreement on Natural Rubber)* [1979] ECR 2871, 2913.

[274] Reg. 3599/85 of 17 Dec. 1985 ([1985] OJ L352/1) applying generalized tariff preferences for 1986 in respect of certain industrial products originating in developing countries and Reg. 3600/85 of 17 Dec. 1985 ([1985] OJ L352/107) applying generalized tariff preferences for 1986 to textile products originating in developing countries.

rather than Article 113, having regard to the 'progressively stronger' link between trade and development.[275]

However, in spite of this evolution in the case law, the reduction of obstacles to international trade remains dependent on achievement of uniformity in the treatment of such trade through harmonization. This is the very kind of situation which was found to be generally unsuitable for securing reduction of obstacles to Community trade[276] and led the Commission to adopt its 'new approach' to harmonization.[277]

Given the limited harmonization achieved or, indeed, achievable within the framework of the common commercial policy, such dependence means that serious obstacles to international trade may remain. To be marketed within the Community products from third states must not only satisfy Community law requirements to be put into free circulation under Article 10(1) of the Treaty.[278] They must also satisfy whatever requirements are stipulated for the marketing of the kind of products concerned by Community harmonization acts or, in the absence of such acts, by the law of the Member State where they are put into free circulation. Thus, for example, the mere fact that a product from a third state complies with the formalities necessary for it to be put into free circulation in a Member State does not entail that it can be marketed, even in principle, in that Member State under a trade mark registered there by another undertaking.[279]

The consequence is that traders from third states, like domestic traders within a Member State, may be disadvantaged in relation to those involved in Community trade. The disadvantages may arise where legal requirements in their own state differ from those laid down in Community harmonization acts

[275] Case 45/86 *EC Commission* v. *EC Council* [1987] ECR 1493, 1521. See, similarly, regarding trade in services, Opinion 1/94 *(Competence of the Community to conclude international agreements on services and the protection of international property)* [1994] ECR I–5267, I–5401. However, while liberalization of trade in services is treated by Art. 59 EC as implying free movement for providers of services and is viewed by the ECJ as also implying free movement for recipients (Joined Cases 186/82 and 26/83 *Graziana Luisi and Giuseppe Carbone* v. *Ministero del Tesoro* [1984] ECR 377), an international agreement concerning movement of such persons is not treated as falling within the scope of Art. 113 of the Treaty ([1994] ECR I–5267, I–5401).

[276] Fundamentally there may be much in common with the question whether in 'less developed countries' liberalization should precede or follow stabilization. See S. Edwards, *On the Sequencing of Structural Reforms* (OECD Working Paper No. 70, Paris, 1989).

[277] *Technical Harmonization and Standards: A New Approach* COM(85)19. See also the Council Resolution of 7 May 1985 ([1985] OJ C136/1) on a new approach to technical harmonization and standards.

[278] These formalities are laid down by Dir. 79/695 of 24 July 1979 ([1979] OJ L205/19) on the harmonization of procedures for the release of foods for free circulation and Dir. 82/57 of 17 Dec. 1981 ([1982] OJ L28/38) laying down certain provisions for implementing Dir. 79/695. See, regarding Art. 10(1) itself, sect. 2.2.2 above.

[279] Case 51/75 *EMI Records Ltd* v. *CBS United Kingdom Ltd* [1976] ECR 811, 846. Warner A. G. tended to obscure this point by apparently merging questions under Art. 30 with those under Art. 36 (*ibid.* 860). See now Reg. 3842/86 of 1 Dec. 1986 ([1986] OJ L357/1) laying down measures to prohibit the release for free circulation of counterfeit goods.

or, in the absence of such acts, in national measures enacted by the Member State in which the products are to be put into free circulation.

The response of third states[280] may be to harmonize their law[281] with that applying within the Community.[282] Where no Community acts have been adopted, harmonization by third states may not be feasible. International traders will need to satisfy the national legal requirements of the particular Member State in which they wish to put their products into free circulation. The fact that their state may have harmonized its legal requirements with those of a different Member State will not assist them.

Such problems, which are inherent in the inverse proportionality between liberalization requirements and need for harmonization, are exaggerated by the particular problems of developing a common commercial policy. Differences in national policies[283] or national conditions[284] within the Community may impede development of this policy.[285] At the same time, its development may

[280] Even the old Soviet Union apparently engaged in such harmonization. See the Opinion of the Economic and Social Committee of 25 Jan. 1995 ([1995] OJ C102/40) on relations between the European Union and Russia, Ukraine, and Belarus, para. 2.1.5.

[281] The 'force exerted by a foreign model on domestic policy can be of two types: push and pull'. See G. Majone, 'Cross-National Sources of Regulatory Policy-Making in Europe and the United States', EUI Working Paper SPS No. 90/6 (Florence, 1990), 47. The force exerted in the present context apparently tends to be of the 'pull' type.

[282] The Community may have reason to be sympathetic to such action. In *A Community Strategy to Develop Europe's Industry*, COM(81)639, 18 the Commission expressed the view that the promotion of norms and standards for a larger market and even the world market might turn out to be advantageous for European industry in sectors where it was in a relatively strong position. On the other hand, there might be concern that Community harmonization would unduly assist traders from third states. See, e.g., *Commission Activities and Community Requirements for the Automobile Industry in 1981–1983*, COM(83)633, 21.

[283] E.g., the German authorities invoked provisions of a bilateral agreement with the USA as a reason not to apply certain Community law rules concerning public procurement. As a result, this and similar agreements between Member States and the USA are excluded from Dec. 91/679 of 6 Dec. 1993 ([1993] OJ L317/61) authorizing the automatic renewal or maintenance in force of provisions governing matters covered by the common commercial policy contained in the friendship, trade, and navigation treaties and in trade agreements concluded between Member States and third countries. See the Commission Joint Reply by Sir Leon Brittan to Written Questions E–2335/93 by Mr Georgios Romeos and E–2392/93 by Mr Sotiris Kostopoulos ([1994] OJ C46/49).

[284] It has been argued that the inadequacy of Community resources to reduce regional disparities explained the 'regionalization' of the common commercial policy and the frequent resort to Art. 115 EC. See J. Bourgeois, 'Les Engagements Internationaux de la Communauté et leurs Implications sur le Plan Interne' in P. Demaret (ed.), *Relations Extérieurs de la Communauté Européenne et Marché Intérieur: Aspects Juridiques et Fonctionnels* (Bruges, 1987).

[285] L. Tsoukalis, n. 234 above, 273. It is not only within GATT practice (see C.-D. Ehlermann and G. Campogrande, 'Rules on Services in the EEC: A Model for Negotiating World-Wide Rules?' in E.-U. Petersmann and M. Hilf (eds.), *The New GATT Round of Multilateral Trade Negotiations* (Deventer, 1991) 481–98, 486) that the 'old approach' is maintained. Such differences may be rendered all the more significant by special ties between some Member States and their colonies or ex-colonies. See, e.g., the Prot. on the Canary Islands and Ceuta and Melilla, annexed to the Portuguese and Spanish Act of Accession. See, regarding such ties generally, H. Dicke and R. J. Langhammer, *The Institutional Framework and External Dimension of the EC Internal Market* (Kiel Working Paper No. 453, Kiel, 1990), 27–8. Particular problems also arose in connection with the division of Germany. See the Prot. on German Internal Trade, annexed to the EC Treaty.

be prejudiced by the impact of various other Community policies in the formulation of which third states may have played no part and the content of which may be unfavourable to their traders. For example, in formulating the common agricultural policy, the Community institutions must take into account, where necessary, the principle of 'Community preference' in favour of Community farmers, which is one of the principles of the Treaty and which in agricultural matters is laid down in Article 44(2).[286] This provision stated that minimum import prices for agricultural products, which Member States might impose during the transitional period, should not be imposed in such a way as to form an obstacle to the development of a natural preference between Member States.

In fact, development of the common commercial policy depends on the interaction of various policies. Sometimes agreements with third states are concluded in execution of a policy fixed in advance, sometimes that policy is defined by the agreements themselves.[287] In practice, however, while there may be concern to avoid the risk of retaliation,[288] demands of other Community policies are likely to prevail over international trade-liberalization considerations.[289] For example, the Treaty may permit the Community to adopt acts restricting international trade, where the adoption of such an act is required by the risk of a serious disturbance endangering objectives of the common agricultural policy.[290] The result is said to be that the common commercial policy has become 'sectoralized by protectionist trade restrictions for the benefit of agricultural, textiles, steel and other lobbies'.[291]

Underlying attitudes also seem to affect interpretation of Community acts which are adopted in implementation of the common commercial policy. Thus, for example, while a licensing system applicable to trade between Member States may be contrary to Articles 30—34 of the Treaty,[292] such a system is not

[286] Case 5/67 *W. Beus GmbH & Co.* v. *Hauptzollamt München* [1968] ECR 83, 98.

[287] Opinion 1/75 *(Draft Understanding on a Local Cost Standard)* [1975] ECR 1355, 1363. See also Opinion 1/94 *(Competence of the Community to conclude international agreements on services and the protection of international property)* [1994] ECR I–5267, I–5398.

[288] Joined Cases 154, 205, 206, 226, and 228, 263, and 264/78, 39, 31, 83, and 85/79 *SpA Ferriera Valsabbia* v. *EC Commission* [1980] ECR 907, 1015–6 and Case 258/80 *SpA Metallurgica Rumi* v. *EC Commission* [1982] ECR 487, 505.

[289] A prot. to an agreement cannot derogate from a fundamental EC Treaty provision, such as Art. 43(2), which provides for establishment of common organizations of agricultural markets. See Case C–280/93 *Germany* v. *EU Council* [1994] ECR I–4908, I–5075.

[290] Case 112/80 *Firma Anton Dürbeck* v. *Hauptzollamt Frankfurt am Main-Flughafen* [1981] ECR 1095, 1119–1120. See also Mayras A. G. in Case 90/77 *Hellmut Stimming KG* v. *EC Commission* [1978] ECR 995, 1016.

[291] E.-U. Petersmann, 'GATT Law as International Legal Framework of the European Free Trade System' in O. Jacot-Guillarmod (ed.), *L'Avenir du libre-échange en Europe: vers un Espace économique européen* (Zürich 1990) 111–29, at 118.

[292] Joined Cases 51 to 54/71 *International Fruit Company NV* v. *Produktschap voor Groenten en Fruit* [1971] ECR 1107, 1116–7.

affected by the prohibition of quantitative restrictions on exports to third states[293] in Article 1 of Regulation 2603/69.[294]

Traders from third states may respond to such limitations to international trade liberalization by establishing subsidiaries or taking over companies in a Member State where they trade on a large scale.[295] Indeed, the Court of Justice considers that imposition of the CCT on goods from third states may 'act as useful incentive' to secure transfer of their production to the Community and that, therefore, exemptions from the tariff should be strictly construed.[296] However, to the extent that traders feel compelled so to transfer their production because of legal obstacles, a trade distortion may be involved. In any case, such a course of action may not be a realistic option for most traders from third states.

That the concomitant of such obstacles to international trade is protection of Community traders receives little attention. According to the Commission, pressing the European market towards internal unity, thereby reaffirming its separate identity *vis-à-vis* the outside world, would help to restore confidence. As the aim was to expand European industry in a way that would create productive employment in the Community, steps must be taken to ensure that it would indeed be European companies that would effectively and in the first place benefit from measures to develop industry within the Community.[297] Such was said to be the thrust of an early Commission document[298] on the internal market.[299] In other words, association of Community trade liberalization with limitations to international trade liberalization may sometimes be thought to be desirable.

The consequences of tolerating, let alone espousing, the protectionism entailed may become increasingly serious. To the extent that completion of the internal market implies scale economies for Community traders, the latter, in the absence of effective exposure to competition from outside the

[293] Jacobs A. G. in Case C–367/89 *Ministre des Finances* v. *Aime Richardt* [1991] ECR I–4621, I–4640.

[294] Of 20 Dec. 1969 ([1969] JO L324/25) establishing common rules for exports. Similarly, Member States may impose a charge for carrying out customs inspections required in connection with the CCT, whereas they may not do so in the case of products benefitting from Community trade liberalization. See Case 340/87 *EC Commission* v. *Italy* [1989] ECR 1483. They may also impose a 'consumption tax' on products from third states. See Joined Cases C–228/90–C–234/90, C–339/90 and C–353/90 *Simba SpA* v. *Italian Foreign Ministry* [1992] ECR I–3713.

[295] F. Capelli, 'Les Relations CE/Etats-Unis et la Réalisation du Marché Intérieur' in J. Schwarze (ed.), *The External Relations of the European Community, in Particular EC–US Relations* (Baden-Baden, 1989), 139–43, 142. The effects of tariffs may be mitigated by the internalizing ability of transnational enterprises. See P. Robson and I. Wooton, 'The Transnational Enterprise and Regional Economic Integration' (1993) *JCMS* 71–89.

[296] Case 236/83 *University of Hamburg* v. *Hauptzollamt München-West* [1984] ECR 3849, 3867.

[297] *A Community Strategy to Develop Europe's Industry*, COM(81)639, 17.

[298] *The State of the Internal Market*, COM(81)313.

[299] *A Community Strategy to Develop Europe's Industry*, COM(81)639, 7.

Community, may internalize these economies and dissipate them through inefficiencies.

More particularly, to the extent that protection has redistributive effects as between import-competing producers and other Community traders, adjustment costs necessitated by developments in international market conditions may be shifted to traders within the Community who have no rational need so to adjust. The costs are not simply static losses associated with misallocations but also efficiency losses in protected firms and the loss of dynamism in the incentive system for performance.[300]

Such distortions are the opposite of what is sought by Community trade liberalization. They reflect, however, the unease with which Community law recognizes the interdependence of the Community market and the markets of third states.[301]

For example, according to the Court of Justice, Articles 85 and 86 of the Treaty apply to conduct of non-Community undertakings which is implemented within the Community.[302] However, it is not clear that the Court has in mind the 'effects doctrine',[303] and it may not be enough that conduct has effects within the Community for it to be prohibited. Trade between Member States must also be affected, because Articles 85 and 86 are interpreted as seeking to secure Community trade liberalization. This interpretation may underlie the Court's idea of 'implementation' within the Community.

More specifically, *EMI Records*[304] concerned the question whether trade mark holders in Member States could use their trade mark rights to prevent importation of goods lawfully manufactured and branded with that mark in the United States. Here the Court referred to a restrictive agreement between traders within the Community and competitors in third states that would bring about an isolation of the common market as a whole and, in the territory of the

[300] Cf. J. Pelkmans, 'The European Community and the Newly Industrializing Countries' in W. Maihofer (ed.), *Noi si Mura* (Florence, 1986), 510–39.

[301] See, regarding the provision of services, Opinion 1/94 *(Competence of the Community to conclude international agreements on services and the protection of international property)* [1994] ECR I-5267, I-5412–4. Cf. the view of the ESA that a tax from which exports were exempted could not affect the international competitiveness of a national producer in Notice 95–002—Norway ([1995] OJ C212/6) concerning aid which Norway proposes to grant in the form of a tax exemption for glass packaging from a basic tax on non-reusable beverage packaging.

[302] Joined Cases 89/85, 104/85, 114/85, 116–117/85, and 125–129/85 *A. Åhlström Osakeyhtiö* v. *EC Commission* [1988] ECR 5193, 5243. Cf., earlier, the ambiguity in the approach of the Court in Case 22/71 *Béguelin Import Co.* v. *S.A.G.L. Import Export* [1971] ECR 949, 959. The potentially broader term 'materialize' is preferred by P. Pescatore, 'The Dynamics and Homogeneity of the European Economic System' (1991) JFT 295–320, at 314.

[303] The Commission favours a broad interpretation of the effects doctrine. Even if the individual participation of a particular undertaking has in itself no appreciable effect within the Community, it is enough that the overall arrangement in which the undertaking participates has such an effect. See Dec. 85/206 of 19 Dec. 1984 ([1985] OJ L92/1) relating to a proceeding under Art. 85 EC (IV/26.870—Aluminium imports from eastern Europe).

[304] Case 51/75 *EMI Records Ltd* v. *CBS United Kingdom Ltd* [1976] ECR 811.

Community, would reduce the supply of products originating in third states and similar to those protected by a trade mark within the Community. Such an agreement might affect trade within the Community. In particular, if the proprietor of the mark in the third state had within the Community various subsidiaries[305] established in different Member States which were in a position to market the products at issue within the common market, such trade might be affected.[306]

Again, in applying Article 92 of the Treaty, the Commission may consider whether state aid to the extra-Community activities of undertakings affects Community trade. These activities may strengthen the position of recipients in such trade. They may also demonstrate the existence of competition between the recipients and other companies and exemplify the export activities of the former.[307]

Commission practice under Article 92 may be supported by the Court of Justice. In *Belgium* v. *EC Commission*,[308] which involved Belgian aid to a steel producer, the Court ruled that the fact that aids for exports to third countries were dealt with in Article 112 of the Treaty, which provided for their progressive harmonization, did not preclude the application of Article 92 to such aids. Given the interdependence of markets, the possibility of distortion of competition in Community trade could not be ruled out *a priori*.[309]

At the same time, the Commission may take account of the impact of producers from third states on the Community market.[310] For example, in

[305] In Case 48/69 *Imperial Chemical Industries Ltd* v. *EC Commission* [1972] ECR 619, 662–3 the doctrine of enterprise unity was employed as a basis of jurisdiction over a parent company which was itself situated in a third country but had subsidiaries within the Community or at least as the ground for rejecting the argument that the actions of the subsidiaries were not imputable to the parent company. See also Case 52/69 *J. R. Geigy* v. *EC Commission* [1972] ECR 787, 835–6; Dec. 74/634 of 29 Nov. 1974 ([1974] OJ L343/19) relating to proceedings under Art. 85 EC (IV/27.095—Franco-Japanese ball-bearings agreement); and Dec. 75/497 of 15 July 1975 ([1975] OJ L228/3) relating to a proceeding under Art. 85 EC (IV/27.000—IFTRA rules for producers of virgin aluminium).

[306] [1976] ECR 811, 848. See also Warner A. G. (*ibid.* 863–4) and the Judgment in Case 71/74 *Nederlandse Vereniging voor Fruit-en Groentenimporthandel, Nederlandse Bond van Grossiers in Zuidruchten en ander Geimporteerd Fruit ' Frubo'* v. *EC Commission and Vereniging de Fruiturie* [1975] ECR 563, 584. The reasoning in such cases might have been influenced by practical considerations. If anti-competitive behaviour is implemented within the Community by means of agreements, the latter will be void under Art. 85(2). If restrictive practices more generally are implemented through subsidiaries, then fines may be imposed on the latter. If neither condition is met, there may be practical problems of enforcing competition law.

[307] Dec. 92/35 of 11 June 1991 ([1992] OJ L14/35) requiring France to suspend the implementation of the aid described below in favour of the Pari Mutuel Urbain (PMU), introduced in breach of Art. 93(3) EC. On the other hand, according to Van Gerven A. G. in Case C–292/90 *British Aerospace plc and Rover Group Holdings plc* v. *EC Commission* [1992] ECR I–493, I–516, state aid to a Community undertaking might be permissible where it was used to finance activities on markets outside the Community.

[308] Case C–142/87 [1990] ECR I–959.

[309] *Ibid.* I–1013.

[310] Dec. 91/305 of 24 Jan. 1991 ([1991] OJ L156/39) concerning investment aid which the Belgian Government plans to grant to Mactac SA, Soignies.

July 1990 the Commission objected to the grant of state aid to a Spanish footwear producer. The Commission noted that the Community footwear industry was subject to steadily increasing import penetration from the developing and newly industrialized countries. Moreover, the industry was extremely fragmented, the average manufacturer being only about a sixtieth of the size of the aid recipients. In these circumstances, the Commission considered that the aid was likely to affect Community trade.[311]

In such practice the application of Community competition law is limited to conduct of undertakings or state aid having a discernible effect on Community trade.[312] Such limitation is consistent with a general tendency of states to exempt from their competition policy any national cartels or monopolies which seek to extract rents from foreign markets.[313] However, the more integrated economies become, the less rational may be the implicit distinction between 'internal' and 'external' competition[314] or between Community trade liberalization and international trade liberalization.

Trade Deflection

To the extent that Community law fails to secure international trade liberalization, Member States remain free to adopt their own rules regarding trade with third states. To the extent that such rules are allowed to vary from one Member State to another, trade may be deflected. Such deflection may result not only from rules governing imports from third states but also from rules governing exports to such states,[315] though it is problems concerning the former kind of rules which appear more prevalent.

A third state trader wishing to sell his products in a Member State with rules

[311] *Twentieth Report on Competition Policy* (EC Commission, Brussels, 1991), 168.

[312] See, e.g., Dec. 69/202 of 25 June 1969 ([1969] JO L168/22) *relative à une procédure au titre de l'article 85 du traité CEE* (IV/597—V.V.V.F.) and Dec. 71/22 of 23 Dec. 1970 ([1971] JO L10/12) *relativa ad una procedura a norma dell'articolo 85 del trattato CEE (IV/337—Supexie).*

[313] See, e.g., R. E. Caves, 'Industrial Policy and Trade Policy: the Connections' in H. Kierzkowski (ed.), *Protection and Competition in International Trade* (Oxford, 1987), 68–85, 81. The ECJ also ruled in Case 91/78 *Hansen GmbH & Co.* v. *Hauptzollamt Flensburg* [1979] ECR 935, 956 that Art. 37 EC, concerning state trading monopolies, did not apply to goods from third states. Cf., however, the view of Capotorti A. G. (*ibid.* 971).

[314] In an early decision the Commission granted a negative clearance to an exclusive distributorship agreement between a French company and a Swiss company, which prohibited the latter from selling within the Community. There was considered to be no distortion of competition within the Community, because, among other reasons, the products had to cross a customs frontier to be sold within the Community. See Dec. 64/233 of 11 Mar. 1964 ([1964] JO 915) *relative à une demande d'attestation négative présentée conformément à l'article 2 du règlement no 17 du Conseil* (IV/A–00061).

[315] In Case 86/85 *Alexander Moksel Import-Export GmbH & Co. Handels-KG* v. *Hauptzollamt-Jonas* [1987] ECR 369, 386 the Court reminded the Commission that restrictions on exports to third states could affect Community trade. Art. 10 of Reg. 2603/69 of 20 Dec. 1969 ([1969] JO L324/25) establishing common rules for exports provided that the principle of freedom of export was not to apply to products listed in the Annex, until the Council introduced common rules for these products.

imposing restrictive requirements may seek to import them into that Member State through a Member State with less restrictive requirements. Such deflection of trade might be accompanied by that of a less direct kind. The imports from the third state into the Member State with less restrictive requirements might displace domestic products from the market of that Member State. The latter might then be exported to the Member State with more restrictive requirements.

The underlying problem is the artificiality of efforts to separate[316] questions of international trade liberalization from those of Community trade liberalization. To the extent of the inability of the common commercial policy to meet the regulatory demands implied for this policy, international trade liberalization may be limited, and the possibility of trade deflection may be inevitable.

Division of the Common Market

Since trade deflection would undermine the pursuit of reciprocity through uniformity in the (separate) treatment of international trade, limitation of Community trade liberalization rather than toleration of trade deflection may be the preferred substitute for a satisfactory common commercial policy. Without such limitation the Community as a whole would, it is said, have to align itself with the policy of the most liberal Member State with a consequent weakening of the Community position in negotiations with third states.[317]

To accept limitation of Community trade-liberalization conflicts with a basic principle of the EC Treaty. Article 9(2) thereof states that the provisions concerning customs duties, quantitative restrictions and charges, and measures having equivalent effect apply to products originating in Member States and to products from third states in free circulation in Member States.[318] Thus 'the Community is not a free trade area but a customs union with a common market, comparable to an internal market, free from trade barriers and different conditions of competition, even in the case of goods from third States which are in free circulation in one of the Member States'.[319]

[316] This separation entails that the Commission considers measures taken in pursuance of agreements with third countries to be acts of commercial policy, which as such lie outside the scope of Art. 85 EC. See Dec. 74/634 of 29 Nov. 1974 ([1974] OJ L343/19) relating to proceedings under Art. 85 of the Treaty establishing the EEC (IV/27.095—Franco-Japanese ball-bearings agreement).

[317] See the approval of the Commission view by Warner A. G. in Case 29/75 *Kaufhof AG* v. *EC Commission* [1976] ECR 431, 448.

[318] Cf., regarding insurance periods completed by workers in a third state, Joined Cases 82 and 103/86 *Giancarlo Laborero and Francesca Sabato* v. *Office de Sécurité Sociale d'Outre-Mer* [1987] ECR 3401, 3428.

[319] VerLoren van Themaat A. G. in Case 59/84 *Tezi Textiel BV* v. *EC Commission* [1986] ECR 887, 904. More particularly, the Court considers it necessary, as a consequence of the customs union and in the mutual interest of the Member States, to acknowledge the existence of a general principle of freedom of transit of goods within the Community. See Case 266/81 *Società Italiana per l'Oleodotto Transalpino (S.I.O.T.)* v. *Ministero delle Finanze* [1983] ECR 731, 779 and Case C–367/89 *Aime Richardt and Les Accessoires SNC* [1991] ECR I–4621, I–4650.

Such thinking has led the Court of Justice to assimilate products from third states to products originating within the Community in connection with the prohibition of fiscal discrimination in Article 95 of the Treaty,[320] even though Article 95 only expressly benefits products of other Member States and Article 9(2) does not mention tax provisions.[321] According to the Court, Article 95 prohibits fiscal discrimination or protectionism against products from third states in free circulation within the Community.[322]

The rationale for such judicial willingness to stretch the ordinary meaning of legal provisions is suggested by case law relating to the ECSC Treaty. This Treaty did not create a Common Customs Tariff. Nevertheless, the Court found that the principle of free movement in Article 4(a) of this Treaty, which required the abolition of import and export duties or charges having equivalent effect and quantitative restrictions on the movement of coal and steel products within the Community, applied to products originating in third states once they had been imported into a Member State.[323] The principle was applied in this way, not for the protection of third country producers, but to prevent the free movement of Community products being itself diminished or impaired by the establishment of obstacles to the movement within the Community of products originating in a third state.[324]

Such concern for Community trade liberalization implies that products from third states which have been put into free circulation in a Member State should be generally assimilated to products originating in that Member State and benefit from Community trade liberalization in the same way as the latter.[325] Indeed, while a total Community quota for imports from third states might be divided into national sub-quotas, such a division could not hinder the free movement of goods subject to the quota once they had been released into free circulation in the territory of one of the Member States.[326]

[320] Case 193/85 *Cooperativa Co-Frutta* v. *Amministrazione delle Finanze dello Stato* [1987] ECR 2085. In contrast, Lenz A. G. maintained that the intention of Art. 95 was to secure undistorted competition in the common market, whereas protection against competition from third states was ensured by the CCT and specific agreements (*ibid.* 2101–2).

[321] Thus in Case 7/67 *Milchwerke H. Wöhrmann und Sohn KG* v. *Hauptzollamt Bad Reichenhall* [1968] ECR 177, 183 the Court had ruled that Art. 95 applied exclusively to products originating in the Member States. See also Case 20/67 *Firma Kunstmühle Tivoli* v. *Hauptzollamt Würzburg* [1968] ECR 199, 204 and Case 148/77 *H. Hansen Jun. and O. C. Balle GmbH & Co.* v. *Hauptzollamt Flensburg* [1978] ECR 1787, 1808.

[322] [1987] ECR 2085, 2112.

[323] Joined Cases 9 and 12/60 *Société Commerciale Antoine Vloeberghs, SA* v. *ECSC High Authority* [1961] ECR 197, 216–7.

[324] Slynn A. G. in Case 36/83 *Mabanaft GmbH* v. *Hauptzollamt Emmerich* [1984] ECR 2497, 2534.

[325] Though they do not, of course, benefit from any greater freedom of movement between Member States than the products to which they are assimilated. See, e.g., Warner A. G. in Case 51/75 *EMI Records Ltd* v. *CBS United Kingdom Ltd* [1976] ECR 811, 860.

[326] Case 218/82 *EC Commission* v. *EC Council* [1983] ECR 4063, 4075; Case 199/84 *Procuratore della Repubblica* v. *Tiziano Migliorini and Tibor Tiburzio Fischl* [1985] ECR 3317, 3331.

However, in *Donckerwolcke*,[327] which concerned French measures to monitor imports of synthetic fibres originating in third states but in free circulation in the Community, the Court stated:

> it results from the system of the Treaty that [such assimilation] . . . is conditional upon the establishment of a common commercial policy. The assimilation to products originating within the Member States of goods 'in free circulation' may only take full effect if these goods are subject to the same conditions of importation both with regard to customs and commercial considerations, irrespective of the State in which they were put in free circulation.[328]

Since the 'equivalence principle' is not part of the common commercial policy, it has been argued in the light of the above passage that this principle is not applicable to goods from third states in free circulation.[329] Support for this argument might be found in the fact that in *Cassis de Dijon*[330] the Court applied the principle in relation to goods 'lawfully produced and marketed' in a Member State. However, the original formula of the principle, introduced in *Dassonville*,[331] was applied to products from third states put into free circulation 'in a regular manner'.[332] Moreover, the principle has been applied in subsequent rulings involving products from third states in free circulation.[333] Therefore, the real significance of the above passage may relate to the absence of a satisfactory common commercial policy. In particular, the Court may have had in mind that assimilation did not affect restrictions on intra-Community trade in goods from third states which, in the absence of a satisfactory policy of this kind, could be applied pursuant to provisions such as Article 115 of the Treaty.[334]

Completion of the internal market logically implies that the only restrictive measures which may now be applied specifically to goods from third states should be applicable to trade between third states and the Community as a whole. However, even to the extent that distortions of competition within the Community do not continue as a result of substitution of Article 115 measures

[327] Case 41/76 *Suzanne Criel, née Donckerwolcke and Henri Schou* v. *Procureur de la République* [1976] ECR 1921. See also Case 59/84 *Tezi Textiel BV* v. *EC Commission* [1986] ECR 887, 923.

[328] [1976] ECR 1921, 1936.

[329] E. L. White, 'In Search of the Limits to Article 30 of the EC Treaty' (1989) 26 *CMLRev.* 235–80.

[330] Case 120/78 *Rewe-Zentral AG* v. *Bundesmonopolverwaltung für Branntwein* [1979] ECR 649, 664.

[331] Case 8/74 *Procureur du Roi* v. *Benoît and Gustave Dassonville* [1974] ECR 837.

[332] *Ibid.* 852. See, later, Case 125/88 *HFM Nijman* [1989] ECR 3533, 3547.

[333] Case 6/81 *BV Industrie Diensten Groep* v. *J. A. Beele Handelsmaatschappij BV* [1982] ECR 707; Case 144/81 *Keurkoop BV* v. *Nancy Keen Gifts BV* [1982] ECR 2853; Case 121/85 *Conegate Ltd* v. *HM Customs and Excise* [1986] ECR 1007; and Case 406/85 *Procureur de la République* v. *Daniel Goffette and Alfred Gilliard* [1987] ECR 2525. However, these were preliminary rulings and the national courts concerned did not ask the ECJ whether there was any legal significance in the fact that such products were involved.

[334] Regarding this provision, see sect. 3.2.3 below.

by less visible measures,[335] more profound distortions than those associated with Article 115 measures may arise from the separation of Community trade liberalization and international trade liberalization. In essence, failure to secure the latter kind of liberalization may still set limits to what can be achieved by way of the former kind and thus undermine the completion of the internal market.

The underlying issues are sometimes touched upon in judicial proceedings. For example, in determining whether scientific equipment from third states could be exempted from the CCT, the Court of Justice considered it 'necessary to balance the needs of Community scientific research against the possibilities of development of the Community industry in the sector of scientific instruments and apparatus'.[336]

However, recognition of underlying issues does not apparently preclude acceptance of distortions of competition. For example, according to the Court, different treatment of Community traders must be regarded as compatible with Community law, where it is merely an automatic consequence of the different treatment accorded to third states with which those traders have entered into commercial relations.[337]

The distortions accepted may be compounded, to the extent that the integration with third states which does take place[338] results in narrower production and export specialization and less import substitution and increases the structural dependence of Member States on states outside as well as within the Community.[339] Controversies concerning local content requirements[340] and 'screwdriver'[341] plants, which confront the basic principle in Article 58

[335] As regards the forms which such measures may take, see *ibid.*

[336] Case 232/86 *Nicolet Instrument GmbH* v. *Hauptzollamt Berlin-Packhof* [1987] ECR 5025, 5038.

[337] Case 52/81 *Faust* v. *EC Commission* [1982] ECR 3745, 3762.

[338] See, regarding the 'globalization process', A. de la Torre and M. R. Kelly, *Regional Trade Arrangements* (IMF Occasional Paper No. 93, Washington, 1992), 46.

[339] U.N. Conference on Trade and Development, *Common European Economic Space* (New York, 1991), 5. According to J. Fagerberg, 'The Process of Economic Integration in Europe: Consequences for EFTA Countries and Firms' (1991) *Co-operation and Conflict* 197–215, at 201, the changing composition of Community trade in recent decades reflects not only European integration but also increasing 'world integration'.

[340] I.e., the requirements that must be met for a product to be regarded as originating within the Community and thus not having to be put into free circulation. 'Simple' assembly work does not confer origin (Case C–26/88 *Brother International* v. *Hauptzollamt Giessen* [1989] ECR 4253), though more substantial assembly work may do so (Case 34/78 *Yashida Nederland BV* v. *Kamer van Koophandel en Fabrieken voor Friesland* [1979] ECR 115).

[341] I.e., plants established within the Community to avoid anti-dumping measures imposed on the finished product entering from a third state. See, in particular, the finding of the GATT Panel in *Re Screwdriver Assembly: Japan* v. *European Economic Community* [1990] 2 CMLR 639. The GATT Director General suggested less demanding requirements than the Community in the context of Uruguay Round negotiations. See the *Tenth Annual Report on the Antidumping and Antisubsidy Activities of the Community*, COM(92)716, 23. No agreement was reached. See the Dec. on Anti-circumvention, in the Final Act Embodying the Results of the Uruguay Round of Multilateral Trade Negotiations.

of the Treaty[342] that subsidiaries of companies from third states having registered offices within a Member State are to be treated in the same way as natural persons who are nationals of that Member State, are symptoms of the conflict between such dependence and the inadequacies of the international trade liberalization secured by Community law.[343] Such symptoms might be treated by 'fundamental external bargains' with countries such as the United States.[344] However, bargains of this kind depend on exceptions being made from the normal decision-making processes of the Community and if they are only made with certain third states, may in overall terms, as well increase as decrease distortions of competition.

In short, therefore, completion of the internal market not only highlights the artificiality of separating international trade liberalization from Community trade liberalization. It also increases the urgency of developing a legal regime tending towards assimilation of the two. The search for such a regime may lead the Community to go beyond the adoption of 'autonomous'[345] commercial policy measures and to conclude 'international anti-trust agreements'[346] with third states,[347] such as that with the United States.[348] More usually, it is sought through conclusion of Free Trade Agreements or Association Agreements.[349]

[342] See, similarly, Art. 34 of the EEA Agreement.

[343] The conflict may be even more pronounced when agreements between the Community and third states embody particularly strict rules of origin. See, e.g., the arguments in the GATT Working Party on the Swedish Free Trade Agreement (BISD, 20th Supp., 183–96).

[344] Cf. W. Sandholtz and J. Zysman, '1992: Recasting the European Bargain' (1989/90)42 *World Politics* 94–128.

[345] I.e., measures deriving their legal force exclusively from the Community legal order.

[346] There is talk of seeking to develop GATT in this regard. See, e.g., *Financial Times*, 4 Feb. 1992. See, more particularly, *A Consistent and Global Approach: A Review of the Community's Relations with Japan*, COM(92)219, 6. It is also considered 'desirable that a genuine body of competition rules should be developed at international level'. See the *Twenty-Fourth Report on Competition Policy*, COM(95)142, 18.

[347] Resolution of 13 Dec. 1991 ([1992] OJ C13/472) on the *Twentieth Report on Competition Policy*, para. 27. See also J. H. J. Bourgeois, 'EEC Control over International Mergers' (1990)10 *YBEL* 103–32, at 132.

[348] [1991] 4 CMLR 823; [1991] ILM 487. It superseded previous, less formal arrangements for consultation. See, e.g., the *Eleventh Report on Competition Policy* (EC Commission, Brussels, 1985), 34. The ECJ however, found the Commission not to be competent to conclude this Agreement in Case C–327/91 *France* v. *EC Commission* [1994] ECR I–3641, and the Commission submitted a Proposal of 12 Oct. 1994 for a Council Dec. concluding the Agreement between the European Communities and the Government of the USA regarding the application of their competition laws, COM(94)430. See also the Draft Agreement between the European Communities and Canada regarding the application of their competition laws (Bull. EU 1/2–1995, 1.3.59).

[349] Agreements with third states may be seen as implementing the principle in Art. 110 EC. See, e.g., the Opinion of the Economic and Social Committee of 25 Jan. 1995 ([1995] OJ C102/40) on relations between the European Union and Russia, Ukraine, and Belarus, para. 3.23. A list of such agreements was given in the Council Reply to Written Question E–182/95 ([1995] OJ C196/16) by Jean-Pierre Raffarin.

2.3 FREE TRADE AGREEMENTS

The Free Trade Agreements concluded between the Community and EFTA States provided for establishment of a free trade area between the Parties in industrial goods.[350] They were thus designed to secure a greater degree of trade liberalization between the Parties thereto than the common commercial policy entails in the case of international trade generally.[351] They were not, however, designed to substitute the pursuit of reciprocity with assimilation of international trade liberalization to Community trade liberalization.[352] On the one hand, there might be 'external' impediments to such substitution. Although Community law did not require that all third states must be treated equally,[353] GATT requirements as to most-favoured-nation status[354] might be influential,[355] and in any case commitment to achieving uniformity in the treatment of products from third states might not easily be abandoned.[356] On the other hand, impediments might result from the unsuitability of Community trade liberalization requirements for transposition into an agreement designed to liberalize trade relations between the Community and a third state.

While they do not seem to have been fully explored in Community practice regarding the Free Trade Agreements, judicial proceedings illustrated aspects of these impediments. In such proceedings these Agreements were treated as forming part of the common commercial policy and not as creating a duty incumbent on Member States to extend to trade with the third states concerned the binding principles of the free movement of goods between Member States.[357] Hence, individual trade-liberalization provisions of these Agreements needed to be interpreted in the light of the 'structure' of the relevant Agreement. The significance of this need was highlighted in the case of provisions governing internal taxation and measures having equivalent effect to quantitative restrictions on imports.

[350] See, e.g., Art. 2 of the Swedish Free Trade Agreement ([1972] JO L300/2).

[351] The traditional response to international externalities has been the formulation of policies for international cooperation. See P. Nicolaides, 'How Fair is Fair Trade?' (1986) *JWTL* 148–62, at 149.

[352] See, regarding EC–EFTA relations, the statement of Commissioner De Clercq in 1987 (Bull. EC 5–1987, 2.2.14); para. 7 of the Declaration of the EFTA Ministerial Meeting in Oslo, 14–15 Mar. 1989 (EFTA Bull. 2/89, 4–7); and the European Parliamentary Resolution of 26 May 1989 ([1989] OJ C158/509) on economic and trade relations between the EEC and EFTA member countries, para. 9.

[353] Case 55/75 *Balkan Import-Export* v. *Hauptzollamt Berlin-Packhof* [1976] ECR 19, 32 and Case 245/81 *Edeka* v. *Federal Republic of Germany* [1982] ECR 2745, 2756.

[354] According to Art. I(1) of GATT, any trade liberalization introduced for one Party to the Agreement must be extended to all other Parties.

[355] See, e.g., the Explanatory Memorandum to the Commission Proposal for a Directive on the Procurement Procedures of Entities Providing Water, Energy, Transport and Telecommunications Services, COM(88)377, 31.

[356] Case 52/77 *Cayrol* v. *Rivoira & Figli* [1977] ECR 2261, 2278–9.

[357] Case 51/75 *EMI Records Ltd* v. *CBS United Kingdom Ltd* [1976] ECR 811, 846–7. EC Treaty provisions 'cannot as such be transposed to relations with non-member countries'. See Case 255/78 *Procureur de la République, Besançon* v. *Bouhelier* [1979] ECR 3151, 3160.

2.3.1 Internal Taxation

In *Kupferberg*,[358] which concerned German taxation of port from Portugal, the Court of Justice had to interpret Article 21(1) of the Portuguese Free Trade Agreement.[359] According to this provision, the Parties should refrain from any measure or practice of an internal fiscal nature establishing, whether directly or indirectly, discrimination between the products of one Party and like products originating in the territory of another Party. It was interpreted as only prohibiting differential treatment of products which had similar characteristics and were manufactured in a similar way.[360]

The reasoning of Advocate General Rozès was that, unlike the EC Treaty, the Portuguese Agreement was not intended to create an area of 'complete neutrality with regard to competition' in an enlarged market.[361] She continued:

> In view of the more restricted purpose of that Agreement, where there is such a non-discrimination clause, the only important question is whether the taxation measures actually have a protectionist effect as regards the importation of goods and thus jeopardise the abolition of obstacles to trade.[362]

In other words, while the EC Treaty seeks to remove obstacles to participation in an enlarged market, the Portuguese Agreement had more a limited objective.[363] The former entailed that taxation should not distort competition, whereas the latter only entailed the prohibition of discrimination against imports.[364] While a simple prohibition of discrimination as between domestic goods and imports would not be considered adequate for the purposes of establishing the common market or 'total equality with regard to competition'[365] required by the EC Treaty, it might satisfy the requirements of a Free Trade Agreement[366] and, indeed, might be regarded as the most practical

[358] Case 104/81 *Hauptzollamt Mainz* v. *CA Kupferberg & Cie KG* [1982] ECR 3641, 3669.

[359] [1972] JO L301/2.

[360] See also Case 253/83 *Sektkellerei C. A. Kupferberg & Cie KG* v. *Hauptzollamt Mainz* [1985] ECR 166, 186. According to the Commission, only 'effective discrimination rather than the mere fact of a difference in taxation' was prohibited by the former provision (Case 104/81 *Hauptzollamt Mainz* v. *C. A. Kupferberg & Cie KG* [1982] ECR 3641, 3652).

[361] *Ibid.* 3676.

[362] *Ibid.* 3676. In other words, taxation measures were only prohibited where they entailed 'the actual economic effect of discrimination' (*ibid.* 3677).

[363] See, similarly, Case 312/91 *Metalsa Srl* [1993] ECR I–3751, I–3774.

[364] Though the prohibition of such discrimination may be imperfect. See, regarding the Austrian Free Trade Agreement, *ibid.*

[365] See the submission of the Commission in Case 253/83 *Sektkellerei C. A. Kupferberg & Cie KG* v. *Hauptzollamt Mainz* [1985] ECR 157, 180.

[366] Though the EFTA Convention (SÖ 1960:198) went further. Art. 6(1)(b) of the Convention prohibited EFTA States from applying fiscal charges to goods from other EFTA States which they did not produce or did not produce in substantial quantities, in such a way as to afford effective protection to domestic goods which, though of a different kind, were substitutable for the domestic goods and in direct competition. For an early comparison of this provision with Art. 95 EC see R. Middleton, 'Some Non-Tariff Barriers to Trade in EFTA and EEC', EFTA Bull. 9/1972, 18–19.

approach to securing reciprocity.[367] Hence, the taxation of port from Portugal was not affected by the Free Trade Agreement, because no similar products were made in Germany.[368] In contrast, Germany would not have been permitted by Article 95 of the EC Treaty to impose any tax on port from a Member State which put such a product at a disadvantage in relation to competing national products.[369] The consequence was that Community trade liberalization and the liberalization required by a Free Trade Agreement were kept separate.[370]

The concepts of discrimination and protectionism may, however, have been invoked too loosely by the Advocate General to express adequately the difference between requirements of the EC Treaty and those of Free Trade Agreements[371] or, more fundamentally, to expose the need for justification of the limited approach adopted to interpretation of liberalization provisions in such Agreements.

The Court itself, apparently seeking a slightly more concrete basis for its approach, stated that Article 21 of the Portuguese Agreement merely aimed to ensure that the liberalization of trade in goods sought by abolition of customs duties and charges having equivalent effect and quantitative restrictions and measures having equivalent effect (which was required by Articles 3–14 of the same Agreement) was not rendered nugatory by fiscal practices of the Parties.[372] Apparently, a conservative approach to abolition of fiscal barriers to trade was felt to be justified by what was assumed to be a conservative approach in the Agreement to abolition of other trade barriers, though the basis for this assumption was not indicated.

[367] However, in relation to banking (Art. 9(4) of Dir. 89/646 of 15 Dec. 1989 ([1989] OJ L124/16) on the co-ordination of laws, regulations and administrative provisions relating to the taking up and pursuit of the business of credit institutions) and public procurement (Art. 29 of Dir. 90/531 of 17 Sept. 1990 ([1990] OJ L297/1) on procurement procedures of entities operating in the water, transport, and telecommunications sectors), the Community is attempting to secure 'comparable and effective' access.

[368] Again, Art. 18(1) of the Austrian Free Trade Agreement ([1972] JO L300/2) was the equivalent of Art. 21(1) of the Portuguese Agreement, but unlike Art. 95 EC (see Case 299/86 *Drexl* [1988] ECR 1213), was not interpreted so as to prohibit national rules punishing offences concerning VAT on importation more severely than those concerning VAT on domestic sales. See Case C–312/91 *Metalsa Srl* [1993] ECR I–3751.

[369] It would only have been permissible where there was no national product capable of being protected by a tax on products imported from another Member State. See Case 27/67 *Firma Finkt-Frucht* v. *Hauptzollamt München-Landsbergerstrasse* [1968] ECR 223, 232–233.

[370] See also, regarding penalties for violation of fiscal rules, Case C–312/91 *Metalsa Srl* [1993] ECR I–3751, I–3775.

[371] Art. 6 of the Swedish Free Trade Agreement prohibited a Member State from levying a charge proportional to the customs value of goods on goods imported from Sweden by reason of their entry into a region of that Member State, notwithstanding the fact that the charge was also imposed on goods entering that region from another part of the territory of the Member State concerned. See Case C–163/90 *Administration des douanes et droits indirects* v. *Léopold Legros, Louise Alidor, épouse Brun, Armand-Joseph Payet, Henri-Michel Techer* [1992] ECR I–5335.

[372] [1982] ECR 3641, 3665.

The underlying concern of the Court may have been to avoid excessive encroachment on the fiscal autonomy of Parties which had not demonstrated in such Agreements the same willingness to contemplate fiscal policy harmonization[373] as had been demonstrated by Parties to the EC Treaty. In particular, the Portuguese Agreement contained no equivalent of Article 99 of the Treaty, which explicitly provides for such harmonization.[374] Because of this provision, interpretation of Article 95 of the Treaty proceeds on the assumption not only that restriction of the fiscal sovereignty of the Member States by Community trade liberalization requirements is compatible with the Treaty[375] but also that fiscal harmonization is necessary for the realization of a common market.[376] While only limited harmonization may have taken place under Article 99 of the Treaty, the accomplishment of harmonization may be less decisive[377] than the implications which may be drawn from its very contemplation in the Treaty.

2.3.2 Quantitative Restrictions and Measures Having Equivalent Effect

Article 13 of the Swedish Free Trade Agreement[378] followed Article 30 of the EC Treaty. The former provision prohibited the introduction of new quantitative restrictions or measures having effect on imports between Sweden and the Community and required the abolition of existing restrictions and equivalent measures, in principle, from the beginning of 1975.

Article 13 of the Swedish Agreement might be contrasted with provisions of certain other agreements, such as the Free Trade Agreement between EFTA States and Turkey,[379] which seek to define the measures prohibited. Article 7(3) of the Turkish Agreement defines quantitative restrictions and measures having equivalent effect as prohibitions or restrictions made effective through

[373] Cf. Case 218/83 *Les Rapides Savoyards* v. *Directeur Général des Douanes et Droits Indirects* [1984] ECR 3105, 3124, where the Court felt obliged to point out that rules in Free Trade Agreements regarding determination of the origin of products did not encroach on fiscal autonomy, because the rules were established on the basis of reciprocal obligations placing the Parties on an equal footing in their relations with each other. Cf. also the concern of GATT organs to avoid interpreting Article III of GATT in such a way as to 'unnecessarily infringe upon the regulatory authority and domestic policy options of contracting parties' (Report on US measures affecting alcoholic and malt beverages, GATT Doc. DS 23/R 95 of 19 June 1992).

[374] Art. 14 of the EEA Agreement substantially embodies the rules of Art. 95 EC, but this Agreement also contains no equivalent of Art. 99 EC. Hence, some doubt might arise as to the likely interpretation of Article 14 of the EEA Agreement.

[375] Lenz A. G. in Case 193/85 *Cooperativa Co-Frutta* v. *Amministrazione delle Finanze dello Stato* [1987] ECR 2085, 2101.

[376] Gand A. G. in Case 28/67 *Firma Mölkerei-Zentrale Wesfalen/Lippe GmbH* v. *Hauptzollamt Paderborn* [1968] ECR 143, 165.

[377] Cf. P. Demaret, 'Le régime des échanges internes et externes de la Communauté à la lumière des notions d'union douanière et de zone de libre-échange' in F. Capotorti *et al.* (eds.), *Du Droit International au Droit de l'Intégration Liber Amicorum Pierre Pescatore* (Baden-Baden, 1987), 139–65, 164–5.

[378] [1970] JO L300/96.

[379] *Regeringens proposition godkännande av avtal rörande handeln mellan EFTA–länderna och Turkiet, m.m.*, prop. 1991/92:23.

quotas, import or export licences, or other administrative measures and requirements restricting trade.

Again, the Canada–US Free Trade Agreement[380] prohibited the maintenance or introduction of standards, related measures, or procedures for product approval that would create 'unnecessary obstacles' to trade between the Parties. Such obstacles would not be deemed to be created if the demonstrable purpose of the measure or procedure was to achieve a legitimate domestic objective and it did not exclude goods of the other Party which met that objective.[381]

No such definition was contained in the Swedish Agreement. In the absence of any such definition, the possibility might be thought to have been left open that Article 13 of the Agreement could operate in the same fashion as Article 30 of the EC Treaty.

However, the possibility was closed by the judgment in *Polydor*.[382] This judgment concerned the importation of gramophone records from Portugal, where they had been purchased from the exclusive licensee for that country, and their sale in the United Kingdom without the consent of the copyright holder or his exclusive licensee in the United Kingdom. In particular, the question was whether the exclusion of such products from the United Kingdom was contrary to the prohibition of quantitative restrictions and measures having equivalent effect in Article 14 of the Free Agreement with Portugal, which corresponded to Article 13 of the Swedish Agreement. The Court of Justice ruled that their exclusion was justified under Article 23 of the same Agreement,[383] which was substantially identical to Article 36 of the EC Treaty.[384] In contrast, within the context of Community trade the 'exhaustion of rights' doctrine would apply to prevent the holder of an industrial or commercial property right from employing his right to exclude from a Member State products marketed in another Member State with his consent.[385] Hence, their exclusion would be prohibited by Article 30 of the EC Treaty and would not be justified under Article 36 of the same Treaty.[386]

Such a contrast between the operation of liberalization provisions in the EC Treaty and the operation of liberalization provisions in the Free Trade Agreements may have been acceptable to national courts in EFTA States. In

[380] [1988] ILM 281.

[381] *Ibid.* Art. 603.

[382] Case 270/80 *Polydor Ltd and RSC Records Inc.* v. *Harlequin Record Shops Ltd and Simon Records Ltd* [1982] ECR 329.

[383] Cf. Case 51/75 *EMI Records Ltd* v. *CBS United Kingdom Ltd* [1976] ECR 811, 847, where the Court implied that liberalization requirements of such Agreements might be more demanding.

[384] See sect. 3.2.1 below, regarding Art. 36 EC.

[385] According to a Joint Declaration concerning Art. 66 of the Polish Agreement, the Parties agree that for the purpose of this Agreement 'intellectual, industrial and commercial property' is to be given a similar meaning as in Art. 36 EC.

[386] See, e.g., Case 119/75 *Terrapin (Overseas) Ltd* v. *Terranova Industrie C. A. Kapferer & Co* [1976] ECR 1039.

Gramola[387] the Austrian Supreme Court found that an Austrian record shop proprietor who imported records from Germany, where they were lawfully marketed, infringed the rights in Austria of the Austrian music society. In so finding, this Court ruled that 'the creation and exercise of copyrights in the widest sense' were not covered by the Austrian Free Trade Agreement,[388] 'at least in so far as the restrictions stipulated by the parties [did] not extend beyond the substance of the property right'.[389]

While the Austrian court did not apparently consider it necessary to justify this interpretation of the Agreement, some reasoning had been provided in *Polydor.*[390] According to the Court of Justice, the scope of the case law regarding Article 30 of the EC Treaty must be determined in the light of Community objectives and activities as defined in Article 2 and 3 of the Treaty, which were concerned with the unification of national markets into a single market having the characteristics of a domestic market.[391] More particularly, the Court observed:

> the instruments which the Community has at its disposal in order to achieve the uniform application of Community law and the progressive abolition of legislative disparities within the common market have no equivalent in the context of relations between the Community and Portugal.[392]

Institutional considerations may also have been influential. Advocate General Rozès noted in the same case:

> whilst with regard to the free movement of goods the structure of the [Portuguese Free Trade] agreement may indeed be comparable to that of the [EEC] Treaty, there are many aspects to the Treaty other than the free movement of goods. Apart from the joint committee, . . . no 'common institution' was established [by the Portuguese Agreement].[393]

Apparently, the liberalization required by a particular provision of a Free Trade Agreement may depend on the generality of the liberalization sought by the Agreement and on the arrangements made therein for harmonization[394] and institutional involvement.[395] Such thinking may partly, though not necessarily

[387] *Austro-Mechana Gesellschaft zur Verwaltung und Auswertung Mechanisch-Musikalischer-Urheberrechte GmbH* v. *Gramola Winter & Co.* [1984] 2 CMLR 626.

[388] [1972] JO L300/2.

[389] *Ibid.* 639. See, more recently, *Mute*, [1989] GRUR Int. 699.

[390] Case 270/80 *Polydor Ltd and RSC Records Inc.* v. *Harlequin Record Shops Ltd and Simon Records Ltd* [1982] ECR 329.

[391] *Ibid.*, 348. See, similarly, in connection with interpretation of Art. 95 EC, Case 15/81 *Gaston Schul* [1982] ECR 1409, 1431–2.

[392] [1982] ECR 329, 349.

[393] *Ibid.* 354.

[394] According to the *Ninth Report on Competition Policy* (EC Commission, Brussels, 1980), 9, the 'metamorphosis of a heterogeneous collection of isolated national markets into a single vast market could not succeed without the establishment of some basic rules'.

[395] Cf. the consequences which the Swiss Supreme Court in *Bosshard Partners Intertrading AG* v. *Sunlight AG* [1980] 3 CMLR 664, 674 attached to the fact that the Free Trade Agreement with Switzerland ([1972] JO L300/189) did 'not aim to create a uniform internal market with supranational regulations governing competition, but merely a free trade area'.

simply, reflect a concern that 'reciprocity is . . . not guaranteed' by Free Trade Agreements.[396] Presumably, in the absence of provisions requiring sufficiently generalized liberalization and making arrangements for harmonization and institutional involvement, application of the same prohibition of measures having equivalent effect to quantitative restrictions in trade between the Community and third states as applies to Community trade would enable undertakings engaged in international trade to exploit differences in competitive conditions which such provisions are designed to preclude. Certainly, the 'complete' free movement of goods sought by the EC Treaty is seen as presupposing, *inter alia*, that the freedom to provide services and freedom of establishment are achieved at the same time.[397] On the other hand, in its case law the Court of Justice implicitly recognizes the inadequacies of harmonization and the work of the Community institutions.[398] The impression is that rulings such as that in *Polydor* reflect underlying assumptions as to the limited degree of integration sought by Free Trade Agreements.

Such rulings might be viewed in terms of a 'pairing' or 'matching' of 'substance' (i.e., trade liberalization requirements) and 'structure' (i.e., institutional involvement), which was successful until integration within the Community 'took a further leap'.[399] Thinking of this kind, however, begs questions why the pairing lacked the dynamism to respond to the real integration taking place between the Parties to the Free Trade Agreements.

It might be argued that, in view of the broad terms of the Preambles to the Free Trade Agreements and their objectives, as outlined in Article 1 of these Agreements and as confirmed by the 'Luxembourg process',[400] such restrictive interpretations of liberalization provisions in these Agreements were not justified.[401] On the other hand, Article 1(b) of these Agreements, according to which they merely aimed 'to provide fair conditions of competition for trade between the Contracting Parties' rather than to create a common market,[402]

[396] [1982] ECR 329, 354.

[397] *Ibid.* 356. See also Joined Cases 55 and 57/80 *Musik-Vertrieb Membran GmbH and K-tel International* v. *GEMA* [1981] ECR 147, 165.

[398] Case 120/78 *Rewe-Zentrale* v. *Bundesmonopolverwaltung für Branntwein* [1979] ECR 649, 662.

[399] See T. Cottier, 'Constitutional Trade Regulation in National and International Law: Structure-Substance Pairings in the EFTA Experience' in M. Hilf and E.-U. Petersmann (eds.), *National Constitutions and International Economic Law* (Deventer, 1993), 409–42, at 423.

[400] I.e., practice following the EC–EFTA Ministerial Declaration of 9 Apr. 1984 (Bull. EC 4–1984, 1.2.1); see sect. 5.3.3 below.

[401] U. Bernitz, 'Sveriges EG-anknyting i rättsligt perspektiv' [1989/90] *JT* 47–69, at 60. Cf., earlier, N. March Hunnings, 'Enforceability of the EEC–EFTA Free Trade Agreements' [1977] *ELRev.* 163–89.

[402] In Case C–312/91 *Metalsa Srl* [1993] ECR I–3751, I–3774–5 the ECJ contrasted the objective of the Austrian Free Trade Agreement (the creation of a free trade area), as indicated in its Preamble, with the objective of creating a common market in Arts 2 and 3 EC. See, similarly, Jacobs A. G. (*ibid.* I–3760)

might have implied that their provisions had to be interpreted more restrictively than corresponding provisions of the EC Treaty.

Moreover, it cannot be assumed that the practical achievements of the Luxembourg process were such as to remove the justification for a restrictive interpretation. For example, in *Bosshard Partners Intertrading AG* v. *Sunlight AG* the Swiss Supreme Court found that a Swiss trade mark holder was entitled to prevent the importation into Switzerland of German-made detergents lawfully branded in Germany with the trade mark concerned. In finding that this entitlement was unaffected by the Swiss Free Trade Agreement[403] the Court observed that the Agreement omitted to establish any institution comparable with the Court of Justice.[404] This omission was not remedied by the Luxembourg process. The absence of any such institution may not simply have rendered 'public good' conceptions of the regime created by these Agreements less appropriate than an approach to interpretation emphasizing the need for reciprocity.[405] It may also have meant that, in practice, reciprocity requirements could not easily be reconciled with a broad interpretation of liberalizing provisions contained therein.

Consequences of major practical importance followed from a narrow interpretation of such provisions. In particular, Free Trade Agreements might allow Parties to adopt policy measures which would be prohibited within the Community by the EC Treaty.

In Sweden, for example, the alcohol policy entailed the prohibition of the sale of strong beers, such as those lawfully brewed and marketed in Belgium. Such a prohibition would have been contrary to Article 30 of the EC Treaty, unless it could have been justified on public health grounds under Article 36[406] or, possibly, on the basis of a 'mandatory requirement' recognized by the Court of Justice.[407] In view of the fact that the sale of spirits was permitted in Sweden, such a justification would not have been easy to establish, and so the prohibition of the sale of strong beers would apparently have been unlawful under this Treaty.[408]

In contrast, provisions of Free Trade Agreements corresponding to Article 30 of the EC Treaty were apparently interpreted merely as prohibiting a Party from discriminating between imports from the other Party and domestic

[403] [1972] JO L300/189.

[404] [1980] 3 CMLR 664, 674. See also Rozès A. G. in Case 104/81 *Hauptzollamt Mainz* v. *C. A. Kupferberg & Cie KG* [1982] ECR 3641, 3674.

[405] According to G. Porro, *L'Integrazione Giuridica nell'Associazione Europea di Libero Scambio* (Milan, 1983), 202–10, the Free Trade Agreements were based on the principle *do ut des* and did not involve the adoption of EC Treaty objectives or the same degree of institutional participation as would an Association Agreement.

[406] See sect. 3.2.1 below.

[407] See sect. 3.2.2 below.

[408] The argument that the prohibition of drinks of intermediate strength is necessary to discourage 'graduation' to strong drinks is, in substance, the same as that which was rejected in *Cassis de Dijon* (663).

goods.[409] Certainly, this interpretation was favoured by the Swiss Supreme Court[410] and was implicitly adopted by the Court of Justice itself in the above *Kupferberg* ruling.[411] In the absence of such discrimination, Parties to such Agreements remained free to pursue domestic policies affecting trade. Apparently, therefore, the prohibition of the sale of strong beers, regardless of origin, was permitted by such Agreements.

On the other hand, a further consequence of a restrictive interpretation of liberalization provisions in the Free Trade Agreements was that most technical barriers to trade between the Parties[412] were unaffected by prohibitions such as that in Article 13 of the Swedish Agreement. Such barriers, which are potentially of significance in relation to any preferential trading arrangements,[413] have increased in importance,[414] as a result of GATT successes in reducing tariffs.[415] To the extent that the relative benefits of tariff preferences decline, traders have to rely more and more on comparative advantage or economies of scale. While comparative advantage, whether natural or man-made, might be sufficient to outweigh the costs associated with non-tariff barriers, the need to maintain multiple 'product lines' implied by such barriers might have a more serious effect in relation to economies of scale and might, indeed, preclude them altogether.

2.4 EUROPE AGREEMENTS

The Europe Agreements follow the Free Trade Agreements in providing for creation of a free trade area in industrial goods between the Parties.[416] More

[409] Cf. Art. III(4) of GATT. The Swiss Supreme Court ruled in *Bosshard Partners Intertrading AG* v. *Sunlight AG* [1980] 3 CMLR 664, 675 that the prohibition of quantitative restrictions and measures having equivalent effect on imports in Art. 13 of the Swiss Free Trade Agreement only covered measures 'directly affecting the import of goods'.

[410] *Maison Godard-Burnet & Fils Sprl* v. *Direction Générale des Douanes*, judgment of the Swiss Sup. Ct. A486/85, 2 Sept. 1986.

[411] Case 104/81 *Hauptzollamt Mainz* v. *C. A. Kupferberg & Cie KG* [1982] ECR 3641. Thus Art. 13 of the Austrian Free Trade Agreement prohibited a Member State from making the marketing authorization for a pharmaceutical product originating in Austria, identical in all respects to a pharmaceutical product already authorized by the health authority of that Member State, subject to the condition that the parallel importer submit documents already made available to that authority by the manufacturer at the time of the first request for a marketing authorization. See Case C–207/91 *Eurim-Pharm GmbH* v. *Bundesgesundheitsamt* [1993] ECR I–3723.

[412] See, generally, H. Ewander, *Avveckling av tekniska handelshinder* (Industriförbundet Arbetsrapport 12, Stockholm, 1989).

[413] In *A Community Strategy to Develop Europe's Industry*, COM(81)639, 16, the Commission noted that the Community preference had declined as CCT duties had fallen. In any case, owing to the increasing relative importance of non-tariff barriers to trade maintained or introduced by the Member States, market unity was not all that it should be.

[414] See, e.g., K. Shigehara, 'External Dimension of Europe 1992: its Effects on the Relationship between Europe, the United States and Japan' [1991] *Bank of Japan Monetary and Economic Studies* 87–102, at 92.

[415] However, low average levels of customs duties may hide significant tariff peaks. See J. Greenwald, 'Negotiating Strategy' in G. C. Hufbauer (ed.), *Europe 1992: An American Perspective* (Washington, 1990), 345–88, at 361.

[416] Art. 7 of the Polish Agreement.

particularly, they apply the asymmetrical principle[417] with a view to ensuring that the Community market is opened up to traders from the other Parties more rapidly than the latter are required to open up their markets to Community traders. However, this principle in itself does not address the fundamental problems which arose in the operation of the Free Trade Agreements, and does not preclude the possibility that similar problems may also arise under the Europe Agreements.

2.4.1 Internal Taxation

In relation to internal taxation, the Europe Agreements follow the Free Trade Agreements. In particular, Article 26 of the Polish Agreement states that the Parties shall refrain from any measure or practice of an internal fiscal nature establishing, whether directly or indirectly, discrimination between the products of one Party and like products originating in the territory of the other Party. Practice under the Free Trade Agreements suggests that this provision may play a more limited role in trade liberalization between the Parties than does Article 95 of the EC Treaty in the context of Community trade liberalization.

2.4.2 Quantitative Restrictions and Measures Having Equivalent Effect

Article 9(4) of the Polish Agreement provides that quantitative restrictions on imports to the Community and measures having equivalent effect shall be abolished on entry into force of the Agreement with regard to products originating in Poland. Article 10(4) of the Agreement provides that quantitative restrictions on imports into Poland of products originating in the Community and measures having equivalent effect shall be abolished on entry into force of the Agreement with the exception of those listed in Annex V, which shall be abolished in accordance with the timetable provided in that Annex.

The terms of these provisions do not go so far as Article 5(1) of the Yaoundé Convention.[418] It provided: 'As regards the elimination of quantitative restrictions, Member States shall apply to imported products originating in associated states rules corresponding to those of the Treaty.' Accordingly, the Court of

[417] Such asymmetry, which is authorized by Art. XXXVI(8) of GATT, may be considered necessary to ensure that the reciprocity required of Association Agreements under Art. 238 EC is real. In relation to agreements with overseas countries and territories of the Member States, asymmetry is envisaged in Art. 131 EC. Note also the conclusions drawn by the ECJ from the 'fundamentally favourable approach of the Community towards the OCT' in Case C–430/92 *Netherlands* v. *EC Commission* (not yet reported).

[418] *Convention d'Association entre la Communauté économique européenne et les Etats africains et Malgache associés à cette Communauté*, 20 July 1963 ([1964] JO 1431).

Justice applied Article 33 of the EC Treaty in relation to trade between the Community and one such associated State.[419]

The possibility might still be thought to be left open that Article 9(4) and 10(4) of the Polish Agreement could operate in the same fashion as corresponding provisions of the EC Treaty, particularly Article 30 thereof. However, practice under the Free Trade Agreements indicates that the concept of measures having equivalent effect may differ in its meaning, depending on the instrument in which it is embodied.[420]

True, Association Agreements generally may be treated as demanding more intensive integration than Free Trade Agreements. For example, the Association Agreement with Greece[421] was said to 'constitute much more than a free trade agreement of the classical type'.[422] Not only did it envisage the future accession of Greece to the Union, but also its structure and content were based on the EC Treaty.[423] However, while the Europe Agreements refer to the possibility of future Union membership for the states concerned,[424] the liberalization sought by these Agreements, which centres on the creation of a free trade area in a transitional period of a maximum of ten years,[425] may not necessarily be regarded as comparable with that sought by the Greek Association Agreement.[426] It is possible, therefore, that the Europe Agreements will be treated as allowing Parties the same kind of freedom to adopt policy measures for themselves as did the Free Trade Agreements,[427] even though trade

419 Case 48/74 *Mr Charmasson* v. *Minister for Economic Affairs and Finance (Paris)* [1974] ECR 1383. Cf., regarding Art. 12 of the Turkish Association Agreement, which provides that the Parties agree 'to be guided by Arts 48, 49, and 50 of the [EC] Treaty for the purpose of progressively securing freedom of movement for workers between them', Case C–434/93 *Ahmet Bozkurt* v. *Staatssecretaris van Justitie* (not yet reported). Here the Court concluded that 'to ensure compliance with that objective, it would seem to be essential to transpose, so far as is possible, the principles contained in those Articles to Turkish workers' who enjoyed rights conferred by an implementing measure adopted by the Association Council.

420 Cf. a Joint Declaration *ad* Ch. II of Title IV of the Polish Agreement, which prohibits treatment by one Party of the nationals or companies of another Party which is either formally or *de facto* less favourable than that accorded to its own nationals or companies.

421 [1963] JO 26.

422 Rozès A. G. in Case 17/81 *Pabst & Richarz KG* v. *Hauptzollamt Oldenberg* [1982] ECR 1331, 1359.

423 The Court itself was rather less expressive (*ibid.* 1350). In Joined Cases 37 and 38/73 *Sociaal Fonds voor de Diamantarbeiders* v. *NV Indiamex and Association de fait De Belder* [1973] ECR 1609, 1619 the Commission distinguished simply between Association Agreements based on a customs union with the Community and Agreements not creating such a union.

424 See the final recital in the Preamble to the Polish Agreement. 'When such a convention looks towards a further accession, the Community must of necessity hold the most extensive powers to conclude agreements with non-member countries in order to cover all the fields of activity contemplated by the EC Treaty.' See Darmon A. G. in Case 12/86 *Meryem Demirel* v. *Stadt Schwäbisch Gmünd* [1987] ECR 3719, 3741.

425 Art. 7 of the Polish Agreement.

426 In connection with the Turkish Association Agreement, Darmon A. G. maintained in Case 12/86 *Meryem Demirel* v. *Stadt Schwäbisch Gmünd* [1987] ECR 3719, 3744 that the 'consensual nature' of such an Agreement might preclude 'the application of provisions without a clearly circumscribed content'.

427 Cf. S. Peers, 'An Ever Closer Waiting Room? The Case for Eastern European Accession to the European Economic Area' (1995) 32 *CMLRev.* 187–213, at 208.

liberalization may be seriously jeopardized thereby.[428] In other words, the Europe Agreements may also fail to overcome the separation of Community trade liberalization from international trade liberalization.[429]

2.5 EEA AGREEMENT

The EEA Agreement constitutes an exceptionally sophisticated attempt not merely to liberalize EC–EFTA trade but to assimilate such liberalization to Community trade liberalization. As far as Sweden was concerned, the Agreement represented the results of a Government policy designed to secure for Swedish citizens, institutions and companies participation in the internal market on the same conditions as Community actors.[430]

Accordingly, Article 1 provides that the aim of the Agreement is to promote a continuous and balanced strengthening of trade and economic relations between the Contracting Parties with equal conditions of competition and respect for the same rules, with a view to creating a homogeneous European Economic Area.

While a Joint Declaration on Political Dialogue, annexed to the Agreement, goes beyond economic matters,[431] the implication in Article 1 that the emphasis is on economic rather than political integration finds confirmation in the Preamble to the Agreement. The fourth recital in the Preamble refers to the objective of establishing a dynamic and homogeneous European Economic Area, based on common rules and equal conditions of competition and providing for adequate means of enforcement including arrangements at the judicial level and entailing equality, reciprocity and an overall balance of benefits, rights and obligations for the Contracting Parties.[432] To achieve this objective, the Agreement reproduces EC Treaty provisions governing the 'four freedoms' (i.e., the free movement of persons, goods, services, and

[428] The only solution may be for countries such as Poland to adapt their legislation to Community rules, if they are to seek to maximize the benefits of these Agreements. See the view of the British Foreign Office in House of Lords Select Committee on the European Communities, *European Agreements with Poland, Hungary and the Czech and Slovak Federal Republic*, (1990–91) HL 35, Minutes of Evidence, 9.

[429] Cf. D. Kennedy and D. E. Webb, 'The Limits of Integration: Eastern Europe and the European Communities' (1993) 30 *CMLRev*. 1095–117, at 1097.

[430] See, e.g., *Europeiska ekonomiska samarbetsområdet*, prop. 1991/92:170, *del* 1, bil. 1, p. 4.

[431] According to this Declaration, the dialogue is to involve informal exchanges of views in the EEA Council (see sect. 6.5.1 below), use of diplomatic channels and informal consultations at conferences and in international organizations. Existing bilateral arrangements are unaffected.

[432] It thus envisages an apparently sophisticated version of what is described by L. A. Winters, 'Reciprocity' in J. M. Finger and A. Olechowski (eds.), *The Uruguay Round* (Washington, 1987), 45–51, at 49 as 'rules reciprocity', though the 'overall balance' envisaged may have more in common with reciprocity by outcome. See, regarding the agreements on agriculture concluded by each EFTA State with the Community at the time of conclusion of the EEA Agreement itself, the Declaration by the European Community on bilateral agreements, annexed to the EEA Agreement.

capital) and competition policy. These provisions are to be interpreted having regard to the case law of the Court of Justice prior to signature of the Agreement,[433] and Community implementing measures listed in Annexes to the Agreement are embodied in EEA law.

To this extent, it is not simply envisaged that the same law will apply to trade relations between EFTA States and the Community as applies within the Community. Rather, it is also apparently envisaged that the same law will apply to relations between each and every Contracting State. Thus, for example, Article 31(1) of the Agreement prohibits 'restrictions on the freedom of establishment of nationals of an EC Member State or an EFTA State in the territory of any other of these States'. Again, according to Article 36, 'there shall be no restrictions on freedom to provide services within the territory of the Contracting States in respect of nationals of EC Member States and EFTA States who are established in an EC Member State or an EFTA State other than that of the person for whom the services are intended'.

Within its scope and for the purposes of the Agreement, EEA law apparently replaces Community law governing trade liberalization between Member States.[434] Such replacement is necessary if the same kind of trade liberalization as that entailed by the EC Treaty is to be extended throughout the EC–EFTA area[435] and, hence, if trade between an EFTA State and a Member State is to be treated similarly to trade between Member States.[436] However, the fact that a customs union is not created and that EFTA States are not required to accept the common agricultural policy[437] or the commercial policy[438] means

[433] Art. 6 of the EEA Agreement.

[434] Nevertheless, reciprocity considerations may remain influential. See the Report of the Committee on Economic and Monetary Affairs and Industrial Policy on the Commission proposal to the Council on the economic situation in 1991–2, EP Doc. A3–0008/92, 10. The EEA Agreement does not require full EFTA participation in the search for reciprocity with non-EEA States. However, Art. 29(6) of Dir. 90/531, n. 434 above, is amended so as to require annual reports on progress achieved regarding access for Community and EFTA undertakings (Annex XVI to the Agreement).

[435] The Commission, however, considered that Swedish accession to the Union would mean that the EEA Agreement 'would cease to be applicable to the bilateral relations between Sweden and the Community'. See *Commission Opinion on Sweden's Application for Membership*, Bull. EC, Supp. 5/92, 17. It will, presumably, continue to apply to relations between Sweden and other EEA States.

[436] Art. 4 of the Agreement reproduces the equality principle contained in Art. 6(1) EC.

[437] EFTA States merely signed bilateral agricultural agreements at the same time as the EEA Agreement. They were 'part of the overall balance of the results of the negotiations'. See the Declaration by the European Community on bilateral agreements, annexed to the EEA Agreement.

[438] In spite of the '*lien indissociable*' between Community trade liberalization and the common commercial policy (see para. 2.3 of the *Communication de la Commission au Conseil portant recommendation de decision du Conseil visant à autoriser la Commission à negocier un accord avec lès pays AELE, portant sur la creation de l'Espace Economique Européen—Commission Communication concerning proposed Council decision authorizing the Commission to negotiate an agreement with the EFTA states on the creation of a European Economic Space*).

[439] Cf. the Joint Declaration by the Governments of the Member States of the EC and the EFTA States on the facilitation of border controls.

that frontier controls[439] and rules of origin[440] remain applicable in EC–EFTA trade.

More fundamentally, according to the Court of Justice in *Opinion 1/91*,[441] where the Court was requested by the Commission pursuant to Article 228(1) of the EC Treaty to give its opinion on the compatibility of the draft EEA Agreement with this Treaty, the fact that provisions of the Agreement and the corresponding Community provisions were identically worded did not mean that they must necessarily be interpreted identically. An international treaty was to be interpreted not only on the basis of its wording but also in the light of its objectives.[442]

The EEA Agreement was concerned with the application of rules on free trade and competition in economic and commercial relations between the Contracting Parties.[443] In contrast, as far as the Community was concerned, the rules on free trade and competition, which the Agreement sought to extend to the whole territory of the Contracting Parties, had developed and formed part of the Community legal order, the objectives of which went beyond that of the EEA Agreement. It followed, *inter alia*, from Articles 2, 7a, and 102a of the EC Treaty[444] that this Treaty aimed to achieve economic integration leading to the establishment of an internal market[445] and economic and monetary union. Article 1 of the Single European Act[446] made it clear, moreover, that the objective of the Treaty was to contribute together to making concrete progress towards European unity.[447] Hence, the provisions of the Treaty on free movement and competition, far from being an end in themselves, were only means for attaining those objectives.

[440] Art. 8(2) of the EEA Agreement and Prot. 4, on Rules of Origin. Such rules may be burdensome both for Community traders and traders from third states. Nevertheless, such rules may still be seen as having importance for 'the trade interests of the Community'. See *Report of the Group of Independent Experts on Legislative and Administrative Simplification*, COM(95)288, 72.

[441] Opinion 1/91 *(Draft Agreement between the Community, on the one hand, and the countries of the European Free Trade Association, on the other, relating to the creation of the European Economic Area)* [1991] ECR I–6079, I–6101.

[442] Art. 31 of the Vienna Convention on the Law of Treaties (1969).

[443] The Part, i.e., Pt. VI, dealing with co-operation beyond the four freedoms was not apparently considered significant. Cf. the argument that the Court underestimated the degree of integration sought by the EEA Agreement in A. Epiney, 'La Cour de justice des Communautés européennes et l'Espace économique européen' [1992] *Revue suisse de droit international et de droit européen* 275–304.

[444] Art. 2 defines the task of the Community, Art. 7a requires the completion of the internal market, and Art. 102a envisages convergence of the economic and monetary policies of the Member States.

[445] I.e. not the common market of *Polydor* (see sect. 2.3.2 above).

[446] However, Art. 31 of the Single European Act provided that the provisions of the Treaties regarding the powers of the ECJ and exercise of these powers did not apply to the part of the Act in which Art. 1 was contained.

[447] Such language echoes that used earlier by Commission President Delors (EP Debs. No. 2–373, 76, 17 Jan. 1989). The French text referred simply to '*l'Union européenne*' without the implication of joint action in use of the word 'together'. Later in the opinion ([1991] ECR I–6079, I–6108) the Court referred in the English version simply to a European Union.

As in *Polydor*,[448] the importance of the objectives of a legal instrument for interpretation of its provisions was stressed by the Court, and these objectives were classified in terms of integration intensities ranging from a free trade area, through an internal market to a union.[449] The reference to 'European unity' may be particularly significant, in that the role of the free movement of persons as a central element of Union Citizenship may be involved.[450] The implication is that this freedom may have to develop more within the Community than within the rest of the EEA. The objective of monetary union may also be relevant for the development of the free movement of goods. For example, devaluation by an EFTA State might be countered by unilateral[451] Community resort to safeguard measures,[452] whereas within the Community problems which might otherwise lead to devaluation are to be tackled within the framework of EMU rules.[453]

The conclusion might be drawn that a solution could have been for the EEA Agreement to have made 'it completely clear that within the scope of this Agreement the objectives are the same as those pursued by the equivalent chapters in the EC Treaty'.[454] The problem is that the relationship between the objectives and the scope of an Agreement may be circular. Objectives may determine scope,[455] but objectives may be only discernible by reference to scope. However, implicit in recognition of this problem is a possible solution. Dynamic interpretation of scope may facilitate expansive definition of objectives.[456]

The underlying concern of the Court of Justice may have been that less than

[448] Case 270/80 *Polydor Ltd and RSC Records Inc.* v. *Harlequin Record Shops Ltd and Simon Records Ltd* [1982] ECR 329.

[449] In referring to such a union, the Court 'moved the goal-posts', and the EC Treaty was regarded as requiring more intensive integration in broader fields than before. According to B. Brandtner, 'The Drama of the EEA: Comments on Opinions 1/91 and 1/92' in O. Jacot-Guillarmod (ed.), *Accord EEE: Commentaires et reflexions* (Bern, 1992), 300–28, at 307, a paradigm shift had taken place.

[450] Sect. 2.2.1 above.

[451] Art. 46 of the EEA Agreement provides for consultations between the Parties regarding monetary policy, but it is stipulated that exchange of views and information 'shall take place on a non-binding basis'. However, Sweden sought some form of 'intervention arrangements' with the Central Banks participating in the Exchange Rate Mechanism. See *Financial Times*, 21 Jan. 1992. Art. 109 EC provides for the Community to conclude formal agreements on an exchange-rate system for the ECU in relation to non-Community currencies.

[452] See sect. 3.5.2 below, regarding the safeguard measures permitted by the EEA Agreement. However, in 1982 the Commission raised the question in the Joint Committee whether Swedish devaluation in that year was compatible with the spirit of the Free Trade Agreement (*Sverige-EG 1982* (Utrikesdepartementets handelsavdelning 1983), 13).

[453] See sect. 3.2.2 below.

[454] O. Due, 'General Introduction to a Discussion on the Principles of Community Law Seen in the EEA Perspective' (1991) *JFT* 288–94, at 290–1.

[455] Cf., regarding the 'revelation' of the objectives of a dir. by its content, the submission of the UK in Case C–295/90 *European Parliament* v. *EC Council* [1992] ECR I–4193, I–4209.

[456] Para. 1 of Prot. 1 to the EEA Agreement, on Horizontal Adaptations, provides that the Preambles to Community acts in the Annexes 'are relevant to the extent necessary for the proper interpretation and application, within the framework of the Agreement, of the provisions contained in such acts'.

dynamic rulings by the EEA Court planned in the draft EEA Agreement[457] might have prejudiced its own freedom to develop Community law in line with the requirements of political union and monetary union. Such a concern does not necessarily entail that the Court of Justice envisages a more conservative approach to development of EEA law than to Community law. Rather, the Court may see itself as having a role to play in ensuring that the potential of the EEA for trade liberalization is realized. In other words, this Agreement, unlike previous Agreements with third states, may embody sufficient Community law that a critical threshold is crossed and that integration developments rather than limitations to integration become cumulative.

The Court was also concerned, however, that the Agreement failed to embrace fundamental tenets of supranationalism. The context in which the objective of the Agreement was situated was said to differ from that in which the Community aims were pursued. The EEA was to be established on the basis of an international treaty which, in essence, merely created rights and obligations as between the Contracting Parties and provided for no transfer of sovereign rights to the intergovernmental institutions which it set up. In contrast, the EC Treaty, albeit concluded in the form of an international agreement, nonetheless constituted the constitutional charter of a Community based on the rule of law. As the Court had consistently held, this Treaty established a new legal order for the benefit of which the states had limited their sovereign rights, in ever wider fields,[458] and the subjects of which comprised not only Member States but also their nationals. The essential characteristics of the Community legal order which had thus been established were in particular its primacy over the law of the Member States and the direct effect of a whole series of provisions which were applicable to their nationals and to the Member States themselves. It followed that legal homogeneity throughout the EEA was not secured by the fact that the provisions of Community law and those of the Agreement were identical in their content or wording.

In effect, the Court may have been concerned that the EEA Agreement did not demonstrate sufficient EFTA acceptance of supranationalism to render the Agreement capable of effectively securing the same kind of trade liberalization as the EC Treaty.

True, the Agreement contains stipulations apparently excluding the possibility that its provisions might have the inherent legal force and supremacy within Member States which, according to the Court, are possessed by directly effective Community law provisions.[459] In particular, Article 7 of the Agree-

[457] See sect. 8.5.1 below.

[458] Cf. Case 26/62 *NV Algemene Transport-en Expeditie Onderneming Van Gend en Loos* v. *Nederlandse Administratie der Belastingen* [1963] ECR 1, 12, where the Court used instead the wording 'albeit within limited fields'.

[459] *Ibid.* and Case 6/64 *Flaminio Costa* v. *ENEL* [1964] ECR 585.

ment provides that Community acts contained in Annexes to the Agreement or in decisions of the EEA Joint Committee[460] must 'be, or be made, part of the internal legal order of the Contracting Parties'. Moreover, Protocol 35 to the Agreement, on the implementation of EEA rules, recognizes that EFTA States may have to introduce statutory provisions to secure the supremacy of implemented EEA rules over conflicting provisions of national law.

However, the grounds which the Court discerned in the EC Treaty for originally asserting the existence of the 'new legal order' in *Van Gend en Loos*[461]—an assertion which may not have been strictly necessary to resolve questions concerning the legal effects of a customs reclassification put to the Court—were far from unambiguous.[462] The lesson to be drawn may thus be that the attitude of EFTA States and their national courts as well as the EFTA Court, established pursuant to the EEA Agreement,[463] to the development of this Agreement could be more important than the terms of its individual provisions[464] and the 'five years of rather futile talks'[465] preceding the adoption of these provisions.

2.6 CONCLUSION

The importance attached by the Court of Justice in *Opinion 1/91* to considerations drawn from the structure of the EC Treaty and the EEA Agreement is typical of its approach to trade liberalization issues under the former Treaty. In order to contain the impact of its case law on the scope for national policy-making, the Court leaves questions of domestic trading activity to the Member States, subject to any rules emerging from the harmonization process in which they participate through the Council of the Union. Removal of obstacles to international trade is, in turn, subordinated to harmonization pursuant to the common commercial policy. Such harmonization may take the form of autonomous Community measures or the conclusion of agreements with third states or international organizations.

Experience of the operation of the Free Trade Agreements raises doubts whether the Europe Agreements concluded with Central and East European states will have significantly greater trade-liberalizing effects on trade between

[460] See sect. 8.5.5 below.

[461] Case 26/62 *NV Algemene Transport-en Expeditie Onderneming Van Gend en Loos* v. *Nederlandse Administratie der Belastingen* [1963] ECR 1, 23.

[462] See sect. 8.2.2 below.

[463] See sect. 8.5.4 below.

[464] Finnish officials apparently felt that embodiment in EEA law of the same kind of freedom of movement of goods as prevails within the Community might require that 'the Cassis de Dijon principle . . . be spelt out more clearly in the EEA context'. See L. Sevøn, 'Legal Issues in the Negotiations on a European Economic Area' [1991] *JFT* 278–87, at 281.

[465] P. Pescatore, 'The Dynamics and Homogeneity of the European Economic System' [1991] *JFT* 295–320, at 318.

the Parties to the latter than preceding arrangements.[466] Most of the Community quantitative restrictions on imports from such states had already been removed prior to their conclusion, and customs duties had generally been reduced, suspended, or eliminated.[467] The Europe Agreements follow this asymmetrical approach, in that they require the Community to eliminate restrictions on trade with these states earlier than is required of the latter in their trade with the Community. The key question is whether the formal asymmetry in these Agreements will result in effective asymmetry in favour of the export trade of these states[468] and will be sufficient to encourage penetration of the Community market by products in which they have a genuine competitive advantage and to attract international investment.[469] The Agreements might have the consequence of rendering more permanent the liberalization steps previously taken by the Community on a unilateral basis,[470] and their mere conclusion might, rather like the '1992 programme' within the Community, also have psychological effects on traders. However, the economies of Central and East European states may not be well-equipped to take full advantage even of the limited liberalization likely to be secured by the Agreements.[471]

The EEA Agreement seeks to secure greater liberalization and to embody the relevant case law of the Court of Justice as well as basic EC Treaty provisions and implementing measures governing the four freedoms and competition policy. However, the Agreement does not require establishment of a common market and does not create at the EEA level an institution comparable with the Commission or the Court of Justice. Consequently, the legal framework provided by this Agreement differs significantly from that

[466] These Agreements replaced the short-term expedient of extending the GSP (General System of Preferences) to these countries. See Reg. 1509/92 of 5 June 1992 ([1992] OJ L159/1) withdrawing Hungary, Poland, and Czechoslovakia from the lists of beneficiaries of the Community generalized preferences scheme as from 1 Mar. 1992.

[467] J. Taraszkiewicz, 'Polish Exports to the EC: Barriers and Stimuli' in A. Evans and P. Falk (eds.), *Transformation and Integration: Polish and Swedish Perspectives* (Umeå, 1992) 11–23.

[468] Otherwise, their trading interests might be better served by liberalization on a most-favoured-nation basis. See A. de la Torre and M. R. Kelly, *Regional Trade Arrangements* (IMF Occasional Paper No. 93, Washington, 1992), 45.

[469] Opinion of the Committee on External Economic Relations for the Committee on Foreign Affairs and Security on the conclusion of an association agreement between the European Community and the Republic of Poland, EP Doc. A3–258/92, 12.

[470] From a Community perspective, they may also be seen as harmonizing the approaches of Member States to trade with the third states concerned and thereby reducing the risk of disruption of the internal market which could have resulted from divergent approaches. Cf. G. Benacchio, 'La CEE e la nuova Europa dell'est: strumenti giuridici' [1992] *Rivista di Diritto Civile* 627–38, at 632, n. 11.

[471] The result may be that 'access to the EC markets may be structured to encourage the development in Eastern Europe of industrial tasks no longer compatible with the highly developed economies of the EC, whether because of environmental or health and safety concerns or the lack of technological or commercial sophistication'. See D. Kennedy and D. E. Webb, 'The Limits of Integration: Eastern Europe and the European Communities' (1993) 30 *CMLRev.* 1095–117, 1110.

provided by the EC Treaty. It cannot, therefore, be assumed that the case law which the Agreement seeks to incorporate will develop in the same way within the framework of this Agreement as it has within the framework of the EC Treaty. Indeed, the determination of the Court of Justice in *Opinion 1/91* to 'insulate' Community law from the EEA Agreement may reflect concerns that the latter would lack the dynamism of the EC Treaty.

On the other hand, interpretation of individual legal provisions by reference to the legal framework within which they are contained seems to offer considerable scope for judicial creativity. Much may depend, therefore, on the approach adopted by third states, their courts, and traders towards realization of the potential of agreements concluded with the Community

3

Requirements Other than Those of Trade Liberalization

3.1 INTRODUCTION

Various requirements other than those of trade liberalization may be embodied, explicitly or implicitly, in legal frameworks for integration and may have an impact on the operation of trade liberalization provisions. The usual approach to assessing the impact assumes that it is necessary first to establish whether a particular measure or activity may be prohibited by a liberalization provision at all and then to determine the possibility of an exception being permissible from the prohibition.[1] Such an approach presumably has much to do with the preference for regarding legal provisions simply as rules which can be divorced from the underlying features of the legal framework within which they operate.

It is true that the 'two-stage test' employed may sometimes be convenient.[2] Where, for example, it is clear that conduct does not fall within the scope of a particular liberalization provision, such an approach avoids the need for a pointless investigation of requirements competing with those with which that provision is concerned.[3] Frequently, however, the position will not be clear-cut, and a choice may have to be made whether trade liberalization requirements or other requirements should be given priority. Here analysis based on the two-stage test may often tend to obscure the complexity and varied nature of the interactions which take place between the different requirements.[4]

3.2 EC TREATY

The EC Treaty expressly recognizes that various requirements, some being of a non-economic character but others being of an economic character, may justify

[1] See, e.g., P. Oliver, *The Free Movement of Goods in the EEC* (London, 1988) and J. Steiner, 'Drawing the Line: Uses and Abuses of Art. 30 EEC' (1992) 29 *CMLRev*. 749–74.

[2] Though there may be controversy as to the order of the two stages. See A. Mattera, 'De l'arrêt "Dassonville" à l'arrêt "Keck": l'obscure clarté d'une jurisprudence riche en principes novateurs et en contradictions' [1994] *Revue du Marché Unique Européen* 117–60, at 129.

[3] See, e.g., Case C–23/89 *Quietlynn and Brian James Richards* v. *Southend Borough Council* [1990] ECR 3059, 3081.

[4] See, regarding the need to reconcile the various objectives of an Association Agreement with each other and with particular provisions thereof, Case C–432/92 *The Queen* v. *Minister of Agriculture, Fisheries and Food, ex parte S. P. Anastasiou (Pissouri) Ltd* [1994] ECR I–3087, I–3132.

trade restrictions. Justification for further trade restrictions may be implicit in the Treaty framework.

3.2.1 Non-Economic Requirements

Trade restrictions may be expressly permitted by the EC Treaty on the basis of various non-economic requirements, notably public policy and security.

Public Policy

Article 36 of the EC Treaty[5] provides that Articles 30–34 thereof shall not preclude prohibitions or restrictions on imports, exports, or goods in transit justified on grounds of public morality, public policy, or public security; the protection of health and life of humans, animals, or plants; the protection of national treasures of artistic, historic, or archaeological value or the protection of industrial and commercial property. It is stipulated, however, that such prohibitions or restrictions shall not constitute a means of arbitrary discrimination or a disguised restriction on trade between Member States.

The Court of Justice has ruled that the reference to 'transit' in Article 36 of the Treaty confirms the general principle of freedom of transit of goods within the Community.[6] An analogy might be drawn with the approach of the Court to interpretation of Article 15 of the Convention on the Transitional Provisions, annexed to the ECSC Treaty. This provision stipulated that if a Member State wished to maintain the same protection against indirect steel imports through Member States with lower tariffs as its own tariffs provided in the case of direct imports, the former Member State had to obtain High Authority authorization. According to the Court, this provision presupposed the applicability of the principle of the free movement of goods to products originating in a third state and imported into a Member State. There would have been no need for such authorization if Member States had been free to adopt unilaterally, within the framework of their own commercial policy,[7] whichever measures were considered most expedient in dealing with indirect imports from third states.[8] Therefore, in relation to Community trade, provisions permitting particular trade restrictions may be interpreted as implying general liberalization requirements.

The EC Treaty framework means that, rather than to imply Community trade liberalization requirements from the terms of provisions permitting trade

[5] Cf. Art. XX of GATT.

[6] Case C–367/89 *Ministre des Finances* v. *Aime Richardt* [1991] ECR I–4621, I–4650. See, earlier, Case 266/81 *Societa Italiana per l'Oleodotto Transalpino (SIOT)* v. *Ministero delle Finanze* [1983] ECR 731, 777.

[7] According to Art. 71 ECSC, the competence of governments of Member States in relation to commercial policy was not affected by this Treaty, unless otherwise provided therein.

[8] Case 36/83 *Mabanaft GmbH* v. *Hauptzollamt Emmerich* [1984] ECR 2497, 2523.

restrictions, the more usual approach of the Court is to promote liberalization through a narrow interpretation of the restrictions permitted by such provisions. In interpreting provisions such as Article 36, the Court has emphasized the importance of establishment of the common market[9] and has characterized such provisions as exceptions from the fundamental principle of free movement.[10] Since they have this character, the Court considers that the scope of such provisions must be strictly construed. Hence, measures based thereon must not simply be necessary to protect the requirements with which the relevant provision is concerned, but they must also be necessary in the particular sense that such requirements could not be as effectively safeguarded by measures less restrictive of Community trade.[11] In other words, the proportionality principle i.e., the principle that a measure must be no more restrictive than is necessary to secure a lawful end, is strictly applied by the Court.

In relation to international trade, the practice of the Court may be modified. In particular, in *Richardt*[12] Advocate General Jacobs considered whether it was compatible with Community law, particularly Regulation 2603/69,[13] for Luxembourg to restrict the transit of electronic equipment being exported from France to the then Soviet Union via Luxembourg. Article 1 of this Regulation prohibited quantitative restrictions on exports to third states, unless the restrictions were covered by its Article 11. The latter provision had similar wording to Article 36 of the Treaty. However, in the view of the Advocate General, the proportionality principle might be less demanding in relation to Article 11 of the Regulation than to Article 36 of the Treaty.[14] Hence, in his view, the former provision might permit restrictions which would go beyond the kinds of restrictions permitted by the latter.

This view is not without support in the case law.[15] For example, in adopting anti-dumping measures against products from third states, the Council and Commission are required by the Court to respect the proportionality principle.[16] However, on the basis of the relevant Community

[9] Note, regarding the establishment of the common market and the need strictly to interpret exceptions from the prohibition of customs duties in Art. 12 EC, Joined Cases 90 and 91/63 *EEC Commission* v. *Luxembourg and Belgium* [1964] ECR 625, 633.

[10] Case 41/74 *Yvonne van Duyn* v. *Home Office* [1974] ECR 1337, 1350.

[11] See, e.g., Case 104/75 *Officier van Justitie* v. *De Peijper* [1976] ECR 613, 636.

[12] Case C–367/89 *Ministre des Finances* v. *Aime Richardt* [1991] ECR I–4621, I–4642.

[13] Of 20 Dec. 1969 ([1969] JO L324/25) establishing common rules for exports.

[14] See also Jacobs A. G. in Case C–312/91 *Metalsa Srl* [1993] ECR I–3751, I–3766. Cf., regarding the operation of this principle in relation to trade between Member States in products in free circulation within the framework of the common commercial policy, Case 52/77 *Cayrol* v. *Rivoira & Figli* [1977] ECR 2261, 2281.

[15] However, the proportionality principle applies so as to limit the possibility of forfeiture of a security lodged in connection with exports to third states of a product covered by a common organization of an agricultural market. See Case 181/84 *The Queen*, v. *Intervention Board for Agricultural Produce (IBAP) ex parte E.D. & F. Man (Sugar) Ltd* [1985] ECR 2889, 2905.

[16] See, e.g., Case 240/84 *NTN Toyo Bearing Company Ltd* v. *EC Council* [1987] ECR 1809, 1850.

legislation,[17] the Court has found that the injury caused to Community industry by dumped products must be assessed as a whole and that it is not necessary (or, indeed, possible) to define separately the share in such injury which is attributable to each of the companies responsible.[18] In contrast, the Court has ruled that persons exercising their freedom of movement within the Community may only be expelled from the host Member State where their own conduct[19] constitutes a 'genuine and sufficiently serious threat' to public policy requirements under Article 48(3) of the Treaty.

The significance of the context within which the acceptability of a restriction falls to be assessed may be all the more pronounced where the Community has enacted legislation on, for example, public health. According to the Court, Member States are not required to show the same degree of confidence towards third states as that which, on the basis of Community legislation, should characterize relations between Member States and which entails the abolition of systematic inspections in Community trade.[20] As a result, restrictions which, in the case of Community trade, are prohibited by such legislation may remain permissible in relation to international trade.

Security

Article 223(1)(a) of the EC Treaty provides that no Member State shall be obliged to supply information the disclosure of which it considers contrary to the essential interests of its security.[21] Moreover, according to Article 223(1)(b) of the Treaty, any Member State may take such measures as it considers necessary for the protection of the essential interests of its security which are connected with the production of or trade in arms, munitions, and war materials;[22] such measures must not adversely affect the conditions of competition in the common market regarding products which are not intended for specifically military purposes. An unpublished list of products covered has been drawn up pursuant to Article 223(2).[23] The products covered are said to

[17] Art. 4 of Reg. 3017/79 of 20 Dec. 1979 ([1979] OJ L339/1) on protection against dumped or subsidized imports from countries not members of the European Economic Community. See now Reg. 3283/94 of 22 Dec. 1994 ([1994] OJ L349/1) on protection against dumped imports from countries not members of the European Community.

[18] Case 255/84 *Nachi Fujikoshi* v. *EC Council* [1987] ECR 1861, 1895.

[19] Case 67/74 *Carmelo Angelo Bonsignore* v. *Oberstadtdirektor der Stadt Köln* [1975] ECR 297, 307.

[20] Case 30/79 *Land Berlin* v. *Wigei, Wild-Geflügel-Eier-Import GmbH & Co. KG* [1980] ECR 151, 166. See, similarly, Rozès A. G. in Case 2/81 *Albert Clément, Gérard Ces* [1981] ECR 3339, 3355.

[21] This provision follows Art. XXI(a) of GATT.

[22] Art. XXI(b)(ii) of GATT also refers to traffic in 'implements of war and . . . in other goods and materials as is carried on directly or indirectly for the purposes of supplying a military establishment'.

[23] The Political Affairs Committee of the European Parliament considers, that in relation to trade with Central and Eastern European countries, the list should be amended or cancelled altogether. See the Interim Report on political developments in Central and Eastern Europe, including the Soviet Union, and the European Community's role, EP Doc. A3–172/90.

be normally products of industries which do not work exclusively on military equipment,[24] and some writers favour an interpretation of this provision broad enough to cover goods, such as uniforms, required by the military even in peacetime.[25] Apparently, however, a narrow interpretation has been adopted.[26] Indeed, the European Parliament favours deletion of this provision and its substitution by common rules on arms exports.[27]

A narrow interpretation of the scope of Article 223 may reflect the fact that one of the original aims of the European Union was so to integrate the coal and steel industries of the Member States that they would be unable to mount a major war against each other.[28] On the other hand, four neutral states have since acceded to the Union, and such an interpretation might be incompatible with their obligations concerning trade with belligerents.[29] It might also exacerbate the difficulties faced by such states in seeking to maintain the economic capability needed to defend themselves in the event of war.[30]

However, in relation to the Common Foreign and Security Policy (CFSP), Article J.4(4) of the Treaty on European Union provides that possible future moves towards a common defence 'shall not prejudice the specific character of the security and defence policy of certain Member States'.[31] A possible

[24] Commission Reply to Written Question 877/89 ([1990] OJ C79/33) by Mr Donnea.

[25] H. von der Groeben *et al.*, *Kommentar zum EWG Vertrag* (Baden-Baden, 1983), i, 664. But cf. *ibid.* ii, 1038.

[26] *Ninth Report on Competition Policy* (EC Commission, Brussels, 1980), 72. Though it is apparently applied to 'sensitive' goods which it was not originally intended to cover. See the Report of the Committee on Foreign Affairs and Security on the Community's role in the supervision of arms exports and the armaments industry, EP Doc. A3–0260/92, 22. The Commission objects that Art. 223(1)(b) is unlawfully invoked by Member States as the basis for exempting imports from the CCT. The Commission view is that Art. 28 EC can provide the only legal basis for such exemption and has drawn up a proposal (Commission proposal of 29 Sept. 1988 ([1988] OJ C265/9) for a reg. temporarily suspending import duties on certain weapons and military equipment) to regulate the matter. See the Reply to Written Question 878/89 ([1990] OJ C171/13) by Mr Donnea.

[27] Resolution of 17 Sept. 1992 ([1992] OJ C284/138) on the Community's role in the supervision of arms exports and the armaments industry, para. 19. See now Reg. 3381/94 of 19 Dec. 1994 ([1994] OJ L367/1) setting up a Community regime for the control of exports of dual-use goods.

[28] See the 5th recital in the Preamble to the ECSC Treaty.

[29] Art. 9 of Convention (No. V) Concerning the Rights and Duties of Neutral Powers in War on Land, The Hague 1907 (SFS 1910:153), provides that a neutral country must not apply discriminatory restrictions to trade with a belligerent. Art. 6 of Convention (No. XIII) Concerning the Rights and Duties of Neutral Powers in Naval War, The Hague 1907 (SFS 1910:153), provides that a neutral country must not supply war material of any kind to a belligerent. See P. Cramér and S. Åström, 'Sverige, EG och neutraliteten' in U. Nordlöf-Lagerkranz (ed.), *Svensk neutralitet Europa och EG* (Stockholm, 1990) 52–75, at 56.

[30] See, regarding the more general impact of completion of the internal market on neutrality, D. Kennedy and L. Specht, 'Austrian Membership in the European Communities' [1990] *Harv. Int. LJ.* 407–61.

[31] Art. J.3 TEU provides for majority decision making by the Council in relation to more general matters of CFSP which the former, on the basis of general guidelines from the European Council, has decided should be subject to joint action. The Commission sought from states applying for Union membership 'specific and binding assurances . . . with regard to their political

implication is that neutrality is not precluded by this Treaty. If this implication is justified, the conclusion might be drawn that Article 223 of the EC Treaty should be interpreted sufficiently broadly to permit neutral Member States to meet neutrality obligations and to maintain the economic capability necessary for their neutrality to be credible.

Support for such a conclusion might be sought in Article 224 of the EC Treaty. According to this provision, Member States shall consult each other with a view to taking together the steps needed to prevent the functioning of the common market being affected by measures which a Member State may be called upon to take in the event of serious internal disturbances affecting the maintenance of law and order, in the event of war, serious international tension constituting a threat of war, or in order to carry out obligations it has accepted for the purpose of maintaining peace and international security.[32] The implication is that measures restricting trade may be permissible under this provision.

More particularly, it might be argued that neutral states have undertaken the obligations of neutrality for the purpose of maintaining peace and international security and, therefore, would be able to rely this provision in the case of measures needed to give effect to these obligations.[33] Such reasoning might offer a justification for the view of the Austrian[34] and Swiss Governments[35] that their neutrality would be compatible with Union membership.[36]

True, the Commission takes the position that the obligations envisaged in Article 224 are exclusively concerned with United Nations operations under

commitment and legal capacity to fulfil the obligations [of CFSP]'. See *Europe and the Challenge of Enlargement*, Bull. EC, Supp. 3/92, 13. See, more particularly, *Commission Opinion on Sweden's Application for Membership*, Bull. EC. Supp. 5/92, 21. The Council envisaged that these states would 'espouse unreservedly' all objectives of the TEU. See Council Reply to Written Question 2408/92 ([1993] OJ C86/20) by Mr Carlos Robles Piquez. The result was a Joint Declaration on Common Foreign and Security Policy, annexed to the Accession Agreement with Austria, Finland, and Sweden.

[32] According to Gand A. G. in Case 15/69 *Württembergische Milchverwertung-Südmilch* v. *Salvatore Ugliola* [1969] ECR 363, 373, Art. 224 permits Member States, in the case of a serious crisis, to take necessary measures without being bound by the Treaty. Even so, it is said that the 'primary focus of Art. 224 is not to protect national jurisdiction but to protect Community interests'. See D. Kennedy and L. Specht, n. 30 above, 429.

[33] T. Muoser, *Finnlands Neutralität und die Europäische Wirtschaftsintegration* (Baden-Baden, 1986), 206 regards this provision as '*ein umfassender Neutralitätsvorbehalt*'—a broad neutrality reservation.

[34] First Report of the House of Lord Select Committee on the European Communities, *Enlargement of the Community*, (1992–3) HL 5, 17. In the Austrian membership application of 17 July 1989 (*Die EG und Österreich* (Vienna, 1989), 464) the view was taken that Union membership was compatible with Austrian neutrality. See *contra* D. Kennedy and L. Specht, n. 30 above.

[35] *Enlargement of the Community*, n. 34 above, 16.

[36] Sweden considers that 'neutrality is no longer an adequate overall term for Sweden's foreign and security policy' (*ibid.* 17). The Swedish membership application of 1 July 1991 (published in SvD, 2 July 1991) made no reference to neutrality. However, the application was made in accordance with a Parliamentary vote approving a Report from the Foreign Affairs Committee which favoured Union membership 'with neutrality policy being retained' (*Sverige och den västeuropeiska integrationen*, 1990/91:UU8).

Chapter VII of the UN Charter,[37] which is headed 'Action with Respect to Threats to the Peace, Breaches of the Peace, and Acts of Aggression'. However, in *Richardt* Advocate General Jacobs adopted a broader interpretation of Article 224 than the Commission. He did not exclude the possibility that application of CoCom[38] rules, which controlled the export of goods of strategic importance to Central and Eastern European countries, by Luxembourg could constitute compliance with the obligations envisaged in this provision.[39] Moreover, this provision was invoked in connection with the imposition of sanctions on Iran,[40] even though the UN Security Council had passed no resolution requiring such action. Therefore, Community practice does not unambiguously support the narrow interpretation of Article 224 obligations adopted by the Commission.[41]

Even if the interpretation of the Commission were justified, account might still be taken of the ruling in *Campus Oil* v. *Minister for Industry and Energy*.[42] This case concerned a requirement in Irish legislation that petroleum importers should purchase a certain proportion of their supplies from the Irish National Petroleum Company. This requirement was designed to protect the viability of the sole oil refinery in the Republic and thereby to secure a supply of petroleum products. The Court of Justice ruled, though without referring to neutrality questions, that the resulting restrictions on the importation of petroleum products might be justified on public security grounds under Article 36 of the Treaty.[43] Possibly, this provision would permit action by a

[37] *Beitrittsantrag Osterreichs, Stellungnahme der Kommission*, SEC(91) 1590, 27, n. 1. See also G. Lysén, 'Some Views on Neutrality and Membership of the European Communities: The Case of Sweden' (1992) 29 *CMLRev.* 229–55, at 249. Art. XXI(c) of GATT expressly adopts this position.

[38] Coordinating Committee for Multilateral Export Controls. Member States rely on Art. 223 of the Treaty to apply these rules. The Commission sought abolition of restrictions on Community trade in the goods concerned. See *Financial Times*, 23 Jan. 1992.

[39] Case C–367/89 *Ministre des Finances* v. *Aime Richardt* [1991] ECR I–4621, I–4643.

[40] Bull. EC 5–1980, 26.

[41] Certain trade restrictions may also be permitted under Arts. 73g(2) and 100c(5) EC. According to the former provision, without prejudice to Art. 224, a Member State may, for serious political reasons and on grounds of urgency, take unilateral measures against a third state with regard to capital movements and payments. According to Art. 100c(5) of the Treaty, harmonization of visa policies regarding nationals of third states shall be without prejudice to the exercise of the responsibilities incumbent upon the Member States with regard to the maintenance of law and order and the safeguarding of internal security. See, similarly, regarding co-operation in the fields of justice and home affairs, Art. K.2 TEU.

[42] Case 72/83 [1984] ECR 2727.

[43] Case 222/84 *Johnston* v. *Chief Constable of the RUC* [1986] ECR 1651. Cf. VerLoren van Themaat A. G. in Case 231/83 *Henri Cullet and Chambre syndicale des réparations automobiles et détaillants de produits pétroliers* v. *Centre Leclerc Toulouse et Centre Leclerc Saint-Orens-de-Gameville* [1985] ECR 305, 313, who maintained that minimum price rules designed to maintain an optimum geographical spread of petroleum supplies for purely individual needs were not covered by Art. 36. See also, regarding essential medical supplies, Case C–324/93 *The Queen* v. *Secretary of State for the Home Dept, ex parte Evans Medical Ltd and Macfarlan Smith Ltd* (not yet reported).

neutral Member State designed to ensure that essential supplies would be maintained in the event of war.[44]

True, objections of the Court of Justice to a broad interpretation of Articles 36, 223, and 224 exclude the possibility of inferring from these provisions that there is inherent in the Treaty a general proviso covering all measures taken for reasons of 'public safety'.[45] Likewise, the fact that Member States may take public security measures against nationals of third states does not mean that the whole field of migration policy in relation to third states falls within the scope of public security.[46] On the other hand, these provisions might justify denial of a right to judicial review before national courts conferred by Community law,[47] where such review was rendered impossible by serious internal disturbances or if measures needed to protect public safety could be deprived of their effectiveness because of such review.[48] More particularly, in *Richardt* the Court ruled that the concept of public security in Article 36 covered both the internal and the external security of a Member State and that restriction of imports, exports, and the transit of goods which could be used for strategic purposes might be justified under this provision.[49] To the extent that neutrality is maintained in the interests of external security, this ruling implies that trade restrictions based on neutrality requirements may be permissible under Article 36.

In short, the meaning of the above provisions is insufficiently clear[50] to resolve such a fundamental question[51] as whether the liberalization require-

[44] Cf., regarding action needed to be taken by a neutral country, P. Cramér, 'Funderingar kring permanent neutralitet och integration i västeuropa' in U. Nordlöf-Lagerkranz (ed.), *Svensk neutralitet Europa och EG* (Stockholm, 1990), 27–51, at 38.

[45] *Ibid.* 1684.

[46] Joined Cases 281, 283, 284, 285, and 287/85 *Germany, France, Netherlands, Denmark, United Kingdom* v. *EC Commission* [1987] ECR 3203, 3253.

[47] Dir. 76/207 of 9 Feb. 1976 ([1976] OJ L39/40) on the implementation of the principle of equal treatment for men and women.

[48] [1986] ECR 1651, 1692. In Case 68/76 *EC Commission* v. *France* [1977] ECR 515, 542 Capotorti A. G. also left open the possibility that unilateral measures by a Member State might be permissible 'as being of unavoidable necessity and urgency'.

[49] Case C–367/89 *Ministre des Finances* v. *Aime Richardt* [1991] ECR I–4621, I–4652.

[50] Particular problems might arise from the fact that use of Arts 223 and 224 can be challenged before the ECJ under Art. 225 of the Treaty. According to the last provision, if measures taken in the circumstances referred to in Arts. 223 and 224 have the effect of distorting competition in the common market, the Commission and the Member State concerned shall examine how these measures can be adjusted to the rules laid down in the Treaty. The Commission or any Member State may bring the matter before the Court if it considers that another Member State is making improper use of these provisions. It has been suggested that such challenges should be excluded where neutrality is invoked as a basis for such use. See W. Hummer and M. Schweitzer, 'Möglichkeiten und Grenzen der Dynamisierung der Beziehungen Österreichs zu den Europäischen Gemeinschaften' [1987] *Europa-Archiv* 343–50, at 349.

[51] In the view of the Commission, difficult problems are raised, which have to be solved in membership negotiations. See, e.g., *Beitrittsantrag Österreichs, Stellungnahme der Kommission*, SEC(91)1590, 25 *et seq.* It is not clear that such problems can be resolved through inclusion of a special derogation in an Accession Agreement. According to the ECJ in Case 231/78 *EC Commission* v. *United Kingdom* [1979] ECR 1447, 1462, regarding such derogations, 'it would be contrary to the principle of the equality of the Member States before Community law to accept that such inequalities could continue indefinitely'.

ments of the EC Treaty are compatible with neutrality.[52] However, the meaning of these provisions does not depend simply on their terms or even on their relationship with liberalization provisions.[53] The demands of 'European unity', mentioned by the Court of Justice in *Opinion 1/91*,[54] are part of the EC Treaty framework and may affect operation of Articles 36, 223, and 224.[55] More particularly, the development of the CFSP under the Treaty on European Union[56] may imply that the scope of application of such provisions should be narrowed.

3.2.2 'Mandatory Requirements'

While the legal framework constituted by the EC Treaty may affect interpretation of the scope of individual provisions expressly permitting trade restrictions on non-economic grounds, the impact of this framework is less immediately obvious, but possibly more profound, in relation to 'mandatory requirements'.

In *Cassis de Dijon*[57] the Court of Justice ruled that national measures necessary to satisfy mandatory requirements, such as those relating to the protection of public health, the defence of the consumer, and the fairness of commercial transactions, as well as the effectiveness of fiscal supervision, escaped the prohibition in Article 30 of the Treaty.

It is clear from the language of the Court in this ruling that the requirements indicated were not to be regarded as constituting an exhaustive enumeration of the grounds on which national measures might be permitted. Thus measures protecting the interests of workers[58] or the well-being of animals,[59] environ-

[52] T. Muoser, n. 33 above, 192–3. See also P. Guggenheim, 'Organisations Economiques Supranationales, Indépendance et Neutralité de la Suisse' [1962] *Zeitschrift für Schweizerisches Recht* 221–343, at 320–1.

[53] It was once thought that specific provisions in a treaty might not be necessary to render performance of neutrality obligations compatible with the treaty concerned. See the dissenting opinion of Judges Anzilloti and Huber in *The S.S. Wimbledon* (PCIJ Series A, No. 1), 36–7.

[54] Opinion 1/91 *(Draft Agreement between the Community, on the one hand, and the countries of the European Free Trade Association, on the other, relating to the creation of the European Economic Area)* [1991] ECR I–6079, I–6102. See also sect. 2.5 above.

[55] See, regarding implications for neutrality, M. Torrelli, 'La Neutralité en Question' [1992] *RGDIP* 5–43.

[56] Cf., regarding earlier developments, J-L. Dewost, 'La Communauté, les Dix et les 'Sanctions' Economiques: de la Crise Iranienne à la Crise des Malouines' [1982] *AFDI* 215–32.

[57] Case 120/78 *Rewe-Zentral AG* v. *Bundesmonopolverwaltung für Branntwein* [1979] ECR 649, 662.

[58] Case 155/80 *Sergius Oebel* [1981] ECR 1993, 2008. Cf., in connection with freedom to provide services, Case 279/80 *Alfred John Webb* [1981] ECR 3305, 3325.

[59] Joined Cases 141 to 143/81 *Gerrit Holdijk* [1982] ECR 1299, 1314. While it is true that this case concerned a common organization of an agricultural market, there is nothing in the terms of the ruling to suggest that similar requirements would not be recognized in the absence of such an organization. Indeed, because common organizations provide for detailed regulation of the relevant activity, it might be thought that the Court would be more willing to recognize such requirements in the absence of a common organization.

mental protection measures,[60] measures to encourage the creation of cinematographic works,[61] and measures based on cultural interests generally[62] have been recognized as permissible. Where such measures 'apply without discrimination to both domestic and imported products',[63] their application will be unaffected by trade liberalization provisions in the Treaty.

However, the measures must be necessary in the sense that the relevant interests are worthy of protection.[64] To determine whether this condition is met, the Court may examine whether these interests are protected by the law of other Member States[65] or by international agreements.[66] More particularly, the Court may investigate whether a product banned pursuant to such measures is consumed[67] or prohibited elsewhere in the Community.[68]

Moreover, the measures must also be necessary in the sense that the relevant interests are not already adequately protected. For example, national rules relating to the general interest may only be imposed on providers of services from other Member States who are not subject to similar rules in the Member State where they are established.[69] An analogous approach may be adopted in relation to goods. For example, *Robertson*[70] concerned Belgian law prescribing hallmarking requirements for silver-plated ware sold in Belgium. Here the Court considered whether hallmarks borne by imported silver-plated articles provided the consumer with equivalent protection to that required by Belgian law.[71]

[60] Case 240/83 *Procureur de la République* v. *Association de Défense des Brûleurs d'Huiles Usagées* [1985] ECR 531, 549; Case 302/86 *EC Commission* v. *Denmark* [1988] ECR 4607, 4630. See also the Commission Communication concerning the Consequences of the Judgment given by the ECJ on 20 Feb. 1978 ([1980] OJ C256/2).

[61] Joined Cases 60 and 61/84 *Cinéthäque* v. *Fédération nationale des cinémas français* [1985] ECR 2605, 2626.

[62] Case C–154/89 *EC Commission* v. *France* [1991] ECR I–659, I–687. Cf., in connection with the free movement of services, Case C–353/89 *EC Commission* v. *Netherlands* [1991] ECR I–4088, I–4094.

[63] Case 788/79 *Herbert Gilli and Paul Andres* [1980] ECR 2071, 2078.

[64] See also, regarding legislative restrictions on advertising, Case C–362/88 *GB-Inno-BM* v. *Confédération du Commerce Luxembourgeois Asbl* [1990] ECR I–667, I–687.

[65] See, e.g., Case 6/81 *BV Industrie Diensten Groep* v. *J. A. Beele Handelsmaatschappij BV* [1982] ECR 707, 717.

[66] See, e.g., the reference to Art. 10*bis* of the Paris Convention for the Protection of Industrial Property (*ibid.* 717).

[67] See, e.g., Case 193/80 *EC Commission* v. *Italy* [1981] ECR 3019, 3035.

[68] See, e.g., Case 53/80 *Officier van Justitie* v. *Koninklijke Kaasfabriek Eyssen BV* [1981] ECR 409, 422.

[69] Joined Cases 110 and 111/78 *Ministère Public and Chambre syndicale des agents artistiques et impresarii de Belgique Asbl* v. *Willy van Wesemael* [1979] ECR 35, 52; Case 279/80 *Alfred John Webb* [1981] ECR 3305, 3325.

[70] Case 220/81 *Timothy Frederick Robertson* [1982] ECR 2349, 2361.

[71] However, Member States may exempt from quality requirements or inspections products intended for export or may not carry out inspections. In practice, therefore, legislative equivalence may offer uncertain protection of the interests concerned. See the Explanatory Memorandum to the Commission Proposal for a Dir. on the official inspection of foodstuffs, COM(86)747. See, generally, G. Brouwers, 'Free Movement of Foodstuffs and Quality Requirements: Has the Commission Got it Wrong?' (1988) 25 *CMLRev.* 237–62, at 251–2.

Public Policy Analogy

It might be thought that recognition of mandatory requirements merely involves acceptance of exceptions from trade liberalization provisions on the basis of public policy, which is itself based on the broad continental civil law concept of *ordre public*.

True, the Court of Justice stipulated in *EEC Commission* v. *Italy*,[72] where the Italian authorities had suspended imports of pigmeat because of a crisis on the pigmeat market, that Article 36 of the Treaty did not permit restrictive measures to be adopted on the basis of economic considerations.[73] A stipulation to the same effect is contained in Article 2(2) of Directive 64/221,[74] which was enacted in order to limit the circumstances in, and procedures by, which a Member State could exclude or expel nationals of other Member States on public policy grounds.

However, the case law concerning industrial and commercial property rights suggests that the mere existence of an economic background to a restrictive measure does not in itself preclude the possibility of the measure being permitted under Article 36. More particularly, there is nothing in the ruling in *EEC Commission* v. *Italy* or in Directive 64/221 to indicate that the Court or the Council meant that measures adopted by Member States would fall outside provisions such as Article 36 simply because of their economic consequences. Indeed, since Treaty liberalization provisions only apply in principle to economic activity,[75] i.e., activity restrictions on which inevitably have such consequences, attribution of such a meaning to the above stipulations would deprive provisions such as Article 36 of effective significance. Hence, the mere fact that national rules, justified by objective circumstances corresponding to the needs of the interests referred to in Article 36, also enable other objectives of an economic nature to be achieved does not exclude the application of that provision.[76]

The real meaning of Community practice is, presumably, that a measure based on a provision such as Article 36 must not simply be justified on one of the grounds specified therein—if it were not so justified, it would in any case constitute what Article 36 expressly prohibits as being a 'disguised restriction on trade between Member States'—but must be so justified independently of

[72] Case 7/61 [1961] ECR 317, 329.

[73] See also Case 352/85 *Bond van Adverteerders* v. *The Netherlands State* [1988] ECR 2085, 2135.

[74] Of 25 Feb. 1964 ([1964] JO 850) on the co-ordination of special measures concerning the movement and residence of foreign nationals which are justified on grounds of public policy, public security, or public health.

[75] Case 36/74 *B. N. O. Walrave and L. J. N. Koch* v. *Union Cycliste Internationale* [1974] ECR 1405, 1417–8. Cf., regarding the 'recreational aspects' of lotteries, Case C–275/92 *Her Majesty's Customs and Excise* v. *Gerhart Schindler and Jörg Schindler* [1994] ECR I–1039, I–1091.

[76] Case 72/83 *Campus Oil Ltd* v. *Minister for Industry and Energy* [1984] ECR 2727, 2752. See also Case 118/86 *Openbaar Ministerie* v. *Nertsvoederfabriek Nederland* [1987] ECR 3883, 3908.

its economic consequences.[77] Thus, for example, it is the function of a trade mark as a guarantee for consumers of the origin of a product rather than as a means of safeguarding the investment of the holder incurred in the promotion of his product which means that use of trade mark rights to exclude products from another Member State may be justified under Article 36 on grounds of the protection of industrial or commercial property.[78] Again, *Thompson*[79] concerned a ban on the export of silver alloy coins from the United Kingdom to other Member States, which was designed to prevent the coins being melted down or destroyed there. The Court found the ban to be justified on public policy grounds within the meaning of Article 36, because it stemmed from the need to protect the right to mint coinage, which was traditionally regarded as involving the fundamental interests of the State. Conversely, Article 36 cannot justify a measure the primary objective of which is budgetary in as much as it is intended to reduce the operating costs of a sickness insurance scheme.[80]

On the other hand, the Court has made clear that, as an exception from the fundamental principle of free movement, the concept of public policy has to be strictly construed,[81] and it was to contribute to a strict construction of the concept in relation to the movement of persons that Directive 64/221 was enacted. Consequently, it would run counter to established Community practice for the Court to treat provisions such as Article 36 as permitting trade restrictions on grounds not expressly laid down in such provisions. In fact, care seems to have been taken to avoid any clear implication being given to the effect that Article 36 might provide the basis for the mandatory requirements recognized by the Court.[82] Moreover, in *EC Commission* v. *Ireland*,[83] which concerned Irish legislation requiring all souvenirs and articles of jewellery imported from other Member States to bear an indication of origin or the word 'foreign', the Court expressly stated that Article 36 did not do so. Subsequently, the Court began to deal separately with questions whether a justification for a restrictive measure could be based on the protection of public health within the meaning of Article 36, on the need to protect consumers, or on the requirements of fair trading.[84] Apparently, therefore, the Court regards the

[77] According to Mancini A. G. in Case 238/82 *Duphar BV* v. *The Netherlands State* [1984] ECR 523, 550, it is enough that the specified grounds have 'a decisive influence' on the restrictive measures adopted by a Member State.

[78] See, e.g., Case 119/75 *Terrapin (Overseas) Ltd* v. *Terranova Industrie C. A. Kapferer & Co.* [1976] ECR 1039, 1061.

[79] Case 7/78 *Regina* v. *Ernest George Thompson, Brian Albert Johnson and Colin Alex Norman Woodiwiss* [1978] ECR 2247, 2275.

[80] Case 238/82 *Duphar BV* v. *The Netherlands State [1984] ECR 523, 542.*

[81] Sect. 3.2.1 above.

[82] See, in particular, Case 8/74 *Procureur du Roi* v. *Benoît and Gustave Dassonville* [1974] ECR 837, 852 and Case 12/74 *EC Commission* v. *Germany* [1975] ECR 181, 199.

[83] Case 113/80 [1981] ECR 1625, 1640–1.

[84] See, e.g., Case 25/88 *Esther Renée Bouchara née Wurmser and Norlaine SA* [1989] ECR 1105.

mandatory requirements recognized in its case law as being distinct from the grounds, including that of public policy, on which provisions such as Article 36 permit trade restrictions.

Despite such rulings, the view persists that provisions such as Article 36 do provide the basis for the mandatory requirements recognized by the Court. This view is supported by the argument that measures otherwise qualifying by reference to such requirements would be treated with undue harshness where they were not equally applicable.[85] Certainly, as the Court continues to rule, such requirements may only cover national measures which are 'applicable without discrimination'.[86] In apparent contrast, provisions such as Article 36 may cover discriminatory measures, provided that the discrimination is not 'arbitrary'. Thus in *Campus Oil*[87] the Court accepted that the public security ground in Article 36 might justify the imposition of restrictions on imported products alone, provided that such restrictions were necessary to preserve the viability of the only oil refinery in the Irish Republic.

However, in *EC Commission* v. *Ireland*[88] the Court was prepared to examine whether the obligation imposed only on imported souvenirs that they be stamped with the country of origin or the word 'foreign' could be justified on grounds of mandatory requirements relating to consumer protection. It was only because imported and domestic souvenirs were found to be comparable that imposition of this obligation on the former alone was held to be discriminatory and, hence, impermissible. Conversely, differentiation between waste from within a particular region and waste from outside that region may be justified and permissible on the basis of mandatory requirements, having regard to the principle in Article 130r(2) of the Treaty that pollution should be remedied at source.[89] In other words, the acceptability of a measure on grounds of a mandatory requirement may depend on whether or not there is 'arbitrary discrimination' of the kind to which Article 36 refers.

The failure of the Court, in recognizing such requirements, to reproduce the language of the Article 36 proviso may be partly attributable to a desire to emphasize that, as regards the possibility of a measure being treated as justified by reference to a mandatory requirement, it is the application rather than the effects of such a measure which is decisive.[90] If it were enough for a measure to be precluded from such treatment that it had the effect of making importation more difficult than the disposal of domestic products, such treatment would be available in respect of few measures which did not anyway fall

[85] See, e.g., P. Oliver, n. 1 above, 92–3.

[86] See, e.g., Case C–353/89 *EC Commission* v. *Netherlands* [1991] ECR I–4088, I–4093.

[87] Case 72/83 *Campus Oil* v. *Minister for Industry and Energy* [1984] ECR 2727, 2753.

[88] Case 113/80 [1981] ECR 1625, 1640.

[89] Case C–2/90 *EC Commission* v. *Belgium* [1992] ECR I–4431, I–4480.

[90] Cf. Van Gerven A. G. in Case 25/88 *Esther Renée Bouchara née Wurmser and Norlaine SA* [1989] ECR 1105, 1118.

outside the scope of Article 30 as currently defined by the case law of the Court. As a result, consideration of the possibility of a mandatory requirement being recognized would be largely pre-empted by determination of whether a measure could be prohibited at all by Article 30, and the willingness of the Court to recognize such requirements would have little real significance.

On the other hand, the fact that the protection of public health is covered by provisions such as Article 36 of the Treaty and has been recognized as a mandatory requirement might be thought to imply that the requirements recognized by the Court have their basis in such provisions. If not, then the Court might be thought to be engaging in unnecessary duplication.[91] However, the purpose of such provisions is simply to enable national interest requirements to be taken into account in the application of trade liberalization provisions. It cannot be assumed that the nature and function of the mandatory requirements recognized by the Court are identical to those of the exceptions provided for in such provisions.

'Reserved Powers'

It has been argued that mandatory requirements reflect recognition by the Court of 'reserved powers' which are provisionally retained by Member States for the implementation of national policies and which are unaffected by Treaty liberalization provisions. Specifically, it has been deduced from the inclusion in the Treaty of various provisions envisaging harmonization of national law and policy[92] that national measures implementing such policies which do not formally discriminate are to be harmonized and, pending such harmonization, cannot be affected by provisions such as Article 30.[93] Some support for this argument might be thought to be provided by judgments such as *Brown*,[94] where the Court ruled that education policy was a matter for Member States and that, therefore, discrimination against nationals of other Member States as regards the award of maintenance grants for university studies was not prohibited by the then Article 7 of the Treaty.[95]

If such an argument really were to have been adopted by the Court in such judgments, the consequence would be that the scope of trade liberalization requirements would vary from Member State to Member State, depending on the extent to which each chose to exercise its reserved powers. The reasonableness or otherwise of such choices would be beyond the control of Com-

[91] Note the clarification in Joined Cases C–1/90 and C–176/90 *Aragonesa de Publicidad Exterior et Publivia* [1991] ECR I–4151, I–4186.

[92] See, e.g., Arts. 99 and 100 EC.

[93] See, e.g., Roemer A. G. in Joined Cases 51 to 54/71 *International Fruit Co. NV* v. *Produktschap voor Groenten en Fruit* [1971] ECR 1107, 1123–4. See also the argument of the German Government in Case 120/78 *Rewe-Zentrale AG* v. *Bundesmonopolverwaltung für Branntwein* [1979] ECR 649, 655.

[94] Case 197/86, *Steven Malcolm Brown* v. *Secretary of State for Scotland* [1988] ECR 3205, 3243.

[95] See now Art. 6 EC.

munity law. Such a situation would run counter to the principle of the uniform application of Community law.[96]

In its refined version this argument might be thought more plausible. According to this version, there is a division of powers between Member States and the Community such that the former may, pending harmonization, enact 'reasonable measures' in the exercise of their powers without falling foul of basic Treaty prohibitions.[97] The Commission might, perhaps, be thought to have proceeded on the basis of such reasoning in drawing up Directive 70/50,[98] where it was accepted that national trading rules which were equally applicable to imports and domestic products were permitted unless their effects exceeded those 'intrinsic' to such rules. The consequence of relying on such reasoning, however, would also render further reduction of trade restrictions dependent on harmonization and, hence, would not be readily reconcilable with the possibility of liberalization requirements being inherently capable of evolution or, in other words, with the autonomy of Community law.[99]

It may have been on these grounds that the Court has avoided adopting such reasoning and has expressly rejected the argument that Article 100 of the Treaty implies that all national law which does not formally discriminate against imports or nationals of other Member States is unaffected by liberalization requirements.[100] This provision envisages the harmonization of national law directly affecting the establishment or functioning of the common market.

More particularly, in *Casagrande*[101] an Italian national, who was a child of an Italian worker in Germany, had been refused an education grant there. The Court observed that competence in the field of education and training policy might not as such have been transferred to the Community institutions. However, exercise of those competences which had been transferred could not be affected by national measures implementing national education or training policy. Hence, such measures could not interfere with the equality of treatment enjoyed by migrant workers and their dependants, and the latter could not be denied education grants available to nationals of the host Member

[96] See, e.g., Case 14/68 *Walt Wilhelm* v. *Bundeskartellamt* [1969] ECR 1, 14.

[97] R. Barents, 'New Developments in Measures Having an Equivalent Effect' (1981) 8 *CMLRev*. 271–308, at 283.

[98] Of 22 Dec. 1969 ([1970] JO L13/29) based on the provisions of Art. 33(7), on the abolition of measures which have an effect equivalent to quantitative restrictions on imports and are not covered by other provisions adopted in pursuance of the EC Treaty.

[99] A Member State 'may not plead a mandatory requirement . . . in order to shield a product from the effects of price competition on the pretext of economic difficulties brought about by the elimination of barriers to intra-Community trade' (see Case 216/84 *EC Commission* v. *France* [1988] ECR 793, 812–3).

[100] Case 193/80 *EC Commission* v. *Italy* [1981] ECR 3019, 3033. See also Capotorti A. G. in Case 120/78 *Rewe-Zentral AG* v. *Bundesmonopolverwaltung für Branntwein* [1979] ECR 649, 655.

[101] Case 9/74 *Casagrande* v. *Landeshauptstadt München* [1974] ECR 773, 779.

State. Again, *Blaizot*[102] concerned French nationals who were in Belgium to study and were charged a supplementary fee by Belgian universities not payable by Belgian students. Here the Court ruled that the development of the common vocational policy under Article 128 of the Treaty meant that university studies fell within the scope of the Treaty. Therefore, discrimination regarding university fees was prohibited by the then Article 7,[103] and the supplementary fee could not be imposed on students from other Member States.

Even so, it might be imagined that the Court, though unwilling to accept the existence of any reserved powers entailing limits to the scope of liberalization provisions, has sought to preserve the availability of such powers by admitting exceptions from such provisions not explicitly envisaged in the Treaty[104] and has merely reversed the burden of proof envisaged by the Commission in Directive 70/50. In fact, however, the only rationale offered by the Court for recognition of mandatory requirements is that the requirements concerned accord with the 'general interest',[105] though some Advocates General have gone further and have maintained that they may be an inherent feature of the Community legal system.[106]

The 'General Interest'

In connection with the 'general interest', rulings concerning the freedom to supply services are particularly notable. For example, *Re Insurance Services': EC Commission* v. *Germany*[107] concerned restrictions on the provision of insurance services in Germany. Here the Court ruled that, regard being had to the particular nature of certain services, specific requirements imposed on the supplier could not be considered to be incompatible with the Treaty where they had as their purpose the application of rules governing such services. However, the freedom to provide services was one of the fundamental principles of the Treaty. Hence, this freedom might only be restricted by requirements which were justified by the general good and applied to all persons or undertakings operating within the territory of the Member State

[102] Case 24/86 *Vincent Blaizot* v. *University of Liège* [1988] ECR 379, 402–5.

[103] See now Art. 6 EC. The same approach was followed with regard to the demographic policies of Member States in Case 65/81 *Reina* v. *Landeskreditbank Baden-Württemberg* [1982] ECR 33, 44–5 and with regard to income tax in Case C–279/93 *Finanzamt Köln-Altstadt* v. *Roland Schumacker* (not yet reported).

[104] Cf. the view of K. Mortelmans, 'Article 30 of the EEC Treaty and Legislation Relating to Market Circumstances: A Time to Consider a New Definition' (1991) *CMLRev*. 115, 116 that the Court has recognized exceptions necessary to take account of 'market circumstances' legislation.

[105] See, e.g., Case 130/80 *Fabriek voor Hoogwaardige Voedingsprodukten Kelderman BV* [1981] ECR 527, 535.

[106] See, e.g., Capotorti A. G. in Case 155/80 *Sergius Oebel* [1981] ECR 1993, 2017.

[107] Case 205/84 [1986] ECR 3755, 3803. See also Case 279/80 *Alfred John Webb* [1981] ECR 3305, 3325 and Joined Cases 110 and 111/78 *Ministère Public and Asbl.* v. *van Wesemael* [1979] ECR 35, 52.

in which the service was provided, in so far as that interest was not safeguarded by the provisions to which the provider of a service was subject in the Member State of his establishment. In addition, such requirements must be objectively justified by the need to ensure that professional rules of conduct were respected and that the interests which such rules were designed to safeguard were protected. Provided these conditions were met, requirements relating to the public interest in protection of the consumer might justify the imposition of certain restrictions on the freedom to provide insurance services.

The Court has been slightly more explicit about the rationale for recognizing such requirements in taxation cases.[108] In such cases the Court has ruled that Article 95 of the Treaty does not prohibit taxation differentiating between similar products on the basis of objective criteria, if it pursues economic policy goals which are themselves compatible with the requirements of the Treaty and secondary legislation and if detailed rules of implementation avoid discrimination or protection.[109]

In fact, the interests with which the mandatory requirements recognized by the Court are concerned appear to be encompassed by the Community objectives, as outlined in Article 2 of the Treaty and the Preamble.[110] In the light of this outline, the Court seems to treat mandatory requirements as implicit in the Treaty framework.[111]

That these requirements have such a basis explains why they must be taken into account not only in judicial application of liberalization provisions but also in legislative harmonization.[112] At the same time, distinctions made by the Court between measures to protect purely national interests and those concerned with the general interest may be explained. For example, monetary compensatory amounts were not levies introduced by some Member States unilaterally but Community measures which might be permissible within the framework of the common agricultural policy.[113] Similarly, as regards charges for health inspections of pigs and bovine animals, which were required by Community legislation,[114] the inspections were not prescribed by each Member

[108] See, e.g., Case 196/85 *EC Commission* v. *France* [1987] ECR 1597, 1615.

[109] See regarding social policy, Case C–132/88 *EC Commission* v. *Greece* [1990] ECR I–1567, I–1592.

[110] An analogy might be drawn with Case 14/68 *Walt Wilhelm* v. *Bundeskartellamt* [1969] ECR 1, 14, where the Court expressly recognized Art. 85(3) EC as being concerned with the promotion of such objectives. Cf. earlier, regarding fishery conservation measures and sustainable development, Joined Cases 3, 4, and 6/76 *Cornelis Kramer* [1976] ECR 1279, 1313.

[111] Community instruments lacking formal legal force, such as the Council Resolution of 19 May 1981 ([1981] OJ C133/1) on a second programme for a consumer protection and information policy, may even be invoked by the Court, at least for the purpose of articulating such requirements. See Case C–362/88 *GB-Inno-BM* v. *Confédération du Commerce Luxembourgeois Asbl* [1990] ECR I–667, I–687–8.

[112] Sect. 5.2 below.

[113] Case 10/73 *Rewe-Zentral* v. *Hauptzollamt Kehl* [1973] ECR 1175, 1192.

[114] Dir. 64/432 of 26 June 1964 ([1964] JO [1977]) on animal health problems affecting intra-Community trade in bovine animals and swine.

State unilaterally in order to protect some interest of its own but by the Council in the general interest of the Community.[115] Hence, the charges might also be permissible.

It is consistent with such distinctions that exceptions expressly provided for in Treaty provisions such as Article 36 and the mandatory requirements recognized by the Court may not operate in identical fashion. An illustration is provided by the manner in which the prohibition of discrimination applies, on the one hand, to Article 36 measures and, on the other hand, to mandatory requirements. Since measures of the former kind are concerned with national interests, criteria for determining the comparability necessary for differential treatment to be characterized as prohibited discrimination must be found in such interests. As the *Campus Oil*[116] judgment illustrates, such interests may mean that imports and domestic products are non-comparable by reason of the very fact that the imports originate from outside the Member State concerned. Since the mandatory requirements recognized by the Court are concerned with the general interest, other criteria must, as in *EC Commission* v. *Ireland*,[117] be found to establish non-comparability. In this sense, provisions such as Article 36 may justify differentiation which cannot be justified on the basis of mandatory requirements recognized by the Court.

The significance of the latter requirements is that their recognition enables the Court to seek to go beyond the limits of the exceptions specifically envisaged in the Treaty, with a view to reconciling[118] trade-liberalization requirements with respect for other Treaty requirements.[119] Such reconciliation is implicit in the condition, employed by the Commission in Directive 70/50 and more recently by the Court,[120] that trading rules may be prohibited where their effects go beyond those intrinsic to such rules.[121]

[115] Case 46/76 *W. J. G. Bauhuis* v. *The Netherlands State* [1977] ECR 5, 17.

[116] Case 72/83 *Campus Oil* v. *Minister for Industry and Energy* [1984] ECR 2727.

[117] Case 113/80 [1981] ECR 1625.

[118] Community legislation, such as Dir. 79/112 of 18 Dec. 1978 ([1979] OJ L33/1) on the approximation of the laws of the Member States relating to the labelling, presentation, and advertising of foodstuffs, may produce different results. E.g., the Commission accepts that indication of fat content is very important as an item of information which enables the consumer to make a distinction between the various types of products on the market. However, for the Netherlands to apply unilaterally measures requiring such an indication would, according to the Commission, be bound considerably to hamper intra-Community trade. Consequently, the Commission acted under Dir. 79/112, so as to require the Netherlands to suspend adoption of the draft measure for 12 months. See Dec. 92/238 of 13 Apr. 1992 ([1992] OJ L121/48) calling upon the Kingdom of the Netherlands to postpone the adoption of a draft Reg. in respect of the labelling of emulsified fats.

[119] Cf., in the agricultural sector, Case 139/79 *Maizena GmbH* v. *EC Commission* [1980] ECR 3393, 3421.

[120] Case C–145/88 *Torfaen Borough Council* v. *B & Q plc* [1989] ECR 3851, 3889.

[121] In order to verify that the restrictive effects on Community trade do not exceed those necessary to attain a legitimate aim, it must be considered whether the effects are direct, indirect, or purely speculative and whether they impede the marketing of imported products more than the marketing of national products. See Case C–169/91 *Council of the City of Stoke-on-Trent, and Norwich City Council* v. *B & Q plc* [1992] ECR I–6635, I–6658–9.

The relationship between trade-liberalization requirements and mandatory requirements entailed by such practice may not necessarily be one of conflict.[122] Consequently, their interaction may not always be reducible to the simple balancing process[123] identified by some writers.[124] The more a measure is justified by reference to mandatory requirements, the less likely it will be to distort competition contrary to trade-liberalization requirements.[125] In *Alsthom Atlantique*,[126] for example, French law concerning the liability of a vendor for defective products was at issue. This law was stricter than that applied in other Member States and embodied an irrebuttable presumption that a trader was aware of any defects in the goods sold. Here the Court of Justice ruled that the presumption 'has been developed in the case law for reasons connected with the protection of buyers and is unlikely to favour or facilitate the adoption of agreements contrary to Article 85'.[127] The question whether a measure has anti-competitive effects on Community trade and the question whether it is justified by reference to a mandatory requirement may thus tend towards merger.[128]

This process may be captured by analysis based on the equality principle more satisfactorily than by one based on the idea of exceptions from a general prohibition. Liberalization requirements may mean that certain likenesses render differential treatment prohibited or that certain differences render like treatment prohibited. Other requirements may mean that certain differences justify differential treatment in the former case or that certain likenesses justify like treatment in the latter case. Hence, recognition of other requirements may

[122] Even if a static conception of competition might suggest conflict, resort to a more dynamic conception might produce different conclusions. For example, imposition of high standards of environmental protection could result in industries in the state concerned becoming more efficient and competitive.

[123] The Commission emphasized the need for a balance to be achieved between high environmental standards and the requirements of free movement in the negotiations for Swedish Accession to the Union. See *Commission Opinion on Sweden's Application for Membership*, Bull. EC, Supp. 5/92, 30–1.

[124] See, e.g., W. P. J. Wils, 'The Search for the Rule in Art. 30EEC Much Ado About Nothing?' (1993) *ELRev*. 475–92, at 478.

[125] Conversely, the less protection a national measure offers to other requirements, the more likely it is to be treated as contrary to liberalization requirements. See, e.g., Case 7/68 *EC Commission* v. *Italy* [1968] ECR 423, 430.

[126] Case C–339/89 *Alsthom Atlantique SA* v. *Compagnie de construction mécanique Sulzer SA* [1991] ECR I–107.

[127] *Ibid.* I–124. The same reasoning may also result in the conclusion that Community measures are acceptable. See, e.g., Joined Cases 424 and 425/85 *Coöperatieve Melkproducentenbedrijven Noord-Nederland BA ('Frico')* v. *Voedselvoorzienings In-en Verkoopbureau* [1987] ECR 2755, 2792.

[128] See also Case C–126/91 *Schutzverband gegen Unwesen in der Wirtschaft* v. *Yves Rocher GmbH* [1993] ECR I–2361, I–2390. Cf. Case C–234/89 *Stergios Delimitis* v. *Henninger Bräu AG* [1991] ECR I–935, I–984, where the Court examined a beer supply agreement by reference to its effect rather than its object, apparently because the restrictions of competition entailed by such agreements were necessary to achieve pro-competitive ends. Cf. also, in the taxation field, Warner A. G. in Case 46/80 *SpA Vinal* v. *SpA Orbat* [1981] ECR 77, 103.

play an organic role in the decision-making on which trade liberalization depends. In essence, there is an interplay of trade liberalization and other requirements—a 'matrix of variables'—embodied in the EC Treaty.

The implications for trade relations between the Community and third states are uncertain. To the extent that objectives other than trade liberalization are pursued in such relations, the need for separation between Community trade liberalization and international trade liberalization may become less important than the need for co-operation. Thus efforts to establish a single trading system with third states, as envisaged in Article 3(b) of the Treaty, and the stabilizing of agricultural markets under Article 39(1)(c) of the Treaty may be treated as complementary.[129] In other words, pursuit of such objectives may tend to soften the contrast between 'internal' and 'external' activities of the Community.[130] However, the Treaty may not necessarily provide an adequate basis for recognition of mandatory requirements in the treatment of international trade and, hence, for reconciliation of liberalization requirements with other requirements.[131]

3.2.3 Economic Requirements

The EC Treaty authorizes or has authorized trade restrictions on the basis of requirements arising from various economic policies.[132] In particular, Article 226 of the Treaty referred to difficulties arising during the transitional period which were serious and liable to persist in any sector of the economy or to bring about serious deterioration in the economic situation of a given area.[133] The 'difficulties' concerned included those attributable to operation of the

[129] See, e.g., Case 135/79 *Gedelfi Großeinkauf GmbH & Co. KG* v. *Hauptzollamt Hamburg-Jonas* [1980] ECR 1713, 1729.

[130] Cf. F. Snyder, 'Ideologies of Competition in European Community Law' (1989) 52 *MLR* 149–78, 160–2. Cf. also, in connection with social policy and immigration from third states, Joined Cases 281, 283–285 and 287/85 *Germany, France, Netherlands, Denmark and the United Kingdom* v. *EC Commission* [1987] ECR 3203, 3252. Characterization of third states as 'outsiders in terms of trade rules' (see P. Pescatore, 'The Dynamics and Homogeneity of the European Economic System' [1991] *JFT* 295–320, at 304) may thus have reduced significance.

[131] Van Gerven A. G. took the view in Case 340/87 *EC Commission* v. *Italy* [1989] ECR 1483, 1502 that equivalent exceptions to those permitted from the free movement of goods within the Community might not be permissible in the case of Community measures designed to harmonize national rules relating to trade with third states because of the demands of the common commercial policy. Cf., regarding the need to balance recognition of exclusive Community competence in relation to international trade under Art. 113 EC with recognition of requirements other than those of trade liberalization in C. W. A. Timmermans, 'Common Commercial Policy (Art. 113 EEC) and International Trade in Services' in F. Capotorti *et al.* (eds), *Du Droit International au Droit de l'Intégration Liber Amicorum Pierre Pescatore* (Baden-Baden, 1987), 675–89.

[132] The relevant provisions may reflect concern about the adjustment costs which can be entailed by regional trade liberalization. See A. Fishlow and S. Haggard, *The United States and the Regionalisation of the World Economy* (OECD, Paris, 1992).

[133] Cf. Art. XIX(1)(a) of GATT. See now the Agreement on Safeguards in Annex 1A to the Agreement establishing the World Trade Organization.

Treaty.[134] However, Article 226 only applied during the transitional period[135] and required Commission authorization of safeguard measures thereunder.[136] Moreover, such measures should be designed to rectify the situation and to adjust the sector concerned to the economy of the common market.[137]

More generally, authorization of trade restrictions is to be gradually replaced by common policies,[138] which may be supposed to offer a more developed solution to 'relative gains'[139] problems in integration. Pending such replacement, their authorization is designed to counter adverse consequences of integration for the interests of the Community[140] rather than for those of individual Member States.[141] As the Court of Justice puts it, a Member State cannot be allowed to avoid the effects of measures provided for in the Treaty by pleading the economic difficulties caused by the elimination of barriers to Community trade.[142] It is for such reasons that the Treaty allocates a central role in the adoption of restrictive measures to the Commission and Council and that the measures adopted may be challenged before the Court of Justice.[143]

[134] See Joined Cases 73 and 74/63 *NV Internationale Crediet-en Handelsvereniging 'Rotterdam' and De Coöperatieve Suikerfabriek en Raffinederij G. A. 'Puttenhoek'* v. *Minister van Landbouw en Visserij* [1964] ECR 1, 25. [135] Art. 226(1) EC. [136] *Ibid.* Art. 226(2).

[137] *Ibid.* Art. 226(1). Art. 226(3) also required that priority should be given to such measures as would least disturb the functioning of the common market.

[138] See, in particular, regarding Art. 46 EC, Joined Cases 80 and 81/77 *Société Les Commissionnaires Réunis Sàrl* v. *Receveur des Douanes; Sàrl Les Fils de Henri Ramel* v. *Receveur des Douanes* [1978] ECR 927, 946. See, regarding Art. 103, Case 154/77 *Procureur du Roi* v. *P. Dechmann* [1978] ECR 1573, 1584 and Joined Cases 88 to 90/75 *Società SADAM* v. *Comitato Interministeriale dei Prezzi* [1976] ECR 323, 338.

[139] J.M. Grieco, *Cooperation among Nations* (London, 1990).

[140] Cf., regarding Art. 67 ECSC, Joined Cases 27 to 29/58 *Compagnie des Hauts Fourneaux et Fonderies de Givors* v. *ECSC High Authority* [1960] ECR 241, 254. According to this provision, the Commission may issue recommendations to a Member State whose action is liable to have appreciable repercussions on competition in the coal or steel industry. Since integration was only partly established by that Treaty, the powers retained by the Member States meant that coal and steel undertakings established in their respective territories remained subject to different legislative provisions. These provisions were liable to operate to the advantage or disadvantage of the coal or steel industry of a Member State in comparison with the same industry coming under the jurisdiction of the other Member States or with other industries in the same Member State. Hence, Art. 67 provided for the Commission to recommend remedial measures. See Case 30/59 *De Gezamenlijke Steenkolenmijnen in Limburg* v. *ECSC High Authority* [1961] ECR 1, 24. Cf., in relation to the agricultural sector, Case 337/82 *St. Nikolaus Brennerei und Likörfabrik, Gustav Kniepf-Melde GmbH* v. *Hauptzollamt Krefeld* [1984] ECR 1051, 1063.

[141] See, e.g., Joined Cases 80 and 81/77 *Société Les Commissionnaires Réunis Sàrl* v. *Receveur des Douanes; Sàrl Les Fils de Henri Ramel* v. *Receveur des Douanes* [1978] ECR 927, 947.

[142] Case 72/83 *Campus Oil* v. *Minister for Industry and Energy* [1984] ECR 2727, 2752.

[143] The burden is on the Member State concerned to establish compliance with procedural requirements for resort to such measures and to show the presence of the material conditions for, and appropriateness of, their adoption. See Roemer A. G. in Joined Cases 6 and 11/69 *EC Commission* v. *France* [1969] ECR 523, 555–6.

Commercial Policy

Article 115 of the EC Treaty provides that in order to ensure that the execution of measures of commercial policy taken in accordance with this Treaty by any Member State is not obstructed by deflection of trade,[144] or where differences between such measures lead to economic difficulties in one or more of the Member States,[145] the Commission shall recommend the methods for the requisite co-operation between Member States. Failing this, the Commission shall authorize Member States to take the necessary protective measures, the conditions and details of which it shall determine.[146] In the selection of such measures, priority shall be given to those which cause the least disturbance to the functioning of the common market.

The Court of Justice sought to interpret Article 115, being an exception from the fundamental freedoms of the common market and from the common commercial policy, as strictly as the Treaty framework was considered to allow.[147] According to the Court, the Commission might, solely for serious reasons[148] and for a limited period, after a full examination of the situation in the Member State seeking a decision under Article 115[149] and having regard to the general interests of the Community, authorize the protective measures which caused the least disruption of Community trade.[150]

[144] Case 1/84R *Ilford* v. *EC Commission* [1984] ECR 423. It was only this, narrower, aim which was apparently regarded as legitimate under the ECSC Treaty. See the Opinion of Roemer A. G. in Joined Cases 9 and 12/60 *Société Commerciale Antoine Vloeberghs SA* v. *ECSC High Authority* [1961] ECR 197, 233.

[145] Case 59/84 *Tezi Textiel BV* v. *EC Commission* [1986] ECR 887, 924.

[146] Prior to its amendment by the TEU, this provision stated that during the transitional period a Member State could itself decide on urgent measures. Even after expiry of the transitional period Member States were empowered under Dec. 71/202 of 12 May 1971 ([1971] JO L121/26) empowering Member States to take interim protective measures with regard to the importation of certain products originating in third countries and put into free circulation in other Member States. The requirement of import authorizations could be introduced and the grant of such authorizations, pending Commission approval of such action could be withheld. Dec. 80/47 of 20 Dec. 1979 ([1980] OJ L16/14) on surveillance and protective measures which Member States may be authorized to take in respect of imports of certain products originating in third countries and put into free circulation in another Member State introduced the requirement of Commission authorization for surveillance measures. See now Dec. 87/433 of 22 July 1987 ([1987] OJ L238/26) on surveillance and protective measures which Member States may be authorized to take pursuant to this provision. See, e.g., Dec. C(90)1712 of 21 Aug. 1990 ([1990] OJ C211/15) authorizing Ireland not to apply Community treatment to blouses, shirts, and shirt-blouses of cat. 7 originating in Hong Kong and in free circulation in the other Member States.

[147] See, e.g., Case 41/76 *Suzanne Criel, née Donckerwolcke and Henri Schou* v. *Procureur de la République* [1976] ECR 1921, 1937.

[148] The Commission breached the proportionality principle if it acted under Art. 115 to authorize restriction of the importation of an 'insignificant' quantity of the products concerned. See, e.g., Case 62/70 *Werner A. Bock* v. *EC Commission* [1971] ECR 897, 902–10.

[149] The Commission might not rely simply on the compatibility of a measure with the Treaty without examining the reasons for the measure. See Case 29/75 *Kaufhof AG* v. *EC Commission* [1976] ECR 431, 443.

[150] Case 41/76 *Suzanne Criel, née Donckerwolcke and Henri Schou* v. *Procureur de la République* [1976] ECR 1921, 1928–9.

Even so, 'complete uniformity' in the treatment of international trade by the various Member States might be necessary to eliminate the need for such measures.[151] To the extent that this condition was not fulfilled, Article 115 measures might fulfil the same kind of function as rules of origin in a free trade area.[152] Indeed, this provision is said to have contributed to fragmentation of the common market along national lines, which made itself felt in wide price differences for identical products.[153] It is not simply that the customs union envisaged in Article 9 of the Treaty may have degenerated into a free trade area but that it degenerated into an imperfect one.

In other contexts a strict interpretation of provisions permitting national measures of commercial policy might not even be attempted, and so the potential for disruption of Community trade might be even greater. In *Schäfer Shop BV* v. *Minister van Economische Zaken*[154] the Court had to interpret paragraph 3 of the Protocol to the EC Treaty on German Internal Trade and Connected Problems. This paragraph permitted Member States to restrict trade in goods from the then German Democratic Republic. The Court pointed out that paragraph 3 was not a measure derogating from the rules of the common market but, on the contrary, was a safeguard measure for Member States against any harm which they might suffer as a result of the exceptional trade between the Federal Republic of Germany and the Democratic Republic. Hence, Member States were entitled to adopt a prior authorization system, even of a general nature, provided that the system constituted in practice the only appropriate means of tackling any disturbance of their economies resulting from German 'internal' trade.

Completion of the internal market might be thought to rule out continued use of any commercial policy measures in respect of Community trade. Its completion logically implies that the only restrictive measures which may now be adopted in pursuit of commercial policy requirements should be applicable to trade between third states and the Community as a whole. In other words, any such measures should be adopted in implementation of the common commercial policy rather than to compensate for its inadequacies. Accordingly, Article 115 measures are no longer authorized.[155]

151 Case 59/84 *Tezi Textiel BV* v. *EC Commission* [1986] ECR 887, 924.

152 Y. Bourdet and G. Hansson, 'The Economics of Trade-Policy Harmonization: with Special Reference to the Passenger Car Industry' [1987] *World Competition* 25–41, at 27. Art. 5(2) of the EFTA Convention referred to amendment of rules of origin as a possible means of dealing with 'deflections of trade' within EFTA. The ECJ has also held that the Community may introduce stricter rules of origin than normal when granting preferential treatment. See Case 385/85 *SR Industries* v. *Administration des Douanes* [1986] ECR 2929, 2942.

153 G. Koopman and H.-E. Scharrer, *Scenarios of a Common External Trade Policy for the EC after 1992* (Institut für Wirtschaftsforschung Report No. 84, Hamburg, 1990), 12.

154 Case 12/88 [1989] ECR 2937, 2962.

155 *The Community Internal Market—1993 Report*, COM(94)55, 56–7. Disparities caused by differing national quantitative restrictions set out in Annex I to Reg. 288/82 of 5 Feb. 1982 ([1982] OJ 435/1) on common rules for imports were eliminated by Reg. 518/94 of 7 Mar. 1994 ([1994] OJ

However, 'regional safeguard measures' may still be permissible in exceptional circumstances.[156] At the same time, 'sectoral back-up measures' have been approved for cars,[157] footwear,[158] and bananas.[159] Textiles are also made subject to special treatment, involving replacement of national quotas with Community quotas, though again regional safeguard measures may still be authorized,[160] and aid is to be provided to Community producers under the Retex Programme.[161] Moreover, in some instances at least, distortions of competition in Community trade may merely take less visible forms,[162] such as 'voluntary export restraints' (VERs) negotiated with third states,[163] even perhaps involving restrictive practices by undertakings sponsored or at least tolerated by Community institutions,[164] than Article 115

L67/77) on common rules for imports and repealing Reg. 288/82. The latter measure has itself been replaced by Reg. 3285/94 of 22 Dec. 1994 ([1994] OJ L349/53) on the common rules for imports and repealing Reg. 518/94. But see, regarding the problems of securing agreement within the Council, the *Eleventh Annual Report on the Community's Anti-Dumping and Anti-Subsidy Activities (1992)*, COM(93)516, 88.

[156] The Commission may exceptionally authorize such measures 'if it considers that such measures applied at that level are more appropriate than measures applied throughout the Community' (Art. 18 of Reg. 3285/94). They must be temporary and must disrupt the operation of the internal market as little as possible. See, similarly, Art. 17 of Reg. 519/94 of 7 Mar. 1994 ([1994] OJ L67/89) on common rules for imports from certain third countries and repealing Regs 1765/82, 1766/82, and 3420/83.

[157] See, regarding Japanese car imports, the *Twenty-Fifth EC General Report* (Brussels, 1992), 331; and Commission Replies to Oral Question 141 by Ms Tongue (EP Debs. No. 3–423, 265, 28 Oct. 1992) and to Written Question 1195/93 by Mr Christian de la Malène ([1994] OJ C32/18).

[158] See, regarding shoes from South Korea and Taiwan, *Financial Times*, 5 Aug. 1991.

[159] Reg. 404/93 of 13 Feb. 1993 ([1993] OJ L47/1) on the common organization of the market in bananas.

[160] See Art. 11 of Reg. 3030/93 of 12 Oct. 1993 ([1993] OJ L275/1) on common rules for imports of certain textile products from third countries and Art. 16 of Reg. 517/94 of 7 Mar. 1994 ([1994] OJ L67/1) on common rules for imports of textile products from certain third countries not covered by bilateral agreements, protocols, or other arrangements, or by other specific Community import rules.

[161] Notice to the Member States laying down guidelines for operational programmes which Member States are invited to establish within the framework of a Community initiative for regions heavily dependent on the textiles and clothing sector ([1992] OJ C142/5). Cf., more particularly, Reg. 852/95 of 10 Apr. 1995 ([1995] OJ L86/10) on the grant of financial assistance to Portugal for a specific programme for the modernization of the Portuguese textile and clothing industry.

[162] E.g., Dec. 95/130 of 27 Mar. 1995 ([1995] OJ L85/44) concerning the import of certain steel products into the new *Länder* of the Federal Republic of Germany from the Russian Federation permits certain duty-free imports of steel into the former GDR and Berlin but in Arts. 1 and 2 requires Germany and the Commission to 'take all the measures necessary to ensure that those products are actually used only' there.

[163] See, regarding Community use of VERs, M. Kelly *et al.*, *Issues and Developments in International Trade Policy* (International Monetary Fund, Washington, 1988). In principle, they are prohibited by Art. 11(1)(b) of the Agreement on Safeguards in Annex 1a to the Agreement establishing the World Trade Organization.

[164] It is envisaged that exclusive distributorship agreements may play a role in preventing trade deflection. See *Financial Times*, 5 Aug. 1991.

measures.[165] In short, therefore, the real effect of completion of the internal market on the use of commercial policy measures in Community trade is uncertain.

In relation to international trade, the development of the Common Foreign and Security Policy (CFSP) may increase the use of commercial policy measures to restrict such trade by reference to CFSP requirements. In particular, Article 113 of the Treaty, which concerns the common commercial policy, has been employed by the Community as a basis for imposing trade boycotts on third states in implementation of agreements reached within the context of European Political Co-operation,[166] and such practice is codified by Article 228a of the EC Treaty, as amended by the Treaty on European Union.[167]

Conjunctural Policy

Article 103 of the EC Treaty provides that Member States shall regard their conjunctural policies as a matter of common concern, and Article 103a(1) of the Treaty provides for the Council to decide what measures should be taken, in particular if serious difficulties arise in the supply of certain products.[168] Where a Member State is in difficulties or is seriously threatened with severe difficulties caused by exceptional occurrences beyond its control,[169] the Council may grant Community financial assistance to the Member State concerned under Article 103a(2).

In the case of shortages of products covered by the ECSC Treaty, it is the Commission which shall, in the absence of a unanimous decision of the Council, allocate the resources among the Member States and impose quotas on exports to third states under Article 59.[170]

[165] Cf. the failure of the Commission to act against a State-sponsored cartel to restrict imports of Japanese cars into France. The CFI found this failure unlawful in Case T–7/92 *SA Asia Motor France* v. *EC Commission* [1993] ECR II–669. See also Case T–37/92 *Bureau Européen des Consumateurs* v. *National Consumer Council* [1994] ECR II–285.

[166] See, e.g., Reg. 945/92 of 14 Apr. 1992 ([1992] OJ L101/53) preventing the supply of certain goods and services to Libya and Reg. 1432/92 of 1 June 1992 ([1992] OJ L151/4) prohibiting trade between the EEC and the Republics of Serbia and Montenegro.

[167] It states that where it is provided in a common position or joint action, according to provisions of the TEU concerning the CFSP, for Community action to interrupt or reduce, in part or completely, economic relations with one or more third countries, the Council shall take the necessary urgent measures. The Council shall act by a qualified majority on a Commission proposal.

[168] E.g., under the original version of this provision, Art. 103(4), Dec. 63/689 of 23 Dec. 1963 ([1963] JO 3108) *autorisant le royaume de Belgique à limiter jusqu'au 31 janvier 1964 les exportations de porcs et de viande de porc à destination des Etats membres* authorized Belgium to restrict exports of pork and live pigs for a fixed period because of the serious shortage of such products in that country.

[169] Cf. Arts. XX(j) and XIX(2)(a) of GATT. Cf. also, regarding provision for reintroduction of visa requirements for nationals of a third country 'in the event of an emergency situation in a third country posing a threat of a sudden inflow of nationals of that country into the Community', Art. 100c(2) EC.

[170] Particular measures have also been adopted in the case of oil shortages. See, e.g., Dec. 77/706 of 7 Nov. 1977 ([1977] OJ L292/9) on the setting of a Community target for a reduction in the consumption of primary sources of energy in the event of difficulties in the supply of crude oil and petroleum products.

It appears that a physical shortage is not necessary for resort to such provisions. According to the Court of Justice, if the price of a raw material is driven up by demand to a level such that a significant part of Community industry is no longer in a position to pay the price demanded, a *prima facie* case exists for a finding that there is a shortage for the purposes of Article 59 of the ECSC Treaty, even though the material may be available in sufficient quantities.[171] Apparently, then, such provisions have the potential to permit serious interference with trade.

However, the involvement of Community institutions may have fundamental implications for the function of such provisions. Given such involvement, these provisions may not so much allow for avoidance of Treaty violations that might otherwise be induced by overly rigid obligations[172] as create the possibility that exercise of the powers conferred on these institutions may entail further integration.

The underlying idea is that of 'Community solidarity'.[173] In accordance with this idea, the Community is to treat the conjunctural problems of a Member State as a matter of 'common concern'[174] and is to adopt measures necessary in the 'common interest'[175] to safeguard Treaty objectives[176] without impeding Community trade.[177] Where such measures have been adopted by the Community, the Member State concerned may not act unilaterally.[178]

Monetary Policy

According to Article 107(2) of the EC Treaty, if a Member State made an alteration in its rate of exchange[179] which was inconsistent with Article 104 objectives[180] and seriously distorted competition, the Commission might authorize other Member States to take measures to counter the consequences of such alteration. However, moves towards monetary union are seen as

[171] Case 25/85R *Nuovo Campsider* v. *EC Commission* [1985] ECR 751, 757.

[172] Cf. A. Manin, 'A propos des clauses de sauvegarde' [1970] *RTDE* 1–42.

[173] Case 77/77 *Benzine en Petroleum Handelsmaatschappij BV* v. *EC Commission* [1978] ECR 1513, 1525. The consequence of such solidarity is by no means unambiguously favourable to trade liberalization. See, e.g., B. M. Hoekman and M. P. Leidy, 'Holes and Loopholes in Regional Trade Arrangements and the Multilateral Trading System' [1992] *Aussenwirtschaft* 325–60.

[174] Case 43/72 *Merkur-Aussenhandels-GmbH* v. *EC Commission* [1973] ECR 1055, 1073.

[175] Joined Cases 9 to 11/71 *Compagnie d'Approvisionnent, de Transport et de Credit SA and Grands Moulins de Paris SA* v. *EC Commission* [1972] ECR 391, 406.

[176] Case 5/73 *Balkan-Import Export* v. *Hauptzollamt Berlin Packhoff* [1973] ECR 1091, 1108 and Case 9/73 *Carl Schlüter* v. *Hauptzollamt Lorrach* [1973] ECR 1135, 1152. See also Case 10/73 *Rewe Zentral AG* v. *Hauptzollamt Kehl* [1973] ECR 1175, 1190.

[177] Reischl A. G. in Case 65/75 *Riccardo Tasca* [1976] ECR 291, 318.

[178] See also Joined Cases 88 to 90/75 *Società SADAM* v. *Comitato Interministeriale dei Prezzi* [1976] ECR 323, 338.

[179] Art. 107(1) EC provided that each Member State was to treat its policy with regard to rates of exchange as a matter of common concern.

[180] I.e., maintenance of a balance-of-payments equilibrium and confidence in the currency, while taking care to ensure a high level of employment and stable prices.

obviating the need for such measures, and so Article 107(2) has been removed by the Treaty on European Union.

At the same time, Article 109h has been introduced.[181] The new provision concerns circumstances where a Member State is in difficulties or is seriously threatened with difficulties as regards its balance of payments either as a result of an overall disequilibrium in its balance of payments, or of the type of currency at its disposal,[182] and where such difficulties are liable in particular to jeopardize the functioning of the common market or the progressive implementation of the common commercial policy. In such circumstances, the Commission is to recommend what action a Member State affected in such a way should take.[183] If such measures prove insufficient, the Council may provide for the grant of mutual assistance.[184] Only if such assistance is not granted or proves insufficient may the Commission authorize protective measures.[185] Article 109i permits a Member State unilaterally to adopt such measures in the case of a sudden crisis, though the Council may decide by majority that these measures should be amended, suspended or abolished.

However, subject to Article 109k(6),[186] Articles 109h and 109i shall cease to apply from the beginning of the third stage of monetary union,[187] i.e., when national currencies are replaced by a common currency. Again, therefore, the policy harmonization implied by establishment of such a union is seen as removing the rationale for protection of national policy-making powers in the field of monetary policy.

On the other hand, provision for resort to safeguard measures in relation to international trade may be considered necessary for implementation of common policies sought through such harmonization. In particular, Article 73f provides that where, in exceptional circumstances, movements of capital to or from third countries cause or threaten to cause serious difficulties for the operation of the monetary union the Council may take safeguard measures with regard to third countries for a period not exceeding six months if such measures are strictly necessary.

Again, according to Article 73g(1), where a boycott against trade with a third country is adopted pursuant to the CFSP and implemented under Article

[181] It replaces Arts 108 and 109 of the Treaty.

[182] Cf. Art. XII of GATT.

[183] Under the original version of this provision, Art. 108(3), the Commission, e.g., authorized France to restrict the imports of cars and certain other products (Dec. 68/301 of 23 July 1968 ([1968] JO L178/15) *autorisant la République française à prendre certaines mesures de sauvegarde conformément à l'article 108 paragraphe 3 du traité*) and Greece to require interest-free deposits to be lodged for the importation of certain goods (Dec. 85/594 of 22 Nov. 1985 ([1985] OJ L375/9) authorizing Greece to take certain safeguard measures under Art. 108(3) EC).

[184] The idea of Community solidarity is thus emphasized. See Joined Cases 6 and 11/69 *EC Commission* v. *France* [1969] ECR 523, 540.

[185] Such authorization must be formally, not tacitly, granted. See Reischl A. G. in Case 27/74 *Demag AG* v. *Finanzamt Duisburg-Süd* [1974] ECR 1037, 1057.

[186] I.e., safeguard measures may still be adopted by Member States with a derogation from participation in the third stage.

[187] Arts. 109h(4) and 109i(4) EC respectively.

228a of the Treaty,[188] the Council may 'take the necessary urgent measures on the movement of capital and on payments as regards the third countries concerned'. Under Article 73g(2) a Member State may take, for serious political reasons and on grounds of urgency, unilateral measures of this kind. However, the Council may decide that the Member State shall amend or abolish such measures.

Competition Policy

The EC Treaty regards competition law as playing a central role in trade liberalization. However, according to the Spaak Report, during the transitional period for establishment of the customs union[189] national anti-dumping measures should be permissible, subject to control by the Commission.[190] Article 91(1) of the Treaty duly provided that, during this period, the Commission could address recommendations to persons engaged in dumping between Member States. If the dumping continued, the Commission could authorize the injured Member State to take protective measures. In the event, little use was made of this provision,[191] and following the 'acceleration decision',[192] it ceased to have legal force on 1 July 1968,[193] though equivalent provisions were included in subsequent Accession Agreements.[194]

Article 91(2) also required that, from the beginning of the transitional period, goods exported from one Member State to another could be re-imported to the former free of customs duties, quantitative restrictions, or equivalent measures.[195] This so-called 'boomerang' clause[196] may have had little practical relevance to problems of intermittent dumping,[197] and even in relation to more persistent dumping may not always have proved effective. It would be expensive for an undertaking faced with dumping by competitors to buy the dumped goods and re-export them to their country of origin, and if all the outlets there were bound by exclusive purchasing agreements, it would be

[188] See n. 143 above. [189] Art. 8 of the original version of the EEC Treaty.

[190] Comité Intergouvernemental Créé par la Conférence de Messine, *Rapport des Chefs de Délégation aux Ministres des Affaires Etrangères* (Brussels, 1956), 54.

[191] *First Report on Competition Policy* (EC Commission Brussels, 1972), 91.

[192] Dec. 66/532 of 26 July 1966 ([1966] JO 2971) *relative à la suppression des droits de douane et à l'interdiction des restrictions quantitatives entre les Etats membres et à la mise en application des droits du tarif douanier commun pour les produits autres que ceux énumérés à l'annexe II du traité.*

[193] Dec. 75/497 of 15 July 1975 ([1975] OJ L228/3 relating to a proceeding under Art. 85 EC (IV/27.000—IFTRA rules for producers of virgin aluminium).

[194] Arts 136 and 137 of the Act of Accession with Denmark, Ireland, and the UK, Art. 131 of that with Greece, and Art. 380 of that with Portugal and Spain.

[195] This provision was implemented by Reg. 8/60 of 11 Mar. 1960 ([1960] JO 597) *pour l'application du paragraphe 2 de l'article 91 du traité instituant la Communauté économique européen*, as amended by Reg. 13/61 of 15 Mar. 1961 ([1961] JO 585).

[196] Cf. Art. 17(2) of the EFTA Convention (SÖ 1960:1).

[197] Such dumping is traditionally regarded as the most dangerous kind. See J. Viner, *Dumping: A Problem in International Trade* (Chicago, 1923), 132 *et seq.*

impossible to market the goods there through normal channels.[198] Such limitations to the effect of the clause seem to have been recognized, and the clause was not included in Accession Agreements.[199]

What may be more important is whether there is sufficient liberalization to enable competitors in the country where the products are dumped to export their own products to the country where the dumping originates. To the extent that this condition is met, undertakings may have less incentive to dump, and states may be deterred from granting certain types of aid, such as those associated with price-support arrangements, which may lead to dumping.

The implicit assumption in the EC Treaty and Accession Agreements that completion of transitional periods was necessary and sufficient for this condition to be met is questionable. The degree of liberalization entailed by Community law at the end of the original transitional period was less than that entailed by such law at the end of the transitional periods applied in the case of acceding Member States.[200] Hence, the assumption may owe more to generalized expectations of the integration processes set in motion by the Treaty than to strictly economic judgment.

3.3 FREE TRADE AGREEMENTS

The Free Trade Agreements contained various provisions permitting trade restrictions. As under the EC Treaty, some restrictions might be permitted on the basis of non-economic requirements and others on the basis of economic requirements.

3.3.1 Non-Economic Requirements

Provisions in the Free Trade Agreements allowing for trade restrictions on non-economic grounds were closely modelled on EC Treaty provisions. During negotiations for the Agreements the former provisions were appar-

[198] Hence, it is argued that differential-price dumping depends on collusion in the exporting industry. See B. Hindley, 'The Economics of Dumping and Anti-Dumping Action: Is there a baby in the bathwater?' in P. K. M. Tharakan (ed.), *Policy Implications of Antidumping Measures* (Amsterdam, 1991), 25–43.

[199] Cf., however, the view that this clause might account for the small number of dumping complaints brought before the Commission in J. Boudant, *L'Anti-Dumping Communautaire* (Paris, 1991), 246.

[200] Art. 46 EC embodies an approach that seems more logical in legal and economic terms. Pending establishment of a common organization of an agricultural market, when the Art. 92 prohibition of state aid is inapplicable, countervailing duties may be employed in relation to intra-Community trade in agricultural products under Art. 46. The latter provision has been interpreted by the ECJ as remaining valid after the end of the original transitional period. See Case 337/82 *St. Nikolaus Brennerei und Likörfabrik, Gustav Kniepf-Milde GmbH* v. *Hauptzollamt Krefeld* [1984] ECR 1051, 1062 and Case 181/85 *EC Commission* v. *France* [1987] ECR 689.

ently of particular interest to EFTA States, while the Community was more interested in provisions permitting trade restrictions on economic grounds.[201]

Public Policy

Article 20 of the Swedish Free Trade Agreement followed Article 36 of the EC Treaty. The former permitted prohibitions or restrictions on imports, exports, or goods in transit justified on various grounds. These grounds were public morality, law and order,[202] or public security,[203] the protection of life and health of humans, animals, or plants, the protection of national treasures of artistic, historic, or architectural value, the protection of industrial or commercial property, or rules relating to gold or silver.[204] The second sentence of Article 20 of the Swedish Agreement also followed Article 36 of the EC Treaty in stipulating that such prohibitions or restrictions must not constitute a means of arbitrary discrimination or a disguised restriction on trade between the Parties.

The similarity between the two provisions was so close that the former provision referred to restrictions which a Party might impose on exports from its territory, even though the original version of the Agreement did not expressly prohibit quantitative restrictions on exports at all. The most likely explanation of this reference was that the authors of the Swedish Agreement simply copied from Article 36 of the EC Treaty, which is designed to permit exceptions not only from Article 30 but also from the Article 34 prohibition of quantitative restrictions and measures having equivalent effect on exports between Member States.[205] Hence, such a reference could not be taken to imply that restrictions on exports were prohibited by the Agreement[206] and, hence, to justify an expansive interpretation of the liberalization requirements of the Agreement.

At the same time, Article 20 of the Agreement might be more permissive in authorizing trade restrictions than its counterpart in the EC Treaty. In particular, the view has been expressed that the proportionality principle[207] could have different effects in the context of a Free Trade Agreement from its effects within the context of the EC Treaty.[208] True, in *HFM*

[201] AiH 4/1972, 22.

[202] This expression presumably corresponded to that of public policy in the EC Treaty.

[203] Such grounds might cover measures needed to be taken by a neutral country during wartime. See P. Cramér, n. 44 above, 38.

[204] Art. 12(f) of the EFTA Convention also refers to such rules. Rules relating to gold and silver are not specifically protected by Art. 36 EC, though the right of a state to mint coinage is protected. See Case 7/78 *Regina* v. *Thompson, Johnson and Woodiwiss* [1978] ECR 2247.

[205] See the criticism of this drafting technique by Capotorti A. G. in Case 225/78 *Procureur de la République* v. *Bouhelier* [1979] ECR 3151, 3166.

[206] Case 174/84 *Bulk Oil (Zug) AG* v. *Sun Oil International Ltd and Sun Oil Trading Co.* [1986] ECR 559, 583. See also Case 225/78 *Procureur de la République* v. *Bouhelier* [1979] ECR 3151, 3160–1.

[207] See sect. 3.2.1 above.

[208] Jacobs A. G. in Case C–312/91 *Metalsa Srl* [1993] ECR I–3751, I–3766.

Nijman,[209] which concerned exclusion from the Netherlands of a Swedish plant-protection product banned by Dutch law, the Court of Justice did not differentiate between the scope of Article 36 of the EC Treaty in relation to Community trade and that of Article 20 of the Swedish Agreement in relation to trade between the Parties. The Court did, nevertheless, maintain that the operation of Article 36 could be affected by 'full harmonization'.[210] In other words, differences in the operation of the two provisions could arise from differences in the harmonization taking place within their respective legal frameworks.

Security

Trade restrictions based on security considerations might be permitted under Article 21 of the Swedish Agreement. Although it was the Community itself rather than the Member States which concluded the Agreement[211] and the Community had no responsibility for the provision of security, Member States were required by Article 228(2) of the EC Treaty[212] to respect agreements concluded by the Community.[213] Presumably, it was thought that the terms of the Agreement might, in the absence of a provision such as Article 21 thereof, have impinged upon the freedom of action of Member States as well as that of Sweden in relation to security.

According to Article 21, the Agreement did not prevent the Parties from taking action in relation to three categories of matters. First, Article 21(a) provided that measures which a Party considered necessary to prevent disclosure of information contrary to its essential security interests were not affected.

Secondly, the Parties remained free under Article 21(b) to take measures relating to trade in arms, munitions, or war materials or to research, development, or production indispensable for defence purposes, provided that such measures did not impair the conditions of competition in respect of products not intended for specifically military purposes.

Article 21(a) and (b) of the Agreement followed Article 223 of the EC Treaty. However, Article 21(b) was apparently somewhat broader than Article 223, which only refers to production of, and trade in, weapons, ammunition, and war materials.

Finally, Article 21(c) of the Agreement provided that the Parties might take measures which they considered essential to their own security in time of war

[209] Case 125/88 [1989] ECR 3533. See also, regarding the Norwegian Free Trade Agreement ([1973] OJ L171/2), Case C–228/91 *EC Commission* v. *Italy* [1993] ECR I–2701 and, regarding the Austrian Free Trade Agreement, Case C–207/91 *Eurim Pharm GmbH* v. *Bundesgesundheitsamt* [1993] ECR I–3723.

[210] [1989] ECR 3533, 3546–57.

[211] In contrast, the Agreement with the ECSC ([1972] JO L350/76) was concluded with the Member States as well as the Community.

[212] See now Art. 228(7) EC.

[213] See, e.g., Case 104/81 *Hauptzollamt Mainz v. C. A. Kupferberg & Cie KG* [1982] ECR 3641, 3662.

or serious international tension. This provision seems to have been a succinctly worded equivalent of Article 224 of the EC Treaty.[214] The former departed from the latter in not referring to measures necessary for a state to meet obligations it had accepted for the purpose of maintaining peace and international security. If such measures were implicitly covered by Article 21(c) of the Agreement, the consequences for neutrality could have been important. Specifically, it might have been argued that Sweden had undertaken the obligations of neutrality for such purposes and, therefore, would have been able to invoke this provision in the case of measures needed to give effect to these obligations.

Article 21(c) was, in fact, invoked by Sweden in November 1975 in order to restrict the importation of shoes,[215] on the ground that maintenance of an adequate level of domestic production was necessary to enable Sweden to maintain its neutrality in the event of war.[216] The Commission, however, objected that Article 21(c) could only be invoked in time of war

[214] Though the former did not impose the same consultation requirement.

[215] There were EFTA objections that the import restrictions were not permitted by Art. 18(1)(b) of the EFTA Convention (SÖ 1960:1) and should be lifted or substituted by other measures. See AiH 3/1976, 9. This provision has similar wording to Art. 21(c) of the Swedish Agreement, but it is stipulated that imposition of customs duties or quantitative restrictions on imports is not permissible. Such restrictions are only permissible on grounds covered by Art. 12 of the EFTA Convention, which is the equivalent of Art. 36 EC. Apparently, state aid to relevant domestic industries might have been permissible. See *Kungl. Maj:ts proposition till riksdagen angående godkännande av Sveriges anslutning till konventionen angående upprättandet av Europeiska frihandelssammanslutningen, m. m., given Stockholms slott den 4 januari 1960* (Government proposal for approval of Swedish accession to the EFTA Convention), prop. 1960:25, 26. See also, regarding shoes and clothing, *Kungl. Maj:ts proposition angående försörjningsberedskapen på beklädnadsområdet m. m. given Stockholms slott den 20 oktober 1972* (Government proposal concerning 'preparedness' for the provision of clothing), prop. 1972:127, 51. Reference was not apparently made to Art. 18(2) of the Convention which authorized action taken by a state to carry out undertakings entered into for the purposes of maintaining international peace and security.

[216] See *Regeringens proposition med förslag till åtgärder för försorjningsberedskapen på beklädnadsområdet m. m.* (Government proposal concerning 'preparedness' for the provision of clothing), prop. 1975/76:57, 15; *Sverige–EG 1975* (Utrikes- och handelsdepartementen, 1976), 21–24. The measures were maintained in 1976. See *Sverige–EG 1976* (Utrikes- och handelsdepartementen, 1977), 22–23. Such action would apparently have been permissible under Art. 3(1)(b) of Ch. 20 of the draft Nordek Treaty, which permitted action necessary on essential security grounds, *inter alia*, to protect production necessary for defence purposes.

[217] This interpretation, which was only clearly supported by the German-language version of the Swedish Free Trade Agreement, seems subsequently to have been accepted by the Swedish Government. See *Svensk utrikeshandel i krislägen* (Swedish foreign trade in wartime) SOU 1989:107, 177. Art. 18(1)(d) of the EFTA Convention (SÖ 1960:1) also refers to measures *adopted in* time of war or other emergency in international relations. Art. XXI(b)(iii) of GATT has the same wording.

[218] See sect. 3.3.2 below, regarding this provision. In the same year Irish restrictions were introduced under Dec. 76/277 of 24 Feb. 1976 ([1976] OJ L58/13) authorizing Ireland to take protective measures in respect of footwear with uppers of leather originating in Sweden, and import surveillance measures were applied by various Member States in the case of several goods covered by the Free Trade Agreement. In these cases Art. 24 or 26 of the Agreement (sect. 3.3.2 below) was invoked. See *Sverige–EG 1975* (Utrikes- och handelsdepartementen, 1976), 21 and 24.

or other critical international situation[217] and that Article 26 of the Agreement[218] should have been invoked.[219]

Commentators also take the view that the Swedish action was contrary to the Agreement, and such a view may be justified in this particular case.[220] On the other hand, the Swedish Government claimed that no country in Europe was less self-sufficient in shoes than Sweden and that an adequate level of shoe production would be essential for a neutral country during a war.[221] In view of the above-mentioned ruling in *Campus Oil*,[222] it seems that Article 20 of the Agreement might have permitted certain action by a neutral country designed to ensure that essential supplies would be maintained in the event of war.

Moreover, a further basis for trade restrictions was introduced by Article 24A of the Agreement, when abolition of quantitative restrictions and measures having equivalent effect on exports between the Parties was provided for in the 1989 protocol to the Agreement.[223] According to this new provision, a Party encountering or likely to encounter 'major difficulties' might restrict exports, where one of two further conditions was met. One condition was met in the case of re-export towards a third country against which the exporting Party maintained, for the product concerned, quantitative export restrictions, export duties, or measures or charges having equivalent effect. Thus non-participation of Sweden in a Community trade boycott need not necessarily have resulted in that boycott being undermined.[224] At the same time, Sweden might have been permitted thereby to meet the obligations of a neutral country not to export war materials to belligerents.

3.3.2 Economic Requirements

The inclusion of safeguard clauses[225] in Free Trade Agreements might be considered necessary simply so that the Parties might prevent encroachment on other requirements by trade liberalization requirements in these Agreements. At the same time, the very limitations to the latter requirements meant that differences in competitive conditions unaffected thereby might have

[219] *Ninth General Report on the Activities of the European Communities* (EC Commission, Brussels, 1976), 252; Bull. EC 11–1975, 2332; *Tenth General Report on the Activities of the European Communities* (EC Commission, Brussels, 1977), 277.

[220] See, e.g., H. Lidgard, 'Tre års frihandelssamarbete med EEC' [1976] *SvJT* 689–714 and U. Bernitz, 'The EEC–EFTA Free Trade Agreements with Special Reference to the Position of Sweden and the Other Scandinavian EFTA Countries' (1986) 23 *CMLRev.* 567–90, 583. The Swedish Board of Trade also considered that the action was contrary to the international obligations of Sweden. See AiH 3/1976. [221] AiH 3/1976, p. 9. [222] Sect. 3.2.1 above.

[223] Supplementary Prot. concerning the elimination of existing and prevention of new quantitative restrictions affecting exports or measures having equivalent effect ([1989] OJ L295/22).

[224] Cf., regarding Swiss arrangements to prevent its territory being used to undermine Community restrictions on trade with South Africa, R. Schwok, *Switzerland and the European Common Market* (London, 1991), 108.

[225] See, regarding the problems of such clauses in international trade generally, P. Merciai, 'Safeguard Measures in GATT' [1985] *JWTL* 41–66.

increased potential for producing distortions of competition.[226] Instead of seeking to reduce such differences through harmonization, such Agreements might include safeguard clauses permitting restriction of the limited liberalization required.[227] As a result, the potential for 'spill-back'[228] in the operation of liberalization requirements was created. Realization of such potential might have been rendered more likely by the absence in the Agreements of provision for independent institutional involvement in relation to safeguard measures.[229] In the absence of such provisions, the operation of such clauses might be largely a matter of economic strength.[230]

Commercial Policy

Article 24 of the Swedish Agreement permitted adoption of safeguard measures where production in the territory of a Party was detrimentally affected by an increase in imports attributable to low customs duties or charges having equivalent effect and where two further conditions were met. First, the increase must result from the reduction or abolition of such duties or charges by the importing Party, as provided for in the Agreement. Secondly, the duties or charges levied by the exporting Party on imports of raw materials or intermediate products used in the manufacture of the product in question must be significantly lower than the corresponding duties or charges levied by the importing Party.

This provision appears to have exemplified difficulties ultimately attributable to the fact that the Agreement did not provide for the establishment of a customs union between the Parties, which would have entailed that both would

[226] Safeguard clauses may thus be said to take the place of more developed liberalization requirements. See, e.g., U. Bernitz, 'Om Statliga Handelsmonopol i EG och enligt Frihandelsavtalen' [1973] *TfR* 514–37. According to T. Heller and J. Pelkmans, id. op., 327, the private adjustment processes and public policy constraints engendered by negative economic integration tend to accentuate the role of national public agents in economic functions still assigned to the national level.

[227] Note the separation between harmonization and use of safeguard measures in Opinion 1/94 *(Competence of the Community to conclude international agreements on services and the protection of international property)* [1994] ECR I–5267, I–5407.

[228] Cf., regarding this process in the context of integration within the Community, L. Lindberg and S. A. Scheingold, *Europe's Would-be Polity* (Englewood Cliffs, New Jersey, 1970).

[229] Cf. T. Heller and J. Pelkmans, n. 226 above, 347.

[230] Certainly, the deterrent effect of possible retaliation would seem to be a function of such strength. See, e.g., *Varuförsörjning i krigstid* (provision of goods in wartime), SOU 1975:57. See, generally, H. Lidgard, 'Sverige-EEG och konkurrensen' [1974] *SvJT* 18–33, 31. Accordingly, during negotiation of the Agreement Sweden sought to ensure that the safeguard clauses contained therein would be as clear and unambiguous as possible (*Utrikesutskottets betänkande med anledning av propositionen 1972:135 angående avtal med de europeiska gemenskaperna m.m. jämte motioner*—Report of the Foreign Affairs Committee of the Swedish Parliament on the Free Trade Agreement (UU1972:20), 27). The effect of such efforts was not readily discernible in the Agreement.

levy the same duties on imports of raw materials or intermediate products from third countries.[231]

The implication of the *Schäfer* ruling[232] is that this provision may have a broader scope of application than that enjoyed by Article 115 of the EC Treaty, even before efforts to complete the single market led to measures designed to remove the need for use of Article 115.[233] As a result, the potential of the former for disrupting trade between the Parties to the Free Trade Agreement may have been greater than that of Article 115 in relation to Community trade.

Conjunctural Policy

Article 26 of the Swedish Agreement[234] was reminiscent of Article 226 of the EC Treaty. The former provided that if serious disturbances arose in any sector of the economy or if difficulties arose which could have brought about serious deterioration in the economic situation of a region, the Party concerned might adopt safeguard measures.[235] This provision was invoked, for example, in 1973[236] and 1982[237] following storm damage to trees in Germany and France respectively and was accepted as a legitimate basis for restricting the importation of Swedish timber.

Moreover, according to Article 24A of the Agreement, a Party encountering or likely to encounter 'major difficulties' might restrict exports, where one of two further conditions was met. One condition was that there must be a serious shortage, or threat thereof, of a product essential to the exporting Party. This provision was somewhat narrower than Article 103(4) of the EC Treaty, which originally covered situations where 'any difficulty should arise in the supply of certain products'.[238]

Monetary Policy

Article 28 of the Swedish Agreement, like Articles 109h and 109i of the EC Treaty, allowed the Parties to protect monetary policy against encroachment by liberalization requirements in the Agreement.[239] It provided that where one or more of the Member States or Sweden was in difficulties or was seriously threatened with difficulties as regards its balance of payments, the Party

[231] Art. 5(2) of the EFTA Convention (SÖ 1960:1) expressly refers to amendment of rules of origin as a possible means of dealing with 'deflections of trade' within the context of trade between EFTA States. [232] See sect. 3.2.3 above. [233] *Ibid.*

[234] See also Art. 3(c) of Prot. 1 to the Agreement, concerning the treatment applicable to certain products where the Community reserved the right to postpone liberalization 'in the event of short-term economic difficulties'. [235] See, similarly, Art. 20(1)(a) of the EFTA Convention.

[236] *Sverige–EG 1973* (Utrikes- och handelsdepartementen, 1974), 23–4.

[237] *Sverige–EG 1982* (Utrikesdepartementet, 1983), 22–3.

[238] See now Art. 103a EC (sect. 3.2.3).

[239] Art. 19 of the EFTA Convention (SÖ 1960:1) has similarities in substance. Cf. the comparison of this provision with Arts 108 and 109 in the original version EC in H. A. H. Audretsch, 'The EEC and EFTA: Two Solutions Regarding Balance of Payments Difficulties' (1966–67) 4 *CMLRev*. 419–39.

concerned might take the necessary safeguard measures. In October 1985, for example, this provision was invoked when Greece imposed a requirement that importers place an interest-free deposit equivalent to a proportion of the value of the imported goods for six months.[240]

Competition Policy

Article 23 of the Swedish Agreement apparently incorporated much of Community competition law into the Agreement and specified anti-competitive conduct which was incompatible with the proper functioning of the Agreement, in so far as trade between the Parties might be affected. The terms of this provision seem to have been capable of a broader construction than Article 15 of the EFTA Convention,[241] which dealt only with 'restrictive business practices' to the extent that they frustrated the benefits expected from liberalization of trade in goods.[242] The former provision might, in fact, be thought to have entailed a broad prohibition of anti-competitive practices in trade between the Parties,[243] and an important contribution to liberalization of such trade might have been expected to result from its application.

(i) Restrictive Practices of Undertakings

Article 23(1)(i) of the Swedish Agreement followed Article 85(1) of the EC Treaty. It provided that all agreements between undertakings, decisions of associations of undertakings, and concerted practices between undertakings which had as their object or effect the prevention, restriction, or distortion of competition as regards the production of, or trade in, goods were incompatible with the Agreement, in so far as trade between the Parties might be affected. Furthermore, Article 23(1)(ii) of the Swedish Agreement followed Article 86 of the EC Treaty. It provided that any abuse by one or more undertakings of a dominant position in the territories of the Parties as a whole or in a substantial part thereof was incompatible with the Agreement, in so far as trade between the Parties might be affected. Although these provisions thus adopted much of the terminology of Articles 85 and 86 of the EC Treaty, in view of the more limited objectives of the Free Trade Agreements, use of equivalent terms does not necessarily mean that Article 23(1) of the Swedish Agreement had the same function as Articles 85 and 86 of the EC Treaty.[244]

[240] *Sverige–EG 1986* (Utrikesdepartementet 1987), 20. See also the Italian measures adopted in 1976 (*Sverige–EG 1976* (Utrikes-handelsdepartementen, 1977), p. 22).

[241] SÖ 1960:1.

[242] An EFTA agreement on restrictive business practices was reached in 1965 (*Sixth Annual EFTA Report 1965* (Geneva, 1965), App.), and an EFTA Council Dec. was adopted in 1968 (EFTA Bull. 9/1968, 8). See also the Lisbon Agreement of 1966 on Art. 14 of the EFTA Convention concerning the practices of public undertakings (EFTA Bull. 2/1967, 2).

[243] See, e.g., N. March Hunnings, 'Enforceability of the EEC–EFTA Agreements' (1977) *ELRev*. 163–9. See also J. Dunlop and R. N. King, 'Regional Economic Integration and GATT: The Effects of the EEC–EFTA Agreements on International Trade' [1974] *Law and Policy in International Business* 207–35, 216.

[244] Cf. M. V. LLavero, 'The Possible Direct Effect of the Provisions on Competition in the EEC–EFTA Free Trade Agreements in the Light of the Kupferberg Decision' [1984/2] *LIEI* 83–101, 96.

Indeed, Article 23(1) of the Swedish Agreement did not expressly prohibit the conduct specified.[245] Like Article 92(1) of the EC Treaty, which provides that state aid distorting competition in trade between Member States is incompatible with the common market and which has been held by the Court of Justice not to be directly effective,[246] Article 23(1) of the Swedish Agreement merely indicated conduct incompatible with the Agreement. The Court of Justice does, however, treat Article 92(1) as entailing a prohibition of the aid indicated therein,[247] and it is enough that aid incompatible with the common market has been granted contrary to Article 92(1) for the Commission to issue a decision requiring its withdrawal.[248] Therefore, too much significance may not have attached to the fact that there was no express prohibition in Article 23(1) of the Swedish Agreement.

A more significant consideration might be that no provision equivalent to Article 85(2) of the EC Treaty, which renders prohibited agreements void, was included in the Agreement. In contrast, Article 24(b) of the Swedish Free Trade Agreement with the ECSC[249] provided for the imposition of penalties for violations of ECSC price and competition rules, which were embodied in Article 20 of that Agreement. The explanation for this contrast might lie in the definition of 'undertakings' in Article 80 of the ECSC Treaty. According to this provision, they are undertakings 'engaged in production in the coal or steel industry within territories' covered by the ECSC Treaty or 'regularly engaged in distribution other than sale to domestic consumers or small craft industries'. This definition might have meant that some restrictive practices of undertakings from Sweden, at least those lacking a subsidiary within the Community, which had anti-competitive effects on trade between Member States could be unaffected by the competition rules in this Treaty.[250] Thus inclusion of Article 24(b) in the Swedish–ECSC Agreement might have been considered necessary to enable such undertakings to be penalized. The implication might be that no equivalent of Article 85(2) of the EC Treaty was included in the Swedish Agreement with the EC, because that provision would itself apply to practices of Swedish undertakings having anti-competitive effects on trade between Member States.[251]

[245] Cf. the possible implication in Dec. 76/159 of 15 Dec. 1975 ([1976] OJ L28/22) relating to a proceeding under Art. 85 EC (IV/847—SABA) that equivalent provisions of the Free Trade Agreements with EFTA States might entail obligations for undertakings at least after 1977, when the free trade area between the Parties was, in principle, to be fully established. Cf., earlier, Dec. 64/233 of 11 Mar. 1964 ([1964] JO 915) *relative à une demande d'attestation négative présentée conformément à l'article 2 du règlement no 17 du Conseil* (IV/A—00061), regarding the significance of customs duties.

[246] Case 77/72 *Carmine Capolongo* v. *Azienda Agricola Maya* [1973] ECR 611, 621–2.

[247] See the reference to 'aid which is prohibited' in Joined Cases 6 and 11/69 *EC Commission* v. *France* [1969] ECR 523, 540 and to 'the prohibition in Art. 92(1)' in Case 78/76 *Firma Steinike und Weinlig* v. *Bundesamt für Ernahrung und Forstwirtschaft* [1977] ECR 595, 608.

[248] *Ibid.*, 609. [249] [1973] OJ L350/76. [250] Arts 65 and 66 ECSC.

[251] In the view of the Commission, the Free Trade Agreements were no obstacle to the application of Art. 85 in these circumstances. See Dec. 89/191 of 21 Dec. 1988 ([1989] OJ L74/21) relating to a proceeding pursuant to Art. 85 EC (IV/31.866, LdPE).

The conclusion drawn by the Swedish Government was that Article 23 of that Agreement merely authorized the Parties to adopt safeguard measures.[252] According to Article 23(2), such measures could be adopted where a Party considered that a given practice was incompatible with Article 23(1). The Commission drew the more particular conclusion that EFTA States were not prohibited by such Agreements from employing their criminal law to penalize persons assisting its investigations of restrictive practices.[253] If Article 23 had prohibited restrictive practices, then, taken together with Article 22, which prohibited the Parties from taking measures jeopardizing achievement of the objectives of the Agreement, such use of the criminal law would also apparently have been prohibited.[254]

Commission thinking seems to have been shared by the Swiss Supreme Court in *Stanley Adams* v. *Staatsanwaltschaft des Kantons Basel-Stadt*.[255] Here this Court dismissed an appeal against a conviction for breach of Swiss law concerning business secrets imposed on an ex-employee of Hoffmann-La Roche who had informed the Commission of involvement by this company in restrictive practices. In dismissing the appeal, the Court ruled that Article 23 of the Free Trade Agreement with Switzerland, which was identical to Article 23 of the Agreement with Sweden, did not prohibit the prosecution or, indeed, anything else. It merely authorized the Parties to take suitable measures against conduct specified therein.[256]

In practice, the measures taken by the Commission in the face of anti-competitive conduct by undertakings from EFTA States involved application of Articles 85 and 86 of the EC Treaty rather than provisions of Free Trade Agreements.[257] Reliance on the former provisions may only have been partly a reflection of the failure of the Agreements to seek to delimit the respective

[252] *Utrikesutskottets betänkande med anledning av propositionen 1972:135 angående avtal med de europeiska gemenskaperna m.m. jämte motioner* (report of the Foreign Affairs Committee of the Swedish Parliament on the Free Trade Agreement) (UU 1972:20), 17–18. Cf. regarding Art. 15 of the EFTA Convention, J. S. Lambrinidis, The Structure, Function and Law of a Free Trade Area (London, 1965), 127.

[253] Commission Reply to Written Question 152/75 ([1975] OJ C209/14) by Mr Cousté.

[254] Cf. the view that Member States may be obliged by Art. 5 EC to employ their criminal law to give effect to the trade liberalization required by this Treaty in Commission Reply by Mr Steichen to Written Question E–1818/94 ([1995] OJ C24/30) by Juan Colino Salamanca.

[255] [1978] 3 CMLR 480.

[256] *Ibid.* 485–6. See also *Bosshard Partners Intertrading AG* v. *Sunlight AG* [1980] 3 CMLR 664, 675. The ECJ may impliedly have adopted a similar approach in Case 53/84 *Stanley George Adams* v. *EC Commission* [1985] ECR 3595. On the other hand in Case C–334/93 *Bonapharma Arzneimittel GmbH* v. *Hauptzollamt Krefeld* (not yet reported) the ECJ recognized that anti-competitive conduct of undertakings might be 'contrary both to the objective and the terms of the [Austrian] Agreement'. Partly for this reason, an exception could be made from the rules governing documentary evidence as to the origin of goods traded between the Parties to this Agreement.

[257] See, e.g., *Sverige–EG 1981* (Utrikes- och handelsdepartementen, 1981), 22. See, generally, M. Haymann, 'Joint Ventures and Mergers as a Test-Mark for a European Competition Law Between EEC and EFTA: Switzerland as an Example' [1990] *World Competition* 5–29.

jurisdictions of the Joint Committees established pursuant thereto,[258] national authorities and the Commission, the lack of direct effectiveness[259] of the relevant provisions in such Agreements[260] or a Commission desire to demonstrate the importance of the Community as an international economic actor.[261] It may also have reflected concern to maintain the uniform application of Community competition law within the Community and to provide traders with a 'one stop shop'[262] where competition therein was distorted by the conduct of undertakings from EFTA States.

The consequence of such concern may have been that the role of competition provisions in Free Trade Agreements became dependent on prior harmonization of competition policy as between the Parties. Unless both the content and the application of their competition law were harmonized—in other words, unless common competition law applied to trade between Parties to such Agreements—uniform application of competition law within the Community could be jeopardized by a Commission failure to apply Article 85 or 86 of the Treaty to restrictive practices affecting trade between the Parties as well as trade between Member States.[263]

The possibility that the presence of an 'extra-Community' element in a restrictive practice might be relevant to its effect on competitive conditions within the Community, which should be taken into account in order to secure real uniformity in the application of Community competition law, and that collaboration between Parties to Free Trade Agreements might be of practical necessity in such circumstances may not have been impressive to the Commission.[264] Even less so may have been the possibility that treatment of restrictive practices having such an element within the framework of a Free Trade Agreement could have made a positive contribution to improving the competitive structure of the Community market.[265]

[258] See sect. 6.3.1 below.

[259] See sect. 8.3.3 below.

[260] Cf. the argument of the Commission in Joined Cases 89/85, 104/85, 114/85, 116–117/85 and 125–129/85 *A. Åhlström Osakeyhtiö* v. *EC Commission* [1988] ECR 5193, 5211 that breach of Art. 23 of the Finnish Free Trade Agreement ([1973] OJ L328/2) could only be invoked by a Contracting Party. According to N. G. van der Pas, 'The European Economic Area: Aspects concerning Free Movement of Goods' in O. Jacot-Guillarmod (ed.), op. cit., 101–14, at 106, 'although allowing Contracting Parties to defend themselves if a dispute cannot be solved in the Free Trade Agreement Joint Committee, the Agreements do not provide the means to act efficiently against illicit behaviour'.

[261] D. P. Fidler, 'Competition Law and International Relations' [1992] *ICLQ* 563–89, at 569.

[262] Cf. the *Twenty-Fourth Report on Competition Policy*, COM(95)142, 17 and 19.

[263] Cf., regarding the related risk of 'forum shopping', the Recommendations by the EEA Joint Parliamentary Committee of 26 and 27 Apr. 1994 ([1994] OJ L247/36), para. II.D.

[264] The attitude of the Commission seems to be changing, now that the 'phenomenon of globalization . . . is becoming more marked'. See the *Twenty-Fourth Report on Competition Policy*, COM(95)142, 17.

[265] 'Rather than contributing to a harmonious exchange of trade, these . . . rules have added an element of confusion and uncertainty to the implementation' of the Free Trade Agreements. See D. Horovitz, 'The Impending "Second Generation" Agreements between the European Community

(ii) State Aid

Article 23(1)(iii) of the Swedish Agreement provided that any public aid which distorted or threatened to distort competition by favouring certain undertakings or the production of certain goods was, in so far as trade between the Parties might be affected, incompatible with the Agreement.[266] The terms of this provision, taken in isolation, seem to have been capable of a broader scope of application than Article 13 of the EFTA Convention,[267] which concerned only the grant of export aid or aid which tended to frustrate the effects achieved through removal of customs duties and quantitative restrictions in trade between EFTA States.[268] Certainly, the Commission seems to have considered that provisions such as Article 23(1)(iii) could make a contribution to removing distortions of competition in trade between the Parties. In particular, the Commission gave an undertaking that if there were specific complaints concerning aid in an EFTA State, it would examine them on a case-by-case basis according to the relevant Free Trade Agreement.[269] The implication might be drawn that the only real difference between Article 23(1)(iii) of the Swedish Agreement and Article 92(1) of the EC Treaty lay in implementation arrangements rather than content.[270] In reality, differences in their respective legal frameworks might entail more fundamental differences in the operation of these provisions.

In the case of an Agreement seeking to establish a free trade area rather than a common market, aid cannot be found to be prohibited merely by reference to the demands of the latter.[271] Parties to such an Agreement may have co-operative incentives to agree to limit their use of aid. More particularly, creation of an agreed surveillance procedure may enable the merits of various claims for special assistance to be evaluated in a non-politicized manner. Such a procedure may also enable governments to turn aside demands from special interest groups that are pursuing goals not in the best interests of the country as a whole.[272] On the other hand, Parties may

and Eastern Europe—Some Practical Considerations' [1991] *JWT* 55–80, 70. However, the logic of Community practice means that the alternative to application of Community competition law may be resort to anti-dumping measures. See R. Kulms, 'Competition, Trade Policy and Competition Policy in the EEC: The Example of Antidumping' (1990) 27 *CMLRev*. 285–313. This alternative may be even more damaging to trade. See below, 128.

[266] See, generally, A. Maag, *Das Verbot Wettbewerbsverfälschender Beihilfen im EWG-Vertrag und im Freihandelsabkommen zwischen der Schweiz und der europäischen Wirtschaftsgemeinschaft* (Bern, 1979).

[267] SÖ 1960:1.

[268] The GATT Agreement on Interpretation and Application of Arts VI, XVI, and XXIII of GATT (BISD, 26th Supp., 56), which supplements Art. XVI of GATT itself, is somewhat broader. A new Agreement is contained in Annex 1A to the Agreement establishing the World Trade Organization.

[269] *Commission policy on sectoral aid schemes*, COM(78)221, 4.

[270] Report of the Committee on External Economic Relations of the European Parliament on economic and trade relations between the EEC and EFTA, EP Doc. 1–1496/84, 23.

[271] See sect. 2.2.2 above regarding the treatment of state aid under the EC Treaty.

[272] R. E. Baldwin, 'Assessing the Fair Trade and Safeguards Laws in Terms of Modern Trade and Political Economy Analysis' [1992] *The World Economy* 185–202, at 195.

also have an incentive to cheat,[273] and fear of such cheating cannot, it seems, easily be allayed.[274] At least, in the absence of a body independent of the Parties to apply the surveillance procedure,[275] the procedure may lack credibility.[276] In these circumstances, defining the kind of aid which has anti-competitive effects contrary to such an Agreement may be problematic.[277] In fact, such a definition implies harmonization of domestic aid policies.

Even if such harmonization were to be achieved, practical difficulties of establishing the existence of the anti-competitive effects of aid would remain. Such effects can only be measured by reference to detailed conditions in the market concerned, the levels of aid to other industries and general equilibrium implications. The difficulties of such measurement are said to cast doubt on the utility of constructing elaborate legal arrangements to curb the use of aid.[278]

It may have been for such reasons that little use was made of Article 23(1)(iii) of the Swedish Agreement. The Commission was willing to engage in general discussions concerning state aid policies.[279] However, less interest was shown in considering complaints about alleged violations of the Agreement by Member States,[280] and anti-dumping proceedings were employed in relation to Swedish companies which might have been receiving state aid.[281] The underlying concern of the Commission may have been to avoid friction at

[273] J. A. Brander and B. J. Spencer, 'Export Subsidies and International Market Share Rivalry' [1985] *Journal of International Economics* 83–100.

[274] Economic theory might suggest that, at least in the case of oligopolistic markets, countervailing duties would be an appropriate response to such cheating. See A. Dixit, 'International Trade Policy for Oligopolistic Industries' [1984] *Economic Journal* 1–16.

[275] The significance of Commission independence for Community competition is often stressed. See, e.g., the *Twenty-Fourth Report on Competition Policy*, COM(95)142, 19 and 94.

[276] Cf. G. Majone, 'Market Integration and Regulation: Europe after 1992', EUI Working Paper SPS No. 91/10.

[277] Problems may be theoretical as well as practical and may relate, e.g., to determination of the relevant product market. See the *Twenty-Fourth Report on Competition Policy*, COM(95)142, 223. See also sect. 2.2.2 above.

[278] J. D. Gaisford and D. L. McLachlan, 'Domestic Subsidies and Countervail: the Treacherous Ground of the Level Playing Field' [1990] *JWT* 55–77.

[279] *Commission policy on sectoral aid schemes*, COM(78)221, 4. According to the Report of Committee on External Economic Relations of the European Parliament on economic and trade relations between the EEC and EFTA (EP Doc. 1–1496/84, 18), the Commission had 'some degree of success' in these discussions.

[280] *Sverige–EG 1980* (Utrikes- och handelsdepartementen, 1981), 23; *Sverige–EG 1981* (Utrikes- och handelsdepartementen, 1982), 23–4; *Sverige–EG 1982* (Utrikesdepartementets handelsavdelning, 1983), 23–4. See also *Att avveckla en kortsiktig stödpolitik*, SOU 1981:72, p. 137.

[281] See 127–9 below. Cf., regarding action to ensure that uranium is imported from the CIS at 'market-related prices', Dec. 94/95 of 4 Feb. 1994 ([1994] OJ L48/45) relating to a procedure in application of the 2nd para. of Art. 53 Euratom.

the official level regarding the aid policies of the Parties,[282] or at least to avoid the difficulties of securing agreement as to what constituted aid incompatible with the Agreement.[283]

It took conclusion of the EEA Agreement, which embodies a commitment to harmonization of state aid policies,[284] to change this practice. Before the new Agreement came into force, Article 23(1)(iii) of the Free Trade Agreement with Austria, which was the equivalent of Article 23(1)(iii) in the Swedish Agreement, was invoked against Austrian aid to General Motors. The Commission objected to this aid on the grounds that it breached Community 'principles', which were to be embodied in the EEA Agreement, regarding regional aid and aid to the automobile sector.[285] In the absence of Austrian acceptance of the Commission position,[286] safeguard measures were adopted under Article 23(2) of the Free Trade Agreement. In accordance with Article 27(3)(a) of the same Agreement, these measures took the form of reintroduction of the CCT in respect of the products concerned.[287] Their reintroduction was apparently designed to secure compliance with 'internal' Community law principles of state aid control in respect of trade between the Parties, no apparent concern being shown for the possibility that such principles might need to be adapted to conditions prevailing in such trade.

[282] R. Kulms, n. 265 above. The possibility of such friction may have been all the greater because of the considerable amounts of aid granted within the Community. The average annual total state aid within the Community between 1986 and 1988 was 82 billion ECUs, which amounted to 2.2% of Community GDP. See the *Second Survey on State Aids in the European Community in the Manufacturing and Certain Other Sectors* (EC Commission, Brussels, 1990). Cf. G. Koopman and H.- E. Scharrer, *Scenarios of a Common External Trade Policy for the EC after 1992* (Institut für Wirtschaftsforschung Report No. 84, Hamburg 1990), 25. The grant of such aid by the Community is often challenged within GATT. See, e.g., *The Community's Anti-Dumping and Anti-Subsidy Activities (1994)*, COM(95)309, 56. More particularly, aid might be authorized under Art. 92(3)(c) EC on the very ground that it attracted investment to the Community rather than to Sweden. See Notice 39/90 (ex N453/90) ([1992] OJ C290/2) concerning aid which the Federal Republic of Germany has decided to grant in favour of Nefab GmbH in Hueckelhoven. Cf, regarding authorization of aid to attract a shipbuilding order, Notice C40/90 (ex N511/90) ([1992] OJ C290/5) concerning draft aid which the Federal Republic of Germany has decided to grant in favour of Chukyo Europe GmbH and Dec. 88/437 of 20 Jan. 1988 ([1988] OJ L211/24) concerning aids planned by the French Government in favour of a shipbuilding contract for which there is no competition between yards in several Member States; and, regarding the authorization of aid to pilot training, which would reduce the need for student pilots to go to third countries for training, Communication C31/93 (NN97/91) ([1993] OJ C293/4) on aid measures involved in the acquisition by KLM of the pilot school RLS.

[283] Cf., regarding the difficulties which have arisen in trade between the Community and the USA, J. M. Finger, 'Subsidies and Countervailing Duties' in P. K. M. Tharakan (ed.), *Policy Implications of Antidumping Measures* (Amsterdam, 1991), 175–89.

[284] See sect. 4.2.2 below.

[285] Annex XV, state aid, to the EEA Agreement.

[286] The Commission secured a 'compromise' concerning aid for a Chrysler car plant in Graz, which entailed a reduction of aid intensity from 33% to 14.4% (*Twenty-Second Report on Competition Policy* (EC Commission, Brussels, 1993), 210).

[287] Reg. 3697/93 of 20 Dec. 1993 ([1993] OJ L343/1) withdrawing tariff concessions in accordance with Art. 23(2) and Art. 27(3)(a) of the Free Trade Agreement between the Community and Austria (General Motors Austria). In the case of aid to Grundig, tariffs were reintroduced

(iii) Dumping

Article 25 of the Swedish Agreement provided that if one of the Parties found that dumping was taking place in trade with the other Party, it might take appropriate measures against this practice in accordance with the Agreement on Implementation of Article VI of GATT.[288] In practice, the Council and Commission, instead of employing Article 23 of the Agreement as a basis for seeking to secure greater equality of competitive conditions in trade between the Parties, relied on Article 25 as authorizing resort to Community anti-dumping legislation to protect Community industry against Swedish traders who may have been in receipt of state aid.[289]

According to Community legislation[290] and GATT,[291] anti-dumping measures can be adopted not only where the export price of a product is below its domestic price but also where the former is below the cost of production. Hence, such measures are not limited to undertakings in third states which are parties to cartels or abuse their dominant positions. They may also be adopted against undertakings which take advantage of state aid to reduce their prices to a level below their real costs.

In 1977, for example, the Commission expressed concern about Swedish aid to the chipboard industry[292] and in the following year secured price undertakings from Swedish exporters of chipboard following commencement of an anti-dumping procedure.[293]

(Reg. 317/94 of 20 Dec. 1993 ([1994] OJ L41/18) withdrawing tariff concessions in accordance with Arts. 23(2) and 27(3)(a) of the Free Trade Agreement between the Community and Austria (Grundig Austria GmbH)), but then lifted following repayment of the aid to which the Commission objected (Reg. 318/94 of 7 Feb. 1994 ([1994] OJ L41/20) repealing Reg. 317/94). It was 'an open question' whether this area could be eligible for state regional aid under Community criteria, and the aid was considered excessive in relation to regional handicaps. See Commission Reply by Mr Van Miert to Written Question E–2771/93 by Gijs de Vries ([1994] OJ C226/53). Cf. Summary of EFTA Surveillance Authority Dec. not to raise objections to the aid which the Austrian Government plans to provide to BMW Motoren Gesellschaft mbH in support of an R & D and investment project in Steyr, Austria ([1994] OJ C250/3).

[288] BISD, 26th Supp., 171. See now the Agreement on the Implementation of Art. VI of GATT, in Annex 1A to the Agreement establishing the World Trade Organization.

[289] US practice in relation to Canadian producers in receipt of regional aid was apparently comparable. See S. A. Baker and S. P. Battram, 'The Canada–United States Free Trade Agreement' [1989] *The International Lawyer* 37–80, at 72.

[290] Art. 2(4) of Reg. 3283/94 of 22 Dec. 1994 ([1988] OJ L209/1) on protection against dumped imports from countries not members of the European Community.

[291] Art. 2(4) of the Agreement on the Implementation of Art. VI of the GATT (BISD, 26th Supp., 171). See now Art. 2.2.1 of the Agreement on the Implementation of Art. VI of GATT, in Annex 1A to the Agreement establishing the World Trade Organization.

[292] *Sverige–EG 1977* (Utrikes- och handelsdepartementen, 1978), 20. See also, regarding aid to the textile industry, *Sverige–EG 1979* (Utrikes- och handelsdepartementen, 1980), 21. See, regarding aid to the paper and pulp industries, *Sverige–EG 1980* (Utrikes- och handelsdepartementen, 1981), 23. Cf., regarding timber, Commission Reply to Written Question 50/83 ([1983] OJ C212/16) by Mr Adam.

[293] Notice of termination of the anti-dumping/anti-subsidies procedure concerning imports of reconstituted wood (wood chipboard) from Spain and Sweden ([1978] OJ C75/3). In the case of

Such practice meant that the effects of aid might be assessed in isolation from consideration of the broader economic policy context in which it was granted.[294] Consequently, not only might the grant of aid in third states lead to the imposition of trade restrictions which could not result within the Community from the grant of aid by a Member State but also these restrictions might be imposed on an undertaking in receipt of aid which might be permissible within the Community.[295]

Such consequences might be thought to have been incompatible with Article 27(2) of the Swedish Agreement. According to this provision, in the selection of safeguard measures priority had to be given to those which least disturbed the functioning of the Agreement. However, the view of the Swedish Government was that the Agreement created no obstacle at all to the application of anti-dumping measures.[296]

This view was not necessarily consistent with GATT. Conclusion of a Free Trade Agreement would seem sufficient under Article XXIV(5) of GATT to remove the need for anti-dumping measures. Certainly, Article VI of GATT, which authorizes anti-dumping measures, is not included in Article XXIV among the provisions justifying restrictions on trade in a free trade area.[297] It might even be argued that anti-dumping rules constitute an example of 'restrictive regulations of commerce [which must be] eliminated on substantially all the trade between the constituent territories in products originating in such territories' under Article XXIV(8)(b) of GATT for a free trade area to be created for the purposes of the Agreement.

Nevertheless, the Community position was that only a very intensive degree of economic integration could justify abandonment or even, it seems, significant limitation of the option to use anti-dumping measures.[298] The frameworks

steel imports, informal pressure in 1984 seems to have been effective. See R. Kulms, n. 265 above, 293. Cf., regarding an agreement with Switzerland concerning steel imports, Joined Cases 154, 205, 206, 226–228, 263, and 264/78, 39, 31, 83, and 85/79 *SpA Ferriera Valsabbia* v. *EC Commission* [1980] ECR 907, 1016.

[294] It has been argued that protective action should only be concerned with those policies which would be economically disastrous if adopted by all countries. See P. Nicolaides, 'How Fair is Fair Trade?' [1986] *JWTL* 148–62, at 159.

[295] Aid may be acceptable within the Community specifically because it enables a producer to sell at a price which is below his real costs. See, e.g., Dec. 88/437 of 20 Jan. 1988 ([1988] OJ L211/24) concerning aids planned by the French Government in favour of a shipbuilding contract for which there is competition between yards in several Member States.

[296] *Tillämpningen av GATT:s Regler för Skydd Mot Dumpad Och Subventionerad Import* (Application of GATT Rules for Protection against Dumped and Subsidized Imports) (Ds UD 1984:6), 15. Cf. the unsuccessful argument in Joined Cases 89/85, 104/85, 114/85, 116–117/85 and 125–129/85 *A. Åhlström Osakeyhtiö* v. *EC Commission* [1988] ECR 5193, 5210.

[297] It has been argued, however, that the list contained in the latter provision is indicative rather than enumerative. See J. J. Allen, *The European Common Market and GATT* (London, 1960), 199 and 224.

[298] A formal justification for this position might be found in the fact that such Agreements, like Community anti-dumping rules, were based on Art. 113 EC and both constituted elements of the common commercial policy.

provided by Free Trade Agreements were treated as securing insufficient integration to remove the need for application of such measures to trade between the Parties.[299]

3.4 EUROPE AGREEMENTS

Many provisions of the Europe Agreements authorizing trade restrictions may formally have much in common with EC Treaty provisions. Certain provisions, however, reflect the asymmetrical approach adopted in these Agreements towards trade liberalization between the Parties.

3.4.1 Non-Economic Requirements

Article 35 of the Polish Agreement follows Article 36 of the EC Treaty. The only formal difference is that the former, like Article XX of GATT, refers to rules regarding gold and silver.

Moreover, Article 112 of the Polish Agreement provides that the Agreement does not prevent the Parties from taking action in relation to three categories of matters. First, Article 112(a) of the Polish Agreement, which is modelled on Article 223(1)(a) of the EC Treaty, provides that measures which a Party considers necessary to prevent disclosure of information contrary to its essential security interests are not affected.

Secondly, Parties remain free under Article 112(b) of the Polish Agreement to take measures relating to the production of, or trade in, arms, munitions, or war materials or to research, development, or production indispensable for defence purposes, provided that such measures do not impair the conditions of competition in respect of products not intended for specifically military purposes. This provision follows, but seems somewhat broader than, Article 223(1)(b) of the EC Treaty.

Thirdly, Article 112(c) of the Polish Agreement reflects Article 224 of the EC Treaty.[300] It provides that the Parties may take measures which they consider essential to their own security in the event of serious internal disturbances affecting the maintenance of law and order, in time of war or serious international tension constituting threat of war or in order to carry out

[299] Similarly, Art. 17 of the EFTA Convention (SÖ 1960:1) provided that nothing in the Convention prevented Parties from taking action against dumped or subsidized goods.

[300] In 1962 the Swedish Minister of Commerce had suggested that a provision like Art. 224 might be included in an Association Agreement and might be drafted in such a way as to allow for Sweden to withdraw from certain obligations or the whole Agreement where neutrality requirements so demanded. See *Utrikesfrågor, Offentliga document m.m. rörande viktigare svenska utrikespolitiska frågor 1962* (Official document concerning major questions of Swedish foreign policy in 1962) (Utrikesdepartementet, 1962), 153.

obligations they have accepted for the purpose of maintaining peace and international security.

Finally, Article 31 of the Polish Agreement permits resort to safeguard measures where the liberalization of exports between the Parties required by this Agreement gives rise to, or is likely to give rise to, 'major difficulties' for the exporting Party and where one of two further conditions is met. One condition is met in the case of re-export towards a third state against which the exporting Party maintains, for the product concerned, quantitative export restrictions, export duties, or measures or charges having equivalent effect.[301] An apparent consequence is that the Agreement need not undermine the effectiveness of Community measures restricting exports to third states pursuant to the CFSP.

However, while the Agreement is to involve a 'political dialogue' between the Community and Poland,[302] formal participation in the CFSP is not envisaged for the latter.[303] Consequently, decision-making from which Poland may be largely excluded could increasingly affect the use made of the above provisions by the Community. Rather than demanding a narrow scope of application for the above provisions, CFSP requirements may imply that they should be given a sufficiently broad interpretation to enable the requirements of this policy to be met. Therefore, development of the CFSP could mean that operation of security exceptions in the Polish Agreement in relation to trade between the Parties and operation of corresponding exceptions in the EC Treaty in relation to Community trade increasingly diverge.

3.4.2 'Mandatory Requirements'

The Polish Agreement refers in rather generalized terms to co-operation in matters such as environmental protection,[304] social policy,[305] and culture.[306] Unless bases for recognition of 'mandatory requirements' can be found in these references, assimilation of trade liberalization requirements in this Agreement with those of the EC Treaty would imply greater trade liberalization between the Parties than is secured between Member States. Such an outcome might not simply be unacceptable politically but would also undermine the effective significance of recognition of 'mandatory requirements'

[301] A similar provision might be thought less necessary in relation to imports, because it is only trade in goods originating in the Community or Poland which is liberalized by the Polish Agreement (Art. 8(1)). Problems may arise, however, in relation to raw materials or components used in the production of such goods.

[302] Art. 1(2) of the Polish Agreement. More detailed arrangements are made in Arts 2–5 of the same Agreement.

[303] Rather, it is envisaged that Poland will have 'the opportunity to come into line with certain CFSP measures'. See the Council Reply to Written Question E–191/95 ([1995] OJ C202/4) by Jean-Pierre Raffarin.

[304] Art. 80 of the Polish Agreement.

[305] *Ibid.* Art. 87.

[306] *Ibid.* Art. 95.

within the context of the EC Treaty. Considerations of this kind militate against a broad interpretation of the liberalization requirements embodied the Agreement. Hence, development of trade liberalization between the Parties might be constrained by the inadequacy of the basis in the Agreement for protecting requirements other than those of trade liberalization.

3.4.3 Economic Requirements

Inclusion of 'defence mechanisms' was considered necessary in the Europe Agreements, particularly because of anti-competitive practices, such as the grant of state aid, associated with the industrial policies of Central and Eastern European countries.[307]

Commercial Policy

Article 27(2) of the Polish Agreement provides that consultations between the Parties shall take place concerning agreements establishing customs unions or free trade areas. Where requested, such consultations shall also take place in relation to other major issues[308] related to their respective trade policy with third states.[309] This provision might facilitate harmonization of tariffs on products from third states and lessen the risk of trade deflection arising from disparities in the treatment of such products. If, however, consultations under this provision do not produce mutually satisfactory results, safeguard measures may be adopted under Article 30 of the Agreement.

Conjunctural Policy

Article 30 of the Polish Agreement has something in common with Article 226 of the EC Treaty. It permits resort to safeguard measures where any product is being imported in such increased quantities and under such conditions as to cause or threaten to cause:

— serious injury to domestic producers of like or directly competitive products in the territory of one of the Parties, or

[307] Opinion of the Economic and Social Committee of 16 Mar. 1990 on the EC's economic relations with the countries of Eastern Europe (CES(90)381, 7). See also the 8th Report of the House of Lords Select Committee on the European Communities, *European Agreements with Poland, Hungary and the Czech and Slovak Federal Republic*, (1990–91) HL 35, 13. Cf., regarding 'less-favoured or developing countries', the Opinion of the Economic and Social Committee of 24 Nov. 1993 ([1994] OJ C34/83) on the Twenty-Second Report on Competition Policy, para. 13.3.

[308] Cf. the complaint that Turkey reduced its tariffs on many goods from third countries to a level below the CCT in the Report of the Committee on External Economic Relations on economic and trade relations between the Community and Turkey, EP Doc. A2–350/88, 12.

[309] Art. 48(4), which falls within the Ch. of the Polish Agreement on establishment, provides that the Agreement does not prejudice the application by each Party of any measure necessary to prevent the circumvention of its measures concerning third country access to its market through the provisions of this Agreement.

— serious disturbances in any sector of the economy or difficulties which could bring about serious deterioration in the economic situation of a region.[310]

More particularly, Article 21 of the Agreement permits safeguard measures in the agricultural sector,[311] and Article 28 permits Poland to increase customs duties to protect infant industries, or certain sectors undergoing restructuring or facing serious difficulties, particularly where these difficulties produce serious social problems.[312]

However, the effectiveness of infant-industry protection is disputed,[313] and support for sectors 'facing serious difficulties' may be even more problematic. In sectors of the latter kind there may be strategic reasons why traders do not exit. The payoff to those leaving may be less than for those remaining, and this will deter any trader from exiting first. The result may be a moribund industry with low rates of return, low investment, and a poor innovation record.[314] Protectionist measures may simply encourage this result.[315] Such thinking would suggest that the measures permitted by Article 28 could be particularly damaging to the development of trade between the Parties.[316]

Finally, problems associated with product shortages are dealt with in Article 31 of the Agreement. This provision, which is reminiscent of Article 103a of the EC Treaty, permits resort to safeguard measures where the liberalization of exports between the Parties required by this Agreement gives rise to, or is likely to give rise to, 'major difficulties' for the exporting Party and where there is a serious shortage, or threat thereof, of a product essential to the exporting Party.

Monetary Policy

Article 64(2) of the Polish Agreement, which is reminiscent of Articles 109h and 109i of the EC Treaty, provides that where one or more Member States or Poland is in serious balance of payments difficulties, or under imminent threat

[310] Community rules for resort to such measures are contained in Reg. 520/94 ([1994] OJ L66/1).

[311] See also the general reservation in favour of measures implementing the agricultural policy of each Party in Art. 25(3). Cf. the special arrangements in Art. 3(1) of Prot. 1, on textile and clothing products.

[312] Under similar conditions Art. 50 provides that Poland may also derogate from the provisions of the Agreement on establishment.

[313] R. E. Baldwin, 'The Case against Infant-Industry Tariff Protection' [1969] *Journal of Political Economy* 295–305. See, more particularly, regarding the impact of such protection on transformation, R. J. Langhammer, *EC Integration Widening Towards Eastern Europe* (Kiel Working Paper No. 524, 1992), 5–6.

[314] S. James, 'Industrial Policy After 1992: Making the Most of the Internal Market' in D. H. Gowland and S. James (eds.), *Economic Policy After 1992* (Aldershot, 1991), 20–45, at 35.

[315] See also J. Waelbroeck, 'The Logic of EC Commercial and Industrial Policy Making' in A. Jacquemin (ed.), *European Industry: Public Policy and Corporate Strategy* (Oxford, 1984), 99–125, at 104.

[316] Cf. the Opinion of the Economic and Social Committee of 26 Jan. 1995 ([1995] OJ C102/40) on relations between the European Union and Russia, Ukraine, and Belarus, para. 3.20.

thereof,[317] the Community or Poland, as the case may be, may, in accordance with the conditions established under GATT,[318] adopt restrictive measures. Such measures may relate to imports,[319] but they must be of limited duration and must not go beyond what is necessary to remedy the balance-of-payments situation.[320]

Competition Policy

The Europe Agreements include provisions concerning restrictive practices by undertakings, state aid, and dumping.

(i) Restrictive practices by undertakings

Article 63(1)(i) and (ii) of the Polish Agreement follow Article 23(1)(i) and (ii) of the Swedish Free Trade Agreement. Safeguard measures may be adopted under Article 63(6) of the Polish Agreement, where the Community or Poland considers that a particular practice is incompatible with the terms of the first paragraph of this Article and is not adequately dealt with under the implementing rules[321] referred to in paragraph 3[322] or, in the absence of such rules, causes or threatens to cause serious prejudice to its 'interest' or material injury to its domestic industry, including its services industry. It cannot be assumed that this provision affects Commission competence to apply the EC Treaty, where trade between Member States is affected, instead of invoking Article 63(1)(i) or (ii) of the Polish Agreement.

If an analogy may be drawn with *Haegeman*,[323] which concerned a countervailing charge imposed pursuant to the common organization of the wine market on imports of Greek wine into Belgium, exercise of such competence

[317] Art. 62 of the Polish Agreement also permits Poland, in exceptional circumstances, to apply exchange restrictions connected with the granting or taking up of short and medium-term credits to the extent that such restrictions are imposed on Poland for the granting of such credits and are permitted according to the status of Poland under the International Monetary Fund.

[318] Art. XII of GATT. Para. 2(a) thereof stipulates that restrictive measures must not exceed those necessary to forestall the imminent threat of, or to stop, a serious decline in its monetary reserves or, in the case of a Party with very low monetary reserves, to achieve a reasonable rate of increase in its reserves.

[319] Art. 10 of Reg. 3492/93 of 13 Dec. 1993 ([1993] OJ L319/4) on certain procedures for applying the Europe Agreement establishing an association between the European Communities and their Member States, of the one part, and the Republic of Poland, of the other, provides that the Regulation does not affect the operation of Arts. 109h and 109i EC. See sect. 3.2.3 above.

[320] Art. 64(3) of the Polish Agreement stipulates that such measures must not apply to transfers related to investment, though an analogy with Joined Cases 286/82 and 26/83 *Graziana Luisi and Giuseppe Carbone* v. *Ministero del Tesoro* [1984] ECR 377, 406 might suggest that Parties could introduce controls to ensure that transfers really were so related.

[321] To be adopted by the Association Council.

[322] See, regarding failure to fulfil obligations more generally, Art. 115(2) of the Polish Agreement. It authorizes a Party to take appropriate measures where it considers that another Party has failed to fulfil an obligation under this Agreement.

[323] Case 181/73 *R. & V. Haegeman* v. *Belgian State* [1974] ECR 449.

would seem to be acceptable to the Court of Justice.[324] Here the Court characterized the imposition of a countervailing charge on Greek wine imports as a stabilization measure essential to the common organization of the wine market, which was permissible under Protocol 12 to the Greek Association Agreement,[325] rather than as a safeguard measure which should have been adopted under Article 41 or 43 of the Agreement itself.[326] In this judgment at least, the Court accepted the legality of Commission action based on an 'internal' Community policy rather than on the legal framework provided by the Agreement.

(ii) State Aid

Article 63(1)(iii) of the Polish Agreement follows Article 23(1)(iii) of the Swedish Free Trade Agreement. Safeguard measures may be adopted by a Party to the former Agreement under Article 63(6) in response to the grant by the other Party of public aid incompatible with Article 63(1)(iii). Such measures may, where GATT applies thereto, only be adopted in conformity with the procedures and under the conditions laid down by GATT and any other relevant instruments negotiated under its auspices which are applicable between the Parties. Moreover, Poland made a unilateral declaration that notwithstanding the provisions of Article 63, the rights of the Parties under the Agreement on Interpretation and Application of Articles VI, XVI, and XXIII of GATT[327] were not impaired. The primary concern of Poland seems to have been to ensure that Article 63(6) would not be used by the Community as a basis for adoption of safeguard measures which would not otherwise be permitted under GATT. Attention did not apparently focus on questions involved in developing a harmonized policy on state aid. However, in the absence of such harmonization, practice under the Polish Agreement might prove to be comparable with that under the Swedish Free Trade Agreement, and Community practice might be to apply anti-dumping measures rather than to invoke Article 63(1)(iii) of the former Agreement.[328]

(iii) Dumping

Article 29 of the Polish Agreement follows Article 25 of the Swedish Free Trade Agreement. The former permits either Party to take appropriate mea-

[324] However, international law may apparently entail certain constraints, at least where 'important interests' of a third state are involved, and the Community law principle of proportionality may be applicable. See J. H. J. Bourgeois, 'EEC Control over International Mergers' [1990] *YBEL* 102–32. [325] [1963] JO 293. [326] [1974] ECR 449, 463.

[327] BISD, 26th Supp., 56. A new Agreement is contained in Annex 1A to the Agreement establishing the World Trade Organization.

[328] The Commission considers that reduction in the use of its commercial defence instruments should be conditional on satisfactory implementation of competition and state aid policies and adoption of other elements of Community law. 'In the short term the Union should offer information to any associated country before the initiation of any anti-dumping or safeguard proceeding'. See *Europe Agreements and Beyond: A Strategy to Prepare the Countries of Central and Eastern Europe for Accession*, COM(94)320, 5.

sures against dumping, in accordance with the conditions and procedures laid down in Article 33[329] and with the Agreement on the Implementation of Article VI of GATT[330] and with related internal legislation.[331]

In the case of countries such as Poland, problems associated with use of anti-dumping measures[332] may in the past have been exaggerated by their classification[333] as non-market economies under Community law.[334] This classification meant that producers from such countries could be subject to anti-dumping duties where their export prices were below those of producers in an analogue third country market economy and, hence, precluded account being taken of 'natural' comparative advantages enjoyed by the former producers.[335] However, Regulation 517/92[336] provided that the Czech Republic, Hungary, Poland, and Slovakia should no longer be so classified. The Preamble to the Regulation justifies this reform on the grounds that 'the Community has signed Europe Agreements aimed at establishing an association with Hungary, Poland and the CSFR, which have embarked on a large-scale programme of reform aimed at ensuring their transition towards a market economy'.[337] The consequence is that, at least in law, problems associated with application of anti-dumping measures to such countries will be no greater than those associated with application of such measures to third countries generally.[338]

329 See sect. 6.4.3 below.

330 BISD, 26th Supp., 171. A new Agreement is contained in Annex 1A to the Agreement establishing the World Trade Organization.

331 Reg. 3492/93 of 13 Dec. 1993 ([1993] OJ L319/4) on certain procedures for applying the Europe Agreement establishing an association between the European Communities and their Member States, of the one part, and the Republic of Poland, of the other part; Dec. 265/94 of 1 Feb. 1994 ([1994] OJ L32/6) on certain procedures for applying the Europe Agreement establishing an association between the European Communities and their Member States, of the one part, and the Republic of Poland, of the other.

332 Such measures 'hardly encourage competition through trade'. See P. Nicolaides, n. 294 above, 155. The essential problem is said to be the emphasis on 'injury' rather than on distortion of competition.

333 Annex I to Reg. 3420/83 of 14 Nov. 1983 ([1983] OJ L346/6) on import arrangements for products originating in state-trading countries, not liberalized at Community level and the Annex to Reg. 1765/82 of 30 June 1982 ([1982] OJ L195/1) on common rules for imports from state-trading countries.

334 Art. 2(5) of Reg. 2423/88 of 11 July 1988 ([1988] OJ L209/1) on protection against dumped or subsidized imports from countries not members of the EEC. See now Art. 2(7) of Reg. 3283/94 of 22 Dec. 1994 ([1994] OJ L349/1) on protection against dumped imports from countries not members of the EC.

335 See, e.g., A. Evans, 'Anti-dumping Law and Third Countries: a Case Study' in A. Evans and P. Falk (eds.) *Integration and Transformation: Polish and Swedish Perspectives* (Umeå, 1992), 219–81.

336 Of 27 Feb. 1992 ([1992] OJ L56/1) amending the autonomous import arrangements for products originating in Hungary, Poland, and the Czech and Slovak Federal Republic (CSFR).

337 The corresponding clause in the Preamble to the Commission Proposal for the new Reg. of 3 Feb. 1992 (COM(92)27) read 'as they move towards a market economy'.

338 In the Opinion of the European Coal and Steel Community Consultative Committee of 28 Jan. 1992 ([1992] OJ C80/2) on the interim Association Agreements on trade and trade related

Such problems will not necessarily diminish. Indeed, completion of the internal market may lead to increased resort by the Community to anti-dumping measures.[339] Economies of scale permitted by completion of the internal market and the resulting lowering of prices within the Community may force traders from third states to reduce the prices of their exports. Such action could be seen as dumping and lead to demands for anti-dumping proceedings. It is also possible that abolition of internal frontier controls within the Community will result in anti-dumping measures[340] being employed to substitute national restrictions which used to be authorized by the Commission under Article 115 of the EC Treaty.[341]

True, Article 33(2) of the Polish Agreement, which follows Article 27(2) of the Swedish Free Trade Agreement, provides that in the selection of measures to be taken under the Agreement priority must be given to those which least disturb the functioning of the Agreement.[342] This provision would seem to embody the principle of proportionality, which the Court of Justice has employed so as to construe narrowly EC Treaty provisions permitting restriction of Community trade.[343] A more particular condition for resort to anti-dumping procedures might be thought to be entailed by this provision, according to which efforts should be made to secure respect for competition provisions in the Agreement before recourse is had to such procedures.[344]

It might further be imagined that the Polish Agreement establishes a framework of such a kind that such efforts could be effective. Not only are customs duties and charges having equivalent effect as well as quantitative restrictions

matters between the European Coal and Steel Community, of the one part, and the Republic of Poland, the Republic of Hungary, and the Czech and Slovak Federal Republic, of the other part fears were expressed about dumping from these countries (para. 5). See also the Resolution of the European Parliament of 7 June 1991 ([1991] OJ C197/3) on the anti-dumping policy of the European Community (para. 5).

339 Indeed, it may be argued that subjection of domestic industry to increased competition from members of a regional trading bloc generally leads to increased demands for protection against non-members. See J. Bhagwati, 'Regionalism versus Multilateralism' [1992] *The World Economy* 535–55.

340 See, e.g., regarding undertakings obtained from exporters to limit their fertilizer sales in the United Kingdom to an amount acceptable to the Commission, *The Community's Anti-dumping and Anti-subsidy Activities* (1994), COM(95)309, 39–40.

341 See, e.g., C. Neme, '1992 et la Clause de l'Art. 115: a Quand une Politique Commerciale Commune?' [1988] *RMC* 578–82.

342 Cf. the effect given to an equivalent obligation in the Association Agreement with Cyprus ([1973] OJ L133/2) in Case C–432/92 *The Queen* v. *Minister of Agriculture, Fisheries and Food, ex parte S. P. Anastasiou (Pissouri) Ltd* [1994] ECR I–3087, I–3133.

343 See above sect. 3.2.1.

344 The Commission, however, insists that anti-dumping measures are necessary to restore fair competition, notes that they are specifically provided for in the Europe Agreements, and concludes that they are compatible with the Community interest in the special relationships sought by these Agreements. See, in connection with the Interim Agreement, Reg. 1189/93 of 14 May 1993 ([1993] OJ L120/34) imposing definitive anti-dumping duties on imports of certain seamless pipes and tubes, of iron and steel, originating in Hungary, Poland, and the Republic of Croatia and definitively collecting provisional anti-dumping duties.

and measures having equivalent effect between the Parties prohibited by the Agreement,[345] but also restrictive practices by undertakings and state aid which distort competition and may affect trade between the Parties are stipulated to be incompatible with the Agreement.[346] In the case of such distortions, provision is made for reference to an Association Council established under the Agreement and composed of representatives of the Polish Government and Community representatives.[347]

Potentially, then, mechanisms are created by this Agreement for co-operative application of competition law to trade between the Parties. While perspectives may differ, both Parties may be expected to welcome such mechanisms. Poland may regard them as offering protection against Community anti-dumping proceedings, and the Community may regard them as offering protection against anti-competitive conduct by Polish undertakings or authorities. As the Commission implicitly accepts, the scope of competition law and anti-dumping law may often be similar.[348] Hence, it may be concluded that for both Parties utilization of these mechanisms would be preferable to reliance on anti-dumping measures.

However, practice under other Association Agreements raises doubts whether the Polish Agreement really will be treated as removing the need for anti-dumping measures. In the case of the Turkish Association Agreement,[349] Article 4 of the Agreement provides for establishment of a customs union with the Community.[350] Moreover, according to Article 16 of the same Agreement, the Parties recognize that principles regarding competition in Title I of Part III of the EC Treaty (i.e., Articles 85–94) are applicable to their relations. Even so, the Community employs anti-dumping measures against imports from Turkey.[351] More particularly, the case law of the Court of Justice entails that the various safeguard clauses in an Association Agreement may be utilized by the Community without observance of any particular priority among them.[352] The apparent conclusion to be drawn is that Article 33(2) of

[345] Ch. I of Title III of the Polish Agreement.

[346] *Ibid.*, Art. 63(1).

[347] See, in particular, *ibid.*, Art. 63(6).

[348] *Seventh Report on Competition Policy* (EC Commission, Brussels, 1978), 40.

[349] [1964] JO 368.

[350] Cf., regarding the operation of a similar provision relating to the movement of persons, Case 12/86 *Meryem Demirel* v. *Stadt Schwäbisch Gmünd* [1987] ECR 3719, 3753–4.

[351] See, e.g., the *Seventh Annual Report on the Community's Anti-dumping and Anti-Subsidy Activities*, COM(90)229.

[352] See Case 40/72 *I. Schroeder K.G.* v. *Germany* [1973] ECR 125, 146, regarding the Greek Association Agreement ([1963] JO 293). The Court did, however, note that the safeguard measures chosen by the Commission seemed less restrictive of trade than the alternative measures available. Warner A. G. considered that the need for 'quick and effective measures' favoured the choice of the Commission (*ibid.* 158). The position may be similar in the case of Commission powers to act against Member States. According to Roemer A. G. in Joined Cases 6 and 11/69 *EC Commission* v. *France* [1969] ECR 523, 553, where parallel powers of such a kind exist, no complaint can be made against the Commission for using those which appear more effective to it.

the Polish Agreement may not be treated as requiring resort to the competition provisions of Article 63 rather than adoption of anti-dumping measures.[353]

Adoption of the latter measures might, indeed, be treated by the Community institutions as being of practical necessity. Difficulties in applying competition law to undertakings from third states could arise from the very fact that such undertakings are established outside the Community. Documentary evidence of the anti-competitive intentions of undertakings might be decisive for the purposes of application of such law to pricing which is felt to be unfairly low,[354] i.e., the very kind of pricing with which anti-dumping law is concerned. Outside the Community the Commission might not secure the necessary assistance from national authorities to obtain such evidence.[355] However, lack of co-operation from exporters may also impede anti-dumping investigations.[356] Increased co-operation between the Parties to the Europe Agreements may mean that practical impediments to the application of competition law to trade between these Parties would be no greater than impediments to the application of anti-dumping law to such trade. More serious impediments may arise from the apparent dependence of application of competition law to trade between the Parties on the harmonization of their respective competition policies.[357]

3.5 EEA AGREEMENT

The EEA Agreement reproduces provisions of the EC Treaty, at least in their form prior to amendment by the Treaty on European Union, authorizing trade restrictions. In addition, the Agreement authorizes certain restrictions which

[353] The Commission has merely committed itself to giving 'on a case-by-case basis, where appropriate, a clear preference to price undertakings rather than duties in order to conclude anti-dumping cases where injury is found'. See the Report from the Council to the Essen European Council on a strategy to prepare for accession of the associated CCEE, *Europe Doc.* No. 1916 (14 Dec. 1994), 3.

[354] Dec. 83/462 of 29 July 1983 ([1983] OJ L252/13) relating to a proceeding under Art. 86 EC (IV/30.698—ECS/Akzo: interim measures).

[355] Reg. 17 of 6 Feb. 1962 ([1962] JO 204) first reg. implementing Arts. 85 and 86 of the Treaty does not even refer to Commission investigations outside the Community. In contrast, Art. 7(2) of Reg. 2423/88 of 11 July 1988 ([1988] OJ L209/1) on protection against dumped or subsidized imports from countries not members of the EEC provided for the Commission to carry out investigations in third states with the consent of the company concerned and provided that the Government concerned had been notified and had raised no objection. These rules followed those in the GATT Agreement on the Implementation of Art. VI (BISD, 26th Supp., 171). A new Agreement is contained in Annex 1A to the Agreement establishing the World Trade Organization. See now Reg. 3283/94 of 22 Dec. 1994 ([1994] OJ L349/1) on protection against dumped imports from countries not members of the EC.

[356] See, e.g., Case 246/87 *Continentale Produkten-Gesellschaft Erhardt-Renken GmbH & Co.* v. *Hauptzollamt München-West* [1989] ECR 1151. See also J. Boudant, *L'Anti-Dumping Communautaire* (Paris, 1991), 259.

[357] The problems of such harmonization are considered in Ch. 4.

reflect the failure of the Agreement fully to embody certain Community policies.

3.5.1 Non-Economic Requirements

Article 13 of the EEA Agreement substantially reproduces Article 36 of the EC Treaty, and Article 123 of the EEA Agreement[358] substantially reproduces Articles 223 and 224 of the EC Treaty.[359]

The extent to which the provisions substantially reproduced allow for maintenance of neutrality is uncertain, and it was presumably with a view to clarifying the legal effects[360] of their counterparts in the EEA Agreement[361] that in negotiations for the Agreement Switzerland and Liechtenstein secured adoption of Protocol 6 thereto. According to this Protocol, the two countries might subject to a scheme of compulsory reserves products which were indispensable for the survival of the population and, in relation to Switzerland, for the army, in times of serious supply shortages, and the production of which in the two countries was insufficient or non-existent and the characteristics and nature of which enabled reserves to be built up. It was stipulated, however, that they would apply this scheme in a manner that did not involve any discrimination, direct or indirect, between the products imported from the other Parties and like or substitute national products.

The very fact that this Protocol was attached to the EEA Agreement might be taken as evidence for the proposition that the measures covered would not otherwise be permitted by the Agreement. On the other hand, the Community responded to certain Declarations by individual EFTA States, such as the Austrian Declaration on Safeguards, by declaring that they were 'without prejudice to the rights and obligations of the Contracting Parties under this Agreement'. The fact that Protocol 6 was agreed between the Parties might suggest that the measures covered would, irrespective of the Protocol, be compatible with the EEA Agreement. In other words, the significance of Articles 13 and 123 of the Agreement for neutrality questions remains unclear.

The significance of Article 31 of the EEA Agreement, which follows Article 31 of the Polish Agreement,[362] may be thought more clear. The former

[358] According to an Agreed Minute *ad* Art. 123 of the EEA Agreement, the Contracting Parties agreed that 'they would not make improper use of provisions in Art. 123 to prevent the disclosure of information in the field of competition'. Art. 123(b) of the EEA Agreement goes further than Art. 223(b) EC and refers to 'other products indispensable for defence purposes'.

[359] Cf. Art. 9 of Prot. 11 to the EEA Agreement, on Mutual Assistance in Customs Matters.

[360] The possibility of withdrawing from the EEA Agreement on 12 months' notice under Art. 127 of the Agreement would be inadequate for this purpose.

[361] No specific provision, like that in Art. 225 EC, for challenges to the use of Art. 123 is made in the EEA Agreement.

[362] A similar provision may be thought less necessary in relation to imports, because it is only trade in products originating within the EEA which is liberalized by the EEA Agreement (Art. 8(3)).

provision apparently means that trade liberalization requirements in the EEA Agreement need neither prevent a neutral EEA State from meeting obligations regarding the export of war materials to belligerents nor jeopardize the effectiveness of CFSP measures. However, the latter measures may affect EC–EFTA trade, even though EFTA States have no real say in their adoption. The EEA Agreement is merely to be accompanied by a political dialogue.[363]

3.5.2 'Mandatory Requirements'

The EEA Agreement contains provisions concerning social policy,[364] consumer protection,[365] environmental protection,[366] and there is also a Joint Declaration on Co-operation in Cultural Affairs. Moreover, while the Commission went into EEA negotiations with the attitude that higher EFTA standards in such areas constituted 'major difficulties',[367] during these negotiations the EFTA States secured adaptations of Community legislation which are consistent with recognition of 'mandatory requirements'.[368]

For example, Austria was allowed to maintain its national legislation governing the maximum weights of vehicles.[369] Moreover, any EFTA State may prohibit on a non-discriminatory basis the placing on their national markets of spirit drinks for direct human consumption which have an alcoholic strength in excess of 60 per cent.[370] Protocol 47 to the Agreement[371] also permitted Austria to maintain its general prohibition of sorbic acid and Sweden its general prohibition of wine containing metatartic acid.

In some cases the situation is to be reviewed in the future. For example, Part II of Annex I[372] to the Agreement permits EFTA States to maintain their

[363] See sect. 2.5 above.

[364] Arts. 66–71 of the EEA Agreement. See also the 11th recital in the Preamble to the Agreement and the Declaration by the Governments of the EFTA States on the Charter of Fundamental Social Rights for Workers.

[365] Art. 72 of the EEA Agreement. See also the 12th recital in the Preamble to the Agreement.

[366] *Ibid.*, Arts. 73–75. See also the 9th recital in the Preamble to the Agreement, regarding environmental protection, and the 10th recital, regarding protection of health, safety, and the environment. The Swedish Government drew a parallel with Art. 100a(3) EC, according to which Art. 100a(1) proposals concerning health, security, protection of the environment, and protection of consumers shall take as their base a high level of protection. See *Europeisk ekonomiska samarbetsområdet*, prop. 1991/92:170, *del* 1, bil. 1, 61.

[367] Para. 2.3 of the Commission Communication concerning a proposed Council decision authorizing the Commmission to negotiate an agreement with the EFTA States on the creation of a European Economic Space.

[368] Thus para. 7 of the Joint EC–EFTA Statement on the State of the Negotiations over the European Economic Area of 14 May 1991 (EFTA Bull. 2/91, 7–9) 'welcomed the pragmatic solutions agreed upon reconciling a high level of protection in the field of health, safety and the environment with the free circulation of goods'.

[369] Pt. II of Annex XIII, Transport, to the EEA Agreement.

[370] *Ibid.*, Pt. XXVII of Annex II, Technical regulations, standards, testing, and certification.

[371] On the abolition of technical barriers to trade in wine.

[372] On veterinary and phytosanitary matters.

national legislation regarding the use of growth promoters in feedingstuffs, and Part XV of the same Annex allows them to maintain their national legislation regarding the marketing and use of dangerous substances.[373] These two matters were to reviewed in 1995.

Therefore, the EEA Agreement provides bases for recognition of 'mandatory requirements'. To the extent that such bases are provided, development of trade liberalization may be reconcilable, at least to the satisfaction of the Court of Justice, with the demands of other requirements.

3.5.3 Economic Requirements

The EEA Agreement authorizes trade restrictions to meet various economic requirements. Article 111(4) of the Agreement provides that disputes regarding the scope or duration of such restrictions may be referred to arbitration.[374] In contrast, the justification for such restrictions is not a matter for such arbitration. Article 114(1) of the Agreement does permit a Party to resort to 'rebalancing' measures in response to adoption of restrictions by another Party. However, an economic balance may not easily be achieved through such measures.[375] Such considerations in themselves suggest that safeguard clauses in the EEA Agreement may operate differently from those in the EC Treaty.

Commercial Policy

Article 22 of the EEA Agreement provides that a Party which is considering the reduction of the effective level of its duties or charges having equivalent effect applicable to third states benefiting from most-favoured-nation treatment, or which is considering the suspension of their application, shall, as far as may be practicable, notify the EEA Joint Committee[376] not less than thirty days before such reduction or suspension comes into effect. It shall take note of any representations by other Parties regarding any distortions which might

[373] In other cases, however, EFTA negotiators seem to have been less successful. E.g., according to Pt. I of Annex II, EFTA States could, until 1 Jan. 1995, apply national legislation prohibiting motorcycles covered by Dir. 78/1015 of 23 Nov. 1978 ([1979] OJ L10/15) on the approximation of the laws of the Member States on the permissible sound level and exhaust system of motorcycles because of their sound level or exhaust system. From 1 Jan. 1995 they could continue to apply their national legislation, but had to allow free circulation according to Community law. According to the Message to the EC on Negotiations of an EES Treaty, adopted by EFTA Ministers on 3 Apr. 1990, 'general European trends should facilitate finding ways of reconciling . . . high standards with the free movement of goods'. However, there was no guarantee that Community law would impose the same standards by Jan. 1995, and the EEA Agreement contains no equivalent of Art. 100a(4) EC. See sect. 5.2.1 below.

[374] See sect. 8.5.2 below.

[375] A similar point may be made in relation to Art. 48(2) of the EEA Agreement. According to this provision, any Party deviating from the standstill clause applicable to discriminatory measures concerning transport in para. 1 shall notify the Joint Committee thereof, and Parties which do not accept the deviation may take corresponding measures.

[376] See sect. 6.5.1 below.

result therefrom.[377] If, however, contacts under this provision do not produce acceptable results, measures restricting trade can be adopted under Article 112 of the Agreement. Thus, even under the EEA Agreement, the failure of the Parties to adopt a common commercial policy may result in restriction of EC–EFTA trade.

Conjunctural Policy

Article 31 of the EEA Agreement follows Article 31 of the Polish Agreement in authorizing safeguard measures to deal with problems of product shortages. More generally, Article 112(1) of the EEA Agreement, which seems broader than Article 30 of the Polish Agreement, provides that if serious economic, societal, or environmental difficulties of a sectoral or regional nature[378] liable to persist arise, safeguard measures may be taken by the Party concerned. Article 112(2) stipulates that such measures shall be restricted with regard to their scope and duration to what is strictly necessary in order to remedy the situation; priority shall be given to such measures as will least disturb the functioning of this Agreement; and, according to Article 112(3), the measures shall apply with regard to all Parties. From the perspective of EFTA States, this provision may have been seen as removing the need for the numerous permanent exceptions[379] from Community law requirements which were originally sought by these states.[380] Its apparent consequence is to allow broad scope for introduction of trade restrictions.

[377] Cf., regarding circumvention on rules on third country access to their markets, Prot. 17, concerning Art. 34. More particularly, according to paras. I(i)(e), 1(iii)(e) and II(i)(a) of Annex IX, on Financial Services, if a third state imposes restrictions on undertakings from EFTA States that it does not impose on Community undertakings, Community authorizations to subsidiaries of parent companies governed by the law of that state shall have validity only within the Community, unless an EFTA State decides otherwise for its own jurisdiction. Cf. also, regarding maritime transport, para. 11(e) of Annex XIV, on Competition. Art. 4(2) of Prot. 28, on Intellectual Property, requires that a Contracting Party which extends the right to protection of topographies and semiconductor products to a non-Contracting Party shall endeavour to ensure that the latter grants equivalent protection to other Contracting Parties, and Art. 4(3) provides for such extension to be respected by other Contracting Parties. If no equivalent grant is obtained, consultations are required by Art. 4(5) regarding the implications for continuation of the free movement of goods under the Agreement, and Pt. VII applies. Cf. also Art. 134 EC, regarding possible deflections of trade arising from the association with overseas countries and territories.

[378] According to an Agreed Minute *ad* Art. 112(1), this provision also covers the situation in a given area.

[379] In May 1990 Norway (DN, 28 May 1990) and Sweden (SvD, 15 May 1990) each envisaged seeking around 50 exceptions or transitional periods. The EC–EFTA Joint Ministerial Declaration of 14 May 1991 (EFTA Bull. 2/91, 7–9) referred in para. 18 to this general safeguard clause as well as to unilateral declarations regarding specific aspects of the application of this clause which could be attached to the EEA Agreement and of which the Parties would take note.

[380] AiH 1/1991, 6. Cf. the Declaration by the Government of Liechtenstein, on the Specific Situation of the Country, regarding Art. 112 and capital inflows liable to endanger access of the resident population to real estate or extraordinary increase in number of nationals from other Contracting Parties or in the number of jobs in the economy, both in comparison with the number of the resident population. See also the Declaration by the Government of Austria on Safeguards,

Monetary Policy

Article 43(4) of the EEA Agreement is modelled on Articles 109h and 109i of the EC Treaty. It provides that where a Member State or an EFTA State is in difficulties or is seriously threatened with difficulties as regards its balance of payments, either as a result of an overall disequilibrium in its balance or the type of currency at its disposal, and where such difficulties are liable in particular to jeopardize the functioning of this Agreement, the Party concerned may take protective measures.[381] Article 43(2) of the Agreement also permits resort to such measures where movements of capital lead to disturbances in the functioning of the capital market in any EEA State. These provisions authorize Parties to prevent encroachment on monetary policy requirements by the operation of trade liberalization provisions in the Agreement.

Other provisions may be designed to permit the consequences of non-harmonization of monetary policies to be countered. Thus Article 43(1) of the Agreement permits resort to safeguard measures where differences between the exchange rules of Member States and EFTA States could lead persons resident in one of these states to use the freer transfer facilities provided for in Article 40[382] to evade the rules of one of those states concerning capital movements to or from third states. Moreover, Article 43(3), like Article 107(2) of the original version of the EC Treaty, provides that if the competent authorities of a Party make an alteration in the rate of exchange which seriously distorts conditions of competition, the other Parties may take for a strictly limited period the necessary measures in order to counter the consequences of such alteration.

Competition Policy

The EEA Agreement reproduces EC Treaty provisions regarding restrictive practices by undertakings and state aid, though it does not entirely exclude the possibility of resort by a Party to anti-dumping measures or to other measures restricting EC–EFTA trade.

(i) Restrictive Practices by Undertakings

Articles 53 and 54 of the EEA Agreement reproduce Articles 85 and 86, respectively, of the EC Treaty.[383] The Agreement also provides for a system

regarding Art. 112 and disturbances on the real estate market. The Community, however, declared that the Austrian Declaration was without prejudice to rights and obligations under the Agreement.

[381] See also Prot. 18, on Internal Procedures for Application of Safeguard Measures. Annex XII introduces transitional periods for EFTA States for implementation of Dir. 88/361 of 24 June 1988 ([1988] OJ L178/5) for the implementation of Art. 67 EC. In addition, Iceland and Norway may continue to restrict foreign ownership of fishing vessels.

[382] This provision prohibits restrictions on capital movements within the EEA.

[383] In addition, Art. 57 of the EEA Agreement provides for Commission application of Reg. 4064/89 of 21 Dec. 1989 ([1989] OJ L395/1) on the control of concentrations between undertakings throughout the EEA.

of surveillance and enforcement equivalent to that of the Community to be established within EFTA[384] and for close co-operation between the EFTA Surveillance Authority (ESA) and the Commission.[385] There is no specific provision for safeguard measures in the event of failure by a Party to apply effectively competition law against restrictive practices by undertakings, presumably because of the role which the Commission and the ESA are expected to play.[386] To the extent that the two achieve consistent application of competition law throughout the EEA, such law could become a means of reducing obstacles to EC–EFTA trade. Even so, Article 56(1)(c) of the Agreement provides for the Commission to decide competition cases affecting EC–EFTA trade, where trade between Member States is also appreciably affected. The possibility cannot be ruled out that the Commission decisions envisaged will reflect the perceived requirements of 'internal' Community competition policy more than conditions of competition in EC–EFTA trade. Article 109(5) merely provides that disagreements between the Commission and the ESA as to the action taken in relation to a complaint or with regard to the result of the examination of a case may be referred by either body to the Joint Committee.[387]

(ii) State Aid

Article 61 of the EEA Agreement substantially reproduces Article 92 of the EC Treaty, and Annex XV lists Commission 'principles' embodying its practice regarding state aid control within the Community. The Commission remains responsible for applying such law within the Community,[388] and the ESA has corresponding responsibility within EFTA.[389] If, however, the practical application of Article 61 of the Agreement is found to be unsatisfactory, Article 64 may be invoked.[390] It permits adoption of safeguard measures[391] where one surveillance authority considers that the other has failed to implement the state aid rules of the Agreement in conformity with the maintenance of equal conditions of competition within the EEA.[392] In other words, even under the EEA Agreement, the grant of state aid by one Party might be met by

[384] *Ibid.*, Art. 108(1). [385] *Ibid.*, Art. 58.

[386] Anti-dumping proceedings may also be available. See below.

[387] The latter is to deal with the matter under Art. 111 of the EEA Agreement. See sects. 6.5.3 and 8.5.2 below, regarding the Art. 111 procedures.

[388] Art. 62(1)(a) of the EEA Agreement. [389] *Ibid.*, Art. 62(1)(b).

[390] Art. 64(1) (*ibid.*) provides that the provisions of this Art. will also apply to state monopolies established after the date of the signature of the Agreement.

[391] The Civil Aviation Agreement ([1992] OJ L200/21) between Norway, Sweden, and the Community went further. It provided for the Commission to request the abolition of state aid. If the request was not met and the Joint Committee did not take a different decision within 6 months, Art. 14(5) provided that the Agreement should cease to be in force.

[392] Uncertainty as to the likely role of Art. 64 of the EEA Agreement is only increased by the failure of this provision to deal with the possibility that the relevant surveillance authority may fulfil its functions properly but a state may still violate the relevant rules.

restrictions on trade[393] rather than implementation of a harmonized aid policy designed to reduce obstacles to EC–EFTA trade. Indeed, resort to anti-dumping measures is not entirely precluded by this Agreement.[394]

(iii) Dumping

Article 26 of the EEA Agreement provides that anti-dumping measures, countervailing duties, and measures against illicit commercial practices attributable to third states shall not be applied in relations between the Parties, unless otherwise specified in this Agreement. However, the first paragraph of Protocol 13 to the Agreement, concerning the Non-Application of Anti-Dumping and Countervailing Measures, provides that the application of Article 26 is limited to the areas covered by the provisions of this Agreement and in which Community law rules are fully integrated into this Agreement.[395]

These limitations suggest that anti-dumping measures may remain permissible to the extent that transitional periods provided for in the Agreement have not expired or that special exceptions from Community law requirements have been secured by one or more EFTA States. Such measures may also become permissible in the future, to the extent that these states fail to adopt amendments to Community legislation. The possibility of such failure is by no means excluded by the EEA decision-making procedures laid down in Part VII of the Agreement.[396]

More particularly, the fact that the Agreement does not require adoption of certain Community policies, such as the common commercial policy, may affect the permissibility of anti-dumping and similar measures. Thus the second paragraph of Protocol 13 provides that unless other solutions are agreed upon by the Parties, the application of Article 26 is without prejudice to any measures which may be introduced by the Parties to avoid circumvention of the following measures aimed at third countries:[397]

- anti-dumping measures;
- countervailing duties;
- measures against illicit commercial practices attributable to third countries.

[393] It is merely stipulated in Art. 64(1) of the Agreement that priority shall be given to measures which least disturb the functioning of the EEA.

[394] This issue seems to have been a difficult one to resolve in negotiations for the EEA Agreement. The EC–EFTA Joint Ministerial Meeting of 19 Dec. 1990 (EFTA Bull. 1/91, 22–5) stated in para. 15 that it remained to be considered whether resort to anti-dumping measures would be permissible within the EEA.

[395] According to N. G. van der Pas, 'The European Economic Area: Aspects concerning Free Movement of Goods' in O. Jacot-Guillarmod (ed.), n. 260 above, 101–14, at 106, Prot. 13 'implies in the Community's understanding also full application of the rules on competition'.

[396] See sect. 6.5.3 below.

[397] Problems that may arise where a Party engages in unfair trading practices in a third state are not addressed.

On the other hand, although the common fisheries policy is not covered by the Agreement, efforts are to be made to exclude the possibility of resort to anti-dumping measures in the fisheries sector. Article 4(3) of Protocol 9, on Trade in Fish and Other Marine Products, provides that the Parties shall endeavour to ensure conditions of competition which will enable the other Parties to refrain from the application of anti-dumping measures and countervailing measures. According to an Agreed Minute *ad* Article 26 of the Agreement and Protocol 13, before the entry into force of the Agreement the Community was, together with the interested EFTA States, to examine whether the conditions were fulfilled in which Article 26 of the Agreement, irrespective of the first paragraph of Protocol 13, would apply between the Community and the EFTA States concerned in the fisheries sector.

The implied reluctance of the Community to commit itself to permanently abandoning use of anti-dumping law in EC–EFTA trade might be attributable to what the 'realist' school of international relations describes as a fear of cheating.[398] This fear is reflected in the attitude of the European Parliament. According to the Parliament, anti-dumping law should only be abolished in such trade after a transitional period, during which sufficient market integration would have to be achieved and agreement on 'accompanying policies', such as competition policy, would have to be reached.[399] Such attitudes, like the above provisions of the EEA Agreement, seem merely to confirm that the role of anti-dumping measures under agreements between the Community and third states depends on more than simply the terms of individual provisions regarding such measures.[400]

3.6 CONCLUSION

The operation of trade liberalization requirements of the EC Treaty cannot be divorced from the operation of other requirements of the Treaty. Differences in the latter requirements as between the Treaty and agreements with third states may thus tend to compound, and be compounded by, differences in liberalization requirements. As an immediate consequence, the likelihood is increased that corresponding provisions in the different legal frameworks will vary in their liberalizing effects.

As a more profound consequence, harmonization may have greater importance for the reduction of trading obstacles within the framework of an

398 J. M. Grieco, *Cooperation among Nations* (London, 1990).

399 Resolution of 14 Dec. 1990 ([1991] OJ C19/633) on the anti-dumping policy of the European Community, para. 22.

400 The Commission insisted in negotiations for the EEA Agreement on '*la nature indissociable des différents éléments de l'acquis communautaire*'. See C.-P. Lucron, 'Vers l'espace économique européen: l'Europe du deuxième cercle' [1990] RMC 527–31, at 528.

agreement between the Community and a third state[401] than within the framework of the EC Treaty. For example, whereas in the Community some harmonization of national policies with which public policy or public security exceptions in the EC Treaty are concerned may effectively result from the strict interpretation given to such exceptions, prior harmonization may be a condition for limiting the scope of corresponding exceptions in agreements with third states. Similarly, whereas Commission application of competition law provisions in the EC Treaty promotes Community trade liberalization, competition provisions within the framework of agreements with third states may be treated as authorizing trade restrictions between the parties, unless there is prior harmonization of competition policy.

Moreover, reduction of trading obstacles may not only be rendered more dependent on harmonization than is the case within the Community. Harmonization may also be rendered more problematic. To the extent that agreements with third states lack the same far-reaching liberalization requirements or the basis for protection of other requirements as the EC Treaty, they may not provide such a developed framework within which harmonization may be pursued.

[401] As the European Parliament puts it, problems of trade with Central and East European states cannot be settled by safeguard clauses alone, but also by taking into account the need of such states for assistance in transforming their economies. See the Resolution of 29 Oct. 1992 ([1992] OJ C305/145) on the situation in the European steel industry, para. 6. See, regarding the safeguard measures being employed, Commission Reply by Sir Leon Brittan to Written Question E–2044/93 ([1994] OJ C234/32) by Robert Delorozoy. Cf., regarding fisheries policy and the possibility of Norwegian accession to the Union, Commission Reply by Sir Leon Brittan to Written Question 1219/93 ([1994] OJ C46/19) by Mr Henry McCubbin.

PART 2
Harmonization

4

Administrative Harmonization: Competition Policy

4.1 INTRODUCTION

Competition law provisions of the EC Treaty concern restrictive practices by undertakings, state aid and state monopolies, and public undertakings. These provisions oppose restrictive practices or State measures which may affect trade between Member States. Hence, they may be regarded as embodying trade liberalization requirements. However, in the elaboration of the requirements so embodied, which is primarily an administrative responsibility of the Commission, account may have to be taken of other requirements also embodied in competition law provisions and in the Treaty more generally.[1] The outcomes of interactions entailed between the trade liberalization and other requirements concerned—and the associated resolutions of policy conflicts—may be expressed as competition policy.

The Free Trade Agreements revealed little concern for such complexities. They merely provided that restrictive practices by undertakings and 'public' aid[2] were incompatible with the Agreements, in so far as trade between the Parties was affected. The Europe Agreements go further and provide for application of Community competition law 'criteria' to trade between the Parties. The EEA Agreement goes even further. It contains provisions substantially identical to those of Community competition law, and the Preamble states that the Agreement is designed to establish a dynamic and homogeneous European Economic Area, based on equal conditions of competition.[3] Hence, uniform interpretation and application of the Agreement and those provisions of Community law substantially reproduced therein are sought, so as to arrive at equal treatment of individuals and economic operators as regards the four freedoms and the conditions of competition.[4] To this end, Article 1(2)(e) of the Agreement provides for the setting up of a system ensuring that competition is not distorted and that the rules thereon are equally respected. This system not

[1] According to the *Twenty-Fourth Report on Competition Policy*, COM(95)142, 23, competition policy is 'an essential instrument in achieving the internal market and economic recovery'.

[2] Presumably, the concept of public aid (as opposed to state aid) covers aid granted by the Community itself. Cf. the Joint Declaration on aid granted through the EC structural Funds or other financial instruments, annexed to the EEA Agreement.

[3] 4th recital in the Preamble to the EEA Agreement.

[4] *Ibid.*, 15th recital in the Preamble. See, similarly, Art. 1(1) (*ibid.*).

only entails that common competition law should apply to trade between the Contracting Parties. It also entails the creation by EFTA States of an independent body, the Surveillance Authority (ESA),[5] which is to have equivalent powers and functions in relation to competition within EFTA to those of the Commission within the Community,[6] and the creation of an EFTA Court to exercise judicial review of the acts of that Authority.[7]

All these frameworks apparently recognize that competition law has a role to play in reducing obstacles to trade. In practice, however, the effective role played by such law depends on features of the particular framework within which it is contained. Under the EC Treaty harmonization of the competition policies pursued by the various Member States results from application of competition law provisions of the Treaty. For example, in applying the provisions governing state aid, the Commission seeks in certain sectors or for certain purposes, such as environmental protection or regional development or for the realization of an important project in the interests of the Community, the reduction of differences in the aids granted by the various Member States rather than the elimination of such aids.[8] Under agreements between the Community and third states operation of the competition law provisions contained in these agreements may be dependent on prior harmonization by the Parties of their respective competition policies.[9] Hence, the capacity of Community competition policy to take account of differences in interests and conditions as between the Community and third states and, ultimately, its adaptability to harmonization with the competition policies of the third states concerned may be critical for the operation of these provisions. However, the very nature of Community competition policy—a reflection of interactions between trade liberalization and other requirements embodied in the EC Treaty but not necessarily reproduced in agreements with such states—means that its adaptability may not be assumed.

4.2 EC TREATY

'Common rules'[10] governing restrictive practices by undertakings and state aid were originally contained in Part Three of the EC Treaty, which was headed

[5] *Ibid.*, Art. 108(1).

[6] The division of responsibilities between the two bodies is intended to accord with the 'one stop shop' principle. See C. Rouam, 'L'Espace economique européen: un horizon nouveau pour la politique de concurrence' (1992) *RMC* 53–7.

[7] Art. 108(2) of the EEA Agreement.

[8] VerLoren van Themaat A. G. in Case 169/84 *Cie Française de l'Azote (COFAZ) SA* v. *EC Commission* [1986] ECR 391, 404–5.

[9] In the case of states which have concluded Europe Agreements with the Community, the Commission sees such harmonization as a condition for securing 'a level playing field' for traders. See *Preparation of the Associated Countries of Central and Eastern Europe for Integration into the Internal Market of the Union*, COM(95)163, Annex, 59.

[10] Title I of Pt. 3 EEC, where the relevant provisions were contained, was so headed.

'Policy of the Community', rather than Part Two, which was headed 'Foundations of the Community' and provided for establishment of the 'four freedoms'.[11] In thus separating competition law from these freedoms, the Treaty implied that operation of the former was to be guided by more than simply the need to eliminate obstacles to Community trade.

4.2.1 Restrictive Practices by Undertakings

Article 85 of the EC Treaty provides that all agreements between undertakings, decisions of associations of undertakings, and concerted practices which may affect trade between Member States and which have as their object or effect the prevention, restriction or distortion of competition within the common market are prohibited. Examples of prohibited practices are given in Article 85(1)(a) to (e). Any agreements or decisions prohibited pursuant to Article 85(1) shall, according to Article 85(2), be automatically void. However, Article 85(3) provides for exemption from the prohibition where four conditions are met.[12] There must be a contribution to improving the production or distribution of goods or to promoting technical or economic progress; consumers must be allowed a fair share of the resulting benefit; restrictions must not be imposed on the undertakings concerned which are not indispensable to the attainment of such objectives; and such undertakings must not be afforded the possibility of eliminating competition in respect of a substantial part of the common market.[13]

Article 86 provides, in turn, that any abuse by one or more undertakings of a dominant position within the common market or a substantial part of it which may affect trade between Member States shall be prohibited. Examples of prohibited practices are given in Article 86(a) to (d).

In assessing the acceptability of restrictive practices by undertakings under these provisions, the Commission may have regard to the competition which the undertakings concerned face from third-country undertakings. For example, in *A Community Strategy to Develop Europe's Industry*[14] the Commission maintained that assessment of the dominant position of an undertaking must

[11] Pts. 2 and 3 have been merged by the TEU. However, the 'Common rules on competition, taxation and approximation of laws' retain a separate title (Title V) from those (Titles I and III) for the 'four freedoms'.

[12] In addition, certain restrictive agreements may fall outside Art. 85(1), where they are consistent with what the ECJ regards as fair competition. See, e.g., Case 161/84 *Pronuptia de Paris GmbH* v. *Pronuptia de Paris Irmgard Schillgalis* [1986] ECR 353. Such competition is seen in structural terms and should enable new entrants to participate in a unified market. See Case 56/65 *Société La Technique Minière* v. *Maschinenbau Ulm* [1966] ECR 235.

[13] See, e.g., A. Evans, 'Art. 85(3) Exemption: 'Allowing Consumers a Fair Share of the Resulting Benefit'' in M. Goyens (ed.), *European Competition Policy and the Consumer Interest* (Bruylant, Brussels, 1985), 99–120.

[14] COM(81)639, 19.

take into account, where necessary, the fact that the undertaking was exposed to actual or potential competition from imports from outside the Community.[15] The implications of Commission thinking are clearer in the *Eleventh Report on Competition Policy*.[16] According to this Report, the Community had to develop strategies to adapt and improve its industrial machinery in order to recover competitiveness where it was lacking. As part of such a strategy, competition policy measures must be analysed in terms of their effects both on economic sectors as a whole and on individual operators therein. Apparently, toleration of certain anti-competitive conduct within the Community may be considered necessary with a view to improving the international competitiveness of Community traders.

Moreover, according to the *Sixth Report on Competition Policy*,[17] developments went hand in hand with developments in other Community policies.[18] In a multiplicity of economic situations, maintained the Commission, competition policy could support 'other measures'.[19] The implication is that the operation of Articles 85 and 86 may be influenced by a range of Community policies.[20]

In short, therefore, Community practice under these provisions is designed to accommodate economic conditions within the Community and various policies pursued by the Community. Such a design may not produce a competition policy which is well adapted to harmonization with the competition policies of third states.

4.2.2 State Aid

Article 92(1) of the EC Treaty provides that, save as otherwise provided in this Treaty, any aid granted by a Member State or through State resources in any form whatsoever which distorts or threatens to distort competition by favouring certain undertakings or the production of certain goods shall, in so far as it affects trade between Member States, be incompatible with the common market.

[15] Community industries are so advanced and specialized that any competition policy choice necessarily has implications for trade with third states. See V. Curzon Price, 'Industrial Trade Policy in a Period of Rapid Industrial Change' [1986] *Aussenwirtschaft* 201–23.

[16] EC Commission, Brussels, 1982, 11.

[17] EC Commission, Brussels, 1977, 10.

[18] Competition policy is an integral part of economic policy. See L. Vogel, *Droit de Concurrence et Concentration Economique* (Paris, 1988), 18–19.

[19] Such an approach to competition policy can find some support in the case law of the ECJ. See Case 14/68 *Walt Wilhelm* v. *Bundeskartellamt* [1969] ECR 1, 14. The approach may, nevertheless, be controversial. See, e.g., S. B. Hornsby, 'Competition Policy in the 80's: More Policy Less Competition?' [1987] *ELRev*. 79–101.

[20] Art. VI(3)(e) of the Agreement between the EC and the Government of the USA regarding the application of their competition laws ([1995] OJ L95/47) envisages that in the enforcement of its competition policy each Party will take account of the 'articulated economic policies' of the other Party.

However, Article 92(2) provides that non-discriminatory aid of a social character granted to individual consumers and aid to make good the damage caused by natural disasters or exceptional occurrences are compatible with the common market.[21] Moreover, Article 92(3) provides that the following may be considered to be compatible with the common market:

(a) aid to promote the economic development of areas where the standard of living is abnormally low or where there is serious under-employment;
(b) aid to promote the execution of an important project of common European interest or to remedy a serious disturbance in the economy of a Member State;
(c) aid to facilitate the development of certain economic activities or of certain economic areas, where such aid does not adversely affect trading conditions to an extent contrary to the common interest.[22]

In addition, Article 92(3)(d), as amended by the Treaty on European Union, provides that the Commission may authorize aid to promote culture and heritage conservation where such aid does not affect trading conditions and competition to an extent contrary to the common interest.[23]

These provisions entail that aid may be authorized by reference to various policies: regional, sectoral and horizontal. A possible implication is that policy conflicts may be more pronounced in the treatment of state aid[24] than in the treatment of restrictive practices by undertakings. As a result, Community treatment of the former may be even less adapted to harmonization with the competition policies of third states than is Community treatment of restrictive practices by undertakings.

Regional Policy

In assessing the acceptability of regional aid, the Commission follows the Treaty and distinguishes between regions covered by Article 92(3)(a) and regions covered by Article 92(3)(c).

[21] Art. 92(2)(c) of the EC also authorizes aid to deal with problems associated with the division of Germany. The Commission is apparently uncertain whether German unification now renders this authorization inapplicable. See Notice C60/91 (ex NN73/91, NN76/91) ([1993] OJ C43/14) regarding the proposal by the German Government to award state aid to the Opel group in support of its investment plans in the new *Länder*.

[22] Art. 92(3)(e), as amended by the TEU, allows for the Council to authorize other categories of aid. It has been employed only for the purpose of adopting Dirs. on shipbuilding aid. See, currently, Dir. 90/684 of 21 Dec. 1990 ([1990] OJ L38/27) on aid to shipbuilding.

[23] The Union itself provides aid in the cultural field, such as that for translations of literary works. See, e.g., the pilot scheme to provide financial aid for translation of contemporary literary works ([1993] OJ C5/12). See now Art. 128 EC, as introduced by the TEU, and the Commission Proposal of 25 Oct. 1994 ([1994] OJ C324/11) for a Dec. establishing a support programme in the field of books and reading (Ariane).

[24] A. Evans and S. Martin, 'Socially Acceptable Distortion of Competition: Community Policy on State Aid' [1991] *ELRev.* 79–111.

(i) Article 92(3)(a) Regions

The Commission relies primarily on GDP figures to identify Community regions covered by Article 92(3)(a) of the Treaty. According to a Commission Communication of 1988,[25] this provision may apply where the majority of NUTS[26] level III regions[27] situated in a level II region have a *per capita* GDP of 75 per cent[28] or less of the Community average in purchasing power parities. These regions, to which Northern Ireland and Teruel have been added for 'special reasons',[29] are listed in Annex I to the Communication. In such regions aid up to 75 per cent net grant equivalent[30] of investment costs may be authorized.[31]

However, not all kinds of aid will necessarily be permitted under Article 92(3)(a), because aid must promote economic development in the regions covered by this provision. In particular, operating aid, which has been defined as aid having a direct effect on production costs and selling prices of recipients,[32] may be objectionable.[33] Such aid includes, for example, aid for transportation and storage,[34] aid for financing shipyard stocks of semi-finished products and finished products, as opposed to raw materials,[35] a ten-year tax exemption on returns from approved investments[36] and aid for the renovation of a float line at a flat-glass factory, which had to be carried out every six to nine years.[37]

It is feared that such aid, instead of leading recipient firms to undertake the

[25] Communication on the method for the application of Art. 92(3)(a) and (c) to regional aid ([1988] OJ C212/2), para. I.1.

[26] Nomenclature of Territorial Units for Statistical Purposes. See Eurostat, *Statistiques Rapides des Régions*, 25 Aug. 1986.

[27] Reference is now to be made to the situation of the level II region as a whole in which the level III region is located. See the Communication on the method for the application of Art. 92(3)(a) to regional aid ([1990] OJ C163/6).

[28] *Per capita* GDP figures are regarded as a better indicator of underemployment than unemployment statistics (para. I.2 of the 1988 Communication).

[29] Teruel, though part of a level II region which did not meet the basic criterion, bordered on other Art. 92(3)(a) regions and was underdeveloped with a sparse population and a high degree of dependence on agriculture (para. I.4 of the 1988 Communication). Northern Ireland was included 'because of its particularly difficult situation' (*ibid.*).

[30] I.e., the discounted post-tax value of total assistance from public sources expressed as a percentage of discounted fixed project costs.

[31] Para. I.5 of the 1988 Communication.

[32] Dec. 82/744 of 11 Oct. 1982 ([1982] OJ L315/23) concerning Italian Law No. 423/81 of 1 Aug. 1981 on measures for agriculture.

[33] Though in sectors such as coal certain types of operating aid may be permissible. See, e.g., *Application of the Community Rules for State Aid to the Coal Industry in 1989*, COM(91)1240.

[34] Communication C25/91 ([1991] OJ C189/5) concerning aids by means of which the Netherlands intend to stimulate an environmentally acceptable disposal of surplus manure.

[35] Dec. 88/281 of 17 Nov. 1987 ([1988] OJ L119/33) on aid for shipbuilding and ship repair in Italy—Art. 10 of Law No. 111 of 22 Mar. 1985.

[36] Dec. 70/304 of 27 May 1970 ([1970] JO L128/33) *relative au projet de loi italien visant la restructuration, la réorganisation et la conversion de l'industrie textile.*

[37] Dec. 87/195 of 3 Dec. 1986 ([1987] OJ L77/47) on a proposal by the Belgian Government to grant aid for investments by a flat-glass producer at Moustier.

restructuring necessary for them to solve their problems,[38] may simply offset such problems[39] and enable the firms to continue uncompetitive activities.[40] In essence, their structural adaptation may be hampered rather than encouraged.[41] More particularly, if such aid is not likely to render the beneficiary viable without permanent aid, it will not be regarded as contributing to the development of a region.[42] For example, as the Court of Justice apparently accepts,[43] aid to support periodic renovation of industrial plant involves no such development.[44]

Accordingly, in the 1979 Principles for the Co-ordination of Regional Aid Systems[45] the Commission expressed reservations in principle about the compatibility of operating aid with the common market and announced its intention to specify the circumstances, if any, in which it might consider such aid to be so compatible.[46] A similar point was made in Article 9(2) of Regulation 1787/84,[47] which provided that Community programmes supported by the European Regional Development Fund (ERDF) might not have as their object the internal reorganization of declining sectors but must, by participating in the establishment of new activities, promote the creation of alternative employment in regions or areas in a difficult situation.

Even so, operating aid may be found to be justified where there is a sufficient threat to the 'social fabric'.[48] For example, exemption from rates in Northern Ireland benefited all enterprises regardless of whether they undertook an initial investment and was, in principle, incompatible with the common market. The Commission considered, however, that in the particular case of Northern Ireland, where the problem of civil unrest accentuated the grave economic difficulties, aid which aimed at maintaining existing industry as well as promoting initial investment was justified.[49] Such a threat may also be perceived to arise, as Directives on, for example, aid to shipbuilding[50] demonstrate, from industrial restructuring in line with Community policies.

Moreover, the accession of Greece and then Portugal and Spain led to 'a

[38] Dec. 73/274 of 25 July 1973 ([1973] OJ L254/14) on Art. 20 of Italian Act 1101 of 1 Dec. 1971 on the restructuring, reorganization, and conversion of the textile industry.

[39] Cf. Case 28/66 *Netherlands* v. *EC Commission* [1968] ECR 1, 15.

[40] See, e.g., the *Programme de politique économique à moyen terme 1966–1970* ([1967] JO 1513), sect. VI.6.

[41] Dec. 79/496 of 2 May 1979 ([1979] OJ L127/50) on the UK scheme of assistance in the form of interest relief grants in favour of the offshore supplies industry (offshore supplies interest relief grant, OSIRG).

[42] Case C-142/87 *Belgium* v. *EC Commission* [1990] ECR I-959, I-1018.

[43] Joined Cases 62 and 72/87 *Executif Régional Wallon and Glaverbel* v. *EC Commission* [1988] ECR 1573. [44] *Ibid.*, 1597. [45] [1979] OJ C31/9.

[46] *Ibid.*, para. 4.

[47] Of 19 June 1984 ([1984] OJ L169/1) on the European Regional Development Fund.

[48] Dec. 85/18 of 10 Oct. 1984 ([1985] OJ L11/28) on the French regional planning grant scheme ('*Prime d'aménagement du territoire*').

[49] *Fourteenth Report on Competition Policy* (EC Commission, Brussels, 1985), 175–6.

[50] See, e.g., Art. 5 of Dir. 81/363 ([1981] OJ L137/39) on aid to shipbuilding.

certain rethinking of the Commission's policy towards regional aid'.[51] As a result, the underdeveloped character of a region may be taken, in certain circumstances, to justify the grant of operating aid.[52] According to the 1988 Commission Communication, undertakings in regions covered by Article 92(3)(a) might face additional costs attributable to their location and infrastructure difficulties, and so operating aid might be beneficial in such regions.[53]

First, there might be serious disadvantages as regards costs and infrastructure, such that the safeguarding of existing investment might be difficult. In order to safeguard such investment, operating aid might be necessary, in earlier stages of development, to attract new investments and to promote economic development. This was particularly so because of the very small undertakings in 'traditional' areas which needed Community market participation.

Secondly, there might be serious structural problems, as for example in the case of peripheral islands. Such problems might also justify the grant of operating aid, provided it was limited in time, was to promote durable and balanced economic development, and would not lead to Community overcapacity in the sector concerned.[54]

In Decision 88/318[55] the Commission found that operating aid provided in the Mezzogiorno fulfilled these criteria and could, therefore, be accepted in those regions which fell within the scope of Article 92(3)(a). This acceptance applied, in particular, to relief from social security contributions; tax concessions; State guarantees; and assistance with transport costs for firms located in Sardinia.

On the other hand, in Decision 92/296[56] the Commission decided that the grant of the last-mentioned category of aid to a Sardinian firm was such as to offset the locational disadvantages of the latter firm and, hence, that no other operating aid was permissible. Moreover, aid to a company 'without a perspective of viability' may be treated as unable to promote durable development for the purposes of Article 92(3)(a).[57] Similarly, continued public investment in loss-making companies in a sector suffering from overcapacity and without a restructuring plan may be prohibited, even in Article 92(3)(a) regions, because it does not favour the economic development of these regions.[58]

[51] *Sixteenth Report on Competition Policy* (EC Commission, Brussels, 1987), 178.

[52] *Eighteenth Report on Competition Policy* (EC Commission, Brussels, 1989), 147.

[53] Para. I.6 of the Communication.

[54] The latter condition implied that Community sectoral policy rules must be respected. See below, 162–70, regarding such rules.

[55] Of 2 Mar. 1988 ([1988] OJ L143/37) on aid to the Mezzogiorno.

[56] Of 27 Nov. 1991 ([1992] OJ L159/46) concerning aid granted by the Italian Government to Nuova Cartiera di Arbatax.

[57] Case C–305/89 *Italy* v. *EC Commission* [1991] ECR I–1603, I–1644.

[58] Case C–303/88 *Italy* v. *EC Commission* [1991] ECR I–1433, I–1481.

Such practice has been primarily designed to cope with problems of underdevelopment associated with dependence on agriculture rather than with problems of declining industrial areas or those of economic transformation. Hence, Belfast was only treated as being covered by Article 92(3)(a) of the EC Treaty because of 'special conditions' in Northern Ireland. However, now that the former German Democratic Republic is also treated as covered by this provision,[59] the need for a fundamental reappraisal of Community practice may be implied.[60]

The Commission has stated that it will apply state aid rules constructively to facilitate the development and full integration of the economy of the former GDR. At the same time, these rules will have to continue to perform their normal function of keeping competitive conditions equal throughout the Community, maintaining a level playing field in the common market, and avoiding any artificial and unjustified advantage for East German companies.[61]

Accordingly, the Commission authorized various aid schemes in the new *Länder*. In particular, extension of the regional aid scheme (Joint Task 'Improvement of Regional Economic Structures') to these *Länder* was authorized, which meant that the granting of regional aid over the whole territory of these *Länder* up to 23 per cent of the investment costs of recipient undertakings was permissible.[62] The Commission also approved the grant of general aid based on the former GDR investment allowance and environmental aid based on a federal programme to support investment aid measures to reduce pollution.[63]

More particularly, in view of 'the unprecedented transformation of a planned economy into a market economy inside the Community', the Commission accepts that aid may be granted to companies in the former GDR 'in order to enable these companies to maintain the manufacturing of products which may become viable after restructuring of the company'[64] or to remedy 'the omissions of the former system to invest in necessary equipment, neglected

[59] Communication C4/94 (ex NN103/93) ([1994] OJ C206/10) concerning aid decided by the German Government in favour of Leuna AG, *Land* Sachsen Anhalt; *Twenty-Fourth Report on Competition Policy*, COM(95)142, 525.

[60] See, generally, M. Schütte and J. -P. Hix, 'The Application of the EC State Aid Rules to Privatizations: The East German Example' (1995) 32 *CMLRev*. 215–48.

[61] *The European Community and German Unification*, Bull. EC, Supp. 4/90, 74–75.

[62] This ceiling is comparatively low, even allowing for the extra 10 per cent permitted in case of cumulation with other aid and was subject to respect for the various aid frameworks in operation in the Community. See below, 162–72.

[63] SG(90)D/90545. The desirability of aid to facilitate 'transition from . . . monopoly arrangements to a free market' seems generally to be recognized by the Commission. See Communication C45/93 (N663/93) ([1994] OJ C100/9) concerning the England and Wales Milk Marketing Board reorganization scheme.

[64] Notice C43/92 (NN131/92) ([1994] OJ C16/6) concerning aid awarded by the German Government to Buna AG. See also, regarding the desirability of aid to maintain research capacity in East German undertakings, the Resolution of the European Parliament of 15 July 1993 ([1993] OJ C255/193) on the Community support framework for the five new *Länder* Germany, para. 9.

maintenance and repair and outdated equipment'.[65] However, the aid should not be used to continue production that cannot be expected to become profitable in a reasonable period of time. If, even for the more modern and most efficient European producers, a certain production is not and cannot be profitable and they will finally be forced to cut back, continued loss-compensation must be stopped. Hence, even if an installation in the former GDR is 'fundamentally competitive', bad sectoral prospects may mean that continued loss-coverage is unacceptable.[66]

Therefore, while accepting that investors in the former GDR face genuine structural and economic handicaps, the Commission seeks to ensure that state aid is appropriate to tackling these handicaps and commensurate with them.[67] A balance is thus sought between permitting the necessary aid to rebuild the economies of the new *Länder* and ensuring that such aid is not disproportionate to their objective, especially relative to aid provided to other disadvantaged areas in the Community.[68]

(ii) Article 92(3)(c) Regions

In the application of Article 92(3)(c) the Commission employs a two-stage test, to determine whether aid may be granted thereunder to facilitate the development of a particular region without trading conditions being adversely affected to an extent contrary to the common interest.

The Commission considers, in the first stage of the test, whether the *per capita* GDP for the area concerned is 85 per cent or less of the national average or structural employment more than 110 per cent of the national average. The rationale is that since aid must facilitate the development of a region, the latter must suffer from a certain backwardness within the Member State concerned.[69]

However, since it would be against the common interest to increase the existing differences between regions within the Community as a whole and the

[65] Notice C61/94 (N375/94) ([1995] OJ C113/5) concerning aid which the German Government intends to grant to Buna GmbH. See also Notice C62/94 (N376/94) ([1995] OJ C113/13) concerning aid which the German Government intends to grant to Sächsische Olefinwerke GmbH, Böhlen.

[66] Notice C43/92 (NN131/92) ([1994] OJ C16/6) concerning aid awarded by the German Government to Buna AG.

[67] Communication C60/91 (NN73/91 and 76/91) ([1992] OJ C68/2) concerning the proposal by the German Government to award state aid to the Opel group in support of its investment plans in the new *Länder*; Communication C61/91 (NN74/91 and 80/91) ([1992] OJ C68/8) concerning the proposal by the German Government to award state aid to the Mercedes-Benz group in support of its investment plans in the new *Länder*; and Communication C62/91 (NN75, 77, 78, 79/91) ([1992] OJ C68/14) concerning the proposal by the German Government to award state aid to the Volkswagen group in support of its investment plans in the new *Länder*.

[68] A further consideration, which might also be applicable in relation to Western aid to countries such as Poland, might be that, in the absence of the discipline provided by competition policy, the risk of inefficient use of aid could be increased.

[69] Para. II.2 of the 1988 Communication.

backwardness of less-favoured regions therein,[70] account must also be taken of the Community context.[71] Hence, the thresholds are modified in the case of the better-off Member States by the application of European indices. Such indices are determined for each Member State and are regularly reviewed[72] in the light of the latest figures,[73] though the maximum for unemployment was originally set at 145. For example, threshold levels for German regions to be eligible for aid under the first stage, i.e., *per capita* GDP less than 76 per cent[74] or average unemployment over the previous five years more than 145 per cent of the national average, were first notified on 31 July 1985.[75]

In the second stage of the test other indicators are considered. According to the 1988 Communication, the indicators include: tendencies and structure of unemployment, evolution of employment, net migration, demographic pressures, population density, levels of activity, productivity, structure of economic activity, especially the importance of declining sectors, investment, geographical situation, topography, and infrastructure.[76]

The second stage may sometimes be decisive. For example, in the case of a German aid scheme for the labour market regions of Aachen and Julich, the Commission considered that although unemployment levels in the area were currently below those normally regarded as serious enough to require regional aid, the closure of the local coal mine was expected to result in significant job losses (around 7,700). For this reason, the Commission decided to approve the scheme, provided that it was time-limited and subject to close monitoring.[77] It would also seem that very low population density—a factor of particular relevance to the northern parts of Finland and Sweden[78]—could be a decisive factor. Certainly, this factor was regarded as justifying exceptional treatment of the Highlands and Islands of Scotland under Article 92(3)(c).[79]

However, even if a region is found to be covered by Article 92(3)(c), the

[70] Note the 5th recital in the Preamble to the EC Treaty.

[71] Para. II.2 of the 1988 Communication.

[72] Communications on the method of application of Art. 92(3)(c) to regional aid ([1989] OJ C78/5; [1990] OJ C163/5; [1992] OJ C114/4).

[73] Dec. 87/15 of 19 Feb. 1986 ([1987] OJ L12/17) on the compatibility with the common market of aid under the German Federal/*Land* Government Joint Regional Aid Programme (Joint Programme for the improvement of regional economic structures) in 6 labour market regions.

[74] The figure is now 75 per cent. See the Communication on the method of application of Art. 92(3)(c) to regional aid ([1992] OJ C114/4). However, in Case 248/84 *Germany* v. *EC Commission* [1987] ECR 4013, 4034 Darmon A. G. considered that a Commission decision should be annulled because it did not explain why aid could not be justified in a German area where *per capita* GDP was 17 per cent below the national average.

[75] Dec. 87/99 of 29 July 1986 ([1987] OJ L40/22) on aid proposed by the Rheinland-Pfalz *Land* Government for a fibre processing firm in Scheuerfeld.

[76] Para. II.3 of the 1988 Communication.

[77] *Eighteenth Report on Competition Policy* (EC Commission, Brussels, 1989), 191.

[78] See sect. 4.5.2 below.

[79] *Tenth Report on Competition Policy* (EC Commission, Brussels, 1981), 123–4 and Bull. EC 5–1980, 2.1.19.

level of permissible aid tends to be lower than in Article 92(3)(a) regions.[80] Moreover, operating aid is not regarded as facilitating the development required by the former provision,[81] and so aid to regions covered thereby must, in principle, be linked to initial investment or job creation.[82]

Sectoral Policy

Treatment of sectoral aid may form part of a common policy, such as that for coal, steel, agriculture, fisheries, or transport, for which the Treaties provide a specific legal basis. Here the acceptability of aid may be determined by the requirements of the common policy concerned. Thus, in the *First Report on Competition Policy*[83] the Commission stated that quite important Commission positions on aid to agriculture or transport could not be separated from the context of the common policies specific to these sectors and within which the purpose aimed at could be more clearly understood.[84] Indeed, the common agricultural policy entails the establishment of rules governing the distribution of Community aid, and these rules are applied by analogy to the grant of state aid in the sectors concerned.[85] In the case of fishing, 'state aid may be granted only if it is consistent with the objectives of the common policy'.[86] In relation to transport, a decisive question has been whether aid is justified by reference to the 'public service' obligations which the transport policy[87] allows Member States to impose on transporters.[88]

However, Community interest is not limited to sectors in relation to which the Treaties provide for a common policy. The Community may also take an interest in a sector because it is in crisis. Crisis sectors generally concern

[80] Para. II.4 of the 1988 Communication and Annex III thereto.

[81] Para. I.6 (*ibid.*) only refers to the possibility of such aid being authorized under Art. 92(3)(a).

[82] *Eighteenth Report on Competition Policy* (EC Commission, Brussels, 1989), 147. See, more particularly, Dec. 86/366 of 10 June 1986 ([1986] OJ L223/30) concerning aid which the Belgian Government has granted to a ceramic sanitary ware and crockery manufacturer.

[83] EC Commission, Brussels, 1972, 132.

[84] See also the *Second Survey on State Aids in the European Community in the Manufacturing and Certain Other Sectors* (EC Commission, Brussels, 1990), 17.

[85] See, e.g., the application of Dec. 90/342 of 7 June 1990 ([1990] OJ L163/71) on the selection criteria to be adopted for investments for improving the processing and marketing conditions for agricultural and forestry products in Notice C6/93 (610/92) ([1993] OJ C179/3) concerning aid which Germany has decided to grant to the modernization of a grain mill in Dresden. See, earlier, 'Competition Policy in Agriculture', *Green Europe* (1987), No. 221, 1. Moreover, authorization of state aid could 'gravely jeopardize' Community efforts under initiatives such as Resider II. See the Resolution of the European Parliament of 3 May 1994 ([1994] OJ C205/108) on the draft notice to the Member States laying down guidelines for operational programmes or global grants which they are invited to establish in the framework of a Community initiative concerning the economic conversion of steel areas (Resider II), para. 2.

[86] Guidelines for the examination of state aid to fisheries and aquaculture ([1994] OJ C260/3), para. 1.3.

[87] Art. 77 EC.

[88] Cf. air transport, where liberalization is seen as necessitating 'a strict policy of control of State aid to avoid any effects which would be contrary to the common interest' (Communication C15/94 (N122/94, NN22/94 and E3/93) ([1994] OJ C93/12) concerning the existing tax exemption and planned recapitalization of TAP).

labour-intensive products, with low intensity of research and development, such as textiles and clothing, footwear and shipbuilding, characterized by growing import penetration by the developing countries. In such sectors it is argued that international trade is close to the Hecksher-Ohlin paradigm of comparative advantage based on different factor endowments.[89] The need may be implied for the Commission strictly to interpret the requirements in Article 92(3)(c) that aid should facilitate the development of the sector concerned and not adversely affect trading conditions to an extent contrary to the common interest.

(i) Textiles and Synthetic Fibres

Strict principles regarding aid to the textiles sector were first notified by the Commission to the Member States in 1971[90] and confirmed in 1977.[91] Similar principles have been introduced regarding aid to the synthetic fibres sector.[92]

The essence of these principles is that only aid designed to encourage conversion to other sectors should be permitted[93] and that aid may not be granted to increase capacity. Thus, e.g., in connection with proposed Irish aid of £IRL 2.9 million in favour of a producer of polyester, the Commission noted that the investment concerned modernization of an obsolete plant which should be effected using the resources of the undertaking concerned without state aid, especially since a large percentage of the output from the plant was exported to other Member States. The Commission also considered that, while the standard of living in the area was very low and it suffered from serious underemployment, the sectoral effects of aid to this particular industry had to be controlled even in the most underdeveloped areas. Taking into account the situation of the polyester sector which was likely to continue in the future, the proposed aid would be likely to distort competition in intra-Community trade without making a contribution to regional development sufficient to compensate for that distortion. The aid would also have the effect of further reducing capacity utilization in the industry concerned. For these reasons, it could not be permitted.[94]

On the other hand, in its assessment of aid to two textile producers in Andalusia, the Commission stated that it would not merely take account of the Community interests in structural adaptation. It would also take account of

[89] A. Jacquemin and A. Sapir, 'European Integration World Integration?' [1988] *Weltwirtschaftliches Archive* 127–39 and 'La Perspective 1992 et l'après Uruguay Round' [1990] *Economie Prospective Internationale* 47–67. [90] SEC(71)363. [91] SEC (77)317.

[92] Aids to the Community synthetic fibres industry ([1985] OJ C171/2); and State Aid—Aid to the EEC synthetic fibres industries ([1989] OJ C173/5).

[93] See, e.g., Dec. 91/391 of 26 Mar. 1991 ([1991] OJ L215/16) on aid granted by the German Government to Deggendorf GmbH, a producer of polyamide and polyester yarns located in Deggendorf (Bavaria).

[94] Dec. 84/498 of 18 July 1984 ([1984] OJ L276/40) on an aid proposal by the Irish Government in favour of a producer of polyester yarn situated in Letterkenny.

the importance of these two producers for the survival of the textile industry in Andalusia.[95] Again, in authorizing Italian aid, the Commission took into account the fact that some recipients were located in an area heavily dependent on the textile industry in which a large number of firms had closed down resulting in significant capacity reductions overall.[96] British aid for reorganization of the wool industry, which would prevent the emergence of social difficulties in certain less well-off regions without an overall increase in capacity, was also authorized.[97]

(ii) Shipbuilding

A series of directives concerning shipbuilding aid has been enacted under what used to be Article 92(3)(d) of the EC Treaty.[98] These directives have authorized, but sought to control, operating aid to shipyards. In particular, Directive 87/167,[99] the Sixth Directive on shipbuilding aid, imposed a common ceiling on such aid within the Community.

However, in the case of shipyards in the former GDR, it was considered likely that these shipyards would need a higher level of operating aid than was permissible in the case of other Community yards, and so Directive 87/167 was amended by Directive 90/652.[100] According to the Preamble to the latter, the shipbuilding industry in the former GDR would require urgent restructuring. The immediate application of the ceiling for operating aid to shipbuilding within the Community generally might not facilitate this process, and particular arrangements should be allowed to enable the shipbuilding industry there gradually to complete restructuring and comply with the aid regime applicable to the Community generally. As a result of this amendment, Article 9(4) of the Directive allowed for operating aid to be granted for shipbuilding and ship conversion in the former GDR, provided that:

—the shipbuilding industry had undertaken a systematic and specific restructuring programme, including capacity reductions, which could be considered capable of allowing it to operate competitively, and

—the aid was being progressively reduced.

Thus, as in the case of Portugal and Spain,[101] a higher rate of assistance could be granted than was permissible in the Community generally.

The inclusion of an identical clause was also envisaged in an amendment[102]

[95] Reply to Written Question 1853/91 ([1991] OJ C323/41) by Mr de los Santos Lopez.

[96] *Sixth Report on Competition Policy* (EC Commission, Brussels, 1977), 116.

[97] *Fourth Report on Competition Policy* (EC Commission, Brussels, 1975), 89. After initial objections the Commission also accepted capacity-increasing textiles aid in Northern Ireland, because it entailed 'investment and employment in a distressed area'. See Notice C20/93 (N29/93) ([1993] OJ C269/8) regarding aid which the UK plans to grant to Hualon Corporation.

[98] See now Art. 92(3)(e) of the Treaty.

[99] Of 26 Jan. 1987 ([1987] OJ L69/55) on aid to shipbuilding.

[100] Of 4 Dec. 1990 ([1990] OJ L353/45).

[101] Art. 9 of Dir. 87/167.

[102] Proposal of 22 Aug. 1990 ([1990] OJ C248/5) amending the proposal for a 7th Directive on aid to shipbuilding currently under discussion in the Council.

to the original Commission proposal for a Seventh Directive on aid to shipbuilding,[103] though no such clause was included in the version adopted by the Council. Instead, in the Council minutes it was declared that the particular problems of the shipbuilding industry in the former GDR might, during a transitional period, necessitate the grant of aid which could not be authorized under the directive. At that stage, however, it was not possible with any certainty to ascertain the aid needed to adapt the shipbuilding industry there to operate at the same level of competitiveness as yards in the remainder of the Community.[104] Only when transparency in relation to such questions was provided could a request from the German Government for a transitional arrangement be considered.[105]

The legal effect of this declaration is uncertain, particularly in view of the ruling in *Antonissen*.[106] In this ruling the significance of a declaration in the Council minutes for the right of residence enjoyed by a job-seeker under Community law was considered. According to Advocate General Darmon, such a declaration could constitute a guide for the interpretation of provisions of a Community enactment the drawing up, or adoption, of which gave rise to that declaration, only in so far as the aim was to clarify the meaning of those provisions which were *ex hypothesi* ambiguous or equivocal. Such a declaration could not serve to fill a *lacuna* in the provisions.[107] According to the Court itself, such a declaration could not be used for the purpose of interpreting a Community enactment where no reference was made to the content of the declaration in the wording of the provision in question.[108]

In practice, such problems as to the legal effects of declarations did not have to be faced in connection with the declaration on shipbuilding aid in the former GDR, because the Seventh Directive was duly amended by Directive 92/69.[109] According to the amendment, a ceiling of 36 per cent for operating aid to be paid by the end of December 1993 (rather than 9 per cent for large vessels and 4.5 per cent for smaller vessels and ship conversion, as in the Community

[103] Proposal of 20 July 1990 ([1990] OJ C223/4) for a Council dir. on aid to shipbuilding.

[104] More particularly, operating aid was prohibited in the Mecklenburg-Vorpommern shipyards pending the outcome of a study designed to establish the ability of these yards to compete on equal terms with other Community yards. The Commission was also concerned to ensure that such aid was not provided under the guise of development aid. See Notice C64/91 (N726/91) ([1992] OJ C36/3) regarding development aid which Germany has decided to grant for a project to build two 1,066 teu container vessels for Indonesia.

[105] *Twentieth Report on Competition Policy* (EC Commission, Brussels, 1991), 131. The European Parliament objected that it was not consulted regarding this declaration. See the Resolution of 13 Dec. 1991 ([1992] OJ C13/472) on the Twentieth Report on Competition Policy, para. 25.

[106] Case C–292/89 *Regina* v. *Immigration Appeal Tribunal, ex parte Gustaff Desiderius Antonissen* [1991] ECR I–745, I–764–5.

[107] It cannot produce an interpretation different from that resulting from the actual wording of a Community act. See Case 429/85 *EC Commission* v. *Italy* [1988] ECR 843, 852.

[108] [1991] ECR I–745, I–778.

[109] Of 20 July 1992 ([1992] OJ L219/54) amending Dir. 90/684.

generally) would apply to East German shipyards, provided capacity reductions of 40 per cent were made by 1995.[110]

This arrangement is reminiscent of past Community efforts to control the use of operating aid to shipbuilding through insisting that such aid should be linked with restructuring.

In particular, Article 3(2) of Directive 72/273[111] made the permissibility of Italian aid conditional upon implementation of a rehabilitation programme securing the competitiveness of Italian shipbuilding at the European level by the end of 1976 at the latest. Article 2(b) of Directive 75/432[112] permitted, in turn, aid in Ireland and Italy after 1975 only on such a condition. Apart from such aid, a price guarantee system in France and credit facilities complying with OECD conditions,[113] all other aid, including investment aid and rescue aid, had to be compatible with the common market under Article 92 of the Treaty.

More generally, Article 6(1) of Directive 78/338[114] provided that operating aid to shipbuilders, as 'crisis aid',[115] must be progressively reduced and could only be granted if linked[116] to the attainment of industrial restructuring objectives with a view to making the industry competitive and able to operate without aid or intervention.[117] Article 6(3) of the same Directive required the Commission to verify that such aid contributed genuinely and in an equitable manner to the adaptation of the industry to the new conditions on the world shipbuilding market. Similar requirements were imposed by Article 6(1) and (4) of Directive 81/363.[118]

Inconsistency of aid schemes with such requirements might sometimes be

[110] The European Parliament favoured a requirement that production aid to East German shipyards should not exceed three times the ceiling for the rest of the Community for 1992 and twice that for 1993. It was also proposed that a capacity reduction of 55 per cent should be required. See the Resolution of 9 July 1992 ([1992] OJ C241/184).

[111] Of 20 July 1972 ([1972] JO L169/28) on aids to shipbuilding.

[112] Of 10 July 1975 ([1975] OJ L192/27) on aid to shipbuilding.

[113] OECD Council Resolution of 18 July 1974 (C(74) 88).

[114] Of 4 April 1978 ([1978] OJ L98/19) on aid to shipbuilding.

[115] I.e., aid 'granted in order to remedy the serious crisis which is causing a substantial reduction in orders on hand in a member state and consequently a decrease in production.'

[116] Art. 5(1) of Dec. 2320/81 of 7 Aug. 1981 ([1981] OJ L228/14) establishing Community rules for aids to the steel industry was rather more demanding and required that in the steel sector such aid must 'form an integral part of a restructuring programme' and stipulated that it could only be granted for a maximum of two years.

[117] In connection with this requirement, the Commission stated that 'three essential elements must be clearly defined . . . the objectives, an assessment of funds involved and a clear link between the two'. See the *Eighth Report on Competition Policy* (EC Commission, Brussels, 1979), 129. See, similarly, the requirements imposed in relation to ship repair yards by Commission practice under Art. 92 of the Treaty (*Ninth Report on Competition Policy* (EC Commission, Brussels, 1980), 99).

[118] Of 21 Apr. 1981 ([1981] OJ L137/39) on aid to shipbuilding. The 7th recital in the Preamble to this Dir. stated that 'the restructuring effort is not confined to reduction of production, employment and production capacity, but includes all other measures enabling the shipbuilding industry to become competitive'.

readily established. For example, in Decision 88/281[119] the Commission considered the acceptability of Italian aid for the building up of shipyard stocks. By its very nature, such aid, which would go primarily to yards without orders so as to enable them to anticipate new work, was tantamount to aid for continued operation pending new orders and would have the effect of delaying capacity cuts and implementation of restructuring measures. Hence, the Commission decided that it was prohibited.

Usually, however, a range of factors had to be assessed. To begin with, it was important that the aid was granted within the context of a restructuring plan. In 1977, for example, the Commission accepted Dutch operating aid, because the aid would be granted in the framework of the general plan for restructuring the shipbuilding industry and would be progressively reduced so as to provide an incentive to the preparation and implementation of more detailed plans by groups of shipyards.[120]

In practice, the Commission apparently experienced some difficulty in securing detailed information about restructuring plans within the context of which aid was supposed to be linked. For example, when the United Kingdom sought to apply a scheme involving aid up to 35 per cent of the contract price, the Commission noted that it 'had received few details of further restructuring measures planned in the United Kingdom industry and considered that aid of this magnitude was liable to remove the pressure for restructuring from the industry and undermine the efforts being made in other Member States to adjust their shipbuilding capacity to market conditions'. Only when the British Government satisfied the Commission as to the restructuring measures involved, and in view of the fact that the losses of nationalized shipyards would be stemmed, did the Commission accept the scheme.[121]

In some cases the Commission accepted the grant of aid, even before a restructuring plan had been completed. For example, an early Commission decision[122] concerned Italian draft legislation altering the aid system for shipbuilding with the aim of ensuring adequate activity in Italian yards during the period considered necessary for them to become competitive. This arrangement was accepted by the Commission, on condition that the Italian Government carried out a rehabilitation programme as planned and submitted a programme to the Commission within six months of the draft becoming law.[123]

A new Italian scheme was challenged by the Commission, because the level of aid was higher (at 30 per cent) than that authorized for other Member States

[119] Of 17 Nov. 1988 ([1988] OJ L119/33) on aid for shipbuilding and ship repair in Italy—Art. 10 of Act 111 of 22 Mar. 1985.

[120] *Seventh Report on Competition Policy* (EC Commission, Brussels, 1978), 143–4.

[121] Notice regarding the UK proposal to assist shipbuilding during the period 1 July 1984 to 1 July 1986 ([1984] OJ C219/3).

[122] Of 8 Mar. 1961 ([1961] JO 582) *concernant une modification du régime d'aides existant en Italie en faveur de la construction navale.*

[123] See also the *EEC Ninth General Report* (EC Commission, Brussels, 1966), 86.

whose aid schemes had recently been approved. There was no clear link between the granting of aid and the achievement of restructuring objectives; since the restructuring plan formulated by the Italian Government had not been approved by the Parliament, it had no official status and it was not clear that the targets established would be worked towards in return for the aid; finally, the scheme was notified to the Commission early in 1980, although its period of application also covered the previous year, and the Commission felt that the retrospective approval for a period of over a year could not be justified unless exceptional grounds could be demonstrated. The scheme was subsequently accepted, however, when the aid level was reduced to 27.5 per cent, the Italian Government convinced the Commission of its firm intention to present to Parliament the restructuring plan discussed with the Commission, and in view of social and regional considerations.[124]

In so far as the Commission was informed about restructuring plans, its tendency was to focus on comparatively simple criteria such as the impact of aid on shipbuilding capacity or on the size of the shipyard work force or whether the aid was to be progressively reduced.

Aid designed to lead to capacity reductions might be favoured. For example, a French scheme was accepted because the Government agreed to reduce the level of aid originally planned and because the aid was 'linked to restructuring measures entailing an accelerated decrease of capacity in shipbuilding and ship repair'.[125] An Irish scheme for up to 30 per cent of the contract price was also authorized 'in order to enable the sole Irish yard, in Cork, to withstand the crisis. The granting of the subsidy [would] go hand in hand with conversion to ship repair and mechanical engineering.'[126]

Similarly, aid designed to produce a reduction in the workforce might be favoured. For example, an Italian yard 'was undertaking an extensive restructuring programme aimed at converting almost half of its workforce to non-shipbuilding activities. [The Government] showed that substantial progress had been made with this programme and that the order [to which the aid related] was important if continuation of this progress was not to be threatened'. Accordingly, aid equivalent to 30 per cent of the contract price was acceptable.[127]

In relation to a German scheme, the assurance of the German Government that it would monitor the industry's progress towards achievement of the

[124] *Eleventh Report on Competition Policy* (EC Commission, Brussels, 1982), 145.

[125] *Sixteenth Report on Competition Policy* (EC Commission, Brussels, 1987), 135–46. See similarly, regarding an earlier French scheme, the *Tenth Report on Competition Policy* (EC Commission, Brussels, 1981), 128–9.

[126] *Eighth Report on Competition Policy* (EC Commission, Brussels, 1979), 130–1. However, ship repair was also a troubled sector (*ibid.* 133–4). The yard's shipbuilding operations were substantially reduced in 1983. See the *Thirteenth Report on Competition Policy* (EC Commission, Brussels, 1984), 164.

[127] *Tenth Report on Competition Policy* (EC Commission, Brussels, 1981), 130.

targets set for workforce reduction by 1982, together with previous implementation of the targets, enabled the Commission to accept that there was an adequate link between the proposed aid and the further restructuring of the industry.[128] A new German scheme, which involved production aid in 1984 of 6 per cent of the contract price and in 1985 4 per cent and which was 'meant to underpin a major restructuring effort involving the closure of yards with the loss of 4,000 jobs and promoting medium-sized facilities specializing in building sophisticated vessels', was also accepted.[129]

It was recognized, however, that capacity reductions in a given Member State might not go too far.[130] Thus, for example, the Irish Government was authorized to grant production aid of 30 per cent in 1983 and 1984 to avert closure of the country's last remaining shipyard.[131] The Commission also allowed the Dutch Government to rescue a repair yard in Amsterdam. The latter rescue was allowed, because closure of the yard would mean Amsterdam losing its repair facilities for ocean-going vessels which were essential for a port of its kind. Even so, given the very difficult position of the ship repair industry in the Community, the Commission took steps to ensure that the rescue was linked to a genuine restructuring of the yard which would give it a prospect of viability, despite the considerable overcapacity in ship repairing on the North Sea coast.[132]

Finally, aid degressivity was important. For example, a United Kingdom scheme was accepted, because it was degressive and in view of the restructuring already achieved.[133] A French scheme was also accepted, because it was degressive in character and was linked to restructuring efforts.[134]

Commission efforts to secure degressivity might, however, be hampered by developments in international market conditions. In 1984, for example, the Commission objected to aid schemes of the United Kingdom, Italy, and the Netherlands, which were said to involve inadequate restructuring arrangements.[135] In the following year, however, these schemes were accepted.[136]

[128] *Ibid.*, 131–2.

[129] *Fourteenth Report on Competition Policy* (EC Commission, Brussels, 1985), 146.

[130] As regards steel production, the ECJ apparently interprets the ECSC Treaty as adopting a more restrictive approach. According to the Court in Joined Cases 63 and 147/84 *Finsider* v. *EC Commission* [1985] ECR 2857, 2882, 'Art. 58 of the Treaty does not require the Commission to guarantee to any one undertaking, to the detriment of other undertakings in the Community, the minimum production which that undertaking considers necessary in accordance with its own criteria of profitability and development'.

[131] *Thirteenth Report on Competition Policy* (EC Commission, Brussels, 1984), 160.

[132] *Ibid.*, 161.

[133] *Eleventh Report on Competition Policy* (EC Commission, Brussels, 1982), 146.

[134] *Ibid.*, 145.

[135] *Fourteenth Report on Competition Policy* (EC Commission, Brussels, 1985), 146.

[136] Application of the degressivity principle had previously been frustrated by the crisis in the international shipbuilding market, which developed in the second half of the 1970s. See the *Seventh Report on Competition Policy* (EC Commission, Brussels, 1978), 139. Note also the successive extensions of the period of validity of Dir. 81/363 ([1981] OJ L137/39) by Dir. 82/880 ([1982] OJ L371/46) and Dir. 85/2 ([1985] OJ L2/13).

Even though the Dutch scheme envisaged additional aid with no further restructuring being involved, it was accepted because of the 'acute worsening of the state of the industry'.[137]

In doubtful cases the Commission might seek to rely on procedural expedients. For example, the Commission accepted an Italian production aid scheme providing up to 30 per cent of the contract price, because it would 'be tied to some adaptation of the industry for it [would] be adjusted by reference to such criteria as the state of the order books of the yard concerned, its specialization and the types of vessel to be subsidised'. However, a requirement of prior notification of each individual application of the scheme was imposed.[138]

In the case of a United Kingdom scheme providing up to 30 per cent of the contract price, the Commission recognized that it had not been possible to prepare a plan to restructure the United Kingdom shipbuilding industry, because it had only just been nationalized. However, the Commission considered that the criteria for selecting the yards to be aided were not sufficiently restrictive to ensure that aid would be limited to yards with a real chance of becoming competitive in the future. In order to ensure that aid was granted on a sufficiently selective basis and that competition between shipyards in the Community was not distorted, the Commission decided to authorize the scheme on condition that each grant of aid was notified for prior approval. This approval would be reviewed after six months.[139]

It is doubtful whether or not such procedural expedients really assisted the Commission in securing an effective link between the grant of state aid and restructuring. Rather, their main significance may have been to increase the administrative burden for the Commission. In short, therefore, precedents do not augur well for the outcome of the approach adopted to control of shipbuilding aid in the former GDR.[140]

Horizontal Policy

Various 'horizontal' policies may affect the treatment of state aid by Community law. Such policies include environmental protection and encouragement of research and development.

[137] *Fifteenth Report on Competition Policy* (EC Commission, Brussels, 1986), 156–7.

[138] *Eighth Report on Competition Policy* (EC Commission, Brussels, 1979), 131.

[139] *Seventh Report on Competition Policy* (EC Commission, Brussels, 1978), 141–2. Again, the Commission considered that a French cost-escalation scheme made no provision for a link with restructuring. In this case the Commission decided that the aid could only be authorized for a short period (*ibid.* 144–5).

[140] See, regarding the 'technical' problems already arising in connection with such aid, Commission Reply by Mr Van Miert to Written Question E–1937/94 ([1995] OJ C24/47) by Niels Sindal.

(i) Environmental Protection

Environmental aid may be accepted as facilitating the development of certain economic activities under Article 92(3)(c) of the Treaty, authorized under Article 92(3)(a) in areas covered by this paragraph or treated as promoting a project of 'common European interest' within the meaning of Article 92(3)(b).[141] Guidelines concerning such aid were introduced in November 1974[142] and were last renewed in 1994.[143]

According to the initial guidelines, firms would normally be expected to bear the cost of investments necessary to comply with environmental laws. However, for a transitional period of five years aid up to a fixed ceiling would be permitted. Aid was only to be permissible after 1980 where there were particular industrial, social, and regional difficulties. The 'polluter pays' principle implicit in such practice is now expressly embodied in Article 130r(2)(i) of the Treaty, though Article 130r(4) requires that in the application of the principle, particular account is taken of the economic and social development of the Community as a whole. The implication in these provisions that application of the principle is problematic has been reflected by successive extensions of the transitional period in the initial guidelines, and it appears that acceptance of environmental aid, particularly that needed by undertakings to meet environmental standards higher than those laid down by law, has become a permanent feature of Commission practice.

(ii) Research and development

The Community approach to research and development aid originated as an aspect of sectoral policies.[144] However, a Framework for control of such aid was adopted in 1986[145] and renewed in 1990.[146] The Framework recognizes that R & D aid may be authorized under Article 92(3)(b) to promote an important project of common European interest[147] or under Article 92(3)(c) to facilitate the development of certain economic activities or certain regions.[148]

The Commission considers that problems arise where aid allegedly granted for R & D purposes is really for general investment and modernization which

[141] Joined Cases 62 and 72/87 *Executif Regional Wallon and Glaverbel* v. *EC Commission* [1988] 1573, 1595.

[142] Commission letter S/74/30.807 of 7 Nov. 1974 (*Competition Law in the European Communities vol. II: Rules Applicable to State Aids* (EC Commission, Brussels, 1990), 124–9). These guidelines were subsequently included in Council Recommendation 75/436 of 3 Mar. 1975 ([1975] OJ L194/1) regarding cost allocation and action by public authorities on environmental matters, which followed the First Programme of Action of the European Community on the Environment ([1973] OJ C112/1).

[143] Community guidelines on state aid for environmental purposes ([1994] OJ C72/3).

[144] See, e.g., Council Resolution of 15 July 1974 ([1974] OJ C86/1) on a Community policy on data processing.

[145] Community framework for state aids for research and development ([1986] OJ C83/2).

[146] SG(90)D/01620. [147] Para. 3.2 of the Framework. [148] *Ibid.*, para. 3.3.

firms should finance from their own resources.[149] The critical distinction is seen as being that between 'genuine innovation' and 'modernization' at Community level. According to the Commission, it is important to recognize the difference between innovation in the sense of the introduction of new products or new production technologies which have not previously existed but respond to future needs and the steady development of existing products and known production techniques which follow automatically from the normal behaviour of undertakings and normal replacement of assets as these wear out.[150]

Thus, for example, aid may be prohibited in the case of investments considered to lack the necessary originality.[151] On the other hand, aid to a costly experiment, designed to develop a system unique within the Community, may be authorized,[152] as may aid for innovative application of existing technology.[153]

4.2.3 State Monopolies and Public Undertakings

Article 37 of the EC Treaty requires the adjustment of state trading monopolies so as to exclude the possibility of discrimination between nationals of Member States, and Article 90(1) provides that, in the case of public undertakings and undertakings to which Member States grant special or exclusive rights, Member States shall neither enact nor maintain in force any measure contrary to the Treaty. These provisions are designed to ensure that trade liberalization is not undermined by the activities of such bodies.[154]

Public undertakings themselves are, in principle, subject to competition law in the same way as private undertakings. For example, a public undertaking, even one exercising powers conferred by legislation to fix charges and conditions of service for customers, is treated as being engaged in 'business activity' for the purposes of Article 86.[155] However, the activities of a public

[149] *Thirteenth Report on Competition Policy* (EC Commission, Brussels, 1984), 141.

[150] *Ibid.*, 144–5. Such aid must encourage additional efforts instead of only supporting current operations. See the *Fifteenth Report on Competition Policy* (EC Commission, Brussels, 1986), 175–6.

[151] Dec. 89/254 of 15 Nov. 1988 ([1989] OJ L106/34) relating to aid which the Belgian Government has granted to a petrochemicals company at Ottignies/Louvain-La-Neuve (SA Belgian Shell).

[152] Dec. 89/305 of 21 Dec. 1988 ([1989] OJ L123/53) concerning aid from the French Government to an undertaking in the motor vehicle sector—Peugeot SA.

[153] Dec. 91/254 of 28 Nov. 1990 ([1991] OJ L123/46) concerning the proposal by the Brussels Regional Authorities (Belgium) to provide aid in favour of Volkswagen Bruxelles SA.

[154] Comité Intergouvernemental Créé par la Conférence de Messine, *Rapport des Chefs de Délégation aux Ministres Etrangères* (Brussels, 1956), 37

[155] Case 41/83 *Italy* v. *EC Commission* [1985] ECR 873, 885. Even where a public body is 'integrated into the State administration", it may still be treated as an undertaking. See Case 118/85 *EC Commission* v. *Italy* [1987] ECR 2599, 2622. Only a public body exercising 'powers . . . which are typically those of a public authority' does not constitute an undertaking for the purposes of Arts. 85 and 86 EC. See Case C–364/92 *SAT Fluggesellschaft mbH* v. *Eurocontrol* [1994] ECR I–43, I–63–4.

body, even if autonomous, in so far as they are adopted in the public interest, lack a commercial character and fall outside the scope of Articles 85 and 86.[156] Hence, Articles 37 and 90 are necessary to prohibit Member States from operating such bodies in a manner contrary to their obligations under the Treaty.[157]

The economic rationale for these provisions, according to the Commission, is that the benefit of the economic rent created for such bodies should be used for delivering public services or accrue to the state as revenue. However, the Commission accepts that it is a delicate task to limit the distortions of competition to what are strictly necessary for such purposes.[158]

Privatization

In so far as the above provisions may reduce the utility of public ownership as an instrument of national economic policy, they might be thought effectively to favour privatization. To the extent that privatization takes place, it might also be thought, competition policy problems may be reduced.[159] In reality, however, complicated issues for competition policy may arise from the privatization process itself, let alone from its aftermath.

Such issues are illustrated by the Commission assessment of aid to the sale of the Rover Group, a company almost entirely owned by the UK Government, to British Aerospace. In 1988 the Commission had authorized the grant of aid to this sale up to a fixed limit.[160] In the event, the British Government subsequently granted three further 'concessions', to which the Commission objected under Article 92 of the Treaty.

First, £9.5 million was paid to British Aerospace to cover part of its costs incurred in acquiring Rover shares from minority shareholders. According to the Commission, under normal market conditions a majority shareholder who sold his stake in a company would not be prepared, without financial consideration, to cover such costs.

Secondly, £1.5 million was paid to Rover to cover the costs it incurred as a result of the sale. The Commission considered that these costs, too, were an expense which normally should be met by the acquiring company. In the absence of any binding stipulation to that effect in the contract of sale, the

[156] Case 94/74 *Industria Gomma Articoli Vari, IGAV* v. *Ente Nazionale per la Cellulosa e per la Carta, ENCC* [1975] ECR 699, 713 (Rec. 714).

[157] For a discussion, see L. M. Pais Antunes, 'L'Art. 90 du Traité CEE: Obligations des Etats Membres et Pouvoirs de la Commission' [1991] *RTDE* 187–209.

[158] See *Preparation of the Associated Countries of Central and Eastern Europe for Integration into the Internal Market of the Union*, COM(95)163, Annex, 50.

[159] The Commission maintains that this may be so in the case of 'recidivists'. See the *Twenty-Fourth Report on Competition Policy*, COM(95)142, 238–9.

[160] Dec. 89/58 of 13 July 1988 ([1989] OJ L25/92) concerning aid provided by the UK Government to the Rover Group.

Commission could see no good reason why such an expense should be borne gratuitously by the vendor.

Finally, the Government agreed to defer payment of the £150 million purchase price from 12 August 1988 to 30 March 1990. The notional benefit to the purchaser was assessed as being £33.4 million. Unless such a deferment formed part of the sale contract and was reflected in the sale price, which was not the case, the Commission considered that a prudent investor, operating in normal market conditions, would not, and would have no good reason to, agree to such a deferment of payment when selling his shareholding.

In these circumstances, the Commission decided that the three concessions constituted aid prohibited by Article 92 of the Treaty and ordered its repayment.[161] The Court of Justice annulled this decision on procedural grounds,[162] though the accepted the characterization of the concessions as aid,[163] and the Commission initiated a new procedure.[164]

Even greater complications arose from the privatization of Volvo Cars BV in the Netherlands. In this case the Dutch state and Volvo Cars Corporation, the principal shareholders in Volvo Cars BV, had advanced interest-free loans to this company. The loans were to be repaid by way of a royalty payment of Dfl. 600 on all cars of a particular model (the 400 series model) sold. These payments would be placed in a separate fund for the shareholders held outside the company. In concluding that this arrangement did not constitute aid, the Commission noted that participation by the Dutch State and Volvo Cars Corporation in the use of the fund and any future re-uses would always be in proportion to their shareholdings in the company. It was also noted that the risk of a shortfall in the repayment of the loans was matched by the possibility of a bonus of surplus repayments. In other words, the participation by the state would be consistent with that of a private investor. However, these arrangements were revised, because the Dutch State wanted to reduce its holding from 70 per cent to 33.3 per cent by selling 33.3 per cent of its holding to Mitsubishi Motors Corporation and 3.3 per cent to Volvo Cars Corporation. Volvo Cars BV was also to be restructured and renamed Nedcar.

The revised arrangements involved termination of the production of the cars on the basis of which the royalty payments were to be made some two years

[161] Communication C8/88 (Ex N119/88) ([1991] OJ C21/2) regarding aid which the UK Government provided to the Rover Group.

[162] Case C–292/90 *British Aerospace plc and Rover Group Holdings plc* v. *EC Commission* [1992] ECR I–493.

[163] *Ibid.* I–514–5.

[164] Communication C5/92 (Ex NN23/92) (OJ [1992] C122/3) concerning aid provided by the UK Government to British Aerospace for its purchase of the Rover Group, subsequent to Commission conditional Dec. 89/58 limiting the aid to this operation. This procedure led to adoption of Dec. 93/349 of 9 Mar. 1993 ([1993] OJ L143/7) concerning aid provided by the UK Government to British Aerospace for its purchase of Rover Group Holdings over and above those authorized in Commission Dec. 89/58 authorizing a maximum aid to this operation subject to certain conditions.

earlier than planned. According to the Commission, a shortfall in repayments was implied. Volvo Cars Corporation would be compensated by its interest as a shareholder in the new and, presumably, more profitable model which was to be introduced. There was nothing, however, to suggest that the Dutch State would be compensated.

The Commission also objected to the price to be paid for the state shares. This price was based on the net book value of the assets of Volvo Cars BV in 1990. The net book value, which took no account of any immaterial assets or goodwill, could be a very crude and misleading measure of the real value of a company. It was particularly so in a case, such as the one at issue, where assets had been rapidly depreciated for accounting purposes but had never been revalued.

Moreover, Mitsubishi was to have no financial responsibility for the 400 series. This exclusion of responsibility arguably warranted a premium on the price per share to be paid *vis-à-vis* that paid by Volvo Cars Corporation for its additional 3 per cent holding from the Dutch State, given that it would retain its 30 per cent responsibility for the 400 series. Far from embodying such a premium, the price was to be frozen. This was difficult to defend in view of the very considerable investments and restructuring of the company planned for the coming years as well as the benefits and synergies likely to arise from the strong presence of an important Japanese producer such as Mitsubishi.

Finally, the Dutch State, like the other two shareholders, planned to provide Nedcar with an interest-free loan of Dfl 700 million. It was difficult to see the justification for the loan when the terms of the arrangement excluded the possibility of the state achieving a return on the loan by way of, for example, a capital appreciation of its holding which would be realizable on sale, interest payments or repayments of principal exceeding Dfl 700 million in the event that the new car sold particularly well. Moreover, the repayments of the loan would be made over the years 1998 to 2004. By this time the real value of the repayments would have eroded considerably. The other two shareholders would, on the other hand, as continuing shareholders with a clear interest in the new car series, enjoy exclusively whatever return was earned on the loan. In these circumstances, the Commission took the view that the grant of state aid might be involved.[165] Subsequently, however, the Commission came to the conclusion that a profitable commercial transaction for the Dutch State was involved and, therefore, lifted its objections.[166]

In short, therefore, the relationship between the requirements of competition law and the privatization process may be problematical.

[165] Notice C3/92 (Ex N645/91) (OJ [1992] C105/16) concerning possible state aid elements contained in agreements between the Dutch State, Volvo Car Corporation and Mitsubishi Motors Corporation.

[166] Bull. EU 9–1994, 1.2.64.

Nationalization

Just as privatization may not necessarily be compatible with the EC Treaty, so the abolition of public undertakings is not necessarily required by this Treaty. Article 222 provides that the rules of the Member States governing the system of property ownership are in no way prejudiced by the Treaty. This provision is said to mean that the Treaty is neutral in the choice a Member State may make between public and private ownership.[167]

More particularly, Article 90(1) of the Treaty presupposes that special or exclusive rights may be granted. Likewise, Article 37 of the Treaty[168] requires the adjustment, but not necessarily the abolition, of state monopolies. Moreover Article 90(2) of the Treaty provides that undertakings entrusted with operation of services of general economic interest or having the character of a revenue-producing monopoly shall be subject to the Treaty rules in so far as application of such rules does not obstruct the performance, in law or in fact, of the particular tasks assigned to them.[169] Hence, there is said to be a strong presumption of legality in favour of public enterprise and the grant of exclusive rights as such.[170]

The Court of Justice considered the underlying issues in *Sacchi*,[171] which concerned the exclusive right of the Italian State to provide television transmissions. According to the Court, nothing in the Treaty prevented Member States, for reasons of public interest of a non-economic nature, from removing radio and television transmissions, including cable transmissions, from the field of competition by conferring on one or more establishments an exclusive right to conduct them.[172] Indeed, according to Advocate General Reischl, the exclusion of purely private groups might be necessary to ensure the appropriate participation of all social groups in the 'freedom of radio reporting'.[173] However, for the performance of their tasks the public bodies concerned remain subject to the prohibition against discrimination[174] and the other requirements of the Treaty.[175]

The conclusion drawn by the Commission is that Member States are free to determine the number and the public or private status of organizations that may be authorized to broadcast television programmes within their territory.

[167] Communication to the Member States—Application of Arts. 92 and 93 EC and of Art. 5 of Commission Dir. 80/723 to Public Undertakings in the Manufacturing Sector (OJ [1991] C273/2), para. 4.

[168] See sect. 2.2.1 above.

[169] It is also provided that the development of trade must not be affected to such an extent as would be contrary to the interests of the Community.

[170] Tesauro A. G. in Case C–202/88 *France* v. *EC Commission* [1991] ECR I–1223, I–1246.

[171] Case 155/73 *Giuseppe Sacchi* [1974] ECR 409.

[172] *Ibid.* 429. See, more recently, Case C–260/89 *Elleniki Radiphonia Tileorassi Anonimi Etaira (ERT AE)* v. *Dimotiki Etaira Pliroforissis (DEP), Sotirios Kouvelas* [1991] ECR I–2951, I–2957.

[173] [1974] ECR 409, 437.

[174] Capotorti A. G. in Case 148/77 *H. Hansen Jun. & O. C. Balle GmbH & Co.* v. *Hauptzollamt Flensburg* [1978] ECR 1787, 1814.

[175] [1974] ECR 409, 430.

However, the authorization procedures and the bodies to which special or exclusive rights have been given must comply with the fundamental principles of freedom of establishment and free movement of persons, services, and capital and with the competition rules laid down in the Treaty.[176]

In essence, the existence of such bodies and the grant of exclusive rights may, depending on the circumstances,[177] be permitted, but the exercise of these rights must be compatible with the Treaty. However, an exclusive right of sale or to import from other Member States[178] has been said to be intrinsically likely to cause discrimination within the meaning of Article 37 of the Treaty[179] and thus to be prohibited.[180]

Alcohol Monopolies

The implications of the EC Treaty for state alcohol monopolies in Finland and Sweden[181] may be particularly controversial. In regard to such monopolies, account may be taken of the ruling in *France* v. *EC Commission.*[182] This ruling concerned exclusive importation and marketing rights in the French telecommunications terminal sector. According to the Court, an exclusive right to import and market, which deprived economic operators of the opportunity of selling their products to consumers, particularly where there was a wide range of technically different products, such that the monopolist might not be able to offer the whole range of products existing on the market, to advise consumers, or to guarantee the quality of the products, might be prohibited by Article 37.[183] A strictly literal interpretation of this ruling would suggest that the Court was simply exemplifying the problems which the prohibition of exclusive rights of importation and marketing sought to eliminate. However, the possibility cannot be discounted that the Court was seeking to justify the prohibition.[184] If the

[176] Reply by Mr Bangemann to Written Question 2225/91 ([1992] OJ C78/41) by Mr Victor Manuel Arbeloa Muru.

[177] Case C–202/88 *France* v. *EC Commission* [1991] ECR I–1223, I–1268–9.

[178] Case 59/75 *Pubblico Ministero* v. *Flavia Manghera* [1976] ECR 91, 101. Indeed, Art. 40 of the Greek Accession Act specifically required Greece to abolish exclusive import rights in the case of copper sulphate, saccharin, and flimsy paper.

[179] Roemer A. G. in Case 82/71 *Pubblico Ministero della Repubblica Italiana* v. *Società Agricola Industria Latte (SAIL)* [1972] ECR 119, 143–4.

[180] On the other hand, according to Reischl A. G. in Case 155/73 *Giuseppe Sacchi* [1974] ECR 409, 440, in the case of a broadcasting undertaking whose whole activity is subject to public control, there are means of excluding the possibility of discrimination. E.g., in relation to advertising, the preparation of advertisements can be carefully separated from broadcasting undertakings, and a clear separation of broadcasting undertakings can be ensured from other commercial undertakings.

[181] The Commission found the Swedish alcohol monopoly 'particularly worrying'. See *Commission Opinion on Sweden's Application for Membership*, Bull. EC, Supp. 5/92, 15.

[182] Case C–202/88 [1991] ECR I-1223.

[183] *Ibid.* I–1268.

[184] Cf., regarding the applicability of Art. 86 to exclusive rights, Case 311/84 *Centre belge d'études de marché Télémarketing (CBEM) SA* v. *Compagnie luxembourgeoise de télédiffusion SA and Information publicité Benelux SA* [1985] ECR 3261.

Court was seeking to do so, the implication is that such rights are not necessarily prohibited.

Certainly, a state monopoly which makes available a wide range of products[185] and facilitates entry onto the market of new products from other countries might well be regarded as improving the competitive structure of the market. Concern for the structure of the market may underlie the abovementioned ruling in *Delimitis*[186] and is a central element in the competition policy developed by the Commission.[187] While such a concern might be said to show insufficient interest even in investigating possible efficiency losses,[188] it need not been seen simply as entailing the sacrifice of efficiency in favour of market integration. Indeed, the best guarantee of efficiency, particularly when viewed in dynamic rather than static terms, may be the competitive structure of the market. Thus in the *Ninth Report on Competition Policy*[189] the Commission referred to the need to maintain 'the right amount of competition in order for the Treaty's requirements to be met and its aims attained'. The logic of the competition policy pursued by the Community in such practice might be favourable to the grant of certain exclusive rights of marketing, or at least that of retailing, if not the exclusive right to import.

However, discussion of the acceptability of alcohol monopolies under the Treaty assumes that they are, in principle, prohibited and concentrates on the question whether an exception from the prohibition can be justified on public health grounds. Public health measures may be covered by Article 36 of the Treaty or by considerations of public health and social policy, which are recognized as 'mandatory requirements' by the Court of Justice.[190] The acceptability of such measures was at issue in *Muller*,[191] which concerned the importation from Germany into France of a preparation used in the manufacture of pastry products containing an additive banned in the latter country. In connection with the protection of public health under Article 36, the Court ruled that Member States were entitled to take into account the consumption habits of their own population and accepted the principle that the uncontrolled consumption of potentially harmful substances should be restricted as far as possible.[192] This ruling may have particular relevance for state alcohol monopolies, because, in practice, regulation of private sector

[185] Cf. the rationale for the block exemption of exclusive dealerships in the 6th recital in the Preamble to Reg. 1475/95 of 28 June 1995 ([1995] OJ L145/25) on the application of Art. 85(3) of the Treaty to certain categories of motor vehicle distribution and servicing agreements.

[186] Case C–234/89 *Stergios Delimitis* v. *Henninger Bräu AG* [1991] ECR I–935.

[187] See also the position taken by the ECJ in Joined Cases C–241/91P and C–242/91P *Radio Telefis Eireann and Independent Television Publications Ltd* v. *EC Commission* [1995] All ER (EC) 416.

[188] See, e.g., B. Hawk, 'The American (Anti-trust) Revolution: Lessons for the EEC' [1988] *ECLRev*. 53–87.

[189] EC Commission, Brussels, 1980, 10.

[190] See sect. 3.2.2 above.

[191] Case 304/84 *Ministäre Public* v. *Claude Muller* [1986] ECR 1511.

[192] *Ibid.* 1528.

outlets for alcoholic drinks, as favoured by the Commission,[193] might not necessarily be as effective in controlling such consumption as the operation of such monopolies.

It is true that Article 36 refers only to Articles 30 to 34 of the Treaty. A literal interpretation might imply that the requirements covered by Article 36 could not justify a restriction on the application of Article 37.[194] On the other hand, in *SAIL*,[195] which concerned the exclusive rights of supply and sale of Italian 'milk centres' within certain geographical limits, Advocate General Roemer was apparently willing to contemplate a less literal interpretation. An analogy might also be drawn with recognition by the Court that a principle embodied in Article 36—respect for industrial and commercial property—may apply in relation to Article 85 of the Treaty.[196]

However, the Commission takes the view that Article 36 cannot justify the exclusive rights of state alcohol monopolies.[197] This view is founded on the ruling in *EC Commission* v. *Germany*,[198] which concerned a German prohibition of additives in beer. The Court ruled that Article 36 only permitted trade restrictions which were 'actually necessary' on public health grounds.[199] In this judgment, however, the Court also confirmed the above mentioned points in the *Muller* ruling[200] and did not refer to the suggestion of Advocate General Slynn that public health might be left to depend on the self-restraint of consumers.[201] Moreover, the Court expressly noted that the restrictive measures at issue entailed the complete exclusion of products from the German market and that their exclusion could not be challenged by traders.[202] A monopoly which arguably provides consumers with a wider choice than would the market left to its own devices might be less objectionable.

In short, therefore, while discriminatory aspects of the operation of state alcohol monopolies may be prohibited, the legal position regarding the exclusive rights of such bodies seems less clear.[203]

193 *Opinion on Norway's Application for EU Membership*, COM(93)142, 30.

194 Art. 36 states that 'the provisions of Arts 30 to 34 shall not preclude' trade restrictions on the grounds specified therein.

195 Case 82/71 *Pubblico Ministero della Repubblica Italiana* v. *Società Agricola Industria Latte (SAIL)* [1972] ECR 119, 147.

196 Case 40/70 *Sirena Srl.* v. *Eda Srl.* [1971] ECR 69, 81.

197 *Opinion on Sweden's Application for Membership*, Bull. EC, Supp. 5/92, 15.

198 Case 178/84 [1987] ECR 1227. 199 *Ibid.* 1274. 200 *Ibid.* 1273 and 1274.

201 *Ibid.* 1257.

202 *Ibid.* 1274. See, similarly, Case 176/84 *EC Commission* v. *Greece* [1987] ECR 1193, 1223.

203 In the event, Accession negotiations led to an exchange of letters between the Commission, on the one hand, and Finland and Sweden on the other. According to these letters, the exclusive rights for wholesale importation, production, and marketing of alcohol monopolies had to be abolished. However, exclusive rights in the retail trade might continue, provided that there was no discrimination. See the *Twenty-Third Report on Competition Policy* (EC Commission, Brussels, 1994), 330–1. It is regarded by the Commission as 'a political agreement'. See the Joint Reply by Mr Monti to Written Questions E–133/95 and E–3134/95 ([1995] OJ C190/6).

Financing of Public Undertakings

In relation to public undertakings generally, problems may arise under Article 92 of the EC Treaty from financing arrangements. Although there are special rules designed to facilitate detection of the grant of aid to such undertakings,[204] prohibited state aid and permissible state investment[205] may not always be readily distinguishable. As the Commission recognizes, state financing of public undertakings is normally dictated by exigencies going beyond the profit motive, but this aspect of state practice is inherent in public ownership, the existence and special nature of which are 'confirmed' by Article 222 of the Treaty, and cannot alone justify the bringing into play of Article 92.[206] Thus, for example, in the case of a publicly owned airline, the provision of capital, loans, or guarantees by the state may constitute an aid, a normal commercial transaction between the owner of an enterprise and that enterprise, or a mixture of the two.[207]

Such thinking may be reflected in Community legislation. In particular, Article 1(4) of Decision 3632/93[208] defines as aid 'financing measures taken by Member States in respect of coal undertakings which are not regarded as risk capital provided to a company under standard market-economy practice'. Similarly, Article 1(2) of Decisions 3855/91[209] defines as aid state financing measures in respect of steel undertakings which the state directly or indirectly owns, where they 'cannot be regarded as a genuine provision of risk capital according to usual investment practice[210] in a market economy'.

The Commission has sometimes gone further and referred to a presumption of state aid, where the state invests in a company.[211] This presumption can

[204] Dir. 80/723 of 25 June 1980 ([1980] OJ L195/35) on the transparency of financial relations between Member States and public undertakings, as amended by Dir. 85/413 of 24 July 1985 ([1985] OJ L229/20) and Dir. 93/84 of 30 Sept. 1993 ([1993] OJ L254/16).

[205] State investment is not automatically contrary to Art. 92. See Case 323/82 *Intermills SA* v. *EC Commission* [1984] ECR 3809, 3830.

[206] The Italian Government, in particular, apparently objects to the treatment of capital injections in industry as constituting aid. See the *Second Survey on State Aids in the European Community in the Manufacturing and Certain Other Sectors* (EC Commission, Brussels, 1990), 9.

[207] *Progress towards the development of a Community air transport policy*, COM(84)72, 37–9. Disputes may arise between Directorate General IV and the Directorate General for Transport, which is responsible for controlling state aid to airlines, on whether state financing measures constitute aid. See, e.g., regarding a French capital injection in Air France, *Financial Times*, 11 July 1992.

[208] Of 28 Dec. 1993 ([1993] OJ L329/12) establishing Community rules for state aid to the coal industry.

[209] Of 29 Nov. 1991 ([1991] OJ L362/57) establishing Community rules for aid to the steel industry.

[210] Art. 1(2) of Dec. 322/89 of 1 Feb. 1989 ([1989] OJ L38/8) establishing Community rules for aid to the steel industry referred to 'standard company practice'. See also Art. 1(d) of Dir. 90/684 of 21 Dec. 1990 ([1990] OJ L380/27) on aid to shipbuilding.

[211] Indeed, such investment might be perceived by other shareholders and actual or potential creditors as reducing the risks of investing in, or dealing with, the company and, in this sense, constitute aid.

only be rebutted where the behaviour of the state is found to be compatible with that of a private investor operating under normal market conditions.[212] Whether or not such a presumption is fully reflected in Community practice, this practice confirms the difficulties of distinguishing between prohibited state aid and permissible state investment.[213]

(i) Private Investor Test

The private investor test is designed to maintain the distinction between prohibited state aid and permissible state investment and thus to uphold the principle of equality of treatment between public and private undertakings.[214] Attempts may be made to base the test on objective considerations, such as the scale and length of the investment.[215] For example, the length of the investment may lead to its being regarded as aid on the assumption that the private sector is not attracted by such long-term investments as the state may be prepared to make.[216] However, such considerations merely enable inferences to be drawn as to the central question—whether the return on the investment would have been such as to attract private investors.[217]

Efforts squarely to face this question may proceed on the basis of simplified conceptions as to the aims of private investors. Thus, for example, a distinction may be made between 'the purchase of shares by the State . . . as an investment for the purposes of obtaining income or capital appreciation, the aim of the ordinary investor' and their purchase 'merely [as] a vehicle for providing financial support for a particular company'.[218] Ultimately, simplified

[212] Notice C3/92 (ex N645/91) ([1992] OJ C105/16) concerning possible state aid elements contained in agreements between the Dutch State, Volvo Car Corporation, and Mitsubishi Motors Corporation.

[213] Lenz A. G. in Case 40/85 *Belgium* v. *EC Commission* [1986] ECR 2321, 2328 and in Case 234/84 *Belgium* v. *EC Commission* [1986] ECR 2263, 2270.

[214] Communication to the Member States—Application of Arts 92 and 93 EC and of Art. 5 of Commission Dir. 80/723 to Public Undertakings in the Manufacturing Sector ([1991] OJ C273/2), para. 11. See, earlier, the *Second Report on Competition Policy* (EC Commission, Brussels, 1972), 125–7. While any aid measure is likely to favour one undertaking in relation to another, the Commission cannot approve aid the grant of which may result in manifest discrimination between the public and private sectors. See Case 304/85 *Acciaierie e Ferriere Lombarde Falck* v. *EC Commission* [1987] ECR 871, 896.

[215] VerLoren van Themaat A. G. in Case 323/82 *Intermills SA* v. *EC Commission* [1984] ECR 3809, 3841.

[216] Reischl A. G. in Joined Cases 188 to 190/80 *France, Italy and the UK* v. *EC Commission* [1982] ECR 2545, 2591. See also Slynn A. G. in Case 84/82 *Germany* v. *EC Commission* [1984] ECR 1451, 1501.

[217] VerLoren van Themaat A. G. in Case 323/82 *Intermills SA* v. *EC Commission* [1984] ECR 3809, 3842; Case 234/84 *Belgium* v. *EC Commission* [1986] ECR 2263, 2286; Case 40/85 *Belgium* v. *EC Commission* [1986] ECR 2321, 2345; Case C–301/87 *France* v. *EC Commission* [1990] ECR I–307, I–361; and Case C–142/87 *Belgium* v. *EC Commission* [1990] ECR I–959, I–1012. See also Dec. 87/515 of 11 Feb. 1987 ([1987] OJ L295/25) on aid granted by the Federal Republic of Germany for the purchase and lease of the Seeadler factory manufacturing fish products in Cuxhaven, Lower Saxony.

[218] Slynn A. G. in Joined Cases 296 and 318/82 *Kingdom of the Netherlands and Leeuwarder Papierwarenfabriek BV* v. *EC Commission* [1985] ECR 809, 811.

conceptions of the relationship between state and market may be revealed. For example, *Belgium* v. *EC Commission*[219] concerned capital subscriptions in a Belgian producer of equipment for the food industry. Here the Court ruled that the question was whether a private shareholder having regard to the foreseeability of obtaining a return and leaving aside all social, regional policy, and sectoral considerations would have made the investment.[220] What seems to have been envisaged is a test based on the conduct of a 'model' private investor.

The underlying rationale for the test is that state financing of public undertakings does not, like financial contributions by private persons to an undertaking, derive from the private property of those persons, which is in all respects subject to commercial risk, but rather directly or indirectly from the resources of the state budget. Hence, there is the danger that in such financing commercial considerations which a businessman would take into account do not always come into play.[221]

In practice, application of the test entails that attention is focussed on the position of the recipient undertaking and, in the case of an undertaking under mixed ownership, on the conduct of private shareholders.

State investment in a company which is basically viable and only has temporary problems pending conversion,[222] which has a sound financial and economic position and good development potential[223] or which is undergoing a rapid financial recovery[224] is not aid. The rationale is that a private shareholder could also be expected to subscribe the capital necessary to secure the survival of an undertaking which is experiencing temporary difficulties but is capable of becoming profitable again, possibly after reorganization. Acceptability of state investment from the perspective of a private shareholder may be confirmed where the investment seeks to promote the development of new activities of high technological quality[225] or by subsequent sale of public shares at a profit.[226]

However, state investment involves aid, where, because of its inadequate cash flow,[227] the company would be unable to raise the funds needed on the

[219] Case 234/84 [1986] ECR 2263, 2286.

[220] Thus aid may be involved where the state acquires holdings in firms to help them until such time as they will have overcome temporary difficulties or to achieve regional policy goals. See the *Second Report on Competition Policy* (EC Commission, Brussels, 1973), 108.

[221] Reischl A. G. in Joined Cases 188 to 190/80 *France, Italy and the UK* v. *EC Commission* [1982] ECR 2545, 2591.

[222] Commission Reply to Question No. 7 put by the Court in Case 84/82 *Germany* v. *EC Commission* [1984] ECR 1451, 1484.

[223] *Eighteenth Report on Competition Policy* (EC Commission, Brussels, 1989), 168. But cf. Slynn A. G. in Case 84/82 *Germany* v. *EC Commission* [1984] ECR 1451, 1501.

[224] *Eighteenth Report on Competition Policy* (EC Commission, Brussels, 1989), 186.

[225] *Ninth Report on Competition Policy* (EC Commission, Brussels, 1980), 112–3.

[226] *Sixteenth Report on Competition Policy* (EC Commission, Brussels, 1987), 155.

[227] According to Dec. 89/43 of 26 July 1988 ([1989] OJ L16/52) on aids granted by the Italian Government to ENI-Lanerossi, aid is present where, in view of the duration and volume of the losses of the recipient, a normal return in dividends or capital gains could not be expected for the capital invested.

capital market.[228] In the case of a loss-making company, there may be serious doubts that a market economy investor would make an investment both covering the company's past losses and restoring the company's capital to its pre-existing level without taking remedial actions in the form of restructuring the company's activities or running down the size of its investment to a level commensurate with the risk and return from the investment.[229]

For example, in Decision 82/312[230] the Commission examined the legality of an acquisition by the Belgian Government of a holding of Bfrs 120 million in a group manufacturing wall coverings, whose combined balance-sheet showed a deficit of Bfrs 500 million. The Commission concluded that the acquisition of the holding could not be justified by reference to the book value of the group concerned.[231] Similarly, in view of the accumulated debts and the costs of the restructuring programme, the Commission considered that no investor apart from the state would be prepared to take part in the restructuring of the Belgian airline, Sabena. Hence, state financing of Sabena was found to have constituted aid within the meaning of Article 92(1).[232]

Such thinking was summarized in the Commission Communication of 17 September 1984.[233] According to this Communication, aid is present where:

—the financial structure and, in particular, the debt structure of the undertaking concerned do not seem such as to produce a normal return;[234]

—the undertaking would be unable, because of the lack of its own financing capacity, to raise on the market the capital needed for investment;

[228] If state investment is not expected to render the undertaking concerned profitable, it is likely to be treated as aid. See Dec. 93/133 of 4 Nov. 1992 ([1993] OJ L55/54) concerning aid granted by the Spanish Government to the Merco company (agricultural processing industry).

[229] Communication C6/92 (ex NN149/91) ([1992] OJ C122/6) concerning contributions by Italimpianti to CMF SUD SpA. Thus public funds cannot be used regularly to offset the losses of firms. See the *Ninth Report on Competition Policy* (EC Commission, Brussels, 1980), 93.

[230] Of 10 Mar. 1982 ([1982] OJ L138/18) concerning the aid granted by the Belgian Government to an industrial and commercial group manufacturing wall coverings.

[231] In Dec. 92/239 of 25 July 1990 ([1992] OJ L183/30) on aid granted by the Italian Government to a manufacturer of ophthalmic products (Industrie Ottiche Riunite—IOR) the Commission considered that a private investor would not have paid almost 11 times his original investment in five years in order to dispose of half of the investment at its nominal price.

[232] Dec. 91/555 of 24 July 1991 ([1991] OJ L300/48) on aid to be granted by the Belgian Government in favour of the air carrier Sabena. See, similarly, Lenz A. G. in Case 40/85 *Belgium* v. *EC Commission* [1986] ECR 2321, 2330, regarding state participation in an undertaking in 'a hopeless financial situation' and where 94 per cent of the new capital came from public funds.

[233] Bull. EC 9–1984, 3.5.1; *Fourteenth Report on Competition Policy* (EC Commission, Brussels, 1985), 124–5. See, earlier, the *Tenth Report on Competition Policy* (EC Commission, Brussels, 1981), 144.

[234] Account may be taken not only of a decision as such to invest but also of the nature of the investment. See, regarding an advance on a future capital injection at a low-risk interest rate, Notice C33/93 (NN32/93) ([1993] OJ C346/7) regarding aid which France has decided to grant to Group Bull.

—the participation involves the taking over or continuation of non-viable activity of an undertaking in difficulty through the creation of a new legal entity;
—there is an obvious imbalance between public and private participation;
—the participation exceeds the real value of the undertaking concerned.

However, in the last two cases, there is no aid where the undertaking concerned is a small or medium-sized one which cannot offer sufficient guarantees for the capital market but whose prospects justify the participation.

In the application of such criteria account may be taken of the viability of restructuring plans for the undertakings concerned. For example, *Belgium* v. *EC Commission*[235] concerned capital subscriptions to a Belgian producer of ceramics. At the time when the capital was subscribed the undertaking had for several years been making very substantial losses relative to its turnover, its survival had already necessitated several injections of capital by the public authorities in order to restore its depleted capital, and its products had to be sold on a market in which there was excess capacity.[236] There was no indication that the restructuring plan for the undertaking was likely to guarantee profitable operations in the future and hence to provide a sufficient basis to attract the requisite private capital. Indeed, the plan had already failed when the capital at issue was subscribed, since a previous subscription of Bfrs 475 million under the first stage of the plan had been almost entirely absorbed by the trading losses incurred in the meantime. Accordingly, the new capital subscriptions had to be regarded as aid.

Similarly, if the state invests in a company on the basis of a restructuring plan, a key aspect of which can no longer be achieved because of developments which should have been known at the time of the investment and no alternative strategy has been adopted, state aid may be involved.[237]

In making such assessments, the Commission may attach decisive importance to the state of the sector in which the company is operating. Thus injection of capital in a public company for new investment and expenditure directly related thereto will not normally be characterized as aid where there is no structural overcapacity in the industry and the company is financially sound.[238] However, the financial position of an undertaking and overcapacity in the sector concerned may be treated as handicaps indicating that the undertaking would have been unable to raise on the private capital markets

[235] Case 40/85 [1986] ECR 2321.
[236] *Ibid.*, 2345. See, similarly, Case 234/84 *Belgium* v. *EC Commission* [1986] ECR 2263, 2286.
[237] Notice C22/92 (N727/91) ([1992] OJ C257/4) concerning aid which Italy plans to grant to Ilva SpA.
[238] Dec. 87/418 of 4 Feb. 1987 ([1987] OJ L227/45) concerning aid to a Belgian steel pipe and tube manufacturer.

the funds essential to its survival.[239] In crisis sectors state participation in undertakings is treated as aid, unless the undertaking concerned is highly competitive[240] or a restructuring plan likely to lead to viability is entailed.[241] For example, the Commission took the view in 1982 that the financial circumstances of virtually all public-sector steel undertakings and the market prospects of the industry as a whole were such that state provision of equity and quasi-equity finance to these undertakings inevitably contained aid elements.[242]

Inferences on the question whether such elements are involved may be drawn from the conduct of private shareholders,[243] existing or potential, in companies only partly owned by public authorities. As regards potential shareholders, aid will be involved where the state purchases shares at a higher price than the former would be prepared to pay. Thus if the undertaking is quoted on the stock exchange, the purchase of its shares by the state at a price above the quoted one would involve the grant of aid.[244] Where the state already owns virtually all the shares of a quoted company, aid may be involved, unless the price paid reflects the present and expected yield of its shares.[245]

More usually, account is taken of the conduct of existing shareholders.[246] For example, in April 1990 the Commission decided to accept the Italian Government's injection of new capital in the steel tube producer, Dalmine, a subsidiary of the publicly-owned Ilva group. The Government had agreed to reduce its contribution to the capital increase to an amount such that the public and private shareholders would contribute in proportion to their original shareholdings and had put forward additional measures for restructuring the

[239] Dec. 83/130 of 16 Feb. 1983 ([1983] OJ L91/32) on aid granted by the Belgian Government to a firm manufacturing ceramic sanitary ware.

[240] *Twelfth Report on Competition Policy* (EC Commission, Brussels, 1983), 120.

[241] *Eighteenth Report on Competition Policy* (EC Commission, Brussels, 1989), 163. See also *ibid.* 165 and Van Gerven A. G. in Case C–305/89 *Italy* v. *EC Commission* [1991] ECR I–1603, I–1626.

[242] *Twelfth Report on Competition Policy* (EC Commission, Brussels, 1983), 120.

[243] Account may even be taken of the conduct of creditors. E.g., French state investment in a company which had taken over a bankrupt trailer manufacturer was acceptable. 40 per cent of the new company was privately owned, and the receiver of the old company had closed part of the latter, rationalized the remainder and reached a settlement with creditors to convert short-term borrowing into medium and long-term loans. See Bull. EC 5–1987, 2.1.82 and the *Seventeenth Report on Competition Policy* (EC Commission, Brussels, 1988), 167.

[244] Dec. 91/555 of 24 July 1991 ([1991] OJ L300/48) on aid to be granted by the Belgian Government in favour of the air carrier Sabena.

[245] However, a higher price might reasonably be paid for the purchase of a blocking minority. See the *Fourteenth Report on Competition Policy* (EC Commission, Brussels, 1985), 137.

[246] Such conduct not only indicates the expectations of private investors as to the profitability of an investment but may also affect its likely profitability. Hence, according to the Commission, a private shareholder would not be prepared to provide financial liquidity to a company in difficulties if its fellow shareholders would not be prepared to contribute in line with their participation in the equity. See Notice C55/94 (ex NN100/94) ([1995] OJ C173/3) with respect to loans granted by Freistaat Bayern to Neue Maxhütte Stahlwerke GmbH, Sulzbach-Rosenberg.

company to restore its viability and ensure a satisfactory return for investors. Also, throughout the period, Dalmine's share price had held up well. The Commission, therefore, took the view that the transaction was in line with what a private investor would do under normal market economy conditions and did not involve aid.[247]

Similarly, the Commission accepted a capital subscription and a participatory loan by the Wallonia Region to Donnay, a company in which the Region was a minority shareholder. As the majority shareholder was also putting money into the company, the Commission concluded that the action of the Region was that of a private investor and did not involve aid.[248]

In the case of a firm under mixed ownership, therefore, aid will not normally be present where the state's subscription of funds is in proportion to its existing holding and is matched by subscriptions by private shareholders,[249] though the latter subscription must have 'economic significance',[250] 'real economic significance'[251] or 'economic relevance'.[252]

The possibility that the conduct of private shareholders may itself be affected by state measures only receives marginal consideration.[253] According to the Commission, where state participation is to be accompanied by an injection of private capital, it is essential to ensure that new shareholders do not enjoy privileges and guarantees. Provision of such guarantees could only be taken as a lack of confidence on behalf of private investors in the possibility of re-establishing long-term viability.[254] Similarly, indirect inducements, such as tax exemptions on sums used by companies to repurchase shares from public bodies, may be considered to entail the grant of aid.[255]

247 *Twentieth Report on Competition Policy* (EC Commission, Brussels, 1991), 153–4.

248 *Ibid.*, 171. Again, Volvo Cars BV received from the Dutch authorities Dfl 155 million in the form of grants or debt write-offs. Since parallel action was taken by other shareholders, the Dutch measure was acceptable. See the *Tenth Report on Competition Policy* (EC Commission, Brussels, 1980), 144.

249 Dec. 87/418 of 4 Feb. 1987 ([1987] OJ L227/45) concerning aid to a Belgian steel pipe and tube manufacturer. In accepting the view of the Commission that aid was involved, the ECJ noted that private investments were much lower than, and followed, state investment (Case C–301/87 *France* v. *EC Commission* [1990] ECR I–307, I–361).

250 Communication C39/93 (NN87/93) ([1993] OJ C334/7) concerning the subscription by CDC–participations to two bond issues of Air France.

251 A shareholding of 4.43 per cent, which has no effect on the management structure of the group concerned and does not enable important decisions to be opposed, lacks such significance. See Notice C33/B/93 (NN12/94) ([1994] OJ C80/4) regarding aid which France has decided to grant to Groupe Bull.

252 Dec. 94/118 of 21 Dec. 1993 ([1994] OJ L54/30) concerning aid to be provided by the Irish Government to the Aer Lingus group.

253 Cf. regarding the 'signals' that state investment may give other interested parties, Notice C38/93 (NN43/93 and NN58/93) ([1994] OJ C31/9) regarding aid, which the Netherlands intends to grant to truck producer DAF.

254 Only the provision of genuine risk capital would sufficiently indicate the commercial viability of the restructuring concept. See Dec. 91/555 of 24 July 1991 ([1991] OJ L300/48) on aid to be granted by the Belgian Government in favour of the air carrier Sabena.

255 *Sixteenth Report on Competition Policy* (EC Commission, Brussels, 1987), 148 and 162.

(ii) Reasonableness

Fundamental problems in Commission practice were highlighted in *Italy* v. *EC Commission*,[256] which concerned capital injections in a nationalized producer of clothing. Here it was argued that the test whether state investment amounted to aid should relate to the actions of the private entrepreneur rather than the 'model' private investor.[257] Advocate General van Gerven accepted that, the relationship between the public and private sectors being so close, a private holding company could not ignore social and regional considerations. Even so, the company would fail in its obligations to shareholders, creditors, and employees if it continued to support a loss-making subsidiary in a sector suffering from overcapacity without adopting a restructuring plan.[258] According to the Court itself, investment in pursuit of a structural policy, general or sectoral, guided by long-term profitability perspectives would not constitute aid. However, aid would be present where the investment was made without any regard to the question of returns, even in the long term.[259]

The evolution of Commission practice seems to have been influenced by such case law. To begin with, the Commission recognizes that investors, public or private, must engage in risk analysis. Such analysis requires the exercise of managerial skills, which necessarily implies a wide margin of judgement by the investor. Within that wide margin the exercise of judgement cannot be regarded as involving the grant of state aid. Only where there are no objective grounds reasonably to expect that an investment will give an adequate rate of return that would be acceptable to a private investor in a comparable undertaking operating under normal market conditions, is state aid involved.[260] No distinction is now made between projects which have short or long-term pay back periods,[261] as long as the risks are adequately and objectively assessed and discounted at the time the decision to invest is made, in the way that a private investor would do.[262]

It is also recognized that a private undertaking may engage in cross-

[256] Case C-303/88 [1991] ECR I-1433, I-1475. Cf. Case C-305/89 *Italy* v. *EC Commission* [1991] ECR I-1603, I-1640.

[257] F. Minneci, 'Le partecipazioni pubbliche al capitale di imprese' [1991] *Diritto Comunitario e degli Scambi Internazionali* 365–72.

[258] [1991] ECR I-1433, I-1459.

[259] *Ibid.* I-1476; Case 305/89 *Italy* v. *EC Commission* [1991] ECR I-1603, I-1640. See also Van Gerven A. G. (*ibid.* 1626) and in Case C-261/89 *Italy* v. *EC Commission* [1991] ECR I-4437, I-4449.

[260] Communication to the Member States—Application of Arts 92 and 93 EC and of Art. 5 of Commission Dir. 80/723 to Public Undertakings in the Manufacturing Sector ([1991] OJ C273/2), para. 27.

[261] It is recognized that the state may have 'a legitimate interest in the long-term viability' of a company where it is the majority shareholder. See the *Twenty-Fourth Report on Competition Policy*, COM(95)142, 512.

[262] Communication to the Member States—Application of Arts 92 and 93 EC and of Art. 5 of Commission Dir. 80/723 to Public Undertakings in the Manufacturing Sector ([1991] OJ C273/2), para. 28.

subsidization, when it has a strategic plan with good hopes of long-term gain or where the cross-subsidy has a net benefit to the group as a whole. The Commission takes account of similar strategic goals where there is cross-subsidization in public holding companies. Such cross-subsidization is treated as aid only where the Commission considers that there is no other reasonable explanation for the flow of funds other than that aid is involved.[263]

Finally, the Commission recognizes the differences in approach a market investor may have between his minority holding in a company on the one hand and full control of a large group on the other.[264] The former relationship may often be characterized as more of a speculative or even short-term interest, whereas the latter usually involves a longer-term interest. Similarly, where a public authority controls an individual undertaking or a group of undertakings, it will normally be less motivated by purely short-term profit considerations than if it had merely a minority/non-controlling holding, and its time horizon will correspondingly be longer. Accordingly, the Commission takes account of the nature of the public authority's holding in comparing its behaviour with the benchmark of the equivalent market economy investor. More particularly, where a decision is made to abandon a line of activity because of its lack of medium/long-term commercial viability, a public group, like a private group, can be expected to decide the timing and scale of its run down in the light of the impact on the overall credibility and structure of the group.[265]

In short, the test employed by the Commission has evolved. It is no longer that of a 'model' private investor,[266] which would entail discrimination against the public sector, but that of a 'reasonable' investor[267] or entrepreneur. As a result, state financing of conversion operations, including redeployment of workers and mitigation of the regional effects of a cutback, may not be treated as prohibited aid. Such operations involve a number of benefits for the companies concerned, such as 'indirect material profit', 'image maintenance' and 'redirection of activities'.[268] However, there must be a 'coherent' restruc-

263 *Ibid.*, para. 29.

264 Transfers within a group of public bodies are, in principle, unobjectionable, but aid may be involved where a transfer takes place 'at rather symbolic terms that do not represent its intrinsic economic value in the light of its economic prospects'. See Notice C6/92 (ex NN141/91) ([1993] OJ C282/5) regarding aid which Italy granted to CMF SUD SpA and CMF SpA.

265 Communication to the Member States—Application of Arts 92 and 93 EC and of Art. 5 of Commission Dir. 80/723 to Public Undertakings in the Manufacturing Sector ([1991] OJ C273/2), para. 30. See, generally, C. -D. Ehlermann, 'Les Entreprises Publiques et le Contrôle des Aides d'Etat' [1992] *RMC* 613–20 and *The Measurement of the Aid Element of State Acquisitions of Company Capital* (Evolution of Concentration and Competition Series: Collection: Working Papers 87).

266 Though the model has not been entirely eliminated from Commission practice. See Dec. 93/133 of 4 Nov. 1992 ([1993] OJ L55/54) concerning aid granted by the Spanish Government to the Merco company (agricultural processing industry).

267 Van Gerven A. G. in Case C–305/89 *Italy* v. *EC Commission* [1991] ECR I–1603, I–1640.

268 Dec. 92/266 of 27 Nov. 1991 ([1992] OJ L138/24) on the conversion activities of French industrial groups outside the steel and coal industries and excluding the Compagnie Générale Maritime, pursuant to Arts 92 to 94 EC.

turing plan,[269] and the financing of 'regional development operations' may still be treated as aid.

4.2.4 Procedures

National administrative and judicial institutions may play a role in the enforcement of competition law under the EC Treaty, but the main role is played by the supranational decision making of the Commission.[270]

National Administrative Enforcement

National administrative enforcement of competition law may be permitted by the EC Treaty.[271] However, national authorities must not act in such a way as to interfere with the uniform application of Community competition law.[272] Rather, they must co-operate with the Commission.[273]

National Judicial Enforcement

According to the case law of the Court of Justice, Article 37(2),[274] Article 85(1) and (2),[275] Article 86,[276] and Article 93(3)[277] of the EC Treaty[278] are directly effective, as may be provisions of implementing regulations and decisions. Hence, the requirements of these provisions may be enforced by national courts,[279] though their role is limited by the lack of direct effectiveness of Articles 85(3) and 92.

[269] Communication C39/93 (NN87/93) ([1993] OJ C334/7) concerning the subscription by CDC–participations to two bond issues of Air France.

[270] According to the Commission itself, 'it is the administrative authority responsible for the implementation and for the thrust of competition policy in the Community' (para. 4 of the Notice on co-operation between national courts and the Commission in applying Arts 85 and 86 EC ([1993] OJ C39/6)). However, because of its limited resources the Commission concentrates on cases 'having particular political, economic or legal significance for the Community' (*ibid.*, para. 14).

[271] Art. 9(3) of Reg. 17 of 6 Feb. 1962 ([1962] JO 204) first reg. implementing Arts 85 and 86 of the Treaty. Prior to adoption of this Reg., national authorities were required by Art. 88 EC to rule on restrictive practices in accordance with their national law and Arts 85 and 86 EC.

[272] Case 14/68 *Walt Wilhelm* v. *Bundeskartellamt* [1969] ECR 1, 14. See, more particularly, Art. 21(2) of Reg. 4064/89 of 21 Dec. 1989 ([1989] OJ L395/1, as corrected by [1990] OJ L257/13) on the control of concentrations between undertakings. It is disputed whether national authorities may apply their national competition law in relation to an agreement exempted by the Commission under Art. 85(3) EC. See J. H. J. Bourgeois, 'EEC Control over International Mergers' [1990] *YBEL* 102–32, at 106. In Joined Cases 253/78 and 1–37/79 *Procureur de la République* v. *Bruno Giry and Guerlain SA* [1980] ECR 2327, 2375 the ECJ held that a 'comfort letter' from the Commission did not preclude application of national competition law.

[273] The Commission intends to draw up a notice explaining the criteria and methods for allocating cases between the national authorities and the Commission. See the *Twenty-Fourth Report on Competition Policy*, COM(95)142, 22.

[274] Case 6/64 *Flaminio Costa* v. *ENEL* [1964] ECR 585, 597.

[275] Case 127/73 *Belgische Radio en Televisie (BRT)* v. *Société Belge des Auteurs, Compositeurs et Editeurs (SABAM)* [1974] ECR 51, 62.

[276] *Ibid.*

[277] See below, 190–4, regarding this provision.

[278] Case 78/76 *Firma Steinike und Weinlig* v. *Germany* [1977] ECR 595, 610.

[279] The Commission is preparing a notice on co-operation with national courts in the state aid field. See the *Twenty-Fourth Report on Competition Policy*, COM(95)142, 276.

For example, the fact that Article 93(3) is directly effective means that national courts may have to determine whether there has been a violation of the aid notification requirements imposed on Member States by this provision.[280] However, to make this determination, such courts must only decide whether aid within the meaning of Article 92(1) has been granted and not whether it distorts competition and affects trade between Member States.[281] In other words, they are not to decide whether or not the aid is compatible with the common market.[282]

Commission Enforcement

The Commission rather than national administrative authorities or national courts plays the main role in securing respect for competition law under the EC Treaty.[283]

(i) Restrictive Practices by Undertakings

Regulation 17[284] outlines the Commission's role in relation to Articles 85 and 86 of the Treaty. In particular, under Article 3 of the Regulation the Commission may require the termination of an infringement of Article 85 or 86 of the Treaty. Alternatively, on application by the undertakings concerned, the Commission may grant a negative clearance, i.e., decide that there are no grounds for action under either Treaty provision. Under Article 6 of the Regulation the Commission may also exempt notified agreements from the prohibition in Article 85(1), provided that the conditions for exemption in

[280] National courts can declare aid which is not notified to the Commission in accordance with these requirements to be unlawful. See Case C–354/90 *Fédération nationale du commerce extérieur des produits alimentaires* [1991] ECR I–5505. See below, 191–2, regarding these requirements.

[281] Lenz A. G. in Case C–44/93 *Namur–Les Assurances du crédit SA* v. *Office national du ducroire et Etat belge* [1994] ECR I–3829, I–3847–8.

[282] The Court (*ibid.*), I–3871. According to Case C–354/90 *Fédération nationale du commerce extérieur des produits alimentaires et Syndicat national des négociants et transformateurs de saumon* v. *France* [1991] ECR I–5505, I–5528, national courts had to ensure that individuals were in a position to enforce rights of action in respect of any disregard of Art. 93(3), from which all the proper consequences would follow, in accordance with their national law, both regarding the validity of acts involving the implementation of aid measures and the recovery of financial support granted in breach of that provision or of any provisional measures. The Commission's final decision could not have the effect of regularizing implementing measures which were invalid for having been effected in breach of Art. 93(3). See also Wolf J in *Regina* v. *Attorney-General, ex parte ICI* [1985] 1 CMLR 588, 608.

[283] Cf. the need, 'if the competition process is to work well in the internal market', for cooperation between the Commission, national competition authorities, and national and European courts (Notice on co-operation between national courts and the Commission in applying Arts. 85 and 86 EC ([1993] OJ C39/6), para. 3).

[284] Of 6 Feb. 1962 ([1962] JO 204) first reg. implementing Arts 85 and 86 of the Treaty.

Article 85(3) are met.[285] The Commission has also acquired merger control powers under Regulation 4064/89.[286]

(ii) State Aid

Article 93(1) of the EC Treaty provides that the Commission shall, in co-operation with Member States, keep under constant review all systems of aid[287] existing in those states.[288] It shall propose to the latter any appropriate measures required by the progressive development or the functioning of the common market.[289] Such proposals may be made in discussions between the Commission and national officials concerning general state aid issues and the annual Report of the Commission on Competition Policy,[290] where a specific legal obligation may merely be one element in negotiations.[291] What is involved is not aid 'authorizations *en bloc*' but the logical consequence of the fact that aid systems crystallize under the provisions of Article 93(1).[292] If, however, the Member State concerned does not undertake to follow a proposal made under this provision, the Commission may initiate the Article 93(2) procedure,[293] which is discussed below.

In the case of planned new aid schemes and non-negligible modifications[294] of existing aid schemes, Article 93(3) obliges Member States to notify their

[285] Where a block exemption has been granted (see, e.g., Commission Reg. 1983/83 ([1983] OJ L173/1)), the requirements of the relevant reg. have to be met.

[286] Of 21 Dec. 1989 ([1989] OJ L395/1) on the control of concentrations between undertakings.

[287] Particular cases of the implementation of an aid scheme already approved by the Commission are not systematically examined by the Commission, unless they concern areas governed by special rules on state aid. See Commission Reply by Sir Leon Brittan to Written Question 2317/92 ([1993] OJ C47/29) by Mr Francesco Speroni.

[288] Aid granted pursuant to a scheme already approved by the Commission and meeting the conditions laid down in the decision of approval constitutes 'existing' aid. See Case C–47/91 *Italy* v. *EC Commission* [1994] ECR I–4635.

[289] E.g., by letter of 19 May 1993 ([1993] OJ C163/5) the Commission proposed that the Portuguese Government abolish the taxation exemption enjoyed by the national airline, TAP. This procedure is said by the Commission to allow account to be taken of changed conditions. See Commission Joint Reply by Mr Van Miert to Written Questions E–2197/93, E–2198/93, and E–2199/93 by Nel van Dijk ([1994] OJ C306/9)

[290] *Agence Europe*, No. 5350 (15/16 Oct. 1990).

[291] F. Snyder, 'The Effectiveness of European Community Law: Institutions, Processes, Tools and Techniques' (1993) 56 *MLR* 19–54, p. 30.

[292] Darmon A. G. in Joined Cases 166 and 220/86 *Irish Cement Ltd* v. *EC Commission* [1988] ECR 6473, 6492–3.

[293] See, e.g., Commission Letter to the German Government ([1993] OJ C289/2) proposing action to be taken in respect of Case E/93 (fiscal aid given to German airlines in the form of a depreciation facility).

[294] Case 177/78 *Pigs and Bacon Commission* v. *McCarren & Co. Ltd* [1979] ECR 2161, 2204 and Joined Cases 91 and 127/83 *Heineken Brouwereijen BV* v. *Inspecteur der Vennootschapsbelasting* [1984] ECR 3435, 3453–4. A modification is considered negligible where it only involves a budget increase not exceeding 20 per cent of the budget initially approved. See the Communication on the accelerated clearance of aid schemes for SMEs and of amendments of existing schemes ([1992] OJ C213/10).

plans to the Commission[295] with enough advance notice[296] to allow the Commission to comment. More specific requirements may be contained in individual decisions,[297] designed to develop or reinforce those in Article 93(3).[298] If the Commission does not act within two months of the notification, the aid may be implemented, and it thus becomes existing aid for the purposes of Article 93(1).[299]

Where aid has not been notified,[300] the Commission can require its suspension[301] as well as information about it. If the Member State complies, the Commission must examine the compatibility of the aid with the common market under Article 93(2). If the Member State does not provide the necessary information, the Commission may reach a decision on the basis of the information in its possession. If the Member State does not suspend the aid, the Commission may bring the violation of the Treaty or a decision requiring suspension before the Court.[302]

[295] See Bull. EC 3–1993, 1.2.39 and the *Twenty-Third Report on Competition Policy* (EC Commission, Brussels, 1994), 243–4, regarding standardized notifications.

[296] Notifications must be made at least two months or 60 days before the intended entry into force of the aid measure, and Art. 169 proceedings may be taken for breach of Art. 93(3). See Notification of State Aids to the Commission pursuant to Art. 93(3) EEC: the failure of Member States to respect their obligations ([1980] OJ C252/2). On 2 Oct. 1974 the Governments had declared in the Council of Ministers that 'the rules of the EEC Treaty regarding aids (Arts 92 and 93) shall be strictly observed both with respect to existing and future aid measures'.

[297] Informal agreements may also be reached. E.g., in 1972 Member States agreed to notify the Commission of all applications of general (including regional) aid schemes to the textiles industry. See the *Second Report on Competition Policy* (EC Commission, Brussels, 1973), 89.

[298] See, e.g., Dec. 75/397 of 17 June 1975 ([1975] OJ L177/13) on the aids granted by the Belgian Government pursuant to the Act of 17 July 1959 introducing and co-ordinating measures to encourage economic expansion and the creation of new industries.

[299] Case 120/73 *Gebr. Lorenz GmbH* v. *Germany* [1973] ECR 1471, 1481–2 and Case 84/82 *Germany* v. *EC Commission* [1984] ECR 1451, 1488. See also Cases 31/77R and 53/77R *EC Commission* v. *United Kingdom* and *United Kingdom* v. *EC Commission* [1977] ECR 921, 923; Case 171/83R *EC Commission* v. *France* [1983] ECR 2621, 2628; and Joined Cases 91 and 127/83 *Heineken Brouwerijen BV* v. *Inspecteur der Vennootschapsbelasting* [1984] ECR 3435, 3454.

[300] The concept is broadly interpreted. Thus legislative provision for aid is treated as unnotified, even if the authorities say that the legislation will only become operative after Commission approval. See Dec. 93/508 of 7 July 1993 ([1993] OJ L238/38) concerning aid granted by the Italian Government in favour of the ceramics industry of Lazio. 'Aid is deemed to have been put into effect as soon as the legislative machinery enabling it to be granted has been set up.' See Dec. 93/627 of 22 July 1993 ([1993] OJ L309/21) concerning aid granted by the Spanish authorities on the occasion of the sale by Cenemesa/Cadmesa/Conelec of certain selected assets to Asea-Brown Boveri. It is not necessary that the aid should have been 'effectively paid'. See Notice C37/93 (NN 63/93) ([1994] OJ C170/5) concerning Art. 29*ter* of the Walloon decree of 25 June 1992 on support for Walloon firms participating in Community industrial programmes which are the subject of specific international agreements. The Commission recommends Member States to include a clause in legislation to the effect that aid can only be paid after it has been cleared by the Commission. See the *Twenty-Third Report on Competition Policy* (EC Commission, Brussels, 1994), 250.

[301] Case C–301/87 *France* v. *EC Commission* [1990] ECR I–307, I–356. The Commission claims similar powers under Art. 88 ECSC. See Notice C22/A/92 (NN53/93) ([1993] OJ C213/6) regarding aid which Italy plans to grant to Ilva SpA.

[302] See, e.g., Dec. 94/220 of 26 Jan. 1994 ([1994] OJ L107/61) requiring France to suspend the payment to Groupe Bull of aid granted in breach of Art. 93(3) EC.

Article 93(2) requires a more elaborate examination than that under Article 93(3).[303] If the Commission has any reason to think that aid could be incompatible with the common market,[304] has serious difficulties in determining whether aid is compatible with the common market[305] or is unable to satisfy itself after a preliminary examination that the aid is compatible, it must initiate the Article 93(2) procedure by addressing a notice to the Member States and to other interested parties,[306] so as to permit them to comment.[307] If the Commission initiates this procedure, it has a reasonable time to complete the procedure.[308] Aid may not be granted before the Commission has reached a final decision under Article 93(2),[309] unless the investments to be aided are 'compellingly urgent'.[310]

If the Commission finds that the aid is incompatible with the common market, it may decide that the state concerned shall abolish or alter it. A decision prohibiting existing aid is constitutive, and so the aid need only be eliminated by the future date specified in the decision.[311] A decision prohibiting unnotified aid is declaratory, and the aid is *ab initio* incompatible with the common market.[312] Unnotified aid is also liable to be subject to a request for recovery,[313] with interest,[314] so as to 'restore the

[303] Mayras A. G. in Case 70/72 *EC Commission* v. *Germany* [1973] ECR 813, 834.

[304] Case C–198/91 *William Cook PLC* v. *EC Commission* [1993] ECR I–2487, I–2529.

[305] Case 84/82 *Germany* v. *EC Commission* [1984] ECR 1451, 1488.

[306] Though Art. 93(2) EC only refers to aid already granted.

[307] Case 84/82 *Germany* v. *EC Commission* [1984] ECR 1451, 1490. Resort to the Art. 93(2) procedure became more automatic after this judgment. There is nothing inherently contentious in resort to this procedure. See J. Flynn, 'State Aid and Self-help' [1983] *ELRev.* 297–312, 299, n. 15. The Commission may not adopt a decision that a Member State has violated conditions laid down in an earlier decision without resort to this procedure. See C–294/90 *British Aerospace and Rover Group Holdings* v. *EC Commission* [1992] ECR I–493.

[308] Case 59/79 *Fédération nationale des producteurs de vins de table* v. *EC Commission* [1979] ECR 2425, 2428. The aim of the Commission is to close the procedure within six months of its commencement. See the *Twenty-Fourth Report on Competition Policy*, COM(95)142, 279.

[309] Communication of 24 Nov. 1983 ([1983] OJ C318/3).

[310] Notice C4/94, C61/94, C62/94, NN2/95, NN3/95 and N467/95 ([1995] OJ C203/6) concerning aid the German Government intends to grant to Sächsische Olefinwerke GmbH, Leuna-Werke GmbH, and Buna GmbH.

[311] Case 70/72 *EC Commission* v. *Germany* [1973] ECR 813, 831.

[312] It has been argued that Art. 93(2) EC is inapplicable to improperly introduced aid and that the Art. 169 procedure is less cumbersome. See Warner A. G. in Case 173/73 *Italy* v. *EC Commission* [1974] ECR 709, 724. Cf. Lagrange A. G. in Case 6/64 *Flaminio Costa* v. *ENEL* [1964] ECR 585, 609.

[313] Case 70/72 *EC Commission* v. *Germany* [1973] ECR 813, 829 and Case 310/85 *Deufil GmbH & Co. KG* v. *EC Commission* [1987] ECR 901, 927. But note the early reticence of the Commission to publicize the fact and its *corrigendum* ([1982] OJ L289/35) to Dec. 82/312 of 10 Mar. 1982 ([1982] OJ L138/18) concerning the aid granted by the Belgian Government to an industrial and commercial group manufacturing wall coverings, which replaced recovery demands with a declaration of incompatibility.

[314] Interest runs from the date of effective payment of the aid. See Dec. 93/349 of 9 Mar. 1993 ([1993] OJ L143/7) concerning aid provided by the UK Government to British Aerospace for its purchase of Rover Group Holdings over and above those authorized in Commission Dec. 89/58 authorizing a maximum aid to this operation subject to certain conditions.

status quo',[315] even though Article 93(2) refers only to the abolition or alteration of such aid.[316] Recovery depends on national law[317] 'in the absence of Community rules',[318] but recovery must not be rendered impossible[319] and there must be no discrimination. The legitimate expectations of recipients are recognized by Community law,[320] though undertakings are responsible for verifying that the aid to be received is lawful.[321] If the state concerned objects to such a decision, it can challenge the legality of the decision by means of an application for annulment brought before the Court of Justice within the period laid down by Article 173 of the Treaty.

(iii) State Monopolies and Public Undertakings

Article 37(6) of the EC Treaty provided for the Commission to make recommendations on the manner in which and the timetable according to which the adjustment of state trading monopolies was to take place. Article 90(3) of the Treaty provides that the Commission shall ensure the application of the provisions of this Article and shall, where necessary, address appropriate directives or decisions to Member States. The Court of Justice has rejected arguments drawn from the structure of the Treaty to the effect that Article 90(3) empowers the Commission only to enact measures dealing with specific situations.[322]

The fact that the Commission thus plays such an important role in the enforcement of Community competition law may have major implications for adaptability of Community competition policy to harmonization with the competition policies of third states. The implication is that, in the absence of a supranational element in enforcement of their competition law, harmonization of their competition law provisions with those of the Community may in itself be inadequate for the purposes of policy harmonization.

[315] Notice C33/B/93 (NN12/94) ([1994] OJ C80/4) regarding aid which France has decided to grant to Groupe Bull.

[316] Darmon A. G. in Joined Cases C–324/90 and C–342/90 *Germany and Pleuger Worthington GmbH* v. *EC Commission* [1994] ECR I–1173, I–1194.

[317] Case C–94/87 *EC Commission* v. *Germany* [1989] ECR 175, 192 and Case C–5/89 *EC Commission* v. *Germany* [1990] ECR I–3437, I–3458.

[318] Joined Cases 205–215/82 *Deutsche Milchkontor* v. *Germany* [1983] 2633, 2665.

[319] An undertaking which could have challenged the Commission decision under Art. 173 EC and fails to do so within the period specified thereby cannot later challenge national implementing measures on grounds of the alleged illegality of the decision. See Case C–188/92 *TWD Textilwerke Deggendorf GmbH* v. *Germany* [1994] ECR I–833.

[320] Case 223/85 *Rijn-Schelde-Verolme (RSV) Maschinenfabrieken en Scheepswerven NV* v. *EC Commission* [1987] ECR 4617, 4659.

[321] Slynn A. G. (*ibid.* 4652).

[322] Joined Cases 188 to 190/80 *France, Italy and the United Kingdom* v. *EC Commission* [1982] ECR 2545, 2572–3.

4.3 FREE TRADE AGREEMENTS

Each Free Trade Agreement provided that restrictive practices of undertakings and public aid were incompatible with the Agreement concerned, in so far as trade between the Parties was affected.

In particular, Article 23(1)(i) and (ii) of the Swedish Agreement was modelled on Articles 85 and 86 of the EC Treaty respectively, though the examples of prohibited practices which are contained in these Treaty provisions were not reproduced. Nor was an equivalent to the Article 85(3) procedure for exemption from the Article 85(1) prohibition reproduced. Again, Article 23(1)(iii) of the Swedish Agreement was modelled on Article 92(1) of the EC Treaty, though no provisions corresponding to Article 92(2) and (3) of the Treaty were included in the Agreement.

On the other hand, as in the case of the other Free Trade Agreements, a declaration by the Community was annexed to the Swedish Agreement.[323] According to this declaration, Article 23(1) of the Agreement would be interpreted and applied by the Commission on the basis of the same 'principles' as Articles 85, 86, 90, and 92 of the EC Treaty.[324] This would be done in 'the autonomous implementation of Article 23(1) of the Agreement which [was] incumbent on the Contracting Parties'.[325] The legal status of this declaration was uncertain,[326] though there may have been agreement on its practical consequences. The Commission considered it to mean that Article 23(1) 'must be applied by each Party on the basis of its own law',[327] and in the Swedish Government Bill to the Parliament proposing ratification of the Agreement the comment was made that the declaration did not prevent Sweden from interpreting Article 23(1) independently.[328] The implication

[323] Declaration by the EEC concerning Art. 23(1) of the Swedish Free Trade Agreement.

[324] An equivalent declaration was attached to the Agreement between Sweden and the ECSC ([1973] OJ L350/76). Both declarations may have been designed to avoid discrimination between undertakings from EFTA States and undertakings from other third states. See E. P. Wellenstein, 'The Free Trade Agreements between the Enlarged European Communities and the EFTA-Countries' (1973) 10 *CMLRev.* 137–49, at 146.

[325] At the same time, the *Second Report on Competition Policy* (EC Commission, Brussels, 1973), 17 stressed the need for 'joint discipline' of competition in relations with the trading partners of the Community.

[326] Art. 1 of Reg. 2839/72 of 19 Dec. 1972 ([1972] JO L300/186) concluding an Agreement between the EEC and the Kingdom of Sweden and adopting provisions for its implementation provided for the texts of the Agreement and the Final Act to be annexed to the Reg. According to the Final Act, the Declaration, which was 'noted' by the representatives of Sweden and the Community, was annexed to this Act. Hence, the Declaration might said to have been part of the Reg.. See, generally, Th. Öhlinger, 'Rechtsfragen des Freihandelsabkommen zwischen Österreich und der EWG' [1974] *ZaöRV* 656–87, at 677.

[327] Reply to Written Question 152/75 ([1975] OJ C209/14) by Mr Cousté.

[328] *Kungl. Maj:ts proposition angående avtal med den europeiska ekonomiska gemenskapen, m.m., given Stockholm slott den 3 november 1972*, (Government proposal on the Free Trade Agreement) prop. 1972:135, 50. Nevertheless, it meant that internal Community practice regarding competition policy was of interest to Sweden. See *Statliga Åtgärder för tekoindustrin* (State measures for the textile and clothing industry), Ds H 1980:8, 8.

was that this provision was intended to apply to restrictive practices and aid affecting trade between the Parties, though there was little apparent interest in securing the harmonization of competition policy necessary for application of this provision to be mutually acceptable.[329]

In practice, rather than employing the Free Trade Agreements as bases for seeking to secure harmonization of competition policy throughout the EC–EFTA area, the Commission was apparently content to rely on application of Article 85 or 86 of the EC Treaty when restrictive practices by EFTA undertakings affected competition in trade between Member States or to adopt anti-dumping measures against EFTA undertakings which may have been in receipt of state aid.[330]

4.4 EUROPE AGREEMENTS

The Europe Agreements provide that restrictive practices of undertakings and public aid are incompatible therewith, insofar as trade between the Parties is affected. They also contain specific provisions regarding state monopolies and public undertakings.

4.4.1 Restrictive Practices by Undertakings

Article 63(1)(i) and (ii) of the Polish Agreement follow Article 23(1)(i) and (ii) of the Swedish Agreement. However, Article 63(2) of the Polish Agreement provides that any practices contrary to this provision shall be assessed on the basis of 'criteria' arising from the application of Articles 85 and 86 of the EC Treaty.[331] Article 63(2) of the Polish Agreement is apparently designed to regulate Polish implementation of the competition law provisions in the Europe Agreement. More particularly, it is apparently envisaged that principles in block exemption regulations in force in the Community 'shall be applied integrally' by Poland.[332] This Agreement may thus be thought to seek closer harmonization of competition policy than the Free Trade Agreements, and such harmonization may be expected to be of major importance for the future development of trading relations between the Parties.[333]

[329] In contrast, the Swedish Free Trade Agreement with the ECSC ([1973] OJ L350/76) provided in Art. 20(1) that Sweden would apply the pricing rules in Art. 60 of the ECSC Treaty even to domestic sales by the Swedish iron and steel industry.

[330] See sect. 3.3.2 above.

[331] A Joint Declaration is also attached to the Polish Agreement to the effect that when applying the criteria arising from the application of the rules of Arts 85, 86, and 92 EC, the notion of affectation of trade between Member States defined in such Arts shall be replaced by the notion of affectation of trade between the Community and Poland.

[332] Cf. Art. 6 of the Commission Proposal of 18 May 1995 concerning implementation arrangements under the Europe Agreement with the Czech Republic, COM(95)157.

[333] Though it is the 'actual implementation' of competition law which, according to the Commission, 'is a prerequisite for the smooth development of trade relations betweeen the two parties'. Cf. the Explanatory Memorandum to the Commission Proposal of 18 May 1995 concerning implementation arrangements under the Europe Agreement with the Czech Republic, COM(95)157, 2.

The search for such harmonization might be seen as a manifestation of a desire to lessen the artificial separation of competition policy from the common commercial policy of the Community or, more fundamentally, to lessen the artificial separation of Community trade liberalization from international trade liberalization. At the same time, such harmonization might have a central role to play in meeting the demand of the European Parliament that the Community should co-operate and assist in developing an efficient system of competition in Central and Eastern Europe.[334] However, very close co-operation between the Parties, involving such consistency in the application of competition law as to impose considerable demands on the emerging private sector in Poland, would apparently be necessary for Article 63(1) of the Polish Agreement to play such a role.

In this connection, particular importance may attach to the use made of Article 63(3) of the Agreement. This provision requires the Association Council to adopt, within three years of the entry into force of the Agreement, the necessary rules for the implementation of Article 63(1).[335] Such rules could provide for imposition of penalties for conduct incompatible with Article 63(1) and stipulate that agreements incompatible therewith are void. If such rules are not adopted, Article 63(1) might be treated simply as preserving Community powers to apply Articles 85 and 86 of the EC Treaty.[336]

4.4.2 State Aid

Article 63(1)(iii) of the Polish Agreement treats as incompatible with the proper functioning of the Agreement, in so far as trade between the Parties may be affected, the kind of state aid which is prohibited by Article 92(1) of the EC Treaty. While the former provision does not reproduce Article 92(2) and (3) of the EC Treaty, Article 63(2) of the Agreement does require that any practices contrary to Article 63(1)(iii) shall be assessed on the basis of criteria arising from the application of Article 92 of the EC Treaty. Further harmonization of competition policy thus seems to be envisaged.

However, the Community approach to state aid has evolved within the context of 'normal structures' and may not necessarily be well adapted to the problems of countries undergoing economic transformation.[337] In the case of such countries, the internationalization of their economies envisaged in the

[334] Resolution of 13 Dec. 1991 ([1992] OJ C13/472) on the Twentieth Report on Competition Policy, *para.* 29.

[335] See, similarly, Art. 8(3) of Prot. 2, on ECSC products, to the Polish Agreement.

[336] In fact, no provision for imposition of penalties seems currently to be envisaged, and Commission competence to apply Arts 85 and 86 EC is carefully preserved. Cf. Arts 1, 2.2 and 9.3 of the Commission Proposal of 18 May 1995 concerning implementation arrangements under the Europe Agreement with the Czech Republic, COM(95)157.

[337] K. Hailbronner, 'Legal Aspects of the Unification of the Two German States' [1991] *EJIL* 18–41, at 40.

Europe Agreements may reproduce the very conditions, notably the inability of national markets to satisfy the demands of technological development and scale economies, which led Western European countries substantially to increase aid programmes to their industry during the 1970s.[338] The pressure which such demands may entail for the authorities of countries such as Poland to grant aid may be all the greater, given that their capital markets may be perceived to be even less efficient than those of Western Europe during the 1970s.[339] In particular, financial institutions in such countries may be unable to make correct judgements about the long-term prospects of credit applicants, and so short-term cash-flow problems may lead to the closure of potentially viable firms.[340] Efforts to compensate for such financial market failures may compound the problems by being unduly responsive to lobbying by special interest groups and various political pressures.[341] The resulting distortions could allow inefficient firms to survive and even to expand.

Therefore, harmonization may require adaptation of Community practice, in order to take account of conditions in countries such as Poland. The problems to be tackled in such adaptation may be all the greater because of the range of policy issues which may be raised.

Regional Policy

According to Article 63(4)(a) of the Polish Agreement, for the first five years after the entry into force of the Agreement any aid granted by Poland shall be assessed taking into account the fact that Poland shall be regarded as an area identical to those areas of the Community described in Article 92(3)(a) of the EC Treaty, i.e., areas where the standard of living is abnormally low or where there is serious underemployment.[342] The Association Council shall, taking into account the economic situation of Poland, decide whether that period should be extended by further periods of five years.

Article 63(4)(a) of the Polish Agreement thus seeks to extend Commission

[338] P. Messerlin, 'Nonborder Measures to Assist Industry' in J. M. Finger and A. Olechowski (eds.), *The Uruguay Round* (Washington, 1987), 127–36, at 129.

[339] See, regarding the significance of such inefficiency for the development of aid programmes, P. Messerlin (*ibid.*).

[340] Lax financial discipline, inter-enterprise arrears and bad loans in the banks' portfolios entailed a chain reaction of liquidity problems making the screening of profitable and non-profitable companies difficult. See the *Third and Fourth Annual Reports on the Implementation of Community Assistance to the Countries of East and Central Europe (PHARE) in 1992 and 1993*, COM(93)13, 19.

[341] Cf., regarding the former GDR, G. Hughes and P. Hare, 'Competitiveness and Industrial Restructuring in Czechoslovakia, Hungary and Poland' in *European Economy* (Spec. Ed. No. 2, The Path of Reform in Central and Eastern Europe, EC Commission, Brussels, 1991) 83–105, at 105.

[342] Art. 29 of the Agreement on Subsidies and Countervailing Measures, in Annex 1a to the Agreement establishing the World Trade Organization, provides in the case of countries 'in the process of transformation from a centrally-planned into a market, free-enterprise economy' a 7-year period for the phasing out of otherwise unlawful subsidies.

practice under Article 92(3)(a) of the EC Treaty to Poland.[343] However, it is envisaged that, in addition to the types of aid allowed in the Community, 'aid designed to combat the specific problems of the associated countries as they undergo reform' may be permissible under the Agreement.[344]

At the same time, competition policy within the Community may be affected, in that conclusion of the Europe Agreements may be seen as necessitating action in favour of certain Community regions. For example, Protocol 1 to the Polish Agreement liberalizes trade in textiles. At the time of agreeing this Protocol, the Commission undertook to adopt measures to improve and modernize the textile industry within the Community and to promote its competitiveness,[345] particularly in the regions most affected by such liberalization.[346]

Sectoral Policy

Competition provisions of the Polish Agreement itself do not apply to products covered by the ECSC Treaty, which are the subject of Protocol 2 to the Agreement.[347] Article 8(2) of the Protocol provides that practices contrary to Article 8(1)(iii) thereof, the equivalent of Article 63(1)(iii) of the Agreement itself, shall be assessed on the basis of the criteria arising from the Community rules on state aid, including secondary legislation.[348]

As regards ECSC steel products, Article 8(4) of the Protocol envisages some relaxation of these criteria. According to this provision, the Parties recognize that during the first five years after the entry into force of the Agreement, and by derogation from Article 8(1)(iii), Poland may exceptionally grant aid for restructuring purposes provided that:

[343] The implication being that countries like Poland are to be treated, at least for 5 years, as belonging to the 'periphery of Europe'. Cf. H. Kramer, 'The EC and the Stabilisation of Eastern Europe' [1992] *Aussenpolitik* 12–21, at 13.

[344] Report from the Council to the Essen European Council on a strategy to prepare for accession of the associated CCEE, *Europe Doc.* No. 1916 (14 Dec. 1994), 4.

[345] Such 'compensation' may be the condition imposed by Member States for the relaxation of 'hard core' national quotas. See G. Koopman and H. -E. Scharrer, *Scenarios of a Common External Trade Policy for the EC after 1992* (Institut für Wirtschaftsforschung Report No. 84, Hamburg, 1990), 13.

[346] *European Report*, No. 1708 (2 Oct. 1991). See, regarding the measures envisaged, *Improving the Competitiveness of the Community's Textile and Clothing Industry*, COM(91)399. The result was the Retex initiative. See Notice to the Member States laying down guidelines for operational programmes which Member States are invited to establish within the framework of a Community initiative for regions heavily dependent on the textiles and clothing sector ([1992] OJ C142/5). Cf., regarding completion of the customs union with Turkey and the question of Community support for the restructuring of the Greek textiles industry, Commission Reply by Mr Bangemann to Written Question E–1169/95 ([1995] OJ C213/37) by Yannos Kranidiotis.

[347] Art. 63(8) of the Polish Agreement.

[348] Dec. 2064/86 of 30 June 1986 ([1986] OJ L177/1) establishing Community rules for state aid to the coal industry, which has been replaced by Dec. 3632/93 of 28 Dec. 1993 ([1993] OJ L329/12) establishing Community rules for state aid to the coal industry; and Dec. 3855/91 of 27 Nov. 1991 ([1991] OJ L362/57) establishing Community rules for aid to the steel industry.

—the restructuring programme is linked to a global rationalization and reduction of steel-producing capacity in Poland;
—it leads to the viability of the recipient firms under normal market conditions at the end of the restructuring period; and
—the amount and intensity of such aid are strictly limited to what is absolutely necessary in order to restore such viability and are progressively reduced.

The Association Council shall, taking into account the economic situation of Poland, decide whether the period of five years may be extended.[349]

This relaxation of Community policy regarding state aid to the steel industry is said to take into account the particular difficulties of Poland in restructuring the steel sector[350] and the fact that this process has been launched very recently.[351] It is comparable with Commission recognition that the steel industry of the former GDR would need to undergo substantial restructuring, if its viability and its integration into the common market were to be ensured.[352] To meet this need, Germany was authorized to grant investment aid on condition that the aim was to render this industry competitive without increasing capacity,[353] though vitally needed reconstruction of the economy should not be used as an excuse artificially to increase production in this sector.[354] The implication is that strict application of the special rules in Protocol 2 to the Polish Agreement will be sought.

Horizontal Policy

No specific reference is made to horizontal aid in the Polish Agreement. However, it seems that control of such aid may have to be relaxed.[355] In the case of environmental aid, the 'polluter pays' principle might be difficult to uphold as a justification for expecting undertakings in Central and East

[349] According to a Declaration by the Community concerning Art. 8(4) of Prot. 2, it is understood that the possibility of an exceptional extension of the 5-year period is strictly limited to the particular case of Poland and does not impair the position of the Community in relation to other cases nor prejudge international commitments. However, the same declaration is also attached to the Agreements with Hungary, the Czech Republic, and Slovakia.

[350] Exceptionally restructuring aid may be permitted within the Community under Art. 95 ECSC. See, e.g., *Restructuring of the Italian Public Steel Industry*, SEC(91)930.

[351] Declaration by the Community concerning Art. 8(4) of Prot. 2 to the Polish Agreement.

[352] It is also comparable with the approach adopted to shipbuilding aid in the former GDR. If, however, respect for restructuring requirements proved difficult to secure within the Community (sect. 4.2.2 above), the difficulty of securing it within the framework of a Europe Agreement may be expected to be all the greater.

[353] *The European Community and German Unification*, Bull. EC, Supp. 4/90, 74–5.

[354] Report of the Committee on Economic and Monetary Affairs and Industrial Policy on the *Twentieth Report on Competition Policy*, EP Doc. A3–0338/91, 18.

[355] Existing Commission practice does take some account of regional considerations in evaluation of the acceptability of horizontal aid. See, e.g., regarding environmental aid in Saxony-Anhalt, Bull. EU 10–1994, 1.2.38 and regarding R & D aid in Berlin, *ibid.* 1.2.44.

European countries[356] themselves to bear the costs of complying with improved environmental standards.[357] In the case of research and development aid, the fact that innovation by Community standards may not be the intended result of aid does not necessarily preclude the possibility that technological development of considerable importance for such countries could result.[358] In other words, 'the high positive externalities', which the Commission accepts as justifying aid within the Community, may be present.[359] At the same time, however, uncontrolled use of horizontal aid in these countries could seriously endanger the competitive position of Community undertakings.

Such problems are merely examples of those which may arise in state aid control under the Europe Agreements. Whether or not Commission decisions concerning aid under the EC Treaty are always consistent with each other, consistency of decision-making under these Agreements may be difficult to achieve, given the economic and other differences between the Parties.

4.4.3 State Monopolies and Public Undertakings

Article 32 of the Polish Agreement requires the Member States and Poland progressively to adjust any state monopolies of a commercial character so as to ensure that, by the end of the fifth year following the entry into force of this Agreement, no discrimination regarding the conditions under which goods are procured and marketed exists between nationals of the Member States and of Poland.

Article 65 of the same Agreement deals, more generally, with public undertakings and undertakings to which special or exclusive rights have been granted. It requires that, as from the third year following the date of entry

[356] Cf. the acceptability of aid to an undertaking in the former GDR to enable the undertaking to meet environmental standards, given 'the former omissions' in Notice C61/94 (N375/94) ([1995] OJ C113/5) concerning aid which the German Government intends to grant to Sächsische Olefinwerke GmbH, Böhlen.

[357] The need for such compliance may have increased importance, because the 'polluter pays' principle may be enforced through the extraterritoriality of legislation in neighbouring countries. See, e.g., regarding new German legislation, W. C. Hoffman, 'Germany's New Environmental Liability Act: Strict Liability for Facilities Causing Pollution' [1991] *Netherlands International Law Review* 27–41.

[358] Certainly, the Commission may authorize 'technical rationalization' aid in the former GDR, given 'the omissions of the former system to invest in necessary equipment, neglected maintenance and repair and outdated equipment'. See Notice C61/94 (N375/94) ([1995] OJ C113/5) concerning aid which the German Government intends to grant to Buna GmbH. Cf. the argument regarding the promotion of technology transfer to less developed regions of the Community in the Opinion of the Economic and Social Committee of 25 Sept. 1991 ([1991] OJ C339/6) on The Regions in the 1990s—Fourth Periodic Report on the Social and Economic Situation and Development of the Regions of the Community, para. 4.11.

[359] *Preparation of the Associated Countries of Central and Eastern Europe for Integration into the Internal Market of the Union*, COM(95)163, Annex, 50.

into force of this Agreement, the principles of the EC Treaty, notably Article 90, and the principles of the concluding document of the April 1990 Bonn meeting of the Conference on Security and Co-operation in Europe[360] (notably entrepreneurs' freedom of decision) should be upheld.

Such provisions may be expected to provide a boost to privatization in countries such as Poland. Commission practice, which may allow for account to be taken of the 'burden of the past', might also be expected to be favourable to such privatization. For example, aid was approved for the Portuguese chemical firm EPSI, because it partially covered an unfavourable financial structure from which the company had suffered since its formation prior to Portuguese accession to the Community.[361] More particularly, aid to 'secure the existence of companies until privatization'[362] or to facilitate adaptation of a company to the market and thus to make its privatization possible may be permissible in the former GDR.[363]

In reality, however, the relationship between the competition law provisions of the Polish Agreement and privatization may be more complicated.[364] Privatization may entail distortions of competition,[365] particularly where productive assets in manufacturing and agriculture[366] are involved and the value of these assets may not easily be determined.[367] A result could be that the economies of Central and Eastern European countries become dominated by a few giant firms, including some of Western European origin.[368] In other words, while such provisions might favour an increased role for the private sector, they do not necessarily mean that this sector will be competitive.

[360] [1990] ILM 1053.

[361] Bull. EC 10–1991, 1.2.32.

[362] Notice C4/94, C61/94, C62/94, NN2/95, NN3/95 and N467/95 ([1995] OJ C203/6) concerning aid the German Government intends to grant to Sächsische Olefinwerke GmbH, Leuna-Werke GmbH, and Buna GmbH.

[363] Notice C62/94 (N376/94) ([1995] OJ C113/13) concerning aid the German Government intends to grant to Sächsische Olefinwerke GmbH, Bohlen.

[364] Cf. the argument that market reforms, at least those which take place within a state which continues to be treated by Community anti-dumping law as a non-market economy, may result in increased exposure of exporters from that state to anti-dumping duties (X. Su, 'EC Anti-dumping Law Applicable to China—A Special Problem', a paper presented at a conference on *Transformation and Integration* in Umeå in June 1992).

[365] Cf., regarding the privatizing activities of the Treuhandanstalt, Notice C58/91 ([1992] OJ C73/2) concerning aid awarded by the German Government to Carl Zeiss Jena Jenoptik and Jenaer Glaswerk.

[366] T. Gruszecki and J. Winiecki, 'Privatization in East-Central Europe: A Comparative Perspective' [1991] *Aussenwirtschaft* 67–100.

[367] House of Lords Select Committee on the European Communities, *European Agreements with Poland, Hungary and the Czech and Slovak Federal Republic*, HL(1990–91) 35, App. 9, Visit of Sub-Committee A to Prague, 17–18 Jan. 1991. See also T. Gruszecki and J. Winiecki, n. 366 above, 80.

[368] Report of the Committee on Economic and Monetary Affairs and Industrial Policy on the Twentieth Report on Competition Policy, EP Doc. A3–0338/91, 19.

4.4.4 Procedures

It is uncertain whether procedural arrangements in the Europe Agreements will enable the Parties satisfactorily to tackle the problems of harmonization in the competition policy field.

National Administrative Enforcement

The Polish Agreement apparently relies heavily on national administrative enforcement of the competition provisions contained therein.[369] In the case of anti-competitive conduct by undertakings, a distinction is made between existing agreements and restrictive practices that may be adopted in the future.

Arrangements regarding the former are contained in a Joint Declaration attached to the Agreement.[370] According to the Declaration, the Association Council shall establish appropriate measures to ensure that all agreements covered by Article 63(1) of the Agreement which affect trade between the Parties and which predate the entry into force of the Agreement will be dealt with in a manner similar to that provided for in Article 7 of Regulation 17.[371]

As regards future restrictive practices, Article 63(3) of the Agreement requires that, within three years of the entry into force of the Agreement, the necessary implementing rules shall be introduced. Until such rules are introduced, the provisions of the Agreement on interpretation and application of Articles VI, XVI, and XXIII of GATT[372] shall be applied.

In the case of aid, Article 63(4)(b) of the Agreement requires each Party to ensure transparency, *inter alia*, by reporting annually to the other Party on the total amount and the distribution of the aid given and by providing, upon request, information on aid schemes. Upon request by one Party, the other Party shall also provide information on particular individual cases of aid. More generally, Article 63(7) provides that, notwithstanding any provision to the contrary adopted in conformity with paragraph 3, the Parties shall exchange information taking into account the limitations imposed by the requirements of professional and business secrecy.[373] Presumably, such reports and information are designed to enable each Party to determine whether the other Party is satisfactorily controlling aid within its jurisdiction. To render such control

[369] See, similarly, the Agreement between the European Communities and the Government of the United States of America regarding the application of their competition laws ([1995] OJ L95/47). The Commission envisages 'sharing the work of enforcement between the parties in accordance with their capabilities'. See *Co-operation with the United States of America regarding the application of their competition rules*, COM(94)430, Annex I, 4.

[370] Joint Declaration No. 11, para. 1.

[371] Of 6 Feb. 1962 ([1962] JO 204) first reg. implementing Arts 85 and 86 of the Treaty. Art. 7 dealt with restrictive practices in existence at the date of entry into force of the Reg.

[372] BISD, 26th Supp., 56.

[373] According to a Joint Declaration annexed to the Agreement, the Parties shall not make improper use of provisions on professional secrecy to prevent the disclosure of information in the field of competition.

feasible in countries such as Poland, the Commission stresses that such countries should 'adopt a system similar to that of the Community with a national authority endowed with monitoring power'.[374]

National Judicial Enforcement

National judicial enforcement is treated as a future possibility in the Polish Agreement. According to a Joint Declaration attached thereto,[375] the Parties may request the Association Council at a later stage, and after the adoption of the implementing rules referred to in Article 63(3), to examine to what extent and under which conditions certain competition rules may be directly applicable in national judicial proceedings, taking into account the progress made in the integration process between the Community and Poland.[376] However, national courts in the Community have only a limited role in enforcing the prohibition of state aid, since Article 92 has been interpreted by the Court of Justice as not being applicable by them.[377] It is unlikely that a greater role for Polish courts is envisaged under the Polish Agreement.

Co-operative Enforcement

The Polish Agreement envisages a role for the Association Council in securing cooperative enforcement of competition law. According to Article 63(3), the Association Council is to adopt implementing rules for Article 63(1) and (2). In relation to aid, the Association Council shall, taking into account the economic situation of Poland, decide whether the period provided for in Article 63(4)(a)[378] should be extended by further periods of five years. In the case of state monopolies of a commercial character, the Council is to be informed about their adjustment under Article 32. In the case of public undertakings, Article 65 requires that the Council is to ensure that EC Treaty principles are upheld as from the third year after entry into force of the Agreement.

More particularly, consultation is to take place in the Association Council prior to adoption by a Party of safeguard measures under Article 63(6).[379] The implication is that questions of the compatibility of a restrictive practice or an aid measure with Article 63(1) of the Agreement may be raised within the Council.

[374] *Preparation of the Associated Countries of Central and Eastern Europe for Integration into the Internal Market of the Union*, COM(95)163, Annex, 53–54.

[375] Joint Declaration No. 11, para. 3.

[376] The Commission considers that 'to a large extent' reliance must be placed on 'viable' national rules. See *Relations with the Associated Countries of Central and Eastern Europe Task Force on Approximation of National Laws*, COM(94)391, 3.

[377] Section 4.2.4 above.

[378] See sect. 4.4.2 above.

[379] Art. 63(7) provides that, notwithstanding any provision to the contrary adopted in conformity with Art. 63(3), the Parties shall exchange information taking into account the limitations imposed by the requirements of professional and business secrecy.

This implication is confirmed by the Commission proposals regarding implementing rules to be adopted under Article 63(6). According to the proposals, when one Party is dealing with a competition case which comes within the competence of both Parties[380] or may affect the important interests of the other Party,[381] the latter is to be notified, and copies of the notifications are to be submitted to the Association Council.[382] If a mutually accetable solution does not emerge, an exchange of views is to take place in the same Council,[383] which 'may make appropriate recommendations for the settlement of these cases'.[384] Moreover, if neither the Commission nor the Polish authorities consider themselves competent to handle a case under their respective legislation, an exchange of views shall take place in the Council, and the latter may again make appropriate recommendations.[385] Similar procedures may be employed where there are 'significant changes' in the competition policy of one of the Parties.[386]

These proposed procedures are designed to avoid prejudicing the existing competences of the Commission. Thus it is expressly stipulated that they are without prejudice to Article 63(6)[387] and to 'any action under the respective competition laws in force in the territory of the Parties'.[388] That their real purpose is to facilitate Polish adaptation to existing Community competition policy is implied by a less formal Commission suggestion. The latter suggestion envisages 'associating the Commission on a voluntary basis with decision shaping' by the authorities of Central and East European countries.[389]

4.5 EEA AGREEMENT

The EEA Agreement goes further than the Free Trade Agreements and the Europe Agreements in seeking to secure harmonization of competition policy.

4.5.1 Restrictive Practices by Undertakings

Article 53 of the EEA Agreement reproduces the terms of Article 85 of the EC Treaty, though 'the territory covered by this Agreement' substitutes 'the common market', and 'trade between Contracting Parties' takes the place of 'trade between Member States'. Similarly, Article 54 of the Agreement

[380] Cf. Art. 2.1.1 of the Commission Proposal of 18 May 1995 concerning implementation arrangements under the Europe Agreement with the Czech Republic, COM(95)157.

[381] *Ibid.*, Art. 3. [382] *Ibid.*, Art. 2.1.3. [383] *Ibid.*, Art. 9.1.

[384] *Ibid.*, Art. 9.2. [385] *Ibid.*, Art. 10. [386] *Ibid.*, Art. 6.

[387] *Ibid.* [388] *Ibid.*, Art. 9.3.

[389] *Preparation of the Associated Countries of Central and Eastern Europe for Integration into the Internal Market of the Union*, COM(95)163, Annex, 51.

embodies the terms of Article 86 of the EC Treaty, though again it is trade between the Contracting Parties to the Agreement which must be likely to be affected and competition within the territory covered by the Agreement which must be distorted. Article 57(1) adds that concentrations which create or strengthen a dominant position as a result of which competition would be significantly impeded within the territory covered by this Agreement or a substantial part of it shall be declared incompatible with the Agreement.

The impact of these provisions on larger EFTA companies may be limited. Because of their trading activity in the Community such companies were, even before entry into force of the EEA Agreement, subject to Community competition law in much the same way as Community companies.[390] Only to the extent that the new provisions result in more account being taken of competitive conditions on the EC–EFTA market in the application of competition policy is there likely to be an impact on such companies.

On the other hand, these provisions may also apply to practices only affecting trade between EFTA States. In accordance with the case law of the Court of Justice embodied in the Agreement,[391] agreements between two undertakings in the same EFTA State and relating only to trade therein will be treated as affecting trade between EFTA States where they are part of a network or networks of agreements effectively 'sewing up' the market in the state concerned and thereby impeding trade with other EFTA States.

In connection with restrictive practices by undertakings, therefore, the EEA Agreement may be expected to be at least as significant in promoting competition within the EFTA area and, more particularly, within individual EFTA States as in promoting competition in EC–EFTA trade.[392] Such states may exhibit a relatively high degree of regulation and weak domestic competition in certain sectors.[393] The EEA Agreement implies the opening up of these sectors to competition. However, adjustment strains might be engendered, which could, in turn, stretch the willingness of such states to participate in developing a harmonized competition policy for the EEA as a whole. If such harmonization does not take place, the application of competition law regarding restrictive practices of undertakings in EC–EFTA trade may remain

[390] See, e.g., Case 238/87 *Volvo AB* v. *Erik Veng (UK) Ltd* [1988] ECR 624.

[391] See sect. 2.2.1 above.

[392] Economic analysis also suggests the importance of the EEA for increasing competition within EFTA States. See, e.g., V. Norman, 'EFTA and the Internal European Market' [1989] *Economic Policy* 423–65. Indeed, it has been argued that for countries such as Norway the main advantage of participation in European integration is that achievement of domestic policy changes and structural adjustments which are needed in any case are made politically easier. See J. I. Haaland, 'Comparative Advantage, Terms of Trade and Welfare Effects of European Integration: Some Preliminary Assessments' [1992] *Scandinavian Journal of Economics* 373–91.

[393] Cf., regarding Sweden, *Commission Opinion on Sweden's Application for Membership*, Bull. EC, Supp. 5/92, 9.

dependent on the perceived requirements of the 'internal' competition policies of the Parties.[394]

4.5.2 State Aid

Article 61(1) of the EEA Agreement is substantially identical to Article 92(1) of the EC Treaty. According to the former provision, any aid granted by Member States, EFTA States, or through state resources in any form whatsoever which distorts or threatens to distort competition by favouring certain undertakings or the production of certain goods shall, in so far as it affects trade between Contracting Parties, be incompatible with the functioning of the Agreement. Moreover, Article 61(2) of the EEA Agreement follows Article 92(2) of the EC Treaty, and Article 61(3) follows Article 92(3) of the EC Treaty.[395] According to a Joint Declaration annexed to the EEA Agreement, the Contracting Parties declare that, in establishing whether a derogation can be granted under Article 61(3)(b) of the Agreement, the Commission shall take the interest of the EFTA States into account and the ESA shall take the interest of the Community into account.[396] Finally, Article 61(3)(d) allows for other categories of aid to be authorized by the EEA Joint Committee.

In addition, various Community enactments relating to state aid and other 'instruments' adopted by the Commission, such as those concerning aid to textiles, environmental aid, and aid to research and development, are included in Annex XV[397] to the Agreement. The latter kind of instruments has an uncertain status within the Community,[398] and they are listed in the Annex as 'acts which the EC Commission and the ESA shall take due account of'.

However, conditions particular to the EFTA States as well as the technical complexities involved in the operation of competition law provisions and the impact of various policy considerations on their operation suggest that the application of EEA law in this area may not be without problems.

Regional Policy

The EEA Agreement seeks a balance between application of competition law and recognition of regional disparities. According to the Preamble to the Agreement, the Parties aim to promote a harmonious development of the European Economic Area and are convinced of the need to contribute to the

[394] Cf. the position of the Commission that aid incompatible with the common market is, for that reason, also incompatible with the functioning of the EEA Agreement in Dec. 95/253 ([1995] OJ L159/21) on aid awarded by the French Government to Allied Signal Fibres Europe SA, Longwy, Meurthe-et-Moselle.

[395] In its version prior to amendment by the TEU.

[396] Joint Declaration on Art. 61(3)(b) of the Agreement.

[397] On state aid.

[398] Darmon A. G. in Case 310/85 *Deufil* v. *EC Commission* [1987] ECR 901, 914.

reduction of the economic and social regional disparities.[399] Article 115 confirms their commitment to reduce such disparities.

To this end, Article 116 provides for the establishment by the EFTA States of a Financial Mechanism, and more detailed provisions governing the mechanism are set out in Protocol 38 to the Agreement.[400] This Protocol, as amended by Article 16 of the Protocol Adjusting the EEA Agreement,[401] provides for the grant of assistance in the form of grants and interest rebates.[402] Over a period of five years the total amount of grants provided is to be ECU 500 million,[403] and the total volume of loans to be eligible for interest rebates[404] over the same period is to be ECU 1,500 million.[405] Finance is to be provided by the EFTA States,[406] and operations are to be administered by the European Investment Bank (EIB).[407] Assistance is to be limited to projects in Greece, the Island of Ireland, Portugal, and the regions of Spain listed in the Appendix to the Protocol.[408] Priority is to be given to projects which place particular emphasis on the environment (including urban development), on transport (including transport infrastructure), or on education and training. Among projects submitted by private enterprises, special consideration is to be given to small and medium-sized enterprises. The maximum grant element for any project supported by the Financial Mechanism shall be fixed at a level which is not inconsistent with Community policies in this regard.[409]

However, just as the Community itself may only grant aid, including aid from the Structural Funds,[410] on condition that competition law requirements in the EC Treaty are respected,[411] so the EFTA Financial Mechanism must

[399] 6th recital. Moreover, in Prot. 42, on Bilateral Agreements concerning Specific Agricultural Products, the Contracting Parties take note that at the same time as this Agreement, bilateral agreements on trade in agricultural products have been signed. These agreements, which develop or supplement agreements made earlier by the Contracting Parties, and reflect, *inter alia*, their agreed common objective to contribute to the reduction of social and economic disparities between their regions, were to enter into force, at the latest, at the time of entry into force of the EEA Agreement.

[400] Art. 117 of the EEA Agreement.

[401] [1994] OJ L1/572.

[402] Art. 1(2) of Prot. 38, on the Financial Mechanism.

[403] *Ibid.*, Art. 3(1).

[404] The percentage fixed for the interest rebates was reduced from 3 per cent to 2 per cent by Art. 16 of the Adjustment Prot.

[405] Art. 2(5) of Prot. 38.

[406] According to an exchange of letters annexed to the EEA Agreement, the EFTA States agreed to calculate their respective contributions to the Financial Mechanism based on the GNP at market price data for the 3 most recent years. See, regarding arrangements for operation of the Co-operation Agreement concluded between the EFTA States and the EIB, EFTA Standing Committee Dec. 4/94 of 10 Jan. 1994 ([1994] OJ L85/79) establishing a financial mechanism committee.

[407] Art. 1(2) of Prot. 38.

[408] *Ibid.*, Art. 4(1). Allocations are to be determined for a 5-year period in the light of the beneficiary region's relative level of economic development and population size and other relevant factors. See Art. 8 of Reg. 2894/94 of 28 Nov. 1994 ([1994] OJ L305/6) concerning arrangements for implementation of the Agreement on the European Economic Area.

[409] Art. 4(2) of Prot. 38.

[410] i.e., the Guidance Section of the EAGGF, the ERDF, and the ESF.

[411] Art. 7(1) of Reg. 2052/88 of 24 June 1988 ([1988] OJ L185/9) on the tasks of the Structural Funds and their effectiveness and on the co-ordination of their activities between themselves and

respect the corresponding requirements of the EEA Agreement. According to a Joint Declaration annexed to the Agreement, the Contracting Parties declare that financial support to undertakings financed by the Community Structural Funds or receiving assistance from the European Investment Bank or from any similar financial instrument or fund[412] shall be in keeping with the state aid provisions of this Agreement. They declare that exchange of information and views on such support shall take place at the request of either surveillance authority.[413]

The challenges which regional problems pose for the application of EEA competition law may, however, be more fundamental than is suggested by the terms of this declaration. For example, regional problems in rural parts of Norway may differ from those on which the regional policy of the Community has traditionally concentrated. They may not necessarily manifest themselves in low GDP figures or even in high unemployment rates in comparison with Community averages. Rather, they may lie in the threat of rural depopulation, if aid to such areas is withdrawn.

The challenges are underlined in the Commission *Opinion on Norway's Application for EU Membership*, where the Commission raised objections to the level of regional aid granted in Norway as well as to the operating character of some such aid.[414] On the other hand, given the accession of Finland and Sweden to the Union, the Commission recognizes that the climatic and demographic features specific to arctic and subarctic regions need to be taken into account in Community structural policies.[415] To the extent that these policies and competition policy must be consistent, the implication is that such features may also have to be taken into account in development of the latter.[416] The further implication is that the harmonization

with the operations of the EIB and the other existing financial instruments, as amended by Reg. 2081/93 of 20 July 1993 ([1993] OJ L193/5), requires that measures financed by Community aid shall be compatible 'with Community policies, including those concerning rules on competition'. This condition may be a source of tension between different Directorates General of the Commission. See, e.g., *Agence Europe* No. 5644 (11 Jan. 1992). See, for an example of modification of competition law requirements to accommodate common agricultural policy requirements regarding the grant of Community aid, the Communication regarding state aid for investments in the processing and marketing of agricultural products ([1995] OJ C71/6).

412 This Declaration presumably applies not only in relation to the new Financial Mechanism but also in relation to financial instruments in the EFTA States, such as the Nordic Industrial Fund.

413 I.e., the European Commission or the ESA.

414 Bull. EC, Supp. 2/93, 24.

415 See, regarding Sweden, the *Opinion on Sweden's Application for EU Membership*, Bull. EC, Supp. 5/92, 14. See, regarding Finland, the *Opinion on Finland's Application for EU Membership*, Bull. EC, Supp. 6/92, 14.

416 The issues were not formally resolved in Accession negotiations, though in relation to agriculture, Art. 142 of the Accession Agreement authorizes operating aid north of the 62nd parallel. Moreover, in connection with distribution of Community aid, a new Objective 6 was agreed for the Structural Funds for regions with a population density of fewer than 8 inhabitants per km^2. See Prot. 6 to the Accession Agreement, as substituted by Art. 52 of Dec. 95/1 of 1 Jan. 1995 ([1995] OJ L1/1) adjusting the instruments concerning the accession of new Member States to the European Union.

of competition policy envisaged in the EEA Agreement may depend on modifications of Community (and not only EFTA) practice.

Confirmation of this implication is provided by a Joint Declaration annexed to the Agreement.[417] In this Declaration the Contracting Parties take note that, even if eligibility of a region for state aid has to be denied in the context of Article 61(3)(a) of the Agreement and according to the first stage of analysis under subparagraph (c), examination according to other criteria, such as very low population density, is possible.

From this Declaration, which relates to the 1988 Commission Communication concerning regional aid within the Community,[418] the ESA draws the conclusion that 'a very low population density' may qualify a region under Article 61(3)(a).[419] It cannot be assumed that this conclusion will be acceptable to the Commission.[420] Rural areas in Scotland, which may have much in common with those in Norway (though not necessarily in terms of *per capita* GDP), have traditionally been treated as being covered by Article 92(3)(c) rather than Article 92(3)(a) of the EC Treaty.[421] In the case of rural Norwegian areas having a higher *per capita* GDP[422] than rural areas of Scotland, it is doubtful whether the Commission would agree to their treatment as being eligible for aid under Article 61(3)(a) of the EEA Agreement. In this connection, therefore, harmonization of competition policy may be problematic.[423]

On the other hand, the ESA has also relied on the Joint Declaration to adapt previous Commission practice to the perceived requirements of Article 61(3)(c) of the EEA Agreement. According to the ESA,[424] a region where the population density is less than 12.5 per square kilometre may, on this

[417] Joint Declaration on Art. 61(3)(c) of the EEA Agreement. The Swedish Government regarded the Declaration as indicating Community recognition of the particular nature of regional problems in Sweden, which would affect future Community treatment of regional aid in this country. See *Europeisk ekonomiska samarbetsområdet*, prop. 1991/92:170, *del* 3, bil. 9, 34.

[418] Sect. 4.2.2 above.

[419] Para. 28.1.3 of Dec. 4/94/COL of 19 Jan. 1994 ([1994] OJ C231/1) on the adoption and issuing of the Procedural and Substantive Rules in the Field of State Aid (Guidelines on the application and interpretation of Arts 61 and 62 of the EEA Agreement and Art. 1 of Prot. 3 to the Suveillance and Court Agreement).

[420] Cf. Changes to the method for the application of Art. 92(3)(a) EC to regional aid ([1994] OJ C364/8), para. 1.1.

[421] Only as their *per capita* GDP has fallen towards the 75 per cent level has the possibility arisen that they may be treated as Art. 92(3)(a) regions. Reg. 2081/93 of 20 July 1993 ([1993] OJ L193/5) amends Annex I to Reg. 2052/88, so as to classify them as Objective 1 regions for the purposes of allocations from the Structural Funds. The possible implication is that they will now also be treated as regions covered by Art. 92(3)(a). However, Hainault in Belgium, which has also become an Objective 1 region, is still treated as being covered by Art. 92(3)(c) of the Treaty. See the *Twenty-Fourth Report on Competition Policy*, COM(95)142, 524.

[422] Cf. the Swedish figures published in *Norbotten inför EG-förhandlingen* (Länstyrelsen Norbottens län, 1992).

[423] Finnmark and the four most northerly municipalities of Troms have been found by the ESA to be covered by Art. 61(3)(a) of the Agreement. See *European Report*, No. 1994 (19 Nov. 1994).

[424] Dec. 88/94/COL of 20 July 1994 ([1994] OJ L240/33) on the second amendment of the Procedural and Substantive Rules in the Field of State Aid, para. 28.2.3.1.

ground alone, be found eligible for aid under the first stage of the test applied under Article 61(3)(c) of the Agreement. The Commission has similarly adapted its own practice under Article 92(3)(c) of the EC Treaty.[425] These adaptations are justified by both the ESA and the Commission on the grounds that the other indicators used in the first stage do not properly reflect regional problems specific to certain Contracting Parties, particularly the Nordic countries. These problems result from geography—the remote northern location of some areas, harsh weather conditions and very long distances inside the borders of the country concerned—and from the very low population density in some parts.

More particularly, it is recognized by both surveillance authorities that such problems may induce firms to relocate to less remote areas or dissuade them from locating in remote areas. Hence, partial compensation for the additional transport costs of undertakings in such areas, provided their population density is less than 12.5 per square kilometre, may be authorized.[426] To this extent, objections to operating aid in regions outside the scope of Article 92(3)(a) of the EC treaty or Article 61(3)(a) of the EEA Agreement have been lifted.[427]

Sectoral Policy

Harmonization of competition policy regarding state aid under the EEA Agreement may be complicated by inclusion in the Agreement of special provisions concerning certain sectors.

(i) Transport

Article 51(1) of the EEA Agreement, which follows Article 80(1) of the EC Treaty, provides that imposition of rates and conditions involving any element of support or protection in the interest of the transport undertakings involved is prohibited unless authorized.[428] According to Article 50(2), in considering whether to grant an authorization, the competent authority, i.e., the Commission or the ESA, is to take account in particular of the requirements of an appropriate regional economic policy, the needs of underdeveloped areas and the problems of areas seriously affected by political circumstances, on the one hand, and of the effects of such rates and conditions on competition on the other. Moreover, Article 49 of the Agreement, which follows Article 77 of the EC Treaty, provides that transport aid shall be compatible with the Agreement

[425] Changes to the method for the application of Art. 92(3)(c) EC to regional aid ([1994] OJ C364/8), paras. 2.5–6.

[426] Changes to the method for the application of Art. 92(3)(c) EC to regional aid ([1994] OJ C364/8), para. 6. According to the Swedish Government, the Commission also agreed that a reduction in employers' social security charges might be authorized in such areas as 'indirect' transport aid (*Sveriges medlemskap i Europeiska unionen*, prop. 1994/95:19, 363) or as aid 'fulfilling the same conditions' (*ibid.* 370).

[427] See sect. 4.2.2 above.

[428] Art. 51(3) of the EEA Agreement provides that the prohibition in paragraph one shall not apply to tariffs fixed to meet competition.

if it meets the needs of co-ordination of transport or if it represents a reimbursement for the discharge of certain obligations inherent in the concept of a public service.

(ii) Fisheries

The EEA Agreement does not, in principle, apply to EC–EFTA trade in agricultural and fisheries products. However, Article 4(1) of Protocol 9 to the Agreement, on Trade in Fish and Other Marine Products, provides that aid granted through state resources to the fisheries sector which distorts competition shall be abolished.[429] According to a Joint Declaration annexed to the Agreement, any distortion of competition in this sector is to be assessed by the Contracting Parties in the context of Articles 92 and 93 of the EC Treaty and in relation to relevant provisions of Community law concerning the fishery policy[430] and the content of the joint declaration regarding Article 61(3)(c) of the Agreement.

(iii) Steel

Article 5 of Protocol 14 to the EEA Agreement, on Trade in Coal and Steel Products, provides that the Contracting Parties shall comply with Community rules for aid to the steel industry.[431] They recognized, in particular, the relevance and acceptance of the rules for aid to the steel industry laid down in Decision 322/89,[432] which expired on 31 December 1991. They also declared their commitment to integrate into the EEA Agreement new Community rules for aid to the steel industry[433] by the entry into force of the Agreement, provided that they were substantially similar to the earlier measure.

Aid to steel firms is strictly limited by such rules. Only research and development aid, environmental protection aid, and certain forms of closure aid may be granted by any Member State. Regional investment aids are prohibited in most Member States, including Italy. Hence, the Commission found in Decision 91/547,[434] which concerned aid granted by the Autonomous Region of Sardinia to Ferriere Acciaierie Sarde, that no regional investment aid could be granted to steel firms located on the island. The fact that Sardinia

[429] Moreover, Art. 4(2) of Prot. 9 provides that legislation relating to the market organization in the fisheries sector shall be adjusted so as not to distort competition.

[430] Note, in particular, Reg. 4028/86 of 18 Dec. 1986 ([1986] OJ L376/7) on Community measures to improve and adapt structures in the fisheries and aquaculture sector.

[431] The framework for certain steel sectors not covered by the ECSC Treaty ([1988] OJ C320/3) is also included among the Community acts listed in Annex XV to the Agreement.

[432] Dec. 322/89 of 1 Feb. 1989 ([1989] OJ L38/8) establishing Community rules for aid to the steel industry.

[433] These new rules are laid down in Dec. 3855/91 of 27 Nov. 1991 ([1991] OJ L362/57) establishing Community rules for aid to the steel industry.

[434] Of 5 June 1991 ([1991] OJ L298/1) concerning aid granted by the Autonomous Region of Sardinia to Ferriere Acciaierie Sarde.

might have had special geographic or socio-economic features did not justify the grant of such aid to one of its steel firms.

(iv) Shipbuilding

The EEA Agreement allows some relaxation of competition law provisions in relation to aid to shipbuilding.[435] According to a Joint Declaration on Shipbuilding, annexed to the Agreement, the Contracting Parties agreed that, until the expiry of the Seventh Directive on shipbuilding,[436] i.e., at the end of 1993, they would refrain from application of the general rules on state aid laid down in Article 61 of the Agreement to the shipbuilding sector, and this Directive was not originally listed in Annex XV. It was also declared, however, that Article 62(2) of the Agreement as well as the Protocols referring to state aid were applicable to this sector. Thus some harmonization was implicitly envisaged.

The implication was confirmed by a Declaration by the European Community on Shipbuilding, also annexed to the Agreement. According to this Declaration, it was the agreed policy of the Community progressively to reduce the level of contract-related production aid paid to shipyards. The Commission was working to lower the ceiling imposed on such aid pursuant to the Seventh Directive as far and as fast as was consistent with this Directive. In deciding whether a new Directive was necessary, the Commission would review the competitive situation in shipbuilding throughout the EEA in the light of progress made towards the reduction or elimination of such aid. When conducting this review the Commission would closely consult with the EFTA States,[437] taking due account of the results of efforts in a wider international context, and with a view to creating conditions which ensured that competition was not distorted.

In the event, following the extension of the period of validity of the Seventh Directive, the latter was integrated into the Agreement by a decision of the EEA Joint Committee.[438]

4.5.3 State Monopolies and Public Undertakings

Article 16 of the EEA Agreement[439] substantially incorporates the terms of Article 37 of the EC Treaty, which concerns state monopolies of a commercial

[435] Continued relaxation would run counter to an OECD Agreement which the Commission wishes to see implemented within the Community. See Agreement respecting normal competitive conditions in the commercial shipbuilding and repair industry, COM(94)460.

[436] Dir. 90/684 of 21 Dec. 1990 ([1990] OJ L38/27) on aid to shipbuilding. It has been extended to 31 Dec. 1994 by Dir. 93/115 of 16 Dec. 1993 ([1993] OJ L326/62).

[437] I.e., the issues raised will be not be left simply to co-operation between the Commission and the ESA.

[438] Dec. 21/95 of 5 Apr. 1995 ([1995] OJ L158/43) amending Annex XV (state aid) to the EEA Agreement.

[439] See also Prot. 8, on state monopolies.

character, and Article 59 substantially incorporates the terms of Article 90 of the EC Treaty, which concerns public undertakings generally. Article 125 of the EEA Agreement follows Article 222 of the EC Treaty.

These provisions might be thought to have serious implications for alcohol monopolies in Iceland and Norway. If the judgment in *EC Commission* v. *Germany*[440] constituted the basis of the Commission position regarding alcohol monopolies in EEA negotiations, the fact that the outcome of these negotiations was inconclusive as to the legality of such monopolies is unsurprising. In particular, a Declaration by the Governments of Finland, Iceland, Norway, and Sweden on Alcohol Monopolies was attached to the EEA Agreement. Without prejudice to the obligations arising under the Agreement,[441] these states recalled in the Declaration that their alcohol monopolies were based on important health and social policy considerations.[442] In response to various other Declarations by one or more EFTA States,[443] the Community responded by declaring that such Declarations should be without prejudice to the rights and obligations of the Contracting Parties under the Agreement. The absence of any such response in the case of the Declaration on alcohol monopolies might imply that such monopolies are, in principle, permissible, though the reference in this Declaration to acceptance of EEA obligations might have been taken to obviate the need for such a response. In other words, harmonization in this field may be jeopardized by uncertainty as to the requirements of EEA law.

4.5.4 Procedures

Enforcement procedures in the EEA Agreement may involve national administrative and judicial authorities, the Commission, and the EFTA Surveillance Authority (ESA).

National Administrative Enforcement

The EEA Agreement makes no provision for national administrative enforcement, though such enforcement may be permitted by the Agreement. According to Part I, Chapter I, Article 9(3) of Protocol 4 to the ESA-Court Agreement,[444] the authorities of the EFTA States shall remain competent to

[440] See sect. 4.2.3 above.

[441] This proviso is said to indicate 'the mainly political motivation behind these statements'. See N. G. van der Pas, 'The European Economic Area: Aspects concerning Free Movement of Goods' in O. Jacot-Guillarmod (ed), *Accord EEE: Commentaires et réflexions* (Bern, 1992) 101–14, at 108.

[442] There was also a Declaration by the Governments of Liechtenstein and Switzerland, which added a reference to agricultural considerations.

[443] Such as the Declaration by the Government of Austria on Safeguards.

[444] Agreement between the EFTA States on the Establishment of a Surveillance Authority and a Court of Justice ([1994] OJ L344/1).

apply certain competition provisions of the Agreement, as long as the ESA has not initiated proceedings under the Protocol. However, national authorities must not act in such a way as to interfere with the uniform application of EEA competition law. Rather, they must co-operate with the Commission and the ESA.[445]

National Judicial Enforcement

The eighth recital in the Preamble to the EEA Agreement states that the Contracting Parties are convinced of the important role that individuals will play in the EEA through the exercise of the rights conferred on them by the Agreement and through the judicial defence of these rights. Thus competition law provisions in the EEA Agreement are to be incorporated into the national law of EFTA States and will become applicable by the national courts of these states[446] to the same extent as corresponding provisions of the EC Treaty.[447]

However, enforcement of EEA competition law is not to be left to depend solely on national institutions. Article 109(1) of the Agreement provides that the fulfilment of the obligations under this Agreement shall be monitored by the Commission acting in conformity with the EC and ECSC Treaties and this Agreement and, on the other, the ESA. More particularly, Article 55 of the Agreement provides that the Commission and the ESA shall ensure the application of the principles laid down in Articles 53 and 54.

Commission Enforcement

The Commission plays an enforcement role under the EEA Agreement which relates both to restrictive practices of undertakings and state aid.

(i) Restrictive Practices by Undertakings

Article 56(1)(c) of the EEA Agreement was added after delivery of *Opinion 1/91*[448] by the Court of Justice and puts existing Commission practice on a more

[445] Art. 10 of Prot. 21, on the Implementation of Competition Rules Applicable to Undertakings, to the EEA Agreement. See also, regarding application of national competition law by national authorities, the ESA Notice on co-operation between national courts and the EFTA Surveillance Authority in applying Arts 53 and 54 of the EEA Agreement ([1995] OJ C112/7), para. 14.

[446] *Ibid.*

[447] See sect. 8.5.5 below. More particularly, Art. 9(2) of the Agreement on Civil Aviation ([1992] OJ L200/21) required the Contracting Parties to ensure that the rights which devolved from Arts 4, 5, 6, 7, and the Regs and Dirs in the Annex to the Agreement might be invoked before national courts.

[448] Opinion 1/91 (*Draft Agreement between the Community, on the one hand, and the countries of the European Free Trade Association, on the other, relating to the creation of the European Economic Area*) [1991] ECR I–6079.

secure legal basis.[449] It provides, with regard to cases falling under Article 53,[450] that the Commission decides on the cases where trade between Member States is affected, though Article 56(3) denies such jurisdiction to the Commission where effects on trade between Member States or on competition within the Community are not appreciable. According to an Agreed Minute, the word 'appreciable' in Article 56(3) is understood to have the meaning it has in the Commission Notice on agreements of minor importance which do not fall under Article 85(1) of the EC Treaty.[451] Within the Community, however, the Notice lacks binding effect, and Annex XIV to the EEA Agreement merely requires that 'due account' is taken of this Notice.[452] The legal effect of the Agreed Minute is also uncertain.[453]

The Commission also decides on cases where EC–EFTA trade, though not trade between Member States, is affected and the turnover of the undertakings concerned in the EFTA States is less than 33 per cent[454] of their total turnover.[455] The Commission thus acquires a new competence in relation to restrictive practices which only affect trade between one Member State and one or more of the EFTA States. It may also be a new competence for the Commission to be entitled to act where only trade between the Community as a whole and one or more EFTA States is affected.[456]

Article 56(2) of the Agreement concerns abuse of a dominant position. It provides for individual cases falling under Article 54 to be decided upon by the surveillance authority within which the dominance is found to exist. If dominance exists in the territories of both authorities, the Commission has

[449] According to the Court in Opinion 1/92 (*Draft Agreement between the Community, on the one hand, and the countries of the European Free Trade Association, on the other, relating to the creation of the European Economic Area*) [1992] ECR I–2821, I–2845, the Community may accept rules made by virtue of an international agreement on the sharing of the respective competences of the Contracting Parties in the field of competition, provided that those rules do not change the nature of the powers of the Community and of its institutions as conceived in the EC Treaty.

[450] This provision substantially reproduces Art. 85 EC. See sect. 4.5.1 above.

[451] [1986] OJ C231/2.

[452] In other cases an apparently even more limited requirement is imposed that the Contracting Parties 'take note of' certain acts. See, e.g., those contained in sects 46 and 47 of Pt. I of Annex II.

[453] Cf. Case C–292/89 *Regina* v. *Immigration Appeal Tribunal, ex parte Gustaff Desiderius Antonissen* [1991] ECR I–745.

[454] This figure was apparently chosen with a view to allowing the ESA sufficient work to justify its establishment. See C. Rouam, 'L'Espace Economique Européen: Un Horizon Nouveau pour la Politique de Concurrence [1992] *RMC* 53, at 55. However, it is reminiscent of Art. 1(2) of Reg. 4064/89 of 21 Dec. 1989 ([1989] OJ L395/1, as corrected by [1990] OJ L257/13) on the control of concentrations between undertakings. According to this provision, a merger lacks the 'Community dimension' necessary for Commission control to be exercised under this measure where each of the undertakings concerned achieves more than two-thirds of its aggregate turnover within one and the same Member State.

[455] Art. 56(1)(c) of the EEA Agreement. See also Prot. 22, concerning the definition of 'undertaking' and 'turnover'.

[456] See sect. 2.2.3 above.

corresponding jurisdiction to that provided for under Articles 56(1)(c) and 56(3) in relation to restrictive agreements.[457]

Article 57(2)(a) provides for the control of concentrations covered by paragraph 1 to be carried out by the Commission in cases falling under Regulation 4064/89[458] in accordance with that Regulation and in accordance with Protocols 21[459] and 24[460] and Annex XIV.[461] The Commission shall, subject to the review of the Court of Justice, have sole competence to take decisions on those cases, i.e., where a merger falling under the Regulation may have anti-competitive effects within the EEA.[462] In return, the EFTA States secured special co-operation arrangements in Protocol 24. The EFTA States also have the right to invoke the existence of a 'distinct national market' under Article 9 of Regulation 4064/89 or 'legitimate interests' under Article 21 of the same Regulation.[463]

These arrangements apparently reflect Community insistence on retention of its recently developed power to control mergers capable of distorting competition within the Community.[464] Since Regulation 4064/89 does not rely on a criterion related to the effect on trade between Member States, there may have been no other readily available formula for fully preserving this power.

The precise extent to which the competences conferred on the Commission by these provisions go beyond its pre-existing competences under the EC Treaty is unclear, because the failure of the Court of Justice unambiguously to adopt the effects doctrine[465] means that the latter competences are themselves uncertain. While the practical significance of this uncertainty within the EEA may be reduced by the EEA Agreement, the uncertainty is not removed by this Agreement. In the Joint Declaration Concerning Rules on Competition, annexed to the EEA Agreement, the Contracting Parties merely declare that the implementation of the EEA competition rules, in cases falling within the competence of the Commission, is based on the existing Community competences, supplemented by the provisions contained in the Agreement.[466] In

457 These criteria are designed to take account of the 'centre of gravity' of the undertakings or activities involved, the need for legal security for economic operators, in particular as to which authority is responsible, and the need for 'automatic' division of responsibilities that will not give rise to serious interpretation problems. See C. Rouam, n. 454 above, 55.

458 Reg. 4064/89 of 21 Dec. 1989 ([1989] OJ L395/1, as corrected by [1990] OJ L257/13) on the control of concentrations between undertakings.

459 On the Implementation of Competition Rules Applicable to Undertakings.

460 On Co-operation in the Field of Control of Concentrations.

461 On Competition.

462 Pt. A of Annex XIV amends Reg. 4064/89 so as to refer to Commission jurisdiction over mergers having a 'Community dimension or an EFTA dimension'.

463 See also C. Rouam, n. 454 above, 56.

464 See, e.g., Dec. 91/535 of 19 July 1991 ([1991] OJ L290/35) declaring the compatibility with the common market of a concentration (Case No IV/M068—Tetra Pak/Alfa-Laval).

465 See sect. 2.2.3 above.

466 Art. 1(1) of the Agreement on Civil Aviation ([1992] OJ L200/21) provided that the Agreement set out rules for the Contracting Parties in the field of civil aviation. However, these rules were to be without prejudice to those contained in the EC Treaty and in particular to existing Community competences under Arts 85 and 86 and the competition rules derived therefrom.

practice, the Commission apparently intends to apply jointly the rules in the EC Treaty and the EEA Agreement, particularly to take account of the effects of anti-competitive conduct on EC–EFTA trade.[467]

The Agreement on Civil Aviation between the EC, Norway and Sweden,[468] which was intended 'to create in the area covered by [the Parties] a set of rules applicable to civil aviation',[469] went somewhat further in strengthening the position of the Commission. It empowered the Commission to apply the competition rules in Articles 4 and 5 of this Agreement, whenever trade between the Parties was affected. There was no need for trade between Member States also to be affected. These rules were substantially identical to those in Articles 85 and 86, respectively, of the EC Treaty and were to be interpreted in accordance with the case law of the Court of Justice at the time of the signature of the Agreement, with due account being paid to future case law.[470]

To facilitate Commission exercise of these competences, Article 8(1) of the Agreement on Civil Aviation required Norway and Sweden to ensure that the Commission was given the information foreseen in the Annex in respect of the application of the rules in Articles 4–5 and the Annex. The Annex included the provisions of Regulation 17[471] laying down general procedural rules for the application of Community competition law to undertakings. It also included provisions of other Community acts containing special procedural rules concerning competition in the civil aviation sector.

More particularly, Article 8(2) of the Agreement on Civil Aviation provided that in instances where the Commission might obtain information directly from undertakings, as provided for in the Annex to this Agreement, Norway and Sweden should upon request provide the Commission with such information and/or arrange, if requested, for a direct visit on a specified date and invite the Commission to participate, while respecting the relevant procedural guarantees laid down by national law.

(ii) State Aid

Article 62(1) of the EEA Agreement requires that all existing aid systems in the territory of the Contracting Parties, as well as plans to grant or alter aid, shall be subject to constant review as to their compatibility with Article 61 of this Agreement. This review shall be carried out, as regards the Member States, by the Commission according to the rules laid down in Article 93 of the EC Treaty. Thus the Commission is empowered to review aid[472] which is

[467] *Twenty-first Report on Competition Policy* (EC Commission, Brussels, 1992), 51.

[468] [1992] OJ L200/21.

[469] 3rd recital in the Preamble to Dec. 92/384 of 22 June 1992 ([1992] OJ L200/20) concerning the conclusion of an Agreement between the EC, Norway, and Sweden.

[470] *Ibid.*, Art. 1(2).

[471] Of 6 Feb. 1962 ([1962] JO 204) first reg. implementing Arts 85 and 86 EC.

[472] According to Art. 62(1)(a) of the EEA Agreement, the Commission is to do so 'according to the rules laid down in Art. 93' EC.

granted by a Member State and may affect trade between EEA States, even where trade between Member States is not affected.

Again, the Civil Aviation Agreement went further. Article 7(2) provided that the Commission should, in co-operation with Norway and Sweden, keep under constant review all systems of aid existing in those states. It should propose to the latter any appropriate measures required by the progressive development or the functioning of this Agreement. If after giving notice to the parties concerned to submit their comments, the Commission found that aid granted by one of those states or through state resources was not compatible with this Agreement having regard to Article 6,[473] or that such aid was being misused,[474] it should inform the state concerned and request that such aid be abolished or altered within a period of time to be determined by the Commission under Article 7(3). Unless the state concerned notified the other Contracting Parties that it was not in agreement with the action requested, it was required by Article 7(4) to take the necessary measures and inform the Commission thereof. If the state concerned was not in agreement with the action requested by the Commission, the matter should within twenty-one days be submitted to the Joint Committee under Article 7(5), and the Committee should meet within fourteen days of the date of submission. Article 14(5) provided that, if the Joint Committee did not take a decision pursuant to Article 7(5) within six months of the date of submission, the Agreement should cease to be in force.

Moreover, under Article 7(6) of the same Agreement the Commission was to be informed, in sufficient time to enable it to submit its comments, of any plans to grant or alter aid. If the Commission considered that any such plan was not compatible with this Agreement having regard to Article 6, it should without delay initiate the procedure provided for in Article 7(3). The state concerned should not put its proposed measures into effect until this procedure had resulted in a final decision.

Such differences between the Civil Aviation Agreement and the EEA Agreement apparently reflect unwillingness on the part of the Community to rely on national enforcement of competition law in third states, even if, as in the case of the former Agreement,[475] national courts of such states may be involved in the enforcement process. Supranational enforcement by a body, established by third states along the lines of the Commission, may, as the EEA Agreement indicates, be more acceptable to the Community.

EFTA Surveillance Authority Enforcement

EFTA States had their own, well established though limited, arrangements for application of competition policy. In particular, an agreement had been

[473] This provision followed Art. 92 EC.

[474] The EC Treaty contains no provision to the effect that the 'misuse' of otherwise lawful aid renders it unlawful.

[475] Art. 9(3) of the Civil Aviation Agreement.

reached in 1968 requiring EFTA States to notify the Secretariat of their annual expenditure on state aid.[476] The Secretariat produced reports in 1979, 1982, and 1983, but in no case was a breach of state aid rules in Article 13 of the EFTA Convention[477] found to have been committed. The lack of such a finding might reflect difficulties of establishing that aid contrary to a provision worded in such generalized terms as Article 13[478] had been granted, the fact that trade between EFTA States was comparatively limited,[479] or even the fact that such a finding could merely have led to a demonstration of EFTA inability to secure compliance with the requirements of Article 13.

In 1984 the EFTA Council sought to go further and established an *ad hoc* committee to carry out an analysis of state aid within EFTA. This committee reported in 1986,[480] and on the basis of this report revised arrangements were introduced by the Council in 1988.[481] According to the revised arrangements, EFTA States have to provide the Secretariat annually with a detailed report of all aid granted. They must also notify any plans to grant new aid or to alter existing aid. The notifications were examined by a Committee of Trade Experts, composed of representatives of EFTA States, and were circulated by the Secretariat to other EFTA States. The latter had the opportunity to comment on and discuss the notifications and even to request an investigation. The Secretariat was itself to produce an annual report on state aid within EFTA as a whole. Moreover, in December 1989 at their Geneva meeting EFTA Ministers considered a proposal to establish special panels[482] to examine the compatibility of existing or planned aid with the EFTA Convention.[483] Aid contrary to the Convention could be prohibited, and repayment might be required.[484] Such arrangements, however, were not apparently designed to establish the kind of supranational element which is central to application of competition law under the EC Treaty.

Introduction of such an element in application of competition policy was apparently not contemplated by EFTA States in early negotiations for the EEA Agreement. Instead, the essential role of national bodies in the enforce-

[476] EFTA Bull. 7/1968, 17.

[477] SÖ 1960:1.

[478] Art. 13(1)(b) of the EFTA Convention prohibits any form of aid 'the main purpose or effect of which is to frustrate the benefits expected from the removal or absence of duties and quantitative restrictions on trade between Member States'.

[479] G. C. Hufbauer, *Procedures for Monitoring and Disciplining Government Aids* (EFTA Occasional Paper No. 30, Geneva, 1989).

[480] Doc. EFTA/EC 11/86.

[481] EFTA Council Dec. No. 10 of 1988. See also *Redovisning av det svenska integrationsarbetet våren 1988–mars 1989* (Report on Swedish 'integration work' from Spring 1988 to March 1989) (Utrikesdepartementets handelsavdelning, 1989), 140.

[482] Involvement of panels in dispute settlement seems to have been favoured generally by EFTA. See, e.g., Art. 10(3) and (4) of the Convention on the Mutual Recognition of Test Results and Proofs of Conformity (1988).

[483] Detailed proposals along these lines were made by G. C. Hufbauer, n. 479 above.

[484] *Sverige – EFTA – EG 1989* (Utrikesdepartementets handelsavdelning, 1990), 45. A planned agreement concerning public procurement also envisaged a system for surveillance and settlement of disputes (*ibid.* 43).

ment of competition rules was discussed.[485] Performance of such a role by national bodies would have been consistent with EFTA traditions[486] and with OECD recommendations regarding co-operation between national authorities in tackling restrictive practices affecting international trade.[487] Accordingly, Sven Norberg, the then Director of the Legal Affairs Division of the EFTA Secretariat, wrote in a scholarly article that, while some multilateral elements might be necessary in the new system demanded by establishment of the EEA, national action and some bilateral action might also be appropriate and that acceptance by EFTA States of the arrangements entailed need not be radically different from acceptance of international obligations in other contexts.[488]

In so far as multilateral arrangements were contemplated, EFTA States spoke only of strengthening EFTA mechanisms for surveillance and enforcement of treaty obligations, so as to ensure their harmonious and uniform application and interpretation throughout the whole of the EEA,[489] or of developing a system as effective as that of the Community.[490] The Swedish Government, for its part, referred vaguely to a general preference for 'channelling' applications and complaints to 'organs with the necessary competence in EES questions'.[491] Such language may have simply envisaged technical improvements to existing EFTA arrangements.

However, the view that such improvements alone would be sufficient for EEA purposes does not seem to have been accepted during the course of negotiations for the EEA Agreement. According to the EC–EFTA Joint Ministerial statement of 19 December 1990,[492] emphasis was placed on the need for equally strong and reliable surveillance and enforcement throughout the whole EEA, comprising an efficient EEA surveillance system and an EEA

[485] P. Lindh, 'Institutional Developments and Linkages—A Response' in M. Robinson and J. Findlater (eds.), *Creating a European Economic Space: Legal Aspects of EC–EFTA Relations* (Dublin, 1988), 109–13, at 112.

[486] Note also the draft Nordek Treaty (NU 1969:11, 79–100).

[487] *Competition Policy and International Trade: OECD Instruments of Co-operation* (OECD, Paris, 1987). See also *Sverige – EG 1984* (Utrikesdepartementets handelsavdelning, 1985), 23–24.

[488] S. Norberg, 'Skapandet av ett Europeiskt Ekonomiskt Samarbetsområde (EES)—rättsliga utmaningar från ett EFTA-perspektiv' ('Creation of the European Economic Space (EES)—Legal Challenges from an EFTA Perspective') [1989] *SvJT* 89–101. Cf. the view that establishment of 'a separate investigating body' might be unnecessary in S. Norberg, 'European Community Anti-Dumping and Competition Laws Their Actual and Potential Application to EFTA Countries: Some Comments from an EFTA Point of View' [1987] *TfR* 638–50.

[489] Para. 17 of the Declaration of the EFTA Ministerial Meeting held in Oslo, 14–15 Mar. 1989 (EFTA Bull. 2/89, 4–7).

[490] *Dagens Industri*, 9 May 1990.

[491] *Sverige – EFTA – EG 1989* (Utrikesdepartementets handelsavdelning, 1990), 134. See also, regarding public procurement, *Redovisning av det svenska integrationsarbetet våren 1988–mars 1989* (Utrikesdepartementets handelsavdelning, 1989), bil. 3, 48.

[492] EFTA Bull. 1/91, 22–5, para. 20.

judicial mechanism.[493] Apparently, more radical arrangements than those embodied in established EFTA practice were envisaged.

What remained to be resolved was the question whether there should be a joint surveillance authority for the EEA as a whole or whether the Community and the EFTA States should have separate authorities.[494] The Commission draft mandate for EEA negotiations referred merely to '*structures collectives*', while the version adopted by the Council required establishment of an '*autorité dotée de pouvoirs*'.[495] In the event, according to the EC–EFTA Joint Ministerial Statement of 13 May 1991, it was agreed that there would be an 'independent EFTA structure (with equivalent powers and similar functions as those exercised by the EC Commission)'.[496]

Article 108(1) of the EEA Agreement duly requires the EFTA States to establish an independent EFTA Surveillance Authority as well as procedures similar to those existing in the Community,[497] including procedures for ensuring the fulfilment of obligations under the Agreement and for control of the legality of acts of the ESA regarding competition.[498] Article 109(1) goes on to provide that the fulfilment of the obligations under this Agreement shall be monitored by, on the one hand, the ESA and, on the other, the European Commission acting in conformity with the EC and ECSC Treaties and this Agreement.

In accordance with these provisions, a single EFTA Agreement[499] established both the ESA and the EFTA Court.[500] Members of the former, like Commissioners, are to be chosen on the basis of their general competence and must be persons whose independence is beyond doubt.[501] Its decisions are to be reached by majority. The competences of the ESA in the competition law field are outlined in Articles 56, 57, and 62 of the EEA Agreement.

(i) Restrictive Practices by Undertakings

Article 56(1)(a) of the EEA Agreement provides, with regard to cases falling under Article 53,[502] that cases where only trade between EFTA States is

493 The Swedish Government considered that a procedure equivalent to that contained in Art. 169 EC would be unproblematic. See *Propositionen om andring i regeringsformen med anledning av ett europeiskt ekonomiskt samarbetsområdet* (Proposal to amend the Constitution for EEA purposes), prop. 1990/91:65, 13.

494 S. Norberg, 'The EEA Surveillance System' [1992] *SvJT* 349–64.

495 Para. 4 of the *Directives de Négotiation.*

496 EFTA Bull. 2/91, 7–9, para. 6.

497 Prot. 21, on the Implementation of Competition Rules Applicable to Undertakings, provides for the ESA to be entrusted with equivalent powers and similar functions to those of the Commission in relation to competition between undertakings. Prot. 26, on the Powers and Functions of the EFTA Surveillance Authority in the Field of State Aid, makes similar provision in the case of state aid.

498 Art. 110 of the Agreement also provides that decisions under this Agreement by the ESA and the Commission which impose a pecuniary obligation on persons other than states shall be enforceable. This provision follows Art. 192 EC.

499 Agreement between the EFTA States on the Establishment of a Surveillance Authority and a Court of Justice ([1994] OJ L344/1).

500 See sect. 8.5.4 below, regarding this Court.

501 It is also to adopt its own Rules of Procedure and to publish an annual report.

502 This provision substantially reproduces Art. 85 EC. See sect. 4.5.1 above.

affected shall be decided upon by the ESA. Moreover, Article 56(1)(b) provides that, without prejudice to Article 56(1)(c), the ESA decides on cases where EC–EFTA trade is affected and where the turnover of the undertakings concerned in the territory of the EFTA States equals 33 per cent or more of their turnover in the territory covered by this Agreement. Article 56(1)(c) means that when trade between Member States is also appreciably affected, the ESA lacks jurisdiction.

Article 56(2) concerns abuse of a dominant position. It provides for the ESA to decide cases under Article 54 where dominance exists only within EFTA. If dominance also exists within the Community, the ESA may still decide the case, provided that the turnover of the undertaking concerned within the territory of EFTA States is 33 per cent or more of its total turnover within the territory covered by the EEA. Again, this latter competence is without prejudice to the competence of the Commission to decide the case where trade between Member States is appreciably affected.

Article 57(2)(b) provides for the control of mergers covered by paragraph 1 to be carried out by the ESA in cases not falling under subparagraph (a)[503] where the relevant thresholds set out in Annex XIV are fulfilled in the territory of the EFTA States in accordance with Protocols 21 and 24 and Annex XIV. This competence is without prejudice to the competence of Member States.

(ii) State Aid

Article 62(1) requires that all existing systems of state aid in the territory of the Contracting Parties, as well as plans to grant or alter state aid, shall be subject to constant review as to their compatibility with Article 61. This review shall be carried out, as regards the EFTA States, by the ESA according to the rules set out in the Agreement between the EFTA States establishing the Surveillance Authority.

These arrangements complete the 'two-pillar' approach to the enforcement of competition policy within the EEA. It is an approach which seeks development of a 'homogeneous' policy without eliminating the internal autonomy of the Parties. As with the EEA construction as a whole, arrangements for co-operation between the two pillars may be of critical significance.

Co-operative Enforcement

The EFTA States had agreed arrangements with the Community in 1988 to increase transparency in the field of state aid through mutual exchange of information.[504] According to these arrangements, the EFTA Secretariat would send to the Commission copies of all state aid notifications which it received

[503] I.e., cases not falling under Reg. 4064/89 of 21 Dec. 1989 ([1989] OJ L395/1, as corrected by [1990] OJ L257/13) on the control of concentrations between undertakings.

[504] EFTA Bull. 1/1988, 10–11.

from, and circulated to, EFTA States. The Commission, for its part, would provide the EFTA Secretariat with copies of notices issued pursuant to the opening of procedures under Article 93(2) of the EC Treaty[505] as well as information notices which it issued on developments concerning state aid policy. The competent EFTA fora as well as the EFTA States concerned would take into consideration any views expressed by the Commission regarding the notification in question, as would the Commission in respect of EFTA views expressed in the course of Commission procedures under Article 93(2) of the Treaty, in which EFTA States might intervene as interested third parties. Exchange of views and information on state aid policy developments would also take place on an annual basis.[506]

The EEA Agreement builds on such arrangements. Article 109(2) of the Agreement requires that to ensure a uniform surveillance throughout the EEA, the ESA and the Commission shall co-operate, exchange information,[507] and consult each other on surveillance policy issues and individual cases. They are to inform each other of complaints received concerning application and implementation of the Agreement.[508] Each is to examine all complaints falling within its competence and pass to the other any complaints which fall outside.[509]

More particularly, Article 59 of the Agreement requires that a uniform surveillance throughout the EEA in the field of competition be developed and maintained and that homogeneous implementation, application, and interpretation of the provisions of this Agreement be promoted. To these ends, the competent authorities shall co-operate in accordance with the provisions set out in Protocols 23 and 24,[510] which concern restrictive practices by undertakings. In particular, each surveillance authority and the states falling within its jurisdiction shall be entitled to be present in the advisory committees of the other authority and to express their views therein, though they do not have the right to vote.[511] Similarly, Article 62(2) provides in relation to state aid for co-operation in accordance with Protocol 27.[512]

These arrangements may not necessarily ensure that competition policy, particularly that concerning state aid, will be identical throughout the EEA. The broad terms of competition law provisions in the EC Treaty have only

505 See sect. 4.2.4 above.

506 EFTA Bull. 3/1988, 8.

507 Note, regarding banking secrecy, the Declaration by the Governments of Liechtenstein and Switzerland on Administrative Assistance, which was attached to the EEA Agreement. The Community, however, responded by declaring that this Declaration was without prejudice to the rights and duties of the Parties under the Agreement.

508 Art. 109(3) of the EEA Agreement.

509 *Ibid.*, Art. 109(4).

510 Prot. 25, on competition regarding coal and steel, also provides for co-operation in relation to competition in the coal and steel sectors.

511 Art. 6 of Prot. 23, concerning the Co-operation between the Surveillance Authorities (Art. 58). See also Ch. 7 below, regarding 'comitology'.

512 See also the Joint Declaration on Para. (c) of Prot. 27 to the Agreement, on Co-operation in the Field of State Aid.

acquired effective meaning in the application of these provisions by the Commission.[513] It is in such application that liberalization, harmonization, and institutional involvement in these processes merge. The ESA might not necessarily apply competition law provisions of the EEA Agreement in the same way. Even where two enforcement authorities apply the same basic concepts and employ the same methodologies of review, they may weigh the evidence differently and reach conflicting conclusions.[514]

There was apparent reluctance in EEA negotiations to confer co-ordinating powers on new EEA bodies, though the Commission referred to the possibility of creating an '*organe paritaire*' with such powers.[515] The Swedish Government, e.g., spoke only of '*någon form av ömsesidigt förfarande*' (some form of reciprocal procedure)[516] or '*et enhetligt sanktions-system . . . i de skilda länderna*' (a uniform sanctions system in the different countries).[517] In the event, Article 109(5) of the EEA Agreement provides that disputes between the ESA and the Commission regarding action to be taken in relation to a complaint or with regard to the result of the examination of a complaint may be referred to the EEA Joint Committee.[518] The latter may settle the dispute under Article 111.

However, the capability of a joint body, like the EEA Joint Committee, which can only act by consensus,[519] to secure application of an identical competition policy as between the Community and EFTA States may be limited. Certainly, the history of the Joint Committees established by the Free Trade Agreements suggests limits as to the likely effectiveness of arrangements for institutional co-ordination of the activities of the Commission and the ESA.[520]

4.6 CONCLUSION

Within the EC Treaty framework competition law plays a role which is both central and, because it assumes the operation of requirements safeguarding

[513] According to the *Twenty-Fourth Report on Competition Policy*, COM(95)142, 93, 'competition law is closely bound up with real economic life, and the principles arrived at cannot therefore be detached from the facts that gave rise to them'.

[514] Cf. D. E. Rosenthal, 'Competition Policy' in G. C. Hufbauer (ed.), *Europe 1992: An American Perspective* (Washington 1990) 293–343, at 342.

[515] Para. 5.2 of the *Commission Communication concerning a proposed Council decision authorizing the Commission to negotiate an agreement with the EFTA states on the creation of a European Economic Space*. Complications for autonomy of decision making would have arisen. See C. Church, 'The Politics of Change: EFTA and the Nordic Countries' Responses to the EC in the Early 1990s' [1990] *JCMS* 401–430, at 407.

[516] *Snabbprotokoll från riksdagsdebatten* 1989/90:101, 22.

[517] *Vissa ekonomisk-politiska åtgärder*, prop. 1988/89:47, 12.

[518] See sect. 6.5.1 below.

[519] Art. 93(2) of the EEA Agreement provides that the Committee shall take decisions by agreement between the Community, on the one hand, and the EFTA States speaking with one voice, on the other.

[520] See sect. 6.3.3 below.

undistorted competition which are established by other Treaty provisions, dependent.[521] In other words, Community competition law is part of the process of spill-over, in which '*mésures de désarmement*'[522] may become cumulative.

At the same time, Commission treatment of state aid in the former GDR demonstrates the adaptability of such law to the diversity of conditions within the Community. Unless there is acceptance under agreements between the Community and third states that diverse conditions as between the Parties may also require modification of competition law on both sides, harmonization of competition policy and its contribution to reduction of trade obstacles are likely to be limited.

Under the Free Trade Agreements the Parties simply relied each on the application of their own rules, including anti-dumping measures. In other words, the response to inadequate harmonization of competition policy was resort to measures restricting trade.

The Europe Agreements do envisage harmonization of competition policy as between the Parties. Indeed, the Commission considers that the Community may provide a policy framework at the 'wider European level, in order to facilitate coherence between different sectoral policies as well as inter-regional co-operation'.[523] However, the requirements of competition law are complicated and are only clarified in the application of such law to individual cases. If they are applied by different bodies, which operate within different legal frameworks and face different economic conditions,[524] their content is likely to vary.

The Europe Agreements apparently seek to rely on co-operation between the Commission and the relevant national authorities responsible for application of competition law under these Agreements and on the possibility of joint bodies

[521] According to the Commission, the obligation of submitting to Community control all aid capable of distorting competition in trade between Member States is the necessary counterpart to the right of Member States to export freely to other Member States and is the basis of a common market. See the Communication to the Member States—Application of Arts 92 and 93 EC and of Art. 5 of Commission Dir. 80/723 to Public Undertakings in the Manufacturing Sector ([1991] OJ C273/2), para. 33. Cf., regarding integration of the textile and clothing sectors into GATT, Commission Reply by Sir Leon Brittan to Written Question E-2152/93 ([1994] OJ C46/43) by Mr Louis Lauga.

[522] The creation of a customs union was described as such a measure by the Court in Joined Cases 90 and 92/63 *EEC Commission* v. *Luxembourg and Belgium* [1964] Rec. 1223, 1234. Use of different terminology in the later English translation of this judgment ([1964] ECR 625, 633) does not necessarily mean that underlying attitudes have changed, though perhaps reticence is greater.

[523] *Europe 2000: Outlook for the Development of the Community's Territory*, COM(91)452, 197.

[524] The European Parliament called upon the Commission and the Council 'to study the possibility, for a transitional period, of allowing derogations from the ban on subsidies which might also help encourage the process of change in Eastern European countries which are undertaking reforms, including the CIS'. See the Resolution of 15 July 1993 ([1993] OJ C255/195) on the Community's response to the problem of restructuring in East Germany and the economic and social crisis, para. 79.

co-ordinating their work. The effectiveness of such co-ordination as a means of securing harmonization of competition policy may be critical for realization of the potential of these Agreements to secure the reduction of obstacles to trade between the Parties.

In the case of Central and Eastern European countries, the radical changes which their economies are undergoing, the generally limited liberalization requirements embodied in the Europe Agreements and the reliance placed on national enforcement of competition law may impose demands which such co-ordination is unable to meet.[525] Whereas the concern of such countries may be to protect their vulnerable industries from increased competition,[526] the Community concern may be to counter possible distortions of competition that may arise from asymmetrical liberalization.[527]

A simple solution to such problems was envisaged in the Civil Aviation Agreement. This Agreement simply empowered the Commission to apply provisions substantially identical to those of Community competition law to any practices affecting competition in trade between the Parties in the civil aviation sector. To confer such powers on the Commission in relation to competition issues arising in trade generally might be perceived to be incompatible with the sovereignty of the third states concerned. To establish a sole body independent of the Parties to exercise such powers might be taken to be as incompatible with Community autonomy as with the sovereignty of third states.

The EEA Agreement may offer a more sophisticated solution, which involves formalization of Commission powers in relation to EFTA companies whose restrictive practices are implemented within the Community, the creation of the ESA and EFTA adoption of EC Treaty provisions and implementing measures governing both the four freedoms and competition policy. The result may be that the separation in Community practice between 'internal' competition policy relating only to trade between Member States and 'external' trade policy issues is reduced. The ESA and the Commission may be expected to apply basically the same competition law requirements, and it may be mutually acceptable for application of these requirements to be differentiated to take account of varying conditions in each EEA State. Indeed, a dialogue between

[525] D. Kennedy and D. E. Webb, 'The Limits of Integration: Eastern Europe and the European Communities' (1993) 30 *CMLRev.* 1095–117, at 1113. 'The Commission considers that for the associated countries . . . the main challenge . . . lies not in the technical adaptation of their legal texts to make them identical to those of the Community but in adapting their administrative machinery and their societies to the framework conditions necessary to make the legislation work'. See *Preparation of the Associated Countries of Central and Eastern Europe for Integration into the Internal Market of the Union*, COM(95)163, Annex, 2.

[526] House of Lords Select Committee on the European Communities, *European Agreements with Poland, Hungary and the Czech and Slovak Federal Republic*, HL(1990–91) 35, Note of a Meeting with Representatives of the Hungarian Government on 20 Nov. 1990, App. 7.

[527] *Ibid.*, Minutes of Evidence, 10. See also the *Twenty-Fourth Report on Competition Policy*, COM(95)142, 283.

the two institutions may be positively beneficial for the development of competition policy.[528] At least, the objections to such differentiation may be insufficient to outweigh the advantages of effective enforcement of basically the same competition policy throughout the EC–EFTA area.

Such considerations may explain the Commission suggestion, as a future possibility, that a 'competition authority' be created along the lines of the ESA by several or all of the states which have concluded Europe Agreements with the Community.[529] In practice, however, the effectiveness of any arrangements of this kind for establishing and developing competition law as an instrument for reduction of obstacles to trade between the Community and third states may depend on acceptance of the need for some degree of pluralism in the elaboration of competition policy.

[528] Cf., regarding the importance of 'effective cooperation' between national competition authorities, national courts, the Court of Justice, the EFTA Court, the Commission, and the ESA, the Notice on co-operation between national courts and the EFTA Surveillance Authority in applying Arts 53 and 54 of the EEA Agreement ([1995] OJ C112/7).

[529] Follow Up to Commission Communication on '*The Europe Agreements and Beyond: a Strategy to Prepare the Countries of Central and Eastern Europe for Accession*', COM(94)361, 7.

5

Legislative Harmonization: The 'Four Freedoms' and Beyond

5.1 INTRODUCTION

Legislative harmonization seeks to reduce obstacles to trade through eliminating differences in state measures which distort the relative costs of trade. Within the EC Treaty framework such harmonization proceeds on the basis of acts, usually Directives, adopted by the Community institutions.[1] According to Article 189(3) of the Treaty, a Directive shall be binding, as to the result to be achieved, upon each Member State to which it is addressed, but shall leave to the national authorities the choice of form and methods.

The substantial difference between such harmonization and operation of trade liberalization provisions lies in the capacity of the two processes to reach different conclusions as to the need for reduction of trade obstacles and as to the appropriate relationship between meeting this need and respecting other requirements embodied in the EC Treaty.[2] Harmonization may not only promote respect for the latter requirements through incorporating them into harmonized national policies. By simultaneously lessening divergences between such policies it may also tend towards equalizing competitive conditions and, hence, towards reducing trade obstacles. In other words, reduction of 'market failures' and reduction of trade obstacles may simultaneously be achieved through harmonization.[3]

More particularly, while sensitivity for national sovereignty may limit the capacity of the Court of Justice to secure domestic trade liberalization through interpretation of liberalization provisions in the Treaty as applying to domestic trade, the same consideration need not inhibit the Community legislature from securing reduction of obstacles to such trade through a harmonization process in which representatives of each Member State participate. As a result, harmonization may go beyond simply prohibiting public or private conduct which makes Community trade more difficult than purely domestic trade and

[1] See sect. 6.2 below, regarding the institutions and procedures involved.

[2] Cf. Joined Cases 80 and 81/77 *Société Les Commissionnaires Réunis Sàrl* v. *Receveur des Douanes* [1978] ECR 927, 944.

[3] As the Commission puts it, there may be 'added value', both for health protection and for industry. See the Explanatory Memorandum to the Commission Proposal for a Directive on in Vitro Diagnostic Medical Devices, COM(95)130, 9.

may tend towards securing the same freedom of trade for everyone[4] within the Community.[5] In this sense, harmonization might be thought to offer a more developed kind of equality than operation of liberalization provisions.[6]

However, harmonization, like liberalization, may be affected by the legal framework within which it takes place. Hence, harmonization under agreements between the Community and third states may not necessarily take place in the same way as does harmonization under the EC Treaty.

5.2 EC TREATY

The EC Treaty contains various provisions envisaging 'Community harmonization', i.e., harmonization[7] of the laws of the Member States. Other Treaty provisions may envisage 'international harmonization', i.e., harmonization as between the Community and third states.

5.2.1 Community Harmonization

The scope of EC Treaty provisions envisaging Community harmonization may, as in the case for example of Articles 100 and 100a, be defined simply by reference to the need to harmonize national law which impedes trade between Member States.[8] The scope of certain other provisions is defined by reference to particular sectors, such as agriculture,[9] and transport,[10] in which harmonization of national policies is sought. Yet other provisions may have their scope of application defined by reference to 'horizontal' policies, such as environmental protection.[11] If the necessary powers cannot be found elsewhere, Article 235 provides for the adoption of acts necessary in the operation

[4] Including, e.g., branches of undertakings from third states, as in Dir. 89/666 of 21 Dec. 1989 ([1989] OJ L395/36) concerning disclosure requirements in respect of branches opened in a Member State by certain types of company governed by the law of another state.

[5] Though the emphasis on minimum harmonization within the context of the 'new approach' (see sect. 7.2.2 below) may do little to realize such potential. See, e.g., Case C–11/92 *The Queen* v. *Secretary of State for Health, ex parte Gallaher Ltd* [1993] ECR I–3545.

[6] For example, Art. 40(3) EC states that common organizations of agricultural markets are to exclude any discrimination between producers or consumers within the Community. Cf., in connection with the iron and steel sectors, Art. 4 of the ECSC Treaty. The affirmative equality sought by financial instruments such as the ERDF might be thought to be even more developed. See Reg. 2052/88 of 24 June 1988 ([1988] OJ L185/9) on the tasks of the Structural Funds and their effectiveness and on the co-ordination of their activities between themselves and with the operations of the EIB and the other existing financial instruments, as amended by Reg. 2081/93 of 20 July 1993 ([1993] OJ L193/5).

[7] Various terms—'approximation', 'co-ordination', and 'harmonization'—are to be found in the Treaty. They appear, however, to be used interchangeably.

[8] These provisions envisage harmonization of national law directly affecting the establishment or functioning of the common market or the internal market, respectively.

[9] Art. 43 EC. [10] *Ibid.*, Art. 84. [11] *Ibid.*, Art. 130s.

of the common market for the attainment of Community objectives. Acts adopted pursuant to such provisions may be complemented, particularly in the case of agricultural and regional policies, by the grant of Community aid,[12] designed to encourage national measures consistent with the acts concerned.

Such Treaty provisions might be seen as enabling the Community to move from 'negative' towards 'positive' integration.[13] The distinction between the two kinds of integration cannot, however, be expressed as if the operation of the former kind were determined solely by the need to secure elimination of barriers to trade between Member States and only the latter recognized other policy goals. A distinction relying essentially on a reformulation of the traditional distinction between liberalism and interventionism[14] would be inadequate for the purposes of analysis of Community harmonization.[15]

On the one hand, the Community legislature may be bound by Treaty liberalization provisions.[16] Hence, the harmonization process must take account of liberalization requirements entailed by such provisions. On the other hand, Member States retain considerable policy-making powers. Even if the Treaty were to require nothing more than the reduction of trade barriers, the drive towards their reduction might still be compromised by the need to make some allowance for the exercise of such powers by Member States. In fact, the Treaty embodies various requirements other than those of trade liberalization, which must also be respected by the Community legislature.[17]

[12] A. Evans, *The Law of the European Community, including the EEA Agreement* (Deventer 1994), ch. 19.

[13] In 1987 G. Sjöstedt, 'Nordic and World Economic-Political Co-operation: Competition, Adaptation or Participation?' [1987] *Cooperation and Conflict* 209–26, at 223 wrote that EC–EFTA relations were in a process of transition from 'negative' to 'positive' integration.

[14] L. Pålsson, *EG-rätt* (Lund, 1976), 16 treats this distinction as being central to Community law. The underlying assumptions remain dominant in Community law studies. See, more recently, W. P. J. Wils, 'The Search for the Rule in Article 30 EEC. Much Ado About Nothing?' [1993] *European Law Review* 475.

[15] L. Tsoukalis, *The New European Economy: The Politics and Economics of Integration* (Oxford, 1991), 251. The relationship between liberalization and harmonization in the Community context is more complex. E.g., it is said that in a mixed economy positive-market-integration-from-above may be a prerequisite of negative-market-integration-from-above. See J. Pelkmans and T. Heller, 'The Federal Economy: Law and Economic Integration and the Positive State—The U.S.A. and Europe Compared in an Economic Perspective' in M. Cappelletti *et al.* (eds.), Integration Through Law (Berlin, 1986), i, 245–412, at 325.

[16] Within its margin of appreciation, the Community legislature must respect Art. 30 EC when adopting harmonization measures. See Case C–39/90 *Denkavit Futtermittel* v. *Land Baden-Württemberg* [1991] ECR I–3099, I–3108. See, similarly, regarding Art. 95 EC, Case 15/81 *Gaston Schul Douane Expediteur BV* v. *Inspecteur der Invoerrechten en Accijnen, Roosendaal* [1982] ECR 1409, 1432. Cf. under the ECSC Treaty, Joined Cases 32 and 33/58 *Société Nouvelles des Usines de Pontlieue—Aciéries du Temple (SNUPAT)* v. *ECSC High Authority* [1959] ECR 127, 143.

[17] Community measures requiring a high standard of protection for such requirements may be envisaged, as by Art. 100a(3) EC. Harmonization measures may also specifically preserve the power of Member States to adopt restrictive measures on 'general good' grounds. See, e.g., Art. 19(6) of Dir. 93/22 of 10 May 1993 ([1993] OJ L141/27) on investment services in the securities field.

Consequently, harmonization, like the operation of liberalization provisions, may reflect the interplay of the underlying requirements.

For example, Article 57 of the Treaty seeks to facilitate exercise of freedom of establishment through providing for the enactment of directives on the mutual recognition of diplomas, certificates and other evidence of formal qualifications[18] and on the harmonization of training requirements and conditions of access.[19] In the case of medical and allied and pharmaceutical professions, the progressive abolition of restrictions shall be dependent upon co-ordination of the conditions for their exercise in the various Member States.[20] This provision is said to be directed towards reconciling freedom of establishment with the application of national professional rules justified by the general good.[21]

The need for such reconciliation in Community harmonization practice generally is recognized in the case law of the Court of Justice. For example, since the protection of the environment is 'one of the Community's essential objectives', harmonization must, according to the Court, take account of environmental protection requirements as well as liberalization requirements.[22] Again, in the agricultural sector harmonization must take account of requirements relating to the public interest, such as the defence of the consumer and the protection of the health and life of humans and animals.[23]

The implications for the Community legislature and, more fundamentally, for the relationship between Community law and national law are underlined by Article 100a(4) of the Treaty.[24] According to this provision, after adoption of a harmonization measure by the Council by a qualified majority a Member State may apply national provisions on grounds of major needs referred to in Article 36 or related to protection of the environment or the working environment. Hence, even if legislation taking inadequate account of such 'needs' may

[18] *Ibid.*, Art. 57(1). [19] *Ibid.*, Art. 57(2). [20] *Ibid.*, Art. 57(3).

[21] Case 71/76 *Thieffry* v. *Conseil de l'Ordre des Avocats à la Cour de Paris* [1977] ECR 765, 776. See, earlier, Case 33/74 *Johannes Henricus Maria Van Binsbergen* v. *bestuur van de bedrijfsvereniging voor de Metalnijverheid* [1974] ECR 1299, 1309. Cf. regarding the need for harmonization to take account of requirements relating to protection of consumers and the health and life of persons, Case C–146/91 *Koinopraxia Enoséon Georgikon Diacheiriséos Enchorion Proionton Syn. PE (KYDEP)* v. *EU Council and EC Commission* [1994] ECR I–4199, I–4239–40 and I–4242–3. Cf. also, regarding the requirements of 'fair trading', Case 249/85 *Albako Margarinefabrik Maria von der Linde GmbH & Co. KG* v. *Bundesanstalt für landwirtschaftliche Marktordnung* [1987] ECR 2345, 2360.

[22] Case 240/83 *Procureur de la République* v. *Association de Défense des Brûleurs d'Huiles Usagées* [1985] ECR 531, 549. Art. 130r(2) EC, as amended by the TEU, provides that environmental protection requirements must be integrated into the definition and implementation of other Community policies.

[23] Case 68/86 *United Kingdom* v. *EC Council* [1988] ECR 855, 896. See also Case C–131/87 *EC Commission* v. *EC Council* [1989] ECR 3743, 3770–1.

[24] See, more particularly, the exhortation to the Community legislature in the Declarations on the Protection of Animals and on Assessment of the Environmental Impact of Community Measures and, in connection with nature conservation, the Declaration on Pt. Three, Title XVI of the Treaty Establishing the European Community, annexed to the TEU.

lawfully be enacted, such legislation risks being ineffective in reducing obstacles to trade.[25]

The implication is that the Community legislature lacks a legal monopoly to determine the requirements with which harmonization is concerned. Consequently, the concept of supremacy may be inadequate to capture and express the variegation and potential dynamism of the relationship between Community law and national law.[26]

More particularly, it may be an oversimplification to regard harmonization only as reintroducing dynamism into a situation rendered static at any given time by exhaustion of liberalization provisions.[27] If the requirements underlying the harmonization process are essentially the same as those which determine liberalization[28] and may be invoked by Member States and others in the context of either process, the two processes may be capable of dynamic interaction.[29] Such interaction may occur in the sense that the approach of one to underlying Treaty requirements may affect the operation of the other.[30]

Recognition of these underlying requirements by the liberalization process cannot ensure that harmonization takes place.[31] However, their recognition may establish guidelines for the Council and Commission 'for defining the

[25] Art. 100a(5) EC also requires that dirs. enacted under Art. 100a 'shall, in appropriate cases, include a safeguard clause authorizing the Member States to take, for one or more of the non-economic reasons referred to in Art. 36, provisional measures subject to a Community control procedure'. See, more particularly, in the environmental field, Art. 130r(2) of the Treaty. Moreover, Art. 130t provides that environmental protection measures adopted by the Community under Art. 130s shall not prevent any Member State from maintaining or introducing more stringent measures. See also, regarding positive discrimination in favour of women, Art. 6(3) of the Agreement on Social Policy Concluded between the Member States of the European Community with the Exception of the United Kingdom.

[26] Cf. the preference for viewing the relationship as one of parallelism in N. Reich, 'Protection of Diffuse Interests in the EEC and the Perspective of "Progressively Establishing" an Internal Market' [1988] *Journal of Consumer Policy* 395–417.

[27] A. McGee and S. Weatherill, 'The Evolution of the Single Market-Harmonization or Liberalization' (1990) 53 *MLR*. 578–96, at 578 begin by 'examining the distinction between lawful and unlawful trade barriers, before considering the ways in which lawful barriers are being treated in the run up to 1992'. In reality, the 'lawfulness' of trade barriers under the EC Treaty may be affected by harmonization. See, e.g., Case 382/87 *Regina Buet and Educational Business Services (EBS) Sàrl* v. *Ministère Public* [1989] ECR 1235, 1252–3.

[28] Harmonization may not necessarily have to be based on Art. 100a, even though trade liberalization is involved. See Case C–70/88 *European Parliament* v. *EC Council* [1991] ECR I–4529; see also Case C–155/91 *EC Commission* v. *EC Council* [1993] ECR I–939.

[29] I.e., their relationship may be more than what J.-M. Sun and J. Pelkmans, 'Regulatory Competition in the Single Market' [1995] *JCMS* 67–89, at 67 describe as 'complementary'.

[30] *Ibid.* Cf. the idea that 'the mere threat of regulatory competition as a realistic alternative to . . . harmonization disciplines the harmonization process itself' (*ibid.* 87).

[31] Cf., regarding the limited amenability to judicial review of choices of policy priorities by the Community legislature under Art. 39 EC, Tesauro A. G. in Case C–204/88 *Ministère Public* v. *Jean-Jacques Paris* [1989] ECR I–4361, I–4372–3.

economic order to be respected by their policies'[32] or may narrow down the area in which Member States can continue to apply national policies.[33] As policy options become narrower, the policy autonomy of each Member State becomes increasingly illusory,[34] and the time needed for completion of Community legislative procedures can be expected to decrease.[35]

On the other hand, harmonization seeks the kind of equality which depends on traders becoming and remaining more alike. To this extent, harmonization risks confronting the dynamism of liberalization and other requirements in the Treaty with a static element.[36] Such dynamism may only partly have been restored by Article 100a(4) of the Treaty, it being disputed whether this provision entitles a Member State to introduce national enactments providing requirements referred to therein with a higher level of protection than that secured by a previous Community measure adopted under Article 100a(1).[37]

Even if threats to dynamism are disregarded, harmonization may remain problematic. The capacity of harmonization to reconcile reduction of trade barriers with other Treaty requirements is not unlimited. Harmonization cannot by its nature be infinitely variegated, and so it necessarily has an impact on the relative costs of traders, depending on their particular circumstances. Limitations to the utility of the process may be implied.

For example, Article 101 of the Treaty provides for harmonization where a difference between the provisions laid down by law, regulation, or administrative action in Member States distorts competition in the common market and the resultant distortion needs to be eliminated. According to the Commission, this provision could not apply to the competitive distortions in horticulture which resulted from the fixing of prices for petroleum products at different levels in the various Member States. It would, in particular, be arbitrary to take

[32] P. VerLoren van Themaat, 'Some Preliminary Observations on the Intergovernmental Conferences: The Relations between the Concepts of a Common Market, a Monetary Union, an Economic Union, a Political Union and Sovereignty' (1991) 28 *CMLRev*. 291–318, at 316.

[33] See, e.g., G. Schricker, 'European Harmonization of Unfair Competition Law—a Futile Venture?' [1991] *International Review of Industrial Property and Copyright Law* 788–801.

[34] It may, however, be an exaggeration to regard the free movement of capital and the common market as 'a first legal argument against a rejection of monetary union for political reasons' (P. VerLoren van Themaat, n. 32 above, 295–96).

[35] T. Sloot and P. Verschuren, 'Decision-Making Speed in the European Community' [1990] *JCMS* 75–85, at 77.

[36] Solutions may be seen in terms of selecting 'the appropriate intensity' of harmonization to be sought by each Community act. See *Report of the Group of Independent Experts on Legislative and Administrative Simplification*, COM(95)288, 53.

[37] L. Krämer, 'Environmental Protection and Art. 30 EEC Treaty' (1993) 30 *CMLRev*. 111–43, at 113 considers that Art. 100a(4) only permits maintenance of existing provisions. On the other hand, D. Wyatt and A. Dashwood, *European Community Law* (London, 1993), 366 consider that the ordinary meaning of this para. is such as to cover new measures. C. D. Ehlermann, 'The Internal Market after the Single European Act' (1987) 24 *CMLRev*. 361–409, at 394 considers that amendments to provisions existing at the time of adoption of a Community measure may be permissible. The Commission certainly accepts consolidation of such provisions. See Dec. 94/783 of 14 Sept. 1994 ([1994] OJ L316/43) concerning the prohibition of PCP notified by Germany.

in isolation one of the general conditions in which the undertakings of a Member State operated (for instance the price of fuels) which handicapped production in that Member State by comparison with other Member States, while ignoring the fact that other general conditions affecting production (for example, social security payments, direct taxation, conditions of credit) resulted in that production enjoying a more favourable position than its competitors.[38] Indeed, adoption of such an approach might lead to treatment of the Member State where undertakings were most handicapped as the norm.[39]

5.2.2 International Harmonization

The EC Treaty may provide for the conclusion of agreements with third states, which may involve 'international harmonization' in specific fields.[40] However, problems of such harmonization may be even greater than those of Community harmonization. On the one hand, reconciliation of the autonomy of the Community with the sovereignty of third states is essential if the circumstances of traders from the latter and the attitudes of their governments are to be taken into account in international harmonization.[41] On the other hand, such reconciliation generally has to be sought in the absence of such a developed framework as that provided by the liberalization and other requirements of the EC Treaty. Such considerations may underlie the tendency for the adoption of Community harmonization acts to be separated from the use of these acts in international harmonization efforts.[42]

However, the Community[43] or at least Member States[44] are involved in various international organizations. Such involvement might be expected to

[38] Distortions of Competition in Hothouse Agriculture, COM(80)306, 33.

[39] Cf. R. H. Snape, 'International Regulation of Subsidies' [1991] *The World Economy* 139–63, at 143.

[40] See, regarding research and technological development, Art. 130m EC and, regarding environmental protection, Art. 130r(4).

[41] Note the recognition of the critical importance of Swedish involvement in Community harmonization work in *De handelspolitiska förutsättningarna för svensk export under 1980-talet*, SOU 1984:6, bil. 6, 58.

[42] Cf. the Explanatory Memorandum to the Commission Proposal for a Directive on in Vitro Diagnostic Medical Devices, COM(95)130, 8.

[43] Art. 127(3) EC requires the Community to foster co-operation with 'the competent international organizations in the sphere of vocational training'. Art. 129(3) imposes the same requirement in relation to public health. See also, regarding research and technological development, Arts 130g(b) and 130m, regarding development co-operation, Art. 130y, and, regarding monetary policy, Art. 109h(2)(a). Art. 130r(4) also requires co-operation with international organizations in the environmental protection field. In this field a list of organizations and their committees in which Sweden participated was given in *Miljopolitiken inför 1990-talet*, prop. 1987/88:85, bil. 9.

[44] According to Art. 116 EC, after the end of the transitional period Member States should 'proceed within the framework of international organizations of an economic character only by common action'. See, in connection with the UN Commission for Europe, Case 22/70 *EC Commission* v. *EC Council* [1971] ECR 263, 280.

create the possibility that separation of Community and international harmonization might be replaced by the participation of the Community and third states in harmonization within the frameworks provided by the organizations concerned, i.e., 'intra-organizational harmonization'.[45]

United Nations

According to Article 229 of the EC Treaty, the Commission is 'to ensure the maintenance of all appropriate relations with the organs of the United Nations [and] of its specialized agencies'.[46] More particularly, Member States are involved with third states in the work of the United Nations Conference on Trade and Development (UNCTAD),[47] the Economic Commission for Europe,[48] and the United Nations has a code of principles and rules for control of anti-competitive practices. The European Commission, Member States and third states participate in the group of experts which follows up the application of the code.[49] Contacts between the Community and third states concerning environmental protection also take place within the context of the United Nations Environmental Programme (UNEP).[50] However, United Nations membership is so heterogeneous that the results of its work are unlikely to reflect the degree of integration taking place between the Community and third states in Europe.

GATT

Article 229 of the EC Treaty provides for the Commission 'to ensure the maintenance of all appropriate relations' with organs of the General Agreement on Tariffs and Trade (GATT).[51] The framework provided by GATT might be thought somewhat more promising for harmonization purposes

[45] See, in relation to competition law, the *Twenty-Fourth Report on Competition Policy*, COM(95)142, 292–3. Cf. *Report of the Group of Independent Experts on Legislative and Administrative Simplification*, COM(95)288, 57.

[46] A Joint Declaration on Co-operation with the States Members of International Organizations was also annexed to the EC Treaty. More particularly, in the field of development co-operation Art. 130u(3) requires the Community and Member States to comply with the commitments and to take account of the objectives they have approved in the context of the UN and other competent international organizations. See also, in connection with the CFSP, the reference to 'the principles of the United Nations Charter' in Art. J.1(2) of the TEU.

[47] For example, Sweden and the Community participated in UNCTAD work concerning sea transport policy. See *Sverige–EG* 1986 (Utrikesdepartementets handelsavdelning, 1987), 47.

[48] *Sverige–EFTA–EG 1989* (Utrikesdepartementets handelsavdelning, 1990), 20. The ECE is also involved in the international harmonization of standards. See *Provning och kontroll i internationell samverkan* (SOU 1988:6), 127.

[49] *Redovisning av det svenska integrationsarbetet våren 1988-mars 1989* (Utrikesdepartementets handelsavdelning), 151.

[50] *Sverige–EFTA–EG 1988* (Utrikesdepartementets handelsavdelning, 1989), 115.

[51] The implication in the 6th recital in the Preamble to the EC Treaty (sect. 2.2.3 above) is that Community activity is to be GATT-consistent.

than the UN.[52] In particular, the GATT notification system means that problems of trade barriers may be tackled within the GATT framework,[53] and solutions can be sought which are consistent with the obligations contained in this framework. To this extent, participation by the Community and third states in GATT may tend to facilitate international harmonization.[54]

OECD

According to Article 231 of the EC Treaty, the Community is to 'establish close cooperation' with the Organization for Economic Cooperation and Development (OECD). While GATT has traditionally been concerned only with trade in goods,[55] the OECD has been concerned with trade relations more generally,[56] as for example in relation to capital movement.[57] To this end, the latter frequently produces recommendations designed to encourage members to harmonize their national law. More particularly, the competition authorities of third states, Member States, and the European Commission co-operate in the Competition Committee of the OECD.[58] OECD work may also be important in relation to environmental matters.[59]

[52] The 2nd recital in the Preamble to the Swedish Free Trade Agreement stressed that the abolition of trading obstacles envisaged therein was to be achieved in accordance with provisions of GATT governing the establishment of free trade areas. This recital reflected concern at the time of the conclusion of the Free Trade Agreements that these Agreements should not be seen as entailing violations of the rights of other Parties to GATT. See the doubts expressed in the GATT Working Party on the Agreement (BISD, 20th Supp., 183–96). Cf. the concern that tariff concessions to Poland and Hungary should be consistent with international obligations of the Community (*Action Plan for Co-ordinated Aid to Poland and Hungary*, COM(89)470, 3).

[53] See, e.g., *Sverige–EFTA–EG 1987* (Utrikesdepartementets handelsavdelning, 1988), 37. More particularly, solutions to problems of trade in relation to certain agricultural products have been negotiated under Art. XXVIII of GATT. See, e.g., Dec. 89/549 of 5 Apr. 1989 ([1989] OJ L299/1) concerning the conclusion of the Agreement in the form of Agreed Minutes between the EEC and the Kingdom of Sweden on apples and pears negotiated under Art. XXVIII of the GATT.

[54] Certainly, at the EFTA Ministerial Meeting in Oslo, 14–15 Mar. 1989 (EFTA Bull. 2/1989, 4–7) the EFTA States stressed their determination to strengthen and further to improve the multilateral trading system and to fight all forms of protectionism. To this end, they pledged their active and constructive support for the efforts being made in GATT and expressed the view that European integration and global liberalization, as pursued in the Uruguay Round, were complementary (para. 20). See also para. 12 of the Joint Communiqué of the Meeting between Ministers of the Member States of EFTA and Willy De Clercq, Member of the EC Commission in Geneva, 29 Nov. 1988 (EFTA Bull. 4/88, 4–5). See, similarly, regarding the Euro-Mediterranean partnership, the Conclusions of the Presidency of the European Council meeting of Dec. 1994 (Bull. EU 12–1994, I.14).

[55] The Agreement establishing the WTO has a wider scope.

[56] See, generally, D. Henderson, 'International Economic Cooperation Revisited' [1993] *Government and Opposition* 11–35.

[57] In para. 23 of the Declaration of the EFTA Ministerial Meeting in Oslo, 14–15 Mar. 1989 (EFTA Bull. 2/1989, 4–7) EFTA States were said to 'value highly' OECD work.

[58] *Sverige och den västeuropeiska integrationen*, prop. 1987/88:66, 51. Sea transport policy issues are discussed within the OECD Sea Transport Policy Committee. See *Sverige–EFTA–EG 1987* (Utrikesdepartementets handelsavdelning, 1988), 39.

[59] See, e.g., *Kemikaliekontroll*, SOU 1984:77.

Council of Europe

Article 230 of the EC Treaty requires the Community to 'establish all appropriate forms of cooperation with the Council of Europe'.[60] The latter[61] may not only influence national legal developments in the Member States of the Community but also Community law-making.[62] For example, the consumer protection policy of the Community was closely modelled on instruments and policy documents produced by the Council of Europe.[63] Such practice may result in the Council of Europe being pictured as providing a 'useful bridge' between the Community and 'other Europeans'.[64] Consistently with this picture, the possibility has been discussed that the Council of Europe might agree to 'extend' Community legislation to those of its members who are outside the Community.[65]

Community involvement in such organizations implies that the rules of the latter and positions reached through contacts therein cannot be disregarded by the Community legislature. On the other hand, the Community may seek to separate its involvement therein from its 'internal' harmonization efforts, with a view to ensuring that the latter are not prejudiced.[66] In any case, Community involvement in such organizations may be so dominant[67] or, because of conflicts of jurisdiction between Member States and Community institutions,

[60] In addition, there are an exchange of letters of 16 June 1987 (Exchange of Letters between the Council of Europe and the European Community concerning the consolidation and intensification of co-operation ([1987] OJ L273/35)) and a Council Dec. of 20 Mar. 1989 (Bull. EC 3–1989, 2.2.51) governing such co-operation. See Commission Reply by Mr Matutes to Written Question 1632/91 ([1992] OJ C38/36) by Mr Yves Verwaerde. See, more particularly, regarding education, vocational training, and youth, Art. 126(3) EC and, regarding culture, Art. 128(3).

[61] Cf., regarding the European Security Conference, *Sverige–EFTA–EG 1989* (Utrikesdepartementets handelsavdelning, 1990), 20.

[62] In the Declaration of the EFTA Ministerial Meeting in Oslo, 14–15 Mar. 1989 the EFTA States stressed the importance of the work of the Council of Europe in promoting closer European co-operation, particularly in the fields of human rights, education, culture and social affairs (EFTA Bull. 2/1989, 4–7, para. 22).

[63] A. Evans 'Council of Europe: Consumer Protection Initiatives' [1980] *JWTL* 454–61. See also *Sverige–EFTA–EG 1988* (Utrikesdepartementets handelsavdelning, 1989), 111, regarding Swedish involvement in Council of Europe work concerning transnational transmission of television programmes.

[64] *Relations between the Community and the Council of Europe*, COM(89)124, 5. See, e.g., the Convention on the Elaboration of a European Pharmacopoeia (ETS(1964) 50), which seeks to harmonize the specifications for the preparation of medicinal substances used throughout Europe.

[65] SEC(87)190; EFTA Group of Legal Experts, 'Possible Models for Cooperation between the EC and EFTA States', EFTA/GLE 4/87, 10.

[66] In connection with Community relations with the Council of Europe, the Commission stressed the 'need to preserve the scope for development of the Community's powers and not to hinder the realization of the objectives of the Treaty and the Single Act'. See *Relations between the Community and the Council of Europe*, COM(89)124, 3.

[67] E.g., concern has been expressed that 'a powerful organization such as the EC is more likely to impose its preferences on the third institution than the smaller EFTA countries'. See EFTA Group of Legal Experts, 'Possible Models for Cooperation between the EC and EFTA States', EFTA/GLE 4/87, 10.

so incoherent[68] or so lacking in credibility[69] that such organizations are unable to provide a satisfactory framework for international harmonization. Hence, provision for harmonization may be made in Free Trade Agreements and Association Agreements concluded between the Community and third States.

5.3 FREE TRADE AGREEMENTS

The Free Trade Agreements formally provided for bilateral harmonization between the Parties. In practice, however, a much greater role was played by voluntary harmonization and inter-organizational harmonization.

5.3.1 Bilateral Harmonization

The Swedish Free Trade Agreement not only contained particular provisions envisaging bilateral harmonization in the agricultural sector. It also contained an 'evolutionary clause', envisaging bilateral harmonization more generally.

Particular Harmonization Clauses

Article 10 of the Swedish Free Trade Agreement provided that if either Party established specific rules as a result of the implementation of its agricultural policy or any alteration of the current rules, that Party might adapt the arrangements resulting from the Agreement in respect of the products which were the subject of those rules or alterations. In such cases the Party in question must take account of the interests of the other Party.[70] To this end, the Parties might consult each other in the Joint Committee, which was created by the Agreement.[71] Moreover, according to Article 15(1), the Parties declared their readiness to foster, so far as their agricultural policies allowed, the harmonious development of trade in agricultural products to which the Agreement did not apply.[72] It was envisaged that this provision would provide a basis for tackling problems concerning traditional Swedish food exports, such

[68] See, e.g., the argument of the Commission in Opinion 1/94 *(Competence of the Community to conclude international agreements on services and the protection of industrial property)* [1994] ECR I–5267, I–5419–20. See also the Report of the Committee on External Economic Relations on Relations between the European Community and the Organization for Economic Cooperation and Development (OECD), EP Doc. A2–313/88, 15. See, generally, C. Schricke, 'La CEE et l'OCDE à l'heure de l'Acte Unique' [1989] *RGDIP* 801–30.

[69] The Commission considers that the credibility of the Community in negotiations with third states may be undermined by failure of Member States fully and rapidly to transpose dirs. into national law. See *Completing the Internal Market: An Area without Internal Frontiers Progress Report Required by Art. 8b of the Treaty*, COM(90)552, 18.

[70] A similar clause was contained in Art. 22 of the EFTA Convention (SÖ 1960:1).

[71] See sect. 6.3 below.

[72] A similar declaration was made in Art. 9(1) of the Agreement between EFTA States and Spain (SÖ 1980:87).

as bacon and butter, to the former EFTA States which joined the Community in 1973.[73]

General 'Evolutionary' Clauses

In the third recital in the Preamble to the Swedish Free Trade Agreement the Parties declared their readiness to examine, in the light of any relevant factor, and in particular of developments in the Community, the possibility of developing and deepening their relations where it would appear to be useful in the interests of their economies to extend them to fields not covered by the Agreement. This recital might be regarded simply as having contemplated possible extension of liberalization provisions to fields other than trade in manufactured goods, such as the supply of services. On the other hand, the idea of 'deepening' the relations between the Parties might be regarded as having envisaged the further possibility of a qualitative change in their relations going beyond simply the removal of trade obstacles.[74] In other words, some kind of legal framework for 'spill-over', albeit rudimentary in comparison with that provided for in the EC Treaty and particularly designed to allow for Community dynamism, may have been envisaged.[75]

Certainly, an 'evolutionary' clause was included in Article 32 of the Swedish Agreement. While this provision did not mention 'deepening', its terms seemed broad enough to be interpreted, particularly in the light of the Preamble, as providing such a framework.[76] According to the first paragraph, where a Party considered that it would be useful in the common interest of both Parties to develop the relations established by the Agreement by extending them to fields not covered thereby, that Party must submit a reasoned request to the other Party. The Parties might instruct the Joint Committee to examine this request and, where appropriate, to make recommendations to them, particularly with a view to opening negotiations.

In the Swedish Agreement, as in the Norwegian Agreement,[77] this procedure was thus to be activated on the basis of the 'common interest' of the Parties. In contrast, the Austrian,[78] Icelandic,[79] and Swiss Agreements[80] required that resort to the procedure must be based on the 'interests of the economies' of the Parties.[81] This contrast implies that considerations other than exclusively economic ones could be taken into account within the framework of the

[73] *Utrikesutskottets betänkande med anledning av propositionen 1972:135 angående avtal med de europeiska gemenskaperna m.m. jämte motioner* (Report of the Foreign Affairs Committee of the Parliament on the Free Trade Agreement) (UU 1972:20), 14–5.

[74] It was presumably because any such change was regarded in Finland as unacceptable at the time that the recital was omitted from the Preamble to the Finnish Free Trade Agreement ([1973] OJ L328/2).

[75] AiH 8/1971, 2.

[76] The same wording was used in Art. 29 of the Swedish Free Trade Agreement with the ECSC ([1973] OJ L350/76).

[77] [1973] OJ L171/2.

[78] [1972] JO L300/2.

[79] [1972] JO L301/2.

[80] [1972] JO L300/189.

[81] See, similarly, the Free Trade Agreement with Israel ([1975] OJ L136/2).

Norwegian and Swedish Agreements. The implication becomes stronger when Article 32 of the Swedish Agreement is taken together with the reference in the first recital in the Preamble to the desire of the Parties to contribute 'to the work of constructing Europe'.

This provision thus seems to have had somewhat more potential significance than Article 30 of the EFTA Convention,[82] which is the nearest equivalent in that Convention. According to Article 30, EFTA States recognize that the economic and financial policies of each of them affect the economies of other such states, and they intend to pursue these policies in a manner which serves to promote the objectives of the association.[83] To this end, they will periodically exchange views on all aspects of these policies, and the EFTA Council may make recommendations to the states on matters relating to these policies to the extent necessary to ensure the attainment of the objectives and the smooth operation of the association.

However, the mere fact that Article 32 of the Swedish Free Trade Agreement had more potential significance than Article 30 of the EFTA Convention did not mean that the potential of the former would necessarily be realized. Indeed, when the Swedish Government suggested that Article 32 could usefully operate in relation to technical or non-tariff barriers to trade, the Commission, concerned to preserve Community autonomy of decision-making, expressed a preference for voluntary harmonization[84] and the mutual recognition of test results.[85]

The Swedish Government also considered that use could be made of Article 32 in relation to questions of public procurement, energy policy, transport policy, environmental policy, and research and development. According to the Government, what was important was that the Agreement contained a procedure for dealing with future co-operation questions in such fields. To this extent, Article 32 was said to compensate for the fact that the Agreement did not itself provide for co-operation in many of the areas of interest to Sweden. During negotiation of the Agreement the Commission accepted that such questions could at least be considered in the future as Community policies began to emerge.[86] Attention was not drawn to the fact that within the framework of an Agreement concluded under Article 113 of the EC Treaty

[82] SÖ 1960:1.

[83] In 1960 the Swedish Government commented, in connection with this provision, that the more far-reaching 'co-operation' envisaged in the EC Treaty seemed neither necessary nor desirable for Swedish purposes. See *Kungl. Maj:ts proposition till riksdagen angående godkännande av Sveriges anslutning till konventionen angående upprättandet av Europeiska frihandelssammanslutningen, m. m., given Stockholms slott den 4 januari 1960* (Royal Proclamation approving Swedish accession to the EFTA Convention), prop. 1960:25, 32.

[84] See, later, the Community suggestion of Apr. 1984 in *En ny kontrollordning för elektrisk materiel, m.m.*, prop. 1987/88:82, 3. See sect. 5.3.2 below, regarding the voluntary harmonization process.

[85] AiH 4/1972, 18.

[86] AiH 4/1972, 22.

the Community could only validly engage in cooperation in relation to that which constituted commercial policy under that provision.[87] Thus, for example, it was considered necessary to base the Financial Protocol to the Portuguese Free Trade Agreement[88] on Article 235 as well as Article 113 of the EC Treaty.

While the permissible scope of action under Article 32 of the Swedish Free Trade Agreement may thus have been problematic, the nature of the procedure by which it was to take place seems to have been even more so. The second paragraph of Article 32(1) of the Swedish Agreement, like that with Norway,[89] provided that recommendations emanating from the Joint Committee might, where appropriate, aim at the attainment of 'concerted harmonization'. The implication of the fact that the harmonization must be concerted was that Sweden was not expected unilaterally to harmonize its rules with Community law.[90] On the other hand, the extent of the concertation envisaged seems to have been limited. It was stipulated, in language anticipating that of the EEA Agreement,[91] that the autonomy of decision of each Party must not be impaired.[92] Thus during negotiation of the Free Trade Agreement the Commission made clear that there could be no question of including a special procedure, as sought by Sweden, for information and consultation relating to Community harmonization efforts.[93] Moreover, since any resulting recommendations would not be binding[94] and would be subject to ratification or approval by the Parties in accordance with their own procedures,[95] it appears that parallel rules, rather than rules deriving direct legal force from a common source,[96] were envisaged in Article 32.

[87] According to the ECJ, procedures such as that in Art. 32 of the Swedish Free Trade Agreement may not affect the competence of the Community under Art. 113 EC. See Opinion 1/94 *(Competence of the Community to conclude international agreements on services and the protection of industrial property)* [1994] ECR I–5267, I–5408. See, regarding evolution of the scope of this policy, sect. 2.2.3 above.

[88] [1978] OJ L274/1.

[89] [1973] OJ L171/2.

[90] H. Danelius, 'Sveriges avtal med de europeiska gemenskaperna—juridiska aspekter' ('Sweden's Agreement with the European Communities—Juridical Aspects') [1973] *SvJT* 97–114, at 110.

[91] See the final clause in the Preamble to the EEA Agreement.

[92] See also the statement of Commission President Delors to the European Parliament in January 1990 (EP Debs. No. 3–385, 111, 17 Jan. 1990).

[93] *Utrikesutskottets betänkande med anledning av propositionen 1972:135 angående avtal med de europeiska gemenskaperna m.m. jämte motioner* (Report of the Foreign Affairs Committee of the Parliament on the Free Trade Agreement) (UU 1972:20), 20 and 28. The Commissioner responsible for the negotiation of the Free Trade Agreements merely described these clauses as '*à la base de progrès futurs*'. See also 'Agreements with the EFTA States not Applying for Membership', Bull. EC 9–1972, 11–21, at 19. See, generally, R. Milas, 'Les Relations entre la Communauté Européenne et les Pays Nordiques' [1984] *RMC* 534–43, at 538.

[94] Art. 29(1) of the Swedish Agreement only required that decisions of the Joint Committee were to 'be put into effect by the Contracting Parties in accordance with their own rules'.

[95] Art. 32(2) of the Swedish Agreement. Cf. Art. 23(3) of the Free Trade Agreement between the EFTA States and Spain (SÖ 1980:87), which provided for a Party to accept a Joint Committee decision subject to fulfilment of constitutional requirements. The decision would enter into force, if no later date was specified therein, on the day the lifting of the reservation was notified.

[96] As in the case, e.g., of Community regs. See Art. 189(2) EC, regarding their 'direct applicability'.

Hence, while the Swedish Agreement clearly laid down a framework for the Parties to engage in harmonization, it might better be described as a framework of an intergovernmental kind rather than one involving supranationalism—in other words, the harmonization envisaged did not require participation by institutions independent of the Parties in adoption of measures having direct legal force within the Parties. In this respect, it seems that the substance, if not the form, of the procedures in the Swedish and Norwegian Agreements differed little from that of the procedures provided for in the Agreements with other EFTA States, which made no express reference to harmonization.

In the case of the Free Trade Agreement with Switzerland,[97] the Swiss Supreme Court took the view not simply that an obligation to harmonize was 'deliberately excluded' from the Agreement, but also that existing legal rules within Switzerland and the Community were mutually recognized and 'approval was given to the unrestricted, independent implementation of these rules'.[98] The Finnish Free Trade Agreement[99] contained no equivalent to Article 32 of the Swedish Agreement at all, and the Preamble stressed that the Parties retained their autonomous power of decision.[100] The absence of an 'evolutionary clause' in this Agreement was sometimes considered worthy of note. For example, the Declaration of the EFTA Ministers at their meeting in Vienna in May 1977[101] expressly noted that the Finnish Agreement contained no such clause and that Finland sought to develop relations with the Community within the framework of the aims of the Agreement. Nevertheless, it is said that the absence of such a clause in the Finnish Agreement did not, in practice, prevent Finnish relations with the Community developing in the same way as relations between other EFTA States and the Community.[102]

In fact, it has been argued that, since no prior commitment to evolution was expressed in such clauses, even in the Swedish Agreement, anything done pursuant to them could also have been done without them.[103]

[97] [1972] JO L300/189.

[98] *Adams* v. *Staatsanwaltschaft des Kantons Basel-Stadt* [1978] 3 CMLR 480, 485. Such thinking, if followed literally, might have led to the non-application of much of the Agreement. Cf., regarding the Competition Agreement with the United States, Tesauro A. G. in Case C–327/91 *France* v. *EC Commission* [1994] ECR I–3641, I–3664.

[99] [1973] OJ L328/2.

[100] Cf. the Soviet memorandum of 18 Aug. 1972 regarding Austrian neutrality and the problem of extension of the Austrian Free Trade Agreement to undefined fields.

[101] EFTA Bull. 5/1977, 4–5, para. 4.

[102] S. Norberg, 'The Free Trade Agreements of the EFTA States with the EC—Experiences and Problems' [1988] *SvJT* 77–107, at 82.

[103] E. P. Wellenstein, 'The Free Trade Agreements Between the Enlarged European Communities and the EFTA-States' (1973) 10 *CMLRev*. 137–49, at 145–6. See also M. Jäger, 'Die sogenannte Entwicklungsklauseln in den Abkommen der EWG mit den Rest-EFTA-Staaten, inbesondere der Schweiz' [1972] *Aussenwirtschaft* 323–39.

Practice

Little use was made of the procedures laid down in Articles 10 and 15[104] or that in 32 of the Swedish Agreement,[105] though the 'evolutionary' clause in the Portuguese Free Trade Agreement[106] was invoked to some effect.[107] At a meeting of officials from EFTA States in 1982 it was noted that co-operation outside the Free Trade Agreements was taking place on an *ad hoc* basis.[108] Evolutionary clauses were rarely invoked as the legal basis for such co-operation, though such clauses are said to have served as expressions of the willingness of the Parties to co-operate in new fields.[109] Certainly, the Preamble to the Protocol to the Swedish Agreement concerning export restrictions,[110] referred both to Article 32 of this Agreement and to what was then described as the European Economic Space.[111] On the other hand, the absence of such a clause in the Finnish Agreement did not prevent adoption of a corresponding Protocol to this Agreement.[112]

At most, the Swedish Agreement provided a formal basis for giving effect to harmonization agreed through contacts outside the framework of the procedures laid down by the Agreement. Such limited use of Article 32 of the Agreement may have been an inevitable consequence of the fact that, according to Community law, the Agreement was simply a commercial policy instrument adopted under Article 113 of the EC Treaty.[113] To the extent that

[104] In the event, trade in unprocessed agricultural products depended on *ad hoc* arrangements made outside the framework of the Swedish Agreement rather than harmonization procedures contained therein. See, e.g., the Agreement in the form of an exchange of letters of 14 July 1986 ([1986] OJ L328/31) between the EC and Sweden concerning non-agricultural and processed agricultural products not covered by the Agreement. The Community concluded this Agreement under Art. 113 EC.

[105] The Agreement between the EC, Norway, and Sweden ([1992] OJ L200/21), concluded by the Community under Art. 84(2) EC, made no reference to the evolutionary clause. No such clause was included in the later Free Trade Agreement between the EFTA States and Spain (SÖ 1980:87).

[106] [1972] JO L301/66.

[107] *EG under första halvåret 1975: Rapport från svenska delegationen i Bryssel* (Utrikes- och handelsdepartementen 1975), 15.

[108] Serious constitutional problems might arise in such co-operation. E.g., Swedish contributions to the budget for the research programme regarding wood, including cork, as a renewable raw material ([1983] OJ L185/20) were proportionate to gross domestic product. In the case of the TEDIS Programme, national budget contributions of EFTA States were passed to the EFTA Secretariat, and the latter passed them on to the Community ([1989] OJ L400/22). In either case Swedish expenditure was ultimately determined by Commission decisions concerning implementation of the relevant programme. Moreover, since Community expenditure was involved in several programmes in which EFTA States participated, the Court of Auditors must be allowed to investigate Swedish accounts relevant to such expenditure.

[109] *Sverige–EG 1982* (Utrikesdepartementets handelsavdelning, 1983), 33. See also H. Lidgard, 'Sverige-EEG och konkurrensen' [1974] *SvJT* 18–33, at 32.

[110] [1989] OJ L295/22.

[111] See also, regarding bilateral agreements between Switzerland and the Community, R. Senti, *EG EFTA Binnenmarkt* (2nd edn., Zurich, 1992), 144.

[112] [1989] OJ L295/2.

[113] This consideration was taken as justifying an approach to trading problems between Parties to such an Agreement different from that applied to such problems within the Community. See Capotorti A. G. in Case 225/78 *Procureur de la République, Besançon* v. *Bouhelier* [1979] ECR 3151, 3165.

the real issues arising in Swedish–Community harmonization efforts were the same as those which arose in Community harmonization efforts and were tackled within the framework of other Community policies, the treatment of the former issues could not be satisfactorily contained within the framework of such an instrument.[114]

5.3.2 Voluntary Harmonization

The Swedish response to the problems of securing bilateral harmonization entailed considerable reliance on 'voluntary harmonization'.[115] Such harmonization takes place where a third state adapts its internal legal provisions to Community law provisions which have no binding force in relation to that state. It may have something in common with that envisaged under the Free Trade Agreement, in that both processes entailed the need for adoption of implementing measures in internal law. The difference is that the measures adopted in Sweden by way of voluntary harmonization were not based on formal recommendations for harmonization under the Agreement.

Institutional Arrangements

To promote voluntary harmonization, an Integration Office was established within the Swedish Government,[116] and a Government directive of June 1988 required that every committee and special investigative body must take account of existing Community rules as well as proposals for further Community legislation and seek to harmonize Swedish draft legislation with them.[117] Any proposed deviation must be justified. Specific instructions were also given to committees preparing draft legislation on, for example, competition policy[118] to produce drafts designed to bring Swedish law more into line with that of the Community.[119]

Practice

Voluntary harmonization means that third states adopt the substance of Community rules in the framing of which they may have had no real

[114] The point may have been missed by the EFTA Group of Legal Experts in 'Possible Models for Co-operation between the EC and EFTA States' (EFTA/GLE 4/87), where it was argued that 'a discussion of the suitability of one or several models for co-operation would have to be based upon a thorough and informed analysis of the EC external relations framework'.

[115] Suggestions for formalizing the process were made in H. Stenberg, 'Sweden and the Internal Market—Situating Some Problems' [1989] *LIEI* 89–107, at 105.

[116] *Riksdagsprotokoll* 1987/88:114, 9.

[117] *Kommittédirektiv till kommittéer och särskilda utredare angående beaktande av EG-aspekter i utredningsverksamheten*, Dir 1988:43.

[118] *Sverige–EFTA–EG 1988* (Utrikesdepartementets handelsavdelning, 1988), 119–20.

[119] It was the systematic character of these arrangements rather than the practice of voluntary harmonization which was novel. Cf. G. Porro, *L'Integrazione Giuridica nell' Associazione Europea di Libero Scambio* (Milan, 1983), 260–1.

participation. Hence, it is said that, by resorting to such harmonization, the EFTA States 'reacted against marginalization, but at the inevitable price of satellization'.[120]

From the Community point of view, voluntary harmonization has the advantage of entailing no legal constraints on its future freedom of action. It was, presumably, for this reason that the Commission felt able to suggest adoption of the practice as a possibility for Sweden during the negotiation of the Free Trade Agreement.[121]

From the point of view of third states, voluntary harmonization may be claimed to entail no loss of sovereignty, the necessary decisions being taken internally.[122] The extent to which the inherent contradictions between such harmonization and formal retention of sovereignty really can be reconciled is questionable. The policy appears, at least in Sweden, simply to have been to seek to avoid attention being drawn to such contradictions. In particular, there was criticism that the reference groups for the working groups within the Integration Office were not regularly called to meet, and, more particularly, industrial representatives were apparently excluded from the working group on institutional questions.[123] It is also notable that neither the working group concerned with trade policy nor that for competition policy and consumer questions reported on questions of public enterprise, despite the obvious importance of such questions in the economy and in Community law.[124]

On the other hand, to the extent that voluntary harmonization takes place, traders from third states will be subject to the same legal conditions as competitors within the Community. In essence, what is involved for the states concerned is 'shadow membership' of the Union without formal acceptance of obligations which may be seen as threatening important national policy interests. Moreover, to the extent that the markets of third states are unified with the Community market, the Community institutions may be inhibited from introducing future divergent rules without consideration of the position of the third states concerned and even consultation at least of an informal kind.

120 P. G. Nell, 'EFTA in the 1990s: the Search for a New Identity' [1990] *JCMS* 327–58, at 352.

121 *Commission Opinion to the Council on the Relations of the Enlarged Community with the Members and Associated States of EFTA not Applying for Admission*, Bull. EC, Supp. 3/71, 12–13.

122 *Redovisning av det svenska integrationsarbetet våren 1988-mars 1989* (Utrikesdepartementets handelsavdelning, 1989), 215. See, similarly, 1989/90:KU30 *med anledning av granskning av statsrådens tjansteutövning och regeringsärendenas handläggning* (Inquiry into the work of the Cabinet and its handling of government affairs), Bil. A 31.

123 The secrecy surrounding the work of the Integration Office was criticised by the Constitutional Committee of the Swedish Parliament (1989/90:KU30 *med anledning av granskning av statsrådens tjansteutövning och regeringsärendenas handläggning*).

124 Such questions were, however, apparently dealt with in an EFTA Working Party and in an internal investigation by Swedish officials. See *Sverige och den västeuropeiska integrationen*, 1990/91:UU8, 62.

Such harmonization is said, however, to be subject to delay and uncertainty, which impede business planning.[125] Moreover, because of the limited liberalization generally secured by the Free Trade Agreements and the informal character of voluntary harmonization, agreements may still have to be concluded between the Community and the third states concerned to secure mutual recognition of voluntarily harmonized law.[126] The prospects of concluding such agreements might be adversely affected by the concern of the Commission that they should not endanger the autonomy of Community decision-making.[127] Indeed, proposals for such agreements might be perceived as attempts by particular third states to secure a *de facto* right of codecision in the event of any changes in the relevant Community law.[128]

Where such agreements are not concluded, the position of third states and their traders may be precarious, in that mutual recognition may be based on a Commission assessment of the equivalence of Community legislation and the national legislation of the third state concerned, subject to the possibility of revocation, should subsequent legislative amendments lead to incompatibility.[129] For example, it was envisaged that EFTA States and the Community would extend their legal protection of semi-conductor products to benefit each others' producers on a reciprocal basis, provided that the protection was accepted to be equivalent. The Swedish Law concerning semi-conductors,[130] which entered into force on 1 April 1987, allowed for the extension of protection to other states on the basis of reciprocity. However, according to the Swedish representatives at the Joint Committee meeting of December 1988, the Commission had not confirmed that this Law gave protection equivalent to that provided in the Community Directive on this subject.[131] Without such confirmation Community law protection would not extend to

[125] L. Ohlsson, *Consequences of the EC for Swedish Manufacturing Industry* (Industriförbundet Working Paper 7, Stockholm, 1988), 14.

[126] *Redovisning av det svenska integrationsarbetet våren 1988-mars 1989*, (Utrikesdepartementets handelsavdelning, 1989), 216–17. While harmonization may mean that mutual recognition is 'automatic' within the Community, an agreement may be necessary between a Member State and a third state. See Case C–154/93 *Abdullah Tawil-Albertini* v. *Ministre des Affaires sociales* [1994] ECR I–451, I–462–3. Cf. the distinction between barriers on the 'internal front' and those on the 'external front' in P. G. Nell, '1992: La Nouvelle Dimension de la Politique d'Intégration de la Suisse' [1989] *RMC* 536–45.

[127] H. G. Krenzler, 'Zwischen Protektionismus und Liberalismus: Europäischer Binnenmarkt und Drittlandsbeziehungen' [1988] *Europa-Archiv* 241–8, at 248.

[128] T. Pedersen, 'EC–EFTA Relations: Neighbours in Search of a New Partnership' in G. Edwards and E. Regelsberger (eds.), *Europe's Global Links* (London, 1990), 97–111, at 104.

[129] See the Commission memorandum summarized in Club de Bruxelles, *EC/EFTA: the Future European Economic Area* (Brussels, 1991), 17–8.

[130] *Lag om ändring i lagen (1986:1145) om skydd för kretsmönster i halvledarprodukter*, SFS 1989:146.

[131] Dir. 87/54 of 16 Dec. 1986 ([1987] OJ L24/36) on the legal protection of topographies of semiconductor products.

Swedish producers, and so to extend the protection of the Swedish Law to Community producers was problematic.[132]

Collaboration between Third States

The practice of voluntary harmonization may be affected by collaboration between third states in this practice. In particular, the Nordic Council introduced reforms in its internal institutional structure so as to promote its work in relation to European integration.[133] In 1989 arrangements were made for dealing with 'European questions' in various committees.[134] Technical barriers to trade in general are considered within a Nordic Council steering group,[135] and more particular problems of barriers to trade in foodstuffs are considered in a permanent committee for such products.[136] Road transport is considered within a special group established by the committee of officials for traffic questions.[137] The committee of officials for environmental protection has established an *ad hoc* group to deal with questions concerning Nordic environmental co-operation and European integration.[138] This group is to suggest initiatives designed not only to promote Nordic co-operation but also to increase Nordic influence over Community environmental policy.[139] The committee of officials for consumer protection treats as priorities questions arising within the Community and European standards organizations.[140] Nordic price and competition authorities meet annually and have established a contact forum with the European Commission and the OECD Competition Committee.[141]

Such institutional reforms are designed, in the first place, to facilitate Nordic Council efforts to co-ordinate voluntary harmonization by its members.[142] For example, work has taken place concerning action to bring their laws more into line with Community law in fields such as financial services[143] and, possibly, taxation.[144] In some respects the role of the Council has tended towards the

[132] In the light of EC–EFTA relations generally, it was subsequently decided that no condition of reciprocity should be imposed in the case of natural or legal persons from Member States (prop. 1988/89:73 *om rättskyddet för kretsmönster i havledarprodukter*, 6).

[133] *The Nordic Council and International Co-operation* (NU 1988:4E), 76–7.

[134] *Redovisning av det svenska integrationsarbetet våren 1988-mars 1989* (Utrikesdepartementets handelsavdelning, 1989), 32.

[135] *Ibid.* 131. Note, in particular, the co-operation programme on the elimination of trade barriers (*Nordisk samarbejds program om afskaffelse af handelshindringer i Norden*, NU 1987:24).

[136] *Redovisning av det svenska integrationsarbetet våren 1988-mars 1989* (Utrikesdepartementets handelsavdelning, 1989), 82. [137] *Ibid.* 95. [138] *Ibid.* 115.

[139] *Europeiska samarbetsfrågor i Nordiska Rådet* (NU 1989:7), 29.

[140] *Redovisning av det svenska integrationsarbetet våren 1988-mars 1989* (Utrikesdepartementets handelsavdelning, 1989), 148–9. See also *Sverige–EFTA–EG 1988* (Utrikesdepartementet, 1989), 117.

[141] *Redovisning av det svenska integrationsarbetet våren 1988-mars 1989* (Utrikesdepartementets handelsavdelning, 1989), 150.

[142] *Europeiska samarbetsfrågor in Nordiska Rådet* (NU 1989:7), 36; *Arbejdsprogram Norden i Europa 1989–92* (NU 1989:50).

[143] *Stronger Nordic States: Economic Action Plan 1989–1992* (NU 1989:4E), 81.

[144] *Ibid.* 49.

creation of a more integrated 'core' within EFTA rather like the Benelux Union within the Community.[145]

At the same time, the Nordic Council seeks to influence harmonization within the Community through strengthening the position of its members in their contacts with the Community.[146] This involves co-ordination of national positions, for which greater resources are sought.[147] Particular importance is attached to contacts between Nordic Parliamentarians and Members of the European Parliament and its committees.[148]

Denmark, as a member of the Union as well as the Nordic Council, has in the past been seen as playing a pivotal role, both in informing Nordic countries of issues being considered within the Community and in putting forward to the Community views agreed upon by Nordic countries.[149] In 1987 a 'deepened information procedure' was established between Denmark and other Nordic states concerning the internal market,[150] and the Nordic Council wished to be involved in these arrangements.[151] Such arrangements may retain importance for Iceland and Norway[152] but may not be without their problems. For example, one of the obstacles to the elimination of frontier controls on the movement of persons within the Community was said to have been Danish involvement in the Nordic free travel area.[153]

5.3.3 Inter-Organizational Harmonization

Inter-organizational harmonization may take place on the basis of agreed procedures between the Community and an organization representing several

[145] Art. 233 EC states that the existence or completion of regional unions between Belgium and Luxembourg or between Belgium, Luxembourg, and the Netherlands shall not be precluded by this Treaty, to the extent that application of the latter does not attain the objectives of these unions. Art. 121(a) of the EEA Agreement states that provisions of this Agreement shall not preclude co-operation within the framework of Nordic Co-operation, to the extent that such co-operation does not impair the good functioning of this Agreement. Cf., regarding Art. 121(b) and the customs union between Liechtenstein and Switzerland, EEA Council Dec. 1/95 of 10 Mar. 1995 ([1995] OJ L86/58) on the entry into force of the EEA Agreement for Liechtenstein.

[146] *Arbejdsprogram Norden i Europa 1989–92* (NU 1989:50).

[147] *The Nordic Council and International Co-operation* (NU 1988: 4E), 76–7.

[148] *Ibid.* 79–82. Contacts with the Council for Mutual Economic Assistance (CMEA) were also envisaged in 1988 (*ibid.* 82).

[149] *Ibid.* 104. The first Nordic–ECSC meeting, e.g., was held in Denmark in 1978. See *Sverige–EG 1978* (Utrikes- och handelsdepartementen, 1979), 27.

[150] *Sverige–EFTA–EG 1987* (Utrikesdepartementets handelsavdelning, 1988), 12.

[151] *The Nordic Council and International Co-operation* (NU 1988:4E), 77.

[152] *The European*, 13–19 Jan. 1995.

[153] *Completing the Internal Market: An Area without Internal Frontiers. Progress Report Required by Art. 8B of the Treaty*, COM(90)552, 9. See, more generally, regarding Danish concern to avoid acceptance of obligations in the Community harmonization process which might conflict with its Nordic Council obligations, N. Reich, 'Protection of Diffuse Interests in the EEC and the Perspective of "Progressively Establishing" an Internal Market' [1988] *Journal of Consumer Policy* 395–417, at 406.

third states. Such procedures may simply facilitate voluntary harmonization. They may also lead to the conclusion of agreements complementing voluntary harmonization or even to the conclusion of agreements establishing substantive rules to be implemented internally by both the Community and members of the international organization concerned.

After the Luxembourg Declaration of April 1984[154] inter-organizational harmonization became increasingly important in EC—EFTA relations.[155] For example, the EFTA Declaration in Oslo on 15 March 1989 envisaged that such harmonization should extend to the 'accompanying policies' to the completion of the internal market.[156] Moreover, the EC–EFTA Declaration in Brussels on 19 December 1989[157] envisaged such harmonization in relation to economic and social policies generally.[158]

Harmonization of this kind might not only be comparatively economical in terms of use of staff resources but might also have had the advantage for the Community of reducing the problem of one EFTA State claiming that another EFTA State was receiving more favourable treatment, possibly in violation of GATT obligations.

Techniques

Techniques of inter-organizational harmonization vary both as to their degree of formality and as to their impact on the policy-making autonomy of the parties.

(i) Information exchanges

The most limited legal technique employed in EC—EFTA harmonization was exchange of information. Experts from EFTA States and the Commission met at least once a year to exchange information on the economic situation in the Community and EFTA States as well as on the economic policies that they implemented. More particular exchanges of information took place regarding, for example, application of indirect taxation to trade across frontiers[159] and the regulation of financial services.[160]

More formal arrangements might be found necessary. Thus EFTA Ministers and the Commission agreed in 1988 to the setting up of a mutual notification system whereby the Commission and EFTA States would make available to

[154] Bull. EC 4–1984, 1.2.1.

[155] See, e.g., regarding consumer protection, *Konsumenterna i ett nytt Europa* (Fakta Europa 1990:1, Utrikesdepartementets handelsavdelning, 1990), 44–9. See, generally, R. Rack (ed.), *30 Jahre danach: Neue Perspektiven für die Beziehungen der EFTA-Staaten zur Europäischen Gemeinschaft* (Baden-Baden, 1987) and P. G. Nell, 'EFTA in the 1990s: the Search for a New Identity' [1990] *JCMS* 327–58.

[156] EFTA Bull. 2/1989, 4–7, para. 12.

[157] EFTA Bull. 4/1989–1/1990, 5–7, para. 5.

[158] Reference was also made to 'a political dialogue' (*ibid.*, para. 8).

[159] *Sverige–EFTA–EG 1987* (Utrikesdepartementets handelsavdelning, 1988), 24.

[160] *Ibid.* 35.

each other as soon as possible, and at the very latest two weeks after their entry into force, full details of any new measures taken affecting agricultural price compensation for products covered by Protocol 2[161] to each Free Trade Agreement. They would also endeavour to keep each other informed at an early stage of any proposals to introduce major amendments to their respective price compensation systems.[162]

Such arrangements did not in themselves secure any harmonization. They were, however, a necessary precondition for those concerned to be in a position to engage in harmonization. For example, EFTA States and the Community co-operated to combat trade in counterfeit goods. It was agreed in 1988 that they would exchange information concerning legislation, including information on implementing measures following the entry into force of Regulation 3842/86,[163] which prohibits the release for free circulation in the Community of counterfeit goods. The EFTA States also agreed to adoption of their own national legislation having equivalent effect to such measures.[164]

(ii) Consultation

Arrangements for exchange of information might be reinforced by procedures for consultation prior to the adoption of legislation. Following a Coreper report of 1979 and a common EFTA approach to the European Commission in January 1980, multilateral EC—EFTA discussions and exchanges of information, within the framework of the GATT Agreement on Technical Barriers to Trade,[165] began to be held.[166]

Moreover, in December 1987, the EFTA Convention was amended, by the insertion of Article 12*bis* so as to require EFTA States to notify proposed new technical rules or changes in existing rules.[167] According to the new arrangements, which were detailed in Annex H to the Convention, EFTA States must notify the EFTA Council of draft technical regulations, certifications, or

[161] Concerning products subject to special arrangements to take account of differences in the cost of agricultural products incorporated therein.

[162] *Redovisning av det svenska integrationsarbetet våren 1988-mars 1989* (Utrikesdepartementets handelsavdelning, 1989), 42.

[163] Of 1 Dec. 1986 ([1987] OJ L134/1) laying down measures to prohibit the release for free circulation of counterfeit goods.

[164] *Sverige–EFTA–EG 1988* (Utrikesdepartementets handelsavdelning, 1989), 123; *Sverige–EFTA–EG* 1989 (Utrikesdepartementets handelsavdelning, 1990), 140.

[165] BISD, 26th Supp., 8. A new Agreement is contained in Annex 1A to the Agreement establishing the WTO.

[166] *Sverige–EG 1980* (Utrikes- och handelsdepartementen, 1981), 24. A joint EC–EFTA expert group on technical barriers to trade was established in 1984. The Community and the Member States are said to have been unenthusiastic in utilizing these arrangements. See O. Keller, *L'Elimination des Entraves Techniques dans la Communauté Européenne* (Berne, 1992), 143.

[167] EFTA Council Dec. No. 15 of 1987; SÖ 1988:52. EFTA States had a well-established system for exchanging information on new or amended regulations for industrial goods, which appeared likely to affect intra-EFTA trade. See the *Fifth Annual EFTA Report 1964/65* (Geneva, 1965), 24 and *Europeiska Frihandelssammanslutningen* (Geneva, 1988), 77–8.

amendments thereto at a stage when changes can still be made to the text concerned. Any deviations from technical specifications worked out by an international or regional body must be reasoned. At least three months must be allowed for other EFTA States to comment. A further notification indicating the extent to which it has been possible to take account of any such comments must be made. If any EFTA State submits a detailed opinion to the effect that the notified draft must be amended in order to prevent or reduce barriers to trade, adoption of the draft must be postponed for a period of six months from the date of notification. If agreement is not reached, the matter can be referred to a committee, which can make recommendations to the EFTA Council. This procedure followed that established within the Community by Directive 83/189[168] and was adopted with the intention of enabling EFTA States to participate in a common notification procedure with the Community. An agreement was duly concluded at the EC—EFTA meeting of December 1989 concerning mutual notification of proposed changes in technical rules and providing for a delay in implementation of such rules to allow adequate consultation.[169]

(iii) Bridging agreements

Even to the extent that arrangements for exchange of information and consultation produced compatibility of legislation, such compatibility might not in itself necessarily be sufficient to secure the goals of EC—EFTA harmonization. As in the case of voluntary harmonization, 'bridging agreements' might also be necessary to give meaning to harmonization of internal legal rules.[170] For example, after a Convention on Mutual Recognition of Test Results and Proofs of Conformity[171] had been adopted by the EFTA States, an EFTA-EC agreement on the same subject was necessary.[172] Agreements such as the

[168] Dir. 83/189 of 28 Mar. 1983 ([1983] OJ L109/8) laying down a procedure for the provision of information in the field of technical standards and regulations, as amended by Dir. 88/182 of 22 Mar. 1988 ([1988] OJ L81/75).

[169] Agreement laying down a procedure for the exchange of information in the field of technical regulations ([1990] OJ L291/2). Far more use was made of this procedure by the Community, which raised objections as to compatibility with Community legislation, than by EFTA States. See *Operation of Dir. 83/189 in 1990 and 1991*, COM(92)565, 19–20.

[170] Statement of the EFTA Ministerial Meeting in Geneva on 2 and 3 Dec. 1986 (EFTA Bull. 4/1986, 2), para. 5 and para. 11 of the Joint Communiqué from the Meeting between Ministers of the Member States of EFTA and Willy De Clercq, Member of the EC Commission in Geneva, 29 Nov. 1988 (EFTA Bull. 4/1988, 4–5). Note, more particularly, the link made by the Commission between adoption of the Lugano Convention (see below) and expert discussions of product liability legislation. (*Redovisning av det svenska integrationsarbet våren 1988-mars 1989* (Utrikesdepartementets handelsavdelning, 1989), 43).

[171] The text is published in Annex 3 to prop. 1988/89:60 *om kontroll genom teknisk provning och om mätning*. Internal EFTA agreements of this kind began to be concluded in the 1960s, and several Community Member States became Parties to them. See B. Hurni, 'EFTA–EC Relations: Aftermath of the Luxembourg Declaration' [1986] *JWTL* 497–506, at 504.

[172] Prop. 1988/89:60 *om kontroll genom teknisk provning och om mätning*.

Convention on the Single Administrative Document,[173] and the Convention on a Common Transit Procedure,[174] might merge the requirement of an internal EFTA agreement and a bridging agreement with the Community.

A particularly sophisticated arrangement is that resulting from the Lugano Convention,[175] signed on 18 September 1988. The Convention lays down rules of international jurisdiction and simplified procedures for recognition and enforcement of judgments and embodies the substance of the 1968 Brussels Convention.[176] Protocol 2 to the Lugano Convention requires that the courts of each Contracting Party, when applying and interpreting the Convention, pay 'due account' to the principles laid down by any decision of the courts of other Contracting Parties concerning the Convention.[177] More particularly, the Member States declared that they would take all measures in their power to ensure respect for the principles of the Convention when Community acts governing jurisdiction and recognition and enforcement of judgments were being drafted. They also considered it appropriate that the Court of Justice when interpreting the Brussels Convention should pay due account to the rulings contained in the case law of the Lugano Convention. Likewise, EFTA States stated that they considered it appropriate that their courts when interpreting the Lugano Convention should pay due account to the rulings contained in the case law of the Court of Justice and of courts of Member States in respect of provisions of the Brussels Convention which were substantially reproduced in the Lugano Convention.

Limitations

Where the substance of 'internal' policies was at stake, there might be limited readiness to move towards harmonization of legal provisions.[178] For example, the desirability of co-operation in relation to environmental protection was recognized in the 1984 Luxembourg Declaration,[179] and various issues for EC—EFTA co-operation were considered at a High Level Contact Group meeting in October 1985.[180] In October 1987, following a meeting of an EC—EFTA expert group earlier in the year, Ministers from the Member States and EFTA States agreed on priorities for co-operation, including: atmospheric pollution, soil protection, water protection, questions concerning climatic change, and co-operation in the event of accidents. They also agreed

[173] [1987] OJ L134/1. [174] [1987] OJ L226/1. [175] [1988] OJ L319/9.

[176] [1978] OJ L304/36. See now [1990] OJ C189/2.

[177] The practical effectiveness of such a requirement is uncertain. See J. H. J. Bourgeois, 'The EFTA States and EC Legal Systems: Is Integration Possible? Comment' in J. J. Jamar and H. Wallace (eds.), *EEC–EFTA: More Than Just Good Friends?* (Bruges, 1988), 299–304, at 301.

[178] Para. 6 of the Declaration of the EFTA Ministerial Meeting in Oslo, 14–15 Mar. 1989 (EFTA Bull. 1/1989, 4–5) said of EC–EFTA co-operation: 'In some respects . . . this broadened co-operation has not quite matched our ambitions and expectations'.

[179] EFTA Bull. 2/1984, 6–7, para. 5.

[180] *Sverige–EG 1985* (Utrikesdepartementets handelsavdelning, 1986), 46.

on the annual convening of meetings of Senior Environmental Officials to exchange views on environmental issues with the aim of establishing joint objectives and common strategies.[181] The Swedish Government maintained that 'in no other field [had] EFTA States and the Community agreed on such far-reaching co-operation' and stressed the opportunities created for Sweden to exert an influence over the early stages of the shaping of Community measures in this field.[182]

In the event, co-operation in relation to environmental protection hardly progressed beyond informal contacts. Reliance on such contacts might often reflect Community rather than EFTA attitudes.[183] The Community, apparently because geographical factors amongst others might render the interests of southern Member States different from those of EFTA States, was reluctant to formalize existing practice.[184] Hence, Sweden was unable to give effect to its preference for the adoption of common rules to protect the environment.

Rather, there was a tendency towards adoption of divergent rules. In the case of vehicle exhaust emissions, the Commission stressed the need for a harmonized approach so as to avoid introducing new obstacles to trade between the Community and EFTA States. However, Sweden,[185] Switzerland, and Austria decided to introduce standards similar to those established in the United States.[186] Such decisions led to criticism from the Community. For example, the Committee on External Relations of the European Parliament insisted that EFTA States must 'apply real reciprocity and not take the attitude of *Alleingang* they took under Sweden's guidance in the affair of exhaust gases'.[187]

Such criticism may reflect general Community concern to secure reciprocity in reduction of obstacles to trade with third states[188] and suggests that the Free Trade Agreements failed to provide a framework for harmonization capable of meeting this concern. This apparent failure of the Agreements may be

[181] *Sverige–EFTA–EG 1987* (Utrikesdepartementets handelsavdelning, 1986), 36–7. See, earlier, the exchange of letters between Sweden and the European Commission of 9 Dec. 1977 (SÖ 1977:86).

[182] *Miljöpolitik inför 1990-talet*, prop. 1987/88:85, 245.

[183] In 1979 H. Romé, 'The Need for More Co-ordination: An Austrian Point of View', EFTA Bull. 4/1979, 4–5, at 5 considered that EC–EFTA relations above and beyond the Free Trade Agreements would probably take place in fields, such as scientific co-operation or environmental policy, which lay 'outside the scope of specific integration measures by the Community'.

[184] *Redovisning av det svenska integrationsarbetet våren 1988-mars 1989* (Utrikesdepartementets handelsavdelning, 1989), 111–13.

[185] *Bilavsgasförordningen* (1987:586).

[186] Cf. the Swiss imposition of a tax on transit traffic following the failure of the Council of Ministers to adopt a common transport policy dealing with transit problems (Report of the Committee on Transport on the Community's relations with certain third countries in the transport sector, EP Doc. A2–69/86, 17–18).

[187] Report on economic and trade relations between the EEC and EFTA countries, EP Doc. 2–32/89/B, 12. Within the Community such action might be permissible under Art. 100a(4) EC.

[188] In some instances, Swedish representatives seem to have responded successfully to Community criticism of domestic policy measures by demonstrating the compatibility of these measures with Community law. See, regarding sea transport policy, *Sverige–EFTA–EG 1988* (Utrikesdepartementets handelsavdelning, 1989), 52.

attributable to the limitations to the trade liberalization and other requirements embodied therein. These limitations meant that reciprocity was sought by reference to the needs of 'internal' policies rather than in terms of 'common' needs as articulated by such requirements.[189] In these circumstances, the significance of policy differences as impediments to harmonization tended to be exaggerated.

5.4 EUROPE AGREEMENTS

The Europe Agreements formally provide for bilateral harmonization between the Parties as well as voluntary harmonization.

5.4.1 Bilateral Harmonization

Article 27(1) of the Polish Agreement provides that the Agreement shall not preclude the maintenance or establishment of customs unions, free trade areas, or arrangements for frontier trade except in so far as they alter the trade arrangements provided for in this Agreement. However, Article 27(2) provides that consultations between the Parties shall take place within the Association Council concerning agreements establishing customs unions or free trade areas and, where requested, on other major issues related to their respective trade policies with third countries. In particular, in the event of a third state acceding to the European Union, such consultations shall take place so as to ensure that account can be taken of the mutual interests of the Community and Poland stated in this Agreement.

Article 25(3) of the same Agreement deals with agricultural policy. It refers to the 'standstill' clauses on customs duties and charges having equivalent effect[190] and quantitative restrictions and measures having equivalent effect on trade between the Parties.[191] These clauses, it is stipulated, shall not restrict in any way the pursuit of the respective agricultural policies of Poland and the Community or the taking of any measures under such policies.[192] However, Article 20(6) takes account of the need for an increased harmony between the agricultural policies in the Community and Poland, as well as Poland's objective of becoming a member of the Community, and provides that both Parties will have regular consultations in the

[189] Certainly, more seems to have been achieved in the context of EEA Agreement negotiations, which took place on the basis of general EC–EFTA consensus about acceptability of Community law in the field covered by this Agreement. See sect. 3.2.2 above.

[190] Art. 25(1) of the Polish Agreement.

[191] *Ibid.*, Art. 25(2).

[192] Art. 25(3) (*ibid.*) provides that this stipulation is without prejudice to concessions granted under Art. 20.

Association Council on the strategy and practical modalities of their respective agricultural policies.[193]

Harmonization in both fields might be expected to be facilitated by the fact that the Europe Agreements were concluded by the Community on the basis of Article 238 rather than Article 113 of the EC Treaty. Conclusion on the basis of the former provision means that there may be no formal legal need to treat harmonization issues under these Agreements as belonging exclusively to the commercial policy field, and thus to separate harmonization efforts between the Parties from harmonization efforts within the Community[194] as there was in the case of the Free Trade Agreements. However, such separation may not merely reflect a legal formality. It may also result from the fact that the Community harmonization process is underpinned by liberalization and other requirements of a kind not entailed by either category of Agreements.[195]

5.4.2 Voluntary Harmonization

Provisions in the Europe Agreements for voluntary harmonization implicitly acknowledge the likely inadequacy of bilateral harmonization. At the same time, however, if the relevant provisions of these Agreements have binding force, the inadequacy of previous voluntary harmonization practice is also implicitly acknowledged, and the contradictions therein are highlighted.

Formal Procedures

Formal provision for voluntary harmonization is made in Article 68 of the Polish Agreement. According to this provision, the Parties recognize that the major precondition for Poland's economic integration into the Community is the approximation of its existing and future legislation to that of the Community. Accordingly, Poland shall use its best endeavours to ensure that its future legislation is compatible with Community legislation. The fields covered include: customs law; company law; banking law; company accounts and taxes; intellectual property; protection of workers at the workplace; financial services; rules on competition; protection of health and life of humans,

[193] Arrangements are also envisaged for participation by Poland in Community framework programmes, specific programmes, projects, or other actions in fields relevant to 'economic and cultural co-operation'. See the Proposal of 13 Dec. 1994 for a Council and Commission Dec. concluding the Additional Protocol to the Europe Agreement between the European Community, of the one part, and the Republic of Poland, of the other part, COM(94)599.

[194] Art. 238 can have the same material scope as the EC Treaty itself. See Case 12/86 *Meryem Demirel* v. *Stadt Schwäbisch Gmünd* [1987] ECR 3719, 3751.

[195] The solution is seen as being the conclusion of mutual recognition agreements. See *Preparation of the Associated Countries of Central and Eastern Europe for Integration into the Internal Market of the Union*, COM(95)163, 5. Cf. sect. 5.5.2 below, regarding organic harmonization under the EEA Agreement.

animals, and plants; consumer protection; indirect taxation; technical rules and standards; transport; and the environment.[196]

It is apparently envisaged that Poland will shape the legal foundations for its new economic system on the Community model.[197] While considerable demands may be imposed on Poland, any obligations on the Community to provide support are expressed only in generalized terms. Article 70 of the Agreement merely envisages that the Community will provide Poland with technical assistance,[198] including the exchange of experts, the provision of information, organization of seminars, training activities, and aid for the translation of Community legislation in the relevant sectors.[199]

More fundamentally, no arrangements are made to secure for Poland any real say in the development of the rules with which it is supposed to harmonize its law. The failure to make such arrangements may be rendered more 'disturbing' by challenges, even within the Community, to the legitimacy of the institutions responsible for the development of such rules.[200]

Institutional Arrangements

Poland has made institutional arrangements to facilitate voluntary harmonization. An Integration Office has been established within the Polish Government to ensure that new legislation is consistent with Community law and to facilitate adaptations of existing legislation to bring it into line with such law.[201] At the same time, informal contacts take place with the Commission, which informs Polish officials of the progress of Community harmonization work.[202] Moreover, specialized sub-committees of the Association Council

[196] Art. 69 of the Polish Agreement. 'Guidelines for the content and organization of an intensive and coherent programme' are provided in *Preparation of the Associated Countries of Central and Eastern Europe for Integration into the Internal Market of the Union*, COM(95)163, 5.

[197] H. Kramer, 'The EC and the Stabilisation of Eastern Europe' [1992] *Aussenpolitik* 12–21, at 15.

[198] Such assistance may be provided through the Phare Programme. See *Follow Up to Commission Communication on 'The Europe Agreements and Beyond: A Strategy to Prepare the Countries of Central and Eastern Europe for Accession'*, COM(94)361, 5.

[199] However, the Community aims to provide similar assistance to most Central and East European countries, and it is doubtful whether its human and financial resources are sufficient to enable the aim effectively to be met. Cf. the Opinion of the Economic and Social Committee of 25 Jan. 1995 ([1995] OJ C102/40) on relations between the European Union and Russia, Ukraine, and Belarus, para. 3.38.

[200] D. Kennedy and D. E. Webb, 'The Limits of Integration: Eastern Europe and the European Communities' (1993)30 *CMLRev*. 1095–117, at 1102, n. 9.

[201] *Europe Report*, No. 1650 (6 Feb. 1991). Such arrangements have apparently been the source of some tensions within the Government. See C. Brzezinski, 'The EC–Poland Association Agreement: Harmonization of an Aspiring Member State's Company Law' (1993) 34 *Harvard International Law Journal* 105–48, 132–4.

[202] S. S. Nello, 'Some Recent Developments in EC–East European Economic Relations' [1990] *JWT* 5–24, 12.

have been given responsibility for 'co-ordination and monitoring' of voluntary harmonization.[203]

Collaboration between Third States

Voluntary harmonization by Poland may be less problematic, if this country collaborates closely with the Czech Republic, Hungary, and Slovakia[204] in such harmonization.[205] Collaboration between such States may be encouraged by the Community.[206] In September 1992, for example, the Heads of the then Czechoslovak, Hungarian, and Polish Delegations to the Community submitted a joint memorandum to the Commission concerning closer co-operation with the Community and prospects for Union membership.[207] The Community response included a call for regional harmonization with the Community.[208]

While collaboration may be difficult to achieve between such states,[209] further encouragement is provided by the Europe Agreements. Article 71(3) of the Polish Agreement, which deals with economic co-operation, provides that special attention must be devoted to measures capable of fostering co-operation between the countries of Central and Eastern Europe with a view to integrated development of the region.[210] To the extent that such co-operation materializes, a framework for inter-organizational harmonization of the kind which used to take place in EC—EFTA relations may emerge.

[203] *Follow Up to Commission Communication on 'The Europe Agreements and Beyond: a Strategy to Prepare the Countries of Central and Eastern Europe for Accession'*, COM(94)361, 5.

[204] Cf. Polish relations with Germany and Polish involvement in the Hexagonal Convention and the Council of Baltic Sea Countries.

[205] See, generally, A. Åslund, *Systemic Change in Eastern Europe and East–West Trade* (EFTA Occasional Paper No. 31, Geneva, 1990), 21.

[206] However, it is the very kind of relationship with the Community about which states such as Poland are said to be least enthusiastic. See *ibid.* 21.

[207] *Agence Europe*, No. 5813 (12 Sept. 1992).

[208] Joint Statement by the Foreign Ministers of the EC and the Visegrad countries of 5 Oct. 1992, Bull. EC 10–1992, 2.3.1. 'Moves to create a Central European Free Trade Area point in the right direction.' See the Report from the Council to the Essen European Council on a strategy to prepare for accession of the associated CCEE, *Europe Doc.* No. 1916 (14 Dec. 1994), 8.

[209] A. Deen and D. A. Westbrook, 'Return to Europe: Integrating Eastern European Economies into the European Market through Alliance with the European Community' (1990) 31 *Harvard International Law Journal* 660–70 and B. Kaminski, 'The Framework of Soviet–East-Central European Economic Relations in the 1990s' in R. F. Staar (ed.), *East-Central Europe and the USSR* (New York, 1991), 37–58.

[210] More particularly, Art. 37 of Prot. 4 to the Polish Agreement, concerning the definition of the concept of 'originating products' and methods of administrative co-operation, provides that the Parties shall take any measures necessary for the conclusion of arrangements with Hungary, the Czech Republic, and Slovakia enabling this Protocol to be applied. The Parties are to notify each other of measures taken to this effect. More generally, the Community encourages the development of a free trade area and co-operation between these companies in fields such as agricultural, environmental and transport policy. See the Council Reply to Written Question E–191/95 ([1995] OJ C202/4) by Jean-Pierre Raffarin.

5.5 EEA AGREEMENT

The EEA Agreement creates a more developed framework for harmonization between the Community and third states than the Free Trade Agreements or the Europe Agreements. It not only formalizes opportunities for EFTA States to participate in the 'shaping' of harmonization measures. It also provides for adoption of such measures by way of 'organic' harmonization.

5.5.1 'Shaping' of Harmonization Measures

Article 99(2) of the EEA Agreement provides that, when transmitting a proposal for legislation in a field covered by this Agreement to the Council of the Union, the Commission shall transmit copies thereof to the EFTA States. More particularly, Article 79(2) of the Agreement provides that the Parties shall exchange information and, at the request of a Party, hold consultations within the EEA Joint Committee in respect of plans or proposals for the establishment or amendment of framework programmes, specific programmes, actions, and projects. Moreover, Article 83 of the Agreement provides that where EC—EFTA co-operation outside the four freedoms takes the form of an exchange of information between public authorities, the EFTA States shall have the same rights to receive, and obligations to provide, information as Member States,[211] subject to the requirements of confidentiality.[212]

5.5.2 'Organic' Harmonization

The EEA Agreement envisages harmonization by way of adoption at EEA level of acts already adopted by the Council of the Union or the Commission. EEA adoption is to take the form of an amendment to the Annex to the Agreement which is directly affected by the new Community act. In the absence of agreement at EEA level to amend the relevant Annex within six months (or the date of entry into force of the Community act in question, if that date is later), the affected part is suspended.[213] Other EEA law, including provisions of the Agreement itself, apparently remains operative. Such arrangements may create the same kind of 'organic' relationship between liberalization and harmonization as the EC Treaty.

[211] Cf. Pt. XIX of Annex II, on Technical Regulations, Standards, Testing, and Certification, which amends Art. 8(1) of Dir. 83/189 of 28 Mar. 1983 ([1983] OJ L109/8) laying down a procedure for the provision of information in the field of technical standards and regulations, so as to introduce a new subparagraph. The new subparagraph provides that the Community, on the one side, and the ESA, on the other, may ask for further information on a draft technical regulation notified.

[212] These requirements are to be fixed by the EEA Joint Committee.

[213] See sect. 6.5.3 below, regarding these procedures. Cf. Art. XXIII(2) of GATT.

On the one hand, a failure of EFTA States to accept a Community act which did not provide such a high standard of, for example, environmental protection as their own legislation or which might prejudice their possibilities to introduce higher standards in the future need not affect the freedom of their traders to export products complying with such legislation to the Community.[214] The Agreement, even if part of an Annex thereto were suspended,[215] would not permit Member States to exclude products meeting a higher standard than that required in the case of their own products.

On the other hand, in such circumstances EFTA States might be entitled, on the basis of mandatory requirements, to exclude products from Member States which failed to comply with their legislation. Any such entitlement would not be affected by possible suspension of part of an Annex to the Agreement. Indeed, Article 75 of the Agreement follows Article 130t of the EC Treaty. The former provides that the environmental protection measures referred to in Article 74 of the Agreement, i.e., those in Annex XX,[216] shall not prevent any Party from maintaining or introducing more stringent measures compatible with this Agreement.

As a result, the liberalization and other requirements embodied in the Agreement may imply for each Party an incentive to take account of the interests of the other Parties in the harmonization process. This implication has formal expression in Article 102(3) of the Agreement. According to this provision, every effort is to be made to find a mutually acceptable solution where a serious problem arises in any area which, in the EFTA States, falls within the competence of the legislator.

True, acts embodied in Annex II to the Agreement, on technical requirements, standards, testing, and certification, on entry into force of the Agreement may present problems where EFTA States wish to provide for the interests involved a higher level of protection than is secured by these acts. For example, Paragraph 4 of this Annex permits EFTA States only to limit access to their markets for certain named substances according to the requirements existing at the date of entry into force of the Agreement. The Agreement contains no equivalent of Article 100a(4) of the EC Treaty,[217] which might have entitled Contracting Parties to 'apply' national rules providing a higher level of protection than that secured by acts referred to in this Annex. Hence, the

[214] In this sense, EFTA States may be in a more favourable position than Member States, if Art. 100a(4) EC only applies to national legislation existing when the relevant Community enactment was adopted.

[215] Indeed, it is fully in accordance with the case law of the ECJ (see sect. 3.2.2 above) that under Art. 102(4) of the EEA Agreement mere equivalence of legislation may be found to be sufficient to avoid the need for suspension.

[216] Environment.

[217] The question whether such a provision should be included was apparently a source of controversy during negotiations of the EEA Agreement. See M. I. A. Cuartero, 'La Protection de l'environment' in O. Jacot-Guillarmod, (ed.), *Accord EEE: Commentaires et réflexious* (Bern, 1992), 459–72.

introduction of legislation by an EFTA State providing a higher level of protection may be found to affect the 'good functioning' of the Agreement contrary to Article 97(1) thereof, though in the case of legislation justified by reference to mandatory requirements embodied in the Agreement such a finding might be questionable. However, these problems arise from the course of the essentially intergovernmental negotiations for the Agreement. Future harmonization under this Agreement need not necessarily produce the same problems.

True also, affected parts of an Annex to the Agreement could be suspended where the EFTA States failed to accept a Community act requiring a higher level of protection than that provided for in previous Community acts or where, without there being any justification of the kind provided by mandatory requirements, they were unwilling to go as far as a Community act in reducing obstacles to trade. In such circumstances, however, suspension would merely prevent such states from taking any advantage from the previous Community acts which was not conferred by the Agreement itself.

Even so, it might be thought that such arrangements, though effective in preserving trade liberalization requirements and permissive in allowing EFTA States to provide a higher level of protection for requirements other than those of trade liberalization, could still, in practice, lead to a lowering of such protection. While an EEA State may retain the legal freedom to impose higher standards internally, provisions of the EEA Agreement itself and implementing acts may permit other EEA States to apply lower standards in their own territories.[218] Hence, the former would effectively be constrained from imposing higher standards, because imposition of such standards on their own companies would increase their costs of production and render their products uncompetitive in EEA States applying lower standards.[219] In other words, the importance of national legislation embodying such standards as a factor of production would be exposed,[220] and EFTA States would feel compelled to compete in making their legislative requirements less costly to producers. The result would be a sub-optimal level of standards. In reality, however, competitiveness is a function of quality as well as price, and enforcement of higher than average standards by a particular EFTA State could operate as a guarantee of the higher quality of the products of companies manufacturing in that state.[221]

[218] Cf., regarding height limits for transport vehicles, Case 241/86 *Openbaar Ministerie* v. *Jacques Bodin and Etablissements Minguet & Thomas* [1987] ECR 2573.

[219] Cf. the argument that such considerations will deter smaller Member States of the Community from making much use of the possibility of adopting national 'safeguard' measures provided for under Art. 100a(5) EC (H. G. Schermers, 'Comment on Weiler's *The Transformation of Europe*' (1991) 100 *Yale Law Journal* 2525–36, at 2535).

[220] Legal arrangements, as growth determinants (see H. Dicke and R. J. Langhammer, *The Institutional Framework and External Dimension of the EC Internal Market* (Kiel Working Paper No. 453, Kiel, 1990), 1), may become more negotiable by economic actors.

[221] Cf., regarding Dutch consumer protection law and 'its effect on the good reputation of Netherlands financial services', Case C–384/93 *Alpine Investments BV* v. *Minister van Financiën* (not yet reported). Moreover, competitive pressures may lead actors to raise their own standards. See Case C–154/89 *EC Commission* v. *France* [1991] ECR I–659, I–687.

It may also be thought, more generally, that states with cheap fixed factors of production will benefit[222] from the EEA and those with higher costs will suffer.[223] However, it is not only the costs of factors of production but also their value which are important for competition.[224] States which fully prepare their 'human capital' for a high-efficiency, high-quality, and high-innovation economy may have a competitive advantage over those which leave human capital formation largely to the limited resources which the individual is able and willing to mobilize to this end.[225]

In other words, it cannot be assumed that the opportunity costs of higher standards imposed on companies will necessarily exceed the increased utility that may be entailed. What EEA States may face, depending on questions of availability of information,[226] is increased pressure to devise efficient means of securing high standards.[227] Greater problems might be faced by companies in EEA States with lower standards, because they could be more exposed to competition from low-cost producers from outside the EEA.[228] In such circumstances, prospects for reaching consensus on EEA harmonization designed to introduce higher standards are apparently improved.

Beyond the scope of the liberalization and other requirements embodied in

[222] R. O. Keohane and S. Hoffmann, 'Institutional Change in the 1980s' in R.O. Keohane and S. Hoffmann (eds.), *The New European Community* (Boulder, 1991), 1–39, at 27.

[223] Reliance on such thinking in relation to the labour market results in the conclusion that implementation of the European Social Charter will render Community industry less competitive internationally and thus lead to increased protectionism against third states. See, e.g., J. T. Addison and W. S. Siebert, 'The Social Charter of the European Community: Evolution and Controversies' [1991] *Industrial and Labor Relations Review* 597–625.

[224] See, e.g., D. Leborgne and A. Lipietz, 'How to Avoid a Two-Tier Europe' [1990] *Labour and Society* 177–99.

[225] A. Pfaller *et al.*, 'The Issue' in A. Pfaller *et al.* (eds.), *Can the Welfare State Compete?* (London, 1991), 1–14, at 10.

[226] A fundamental difficulty for regulators is that they know less about the costs of complying with regulations than firms themselves. See S. Barrett, 'Environmental Regulation for Competitive Advantage' [1991] *Business Strategy Review* 1–15.

[227] At least, the resulting legislation might not be as inefficient as that derived from bargains struck between special interest groups. Cf. the argument that governments will be under pressure to use tax revenues efficiently to provide public goods in H. Siebert, *The New Landscape in Europe* (Oxford, 1991), 21. Cf. also, regarding the 'market for incorporation', D. Charney, 'Competition among Jurisdictions in Formulating Corporate Law Rules: an American Perspective on the "Race to the Bottom" in the European Communities' (1991) 32 *Harvard International Law Journal* 423–56.

[228] Cf. the Commission concern that concentration of the less developed regions of the Community on labour intensive industries with a low technological content would leave them 'extremely vulnerable to increased competition from developing countries and Eastern Europe' (*Fourth Periodic Report on the Social and Economic Situation and Development of the Regions of the Community*, COM(90)609, 80). See, more particularly, regarding the textiles industry, 'The Impact of the Single Market on Women's Employment in the Textile and Clothing Industry', *Social Europe*, Supp. 2/91. Adjustment problems tend to be greater where integration leads to inter-industry rather than intra-industry specialization. See L. Lundberg, 'Economic Integration, Inter- and Intra-Industry Trade: The Case of Sweden and the EC' [1992] *Scandinavian Journal of Economics* 393–408.

the Agreement harmonization prospects seem less certain. Articles 78–88 of the Agreement provide for 'co-operation outside the four freedoms'.[229] To this end, Article 79 requires that the Parties shall strengthen the dialogue between them by all appropriate means, in particular, through the procedures provided for in Part VII,[230] with a view to identifying areas and activities where closer co-operation outside the four freedoms could contribute to the attainment of their common objectives in the fields referred to in Article 78. These fields are: research and technological development; information services; the environment; education, training, and youth; social policy; consumer protection; small and medium-sized enterprises; tourism; the audiovisual sector; and civil protection. In other words, arrangements are made in the Agreement to put earlier EFTA involvement in various Community activities[231] outside the four freedoms on a more systematic basis.[232] However, Article 88 states that nothing in these provisions shall preclude the ability of any Party to prepare, adopt and implement measures independently.

Such co-operation, like resort to the evolutionary clause in Article 118, which deals with the situation where a Contracting Party considers that it would be useful in the interests of the Parties to develop the relations established by the Agreement by extending them to fields not covered thereby,[233] may lie outside the scope of the organic harmonization envisaged in the Agreement. To this extent, it may lack the supportive framework available to organic harmonization and, hence, may face problems comparable with those which arose under the Free Trade Agreements.

5.6 CONCLUSION

Harmonization issues arising in relation to international trade may not be qualitatively different from those arising in relation to Community trade, and neither the case law of the Court of Justice[234] nor the EC

[229] The EC–EFTA Joint Ministerial Meeting of 19 Dec. 1990 (EFTA Bull. 1/1991, 22–5, para. 13) considered, with regard to such co-operation, that the Agreement should provide a firm legal basis for comprehensive and dynamic co-operation and should also promote the development of actions of common interest.

[230] See sect. 6.5.3 below, regarding these procedures.

[231] EFTA States had favoured joint negotiation of new EEA programmes rather than mere participation in Community programmes. See C. Church, 'The Politics of Change: EFTA and the Nordic Countries' Responses to the EC in the Early 1990s' [1990] *JCMS* 401–30, at 405.

[232] 'Global contributions' by EFTA States to Community programmes are envisaged, which will be 'unaffected by the legal notion of a "fair" return'. See Court of Auditors, Opinion 3/92 ([1992] OJ C342/1) on a proposal for a Council Reg. amending the Financial Reg. of 21 Dec. 1977 applicable to the general budget of the EC, para. 16.

[233] It is intended also to allow for future extension of the Community customs union to include EFTA States. See para. 9 of the *Directives de Négociation*, approved by the Council of Ministers on 18 June 1990.

[234] Case 22/70 *EC Commission* v. *EC Council* [1971] ECR 263, 274; and Opinion 1/94 *(Competence of the Community to conclude international agreements on services and the protection*

Treaty[235] necessarily requires separation of the two categories of issues. Nevertheless, the former issues tend to be approached by the Community within a separate substantive law framework and on the basis of procedures not specifically concerned with their subject-matter.

Practice under the Free Trade Agreements raises serious doubts whether harmonization arrangements in the Europe Agreements will effectively counter such tendencies. Although the latter Agreements were concluded on the basis of Article 238 rather than Article 113 of the EC Treaty, the more limited liberalization and other requirements embodied in these Agreements may not provide the same support for harmonization[236] as the EEA Agreement. Moreover, as regards inter-organizational harmonization, countries such as Poland seem to be in a less advantageous position than were EFTA States.[237] As a result, Poland may depend heavily on its own efforts at voluntary harmonization. However, differences in economic conditions as between Poland and the Community may be such that harmonization of this kind may be even less appropriate to Polish needs than it may have been to the needs of EFTA States.

In contrast, to the extent that EEA law reproduces liberalization and other requirements embodied in the EC Treaty provisions, separate development of policies within the Community and within EFTA States may be replaced by joint efforts to manage these requirements. More particularly, these requirements provide an incentive for each EEA State to take account of the interests of other EEA States in efforts to reconcile conflicting requirements. None has the option of limiting liberalization in relation to others simply because of

of industrial property) [1994] ECR I–5267, I–5402 and I–5405. Indeed, the latter ruling might be taken to suggest that commercial policy measures are only considered appropriate for tackling international trade problems where the main Community concern is the reduction of obstacles to such trade. The ruling may be criticized on the grounds that its approach to treatment of the 'constitutional' relationship between Community powers and state powers was inconsistent both internally and in relation to precedent. See J. H. J. Bourgeois, 'The EC in the WTO and Advisory Opinion 1/94: An Echternach Procession' (1995) 32 C*MLRev.* 763–87. However, it seems that the perspective adopted by the Court was that of law as an instrument of economic policy and that treatment of constitutional issues, as perhaps in Opinion 1/91 (*Draft Agreement between the Community, on the one hand, and the countries of the European Free Trade Association, on the other, relating to the creation of the European Economic Area*) [1991] ECR I–6079, was determined by this perspective.

235 In particular, Art. 130m EC provides for the conclusion of agreements with third states within the context of research and technological development policy, and Art. 130r(4) provides for the conclusion of such agreements within the context of environmental policy. See also, regarding development co-operation, Art. 130y. See, regarding 'co-operation' with third states, Arts 126(3) (education, training, and youth), 127(3) (vocational training), 128(3) (culture), 129(3) (public health), and 129c(3) (transport networks). Note also the Declaration on Monetary Co-operation with Non-Community Countries, annexed to the TEU.

236 According to Mayras A. G. in Case 96/71 *R. & V. Haegeman* v. *EC Commission* [1972] ECR 1005, 1023–4, a country having an Association Agreement was 'a third country and must be treated as such, save insofar as particular and mandatory provisions of the agreement or its annexes authorize[d] it to claim privileged treatment on certain points'.

237 Cf. the declarations of EFTA States and the then Czechoslovakia, Hungary, and Poland regarding co-operation (EFTA Bull. 3/1990, 22–3)

differences in attitudes to such requirements. To this extent, therefore, harmonization procedures included in an instrument such as the EEA Agreement may be expected to be more effective than those in the Free Trade Agreements and the Europe Agreement

PART 3

Institutional Involvement

6
Joint Decision-Making

6.1 INTRODUCTION

Joint decision-making denotes the process whereby legally binding decisions under an international agreement are adopted by bodies representing the parties to that agreement. Arrangements for such decision-making are made in the EC Treaty and in agreements between the Community and third states. The implicit assumption in these arrangements is that integration simply entails obligations between these parties, which can satisfactorily be determined and developed by such bodies. In other words, it is implicitly assumed that issues of trade relations between the parties can be separated from issues of trade relations within each party.[1] Such separation may be consistent with ideas of Community autonomy and national sovereignty, but may not adequately reflect the economic integration taking place between the parties. The resultant risk is that there may be a legal vacuum, inconsistent with real relations between the parties.

Under the EC Treaty the Council of the Union, composed of representatives of the governments of Member States, engages in joint decision-making. In its decision-making this institution is intended to secure reconciliation of positions formulated by each Member State independently of the other.[2] Such reconciliation may be problematic, because independent formulation of its position by each Member State may tend to exaggerate differences between these positions.[3] However, this tendency in the work of the Council may not only be affected by the operation of the trade liberalization and other requirements in the Treaty but is also intended to be countered by the supranation-

[1] Cf. the view that the legality of a 'delegation' of Community powers to such a body may depend on whether the powers relate to 'internal' or 'external' Community policies in K. Lenaerts, 'Regulating the Regulatory Process: "Delegation of Powers" in the European Community'(1993) *ELRev.* 23–49, at 26.

[2] It is said that institutionalized dialogue permits individual issues to be examined in their broader context and provides mechanisms for earlier consultations on potential subjects of conflict. See H. G. Krenzler, 'The Dialogue between the European Community and the United States of America: Present Form and Future Prospects' in J. Schwarze (ed.), *The External Relations of the European Community, in Particular EC–US Relations* (Baden-Baden, 1989), 91–103, at 102. However, joint decision-making may not necessarily foster such a dialogue.

[3] A consequence of the institutional structure established by the EC Treaty is said to be that different, conflicting, and often contradictory interests may be expressed as 'unified' national interests. See F. Snyder, 'Ideologies of Competition in European Community Law' (1989) 52 *MLR* 149–78, at 172.

alism of other institutions created by the Treaty. In particular, the Treaty envisages close co-operation between an institution independent of national governments—the European Commission[4]—and the Council.[5]

Joint bodies established by agreements between the Community and third states are supposed to reconcile the Community position with that of the third state or states concerned. However, the Community position expressed in such bodies will be the result of 'internal' Community negotiations and compromises and thus may not easily be modified to accommodate the needs of such reconciliation.[6] Therefore, joint decision-making may be more problematic within the context of agreements with third states than in the context of the EC Treaty, though such agreements rely more heavily on joint decision-making than the latter Treaty.

In particular, each EC–EFTA Free Trade Agreement provided for the establishment of Joint Committees,[7] composed of Community representatives and representatives of the EFTA State concerned. The Europe Agreements provide, in turn, for the establishment of Association Councils and Association Committees. The EEA Agreement goes further. It not only provides for the establishment of an EEA Council and an EEA Joint Committee. It also provides for the EFTA States to establish a Surveillance Authority (ESA)[8] to apply the principles of Community competition law within the EFTA area. Not even this Agreement, however, provides for the establishment of a body independent of all the Contracting Parties at the EEA level.[9] This Agreement thus poses a major challenge for integration theory. It envisages considerable integration without creating a supranational institution at the EEA level.[10]

6.2 EC TREATY

The EC Treaty and the Treaty on European Union establish institutions—the Council of the Union and the European Council—responsible for joint

[4] See, in particular, Art. 157(2) EC, regarding Commission independence. Cf., in connection with the planned European Central Bank, Art. 107.

[5] According to Art. 162(1) EC, the Council and Commission shall consult each other and settle by common accord their methods of co-operation.

[6] In the case of the EEA Agreement, the same may be said of positions expressed by EFTA representatives in the joint bodies established thereby.

[7] The importance of the Joint Committees was stressed in the Report of the Committee on External Economic Relations on the agreements negotiated between the Community and the EFTA Member and Associated States which have not applied to join the Community, EP Doc. 322/72, 7.

[8] Art. 108(1) of the EEA Agreement.

[9] Moreover, the ESA will not participate in EEA decision-making in the way that the Commission participates in Community decision-making. See *EES–Avtalets införlivande m. m.* (Ds 1992:14), 19.

[10] E.g., according to O. Due, 'General Introduction to a Discussion on the Principles of Community Law Seen in the EEA Perspective' [1991] *JFT* 288–94, at 289, the dynamism of an organization depends on majority decision-making by independent institutions.

decision-making and lay down rules governing the composition, procedures, and functions of these institutions.

6.2.1 Institutions

According to Article 2 of the Merger Treaty, members of the Council of the Union were delegated by their governments.[11] Article 146 of the EC Treaty, as amended by the Treaty on European Union, now provides that the Council shall consist of a representative of each Member State at ministerial level. The representative must be authorized to commit the government of that State.[12]

Council meetings may be attended by national officials other than ministers,[13] but only ministers may vote.[14] Article 150 of the Treaty does permit proxy voting. However, with a view to curbing excessive absenteeism, this provision stipulates that a minister may not vote on behalf of more than one Member State in addition to his own.

Further Article D of the Treaty on European Union states that the European Council shall bring together the Heads of State or of Government of the Member States and the President of the Commission. They shall be assisted by the Ministers for Foreign Affairs of the Member States and by a Commissioner.[15]

6.2.2 Procedures

The EC Treaty provisions governing the procedures of the Council of the Union lay down rules on the internal organization of this Council, the kinds of acts it may adopt and the conditions under which they may be adopted and makes arrangements for democratic control.

Internal Organization

According to Article 147 of the EC Treaty, the President convenes the Council on his own initiative or at the request of one of the members or of the

[11] See, generally, F. W. Scharpf, 'The Joint–Decision Trap: Lessons from German Federalism and European Integration' [1988] *Public Administration* 239–78.

[12] The European Parliament has called on Member States which, because of their constitutional provisions, have regions with exclusive legislative powers to facilitate the participation of representatives of these regions in meetings of the Council when matters falling within their competence are being considered. See the Resolution of 18 November 1993 ([1993] OJ C329/279) on the participation and representation of the regions in the process of European integration: the Committee of the Regions, para. 11.

[13] Art. 6(3) of Dec. 93/662 of 6 Dec. 1993 ([1993] OJ L304/1) adopting the Council's Rules of Procedure.

[14] Art. 7(3), *ibid.*, provides that the right to vote may be delegated only to another member of the Council.

[15] According to the same provision, the European Council shall provide the Union with the necessary impetus for its development and shall define its general political guidelines thereof. The European Council shall meet at least twice a year, under the chairmanship of the Head or State or Government of the Member State which holds the Presidency of the Council.

Commission. Neither the Treaty nor the Rules of Procedure of the Council specify the frequency of Council meetings. In practice, they are held with considerable frequency. For example, ninety-five meetings were held in 1994.[16] Moreover, the Rules of Procedure of the Council provide for decisions to be reached by written procedure.[17] The Presidency of the Council, held for six months, is to be rotated among Member States in turn.[18]

Article 151(3) of the Treaty provides for the Council to adopt its own Rules of Procedure.[19] These Rules provide that in the absence of a unanimous vote to the contrary, meetings take place in camera.[20] The secrecy thus surrounding Council debates and even Council minutes, except in the case of a resolution, apparently renders the Council less sensitive to public opinion.[21] Responses to such problems have included adoption of a code of conduct concerning public access to Council and Commission documents[22] and a decision on public access to Council documents.[23]

Acts

Article 189 of the EC Treaty provides that, in order to carry out its task and in accordance the provisions of this Treaty, the Council may make regulations and issue directives, take decisions, make recommendations, or deliver opinions. Further, it is provided that regulations shall have general application. They shall be binding in their entirety and directly applicable in all Member States. Directives shall be binding, as to the result to be achieved, upon each Member State to which they are addressed, though the latter may choose the form and method of complying with obligations contained therein. Decisions are binding in their entirety on the persons addressed. Recommendations and opinions lack binding force, though they may cast light on the interpretation of law having such force.[24] A Declaration on the Hierarchy of Community Acts, annexed to the Treaty on European Union, contemplates a review of 'the classification of Community acts with a view to establishing an appropriate hierarchy between the different categories of acts'.

Usually, the Treaty provisions empowering the Council to adopt particular acts require that the latter must be based on a Commission proposal. Where the

[16] *EU General Report 1994* (EC Commission, Brussels, 1995), 419.

[17] Art. 8 of Dec. 93/662 of 6 Dec. 1993 ([1993] OJ L304/1) adopting the Council's Rules of Procedure.

[18] See now Dec. 95/2 of 1 Jan. 1995 ([1995] OJ L1/220) determining the order in which the office of President shall be rotated.

[19] Dec. 93/662 of 6 Dec. 1993 ([1993] OJ L304/1) adopting the Council's Rules of Procedure.

[20] *Ibid.*, Art. 4(1) and 6(2). See also Art. 6(1) regarding 'policy debates'.

[21] Note the Declaration on the Right of Access to Information, annexed to the TEU.

[22] [1993] OJ L340/41.

[23] Dec. 93/731 of 20 Dec. 1993 ([1993] OJ L340/43).

[24] Case 113/75 *Giordano Frecassetti* v. *Amministrazionedelle Finanze dello Stato* [1976] ECR 983; Case C–322/88 *Salvatore Grimaldi* v. *Fonds des maladies professionnelles* [1989] ECR 4407.

act must be so based, Article 189a(1) provides that unanimity shall be required for the Council to amend the proposal.[25] In some cases the Council may adopt acts on the basis of a Commission recommendation[26] or merely has to consult the Commission[27] or to receive its opinion.[28] In other cases the Council may adopt acts on a recommendation from the European Central Bank.[29] In a few cases the Council may adopt acts on its own initiative[30] or on application by a Member State.[31]

Unanimity Requirements

Many provisions of the EC Treaty require unanimous Council approval of acts to be adopted thereunder.[32] Where unanimity is required, Article 148(3) of the Treaty provides that abstentions by members present in person or represented in the Council shall not prevent adoption of the act concerned.[33] More usually, the Council may act by a qualified majority,[34] where the votes of Member States are weighted to take some account of differences in population sizes,[35] or even by a simple majority of its members.[36] However, if the Council wishes to amend a Commission proposal, it generally has to act unanimously, and in some circumstances it may have to act unanimously where it is opposed by the European Parliament.[37]

[25] However, this rule is subject to exceptions under Art. 189b(4) and (5), where the Council codecides with the European Parliament. See sect. 6.2.2 above, regarding the codecision procedure.

[26] Arts 100c(2), 103(2) and (4), 104c, 109(1) and (2), 109h(1), 109i(2), and 109k(1).

[27] Art. 106(5) and (6). [28] Art. 109i(3). [29] Arts 106(5) and (6) and 109(1) and (2).

[30] Article 73g. [31] Art. 93(2).

[32] See, e.g., Arts 8a(1), 8b(1) and (2), 8e, 7(2), 73c(2), 75(3), 99, 100, 100c, 103a, 104c(11) and (14), 105(6), 106(5) and (6), 109(1), 130(3), 130b, 130d, and 130o EC, as amended by the TEU. In Arts 130i(1) and 128(5) the unanimity requirement applies, even though the codecision procedure (see below) is otherwise to be followed.

[33] In Arts 109k(4) and 109l(5) the requirement is modified to exclude Member States 'with a derogation' from participation in the third stage of monetary union.

[34] Art. 148(2). Such a majority is required, e.g., under Arts 73c(2), 73g, 94, 100(2) and (3), 103(2) and (4), 104c(6) and (14), 106(5) and (6), 109(1) and (2), 113(4), 126(4), 129(4), 130i(4), and 228a. The requirement is modified in Art. 109k(1), (2), and (5) to suspend the voting rights of Member States 'with a derogation' from participation in the third stage of monetary union. See also Art. 104c(13), where the voting rights of a Member State with 'an excessive budget deficit' are suspended. See, similarly, the Prot. on Social Policy, annexed to the EC Treaty.

[35] The current weightings are set out in Art. 15 of the Austrian, Finnish, and Swedish Accession Act, as substituted by Art. 8 of Dec. 95/1 of 1 Jan. 1995 ([1995] OJ L1/1) adjusting the instruments concerning the accession of new Member States to the EU.

[36] While it rarely applies, according to Art. 148(2) EC, this is the general rule. Hence, Art. K.9 of the TEU seems problematic. According to this provision, the Council may decide to apply Art. 100c EC, which concerns immigration from third states, to action in areas covered by Art. K.1(1) to (6) of the former Treaty, which concern co-operation in justice and home affairs. If the Council so decides, it may also determine the voting rules to apply.

[37] See below.

Democratic Control

The Council is usually required by the EC Treaty to consult,[38] co-operate,[39] or co-decide[40] with the European Parliament.[41] Where consultation is required, the opinion of the Parliament is not binding on the Council, but the latter must obtain such an opinion, except in cases of urgency.[42] Where the co-operation procedure operates, the Council may only adopt an act opposed by an absolute majority of Members of the European Parliament (MEPs), if the act has unanimous Council support. Where the co-decision procedure applies, the Parliament may, also by an absolute majority of MEPs, reject an act approved by the Council.[43] In other cases the Council may merely be required to inform[44] or to report to the Parliament,[45] though occasionally no contact at all with the Parliament may be required.[46] In cases where the Council, 'meeting in the composition of the Heads of State or Government', is empowered to act, it may also be required to consult[47] and even to 'take account' of the opinion of the Parliament.[48] Efforts to strengthen such arrangements for democratic control envisage, *inter alia*, an enhanced role for national parliaments.[49]

The Council may also be required to consult the Economic and Social Committee[50] or the Committee of the Regions.[51] The former Committee was established by Article 193 of the Treaty.[52] Its function is to advise the Council and Commission on the solutions to be adopted with regard to practical problems of an economic and social nature and to deliver opinions based on its specific competence and knowledge.[53] The Committee of the

[38] See, e.g., Arts 8b(1) and (2), 8e, 57(2), 94, 99, 100, 100c(1) and (3), 106(5) and (6), 109(1), 109f(6), 109j(5), 109k(2), 130(3), 130b, 130i(4), 130o, and 130s(2).

[39] Art. 189c. This procedure applies, e.g., under Arts 6(2), 75(1), 103(5), 104a(2), 104b(2), 105a(2), 118a(2), 125, 127(4), 129d, 130e, 130o, 130s(1), and 130w.

[40] Art. 189b. This procedure applies, e.g., under Arts 49, 54(2), 57, 126(3), 128(5), 129(4), 129a(2), 129d, 130i and 130s(3).

[41] Moreover, according to Art. 138b, the European Parliament may request the Commission to submit any appropriate proposal on matters on which it considers that a Community act is required for the purpose of implementing the Treaty.

[42] Case 138/79 *SA Roquette Frères and Maizena* v. *EC Commission* [1980] ECR 3333; and Case C–65/93 *European Parliament* v. EU *Council* (not yet reported).

[43] In a few cases the assent procedure applies, which means that a measure may only come into force if it has been approved by the Parliament. See, e.g., Arts 8a(2), 105(6), 106(5), and 130d.

[44] Arts 103(2), 103a(2), 104c(11), and 109(1). [45] Art. 103(4).

[46] See, e.g., Arts 73c(2), 100c(2), 103a(1), 109(2) and (4), 109i(3), 109l(4) and (5), and 126(4) (recommendations). [47] Art. 109j(2). [48] Art. 109j(3) and (4).

[49] See the Declarations on the Conference of the Parliaments and on the Role of National Parliaments in the EU, annexed to the TEU.

[50] See, for example, Arts 49, 54(2), 75(1) and (3), 99, 100, 105(4), 105a(2), 118a(2), 125, 126(3), 127(4), 129(4), 129a(2), 129d, 130(3), 130b, 130d, 130e, 130i(1) and (4), 130o, and 130s(2) and (3).

[51] Arts 129d, 130b, 130d, and 130e.

[52] A Consultative Committee was also established by Art.18 ECSC.

[53] Joined Cases 281, 283–285 and 287/85 *Germany, France, Netherlands, Denmark and the UK* v. *EC Commission* [1987] ECR 3203, 3256.

Regions was established by Article 198c of the EC Treaty, as amended by the Treaty on European Union. Its function is comparable with that of the Economic and Social Committee, but relates to regional issues.

6.2.3 Functions

The Council of the Union is required by Article 4(1) of the EC Treaty, like the other Community institutions, to collaborate in the achievement of Community objectives. In so collaborating, the Council is to perform the functions laid down in Article 145 of the Treaty. These functions involve the coordination of national economic policies and the power to adopt legally binding acts. Such acts concern both liberalization and harmonization.

Liberalization

The Council originally played a role in relation to implementation of trade liberalization associated with the progressive establishment of the common market.[54] It continues to play a role in relation to disputes relating trade liberalization and use of safeguard measures.

(i) Disputes

Under Article 93(2) of the EC Treaty, the Council, on application by the Member State concerned,[55] may authorize state aid which the Commission opposes.[56] This procedure has been employed, for example, in relation to French aid to the paper industry[57] and Danish aid for the slaughter of hens.[58] However, such an authorization must be 'justified by exceptional circumstances'. For example, when German farmers were already recovering from the Community 80 per cent of their loss of income due to the dismantling of positive monetary compensatory amounts,[59] the discovery of the shortfall did not constitute an exceptional circumstance[60] such as to justify the authorization of state aid.[61]

[54] Art. 8 of the EEC Treaty.

[55] Applications are not always successful. See, e.g., regarding Italian textile aid, the *Second Report on Competition Policy* (EC Commission, Brussels, 1973), 89.

[56] Again, under Art. 109h(3) EC, as amended by the TEU, the Council may revoke Commission authorization of protective measures in the monetary policy field. See also Art. 109i(3).

[57] Dec. of 19 December 1960 ([1960] JO 1972) *portant sur le regime des aides existant en France en faveur de certain categories de pâtes à papier.*

[58] Dec. 76/556 of 22 June 1976 ([1976] OJ L168/12) on the system of aid applicable to the slaughter of hens in Denmark.

[59] Reg. 855/84 of 31 Mar. 1984 ([1984] OJ L90/1) on the calculation and the dismantlement of the monetary compensatory amounts applying to certain agricultural products.

[60] Slynn A.G. in Case 253/84 *Groupement agricole d'exploitation en commun (GAEC) de la Ségaude* v. *EC Council and Commission* [1987] ECR 123, 147.

[61] Dec. 84/361 of 30 June 1984 ([1984] OJ [1984] L185/41) concerning an aid granted to farmers in the Federal Republic of Germany.

(ii) Safeguard Measures

Occasionally the Council may authorize safeguard measures on its own initiative. According to Article 73g(1) of the EC Treaty, where a boycott against trade with a third country is adopted pursuant to the CFSP and implemented under Article 228a of the Treaty,[62] the Council may 'take the necessary urgent measures on the movement of capital and on payments as regards the third countries concerned'.[63]

More usually, the initiative is taken by the Commission. According to Article 103a(1), the Council, acting on a Commission proposal, may decide on conjunctural policy measures, in particular if severe difficulties arise in the supply of certain products. Under Article 103a(2) the Council, again acting on a Commission proposal, may grant Community financial assistance to a Member State in difficulties or seriously threatened with severe difficulties caused by exceptional occurrences beyond its control.

The Council may, instead, be required to act on a Commission recommendation. In the event of an emergency situation in a third country posing a threat of a sudden inflow of nationals from that country into the Community, the Council may, acting on a Commission recommendation under Article 100c(3), introduce a visa requirement for nationals from the country concerned.

In certain cases the European Central Bank may have to be consulted. Article 73f provides that where, in exceptional circumstances, movements of capital to or from third countries cause or threaten to cause serious difficulties for the operation of European Monetary Union the Council, acting on a Commission proposal and after consulting the Bank, may take safeguard measures with regard to third countries for a period not exceeding six months if such measures are strictly necessary.[64]

Harmonization

The Council adopts harmonization acts under provisions such as Article 100a of the EC Treaty.[65] Again, however, its role is tempered by the involvement of institutions independent of Member States, notably the Commission and the European Parliament, in this process.

Moreover, Article C of the Treaty on European Union provides that the 'Union shall be served by a single institutional framework which shall ensure the consistency and the continuity of the activities carried out in order to attain its objectives while respecting and building upon the acquis *communautaire*'. In other words, the Council must respect the trade liberalization and other

[62] See sect. 2.2.1 above.

[63] Under Art. 73g(2) a Member State may take, for serious political reasons and on grounds of urgency, unilateral measures of this kind. However, the Council, acting on a Commission proposal, may decide that the Member State shall amend or abolish such measures.

[64] See also Arts 109h and 109i EC.

[65] See sect. 5.2.1 above.

requirements embodied in the EC Treaty. To the extent that these requirements limit the uncertainty and negotiation costs which might otherwise inhibit joint decision-making,[66] the capacity of this institution to perform its harmonization functions may be enhanced.

However, there are limits to the possibility of developing Community law through Council acts. While these limits may not be readily identifiable with precision, their existence is reflected by the frequency with which intervention by the European Council or even an intergovernmental conference of the Member States under Article N of the Treaty on European Union, for the purposes of amending the EC Treaty, is felt to be necessary.[67] The necessity for such intervention may reflect limitations to networking arrangements[68] and, hence, to spill-over within the EC Treaty framework.

Joint decision-making in the Council may be even more problematic in the context of relations between the Community and third states. Participation in such decision-making is treated by the EC Treaty as implying membership of the Union, and so by definition third states are excluded from such participation. According to Article 146, it is each Member State which is to be represented in the Council. To maintain the effectiveness of the exclusion of third states, restrictions may also be imposed on the development of relations between a Member State and third states outside the Council. Thus the former may be said to have a 'duty of loyalty' under Article 5[69] not to undertake formal or informal commitments to third states which could have the effect of limiting its freedom to vote in the Council or of prejudicing the possibility of the Council reaching a decision relating to the subject matter of such commitments.[70]

The implication might been drawn from such practice that separate institutions must be created for joint decision-making as between the Community and

[66] Cf., regarding 'the link between policy dynamics and institutional behaviour', H. Wallace, 'The Council and the Commission after the Single European Act' in L. Hurwitz and C. Lequesne, *The State of the European Community* (London, 1991), 19–31, at 20.

[67] Cf. Art. 109j(3) and (4), which provide for the Council, 'acting in the composition of Heads of State or Government', to take decisions under the EC Treaty. See also the provision in Art. 103(2) for the adoption of European Council 'guidelines' for the Community institutions.

[68] The Community political system can best be visualized as an elaborate set of networks, closely linked in some ways, particularly decomposed in others, whose results depend on the political style in ascendancy at the moment. When conditions are propitious and leadership strategies appropriate, as they became in 1985, the political style of supranationalism enables connections to be made among points in the network, and allows for an expanded conception of tasks. When conditions are less benign or strategies inappropriate, the results are policy stagnation and separation of policy spheres. See R. O. Keohane and S. Hoffmann, 'Institutional Change in Europein the 1980s' in R. O. Keohane and S. Hoffmann (eds.), *The New European Community Decisionmaking and Institutional Change* (Boulder, 1991), 1–39, at 15.

[69] According to Case 208/80 *Rt. Hon. Lord Bruce of Donington* v. *Eric Gordon Aspden* [1981] ECR 2205, 2219, Art. 5 entails for Member States a 'duty not to take measures which are likely to interfere with the internal functioning of the institutions of the Community'.

[70] *Relations Between the Community and EFTA*, 14th Report of the House of Lords Select Committee on the European Communities, HL(1989–90) 55–2, 144.

third states. Such institutions have duly been established by Free Trade Agreements and Associated Agreements.

6.3 FREE TRADE AGREEMENTS

Each Free Trade Agreement established a Joint Committee, composed of representatives of the Community and the EFTA State concerned and empowered to engage in joint decision-making.

6.3.1 Institutions

Article 29(1) of the Swedish Free Trade Agreement established a Joint Committee, which was to consist of representatives of the Community,[71] on the one hand, and representatives of Sweden, on the other.[72] There was no requirement that the representatives be of ministerial rank and authorized to commit the Party concerned. In practice, the Committee was composed only of officials,[73] who lacked the competence formally to bind their respective Party as regards matters of any significance, and the Community position in the Committee was determined according to the 'Article 113 procedure',[74] i.e., the procedure employed for negotiation of agreements under Article 113 of the EC Treaty.[75] Hence, real discussions necessarily took place outside the Committee.

It may have been for this reason that from 1981 the summer meeting of the EC–Swedish Joint Committee (as well as that of the Joint Committee for coal and steel[76]) was replaced by a bilateral meeting between Swedish Ministers and the Commission. Norway and the Commission made similar arrangements in the same year.[77] The initiative for these changes apparently came from the

[71] According to Art. 3 of Reg. 2838/72 of 19 Dec. 1972 ([1972] JO 300/96) concluding an Agreement between the EEC and the Kingdom of Sweden and adopting provisions for its implementation, the Community was to be represented by the Commission, assisted by representatives of the Member States.

[72] Art. 30 of the Swedish Free Trade Agreement.

[73] H. Lidgard, 'Sverige–EEG och konkurrensregler' [1974] *SvJt* 18–33, at 30. The Swedish representatives were led by the Head of the Swedish Delegation to the Community and the Community representatives by the Director General for External Relations. See AiH 4/1990, 20.

[74] J. V. Louis *et al.*, *Le Droit de la Communauté Economique Européenne* (Brussels, 1980), xii, 152.

[75] According to this provision, the Commission is to negotiate in consultation with a special committee appointed by the Council to assist the Commission in this task and in accordance with directives issued by the Council.

[76] The latter body was established by Art. 26 of the Swedish–ECSC Agreement ([1973] OJ L350/76).

[77] The EC/US Transnational Declaration of 22 Nov. 1990 (Bull. EC 11–1990, 1.5.3) goes further in providing for informal contacts. It provides for biannual consultations between the US President and the Presidents of the Council and Commission. In addition, biannual meetings between the Foreign Ministers of the Member States, the Commission, and the US Secretary of State are

Community, which did not consider the work of the Joint Committees sufficiently important to justify the amount of 'red tape' involved.[78] The first such Sweden–Community meeting was attended by the Swedish Trade Minister, Björn Molin, and Commission Vice-President Wilhelm Haferkamp.[79] The economic situation in Sweden and the Community as well as certain global trade policy questions were discussed.[80] Questions are begged, however, why the Parties favoured informal contacts of this kind[81] rather than higher-level representation in the Joint Committee.

In addition to these bilateral contacts, meetings came to be held each year between EFTA Ministers and the Commissioner for External Relations, and meetings might also be held between EFTA Ministers and Ministers from Member States. However, both practical considerations, such as the difficulties of adequate preparation of such meetings associated with the overloaded agenda of the Council of the Union, and, more fundamentally, an internal decision-making process which might leave the Community little room for manœuvre in such meetings may have endangered the usefulness of these multilateral meetings.[82]

6.3.2 Procedures

Procedural rules governing joint decision-making under the Free Trade Agreements concerned the internal organization of the Joint Committees as well as the kind of acts the latter might adopt and the conditions under which the acts might be adopted. Little was apparently done to ensure democratic control of the decision-making involved.

Internal Organization

Article 31 of the Swedish Free Trade Agreement provided that the Joint Committee established thereunder should meet at least once a year in order

foreseen as well as biannual Commission–US consultations at cabinet level and *ad hoc* consultations at ministerial level. See also Commission Reply by Mr Andriessen to Written Question1900/91 ([1992] OJ C112/20) by Mr Miguel Arias Canete *et al.*

[78] P. Luif, 'Decision Structures and Decision-Making Processes in the European Communities' Relations to the EFTA Countries: A Case Study of Austria' [1983] *Österreichisches Zeitschrift für Aussenpolitik* 139–60, at 154.

[79] It is said, however, that similar Community–US meetings suffered from 'long agenda and cumbersome bureaucratic preparations and, because of [their] ritual character, ultimately had no impact on the solving of bilateral problems'. See H. G. Krenzler, n. 2 above, 97.

[80] Sverige–EG 1981 (Utrikes–och handelsdepartementen, 1982), 13.

[81] Cf. the argument that formalization of institutional relations between the Community and the USA will increase internal bureaucratic struggles and (undesirable) litigation, at least in the USA in B. E. Carter, A Code of Conduct for EC–US Relations' in J. Schwarze (ed.), n. 2 above, 131–9, at 132.

[82] Cf. A. von Stechow, 'The Council of Ministers: the Constraint on Action' in G. Edwards and E. Regelsberger (ed.), *Europe's Global Links* (London, 1990) 161–8. Cf. also G. Edwards, 'The Relevance of Theory to Group-to-Group Dialogue' *ibid.*, 201–18, at 212–3.

to review the general functioning of the Agreement. Each Party should preside in turn over the Committee, in accordance with arrangements to be laid down in its Rules of Procedure.[83] The Committee might also meet at other times whenever special circumstances so required, at the request of either Party, in accordance with the conditions to be laid down in its Rules of Procedure. In 1983, for example, a special meeting was requested by the Community to discuss Commission anti-dumping action against Swedish hardboard exporters.[84] However, only limited use was made of the option to request such meetings.

The Rules of Procedure of the Joint Committee[85] were, according to Article 29(3) of the Agreement, to be adopted by the Committee itself. To this extent, the Committee had the same kind of freedom of internal organization[86] as that enjoyed by the Council under the EC Treaty[87] and which used to be denied to the Economic and Social Committee.[88] The conclusion might be drawn that the Parties to the Free Trade Agreements intended that the Joint Committees should become important bodies. An alternative explanation is that they considered questions of their internal organization too unimportant to regulate or to provide a more detailed framework for regulation of such questions in the Agreements themselves.

Acts

Article 29(1) of the Swedish Agreement provided that the Joint Committee might take decisions in the cases provided for in the Agreement and make recommendations. The former were to 'be put into effect by the Contracting Parties in accordance with their own rules'. Provided there was a direct connection with the Agreement, such decisions might become part of Community law.[89] Recommendations, on the other hand, were not binding, though

[83] Dec. 1/73 of Feb. 1973. See *Sverige–EG 1973* (Utrikes–och handelsdepartementen, 1974), bil. 5.

[84] *Sverige–EG 1983* (Utrikesdepartementetshandelsavdelning, 1984), 23.

[85] Dec. 1/73 of Feb. 1973. See *Sverige–EG 1973* (Utrikes–och handelsdepartementen 1974), bil. 5.

[86] The Committee established by the Agreement on Trade and Commercial and Economic Cooperation between Poland and the Community ([1989] OJ L339/2) was also to adopt its own Rules of Procedure and work programme, and it might establish sub-committees to assist it in the performance of its tasks. It was to meet once a year in Brussels and Warsaw alternately. Special meetings might be convened by mutual agreement at the request of either Party. The office of chairman was to be held alternately by each Party. Wherever possible, the agenda for meetings of the Committee were to be agreed beforehand.

[87] See sect. 6.2.2 above. See also, in the case of the European Commission, Art. 162 EC.

[88] According to Art. 196 of the EEC Treaty, the Rules of Procedure of the Economic and Social Committee had to be approved by the Council. The TEU amended Art. 196, so as to empower the Committee to adopt its own Rules of Procedure.

[89] Case C–188/91 *Deutsche Shell AG* v. *Hauptzollamt Hamburg-Harburg* [1993] ECR I–363, I–388. The ECJ may be reluctant to interfere with the exercise of such decision-making power. See Van Gerven A. G. *ibid.*, I–380.

national courts of Member States might have to take account of the recommendations of such bodies for interpretative purposes.[90]

More particularly, Article 12A, which was added to the Agreement in 1978, empowered the Committee to take decisions adapting the Agreement to changes in the common customs nomenclature.[91] The Committee also took decisions under Article 28 of Protocol 3 to the Agreement,[92] which concerned rules of origin, amending this Protocol.[93] In such instances the Committee might exercise what amounted to legislative power at the international level.

Unanimity Requirements

Just as unanimity requirements in the EC Treaty may be seen as preserving the sovereignty of Member States, so in the context of agreements with third states such requirements may be seen as preserving Community autonomy.[94]

Accordingly, Article 30(2) of the Swedish Agreement stipulated that the Joint Committee should act by mutual agreement.[95] More particularly, Article 5 of the Rules of Procedure of the Joint Committee followed a precedent set by the Rules of Procedure of the Council of the Union[96] and of the Commission[97] and permitted decisions to be taken by a written procedure, if both Parties agreed. This procedure was first employed in 1973 regarding adoption of a safeguard measure under Article 26 of the Agreement[98] limiting imports of Swedish timber at a time when storm damage to trees in Germany had led to a surplus of timber there. Sweden expressed a preference for oral discussion in the Joint Committee, but agreed to the use of the written procedure on condition that the matter was examined at the next meeting of the Committee.[99] However,

[90] *Ibid.* I–388.

[91] Agreement in the form of an exchange of letters amending the Agreement between the European Economic Community and the Kingdom of Sweden ([1978] OJ L303/15).

[92] See, e.g., Dec. 5/1988 of 5 Dec. 1988 ([1988] OJ L381/18) of the EEC–Sweden Joint Committee modifying Prot. 3 on the concept of 'originating products' and methods of administrative co-operation in order to simplify the cumulation rules. See, similarly, regarding the role of the Joint Committee established by the Agreement between the EEC and the Socialist Republic of Romania on the establishment of the Joint Committee ([1980] OJ L352/2), C. Flaesch-Mougin, 'Les Accords Externes de la CEE (1 juillet 1986/31 octobre 1989)' [1990] *RTDE* 457–518, at 471, n. 53.

[93] Art. 16 of Prot. 3 to the Swedish Free Trade Agreement also provided for the Joint Committee to take decisions on methods of administrative co-operation to be applied in the Community and Sweden, and Art. 3 of Prot. 2 to the Agreement, concerning products subject to special arrangements to take account of differences in the cost of agricultural products incorporated therein, provided for the Committee to take decisions regarding tariff reductions for alcoholic beverages.

[94] Cf. K. Lenaerts, 'Regulating the Regulatory Process: "Delegation of Powers" in the European Community' (1993) *ELRev.* 23–49, at 38–9.

[95] The same stipulation was contained in Art. 23(2) of the Free Trade Agreement (SÖ 1980:87) between the EFTA States and Spain in the case of the multilateral Joint Committee established by that Agreement.

[96] See sect. 6.2.2 above.

[97] Art. 11 of the Rules of Procedure (Dec. 93/492 of 17 Feb. 1993, [1993] OJ L230/15).

[98] See sect. 3.3.2 above.

[99] *Sverige–EG 1973* (Utrikes–och handelsdepartementen, 1974), 23–4. Among the reforms of Joint Committee practice advocated in a Coreper report of 1983 on EC–EFTA relations was the shortening of time limits for consultation. See *Sverige–EG 1983* (Utrikesdepartementets handelsavdelning, 1984), 38.

although resort to this procedure might have done something to compensate for the fact that only infrequent regular meetings of the Joint Committee were required by the Agreement, in practice, only limited use was made of the procedure. The implication is that the formal decision-making competence of the Committee was not regarded as important for the day-to-day functioning of the Agreement. The reason might be thought to lie, at least partly, in the fact that unanimity requirements were such as to limit prospects of decisions being reached within the Committee on contentious issues.

Democratic Control

The impact of unanimity requirements on decision-making under the Free Trade Agreements had little public exposure. Article 4 of the Rules of Procedure of the Swedish–EC Joint Committee stated that meetings of the Committee were not public except in so far as a decision was adopted. This language was interpreted as meaning that only formal decisions should be published. The implication might be that the Committee was expected to engage in consideration of sufficiently important and sensitive issues as to demand such secrecy. On the other hand, this provision exemplified the secrecy which generally surrounded EC–EFTA institutional relations and which may have seriously impeded democratic control of decision-making.[100]

6.3.3 Functions

The Free Trade Agreements tended to use generalized language to define the functions of the Joint Committees established thereunder. They envisaged that these Committees would be responsible for the administration of the Agreements and ensuring their proper implementation.[101] This responsibility related both to liberalization and to harmonization.

Liberalization

It was in connection with control of resort to safeguard measures that the Joint Committees established by the Free Trade Agreements were regarded as

[100] Cf. the criticism of the work of the Integration Office within the Swedish Government by the Constitutional Committee of the Swedish Parliament (1989/90: KU30 *med anledning av granskning av statsrådens tjansteutövning och regeringsärendenas handläggning* (Inquiry into the work of the Cabinet and its handling of government affairs).

[101] Art. 29(1) of the Swedish Free Trade Agreement. Art. 29(2) provided that, for the purpose of the proper implementation of the Agreement, the Parties were to exchange information. At the request of either Party consultations were to be held in the Joint Committee. Cf. Art. 20(2)(a) of the Polish–EC Agreement on Trade and Commercial and Economic Co-operation ([1989] OJ L339/2), which provided that the Joint Committee established thereunder was to ensure the proper functioning of the Agreement and devise and recommend measures for achieving its objectives, keeping in view the economic and social policies of the Parties.

having their most important function.[102] As the Court of Justice noted in *Kupferberg*,[103] such measures could only be adopted 'in specific circumstances and as a general rule after consideration within the Joint Committee in the presence of both Parties'. Certainly, the Swedish Agreement usually required compliance with procedures involving consultation of the Joint Committee prior to adoption of safeguard measures.[104] In other words, such bodies were seen as having the function of upholding liberalization requirements against unjustified use of such measures. Article 22(1) of the Swedish Agreement might be thought to have implicitly reinforced the obligation of each Party to co-operate in the performance of this function by the Joint Committee. According to this provision, Parties should refrain from any measure likely to jeopardize the fulfilment of the objectives of the Agreement and should take all general or specific measures required to fulfil their obligations under the Agreement.

In reality, practice concerning adoption of anti-dumping measures and anti-trust measures suggests that the above function might not be effectively performed by the Joint Committees.

(i) Anti-dumping Measures

Article 27 of the Swedish Agreement laid down the procedures in accordance with which the Parties could adopt anti-dumping measures under Article 25. In particular, Article 27(3)(c) of the Agreement stipulated that the Joint Committee should be consulted prior to the adoption of such measures.

This stipulation seems to have been of little practical significance. For example, in 1978 the Commission investigated Swedish exporters of five different products for suspected dumping without invoking Article 25 of the Agreement[105] or involving the Swedish authorities in any way.[106] The Swedish

[102] Rozès A. G. in Case 270/80 *Polydor Ltd and RSC Records Inc.* v. *Harlequin Record Shops and Simon Records Ltd* [1982] ECR 329, 354.

[103] Case 104/81 *Hauptzollamt Mainz* v. *C. A. Kupferberg & Cie K. G.* [1982] ECR 3641, 3664. See sect. 2.3.1 above.

[104] Arts 23(2), 24, 25 and 26 of the Swedish Free Trade Agreement. Art. 22(2) provided, more generally, that if either Party considered that the other had failed to fulfil an obligation under the Agreement, it might take appropriate measures in accordance with the procedures laid down in Art. 27, which specified the role of the Joint Committee. However, Art. 28 merely required a Party to inform the other Party of safeguard measures adopted thereunder 'forthwith'.

[105] Art. 3 of Reg. 2839/72 of 19 Dec. 1972 ([1972] JO L300/186) on the safeguard measures provided for in the Agreement between the European Economic Community and the Kingdom of Sweden provided that in the case of a practice that might justify application of Art. 25 of the Agreement, the procedures established by Reg. 459/68 of 5 April 1968 ([1968] JO L93/1) on protection against dumping or the granting of bounties or subsidies, by countries which are not members of the EEC, should be applicable.

[106] In relation to kraft liner (Notice of termination of the anti-dumping/anti-subsidies procedure concerning imports of kraft liner paper and board from Finland, Portugal, Sweden, and Austria ([1978] OJ C61/2), wood chipboard (Notice of termination of the anti-dumping/anti-subsidies procedure concerning imports of reconstituted wood (wood chipboard) from Spain and Sweden

representative complained in the Joint Committee that undue pressure was being applied to Swedish companies by such a means of proceeding.[107] It might be, however, that a Commission decision to open an investigation did not constitute a 'measure' for the purposes of Article 27(3)(c). Certainly, similar action was taken the following year,[108] but this time there was no official Swedish comment.[109]

The question whether a price undertaking, i.e., an undertaking from exporters that they will maintain minimum prices considered by the Commission appropriate to remove the injury attributed to dumping,[110] could constitute such a measure might be thought more problematic. In 1981 the Commission secured such an undertaking from a Swedish firm suspected of dumping without prior discussion in the Joint Committee.[111] Rather, a general discussion of Commission anti-dumping practice took place between Swedish and Commission officials outside the Committee.[112] Apparently the Commission interpreted 'measures' as only covering the imposition of anti-dumping duties.

([1978] OJ C75/3) and rosin (Notice of termination of the anti-dumping/anti-subsidies procedure concerning imports of certain rosin originating in Sweden ([1978] OJ C112/4), price undertakings by the exporters concerned were accepted by the Commission. In the case of wood pulp, the investigation (Notice of initiation of anti-dumping/anti-subsidy procedure concerning certain chemical wood pulp originating in Canada, Finland, Sweden, and the USA ([1978] OJ C89/2) was terminated without any further action being taken (Notice of termination of the anti-dumping/ anti-subsidies procedure concerning certain chemical wood pulp originating in Canada, the USA, Finland, and Sweden ([1978] OJ C303/10). In the case of ferro–chromium, the investigation (Notice of initiation of anti-dumping/anti-subsidy procedure concerning imports of ferrochromium originating in the Republic of South Africa and Sweden ([1978] OJ C90/3) led initially to a provisionalanti-dumping duty and then to price undertakings, whichwere replaced in 1983. See Dec. 83/306 of 16 June 1983 ([1983] OJ L161/15) accepting undertakings given inconnection with the anti-dumping proceeding concerning imports of low ferro–chromium originating in South Africa, Sweden, Turkey, and Zimbabwe, and terminating that proceeding.

107 *Sverige–EG 1978* (Utrikes–och handelsdepartementen, 1979), 21–2.

108 The investigations concerned fibreboard (Notice of initiation of anti-dumping/anti-subsidy procedure concerning fibre building board from Sweden, Norway, Finland, and Spain ([1979] OJ C116/2) and anchor chains (Notice of initiation of anti-dumping/anti-subsidy procedure concerning studded welded link chain originating in Spain and Sweden ([1979] OJ C303/5). See also Dec. 80/ 1094 of 25 May 1980 ([1980] OJ [1980] L320/41) terminating the anti-dumping proceeding concerning imports of edible and pharmaceutical gelatine originating in Sweden, where Swedish representatives were merely said to have been given 'the opportunity to inspect non-confidential information made available to the Commission'.

109 *Sverige–EG 1979* (Utrikes–och handelsdepartementen, 1980), 20.

110 See now Art. 8 of Reg. 3283/94 of 22 Dec. 1994 ([1994] OJ L349/1) on protection against dumped imports from countries not members of the EC.

111 See also Dec. 80/783 of 27 Aug. 1980 (OJ [1980] L231/10) accepting undertakings in connection with the anti-dumping proceeding concerning imports of studded welded-link chains, originating in Spain and Sweden and terminating these proceedings and Dec. 80/1094 of 25 Nov. 1980 ([1980] OJ L320/41) terminating the anti-dumping proceeding concerning imports of edible and pharmaceutical gelatine originating in Sweden.

112 *Sverige–EG 1981* (Utrikes-och handelsdepartementen, 1982), 22.

Hence, it only consulted the Committee[113] prior to imposition of such duties[114] and did not consult[115] prior to seeking price undertakings.[116]

In 1985, however, the Commission imposed provisional duties without prior consultation in the Joint Committee.[117] This action was, presumably, based on Article 27(3)(e) of the Swedish Agreement, which allowed for the possibility that exceptional circumstances might make prior examination in the Committee impossible.[118]

Such practice may explain why introduction of more developed rules governing consultation of such Committees was sought.[119] At one stage an EC–EFTA working group was mandated to discuss concertation procedures and the ways of calculating injury as a result of dumping.[120] According to one proposal,[121] co-operation between competition authorities of the Parties would take place, whenever the Commission suspected an EFTA company of dumping. The national authorities of the EFTA State concerned would investigate whether the company was selling below cost, and it was envisaged that the

[113] See, e.g., *Sverige–EG 1983* (Utrikesdepartementets handelsavdelning, 1984), 23. The consultation, however, was inconclusive, and the Swedish representatives merely expressed the view that such problems should be tackled within the context of the development of closer trade policy relations between Sweden and the Community.

[114] Reg. 2444/83 of 29 Aug. 1983 ([1983] OJ L241/9) imposing a provisional anti-dumping duty on certain imports of hardboard originating in Czechoslovakia, Poland, and Sweden and reopening the anti-dumping proceedings concerning these imports and Reg. 3648/83 of 19 Dec. 1983 ([1983] OJ L361/6) imposing a definitive anti-dumping duty on imports of hardboard originating in Sweden.

[115] See, e.g., *Sverige–EG 1983* (Utrikesdepartementets handelsavdelning, 1984), 22–3.This practice was accepted by the Swedish Government in *Tillämpningen av GATT:s Regler för Skydd mot Dumpad och Subventionerad Import* (Application of GATT Rules for Protection against Dumped and Subsidized Imports) (Ds UD 1984: 6), 16.

[116] See also Dec. 83/306 of 16 June 1983 ([1983] OJ L161/15) accepting undertakings given in connection with the anti-dumping proceeding concerning imports of low carbon ferro–chromium originating in South Africa, Sweden, Turkey, and Zimbabwe, and terminating that proceeding.

[117] *Sverige–EG 1985* (Utrikesdepartementets handelsavdelning, 1986), 25. In Reg. 2823/85 of 7 Oct. 1985 ([1985] OJ L268/11) imposing a provisional anti-dumping duty on imports of certain clogs originating in Sweden it is recorded that Swedish representatives were 'officially advised' of the opening of the investigation. This seems to have been the usual practice. See also, e.g., Dec. 86/35 of 21 Feb. 1986 ([1986] OJ L46/23) accepting undertakings given in connection with the anti-dumping proceeding concerning imports of fibre building board from Finland and Sweden and terminating the investigation. Moreover, after the imposition of provisional duties on the clogs 'representatives of the Swedish authorities acting on behalf of the Swedish clog industry as a whole made written and oral submissions to the Commission on both dumping and injury'. See Reg. 264/86 of 4 Feb. 1986 ([1986] OJ L32/1) imposing a definitive anti-dumping duty on imports of certain clogs originating in Sweden and definitively collecting the provisional anti-dumping duty.

[118] In the same circumstances this provision also permitted adoption of safeguard measures without prior consultation on the basis of Arts 24, 24A, or 26 or in the case of export aids having a direct and immediate incidence on trade.

[119] *Redovisning av det svenska integrationsarbetet våren 1988–mars 1989* (Utrikesdepartementets handelsavdelning, 1989), 59.

[120] B. Hurni, 'EFTA–EC Relations: Aftermath of the Luxembourg Declaration' [1986] *JWTL* 497–506, at 502–3.

[121] M. Bronckers in J. Jamar and H. Wallace (eds.), *EEC–EFTA: More Than Just Good Friends?* (Bruges, 1988), 61–8, at 67–8.

Commission would take account of the results of the investigation. However, the Commission and the Council have proved willing to take only limited account of competition policy considerations in the context of anti-dumping proceedings,[122] and it may be that the problems raised by the use of anti-dumping measures in EC-EFTA trade were not such as to be amenable to a purely procedural solution.[123]

(ii) Anti-trust Measures

Article 27(3)(a) of the Swedish Agreement provided that either Party might refer a restrictive practice to the Joint Committee if it considered that the practice was incompatible with the proper functioning of the Agreement within the meaning of Article 23(1). The Parties should provide the Joint Committee with all relevant information and give it the assistance it required to examine the case and, where appropriate, to eliminate the practice. If the Party concerned failed to put an end to the practice within the period fixed by the Joint Committee, or in the absence of agreement in the Committee within three months of the matter being referred to it, the other Party might adopt any safeguard measures it considered necessary to deal with the serious difficulties resulting from the practice; in particular, it might withdraw tariff concessions.

It might be argued that the principal significance of Article 27(3)(a) was that it defined the conduct in relation to which the special procedures established by the Agreement might come into operation. If so, then the *lex specialis* principle might be taken to mean that such procedures should be utilized in the event that trade between the Parties to the Agreement was affected, even though trade between Member States might also be affected.[124]

On the other hand, the Commission, like other Community institutions, may only 'act within the limits of the powers conferred on it' by the EC Treaty.[125] Article 89 of the Treaty requires the Commission to ensure the application of the principles laid down in its Articles 85 and 86 thereof but makes no reference to conduct of undertakings incompatible with agreements with third states. More particularly, Article 3(2) of Regulation 17[126] does not even provide for third states to complain to the Commission concerning anti-competitive conduct.[127] The question is begged, however, why the Council

[122] See, e.g., Reg. 997/85 of 18 April 1985 ([1985] OJ L107/8) imposing a provisional anti-dumping duty on imports of glycene originating in Japan and Reg. 2322/85 of 12 Aug. 1985 ([1985] OJ L218/1) imposing a definitive anti-dumping duty on imports of glycene originating in Japan. [123] Cf. sect. 6.5.3 below, regarding the solution sought in the EEA Agreement.

[124] It was suggested, however, that the Commission need not resort to the provisions of a Free Trade Agreement where restrictive practices might affect trade between the Parties but the other Party had not complained to the Commission. See M. Waelbroeck, 'Enforceability of the EEC–EFTA Free Trade Agreements: A Reply' (1978) *ELRev.* 27–31, at 31 n. 15.

[125] Art. 4(1) EC.

[126] Reg. 17 of 6 Feb. 1962 ([1962] JO 204), first reg. implementing Arts 85 and 86 EC.

[127] Cf. Tesauro A. G. in Case C–327/91 *France* v. *EC Commission* [1994] ECR I–3641, I–3662–4.

did not act under provisions such as Articles 87[128] and 113 of the Treaty to confer the necessary powers on the Commission to act against conduct incompatible with the Free Trade Agreements.

Procedures under these Agreements might still be seen as having some role to play in efforts to curb restrictive practices. For example, in 1975 the Commission instituted concurrent procedures against Hoffmann-La Roche under Regulation 17:[129] one was for presumed breaches of Articles 85 and 86 of the EC Treaty, and the other took the form of a reference to the Joint Committee under Article 27 of the Swiss Free Trade Agreement[130] in respect of effects on trade between the Community and Switzerland.[131] On the other hand, discussion of the possibility that the Swedish Joint Committee should establish a sub-committee on restrictive practices came to nothing.[132]

In fact, rather than seeking to develop the Joint Committees as institutions which might assist enforcement of competition law throughout the EC–EFTA area, the Commission tended to rely on application of Article 85 or 86 of the EC Treaty where anti-competitive conduct affecting EC–EFTA trade also affected trade between Member States. The Commission apparently considered that it thereby avoided the need to give the Joint Committee the opportunity provided for in provisions such as Article 27(3)(a) of the Swedish Agreement to tackle the problem.

Thus, for example, in May 1979 the Commission took proceedings against three Swedish companies for breach of Article 85 of the Treaty. The matter was not referred to the Joint Committee, the Free Trade Agreement was not invoked, and it was not shown that trade between the Community and Sweden was affected. Instead, informal consultations took place.[133] In fact, while confidentiality requirements imposed by Article 20 of Regulation 17[134] might have constrained the Commission,[135] the latter seems generally to have been willing to hold consultations with Swedish officials outside the Joint Committee,[136] in accordance with an OECD Recommendation of 1979.[137]

In the *Wood Pulp* case,[138] where wood pulp producers established in

[128] According to Art. 87 EC, the Council is to adopt any appropriate measures to give effect to the principles set out in Arts 85 and 86 of the Treaty.

[129] Reg. 17 of 6 Feb. 1962 ([1962] JO 204), first reg. implementing Arts 85 and 86 EC.

[130] [1972] JO L300/191.

[131] Commission Reply to Written Question 152/75 ([1975] OJ C209/14) by Mr Cousté

[132] H. Lidgard, 'Tre års frihandelssamarbete med EEC' [1976] *SvJT* 689–714, at 702.

[133] *Sverige–EG 1981* (Utrikes-och handelsdepartementen, 1981), 22.

[134] Reg. 17 of 6 Feb. 1962 ([1962] JO 204), first reg. implementing Arts 85 and 86 EC.

[135] Cf. *Co-operation with the United States of America regarding the Application of their Competition Rules*, COM(94)430, 2 and Annex I, 6.

[136] *Sverige–EG 1984* (Utrikesdepartementetshandelsavdelning 1985), pp. 23–24.

[137] *Competition Policy and International Trade: OECD Instruments of Co-operation* (OECD, Paris, 1987) and the *Ninth Report on Competition Policy* (EC Commission, Brussels, 1980), 35.

[138] Joined Cases 89, 104, 114, 116, 117, 125–129/85 *A. Åhlström Osakeyhtiö* v. *EC Commission* [1988] ECR 5193.

Canada, Finland, and the United States had engaged in price-fixing arrangements which affected the prices paid by purchasers in the Community, the Court of Justice did not object to Commission reliance on such practice. However, the point does not seem to have been put squarely to the Court that the Commission might have been interfering with the trade which the Free Trade Agreement with Finland sought to liberalize without satisfying the procedural conditions laid down in the Agreement for resort to safeguard measures.[139]

If such Agreements did not operate to constrain the Commission, the latter might have felt little practical or legal need to rely on greater Joint Committee involvement. Since most of the larger Swedish companies had subsidiaries within the Community, the Commission might, in practice, often have had the same opportunities for investigation of anti-competitive practices and imposition of sanctions on offenders as if Sweden had already been a Member State. Moreover, although Regulation 17[140] does not refer to Commission investigations outside the Community,[141] such investigations would seem to be permitted by international law with the consent of the state concerned. Consent would apparently have been forthcoming from the Swedish Government, which stated that co-operation between Swedish competition authorities and the Commission was close.[142] As for Swedish companies themselves, they apparently tended to be compliant so as to maintain 'good relations' with the Commission.[143]

Problems of 'Success'

It might be argued that the simple reason for the failure of the Swedish–EC Joint Committee to play a more prominent role in tackling trading problems between the Parties was the success of the Free Trade Agreement. In other words, the Committee did not need to take on a more prominent role, because the Agreement worked smoothly and the problems that arose were not such as appreciably to affect trade between the two.[144]

[139] Arts 23(2) and 27 of the Finnish Agreement. Cf. the provision for Commission negotiations under Council authorization with third states where application of Reg. 4056/86 of 22 Dec. 1986 ([1986] OJ L378/4) laying down detailed rules for the application of Arts 85 and 86 of the Treaty to maritime transport (Art. 9) is liable to conflict with the laws of such states.

[140] Reg. 17 of 6 Feb. 1962 ([1962] JO 204), first reg. implementing Arts 85 and 86 EC .

[141] Within the Community, Reg. 17 requires the Commission to exercise its powers to investigate undertakings suspected of anti-competitive conduct after notifying the authorities of the Member State concerned (Art. 14(2)).

[142] *Redovisning av det svenska integrationsarbetet våren 1988–mars 1989* (Utrikesdepartementets handelsavdelning 1989), 150–1.

[143] *Industri och EG* (Industriförbundet Arbetsrapport 11, Stockholm, 1988), 8. Exchange of confidential information may apparently be 'authorized' by the underraking concerned. See the *Twenty-Fourth Report on Competition Policy*, COM(95)142, 18.

[144] But see, regarding the trade problems unaffected by the Agreement, the Commission memorandum summarized in Club de Bruxelles, *EC/EFTA: The Future European Economic Area* (Brussels, 1991), 13–15.

However, trade statistics show a general trend for the Swedish share of manufactured goods imported by the Community of Nine to fall substantially from the beginning of the 1970s to the early 1980s.[145] Besides, such reasoning does not explain the need felt by the Swedish Government itself to resort to other arrangements for tackling problems which arose within the field covered by the Agreement. There was, in fact, a tendency for such problems to be channelled through the Board of Trade (*Kommerskollegium*),[146] within which there was a reference group for Community questions where industry and labour were represented, to the Swedish Delegation in Brussels.[147] The latter then made direct contact with the Commission. As early as 1974 the Report from the Swedish Delegation in Brussels recorded that a series of informal bilateral discussions had been held with the Commission to discuss the general application of the Agreement.[148]

Problems of Bilateralism

It might be thought that problems arising in trade between the Community and a third state are often not such as to be capable of a purely bilateral solution between the two. For example, when the failure of the Commission to consult the Finnish–EC Joint Committee was challenged before the Court of Justice in the *Wood Pulp* case, the Court pointed out that Canadian and United States companies as well as Finnish companies were involved in the restrictive practices to which the Commission objected. In these circumstances, bilateral action through the Joint Committee could not alone have provided a solution.[149]

Certainly, there has been a general tendency for multilateral solutions to be sought. Even before entry into force of the EEA Agreement, problems arising under the Free Trade Agreements were tackled in EC–EFTA bodies. For example, in 1974 problems concerning rules of origin began to be referred to informal meetings between representatives of the Commission and EFTA States,[150] and in 1980 informal multilateral meetings of customs experts from EFTA States and Member States began to be held in association with meetings of the Customs Committees established by the Joint Committees.[151] More generally, because the Free Trade Agreements were virtually identical and

[145] Diagram 2.2 in *Med sikte på 2000-talet*, SOU 1990:14.

[146] Note also the instructions given to the Board regarding TBTs by the *Förordning om ändring i förordningen (1988:570) med instruktion för kommerskollegium* (SFS 1989:916).

[147] This Delegation was established in 1959, and the Commission subsequently established a Delegation in Stockholm. See the Agreement of 19 Oct. 1989 (SÖ 1990:8). Cf., generally, *Report on the functioning of the Commission's External Delegations*, COM(95)68.

[148] *EG under första halvåret 1974: Rapport från svensk delegationen i Bryssel* (Utrikes-och handelsdepartementen, 1974), 26.

[149] Joined Cases 89, 104, 114, 116, 117, 125–129 *A. Åhlström Osakeyhtiö* v. *EC Commission* [1988] ECR 5193, 5246.

[150] *Sverige–EG 1974* (Utrikes-och handelsdepartementen, 1975), 11.

[151] *Sverige–EG 1980* (Utrikes-och handelsdepartementen, 1981), 13.

matters discussed in the Joint Committees usually concerned all the Agreements, co-ordination of the positions of the EFTA States took place prior to meetings of these Committees.[152] Such practice resulted in the creation of the High Level Contact Group, within the framework of the Luxembourg process,[153] to provide a forum for multilateral EC–EFTA contacts.[154] The Joint Committees then played the purely formal role of implementing agreed solutions in the form of decisions.[155]

Formal developments of this kind also occurred. For example, a Joint Committee was established by the Convention on the Simplification of Formalities in Trade in Goods,[156] concluded between the Community and the EFTA States multilaterally.[157] Each Contracting Party was represented in the Committee, which acted by mutual agreement.[158]

It cannot be assumed, however, that the bilateral character of the Joint Committee established by the Swedish Free Trade Agreement was the only reason for its failure to take on a more prominent role. For example, in 1985 the Commission imposed provisional anti-dumping duties on Swedish clogs[159] imported into the Community without prior consultation taking place in the Joint Committee.[160] It is not immediately apparent why the bilateral character of the Committee should have rendered it an unsuitable body for consultation in such a case.

Problems of 'Political' Bodies

According to the Swedish Government, the real problem was that the Joint Committee was a 'political'[161] rather than 'legal' body. A distinction was also

[152] An EFTA Committee of Origin and Customs Experts was established by EFTA Council Decision No. 8 of 1974. See also F. Weiss, 'The European Free Trade Association After Twenty-five Years' [1985] YBEL 287–323.

[153] I.e., developments in EC–EFTA relations following the Luxembourg Declaration of April 1984 (Bull. EC 4–1984, 1.2.1).

[154] *Sverige–EG 1984* (Utrikesdepartementets handelsavdelning, 1985), 39; EFTA Bull. 3/1984, 17.

[155] To this extent, the Joint Committees implemented coordinated regulation of EC–EFTA trade. See EFTA Secretariat, *The European Free Trade Association* (Geneva, 1980), 90.

[156] [1987] OJ L134/2.

[157] EFTA itself provided a precedent for such an arrangement in 1978, when a multilateral Joint Committee was established with Yugoslavia. Similarly, an EFTA–Spain Joint Committee was established in 1980 by the Agreement between EFTA States and Spain (SÖ 1980:87). See, regarding this Agreement generally, F. A. Blankart, 'Die Bedeutung des Abkommens zwischen den EFTA-Ländern und Spanien im Rahmen der europäischen Integration' [1981] *Aussenwirtschaft* 88–99.

[158] Art. 10 of the Convention on the Simplification of Formalities in Trade in Goods.

[159] Reg. 2823/85 of 7 Oct. 1985 ([1985] OJ L268/11) imposing a provisional anti-dumping duty on imports of certain clogs originating in Sweden.

[160] *Sverige–EG 1985* (Utrikesdepartementets handelsavdelning, 1985), 25.

[161] *Redovisning av det svenska integrationsarbetet våren 1988–mars 1989* (Utrikesdepartementets handelsavdelning, 1989), 132. U. Bernitz, 'Sveriges EG–Anknuting i rättsligt perspektiv' [1989/90] JT 47–69, at 54 described the Joint Committee established by the Swedish Agreement as '*ett diplomatiskt organ*' (a diplomatic organ).

made between 'diplomatic settlement' and 'legal or judicial settlement' in a report from the EFTA Group of Legal Experts.[162] Similarly, in *Kupferberg* Advocate General Rozès referred to the 'political procedure' of the Joint Committee established by the Free Trade Agreement with Portugal.[163] The conclusion drawn by the Swedish Government was that '*mer rättsligt präglade tvistlösnings-procedurer*' (dispute-solving procedures of a more legal character) were needed.[164]

Clear-cut distinctions of this kind may not be easy to make,[165] let alone to apply to the Joint Committee. Apparently much may depend on whether such a body is involved in a dispute before the Parties have reached a political *impasse*, which may affect its proceedings.[166] In the absence of such a situation, the Committee might exercise what amounted to legislative power at the international level.[167]

However, the fact that to describe the Joint Committee as a 'political body' may be an oversimplification does not in itself mean that the Committee could have provided a legal means of settling disputes. In view of the limited liberalization secured by the Free Trade Agreement, the latter may rarely have been treated as providing a satisfactory legal framework for tackling trade problems arising between Sweden and the Community. In fact, GATT successes in securing tariff reductions meant that the elimination of tariffs secured by the Free Trade Agreement lost much of its significance and that non-tariff barriers to trade, which were largely unaffected by the liberalization requirements in the latter Agreement, became more important.[168] Consequently, the limitations to the liberalization requirements entailed by the Agreement and reliance on joint decision-making to secure consistent opera-

[162] *The Settlement of Disputes in the Free Trade Agreements and Other Agreements Between the EFTA Countries and the European Communities*, EFTA/GLE 3/87.

[163] Case 104/81 *Hauptzollamt Mainz* v. *C. A. Kupferberg & Cie K. G.* [1982] ECR 3641, 3674. See sect. 2.3.1 above. According to Van Gerven A. G. in Case C–188/91 *Deutsche Shell AG* v. *Hauptzollamt Hamburg-Harburg* [1993] ECR I–363, I–377, such bodies are '*une sorte de forum où les parties contractantes peuvent se concerter et échanger les expériences*' in the application of the agreement concerned.

[164] *Sverige–EFTA–EG 1988* (Utrikesdepartementets handelsavdelning, 1989), 126.

[165] Cf., regarding dispute-settlement within the GATT framework, M. Hilf, 'Settlement of Disputes in International Economic Organizations: Comparative Analysis and Proposals for Strengthening the GATT Dispute Settlement Procedures' in E-U. Petersmann and M. Hilf (eds.), *The New GATT Round of Multilateral Trade Negotiations* (Deventer, 1991), 285–322, at 289–90.

[166] Cf. J. H. Bello, 'Midterm Report on Binational Dispute Settlement Under the United States-Canada Free-Trade Agreement' (1991) 25 *The International Lawyer* 489–516.

[167] See sect. 6.3.2 above. Cf. the view expressed in relation to the Joint Committees established by the Trade and Commercial and Economic Co-operation Agreements, such as that with Poland ([1989] OJ L339/2), that 'the Committee's nature as a recommending body, and its duty to reach consensus prior to any further act, deprives it of effective and binding legal powers' (D. Horovitz, 'EC–Central/East European Relations: New Principles for a New Era' (1990) 27 *CMLRev.* 259–84, at 271).

[168] See, e.g., *De handelspolitiska förutsättningarna för svensk export under 1980-talet*, SOU 1984:6, bil. 6.

tion of these requirements throughout the territories of the Parties may have tended to be mutually reinforcing in impeding effective Joint Committee involvement in securing trade liberalization.

Harmonization

Harmonization under the Free Trade Agreements might be thought to have entailed opportunities for the 'politically weak bodies'[169] established by such Agreements to contribute effectively to tackling trade problems between the Parties.[170]

(i) Bilateral Harmonization

As soon as the Swedish Agreement came into force, Swedish representatives, conscious of the 'evolutionary clause' in Article 32 of the Agreement, sought to utilize the Joint Committee as a forum for consideration of matters relating, for example, to transport policy and environmental policy. However, while Community representatives are said to have noted the aims and interests of Sweden, it was reported that nothing was decided in the Committee.[171]

Three years later Sweden suggested that the Joint Committee should be used as a forum in which co-operation concerning matters of common interest generally should be discussed. The Community accepted the desirability of such discussion but expressed uncertainty whether the Committee was the appropriate forum. Administration of the Free Trade Agreement was said to be the main task of the Committee,[172] and consultation therein was only considered obligatory in relation to matters concerning the dismantling of tariffs on industrial products and certain processed agricultural products.[173] Such a view apparently relied on an interpretation of the role of the Committee that might have been more strict than was required by the aims of the Agreement or by Article 113 of the EC Treaty, pursuant to which the Agreement was concluded by the Community.[174]

Matters beyond the scope of the liberalization requirements contained in the

[169] The importance attached to legislative harmonization in Community practice is said to reflect the Commission's 'depoliticised position in the structure of the Community organs'. See K.-H. Ladeur, 'European Community Institutional Reforms: Extra-National Management as an Alternative Model to Federalism' (1990/2) *LIEI* 1–21, 9.

[170] In the event, the operation of the Joint Committees apparently varied from one Agreement to another. Thus, e.g., the Joint Committee established by the Portuguese Free Trade Agreement is said to have played a more important role in the broadening of relations between the Community and Portugal (see *EG under första halvåret 1975: Rapport från svenska delegationen i Bryssel* (Utrikes-och handelsdepartementen 1975), 15) than did the Joint Committees established by other Free Trade Agreements in the case of relations with the Community and the third states concerned.

[171] *Sverige–EG 1973* (Utrikes-och handelsdepartementen, 1974), 10 and 25.

[172] *Sverige–EG 1976* (Utrikes-och handelsdepartementen, 1977), 12–13. See also *EC Ninth General Report* (EC Commission Brussels, 1976), 27.

[173] Reply to Written Question 491/74 ([1975] OJ C28/19) by Lord O'Hagan.

[174] See sect. 2.2.3 above, regarding the permissible scope of action under this provision.

Agreement could, according to the Commission, only be discussed in the Committee where both Parties consented to their discussion.[175] This attitude reflected a strict interpretation of the stipulation in Article 32 that the Committee could only act thereunder at the request of both Parties. Apparently a rigid distinction was favoured between the function of the Committee in relation to application of liberalization requirements established by the Agreement and its function in relation to harmonization under Article 32.

In 1977, however, when the customs duties on most industrial goods traded between EFTA and the Community had been eliminated pursuant to the Free Trade Agreements, the EFTA Ministers at their meeting in Vienna declared themselves in favour of broadening co-operation with the Community,[176] and the first informal meeting was held between experts from *ekonomi-departementet* (the Swedish Ministry for Economic Affairs) and the Commission in Brussels to discuss general economic policy matters.[177] This new practice, presumably combined with development of Community policies[178] in many of the fields of interest to EFTA States,[179] apparently rendered the restrictions previously imposed on the topics which might be discussed by the Joint Committee itself less meaningful.[180] Thus in 1983, for example, the Commission representatives in the Joint Committee expressed interest in harmonization of technical rules, such as those concerning exhaust emissions, and exchanges of views and information took place concerning economic and monetary policy, transport and environmental questions, and consumer protection and advice.[181] Nevertheless, little use was made of the procedure laid down in Article 32,[182] and the failure of the Joint Committees to play an effective role in promoting bilateral harmonization between the Parties continued.

[175] Reply to Written Question 491/74 ([1975] OJ C28/19) by Lord O'Hagan. See, similarly, the Reply to Written Question 553/74 ([1975] OJ C86/8) by Lord O'Hagan.

[176] EFTA Bull. 1977/5, 4–5, para. 5.

[177] *Sverige–EG 1977* (Utrikes-och handelsdepartementen, 1978), 11.

[178] Where a policy in a given field beyond the scope of the common commercial policy was 'not yet sufficiently developed, power to conclude' agreements with third states lay with the Member States. See Case 22/70 *EC Commission* v. *EC Council* [1971] ECR 263, 281.

[179] Cf. Capotorti A. G. in Case 181/80 *Procureur Général prés la Cour d'Appel de Pau* v. *José Arbelaiz-Emazabel* [1981] ECR 2961, 2989, regarding the significance of the emergence of a common fisheries policy for Community efforts to develop legal frameworks to govern relations with third states in this sector.

[180] There is little for the Community to negotiate with third states, if the Community has no common internal policies. See L. Tsoukalis, *The New European Economy: The Politics and Economics of Integration* (Oxford, 1991), 257.

[181] *Sverige–EG 1983* (Utrikesdepartementets handelsavdelning, 1984), 16.

[182] The more particular arrangements in Arts 10 and 15(1) of the Swedish Agreement (sect. 5.3.1 above) also failed to secure for the Joint Committee an effective role in bilateral harmonization, as did the notification requirements in Art. 12, regarding changes in customs duties applied to products from third states, and the information requirements in Art. 14, regarding Community modifications of duties on petroleum products pursuant to Community decisions under the common commercial policy or establishment of a common energy policy.

(ii) Voluntary Harmonization

The Swedish Government sought in negotiations for the Free Trade Agreement arrangements which might have mitigated problems raised by voluntary harmonization. The arrangements sought were designed, without jeopardizing the autonomy of decision-taking of the Parties, to secure provision of information and consultation between the Parties in the general field covered by this Agreement.[183] Presumably, such consultation would have taken place in the Joint Committee. The Commission view, however, was that such Committees should only decide technical matters arising from trade and should have no involvement in Community policy-making.[184] Accordingly, the Commission made clear that there could be no question of including in the Agreement a special procedure for information and consultation of the kind sought by Sweden.[185] The Commission, concerned to preserve Community autonomy of decision-making, particularly at a time when the Community was not 'in full possession of its powers',[186] apparently considered that such arrangements were not necessary to enable EFTA States 'voluntarily' to adapt their national law to Community law.[187]

Soon after the Free Trade Agreement came into force, the Swedish Government raised these issues again and stressed in the Joint Committee the need to receive information at an early stage concerning Community legislative work.[188] The Committee might have been considered an appropriate body through which such information could have been provided. However, the Community remained reluctant to introduce formal arrangements, and at the beginning of 1989 the Swedish Government was still complaining about the lack of formal opportunities for it to influence such work.[189] Apparently, therefore, the Joint Committees established by the Free Trade Agreements failed to mitigate problems raised by voluntary harmonization.

6.4 EUROPE AGREEMENTS

The institutional arrangements for joint decision-making in the Europe Agreements are typical of those in Association Agreements and thus more elaborate than those in the Free Trade Agreements.

[183] *Commission Opinion to the Council on Relations of the Enlarged Community with the EFTA Member and Associated Countries which have not Asked to Join the EEC*, Bull. EC, Supp. 3/71, 6.

[184] Swedish Government memorandum of 6 Sept. 1971, which is reproduced in Annex 3 to D. Viklund, *Spelet om Frihandelsavtalet* (Stockholm, 1977).

[185] *Utrikesutskottets betänkande med anledning av propositionen 1972:135 angående avtal med de europeiska gemenskaperna m.m. jämte motioner* (Report of the Foreign Affairs Committee of the Parliament on the Free Trade Agreement) (UU 1972:20), 20 and 28.

[186] *Commission Opinion to the Council on Relations of the Enlarged Community with the EFTA Member and Associated Countries which have not Asked to Join the EEC*, Bull. EC, Supp. 3/71, 12–13.

[187] AiH 4/1972, 18.

[188] *Sverige–EG 1974* (Utrikes-och handelsdepartementen, 1975), 21.

[189] *Redovisning av det svenska integrationsarbetet våren 1988–mars 1989*, (Utrikesdepartementets handelsavdelning, 1989), 215.

6.4.1 Institutions

An Association Council, an Association Committee, and an Association Parliamentary Committee are established by the Polish Agreement. The Association Council consists of the members of the Council of the Union and members of the European Commission, on the one hand, and members of Polish Government, on the other.[190] Members of the Association Council may arrange to be represented, in accordance with arrangements to be laid down in its Rules of Procedure.[191] The Association Committee is to be composed of representatives of the Council of the Union and members of the Commission on the one hand, and representatives of the Polish Government on the other, normally at senior civil servant level.[192] The Association Parliamentary Committee is to comprise Members of the European Parliament, on the one hand, and Members of the Polish Parliament, on the other.[193]

The composition of the Association Council[194] and the importance attached by the Agreement to political dialogue[195] might be thought to imply an effective role for this Council, though problems may remain in the case of the Association Committee. There may also be an element of unreality in the work of bodies where fifteen Member States, on the one hand, and a single third state, on the other, are equally represented.[196] More fundamentally, the supposed benefits of inter-organizational co-operation—the tendency for the edge to be taken off national ambitions[197] and for the actions of a greater number of participants to become more transparent and calculable[198]—may be secured in a one-sided way at most.[199]

[190] Art. 103(1) of the Polish Agreement.

[191] *Ibid.*, Art. 103(2).

[192] *Ibid.*, Art. 106(1).

[193] *Ibid.*, Art. 106(1).

[194] *Ibid.*, Art. 3 also provides for consultations to take place, as appropriate, between the President of the European Council, the President of the Commission, and the President of Poland. In practice, multilateral summits with the Presidents of Parties to the Europe Agreements will be held annually, and there will be biannual meetings between foreign ministers. See Annex II to the Conclusions of the Presidency (Bull. EC 6–1993, I.26).

[195] Title I of the Polish Agreement.

[196] Possibly in recognition of such problems, the European Council agreed in Dec. 1994 that there would be annual summit conferences with the Parties to the Europe Agreements as well as two meetings each year at the level of foreign ministers (Bull. EU 12–1994, I.40, Conclusions of the Presidency, Annex IV).

[197] S. Nuttall, 'The Commission: Protagonists of Inter-regional Co-operation' in G. Edwards and E. Regelsberger (eds.), *Europe's Global Links* (London, 1990), 143–57, at 156.

[198] E. Regelsberger, 'The Dialogue of the EC/Twelve with Other Regional Groups: A New European Identity in the International System' in G. Edwards and E. Regelsberger (eds.), n. 197 above, 3–26, at 9. 'Third parties' to negotiations, such as traders, may also welcome the relative ease with which they can discover which commitments have been made by which state. See S. Peers, 'An Ever Closer Waiting Room? The Case for Eastern European Accession to the European Economic Area' (1995) 32 *CMLRev.* 187–213, at 204.

[199] The Community apparently seeks to tackle such problems through introduction of informal arrangements for 'multilateral dialogue'. See the Council Reply to Written Question E–192/95 ([1995] OJ C202/5) by Jean-Pierre Raffarin.

6.4.2 Procedures

Procedural rules governing joint decision-making under the Europe Agreements concern the internal organization of the joint bodies created as well as the kind of acts the latter may adopt and the conditions under which the acts may be adopted and include arrangements for democratic control.

Internal Organization

According to the Polish Agreement, the Association Council is to meet at ministerial level once a year and when circumstances require.[200] The Presidency of the Association Council is to be held in turn by a member[201] of the Council of the Union and a member of the Government of Poland, in accordance with the provisions to be laid down in its Rules of Procedure.[202] According to Article 103(3) of the Agreement, these Rules are to be drawn up by the Association Council itself. These Rules are to determine the duties of the Association Committee,[203] which shall include the preparation of the meetings of the Association Council, and how the Committee shall function.[204]

Acts

The Polish Agreement provides that decisions taken by the Association Council[205] and the Association Committee[206] shall be binding on the Parties, which shall take the measures necessary to implement them. Within the Community decisions of such kinds, which are now regularly published by the Community,[207] may be directly effective in accordance with the same criteria as may provisions of the relevant Agreement itself.[208] These bodies may also make appropriate recommendations, which are not binding.

Unanimity Requirements

Article 104 of the Polish Agreement requires that the Association Council shall draw up its decisions and recommendations by agreement between the Parties. Article 106(2) renders the unanimity requirement equally applicable to the

[200] Art. 102 of the Polish Agreement.

[201] Article 1 of the Hungarian-EC Association Council Dec. 1/94 of 7 Mar. 1994 ([1994] OJ L242/23) on its Rules of Procedure refers to a 'representative' of the Council of the Union and a 'representative' of the Hungarian Government.

[202] Art. 103(4) of the Polish Agreement.

[203] The Hungarian Association Committee is to meet when circumstances require and with the agreement of both Parties (Art. 2 of the Rules of Procedure of the Committee, annexed to the Hungarian-EC Association Council Dec. 1/94 of 7 Mar. 1994 ([1994] OJ L242/23) on its Rules of Procedure).

[204] Art. 106 of the Polish Agreement. Art. 13(2) of the Rules of Procedure of the Hungarian–EC Association Council provides that the Committee shall consider any matter referred to it by the Association Council as well as any other matter which may arise in the course of the day-to-day implementation of the Agreement.

[205] Art. 104 of the Polish Agreement.

[206] *Ibid.*, Art. 106(2).

[207] Commission Reply by Mr Delors to Written Question E–260/93 ([1994] OJ C352/1) by Anita Pollack.

[208] See sect. 8.4.2 below.

Association Committee, when the latter exercises powers delegated by the Association Council.

Democratic Control

Article 110 of the Polish Agreement provides that the Association Council must supply the Association Parliamentary Committee with any information requested regarding implementation of the Agreement. In addition, the latter Committee is to be informed of decisions of the Association Council[209] and may make recommendations to the latter.

6.4.3 Functions

Article 102 of the Polish Agreement provides that the Association Council shall supervise the implementation of the Agreement. Its powers, which may be delegated to the Association Committee,[210] are to be exercised for the purposes of attaining the objectives of the Agreement.[211] The Association Council is also to examine any major issues arising within the framework of the Agreement and any other bilateral or international issues of mutual interest.[212] In essence, these functions concern liberalization and harmonization.

Liberalization

The functions of the joint bodies created by the Polish Agreement are apparently to involve both detailed implementation of trade liberalization requirements in the Agreement and the settlement of disputes, especially those arising from the adoption of safeguard measures, anti-dumping measures and anti-trust measures. The duty of each Party to take account of the legitimate interests of the other Party to the Agreement and the contractual obligation to refrain from jeopardizing achievement of the aims of the Agreement in Article 115(1) thereof[213] apparently mean that in interpreting and applying the Agreement the Parties should facilitate performance of such functions by these bodies.[214]

[209] Art. 7 of the Rules of Procedure of the Hungarian–EC Association Council provides that, unless otherwise decided, the meetings of the Association Council shall not be public. See, similarly, Art. 5 of the Rules of Procedure of the Hungarian–EC Association Committee.

[210] Art. 106(2) of the Polish Agreement.

[211] *Ibid.*, Art. 104.

[212] *Ibid.*, Art. 102. With regard to political dialogue, the Association Council shall have general responsibility for any matters the Parties might wish to put to it (*ibid.*, Art. 3(2)).

[213] This provision requires the Parties to take any general or specific measures required to fulfil their obligations under the Agreement. They must see to it that the objectives set out in the Agreement are attained.

[214] See Case C–432/92 *The Queen* v. *Minister of Agriculture, Fisheries and Food, ex parte S.P. Anastasiou (Pissouri) Ltd* [1994] ECR I–3087, I–3133, regarding the Association Agreement with Cyprus.

(i) Implementation

Article 6(2) of the Polish Agreement provides for the Association Council regularly to examine the application of the Agreement and Poland's accomplishments in the process leading to a market economy system. Article 6(3) provides that the results of such examination will be taken into account by this Council, when it decides on transition from the first to the second stage of the transitional period for creation of a free trade area between the Parties under Article 7(1).[215]

More particularly, Article 63(3) of the Agreement concerns competition law. It provides for the Association Council, within three years of the entry into force of the Agreement, to adopt by decision the necessary rules for implementation of paragraphs 1 and 2 of that provision. Thereafter, according to a Joint Declaration attached to the Agreement,[216] the Parties may request the Association Council to examine to what extent and under what conditions certain competition rules may be directly applicable. The Association Council is also to decide whether the five-year period for treating Poland as an area identical to those Community areas covered by Article 92(3)(a) of the EC Treaty for the purposes of assessing compatibility of public aid with the Agreement should be extended by further periods of five years.[217] Finally, the Association Council is to be informed of the measures adopted for adjustment of State monopolies pursuant to Article 32 of the Agreement.

(ii) Disputes

In the event of a dispute relating to the application or interpretation of the Polish Agreement, Article 105 of the Agreement provides that each of the two Parties may refer the dispute to the Association Council. This Council may settle the dispute by means of a decision,[218] and each Party will be bound to take the measures necessary for carrying out such a decision.[219]

(iii) Safeguard measures

Article 115(2) of the Polish Agreement provides that if either Party considers that the other Party has failed to fulfil an obligation thereunder, it may take appropriate measures. Before doing so, it shall supply the Association Council with all relevant information required for a thorough examination of the situation with a view to seeking a solution acceptable to the Parties. The measures adopted shall be notified immediately to the Association Council and shall be the subject of consultations within the Council, if the other Party so requests.

[215] Such conditionality is seen as 'serving the twin aims of preserving the EC's flexibility and providing it with a basis to influence internal policy'. See D. Kennedy and D.E. Webb, 'The Limits of Integration: Eastern Europe and the European Communities' (1993) 30 *CMLRev.* 1095–117, at 1105.

[216] Joint Declaration 11.3.

[217] Art. 63(4)(a) of the Polish Agreement.

[218] *Ibid.*, Art. 39(2).

[219] *Ibid.*, Art. 39(3).

More particularly, Article 28 of the Agreement provides that Poland shall inform the Association Council of any customs duties it intends exceptionally to introduce thereunder.[220] At the request of the Community, consultations shall be held in the Council on such duties and the sectors concerned before they are applied. When introducing the duties, Poland shall provide the Council with a schedule for their elimination. This schedule shall provide for a phasing out of the duties starting at the latest two years after their introduction at equal annual rates. The Council may, however, decide on a different schedule.

Moreover, before taking safeguard measures under Articles 29, 30, and 31 of the Agreement,[221] the Party concerned must, according to Article 33(2), supply the Association Council with all relevant information with a view to seeking a solution acceptable to the two Parties. In particular, measures may only be taken under Article 30 if the Council or the exporting state has not put an end to the difficulties or no other satisfactory solution has been reached within thirty days of the matter being referred to the Council.[222] Similar arrangements are made in relation to Article 31 measures.[223] In the event that precautionary measures are adopted under Article 33(3)(d), the Council shall be supplied with all relevant information as soon as possible. All definitive measures shall be notified immediately to the Council and shall be the subject of periodic consultations therein, particularly with a view to establishing a timetable for their abolition as soon as circumstances permit.[224]

The operation of these arrangements may be particularly problematic in the case of anti-dumping measures. Article 33(3)(b) specifies that the Association Council shall be informed of the dumping case as soon as the authorities of the importing Party have initiated an investigation. When no end has been put to the dumping or no other satisfactory solution has been reached within thirty days of the matter being referred to the Council, the importing Party may adopt the appropriate measures. Any measures adopted shall, according to Article 33(2), be notified immediately to the Council and shall be the subject of periodic consultations within that body, particularly with a view to establishing a timetable for their abolition as soon as circumstances permit. However, Article 33(3)(d) of the Agreement provides that, where exceptional circumstances requiring immediate action make prior information or examination impossible, a Party may apply forthwith the precautionary measures strictly necessary to deal with the situation. Article 33(3)(d) thus offers a basis for

[220] I.e., imposition of customs duties on Community products in order to protect infant industries or certain sectors undergoing restructuring or facing serious difficulties in Poland.

[221] See, regarding the measures permitted, sect. 3.4 above.

[222] Art. 33(3)(a) of the Polish Agreement.

[223] *Ibid.*, Art. 33(3)(c).

[224] *Ibid.*, Art. 62 also requires Poland to inform the Association Council promptly of any exchange restrictions introduced for the purpose of obtaining short and medium-term credits.

imposition of provisional anti-dumping duties without prior consultation in the Association Council.

Indeed, the Community institutions apparently consider the presence of material injury sufficient to entail a need for urgency, such as to justify imposition of provisional duties without even informing such bodies beforehand.[225] However, the presence of such injury is laid down in Community legislation[226] as a substantive condition for imposition of provisional duties. Therefore, whenever the substantive conditions in such legislation for the imposition of such duties are met, the urgency condition in Article 33(3)(d) will also be met. In other words, Community practice seems to render the latter condition effectively meaningless in relation to provisional duties. If this practice is maintained, no effective role is likely to be played by the Association Council in relation to such duties.

Again, Article 63(6) of the Agreement provides for either Party to take appropriate measures against anti-competitive practices affecting Polish–Community trade which are not considered to be satisfactorily tackled by the other Party after consultation within the Association Council or after thirty working days following referral for such consultation. However, practice under the Free Trade Agreements raises the possibility that the Commission may simply apply the EC Treaty where such practices also affect trade between Member States without complying with the procedures laid down in Article 63(6) of the Polish Agreement. Certainly, it is expressly stated in the proposed implementing rules[227] that procedures within the Association Council 'are without prejudice to any action under the respective competition laws in force in the territory of the Parties'.[228]

Harmonization

The Polish Agreement implicitly acknowledges the difficulties of securing an effective role for joint bodies in bilateral harmonization, but it does not seek to overcome these difficulties. The Agreement deals in some detail with economic co-operation,[229] cultural co-operation,[230] and financial co-operation between the Parties.[231] However, only limited provision is made for Association Council involvement in such co-operation,[232] though a proposed Protocol

[225] Cf., regarding Art. 27(3)(b)—the equivalent provision in the Interim Agreement between Poland and the Community, Reg. 1189/93 of 14 May 1993 ([1993] OJ L120/34) imposing definitive anti-dumping duties on imports of certain seamless pipes and tubes, of iron and steel, originating in Hungary, Poland, and the Republic of Croatia and definitively collecting provisional anti-dumping duties.

[226] Art. 3 of Reg. 3283/94 of 22 Dec. 1994 ([1994] OJ L349/1) on protection against dumped imports from countries not members of the EC.

[227] Cf. Commission Proposal of 18 May 1995 concerning implementation arrangements under the Europe Agreement with the Czech Republic, COM(95)157.

[228] *Ibid.*, Art. 9.3.

[229] Arts. 71–94 of the Polish Agreement.

[230] *Ibid.*, Art. 95.

[231] *Ibid.*, Arts. 96–101.

[232] *Ibid.*, Arts. 75(2), 98, and 99.

to the Agreement[233] envisages in Article 2 that the Association Council shall decide the terms and conditions for the participation of Poland in Community framework programmes, specific programmes, projects, or other actions in such fields.

At the same time, while Articles 68 and 69 of the Agreement envisage voluntary harmonization by Poland and technical assistance from the Community, no formal provision is made for the involvement of the Association Council in such harmonization. Apparently, voluntary harmonization with Community legislation is supposed to take place without any institutional arrangements to ensure that Poland will have the opportunity to influence the content of the legislation.[234]

6.5 EEA AGREEMENT

The EEA Agreement departs from the Free Trade Agreements and the Europe Agreements, in that it provides for the establishment of multilateral rather than bilateral institutions.

6.5.1 Institutions

Article 89 of the EEA Agreement establishes an EEA Council, composed of members of the Council of the Union, members of the European Commission, and one member of the Government of each of the EFTA States.[235] An EEA Joint Committee is also established.[236] The precise composition of the Joint Committee and its relationship with the EEA Council are not specified in the Agreement.[237] Apparently, however, the Community is to be represented in this body not by the Commission alone,[238] as was originally envisaged by the

[233] Proposal of 13 Dec. 1994 for a Council and Commission Decision concluding the Additional Protocol to the Europe Agreement between the European Community, of the one part, and the Republic of Poland, of the other part, COM(94)599.

[234] Cf., however, in the competition law field, sect. 4.4.4 above.

[235] Art. 90(1) of the EEA Agreement. The Community's position in the EEA Council is to be adopted by the Council of the Union. See Art. 2 of Reg. 2894/94 of 28 Nov. 1994 ([1994] OJ L305/6) concerning arrangements for implementing the Agreement on the European Economic Area.

[236] Art. 92 of the EEA Agreement. A precedent for the EEA Joint Committee was the Joint Committee established by the Agreement between the EC, Norway, and Sweden on Civil Aviation ([1992] OJ L200/21).

[237] On 15 Jan. 1992 it was stated that the composition of the Joint Committee and its 'ranking' in relation to the Association Council were 'still to be negotiated'. See Council Reply to Written Question 192/91 ([1992] OJ C38/3) by Mr Marc Galle.

[238] According to A. T. Laredo, 'The EEA Agreement: An Overall View' (1992) 29 *CMLRev.* 1199–213, at 1208, the Committee 'is normally composed of representatives of the Commission and of each of the EFTA States'.

latter,[239] but also by the Permanent Representatives of the Member States[240] or at least the Council Presidency.[241]

This view is suggested by a comparison of Articles 93(1) and 94(1) of the Agreement. Whereas Article 93(1) provides for the Joint Committee to consist of representatives of the Contracting Parties, Article 94(1) refers to the Commission as the representative of the Community in the Committee. As far as the Community is concerned, Article 2(2) of the Agreement provides that, depending on the context, the term 'Contracting Parties' may mean the Community on the one hand, and the Member States on the other, the Community alone, or the Member States alone. The apparent implication is that Article 93(1) requires both the Community and the Member States to be represented in the Committee and that, while the Commission represents the Community itself, Member States are also to have their own representatives in the Committee.

In practice, the Commission alone states the Community's position in the Committee where a simple extension of a Community act to the EEA is involved or where the Commission is responsible for adopting the Community act in question.[242] Where more than technical changes to the Community act are involved and in cases other than those where extension of a Community act is involved, the Community position in the Committee is to be established by the Council of the Union, in accordance with the procedures laid down in the corresponding Treaty provisions.[243] However, the Commission mandate for EEA negotiations, as approved by the Council, insisted that such arrangements must not affect the principle that the Community would 'speak with one voice'.[244] In other words, the Community position is to be determined in advance and possibilities of its modification in the Joint Committee might be expected, in practice, to be limited.

Establishment of these bodies is accompanied by introduction of arrange-

[239] Para. 5.3 of the Commission Communication concerning a proposed council decision authorizing the Commission to negotiate an agreement with the EFTA States on the creation of a European Economic Space, and para. 11 of the annexed Directives de Négociation. At one stage it was suggested that this body should only contain a Commission representative and a representative from the country holding the EFTA Presidency. See SvDN, 10 Oct. 1989.

[240] However, it is said that they will only act as observers. See D. Felder, 'Structure Institutionnel et Procédure Décisionnelle de l'EEE' in O. Jacot-Guillarmot (ed.), *Accord EEE: Commentaires et Réflexions* (Bern, 1992), 571–81, at 574.

[241] Council Declaration *ad* para. 11 of the Directives de Négociation. See, generally, C-P. Lucron, 'Vers l'Espace Economique Européen, L'Europe du Deuxième Cercle' [1990] *RMC* 527–31. Some Member States, notably Denmark, Greece, and Portugal, sought thereby a permanent role in EEA decision making. Such an arrangement was earlier suggested at an academic conference in Geneva. See H. Mayrzedt, 'Beziehungen zwischen EWG und EFTA Kritischer Rückblick und Ausblick' in P. du Bois and B. Hurni (eds.), *L'AELE d'Hier à Demain* (Geneva, 1987), 139–147, at 146.

[242] Art. 1(2) of Reg. 2894/94 of 28 Nov. 1994 ([1994] OJ L305/6) concerning arrangements for implementing the Agreement on the European Economic Area.

[243] *Ibid.*, Art. 1(3).

[244] Directives de Négociation.

ments for popular representation at the EEA level. Article 95(1) of the EEA Agreement and the Agreement on a Committee of Members of Parliament of the EFTA States[245] established the EEA Joint Parliamentary Committee. It shall be composed of equal numbers of, on the one hand, Members of the European Parliament (MEPs) and, on the other, Members of the Parliaments of the EFTA States.[246] The total number of members of the Committee[247] is laid down in the Statute in Protocol 36.[248]

Such an arrangement is far from novel. The first meeting of Members of the European Parliament and EFTA parliamentarians was held in 1981.[249] More particularly, meetings were held between the Committee for External Trade Relations of the European Parliament and the EFTA Parliamentary Committee.[250]

Arrangements equally lacking in novelty are envisaged for the social partners.[251] Article 96(1) of the EEA Agreement requires that members of the Economic and Social Committee and other bodies representing the social partners in the Community[252] and the corresponding bodies in the EFTA States shall strengthen their contacts and co-operate in an organized and regular manner in order to enhance the awareness of the economic and social aspects of the growing interdependence of the economies of the Parties and of their interests within the context of the EEA. Accordingly, an EEA Consultative

[245] *Europeiska ekonomiska samarbetsområdet*, prop. 1991/92:170.

[246] The Rules of Procedure of the Joint Parliamentary Committee ([1994] OJ L247/34) provide that any parliament of an EFTA State which does not 'take part in the EEA Agreement' may obtain observer status during sessions of this Committee.

[247] The European Parliament considered that the number of members of the Committee should be laid down in the Prot., with account being taken of the Committee's ability to function and its wide-ranging tasks, and that the Committee should itself determine its calendar of sittings in the light of actual requirements. See the Resolution of 14 Feb. 1992 (OJ [1992] C67/197) on the European Economic Area, para. 10.

[248] It provides for the Committee to be composed of 66 members, equally divided between the European Parliament and the Parliaments of the EFTA States (Art. 2) and to hold plenary sessions twice a year (Art. 4). Originally the Parliaments of Austria, Sweden, and Switzerland were each to designate 6 members, the Finnish and Norwegian Parliaments 5 members each, the Icelandic Parliament 3 members and the Liechtenstein Parliament 2 members.

[249] EFTA Bull. 5/1981, 16. See generally A. Teschl, 'EFTA–EG och framtiden: ur en EFTA-parlamentarikers synvinkel', EFTA Bull. 3/1985, 1–2. Representatives of Swedish political parties also attended meetings of the relevant political groups within the European Parliament as observers. See *Sverige och den västeuropeiska integrationen*, 1990/91:UU8, 26.

[250] *Sverige–EFTA–EG 1988* (Utrikesdepartementets handelsavdelning, 1989), 14–15. The latter body was reformed by the EFTA Agreement on a Committee of Members of Parliament of the EFTA States (*Europeiska ekonomiska samarbetsområdet*, prop. 1991/92:170).

[251] Even so, the arrangements may be seen as a model to be adopted in relations between the Community and Central and East European countries. See the Opinion of the Economic and Social Committee of 26 Jan. 1995 ([1995] OJ C102/40) on relations between the EU and Russia, Ukraine, and Belarus, para. 3.18.

[252] No reference to representation of the ECSC Consultative Committee or the Committee of the Regions (see sect. 6.2.2 above) is made in Art. 96(2) of the EEA Agreement, though they might perhaps qualify for observer status under Art. 4 or 5 of the Rules of Procedure of the EEA Consultative Committee ([1994] OJ L301/10).

Committee is established by Article 96(2) of the Agreement. It shall be composed of equal numbers of, on the one hand, members of the Economic and Social Committee and, on the other, members of the EFTA Consultative Committee.[253] These arrangements formalize established practice, according to which representatives from the Economic and Social Committee and the EFTA Consultative Committee had been meeting regularly since 1975.

6.5.2 Procedures

Procedural rules governing joint decision-making under the EEA Agreement concern the internal organization of the EEA Council and the EEA Joint Committee as well as the kind of acts these bodies may adopt and the conditions under which the acts may be adopted, and arrangements are made for democratic control.

Internal Organization

The EEA Council is to be convened twice a year by its President.[254] It shall also meet whenever circumstances so require, in accordance with the Rules of Procedure. These Rules make it clear that the words 'whenever circumstances so require' cover the situation where a Party makes use of its '*droit d'évocation*', i.e., its right to raise 'any issue giving rise to a difficulty',[255] in conformity with Article 89(2) of the EEA Agreement.[256] The Presidency shall be held alternately, for a period of six months, by a member of the Council of the Union and a member of the Government of an EFTA State.[257] The EEA Council adopts its Rules of Procedure under Article 89(3) of the Agreement.[258]

The EEA Joint Committee shall meet, in principle, at least once a month.[259] It shall also meet on the initiative of its President or at the request of one of the Parties in accordance with its Rules of Procedure.[260] The office of President shall be held alternately, for a period of six months, by the representative of the Community, i.e., the Commission, and the representative of one of the EFTA States.[261] The EEA Joint Committee also adopts by decision its own Rules of Procedure under Article 92(3) of the Agreement.[262]

[253] This body was originally established by EFTA Council Dec. No. 5 of 1961.

[254] Art. 91(2) of the EEA Agreement.

[255] Cf. Art. 5, which refers to a 'matter of concern', and Art. 92(2), which refers to 'any point of relevance to the Agreement giving rise to a difficulty'.

[256] Agreed Minute *ad* Art. 91(2). See now Art. 1(2) of Dec. 1/94 of 17 May 1994 ([1994] OJ L138/39) adopting the Rules of Procedure of the EEA Council.

[257] Art. 91(1) of the EEA Agreement.

[258] Dec. 1/94 of 17 May 1994 ([1994] OJ L138/39) adopting the Rules of Procedure of the EEA Council.

[259] Art. 94(2) of the EEA Agreement.

[260] The fact that frequent meetings are envisaged for the EEA Joint Committee might be expected to contribute to securing for this Committee an active role in relations between the Parties.

[261] *Ibid.*, Art. 94(1).

[262] Dec. 1/94 of 8 Feb. 1994 ([1994] OJ L85/60) adopting the rules of procedure of the EEA Joint Committee.

Acts

The EEA Council is to take 'the political decisions leading to amendments of the Agreement' under Article 118(1)[263] of the EEA Agreement.[264] According to Article 92(1), the EEA Joint Committee shall take decisions in the cases provided for in this Agreement.[265] Article 104 provides that decisions taken by this Committee in the cases provided for in the Agreement shall, unless otherwise provided for therein, upon their entry into force be binding on the Parties. The latter shall take the necessary steps to ensure their implementation and application. If constitutional obstacles prevent ratification of such a decision, the 'affected part' of EEA law may be suspended under Article 102(5).[266]

Unanimity Requirements

The EEA Council and Joint Committee may only act unanimously, though the EEA Agreement seeks to adapt unanimity requirements to the needs of a 'twin-pillar' construction, with the Community being the one pillar and the EFTA States the other. Both bodies, unlike the EFTA Council,[267] the EFTA Standing Committee,[268] and the EFTA Surveillance Authority,[269] are unable to take decisions by majority. Thus Article 90(2) of the Agreement provides that decisions of the EEA Council shall be taken by agreement between the Community, on the one hand, and the EFTA States, on the other. According to an agreed minute, the Rules of Procedure of the Council will make it clear that, when taking decisions, EFTA Ministers speak with one voice.[270] Similarly, Article 93(2) provides that the EEA Joint Committee shall take decisions

[263] See sect. 6.5.3 below.

[264] Art. 89(1) of the EEA Agreement. It is also to take decisions on its Rules of Procedure under Art. 89(3).

[265] See, e.g., Arts 61(3)(d), 82(1)(b) and (c), 83, 86 and 102(1) and (5) of the EEA Agreement. No formal power to take decisions is conferred on the EEA Council. In this sense, therefore, the latter has more in common with the European Council than the Council of the Union.

[266] *Ibid.*, Art. 103(2). According to a Joint Declaration on Art. 103 of the Agreement, there are 'no practical implications for internal Community procedures'.

[267] See, in particular, Art. 31 of the EFTA Convention (SÖ 1960:1). Majority voting in the EFTA Council was apparently only acceptable to the Swedish Government, because it was limited to 'certain clearly defined cases'. See *Kungl. Maj:ts proposition till riksdagen angående godkännande av Sveriges anslutning till konventionen angående upprättandet av Europeiska frihandelssammanslutningen, m. m., given Stockholms slott den 4 januari 1960* (Government proposal for parliamentary approval of Swedish accession to the EFTA Convention), prop. 1960:25, 46.

[268] Art. 6(2) of the EFTA Agreement on a Standing Committee of EFTA States (*Europeiska ekonomiska samarbetsområdet*, prop. 1991/92:170). See also Dec. 1/94 of 10 Jan. 1994 ([1994] OJ L85/72) adopting the Rules of Procedure of the Standing Committee of the EFTA States.

[269] Art. 15 of the Agreement Between the EFTA States on the Establishment of a Surveillance Authority and a Court of Justice ([1994] OJ L344/1).

[270] Art. 4 of the Rules of Procedure. The official Swedish position was that EFTA States would decide '*gemensamt*'. This expression is reminiscent of that of 'common accord' in Art. 158 EC, which, unlike unanimity as defined in Art. 149 of the same Treaty, cannot be achieved if one or more representatives abstain from voting.

by agreement between the Community, on the one hand, and the EFTA States speaking with one voice on the other. The apparent consequence is that while EFTA States may agree[271] to veto EEA decisions,[272] individual EFTA States will lack an 'opting-out' right.[273]

Democratic Control

The EEA Joint Parliamentary Committee is intended to contribute, through dialogue and debate, to a better understanding between the Community and EFTA States in the fields covered by the EEA Agreement.[274] This Committee, which adopts its own Rules of Procedure,[275] may express its views in the form of reports or resolutions, as appropriate.[276] It is to meet at least twice a year, with the Presidency being held for one year alternately by an MEP and a member of a Parliament of an EFTA State. It shall, in particular, examine the annual report, which the EEA Joint Committee is to issue on the functioning and development of the Agreement.[277] The President of the EEA Council may also appear before the Committee in order to be heard by it.[278] The Committee, however, has no powers to participate in EEA decision-making, apparently

[271] Minute of the Council and Commission *ad* para. 12 of the *Directives de Négociation*.

[272] The original EFTA negotiating position was apparently that unanimity amongst its members should be necessary for adoption of EEA decisions. See the Interim Report of the Political Affairs Committee on the Community's future political relations with the EFTA countries, EP Doc. A 3–116/90, 17. Such unanimity is not required by the EEA Agreement, and the position continues to depend on EFTA rules. In practice, individual EFTA States may be under pressure from other EFTA States to side with the majority. See, e.g., M. Hösli, 'Decision-making in the EEA and EFTA States' Sovereignty' [1990] *Aussenwirtschaft* 463–94.

[273] This right was apparently sought by Switzerland in particular. See SvD, 17 June 1991. Cf. sect. 6.5.3 below, regarding the right of each EFTA State to take a matter of concern to the EEA Council and thereby 'block' a decision in the Joint Committee. However, whereas a blocking minority of Member States may prevent adoption of a Community act, a minority of EFTA States can merely prevent extension of the act throughout the EEA. Apparently EFTA States may also agree amongst themselves and with the Community in the Joint Committee that the latter should decide under Art. 102 of the EEA Agreement on differentiated application of the act concerned, possibly with differentiated suspension or rebalancing measures under Art. 114 of the Agreement.

[274] Art. 95(3) of the EEA Agreement.

[275] *Ibid.*, Art. 95(6). The Rules are published in [1994] OJ L247/34.

[276] According to Rule 10 of the Rules of Procedure (n. 275 above), all Community legislation applying to the EEA as well as its implementation shall be subject to scrutiny by the Joint Parliamentary Committee.

[277] Arts 94(4) and 95(4) of the EEA Agreement.

[278] *Ibid.*, Art. 95(5). According to the Committee on External Economic Relations, it should be made explicit, if only in a Council declaration, that this may also occur at the request of the Committee. See the Report on economic and trade relations between the European Community and the EFTA countries in the European Economic Area, EP Doc. A3–306/92, 12. Rule 10 of the Rules of Procedure provides that the President of the Council and representatives of the EEA Joint Committee will be invited to participate actively in the work of the Joint Parliamentary Committee, while under Rule 16 Members of the Joint Parliamentary Committee have the right to put oral and written questions to the representatives of the EEA Council and the EEA Joint Committee. The European Parliament considers that the President of the EEA Council should attend meetings of the Joint Parliamentary Committee, when the latter so requests. See the Resolution of 30 Oct. 1992 ([1992] OJ C305/586) on economic and trade relations between the European Community and the EFTA countries in the European Economic Area, para. 23.

because there is supposed to have been no transfer of legislative competence[279] which could affect the powers of the national Parliaments of the EFTA States.

The contrast between formal arrangements for democratic control in the EEA Agreement and those in the Europe Agreements does not reflect the greater degree of integration envisaged by the former Agreement. Indeed, the European Parliament objected[280] that the lack of powers accorded to the EEA Joint Parliamentary Committee was incompatible with the democratic principles outlined in the Preamble to the EEA Agreement.[281]

There might even be a risk, given the arrangements for involvement of EFTA States in Community decision-making,[282] that the existing role of the European Parliament in relation to such decision-making could be jeopardized. Such involvement means, in particular, that experts of EFTA States may be consulted by the Commission on a proposal before the Parliament is consulted by the Council of the Union. Hence, effective EC–EFTA agreement may be reached before the proposal reaches the Parliament.[283]

Consequently, new institutional procedures were demanded to ensure that the European Parliament was kept constantly informed of proposals from the outset.[284] Specifically, it was demanded that the documents forwarded by the Commission to the Council of the Union and the EFTA States should be sent at the same time to the Parliament, as should the various documents exchanged between the Commission and EFTA States in the ongoing information and consultation procedure required by the Agreement. Such arrangements were considered necessary to ensure that the Parliament was not presented with *faits accomplis* or did not consider texts which had been superseded.[285]

In response, the Commission has undertaken to keep the competent bodies of the Parliament informed of the adoption of all proposals and measures relating to the EEA and, if necessary, to introduce new procedures for keeping Parliament abreast of these developments in the light of the practical experience of implementing the EEA Agreement.[286] More particularly, when a

[279] See, in particular, Prot. 35 to the EEA Agreement, on the implementation of EEA rules.

[280] See the observations of the Parliament in Opinion 1/92 *(Draft Agreement between the Community, on the one hand, and the countries of the European Free Trade Association, on the other, relating to the creation of the European Economic)* [1992] ECR I–2821, I–2837.

[281] First recital in the Preamble. Cf., regarding constitutional problems in the budgetary field, the Report of the Committee on Foreign Affairs and Security on the Commission proposal to the Council on the conclusion of the agreement on the European Economic Area, EP Doc. A3–0316/92, 10.

[282] See sect. 6.5.3 below and Ch. 7.

[283] Cf. the Resolution of the European Parliament of 16 Dec. 1993 ([1994] OJ C20/174) on the role of national experts and the Commission's right of initiative, para. 6.

[284] Report of the Committee on External Economic Relations on economic and trade relations between the EC and the EFTA countries in the European Economic Area, EP Doc. A3–306/92, 14.

[285] Resolution of 14 Feb. 1992 ([1992] OJ C67/197) on the European Economic Area, para. 8.

[286] Report of the Committee on Foreign Affairs and Security on the Commission proposal to the Council on the conclusion of the agreement on the European Economic Area, EP Doc. A3–316/92, 14.

proposal is forwarded to the Parliament for Community legislation in an area covered by the Agreement, the Parliament will be requested simultaneously to adopt a position on extension of the proposed legislation to the EEA.[287] Through utilizing such arrangements the Parliament will seek to ensure that measures which would normally presuppose the conclusion of an international agreement by the Community[288] and would thus be subject to Parliamentary scrutiny cannot adopted without such scrutiny.[289]

While the European Parliament may be able to use its existing powers over the Commission[290] to secure and to safeguard such opportunities to participate in EEA decision-making,[291] the Joint Parliamentary Committee itself is apparently less well placed to secure such opportunities. Similarly, while the EEA Consultative Committee may also express its views in the form of reports or resolutions as appropriate, and adopts its own Rules of Procedure,[292] no powers are conferred on it. These two committees may still be expected to contribute to lessening the tendency for Parties to develop separate positions which are not easily reconcilable in joint bodies that can only act unanimously. Nevertheless, the EEA Agreement raises serious problems of democratic control and could, indeed, exacerbate problems associated with the 'democratic deficit' within the Community.[293]

6.5.3 Functions

While the EEA Joint Committee is to be responsible for the implementation and operation of the EEA Agreement,[294] the EEA Council is responsible for laying down general guidelines and giving the political impetus in the implementation of the Agreement.[295] Both trade liberalization and harmonization are involved.

[287] Art. 3(1) of Reg. 2894/94 of 28 Nov. 1994 ([1994] OJ L305/6) concerning arrangements for implementing the Agreement on the European Economic Area. [288] Art. 228(1) EC.

[289] Report of the Committee on External Economic Relations on economic and trade relations between the European Community and the EFTA countries in the European Economic Area, EP Doc. A3–306/92, 14. In practice, the Council consults the Parliament on proposed decisions of the EEA Joint Committee under Art. 228(1) EC. See, e.g., the Resolution of 17 Nov. 1994 ([1994] OJ C341/126) on the proposal for a decision of the EEA Joint Committee amending Prot. 31 to the EEA Agreement on cooperation in specific fields outside the four freedoms.

[290] The censure procedure in Art. 144 EC establishes the principle of Commission responsibility to the Parliament.

[291] Cf. the Resolution of 30 Oct. 1992 ([1992] OJ C305/586) on economic and trade relations between the EC and the EFTA countries in the European Economic Area, para. 20.

[292] Art. 96(3) of the EEA Agreement. It adopted its Rules of Procedure at its Constituent Meeting held on 8 Feb. 1994 ([1994] OJ L301/10).

[293] See, e.g., A. Evans and P. Falk, *Law and Integration: Sweden and the European Community* (Stockholm, 1991). [294] Art. 92(1) of the EEA Agreement. [295] *Ibid.*, Art. 89(1).

Liberalization

The work of the joint bodies established by the EEA Agreement concerns both the settlement of disputes related to the trade liberalization sought by the Agreement and, more particularly, the use of safeguard measures.

(i) Disputes

Article 5 of the EEA Agreement provides that a Party may at any time raise a matter of concern at the level of the EEA Joint Committee or the EEA Council according to the modalities laid down in Articles 92(2) and 89(2) respectively.[296] Article 92(2) requires the Parties to hold consultations in the Joint Committee on any point of relevance to the Agreement which gives rise to a difficulty and is raised by one of them. Article 89(2) provides that after having discussed it in the EEA Joint Committee, or directly in exceptionally urgent cases, a Party may raise in the EEA Council any issue giving rise to a difficulty.

More particularly, the Community or an EFTA State may bring a matter under dispute which concerns the interpretation or application of the Agreement before the EEA Joint Committee under Article 111(1).[297] Article 111(2) provides that the Committee may settle the dispute. It shall be provided with all information which may be of use in making possible an in-depth examination of the situation, with a view to finding an acceptable solution. To this end, the Committee shall examine all possibilities to maintain the good functioning of the Agreement.

(ii) Safeguard Measures

In the event that safeguard measures are contemplated, under Article 112 of the EEA Agreement,[298] Article 113 thereof requires that, save in exceptional circumstances requiring immediate action, a Party must notify the Joint Committee and enter into consultations within the Committee before adopting such measures. Consultations must be held within the Committee concerning such measures every three months, and each Party may at any time request the Committee to review such measures.[299]

More particularly, Article 45(2) requires that safeguard measures relating to capital movements shall be the subject of prior consultations and exchange of information within the Joint Committee. However, exceptions are allowed under paragraphs (3) and (4) of Article 45. Article 45(3) refers to Article

[296] See also in the competition field Art. 64(1) (*ibid.*) and, in relation to state trading monopolies, Art. 64(2) (*ibid.*).

[297] See also Art. 35 of Prot. 4 to the EEA Agreement, on Rules of Origin. There may be an overlap with the role of the EEA Council when the *droit d'évocation* is exercised under Art. 89(2) of the Agreement.

[298] See sect. 3.5.3 above.

[299] See also sect. 3.5.3 above, regarding notification requirements under Art. 22 of the EEA Agreement.

43(2), which permits protective measures where capital movements lead to disturbances in the functioning of the capital market in any Member State or EFTA State. In such a situation Article 45(3) permits the Party concerned, on grounds of secrecy and urgency, to take such measures, where this proves necessary, without prior consultations and exchange of information. Article 45(4) provides that where a sudden crisis in the balance of payments occurs and the procedures in Article 45(2) cannot be followed, the Party concerned may, as a precaution, take the necessary protective measures. Where measures are taken in accordance with paragraphs (3) and (4), notice thereof shall be given at the latest by their date of entry into force, and the exchange of information and consultation as well as notification to the Joint Committee shall take place as soon as possible thereafter.[300]

The effects of adoption of any such safeguard measures may be countered by other Parties through resort to 'rebalancing' measures under Article 114. Adoption of the latter measures must follow the procedures laid down in Article 113.[301] More particularly, Article 48(2) provides that any Party deviating from the standstill clause applicable to discriminatory measures concerning transport in paragraph 1 shall notify the Joint Committee thereof, and Parties which do not accept the deviation may take corresponding measures.

More particularly, as regards anti-dumping measures, the EEA Agreement is designed to secure such a degree of integration between the Parties as to render resort to such measures unnecessary. In other words, the Agreement seeks to rely on reform of 'substantive' law. However, even to the extent that such reform is achieved, safeguard measures other than anti-dumping measures may still be available. In effect, the problem of securing an effective role for the EEA Joint Committee may merely be shifted to a related substantive law context.

According to Article 64(1), if one of the surveillance authorities considers that the implementation by the other surveillance authority of state aid rules in Articles 61 and 62 of the Agreement and Article 5 of Protocol 14[302] thereto is not in conformity with the maintenance of equal conditions of competition within the territory covered by this Agreement, exchange of views shall take place between the Commission and the ESA within two weeks according to the procedure of Protocol 27, paragraph (f), which deals with co-operation in the field of state aid. If a commonly agreed solution has not been found by the end of these two weeks, the competent authority of the affected Party may immediately adopt appropriate interim measures in order to remedy the resulting distortion of competition.[303] Consultations shall then be held in the

[300] Art. 45(5) of the EEA Agreement.

[301] *Ibid.*, Art. 114(2).

[302] On Trade in Coal and Steel Products.

[303] Adoption of such measures is not subject to the possibility of arbitration under Art. 111(4) of the EEA Agreement.

Joint Committee with a view to finding a commonly acceptable solution. If within three months the Committee has not been able to find such a solution, and if the practice in question causes or threatens to cause distortion of competition affecting trade between the Parties, the interim measures may be replaced by definitive measures, strictly necessary to offset the effect of such distortion.[304]

Again, as regards anti-trust measures, Article 56(1)(c) and (2) of the EEA Agreement preserves for the Commission the competence to act under Articles 85 and 86 of the EC Treaty against restrictive practices by undertakings which appreciably affect trade between Member States. Co-operation is to take place between the Commission and the ESA[305] in accordance with Protocols 23[306] and 24,[307] and Article 109(5) of the Agreement deals with the problem of disagreements between the two in the competition policy field. It provides that, in the case of disagreement regarding action to be taken on a complaint or regarding the result of the examination of the complaint, either body may refer the matter to the EEA Joint Committee which shall deal with it in accordance with the dispute-solving procedures in Article 111.[308] However, such a reference seems to have no suspensive effect, and so these procedures in themselves need not necessarily have any real impact on Commission practice under the EC Treaty.

The EEA Agreement seems, therefore, to confirm the difficulties of securing an effective role for joint bodies in relation to major trading problems. On the other hand, to the extent that the EEA Agreement reproduces trade liberalization and other requirements embodied in the EC Treaty, a far wider range of trading problems may take on a legal character[309] under this Agreement than under the Free Trade Agreements or Europe Agreements. Moreover, the Agreement embraces supranationalism, to the extent that a body independent

[304] Presumably, such measures could take the form of anti-subsidy duties imposed by the Community under Art. 11 of Reg. 3284/94 of 22 Dec. 1994 ([1994] OJ L349/22) on protection against subsidized imports from countries not members of the EC.

[305] Art. 58 of the EEA Agreement.

[306] Concerning the Co-operation between the Surveillance Authorities (Art. 58).

[307] On Co-operation in the Field of Control of Concentrations.

[308] Art. 11(1) of the Agreement on Civil Aviation between Norway, Sweden, and the EC ([1992] OJ L200/21) provided that whenever a Joint Committee decision contained a request for action to be taken by Norway and/or Sweden pursuant to the Regs and Dirs specified in the Annex then, unless the state concerned notified the other Parties that it was not in agreement with the action requested, it should take the necessary measures and inform the Commission. If the state concerned was not in agreement with the action requested by the Commission, Art. 11(2) provided that the matter should within 21 days be submitted to the Joint Committee which should meet within 14 days of the date of submission.

[309] In other words, what may be termed 'constitutional norms' (see T. Cottier, 'Constitutional Trade Regulation in National and International Law: Structure–Substance Pairings in the EFTA Experience' in M. Hilf and E.-U. Petersmann (eds.), *National Constitutions and International Economic Law* (Deventer, 1993), 409–42, at 411) become applicable.

of the EFTA States, the ESA,[310] is to be involved in securing respect for EEA law. To the extent that this Authority secures respect for such law, the Commission may have less justification for resorting to unilateral safeguard measures rather than seeking solutions to problems arising in EC–EFTA trade within the EEA Joint Committee. In these circumstances, the Committee may be able effectively to contribute to trade liberalization between the Parties, and Article 3 of the Agreement may have real significance. According to this provision, the Parties shall take all appropriate measures, whether general or particular, to ensure fulfilment of the obligations arising out of the Agreement, abstain from any measure which could jeopardize Agreement objectives and facilitate co-operation within the framework of the Agreement.

Harmonization

The EEA Joint Committee is to be involved in organic harmonization under Part VII of the EEA Agreement.[311] According to Article 97 of the Agreement, Parties which amend their internal legislation in areas covered by the Agreement[312] must respect the principle of non-discrimination, and the other Parties must be informed beforehand. Moreover, unless the Joint Committee concludes that the legislation as amended does not affect[313] the good functioning of this Agreement, the procedures referred to in Article 98,[314] notably those of Articles 99 and 102, must be completed.[315] While these procedures mean that the Community, though not an EFTA State, may enact legislation which does affect the good functioning of the Agreement, they must still be carried out.

[310] See, regarding the requirements of independence applicable to the Authority, Art. 8 of the Agreement between the EFTA States on the Establishment of a Surveillance Authority and a Court of Justice ([1994] OJ L344/1).

[311] Such involvement extends to financial decision making. Art. 81(c) of the EEA Agreement, taken together with Art. 79(3) thereof, entails that decisions by the Community, other than those relating to the general budget of the Community, which affect directly or indirectly a framework programme, specific programme, project, or other action, in which EFTA States participate by a decision under this Agreement, shall be subject to the procedures set out in Part VII. Decisions regarding the financial contributions of Parties are, according to Art. 82(1)(c), to be taken by the EEA Joint Committee, and Art. 86 entails that, in taking such decisions, the Committee shall act in accordance with Part VII.

[312] Where it has been decided by the EEA Joint Committee that co-operation in relation to the environment shall take the form of parallel legislation of identical or similar content by the Parties, the procedures in Part VII of the EEA Agreement shall also apply. See Art. 3(3) of Prot. 31 to the Agreement, on Co-operation in Specific Fields outside the Four Freedoms.

[313] In the Swedish version the terminology '*negativt påverkar*' is employed.

[314] According to this provision, the Annexes to the Agreement and Prots 1 to 7, 9 to 11, 19 to 27, 30 to 32, 37, 39, 41 and 47, as appropriate, may be amended by a decision of the EEA Joint Committee in accordance with Arts 93(2), 99, 100, 102, and 103 of the Agreement.

[315] Art. 12(1) of the Civil Aviation Agreement between Norway, Sweden, and the EC ([1992] OJ L200/21) provided that the Agreement should be without prejudice to the right of each Party, subject to compliance with the principle of non-discrimination and the provisions of this Art. and of Art. 13(2), unilaterally to amend its domestic legislation on a point regulated by this Agreement.

The EEA Agreement contains no straightforward provision, such as Article 27(2) of the Convention of the Member States of the Council of Europe and the Member States of the OECD regarding mutual administrative assistance in tax matters[316] or Protocol 3 to the Lugano Convention,[317] designed to preserve the absolute autonomy of Community decision-making.[318]

Article 99 of the EEA Agreement concerns 'joint decision shaping'.[319] According to this provision, when the Commission submits a proposal to the Council of the Union, at the request of one of the Parties, a preliminary exchange of views takes place in the Joint Committee on the proposal.[320] During the phase preceding the decision of the Council of the Union, in a continuous information and consultation process,[321] the Parties will consult each other again in the Joint Committee at 'the significant moments' at the request of one of them.[322] The Parties shall co-operate in good faith during this process with a view to facilitating, at the end of the process, 'decision taking' in the Joint Committee.[323]

Article 102(1) deals with such decision-taking. It provides that in order to guarantee the legal security and the homogeneity of the EEA, the Joint Committee shall take a decision concerning the amendment of an Annex to the EEA Agreement as closely as possible to the adoption by the Community of the corresponding new Community legislation, with a view to permitting a simultaneous application of the latter as well as amendments of the Annexes to the Agreement.[324] To this end, the Community shall, whenever adopting a

[316] ETS(1988) 127.

[317] [1988] OJ L319/9.

[318] Prot. 3 to the Lugano Convention, taken together with Art. 57(1) of the same Convention, means that its terms do not affect the freedom of the Community to legislate in relation to matters covered by the Convention. Cf. Art. 27(1) of the Council of Europe Convention on Transfrontier Television (ETS(1989)132), which entails that in their mutual relations Union Member States will only apply the provisions of the Convention to the extent that there is no Community rule governing the particular matter concerned.

[319] The EC–EFTA Joint Ministerial Statement of 19 Dec. 1990 (EFTA Bull. 1/1991, 22–5) referred in para. 7 to a 'continuous information and consultation process in the decision-shaping phase'.

[320] Art. 99(2) of the EEA Agreement. Art. 79(2) also provides that the Parties shall exchange information and, at the request of a Party, hold consultations within the Committee in respect of plans or proposals for the establishment or amendment of framework programmes, specific programmes, actions, and projects in the fields referred to in Art. 78.

[321] The Joint EC–EFTA Ministerial Statement of 13 May 1991 (EFTA Bull. 2/1991, 7–9) referred in para. 19 to 'an ongoing process of information and consultation'. Cf. Art. 39(2) of the Agreement between the EEC and the Swiss Confederation on Direct Insurance other than Life Insurance ([1991] OJ L205/3), which provides for consultation, once a Party has begun the legislative process.

[322] Art. 99(3) of the EEA Agreement.

[323] *Ibid.*, Art. 99(4).

[324] More particularly, Prot. 17 to the EEA Agreement, concerning Art. 34, provides that any legislation concerning third country access to their markets in a field governed by the Agreement shall be dealt with according to the procedures laid down in this Agreement and the Parties shall endeavour to elaborate corresponding EEA rules.

legislative act on an issue which is governed by this Agreement, as soon as possible inform the other Parties in the Joint Committee.[325]

This arrangement departs from that sought by the Swedish Government. The latter apparently considered that both sides should have the right to put proposals for legislation to the Committee. Such a right was said, indeed, to follow from general international law rules.[326] However, although EFTA States may apparently suggest to the Commission potential subjects for legislation,[327] no right to do so is formally recognized by the Agreement. Presumably, the Swedish position was rejected by the Community, partly because a formal right of the kind sought for EFTA States is not enjoyed by Member States themselves.[328]

More fundamental issues were also at stake. EFTA States, with some support from early remarks of Commission President Delors[329] and a report[330] by officials in the High Level Steering Group,[331] sought establishment of EEA institutions which would effectively have assumed the decision-making powers of Community institutions in relation to matters covered by the EEA Agreement.[332] A modified version of this position, though one which was still in line with a 'three-pillar' construction,[333] was that there should be a joint decision-making mechanism in substance and form,[334] but that if a joint

[325] Art. 12(2) of the Agreement on Civil Aviation ([1992] OJ L200/21) provided that as soon as a Party had adopted an amendment of its domestic legislation it should inform the other Parties via the Joint Committee, 8 days after adoption at the latest. The Joint Committee should within 14 days thereafter hold an exchange of views on the implications of such an amendment for the proper functioning of the Agreement.

[326] *Europeiska ekonomiska samarbetsområdet,* prop. 1991/92:170, *del* 1, bil. 1, 43.

[327] *Relations Between the Community and EFTA*, n. 70 above, 25.

[328] Under Art. 152 EC the Council (but not individual Member States) may request the Commission to undertake any studies the Council considers desirable for the attainment of the common objectives and to submit to it any proposals.

[329] Commission President Delors had referred to '*organes communs et de décision et de gestion*' in his speech to the European Parliament in Jan. 1989 (EP Debs. No. 2–373, 86, 17 Jan. 1989).

[330] An unpublished report of the results of the HLSG meeting of 20 Mar. 1990 referred to the idea of a '*décision commune* by consensus as the result of osmosis'.

[331] This was an EC–EFTA body responsible for co-ordinating the activity of the 5 working groups which prepared the ground for formal EEA Agreement negotiations.

[332] Para. 9 of the EFTA Ministerial Declaration of 15 Mar. 1989 (EFTA Bull. 2/1989, 4–7) referred to 'common decision-making and administrative institutions'. See, similarly, the Statement of Members of Parliament of the EFTA Countries, 26 May 1989 (EFTA Bull 2/89), para. 8. Cf. the idea that the CEN/CENELEC voting system might be employed in relation to EEA decision-making in H. Wallace, 'Comment on Per Kleppe's Presentation' in F. Laursen (ed.), *Europe 1992: World Partner* (Maastricht, 1991), 81–7, at 84.

[333] The pillars being the EEA, the Community and EFTA.

[334] Para. 6 of the EFTA Ministerial Declaration of 14 June 1990 (EFTA Bull. 3/1990, 11–12) sought provision for 'the right of both sides to launch EES initiatives, for joint shaping of EES rules and joint decisions thereon' and 'a genuine joint decision-making mechanism in substance and form'. See also *Relations Between the Community and EFTA*, n. 70 above, 84. Similarly, the Message of the EFTA Ministers to the Community regarding negotiation of the EEA Agreement, of 23 Oct. 1990 (EFTA Bull. 1/91, 20), referred to 'a genuine common decision-making mechanism' and maintained that 'there is, between substance and institutions, an inextricable link and a balance still to be found which has to correspond to the broad scope of our future cooperation on equal footing'.

decision could not be made within a given time limit,[335] each side would be free to proceed according to its own procedures.[336]

However, homogeneity requirements would have entailed that new Community legislation, in so far as it fell within the scope of the EEA Agreement, would have had to be compatible with EEA decisions. In other words, these requirements would have meant, within the scope of this Agreement, the subordination of Community institutions to EEA institutions. Therefore, homogeneity and internal autonomy of Community decision-making[337] could not easily be reconciled by the procedures which EFTA States sought.[338] Hence, the Commission considered that each side should preserve its decision-making autonomy throughout the process; that the EFTA structure should be reinforced, in line with the 'two-pillar' approach;[339] and that the 'decision-taking' procedures of the Community should be separated from those of the EEA as a whole.[340] Such thinking underlies the arrangements made in Articles 99 and 102 of the EEA Agreement.

These arrangements might be thought to entail merger of the processes of voluntary harmonization and conclusion of 'bridging' agreements in earlier EC–EFTA practice. The difference is that the Joint Committee has broad powers to amend the Annexes to the EEA Agreement and, hence, the obligations of EFTA States, without the need for these States individually to ratify a new agreement or amendments to an Annex.

A partial precedent might be said to have been provided by EFTA itself. The FINEFTA Joint Council, established under the 1961 Association Agreement with Finland, was composed of representatives of the EFTA States and of Finland and invariably met simultaneously with the EFTA Council, exercising almost identical powers. A decision by the EFTA Council would be referred to the Joint Council for immediate adoption without further discussion. However, this arrangement was apparently facilitated by *de facto* treatment of Finland as

[335] It was apparently envisaged that Community decision-making would be held in abeyance for a limited period to allow for a common EEA decision to be reached. See B. Spinner, 'Institutional Development and Linkages—a Response' in M. Robinson and J. Findlater (eds.), *Creating a European Economic Space: Legal Aspects of EC–EFTA Relations* (Dublin, 1990), 91–8, at 96.

[336] In contrast, in its Statement of 7 Apr. 1989 (EFTA Bull. 2/89) the EFTA Consultative Committee merely envisaged 'negotiation of multilateral framework or bridging agreements (with subsequent parallel agreements) between EFTA Countries and the Community' (para. 7).

[337] The need for such autonomy had been emphasized by Commissioner de Clercq at the EC–EFTA meeting in Interlaken on 20 May 1987 (Bull. EC 5–1987, 2.2.14) as one of the principles which should govern EC–EFTA relations.

[338] According to Commission President Delors (EP Debs. No. 3–385, 111, 17 Jan. 1990), joint decision-taking would imply Union membership.

[339] Results of the Commission/EFTA High-Level Steering Group Meeting of 20 Oct. 1989 (published in O. Jacot-Guillarmod (ed.), *L'Avenir du libre-échange en Europe: vers un Espace économique européen* (Zürich, 1990), 521–4).

[340] Para. 5.3 of the *Communication de la Commission au Conseil portant recommendation de decision du Conseil visant à autoriser la Commission à negocier un accord avec les pays AELE, portant sur la creation de l'Espace Economique Européen.*

a full negotiating partner in the first and only substantive negotiations taking place in the EFTA Council.[341]

Part VII of the EEA Agreement by no means ensures that EFTA States will be so fully involved in Community negotiations.[342] On the other hand, the effectiveness of the involvement formally required by Article 99 may be increased by the impact of the requirements imposed in Article 102(3) to (5). The Parties are required by Article 102(3) to make all efforts to arrive at an agreement on matters relevant to the EEA Agreement. The Joint Committee shall, in particular, make every effort to find a mutually acceptable solution where a serious problem arises in any area which, in the EFTA States, falls within the competence of the legislator.[343] This requirement reflects the fact that, in the case of dualist countries, the homogeneity of EEA law would be endangered by Joint Committee adoption of acts which national Parliaments were not willing to incorporate into national law.[344]

If agreement on an amendment of an Annex to the Agreement cannot be reached, the Joint Committee shall examine all further possibilities of maintaining the good functioning of this Agreement and adopt any decision necessary to this effect,[345] including the possibility to take notice of the equivalence of legislation. Such a decision shall, according to Article 102(4), be adopted at the latest at the expiry of a period of six months from the date of referral to the Joint Committee or, if that date is later, on the date of entry into force of the corresponding Community legislation.

In the absence of any such solution, EFTA States will not be bound by the Community act concerned. In this sense, such States together may be in a more advantageous position than individual Member States, which may be bound by a Community act adopted in the Council of the Union by majority. This advantage reflects the fact that EFTA States are not fully involved in the negotiations for adoption of a Community act. However, the Agreement seeks

[341] *Relations Between the Community and EFTA*, n. 70 above, 145. Cf. the idea that EFTA States might be heard by the Council of the Union prior to the formal opening of a session of the latter in C.-P. Lucron, n. 241 above, 531.

[342] The Commission considered that direct EFTA participation in the shaping of Community decisions would require amendment of the EC Treaty (Communication to the Council of 22 Nov. 1989 on future relations between the Community and EFTA). However, Art. 238 EC envisages partial participation by third states. See Darmon A. G. in Case 12/86 *Meryem Demirel* v. *Schwäbish, stadt Gmünd* [1987] ECR 3719, 3741 and the Court itself (3751).

[343] Art. 102(3) of the EEA Agreement.

[344] The apparent implication is that the Joint Committee might decide on the differentiated application of the relevant act to EFTA States.

[345] Similarly, Art. 12(3) of the Civil Aviation Agreement ([1992] OJ L200/21) provided that the Joint Committee should: either adopt a decision revising the provisions of the Agreement so as to integrate therein, if necessary on a basis of reciprocity, the amendments made to the legislation in question; adopt a decision to the effect that the amendments to the legislation in question shall be regarded as in accordance with the Agreement; or decide any other measure to safeguard the proper functioning of the Agreement.

to ensure that there are effective disincentives to irresponsible exploitation of their position.[346]

Article 102(5) provides that if, at the end of the time limit set out in paragraph 4, the Joint Committee has not adopted a decision on an amendment of an Annex to this Agreement, the affected part thereof, as determined by the Committee in accordance with paragraph 2, is regarded as provisionally suspended,[347] subject to a decision to the contrary by the Committee.[348] Such a suspension shall take effect six months after the end of the period referred to in paragraph 4, but in no event earlier than the date on which the corresponding Community act is implemented in the Community. The Committee shall pursue its efforts to agree on a mutually acceptable solution in order for the suspension to be terminated as soon as possible.[349]

The practical consequences of such suspension are to be discussed in the Committee,[350] and the Parties shall, as appropriate, decide on the adjustments necessary due to the suspension. However, the rights and obligations which individuals and economic operators have already acquired under this Agreement shall remain.[351] More particularly, such suspension can only apply in relation to parts of an Annex or certain Protocols.[352] The trade liberalization and other requirements embodied in the Agreement itself will continue to operate,[353] and so the consequences of suspension will also depend on the operation of these requirements. In other words, failure to reach agreement within the Joint Committee means that EC–EFTA trade relations will depend on requirements beyond the control of the individual Parties. In contrast, reaching agreement within the Committee offers them the possibility of contributing to the development of these requirements and thus of managing their relations having regard to their perceived interests. In these circum-

[346] *Relations Between the Community and EFTA*, n. 70 above, 26. Cf. the idea of penalties as an effective means of curbing protectionism in international trade (J. Waelbroeck, 'The Logic of EC Commercial and Industrial Policy Making' in A. Jacquemin (ed.), *European Industry: Public Policy and Corporate Strategy* (Oxford, 1984), 99–125).

[347] This provision may, in one sense, be a response to the EFTA position that provisions of agreements with the Community were not, in the absence of express provision, affected by internal developments in Community law. See B. Spinner, 'Les travaux du groupe d'experts juridiques de l'AELE (1987–1988)' in O. Jacot-Guillarmod (ed.), *L'Avenir du libre-échange en Europe: vers un Espace économique européen* (Zürich, 1990), 87–93, at 89.

[348] Opting out by an individual EFTA State might be the agreed solution with suspension arrangements or rebalancing measures.

[349] The Swedish Government considered that EEA rules might be applied in Sweden, even if other EFTA States did not wish to apply them. See *EES-Avtalets införlivande m. m.* (Ds 1992:14), 40.

[350] Art. 102(6) of the EEA Agreement.

[351] Mere expectations are not covered. Examples of the rights which are protected are given in an Agreed Minute *ad* Art. 102(6).

[352] Art. 98 of the EEA Agreement.

[353] The Agreement on Civil Aviation ([1992] OJ L200/21) went further. Art. 14(5) provided that if the Joint Committee did not take the decisions pursuant to Arts 1(2), 7(5), 9(1), 11(2) and 12(3) within 6 months of the date of referral, the Agreement should cease to be in force. Cf. Art. 39 of the Agreement between the EEC and the Swiss Confederation concerning direct insurance other than life insurance ([1991] OJ L205/48).

stances, all Parties may have an incentive to modify their positions, both in the 'decision-shaping' and 'decision-taking' stages, so as to reach agreement, and so their relations may be rendered less unequal[354] than might otherwise be the case.[355]

As a result, the potential of joint decision-making to promote harmonization in relations between the Community and third states may be more fully realized than in the case of such decision-making under the Free Trade Agreements or the Europe Agreements.

Beyond the scope of the trade liberalization and other requirements embodied in the EEA Agreement, the potential role of such decision-making is less clear. Article 118 of the Agreement is based on the 'evolutionary clauses' in the Free Trade Agreements.[356] It provides that where a Party considers that it would be useful in the interests of all the Parties to develop the relations established by the Agreement by extending them to fields not covered thereby, it shall submit a reasoned request to the other Parties within the EEA Council. Hence, in contrast to the arrangements made by the Free Trade Agreements, the procedure and the involvement of a joint body may be invoked unilaterally by a Party. However, the EEA Council alone may instruct the Joint Committee to examine all aspects of this request and to issue a report and, where appropriate, take the political decisions with a view to opening negotiations between the Parties. In essence, what seems to be envisaged is the kind of procedure which had such limited effectiveness under the Free Trade Agreements.

6.6 CONCLUSION

Not only the supranationalism of institutions independent of Member States but also the framework provided by the trade liberalization and other requirements in the EC Treaty may facilitate joint decision-making under this Treaty. Such decision-making may benefit from a virtuous circle of the operation of legal provisions and institutional conduct. It is said that, while institutions

[354] If attention is directed only to the 'Institutional Provisions' in Part VII of the EEA Agreement, it may be natural to follow the view expressed by P. Pescatore in 'The Dynamics and Homogeneity of the European Economic System' [1991] *JFT* 295–320, at 317 that the relationship between the Parties is so 'unequal [as] to be incompatible with one of the basic assumptions of international law.'

[355] At the same time, the dynamism may be such as to counter the risk that joint decision-making may lead to stagnation. Cf. F. W. Scharpf, n. 11 above.

[356] Para. 3.4 of the Commission Communication concerning a proposed council decision authorizing the Commission to negotiate an agreement with the EFTA states on the erection of a European Economic Space.

influence the development of law, the evolution of institutions is, in turn, 'fundamentally influenced' by the legal framework.[357]

The Europe Agreements, like the Free Trade Agreements before them, may embody insufficient liberalization requirements to offer such a developed framework as the EC Treaty for tackling trade problems between the Parties. Hence, the contribution of joint decision-making to the resolution of problems seriously affecting such trade may, as in the case of the Free Trade Agreements, be very limited.

In contrast, to the extent that the EEA Agreement embodies the same trade liberalization and other requirements as the EC Treaty, joint decision-making under the former may be facilitated. More particularly, previous tendencies towards separation of harmonization efforts within the Community from harmonization efforts in relations between the Community and EFTA States may be reduced. As a result, EEA joint bodies may be more able to perform the role expected of them than those established by the Free Trade Agreements.[358]

Although the EEA decision-making process may still prove fragmented, the fragmentation may not be such as to preclude networking[359] and incremental decision-making on the basis of Community law requirements reproduced in the EEA Agreement.[360] Once a development path is set on a particular course, it is said, the network externalities, the learning process of organizations, and the historically derived subjective modeling of the issues reinforce the course.[361]

[357] Cf. D.C. North, *Institutions, Institutional Change and Economic Performance* (Cambridge 1990), 5. In other words, effective participation in decision-making, which requires equality in relation to mechanisms of issue presentation and resolution, may be at least as dependent on the rules to be applied to the issue concerned as on the rules governing the institutions involved. J.-M. Sun and J. Pelkmans, 'Regulatory Competition in the Single Market' [1995] *JCMS* 567, consider the dependence of regulatory competition on 'business–government interactions' (572), but not the impact of trade liberalization and other requirements on the operation of rules governing such interactions.

[358] Indeed, as in the Community, policy demands may favour institutional strengthening, at least of an informal kind. Cf. H. Wallace, 'The Best is the Enemy of the "Could": Bargaining in the European Community' in S. Tarditi *et al.* (eds.), *Agricultural Trade Liberalization and the European Community* (Oxford, 1989), 193–206.

[359] Formal structures and boundaries, once set up, allow and encourage the strengthening of informal interactions along the channels created—or across the space thus cleared and enclosed. See W. Wallace, *The Transformation of Western Europe* (London, 1990), 83. However, major intergovernmental bargaining may be necessary for more fundamental change. Cf. R. O. Keohane and S. Hoffmann, 'Institutional Change in the 1980s' in R.O. Keohane and S. Hoffmann (eds.), *The New European Community* (Boulder, 1991), 1–39.

[360] Cf. C. Leman, 'Patterns of Policy Development: Social Security in the United States and Canada' [1977] *Public Policy* 261–91.

[361] D. C. North, n. 357 above, 99.

7

Committee Work

7.1 INTRODUCTION

'Comitology'[1] denotes the involvement of various kinds of committees in decision-making. Such committees are distinct from the bodies discussed in the previous chapter, since the former do not formally make decisions. Nevertheless, not only may the range of interests taken into account by decision-makers tend to be broadened by their involvement, but also responsiveness of decision makers to network relationships, which reflect the reality of integration, may tend to be facilitated. In other words, the vacuum which might otherwise result from reliance on decision-making in bodies such as the Council of the Union may tend to be filled.

Formal legal support for such tendencies is provided by the EC Treaty and the EEA Agreement. To the extent that possibilities for one Party effectively to participate in the internal decision-making of another Party are entailed, the latter Agreement implicitly rejects strict commitment to ideas of national sovereignty and Community autonomy. Such commitment seems to have been more resistant in the Europe Agreements, which are more reticent than the EEA Agreement in formalizing 'comitology'.[2] However, as practice under the EC Treaty and the Free Trade Agreements illustrates, development of 'comitology' is not dependent on formal legal provisions alone.[3]

7.2 EC TREATY

Within the EC Treaty framework 'comitology' may be associated with the work of privately established bodies or of bodies established under the Treaty.

[1] See, generally, K. St Clair Bradley, 'Comitology and the Law: Through a Glass Darkly' (1992) 29 *CMLRev*. 693–721.

[2] In the course of the negotiations for the EEA Agreement the Commission produced a document entitled 'Mutual Information Procedures and Comitology concerning Community Decisions' (*Agence Europe*, No. 5356 (24 Oct. 1990)).

[3] The very nature of Community decision-making is such that there may be a range of informal links with different actors. Cf., regarding problems of negotiating with the USA, M. Hart, 'A North American Free Trade Agreement: the Elements Involved' (1991)14 *The World Economy* 87–102, at 100.

7.2.1 Lobbying Bodies

Article 138d of the EC Treaty, which was introduced by the Treaty on European Union, provides that any Union Citizen and any natural or legal person residing or having his registered office in a Member State shall have the right to address, individually or in association with other Citizens or persons, a petition to the European Parliament on a matter which comes within the Community's fields of activity and which affects him directly. This provision seems to treat lobbying of the European Parliament as a constitutional right.[4]

Lobbying, as a response to trading problems, and the operation of Community law may be interrelated processes. In particular, lobbying constitutes a response on the political market as an alternative to an exit response on the economic market and may be at least as likely as the latter to determine the extent to which the operation of trade liberalization provisions really leads to regulatory competition between Member States.[5] At the same time, in so far as 'integration management' leads the Community to adopt harmonization acts, lobbying may be regarded as an instrument of 'participatory democracy', according to which those more directly affected by such an act should have a proportionally greater input in its preparation than others.[6] The implication is that the content of such acts may be affected by lobbying.

However, lobbying may be both controversial, because of fears that decision-making may be 'distorted' thereby,[7] and of variable effectiveness.[8] For example, Article 118b of the Treaty requires the Commission 'to endeavour to develop the dialogue between management and labour at European level which could, if the two sides consider it desirable, lead to relations based on agreement'.[9] In practice, this dialogue has made little progress.[10]

[4] Cf. the role of 'representative organizations' in appointing members of the ECSC Consultative Committee under Art. 18 ECSC. Art. 195 EC provides that, in making appointments to Economic and Social Committee, the Council may obtain the opinion of European bodies which are representative of the various economic and social sectors to which the activities of the Community are of concern. According to Case 297/86 *Confederazione Italiana Dirigenti di Azienda (CIDA)* v. *EC Council* [1988] ECR 3531, 3557, no requirement to consult such bodies is implied.

[5] J.-M. Sun and J. Pelkmans, 'Regulatory Competition in the Single Market' [1995] *JCMS* 567.

[6] K. Lenaerts, 'Regulating the Regulatory Process: 'Delegation of Powers' in the European Community' (1993) *ELRev.* 23–49, at 24.

[7] See, regarding plans for a register of interests of assistants of MEPs, *The European*, 10–16 Feb. 1995 and 31 Mar.–6 Apr. 1995. Cf. the application of the idea of comparative advantage to situations where a Member State has nationals well placed in committees of the European Parliament in J.-M. Sun and J. Pelkmans, n. 5 above, 80, n. 11.

[8] See, generally, C. Harlow, 'A Community of Interests? Making the Most of European Law' (1992) *MLR* 331–50.

[9] See also Art. 3 of the Agreement on Social Policy, annexed to the EC Treaty, regarding consultation of management and labour at Community level.

[10] W. Streeck and P. C. Schmitter, 'From National Corporatism to Transnational Pluralism: Organised Interests in the Single European Market' [1991] *Politics and Society* 133–64.

Lobbying of the Commission by undertakings may be better established.[11] In this connection, the work of the Union of Industrial and Employers' Confederations of Europe (UNICE), which may be open to representative organizations from third states as well as Member States, is prominent.[12] Through such bodies traders from third states may apparently take advantage of opportunities for their counterparts within Member States to seek to influence Community decision-making.[13]

7.2.2 International Standards Bodies

The significance of international standards bodies, such as the Comité Européen de Normalisation (CEN), the Comité Européen de Normalisation Electronique (CENELEC),[14] and the European Conference of Postal and Telecommunications Administrations (CEPT), has grown along with increasing use by the Commission of 'the new approach' to harmonization.[15] According to this approach, Community directives harmonizing national law seek simply to lay down 'essential requirements'.[16] The technical specifications needed to meet these requirements are, as for example in the case of Directive 88/378 on toy safety,[17] left to the relevant standards bodies.[18] Such an approach was foreseen as a possibility in the Draft General Programme for the Elimination of Technical Barriers to Trade of 7 March 1968[19] and was first employed by the Community legislature in 1973.[20] Its increased use reflects a

[11] Large Swedish companies, e.g., might have their own representatives in Brussels. See, regarding contacts between Swedish paper producers and the Commission, *Sverige–EFTA–EG 1987* (Utrikesdepartementets handelsavdelning, 1988), 15.

[12] Since 1974 the Swedish Employers' Association (SAF) and the Confederation of Swedish Industries (*Industriförbundet*) had been represented in UNICE. Cf. the representation of the Swedish labour organizations, *Landsorganisationen* (LO) and *Tjänstemännens centralorganisation* (TCO) in the European Trade Union Confederation (ETUC). Further contacts developed at a variety of levels and included, e.g., those between the Chamber of Commerce in Gothenburg and the Bureau for Small and Medium-Sized Enterprises (*Sverige–EFTA–EG 1987* (Utrikesdepartementets handelsavdelning, 1988), 34).

[13] Again, the European Trade Union Technical Bureau for Health and Safety, attached to ETUC and financed by the Community and EFTA States, is intended to influence CEN-CENELEC work. See *Standardiseringens roll i EFTA-EG-samarbetet*, SOU 1989:45, 65.

[14] CEN and CENELEC are listed in List I to Dir. 83/189 of 28 Mar.1983 ([1983] OJ L109/8) laying down a procedure for the provision of information in the field of technical standards and regulations.

[15] *Technical Harmonization and Standards: A New Approach* (COM(85)19) and the Council Resolution of 7 May 1985 ([1985] OJ C136/1) on a new approach to technical harmonization and standards.

[16] See, generally, R. Hayder, 'Neue Wege der europäischen Rechtsangleichung?' [1989] *Rabels Zeitschrift für ausländisches und internationales Privatrecht* 622–98.

[17] Of 3 May 1988 ([1988] OJ L187/1) on the approximation of the laws of the Member States concerning the safety of toys, Arts 3 and 5.

[18] The legality of such an approach was accepted in Case 815/79 *Gaetano Cremonini and Maria Luisa Vrankovich* [1980] ECR 3583.

[19] [1968] JO C48/24, Pt IV.

[20] Dir. 73/23 of 26 Mar.1973 ([1973] OJ L77/29) on the harmonization of the laws of Member States relating to electrical equipment designed for use within certain voltage limits.

general tendency for non-governmental agents to become more closely involved in the formulation of economic policy and legal provisions,[21] and it may operate in such a way as to overcome reluctance of traders to devote resources[22] to developing rules which simply constrain them.[23]

More fundamentally, the consequences of transition from industrial society to information society may be reflected. That traders may acquire a capacity to develop new products and services which is greater than the capacity of decision makers to draw up standards[24] is not the only consequence. The further consequence is that the effects of a standard may depend less on its formal legal force than on its informal, but strategically significant,[25] components—information, coordination and mobilization of values and aims.[26]

Equally, the impact on the law of globalization tendencies may be reflected, in that opportunities may be entailed for participation by representatives of third states in Community decision-making which goes beyond mere issue presentation (through lobbying) and concerns issue resolution.[27] The first EC–EFTA common mandate was given to CEN in 1982,[28] and there is a common working group within CEN and CENELEC.[29] Framework agreements were signed with CEN and CENELEC in January 1986,[30] which made it possible for EFTA States to take part in an advance information procedure concerning draft standards and standardization programmes.[31]

[21] UN Conference on Trade and Development, *Common European Economic Space* (New York, 1991), 5.

[22] Though financial aid is provided by the Community. See the Council Resolution of 18 June 1992 ([1992] OJ C173/1) on the role of European standardization in the European economy, para. 24. See also the Commission Communication to the Council of 20 Dec. 1991 ([1992] OJ C96/2) on standardization in the European economy, paras 66 and 67.

[23] M. Andrieu, 'La normalisation europėenne instrument du cohėsion' [1992] *RMC* 627–30.

[24] S. Woolcock, id. op., 92.

[25] The Commission Communication of 16 Oct. 1990 ([1991] OJ C20/1) on the Development of European Standardization highlighted the strategic significance of standardization for the European market, para. 10.

[26] K.-H. Ladeur, 'European Community Institutional Reforms: Extra-National Management as an Alternative Model to Federalism' (1990/2) *LIEI* 1–21, at 10. Industrial and commercial property rights may be particularly well suited to such mobilization. See R. Joliet, 'Droit des marques et libre circulation des marchandises: l'abandon de l'arràt Hag I' [1991] *RTDE* 169–85. But cf. the Commission Communication of 16 Oct. 1990 ([1990] OJ C20/1) on the Development of European Standardization, para. 92.

[27] See, generally, *Europastandardiseringens betydelse för Sverige och för integration i Västeuropa* (Fakta Europa 1989:2, Utrikesdepartementet, 1989).

[28] EFTA States are full members of the standards organization for steel (ECISS), which is attached to CEN. See *Sverige–EFTA–EG 1989* (Utrikesdepartementets handelsavdelning, 1990), 47.

[29] *Sverige–EG 1982* (Utrikesdepartementets handelsavdelning, 1983), 25.

[30] EFTA Bull. 1/1986, 19. See, generally, B. Hurni, 'EFTA–EC Relations: Aftermath of the Luxembourg Declaration' [1986] *JWTL* 497–506, at 501. In the same month EFTA States also signed an agreement for the creation of a Comparative Index of European and National Standards (ICONE), which serves as a central data base on all national standards in EFTA and Community countries.

[31] A common declaration was also made by EFTA and CEPT in 1985 (*Sverige–EG 1985* (Utrikesdepartementets handelsavdelning, 1986), 38).

In practice, however, reaching agreement on new standards in such bodies and securing transposition of agreed standards at national level may not be without difficulty.[32] To avoid exacerbating such difficulties, the Commission wishes to limit involvement by non-EEA states.[33] Even if a standard is agreed, its effectiveness may be limited where Member States introduce diverse legislation in the field concerned.[34]

At the same time, judicial control problems may arise. For example, an agreement between national associations which are 'governed by private law and act within the framework of the functions attributed to them by their statutes and the national legislation to which they are subject' cannot be considered an act of a Community institution for the purposes of review of its legality by the Court of Justice, since no such institutions take part in its conclusion. The fact that the conclusion of such an agreement[35] may be a precondition for the entry into force of a Council enactment and that the length of time for which the enactment applies may be determined by the duration of the agreement does not affect the nature of the agreement as a measure adopted by private bodies.[36]

Such problems may be all the greater because consumer interests may not be represented in standards bodies.[37] More fundamentally, constitutionally undesirable privatization of public functions may be said to be involved,[38] though it is not clear that the problems are any greater than those of arrangements dominated by officials within Coreper working groups.[39]

[32] Commission Communication on the Development of European Standardization ([1991] OJ C20/1), para. 22. See also *Report of the Group of Independent Experts on Legislative and Administrative Simplification*, COM(95)288, 71.

[33] However, the American National Standards Institute (ANSI) has close contacts with CEN and CENELEC, and US firms and associations can participate as observers in the work of the European Telecommunications Standards Institute (ETSI). See G. C. Hufbauer, 'An Overview' in G. C. Hufbauer (ed.), *Europe 1992: An American Perspective* (Washington, 1990), 1–64, at 39. See also, regarding contacts between European and other international standards bodies, House of Representatives Committee on Small Business, *European Community Approach to Testing and Certification: Should the US Government Play a Role?* (Serial No. 101–56, Washington, 1990). Nevertheless, the 'interface' between European-level and international-level standardization may be problematic. See J. Pelkmans and M. Egan, *Fixing European Standards: Moving Beyond the Green Paper* (CEPS Working Document No. 65, Brussels, 1992), 16–18.

[34] Explanatory Memorandum to the Commission Proposal for a Dir. on *in Vitro* Diagnostic Medical Devices, COM(95)130, 7.

[35] See, e.g., the Supplementary Agreement between National Bureaux of 12 Dec. 1973 ([1973] OJ L87/15), regarding car insurance.

[36] Case 152/83 *Marcel Demouche* v. *Fonds de Garantie Automobile and Bureaux central français* [1987] ECR 3833, 3852–3.

[37] According to the Commission, greater openness in the process of European standardization is necessary in order to increase public interest and confidence in European standards. See the Communication on the Development of European Standardization ([1991] OJ C20/1), para. 63. See, earlier, Commission Recommendation 88/41 of 10 Dec. 1987 ([1988] OJ L23/26) on the involvement and improvement of consumer participation in standardization.

[38] See, e.g., the position of the Swedish Environment Party (*Sverige och den västeuropeiska integrationen*, prop 1988/89:19, 28).

[39] See sect. 7.2.3 below.

As a result, participation by representatives of third states and traders therefrom in international standards bodies entails for them the challenge of seeking to tackle deficiencies in the Community harmonization process[40] as well as the opportunity to develop the legal framework for their trade relations with the Community.[41] In the case of third states not represented in such bodies the risk is that their traders will see standards bodies and the rules within which standards are embodied 'captured' by their competitors.[42] In other words, such traders may become marginal to partnership strategies between public and private actors designed to create comparative advantage in rapidly-changing and oligopolistic global markets.[43]

7.2.3 Coreper

Article 151(1) of the EC Treaty provides that a committee consisting of the Permanent Representatives of the Member States (Coreper)[44] shall be responsible for preparing the work of the Council and for carrying out the tasks assigned to it by the Council.[45] Coreper is divided into the First Part, which is

[40] Note the concern to increase the role of consumer and labour representatives in the work of these bodies in *Standardiseringens roll i EFTA-EG-samarbetet*, SOU 1989:45, 60. EFTA States favour creation of an EC–EFTA consumer policy committee attached to CEN and CENELEC. See *Europa utsikt* 6/1989.

[41] Cf. the insurance associations from third states which were party to the agreement annexed to Dec. 74/167 of 6 Feb. 1974 ([1974] OJ L87/14), 2nd Commission Dec. relating to the application of Council Dir. 72/166 of 24 Apr. 1972 on the approximation of the laws of the Member States relating to insurance against civil liability in respect of the use of motor vehicles, and to the enforcement of the obligation to insure against such liability.

[42] Cf. G. Koopman and H.-E. Scharrer, *Scenarios of a Common External Trade Policy for the EC after 1992* (Institut für Wirtschaftsforschung Report No. 84, Hamburg, 1990), 30.

[43] W. Wallace, *The Transformation of Western Europe* (London, 1990), 89.

[44] In Feb. 1953 the ECSC Special Council of Ministers established a Co-ordinating Committee (CoCor) under Art. 10 of its Rules of Procedure (JOCECA, 12 Feb. 1953, 7), which provided for establishment of committees. This committee was composed of senior officials drawn from the national administrations of the Member States and met about once a month to carry out the preparatory work for Council meetings. Following this precedent, the EEC and Euratom Treaties provided that the Rules of Procedure of the two new Councils established thereby might 'provide for the setting up of a committee consisting of representatives of the Member States, the powers and tasks of which [were] to be determined by the Council' (Art. 151 EEC and Art. 121 Euratom). Accordingly, a Committee of Permanent Representatives was established for the EEC and Euratom Communities. This development was implicitly approved in Art. 4 of the Merger Treaty, which provided that a committee consisting of the Permanent Representatives of the Member States should be responsible for preparing the work of the Council and for carrying out the tasks assigned to it by the Council. Consequently, CoCor was abolished, and a single Committee of Permanent Representatives took over such responsibilities under all three Treaties.

[45] Art. 151(2) EC provides that the Council is also to be assisted by a Secretariat General. More particularly, without prejudice to Art. 151, a Co-ordinating Committee of senior officials was established under Art. K.4 of the TEU to prepare meetings regarding co-operation in the fields of justice and home affairs. See also Art. 100d EC. Art. J.8(5) of the TEU also provides for a Political Committee, consisting of Political Directors, for the CFSP. According to the Declaration on Practical Arrangements in the Field of the Common Foreign and Security Policy, which was attached to the TEU, the division of work between the Political Committee and Coreper would

composed of Deputy Permanent Representatives and deals with what are regarded as technical matters, and the Second Part, which is composed of the Permanent Representatives themselves and deals with more controversial matters.[46] It meets at least once a week and maintains close contacts with the Council Presidency—indeed the latter and the Coreper Presidency rotate simultaneously. Presumably, the effectiveness of its work benefits from the comparative frequency of its meetings and the comparative permanence of its members.[47]

The detailed work of Coreper is devolved to working groups covering each field of Community activity as well as *ad hoc* groups that may be created.[48] These bodies, whose work is co-ordinated by Coreper, are composed of officials from Member States as well as a Commission representative and are chaired by the Member State holding the Council Presidency. Their work may be important not only in a technical sense but, more generally, in encouraging the development of networks between Commission officials and national officials.

Council activity may be significantly affected by such arrangements. In particular, Council agendas are divided into 'A items' and 'B items'. The former items are those on which provisional agreement has been reached within Coreper. Formal Council approval in relation to such items is still required, though such approval is rarely delayed. Thus the preparatory work for which Coreper has responsibility is capable of compensating for the relative infrequency of Council meetings and expediting Council decision-making. Indeed, if all the Council members agree and, where the decision is to be taken on the basis of a Commission proposal, the Commission gives its consent, urgent matters may be decided by a written procedure.[49] Resort to this procedure is common where a Council meeting is not scheduled early enough for an A item decision to be taken by the date required. As for B items, these relate to matters on which, despite the preparatory work, disagreement persists. Protracted discussion of such matters in the Council itself may be necessary.

7.2.4 Working Groups of Experts

Like Coreper, the Commission establishes working groups. These groups, which are responsible for the preliminary work on Commission proposals,

be examined at a later stage, as would the practical arrangements for merging the Political Co-operation Secretariat with the Secretariat General of the Council and for co-operation between the latter and the Commission.

[46] Art. 19 of Dec. 93/662 of 6 Dec. 1993 ([1993] OJ L304/1) adopting the Council's Rules of Procedure.

[47] In the agricultural sector the Special Committee on Agriculture was established to carry out the functions which would otherwise have been the responsibility of Coreper (Art. 5 of the Dec. of 12 May 1960 ([1960] JO 1217) *concernant l'accéleration du rythme de réalisation des objets du traité*).

[48] Art. 19(2) of the Rules of Procedure of the Council (Dec. 93/662 of 6 Dec. 1993 ([1993] OJ L304/1) adopting the Council's Rules of Procedure).

[49] *Ibid.*, Art. 6.

are composed of experts from Member States.[50] Although these experts are expected to act independently, they include civil servants, who will be in a position to advise the Commission of the acceptability of its proposal to their respective national governments.

7.2.5 Management Committees

Article 145 of the EC Treaty provides for the Council to empower the Commission to enact measures implementing acts adopted by the former. In exercising such power the Commission is usually 'assisted' by committees. A declaration annexed to the Final Act to the Single European Act requested the Council to give a predominant role to advisory committees.[51] Accordingly, Commission proposals may sometimes be submitted to a purely advisory committee.[52] However, in spite of the declaration, the Commission is often required to submit draft measures to a management committee,[53] composed of representatives of the Member States. If the committee objects to the draft concerned, the Council may effectively take back the power delegated to the Commission and itself take a decision.

Such committees favour network-building by officials from different Member States. Hence, their creation is said to have done much to overcome bureaucratic resistance within Member States to Community decision-making.[54]

7.2.6 Programme Committees

Various committees are involved with the Commission in the implementation of Community programmes, such as those for science and technology and for education and training. For example, the Committee for the European Development of Science and Technology was established by Decision 82/835.[55] Its task was to assist the Commission in the preparation and implementation of its policy in regard to the stimulation of the Community's science and technical potential.[56] It has been replaced by the European Science and Technology

[50] See, generally, M. Ayral, 'Essai de classification des groupes et comités' [1975] *RMC* 330–42. See, regarding the origins of these arrangements under the ECSC Treaty, D. Vignes, *Communauté Européenne de la Charbon et de l'Acier* (Paris, 1956), 24.

[51] Declaration on the powers of implementation of the Commission.

[52] 'Procedure I' in Art. 2 of Dec. 87/373 of 13 July 1987 ([1987] OJ L197/33) laying down procedures for the exercise of implementing powers conferred on the Commission.

[53] 'Procedure II' (*ibid.*). Occasionally the draft may have to be submitted to a 'regulatory' committee ('Procedure III' (*ibid.*)). Management committees are concerned with management of common policies, while regulatory committees are concerned with regulation of a given sector which has already been the subject of a basic measure. See C. Lassalle, 'Les comités et l'évolution institutionnelle de la CEE' [1968] *CDE* 395–420, at 407–8.

[54] H.G. Schermers, 'Comment on Weiler's *The Transformation of Europe*' (1991) 100 *Yale Law Journal* 2525–36, at 2527.

[55] Of 6 Dec. 1982 ([1982] OJ L350/45) on the creation of the Committee for the European Development of Science and Technology.

[56] *Ibid.*, Art. 2(1).

Assembly.[57] The latter is composed of 'high-level' persons in European organizations representing exact and natural sciences.[58]

For the implementation of Comett II (the Community Action Programme on Education and Training), Article 5(2) of Decision 89/27[59] provides for the Commission to be assisted by a committee consisting of two representatives from each Member State and chaired by a Commission representative. In relation to general guidelines regarding the programme, general guidelines regarding Community financial assistance, and questions regarding the general balance of the programme,[60] the committee acts as a management committee. If Commission proposals regarding such guidelines or questions are not approved by the committee, the Council may take a different decision.[61] In the case of measures governing the procedure for selecting the various types of projects to be supported,[62] the Commission is to 'take utmost account' of committee opinions.[63] In addition, Article 5(8) of the same Decision provides for a group of experts to advise the Commission and the committee.

7.3 FREE TRADE AGREEMENTS

Formal arrangements for 'comitology' were made in the Free Trade Agreements. These arrangements might be complemented by informal developments and by arrangements adopted pursuant to other EC–EFTA agreements. Creation of new bodies or simply enlargement of existing Community bodies might be entailed.

7.3.1 Joint Committee Working Parties

The Free Trade Agreements provided that the Joint Committees established thereby might decide to set up any working party that could assist them in carrying out their duties.[64] This option was used once under the Swedish Agreement. A committee, composed of customs officials from the Member States, Commission officials, and Swedish customs officials, was established by Joint Committee Decision 2/73 of February 1973[65] and met regularly twice

[57] Dec. 94/204 of 16 Mar. 1994 ([1994] OJ L98/34) on the creation of the European Science and Technology Assembly.
[58] *Ibid.*, Art. 3(2).
[59] Of 16 Dec. 1988 ([1989] OJ L13/28) adopting the second phase of the programme on cooperation between universities and industry regarding training in the field of technology (COMETT II 1990–4).
[60] *Ibid.*, Art. 5(3)(a).
[61] *Ibid.*, Art. 5(4).
[62] *Ibid.*, Art. 5(3)(b).
[63] *Ibid.*, Art. 5(5).
[64] Art. 31(3) of the Swedish Free Trade Agreement.
[65] *Sverige–EG 1973* (Utrikes- och handelsdepartementen, 1974), bil. 6.

a year. The practice of mandating officials of both Parties to consider problems and produce proposals to be discussed by the Joint Committee was also established in 1974.[66] However, this practice was not formalized through the formal creation of further committees.[67]

7.3.2 Working Groups of Experts

Informal, multilateral contacts between experts seem to have been favoured in practice under the Free Trade Agreements. Thus EC–EFTA expert meetings might be held to discuss Commission draft proposals.[68] Similar meetings were held at least once a year to exchange information on the economic situation in the Community and EFTA States as well as on their respective economic policies. More particular exchanges of information took place regarding, for example, application of indirect taxation to trade across frontiers[69] and the regulation of financial services.[70]

7.3.3 Programme Committees

The commitment to closer integration expressed in the Free Trade Agreements was reflected in the conclusion of numerous Co-operation Agreements providing for participation by EFTA States in Community programmes and, more particularly, for the representation of these States in the relevant programme committees. For example, the Co-operation Agreement regarding research in the field of wood, including cork, as a renewable raw material[71] provided for the enlargement of the Management, Co-ordination, and Advisory Committee on Raw Materials, which assisted the Commission in implementation of the Agreement, to include three Swedish representatives.[72] However, those representatives might only attend discussions concerning wood, including cork, as a renewable raw material.

Again, a Co-operation Agreement was concluded between Sweden and the Community designed to increase the international co-operation and the exchange of research scientists between the Parties. According to Article 4

[66] *Sverige–EG 1974* (Utrikes- och handelsdepartementen, 1975), bil. 6.

[67] Cf., regarding possible enlargement of Coreper to include EFTA representatives, the suggestions made in the Swedish Government memorandum of 6 Sept. 1971 presented to the Commission during negotiation of the Free Trade Agreement. The memorandum is reproduced in Annex 3 to D. Viklund, *Spelet om Frihandelsavtalet* (Stockholm, 1977).

[68] See, e.g., *Redovisning av det svenska integrationsarbetet våren 1988-mars 1989* (Utrikesdepartementets handelsavdelning, 1989), 37.

[69] *Sverige–EFTA–EG 1987* (Utrikesdepartementets handelsavdelning, 1988), 24.

[70] *Ibid.*, 35. [71] [1988] OJ L276/5. [72] Art. 4 of the Co-operation Agreement.

of the Agreement,[73] Sweden was entitled to send a delegate[74] to the Committee for European Development of Science and Technology.[75]

However, such arrangements might not secure for EFTA States any real say in the operation of Community programmes, and these States might not be represented at all in some programme committees, such as that for COMETT II.[76] Apparently, the Community considered that their representation would jeopardize its decision-making autonomy and, more particularly, would have prejudiced EEA negotiations.[77]

7.4 EUROPE AGREEMENTS

The Europe Agreements formally recognize the importance of participation by the Parties in international standards bodies. For example, Article 74 of the Polish Agreement provides for co-operation between the Parties to encourage the participation of Poland in such bodies as CEN and CENELEC. The implication is that economic and political transformation of countries such as Poland sufficient to permit their full participation therein may be an essential element in their closer integration with the Community.

The Europe Agreements also provide for subcommittees to be established by the Association Councils. For example, Article 107 of the Polish Agreement provides that the Association Council may establish subcommittees to assist it.

[73] Co-operation Agreement between the Community and Sweden on a programme to stimulate the international cooperation and interchange needed by European research scientists (Science) ([1990] OJ L50/22).

[74] The delegate was only to participate in the definition and outline of plans for the stimulation of the international cooperation and interchange needed by European research scientists and in the examination of applications submitted under the stimulation plan (*ibid.* Art. 4). The delegate was not apparently to participate in the more general work of the Committee and was not a member. According to Art. 8 of Dec. 82/835 of 6 Dec. 1982 ([1982] OJ L350/45) on the creation of the Committee for the European Development of Science and Technology, where an opinion or topic 'bears upon a question of a confidential nature', only members of the Committee and Commission representatives may take part in meetings.

[75] Moreover, according to Art. 2 of the Co-operation Agreement in the Field of Medical and Health Research ([1990] OJ L74/2), the Management and Co-ordination Advisory Committee on Medical and Health Research was enlarged to include two Swedish representatives, who could also attend relevant meetings of experts within the concerted action committees established to assist the former body. Likewise, Art. 4 of the Agreement for co-operation between Euratom and Sweden in the field of controlled thermo-nuclear fusion and plasma physics ([1976] OJ L162/28) provided for Sweden to be represented in the Liaison Group set up within the framework of the Euratom programme.

[76] See sect. 7.2.6 above. Instead, Art. 7 of the Agreement between the Community and Sweden establishing Co-operation in the field of training in the context of the implementation of COMETT II (1990–4) ([1990] OJ L102/42) established a Joint Committee to represent Sweden in matters relating to this country. Art. 9 also required the Commission to ensure that the composition of the expert group (established pursuant to Art. 5(8) of Dec. 89/27) was such as to enable it to give any advice required in regard to the participation of universities and industry from Sweden.

[77] SvDN, 18 Dec. 1989.

More particularly, according to Article 10 of Protocol 2 to the Agreement, which concerns ECSC products, the Parties agreed that the Association Council should establish a contact group[78] to discuss implementation of this Protocol.[79] Article 33 of Protocol 4 to the Agreement, concerning the definition of the concept of 'originating products' and methods of administrative co-operation, also provides for the establishment of a Customs Co-operation Committee.

Committee work within the Community suggests that the potential of such work for promoting integration between the Parties to the Europe Agreements should not be disregarded. At the same time, however, encouragement of 'government by experts' and demands that Central and Eastern European countries 'democratize' may not be entirely consistent.[80]

7.5 EEA AGREEMENT

During negotiations for the EEA Agreement the possibility was discussed of enlarging the Community institutions to include EFTA representatives whenever these institutions dealt with matters related to the EEA.[81] In particular, there were suggestions that Coreper and the Commission[82] should be enlarged to include persons appointed by EFTA States.

However, Article 4 of the Merger Treaty only provided for Coreper to include representatives of Member States,[83] and Article 10(1) of the Merger Treaty[84] expressly provided that only nationals of Member States might be Commissioners. Hence, Treaty amendments would apparently have been necessary for the suggested enlargements to be permissible. On the other hand, arrangements for close involvement of non-members of the Commission in Commission work would not have been entirely without precedent.

[78] Cf. the role envisaged for Coreper and for 'preparatory talks in the form of joint meetings in Brussels, in particular at ambassadorial level' in the Report from the Council to the Essen European Council on a strategy to prepare for the accession of the associated CCEE, *Europe Doc*. No. 1916 (14 Dec. 1994), 2–3.

[79] Sub-committees on customs co-operation, transport, agriculture, approximation of legislation, science and technology, an *ad hoc* group on ECSC matters, and a working group on implementation of competition rules have been established under the Hungarian Agreement (Annex II to the Hungarian–EC Association Council Dec. 1/94 of 7 Mar. 1994 ([1994] OJ L242/23) on its Rules of Procedure). However, the 'efficiency' of such groups is disputed. See the Opinion of the Economic and Social Committee of 25 Jan. 1995 ([1995] OJ C102/40) on relations between the EU and Russia, Ukraine, and Belarus, para. 3.25.

[80] D. Kennedy and D. E. Webb, 'The Limits of Integration: Eastern Europe and the European Communities' (1993) *CMLRev*. 1095–117, at 1102, n. 9.

[81] Arrangements made for representation of Finland in EFTA organs prior to her admission to full EFTA membership could, perhaps, have been taken as a suitable model. See, generally, *Den Europeiska frihandelssammanslutningen* (EFTA Secretariat, Geneva, 1988), 34.

[82] SvDN, 10 Oct. 1989.

[83] See now Art. 151(1) EC, as amended by the TEU.

[84] See now Art. 157(1) EC, as amended by the TEU.

Originally, the EEC Commission, like the ECSC High Authority, had nine members.[85] The Euratom Commission, in contrast, had only five, though Article 133 of the Euratom Treaty provided that the Council, acting unanimously, could agree that the government of a Member State[86] might accredit to the Commission a qualified representative to undertake permanent liaison duties. Such an arrangement might perhaps have been treated as constituting some kind of precedent for securing EFTA 'liaison' with the Commission. In the event, however, the idea of reforming the Commission to accommodate EFTA involvement does not seem to have been pursued in negotiations for the EEA Agreement.

Instead, it was suggested that EFTA observers might be admitted to meetings of Coreper and even the Council,[87] when matters of relevance to the EEA were discussed. The grant of observer status was apparently given serious consideration by the Community[88] and would have been consistent with treating the EEA Agreement as entailing 'affiliate' membership of the Union for EFTA States.[89] However, the established Community position is that only Member States can 'exert an effective influence on the life of the Community'.[90] Hence, it was never envisaged that representatives of EFTA States would be entitled to vote in the Council,[91] let alone enjoy a veto.[92]

Even so, such suggestions proved extremely controversial.[93] In particular, the European Parliament, which must approve the conclusion of Association Agreements under Article 238 of the EC Treaty, insisted that its own prerogatives and the autonomy of Community decision-making must not be jeopardized.[94]

As a result, ideas of formal arrangements for EFTA involvement in the Commission, Council, or Coreper were abandoned early in the negotiations for the EEA Agreement.[95] Instead, arrangements were made for establishment of EEA committees or, more usually, for enlargement of existing Community committees.

[85] Art. 157 of the EC Treaty.

[86] In practice, Luxembourg.

[87] Cf. the Commission suggestion regarding arrangements 'to associate other European countries as "partner-members" in specific Community policies, with the possibility to participate (but not to vote) in certain Community meetings on subjects of trans-European interest' in *Europe and the Challenge of Enlargement*, Bull. EC, Supp. 3/92, 18–19.

[88] *European Report*, No. 1485 (5 Apr. 1989).

[89] Such affiliation was, at one stage of the negotiations for the EEA Agreement, mooted as a possible option for EFTA States. See SvD, 21 July 1991.

[90] *Opinion on Problems Raised by Applications for Membership from the United Kingdom, Ireland, Denmark and Norway*, Bull. EC, Supp. 4/68, 9.

[91] Cf. the admission of Sweden as an observer to the Interim Committee established to represent Parties under the European Patent Convention (SÖ 1980:2).

[92] A. Gradin, *Europa utsikt* 4/1990, 2.

[93] *Financial Times*, 23 Nov. 1989 and 23 Mar. 1990.

[94] Resolution of 14 Dec. 1989 ([1990] OJ C15/336) on relations between the EC and the EFTA States, paras 8 and 9.

[95] SvDN, 21 Nove. 1989.

7.5.1 Sub-committees and Working Groups of the EEA Joint Committee and EEA Council

Article 94(3) of the EEA Agreement provides that the EEA Joint Committee may establish subcommittees or working groups to assist it with its tasks.[96] In the event, sub-committees, composed of representatives of the Contracting Parties,[97] have been established for the free movement of goods, competition, state aid, state monopolies, intellectual property, and procurement; free movement of capital and services; free movement of persons; 'flanking and horizontal policies', such as research and development and environmental protection; and legal and institutional matters.[98] They are to prepare decisions to be taken by the EEA Joint Committee,[99] and consultations are to take place in these sub-committees, unless a Party requests consultation in the Joint Committee itself.[100]

Presumably, the EEA Council could also create what might amount to an enlarged version of Coreper to include EFTA representatives. Certainly, an Agreed Minute *ad* Article 91 of the Agreement stated that the EEA Council should, if necessary, provide in its Rules of Procedure for the possibility of establishing subcommittees or working parties.[101] More particularly, according to an Agreed Minute *ad* Article 14(3) of Protocol 11, on Mutual Assistance in Customs Matters, the Community, while fully complying with the coordinating role of the Commission, will develop direct contacts with EFTA States, where such contacts may grant flexibility and efficiency to the functioning of the Protocol, though only on a reciprocal basis.

7.5.2 Working Groups of Experts

Article 99(1) of the EEA Agreement provides that as soon as new legislation is being drafted by the Commission in a field which is governed by this Agreement, the Commission shall informally seek advice from experts of the EFTA States in the same way as it seeks advice from experts of the

[96] According to an Agreed Minute *ad* Art. 94(3), the Joint Committee would at one of its first meetings, when adopting its Rules of Procedure, decide on the setting up of subcommittees or working groups particularly needed to assist it in carrying out its tasks, e.g. in the field of origin and other customs matters.

[97] Art. 16(1) of Dec. 1/94 of 8 Feb. 1994 ([1994] OJ L85/60) adopting the Rules of Procedure of the EEA Joint Committee. [98] *Ibid.*, Art. 15(1). [99] *Ibid.*, Art. 15(2).

[100] *Ibid.*, Art. 15(3). The Joint Committee may also establish working groups for individual tasks.

[101] Art. 11 of Dec. 1/94 of 17 May 1994 ([1994] OJ L138/39) adopting the Rules of Procedure of the EEA Council duly makes such provision. EFTA States have also established their own Standing Committee. See the EFTA Agreement on a Standing Committee of EFTA States (*Europeiska ekonomiska samarbetsområdet*, prop. 1991/92:170).

Member States for the elaboration of its proposals.[102] This provision puts pre-existing EC–EFTA practice on a formal and more systematic basis.[103]

7.5.3 Management Committees

Article 100 of the EEA Agreement provides that the Commission shall ensure experts of the EFTA States as wide a participation as possible, according to the areas concerned, in the preparatory stage of draft measures to be submitted subsequently to the committees which assist the Commission in the exercise of its executive powers.[104] Each EFTA State will designate its own experts, who will be involved on an equal footing with experts from the Member States in the preparatory work. The Commission will pursue consultations as long as deemed necessary, until submitting its proposal to a formal meeting of the relevant committee.[105]

When submitting its proposal, the Commission is to transmit to the Council the views of the experts of the EFTA States. These arrangements mean that EFTA experts have a more limited role than representatives of Member States. However, it was thought that to go further and to permit EFTA States to vote in management committees, as was sought by these States,[106] would conflict with Community retention of decision-making autonomy.[107]

7.5.4 Programme Committees

Article 81(b) of the EEA Agreement provides, in connection with co-operation outside the four freedoms, that the status of EFTA States in the committees which assist the Commission in the management or development of a Community activity to which these States may be contributing financially by virtue

[102] Although such arrangements were apparently criticized by the External Relations Committee of the European Parliament (*Agence Europe*, No. 5221, 24 Mar. 1990), the Parliament as a whole considered that for EFTA experts to give their opinions prior to the drafting of proposals would be acceptable. See the Resolution of 5 Apr. 1990 ([1990] OJ C113/172) on relations between the EEC and EFTA, para. 5 and the Resolution of 12 June 1990 ([1990] OJ C175/51) on economic and trade relations between the EC and the EFTA countries, para. 10.

[103] Section 7.3.2 above.

[104] In addition, Pt. XXI of Annex II, on Technical Regulations, Standards, Testing and Certification, provides that Art. 100 shall apply to the participation of EFTA States in the work of the European Organization of Technical Approval.

[105] Declaration by the EC on the Participation of the EFTA States' Experts in EEA Relevant EC Committees in Application of Art. 100 of the Agreement. An exchange of letters, attached to the EEA Agreement, deals, more particularly, with the Banking Advisory Committee.

[106] EFTA States insisted on the close link between the acceptability of the substance of Community legislation and arrangements for its implementation within the framework of the powers delegated to the Commission. See para. 2.1 of the Commission Communication concerning a proposed Council decision authorizing the Commission to negotiate an agreement with the EFTA States on the creation of a European Economic Space.

[107] *Relations Between the Community and EFTA*, 14th Report of the House of Lords Select Committee on the European Communities, HL(1989–90) 55–2, 26.

of their participation therein shall take full account of that contribution. More details are provided by Protocol 31 to the Agreement, on Co-operation in Specific Fields Outside the Four Freedoms.[108]

Article 1 of the Protocol deals with co-operation in relation to research and technological development. Article 1(3) provides for EFTA States to participate fully in all the Community committees which assist the Commission in the management, development, and implementation of the Framework Programme of Community activities[109] and its specific programmes.[110] Moreover, given the particular nature of the co-operation foreseen in this field, representatives of EFTA States shall be associated with the work of the Scientific and Technical Research Committee (Crest) and other Community committees which the Commission consults in this field, to the extent necessary for the good functioning of that co-operation.[111] According to an exchange of letters attached to the Agreement, this 'association' means that EFTA States should be invited to send experts to participate in Crest meetings when it is advising the Commission on matters relevant to the EEA, though not when it is advising the Commission on internal Community matters or is advising the Council.

As regards programmes in the field of education, training, and youth generally, Article 4(4) of the Protocol provides that the EFTA States shall, as from the start of co-operation in programmes to which they contribute financially,[112] participate fully in all Community committees which assist the Commission in the management or development of these programmes. They shall also participate in the various activities of the Community involving the exchange of information including, where appropriate, contacts and meetings of experts, seminars, and conferences.[113]

Finally, Article 5(3) of the Protocol provides for EFTA States to participate fully in the Community committees which assist the Commission in the management or development of the social programme, except for matters relating to the distribution of Community financial resources between Member States.

According to a Joint Declaration annexed to the EEA Agreement,[114] the

[108] As amended by EEA Joint Committee Dec. 10/94 of 12 Aug. 1994 ([1994] OJ L253/32). Art. 3(1) of Prot. 31 also provides for the adoption of the necessary decisions to ensure the participation of EFTA States in the European Environmental Agency.

[109] Dec. 90/221 of 23 Apr. 1990 ([1990] OJ L117/28) concerning the framework programme of Community activities in the field of research and technological development (1990–4).

[110] Art. 1(1)(c) of Prot. 31. There is concern in the European Parliament that its budgetary powers may be prejudiced. See the Opinion of the Committee on Budgets in the Report of the Committee on Foreign Affairs and Security on the Commission Proposal to the Council on the conclusion of the Agreement on the EEA, EP Doc. 3–0316/92, Annex I, 10.

[111] Art. 1(1)(d) of Prot. 31.

[112] In accordance with Art. 82(1)(a) of the EEA Agreement.

[113] Art. 4(5) of Prot. 31.

[114] Joint Declaration on Applicable Procedures in Cases where, by virtue of Art. 76 and Pt. VI of the Agreement and Corresponding Protocols, EFTA States Participate Fully in EC Committees.

EFTA States shall have the same rights as Member States within such committees,[115] except in respect of voting procedures, if any. In reaching its decision on matters with which the committees are concerned, the Commission shall take due account of the views expressed by the EFTA States in the same manner as of the views expressed by the Member States before voting. In cases where the Member States have the possibility of appealing to the Council of the Union against the decision of the Commission, the EFTA States may raise the issue in the EEA Joint Committee in conformity with Article 5 of the Agreement.

7.5.5 Committees Relevant to the Good Functioning of the Agreement

Article 101(1) of the EEA Agreement provides that, in respect of committees which are covered neither by Article 100 nor by Article 81(b) of the Agreement, experts from EFTA States shall be associated with their work when such association is called for by the good functioning of the Agreement. These committees are listed in Protocol 37[116] to the Agreement.[117] They include the Scientific Committee for Food,[118] the Pharmaceutical Committee, the Scientific Veterinary Committee, the Committee on Transport Infrastructure, the Administrative Commission on Social Security for Migrant Workers,[119] the Contact Committee on Money Laundering, the Advisory Committee on Restrictive Practices and Dominant Positions, and the Advisory Committee on Concentrations.[120] The modalities of such association are set out in the relevant sectoral Protocols and Annexes. If it appears to the Contracting Parties that association should be extended to other committees which present

[115] The Declaration also applies to statistics committees. See below sect. 7.5.6.

[116] Containing the List Provided for in Art. 101.

[117] In addition, Art. 14 of Prot. 10, on Simplification of Inspections and Formalities in Respect of Carriage of Goods, provides that Contracting Parties may establish 'consultation groups'.

[118] Pt. XII of Annex II, on Technical Regs, Standards, Testing and Certification, provides that the Commission nominates from highly qualified scientific persons from the EFTA States at least one person who will be present in the Scientific Committee for Food and who will be able to express his views therein. His position will be recorded separately.

[119] Annex VI, on Social Security, stipulates that each EFTA State may send a representative who will be 'present in an advisory capacity (observer)'.

[120] Art. 6 of Prot. 23, concerning the Co-operation between the Surveillance Authorities, provides that each surveillance authority and the states falling within its competence shall be entitled to be present in the advisory committees of the other surveillance authority and to express their views therein. They shall not, however, have the right to vote. An Agreed Minute *ad* Prot. 37 indicates that such entitlement applies not only in relation to the Advisory Committee on Restrictive Practices and Dominant Positions but also in relation to the Advisory Committee on Restrictive Practices and Monopolies in the Transport Industry, the Advisory Committee on Agreements and Dominant Positions in Maritime Transport, and the Advisory Committee on Agreements and Dominant Positions in Air Transport. Art. 5(3) of Prot. 24, on Co-operation in the Field of Control of Concentrations, provides the same rights in relation to the Advisory Committee on Concentrations.

similar characteristics, Article 101(2) provides that the EEA Joint Committee may amend Protocol 37.[121]

According to a Joint Declaration annexed to the Agreement, having regard to the association of experts of the EFTA States with the work of the Community committees listed in Protocol 37, Community experts shall on the same basis be associated, at Community request, with the work of any corresponding bodies among the EFTA States or set up by the EFTA Surveillance Authority relating to the same subject matter as is covered by the Community committees concerned.

7.5.6 Statistics Committees

Article 76 of the EEA Agreement and Protocol 30, on Specific Provisions on the Organization and Co-operation in the Field of Statistics, deal with co-operation in the field of statistics. Article 1 of this Protocol provides that a conference of representatives of national statistical organizations of the Contracting Parties, the Statistical Office of the European Union (Eurostat), and the Office of the Statistical Adviser of the EFTA States shall be created. Moreover, Article 2 of the same Protocol provides that the EFTA States shall participate fully in the Community committees which assist the Commission in the management or development of actions in the field of statistics in so far as the subjects dealt with are covered by the Agreement. The following committees are involved: the Committee on the Statistical Programmes of the European Communities; the Committee on Monetary, Financial, and Balance of Payments Statistics; the Committee on Statistical Confidentiality; the Committee on the Harmonization of the Compilation of GNP at Market Prices; and the Committee on Economic and Social Statistics.[122]

7.6 CONCLUSION

Committee work offers a potential basis for the involvement of third states and traders therefrom in Community decision-making. However, serious impediments to realization of this potential may be implicit in practice under the EC Treaty.

Such practice is affected by relations between Community institutions. In particular, the preference of the Commission[123] for treating issues arising in

[121] In an Agreed Minute *ad* Prot. 37 the Coordinating Group on Mutual Recognition of Higher-Education Diplomas was added to the list in this Prot. According to EEA Joint Committee Dec. 5/94 of 8 Feb. 1994 ([1994] OJ L85/71) amending Prot. 37 and Annex VII to the EEA Agreement, each EFTA State may designate one observer to the Committee.

[122] Agreed Minute *ad* Prot. 30.

[123] In itself the formal question of the particular EC Treaty provision on which a Community measure is based may be of less concern to the Commission, and also the Council, than to the Court. See Case 78/77 *Firma Johann Lührs* v. *Hauptzollamt Hamburg-Jonas* [1978] ECR 169.

trade with third states as commercial policy issues[124] may reflect the exclusivity of Community powers in this policy field[125] and the desire of the Commission to strengthen its position in the Community institutional system by invoking these powers. At the same, attitudes within the Commission may differ, as other Directorates General may be less willing than Directorate General I, which is responsible for commercial policy, to accept resolution of such issues solely in commercial policy terms.[126] In short, Community practice may be determined by complex inter-institutional and intra-institutional relations.[127]

Such relations may have affected committee work under the Free Trade Agreements. For example, in the field of environmental protection the Swedish Government preferred to hold direct talks with Directorate General XI, which has responsibility for environmental policy. The Commission, however, might treat environmental issues arising in the context of relations with third states as matters of commercial policy, and so talks tended to be held with Directorate General I.

Committee work under the Europe Agreements may be similarly affected. In contrast to the ideas aired in connection with discussion of affiliate membership or 'partner-membership' of the Union, these Agreements do not provide for third state participation, even on a non-voting basis, in 'Community meetings'.[128] While informal contacts between States such as Poland and Community bodies may be expected to increase in accordance with the 'structured relationship' envisaged at the June 1993 meeting of the European Council,[129] the development and effectiveness of these contacts may be limited by the same factors that used to affect informal EC–EFTA contacts.[130] In essence, such

[124] Case 275/87 *EC Commission* v. *EC Council* [1989] ECR 259. However, the Court may be concerned that action under Art. 113 EC should not disturb 'internal' Community activity. See Opinion 1/94 *(Competence of the Community to conclude international agreements on services and on the protection of intellectual property)* [1994] ECR I–5267. See also, regarding transport policy, Opinion 2/92 *(Third Revised Decision of the OECD on Internation Treatment)* (not yet reported).

[125] Cf. G. Close, 'External Relations in the Air Transport Sector: Air Transport Policy or the Common Commercial Policy?' (1990) 27 *CMLRev.* 107–27. See, more particularly, the Explanatory Memorandum to the Commission Recommendation for a Council Dec. on the opening of negotiations between the EEC and EFTA countries on scheduled air passenger services, COM(90)18.

[126] Cf., in the case of shipping, A. Bredima-Savopoulou and J. Tzoannos, *The Common Shipping Policy of the EEC* (Amsterdam, 1990), 235–6.

[127] See, regarding objections on the impact on Community policies other than commercial policy, the Opinion of the Economic and Social Committee of 27 Nov. 1991 ([1992] OJ C40/20) on the Commission proposal for a Council Dec. concerning an Agreement between the EEC, the Kingdom of Norway, and the Kingdom of Sweden on Civil Aviation., para. 2.2.3.

[128] See, regarding these ideas, *Europe and the Challenge of Enlargement*, Bull. EC, Supp. 3/92, 18–19.

[129] Annex II to the Conclusions of the Presidency (Bull. EC 6–1993, I.26).

[130] According to *Europe Agreements and Beyond: A Strategy to Prepare the Countries of Central and Eastern Europe for Accession*, COM(94)320, 2, only limited progress in the development of the 'structured relationship' had been achieved by July 1994.

states may be unable effectively to influence relations within the Community which determine approaches of the latter to issues arising under the Europe Agreements.[131]

The EEA Agreement creates a much more developed basis for committee work in the context of EC–EFTA relations. EFTA States may lack voting rights in enlarged Community committees, but the trade liberalization and other requirements embodied in the Agreement apparently mean that the interests they express and positions they adopt in such committees have to be given serious attention. Opportunities may thus be presented for their participation in networking and even coalition-building. In other words, for such states committee work may entail opportunities to influence the internal Community relations which determine Community approaches to issues arising under the Agreement. To the extent that the opportunities are exploited, such approaches may become more readily reconcilable with their own, and so achievement of the integration sought by the EEA Agreement may be facilitated.

[131] Such states may 'remain squarely on the EC's external affairs agenda, which is shaped by a variety of internal political considerations over which they have no influence'. See D. Kennedy and D. E. Webb, 'The Limits of Integration: Eastern Europe and the European Communities' (1993) 30 *CMLRev*. 1095–117, at 1109.

8

Judicial Control

8.1 INTRODUCTION

Judicial control may play an important role in integration processes, at least where, as in the case of the European Court of Justice, the judiciary has a formal obligation to promote integration. Such control may not simply be central to the interpretation of trade liberalization and other requirements embodied in the EC Treaty. To the extent that the other Community institutions and national institutions must respect such requirements, the natural implication is that the work of these institutions and, hence, their treatment of trade issues may be affected by judicial interpretation of the same requirements. As a result, the operation of provisions governing trade may not only be affected by, but may also affect, the operation of provisions governing the presentation and resolution of trade issues.

Recognition of the importance of judicial control for integration processes seems to have been more influential in negotiations for the EEA Agreement[1] than in negotiations for the Free Trade Agreements and the Europe Agreements. Indeed, the draft EEA Agreement envisaged the creation of two new judicial bodies: the EEA Court of Justice and the EEA Court of First Instance. These courts were designed to go further in reconciling institutional separation with application of common rules than the arrangements for joint decision-making and committee work also made in the Agreement. In the view of the Commission, such reconciliation was achieved by the draft Agreement without the role of the existing Court of Justice being prejudiced. According to the Commission, the draft Agreement meant that no court other than the Court of Justice would have jurisdiction to give preliminary rulings on the interpretation of the EC Treaty, that the EEA Court would not apply the EEA Agreement in ignorance of Community law or the case law of the Court of Justice, that the competition rules would not be applied in a disorganized manner, that economic agents would not be denied access to judicial review by the procedure for preliminary rulings, and that the EFTA States would not be made

[1] At the first meeting in July 1989 of EC–EFTA Working Group V, on Legal and Institutional Questions, it was agreed that procedures for uniform interpretation and dispute settlement within the EEA would be needed. References were made to a future EEA judicial body and to a formula based on Prot. 2 to the Lugano Convention (*Present stage of discussions in EC–EFTA Working Group V with regard to a Future EEA Judicial Body*).

subject to foreign judges.[2] However, as *Opinion 1/91*[3] of the Court of Justice underlined, judicial arrangements cannot so easily secure reconciliation of perceived contradictions in legal frameworks for integration between the Community and third states.

8.2 EC TREATY

The Court of Justice is required by Article 4(1) of the EC Treaty to contribute to the achievement of Community tasks.[4] The contribution expected of the Court is indicated in Article 164 of the Treaty, according to which it is to ensure that in the interpretation and application of this Treaty the law is observed.

In particular, the Court is to uphold the 'rule of law' enshrined in Article 4(1) of the Treaty, which states that each Community institution is to act within the limits of the powers conferred on it by the Treaty. It also interprets Community law to be applied by national courts. By interpreting many provisions of Community law as having direct effects before such courts, it has ensured that its judicial control function within the EC Treaty framework is shared with the latter.

8.2.1 European Court of Justice

The Court of Justice has plenary jurisdiction to ensure that the Community institutions do not act or fail to act in breach of Community law and to rule on complaints that Member States are violating Community law.[5] It also has jurisdiction to deliver preliminary rulings requested by national courts under Article 177 of the EC Treaty.

Plenary Jurisdiction

Member States and Community institutions have privileged standing to invoke the plenary jurisdiction of the Court of Justice, but the standing of private persons is more limited. Opportunities for the latter to bring proceedings before the Court tend to be limited, according to the case law of the Court, to issues raised by detailed decisions rather than broader policy issues.

In particular, the admissibility of proceedings by a private person for

[2] Submission of the Commission in Opinion 1/91 (*Draft Agreement between the Community, on the one hand, and the countries of the European Free Trade Association, on the other, relating to the creation of the European Economic Area*) [1991] ECR I–6079, I–6093.

[3] *Ibid.*

[4] See also Art. E of the TEU.

[5] Arts 169 and 170 EC. According to Art. 219 of the same Treaty, the Member States undertake not to submit a dispute concerning the interpretation or application of the Treaty to any method of settlement other than those provided for therein.

annulment of a Council or Commission act under Article 173 of the EC Treaty depends on the act in question being of direct and individual concern to him. Hence, such proceedings are not admissible against an act having general application. They will only be admissible against an act which affects the legal position of a private person because of a factual situation which differentiates him from all other persons in the same way as would an act addressed to him.[6] Thus, for example, an importer might be unable to challenge a Commission decision authorizing a Member State to apply intra-Community surveillance to products originating in third states.[7] Similarly, a private person may only bring Article 175 proceedings against the Council or Commission for failure to act where one of these institutions has failed to address an act to him.[8] Even in the case of an application for damages under Article 215(2), these may only be awarded in respect of a legislative act, where there has been a serious breach of a general principle of law designed to protect the interests of individuals.[9]

As explained below, these limitations on the possibilities for private persons to take advantage of the plenary jurisdiction of the Court of Justice seriously affect the significance of the rights enjoyed by third states to intervene in proceedings before the Court.

Preliminary Rulings

The Court of Justice may deliver a preliminary ruling on questions of Community law referred to it by a national court under Article 177 of the EC Treaty. National courts of last resort are formally obliged by Article 177(3) to request a ruling on questions of this kind raised before them.[10]

It is through preliminary rulings, such as *Cassis de Dijon*,[11] that the Court of Justice has made its main contribution to the development of trade liberalization and other requirements in the Treaty.[12] More particularly, much

[6] Case 26/86 *Firma Deutz und Geldermann, Sektkellerei Breisach/Baden GmbH* v. *EC Council* [1987] ECR 941, 952.

[7] Case 82/87R *Autexpo* v. *EC Commission* [1987] ECR 2131.

[8] See, e.g., Case 246/81 *Nicholas William, Lord Bethell* v. *EC Commission* [1982] ECR 2277.

[9] See, e.g., Case 153/73 *Holtz and Willemsen* v. *EC Council* [1974] ECR 675, 693.

[10] According to J. Weiler, 'The Transformation of Europe' (1991) *Yale Law Journal* 2403—83, at 2426, 'the ingenious nature of Art. 177 ensured that national courts did not feel the empowerment of the European Court of Justice was at their expense'. However, the insistence of the ECJ that questions referred must be related to a real dispute means that the factual background must be indicated. See Case C/378/93 *La Pyramide Sàrl* [1994] ECR I–3999, I–4008. Apparently, therefore, the process of 'applying law to fact' is not wholly reserved to the national court making the reference, and so the position of the latter is not wholly unimpaired.

[11] Case 120/78 *Rewe-Zentral* v. *Bundesmonopolverwaltung für Branntwein* [1979] ECR 649.

[12] It may be something of an oversimplification to say (see K.-H. Ladeur, 'European Community Institutional Reforms: Extra-National Management as an Alternative Model to Federalism' (1990/2) LIEI 1–21, 6) that dependence of the Court on the initiative of plaintiffs seeking to assert their rights limits its decision-making resources and thus imposes a 'political constraint' with regard to judgments concerning more complex integration problems.

decision-making in implementation of harmonization acts adopted by the Community is left to national authorities, and the new approach of the Commission to harmonization[13] implies an expanded role for such authorities in decision-making of this kind. Their decisions can be challenged before national courts, which may request a preliminary ruling from the Court of Justice[14] on the interpretation or validity of the act concerned.[15] Such rulings may enable this Court also to contribute to determining detailed requirements of harmonization acts.

The impact of preliminary rulings might have been limited if their function had been treated as being only that of an advisory opinion.[16] However, as the Court of Justice insists, 'the purpose of a preliminary ruling is to decide a question of law'.[17] Indeed, provided that there is a 'genuine dispute', the Court of Justice will deliver a preliminary ruling which enables a national court of one Member State effectively to determine whether the legal provisions of another Member State are compatible with Community law.[18] Thus national courts may be able to contribute to securing respect for Community law beyond their own Member State.

On the other hand, the possibility of a preliminary ruling being requested is dependent on national law, to the extent that access to national courts is a matter for national law. Member States must merely ensure that their law in this regard is non-discriminatory and does not render the exercise of rights conferred by Community law impossible in practice.[19]

Moreover, Article 177 does not expressly state that preliminary rulings are binding. In practice, their binding character may never have been seriously

[13] See sect. 7.2.2 above.

[14] Joined Cases 133/136/85 *Walter Rau Lebensmittelwerke* v. *Bundesanstalt für landwirtschaftliche Marktordnung* [1987] ECR 2289, 2338.

[15] The fact that the national court is empowered to determine which questions it intends to submit to the Court is an inherent feature of the system of means of redress established by the Treaty. It is not, therefore, an argument capable of justifying a broad interpretation of the conditions of admissibility laid down in Art. 173 of the Treaty. See Case 97/85 *Union Deutsche Lebensmittelwerke GmbH* v. *EC Commission* [1987] ECR 2265, 2287.

[16] Case 244/80 *Pasquale Foglia* v. *Mariella Novello* [1981] ECR 3045, 3062.

[17] Case 52/76 *Benedetti* v. *Munari* [1977] ECR 163, 183. Hence, the jurisdiction of the Court to reply to a request for a preliminary ruling is subject to the requirement that the request emanate from a court or tribunal which has acted in the general framework of its task of judging, independently and in accordance with the law, cases coming within the jurisdiction conferred on it by law. See Case 338/85 *Fratelli Pardini SpA* v. *Ministero del Commercio con l'Estero and Banca Toscana (Lucca branch)* [1988] ECR 2041, 2074. See also Case 14/86 *Pretore di Salò* v. *Persons unknown* [1987] ECR 2545, 2567.

[18] Case C–150/88 *KG Eau de Cologne and Parfumerie-Fabrik Glochengasse No. 4711* v. *Provide Srl* [1989] ECR I–3891. This ruling did not refer to the difficulties which might be raised for national courts and which were previously noted in Case 244/80 *Pasquale Foglia* v. *Mariella Novello* [1981] ECR 3045, 3064, though in the latter ruling the ECJ took the view that there was no 'genuine dispute' before the national court concerned (3059).

[19] Case 130/79 *Express Dairy Foods* v. *Intervention Board for Agricultural Produce* [1980] ECR 1887, 1900. See also Case 811/79 *Amministrazione delle Finanze dello Stato* v. *Ariete* [1980] ECR 2545, 2554–5.

doubted, and there may be little reason why national courts should not feel bound by such a ruling once they have decided to request one.[20] Even so, in the *Fifth Annual Report to the European Parliament on its Monitoring of the Application of Community Law*[21] the Commission noted that problems could arise because rules regarding costs for the parties varied between Member States.[22] More fundamentally, the Commission asserted that misuse by national courts of last resort of the *acte clair* doctrine,[23] according to which preliminary rulings need not be sought on questions of Community law where the answer is 'clear', had the effect of emasculating the Article 177 procedure.[24]

The Court of Justice implicitly seeks to overcome the latter problem through co-operation with national courts.[25] Thus the Court of Justice accepts that the national court to which a preliminary ruling is addressed may properly consider a further such ruling to be necessary before giving judgment in the main proceedings. In particular, a national court may be justified in doing so when it encounters fresh difficulties in understanding or applying the preliminary ruling, when it refers a fresh question of law to the Court, or when it submits new considerations which may lead the Court to give a different answer to a question submitted earlier. However, it is not permissible to use the right to refer further questions to the Court as a means of contesting the validity of the preliminary ruling delivered previously, as this would call in question the allocation of jurisdiction as between national courts and the Court of Justice under Article 177.[26]

If a national court does not demonstrate the co-operative attitude expected by the Court of Justice, it may be formally possible for the Commission to obtain from the Court of Justice a ruling under Article 169 of the Treaty[27] to the effect that the national court had misinterpreted Community law. At the very least, it may be possible to obtain a ruling that a national court of last resort had violated its obligation in Article 177(3) to refer questions of Community law for a preliminary ruling. However, prior to its amendment

[20] H. G. Schermers, 'Opinion 1/91 of the Court of Justice of Justice, 14 December 1991: Opinion 1/92 of the Court of Justice, 10 April 1992' (1992) 29 *CML Rev.* 991, 1007. See also the research reported in J. Korte, *Primus Inter Pares: The European Court and National Courts* (Baden-Baden, 1991), 86–7.

[21] COM(88) 425.

[22] The real effectiveness of the procedure may also vary depending on the delays arising in judicial procedures in the different Member States. See, regarding the variations that may arise, *Financial Times*, 13 Jan. 1992.

[23] See, generally, M. Lagrange, 'The Theory of the Acte Clair: A Bone of Contention or a Source of Unity?' (1971) 8 *CMLRev.* 313–24.

[24] COM(88)425, 6.

[25] The importance of the attitudes of such courts is stressed by H. G. Schermers, 'Comment on Weiler's *The Transformation of Europe*' (1991) 100 *Yale Law Journal* 2525–36.

[26] Case 69/85 *Wünsche Handelsgesellschaft GmbH & Co.* v. *Germany* [1986] ECR 947, 953.

[27] Under Art. 169 the Commission can bring default proceedings against a Member State before the ECJ after having given the Member State concerned the opportunity to submit its observations and after having delivered a reasoned opinion.

by the Treaty on European Union, there was no provision in the EC Treaty for sanctions to be imposed on a Member State that failed to respect such a ruling from the Court.[28] In any case, concern to avoid appearing to threaten judicial independence and jeopardizing continuation of the co-operative attitude generally demonstrated by national courts in the development of Community law has limited the Commission to purely informal contacts with the governments of Member States whose courts commit such apparent violations of the Treaty.[29]

Intervention Rights for Third States

Third states are entitled to intervene in plenary proceedings before the Court of Justice, provided that the necessary interest in the result of the case can be established under Article 37 of the Statute of the Court.[30] However, this provision stipulates that the entitlement does not apply in relation to cases between Member States, between Community institutions, or between Member States and Community institutions.[31] Hence, the rights of third states to intervene are limited to proceedings brought by private persons against Community institutions. It is for this reason that limitations to the possibilities for private persons to take advantage of the plenary jurisdiction of the Court of Justice seriously affect the significance of the intervention rights of third states.

In the case of preliminary rulings, Article 20 of the Statute of the Court provides that when a reference for such a ruling is made to the Court, Member States and the Commission are to be notified. Where the validity or interpretation of a Council act is involved, the Council is also to be notified. Moreover, the parties, the Member States, and, where appropriate, the Council, are entitled to submit statements of case or written observations to the Court. However, no such entitlement is conferred on third states,[32] and this provision has been strictly interpreted by the Court.[33] As a result, third states may be excluded from Court of Justice proceedings leading to the delivery of preliminary rulings.

[28] See now Art. 171 EC, as amended by the TEU.

[29] A. Evans, 'The Enforcement Procedure in Art. 169 EEC: Commission Discretion' (1979) *ELRev.* 442–56.

[30] Joined Cases 91 and 100/82 *Chris International Foods Ltd* v. *EC Commission* [1983] ECR 417. In Case 266/81 *Società Italiana per l'Oleodotto Transalpino (SIOT)* v. *Ministero delle Finanze, Ministero della Marina Mercantile, Circoscrizione Doganale di Trieste and Ente Autonomo del Ponte di Trieste* [1983] ECR 731, 769 Germany referred the Court to a memorandum and a letter from the Austrian Embassy to the German Government.

[31] The stipulation has been relaxed in favour of EFTA States. See sect. 8.5.3 below.

[32] See, however, sect. 8.5.3 below, in the case of EFTA States.

[33] Case 19/68 *Giovanni De Cicco* v. *Landesversicherungsanstalt Schwaben* [1968] ECR 473, 479.

8.2.2 National Courts

In *Van Gend en Loos*[34] the Court of Justice noted that the establishment of a common market implied that the EC Treaty did more than simply create a system of mutual rights and obligations for contracting states. Rather, the concern of the Treaty was with participation in the common market by private persons. Such persons also had the opportunity to participate in the work of the Community through representation in the European Parliament and the Economic and Social Committee. More particularly, the procedure in Article 177 of the Treaty, whereby national courts might refer questions of Community law to the Court of Justice for a preliminary ruling, implied that Community law was to be applied to individuals within the Member States. On the basis of such considerations the Court concluded that 'a new legal order' had been created and that individuals as well as Member States were the subjects of this order.

This conclusion was apparently designed not so much to enable the national court which had requested the preliminary ruling to give judgment in the case before it,[35] but rather to give some legal solidity to a Community which at the time was in danger of political disintegration.[36] This solidity took the specific form of a finding by the Court that within this legal order Community law might have direct effects before national courts, i.e., rights might be entailed for individuals which national courts had to enforce.

Direct Effectiveness

Where a provision of the EC Treaty is sufficiently clear and precise for judicial application and establishes an unconditional obligation, the obligation is complete and legally perfect and its implementation is not dependent on measures being subsequently taken by Community institutions or Member States with discretionary power in the matter,[37] the provision must be applied directly by national courts to the situations with which the provision is concerned. Direct effects may arise for individuals in the form of rights enforceable by these courts.

Direct effects may also arise from Community acts. According to Article 189(2) of the EC Treaty, a regulation shall be 'directly applicable in all Member States'. Provisions of regulations, like Treaty provisions, which are sufficiently precise must be applied directly by national courts to the situations with which those provisions are concerned. Direct effects may arise for individuals.[38]

[34] Case 26/62 *NV Algemene Transport- en Expeditie Onderneming van Gend en Loos* v. *Nederlandse Administratie der Belastingen* [1963] ECR 1, 12.

[35] See sect. 2.5 above.

[36] See, regarding the impact of the collapse of UK accession negotiations, PE Débs, No. 61, 29 ff., 5 Feb. 1963.

[37] A. G. Mayras in Case 2/74 *Jean Reyners* v. *Belgian State* [1974] ECR 631, 659–61.

[38] Case 93/71 *Leonesio* v. *Italian Ministry for Agriculture and Forestry* [1972] ECR 287, 293.

According to Article 189(3), a directive shall be binding, as to the result to be achieved, upon each Member State to which it is addressed, but shall leave to the national authorities the choice of form and methods. After expiry of the period within which national law must be introduced for their implementation,[39] provisions of directives which are sufficiently precise may have direct effects entailing rights for individuals against the state, though they entail no rights which the state may invoke against individuals. Since they also entail no rights in the context of relations between individuals, their direct effects are said to be 'vertical' but not 'horizontal'.

However, when a dispute concerns a matter within the sphere of application of a directive, national courts must, as far as possible, interpret national legislation in the light of the wording of the directive.[40] Moreover, Member States may be liable in damages for harm caused to private persons by their violations of Community law, including failures to implement directives.[41] As a result, the practical significance of the lack of horizontal effects of directives is reduced and, hence, the distinction between directives and regulations is further blurred. Difficult constitutional issues within Member States may be raised.[42]

Supremacy

Where Community law has direct effects, national courts must not apply conflicting provisions of national law.[43] In this sense, Community law enjoys supremacy over national law. According to the Court of Justice, such supremacy is an inherent feature of the Community legal system,[44] though the intergovernmental conference which adopted the Treaty on European Union found it necessary to make a Declaration on the Implementation of Community Law.

In essence, what is entailed is an 'autocontrol' system, whereby national courts control the compliance of their own national authorities with Community law. The system is activated by what the Court of Justice described in *Van*

[39] There may be considerable delay in the 'transposition' of directives into national law. See, e.g., *Completing the Internal Market: An Area Without Internal Frontiers*, COM(90)552, 16–17. See also the Report of the Committee on Legal Affairs and Citizens Rights on the *8th Annual Report on Commission Monitoring of the Application of Community Law* (EP Doc. A3–0143/92), 13 ff.

[40] Case C–106/89 *Marleasing* v. *La Comercial International de Alimentacion SA* [1990] ECR I-4135, 4159. See, earlier, Case 14/83 *Sabine von Colson and Elisabeth Kamann* v. *Land Nordrhein-Westfalen* [1984] ECR 1891, 1909.

[41] Joined Cases C–6/90 and C–9/90 *Francovich and Bonifaci* v. *Italy* [1992] ECR I–5357. National legislation limiting the amount of damages that may be awarded may be inapplicable. See Case C–271/91 *M. H. Marshall* v. *Southampton and South West Hampshire Area Health Authority (Teaching)* [1993] ECR I–4367.

[42] See, e.g., C. F. Mancini, 'L'Incorporazione del Diritto Comunitario nel Diritto Interno degli Stati Membri delle Comunità Europee' [1988] *RDE* 87–100.

[43] Case 14/68 *Walt Wilhelm* v. *Bundeskartellamt* [1969] ECR 1, 14.

[44] Case 6/64 *Flaminio Costa* v. *ENEL* [1964] ECR 585, 594.

Gend en Loos as 'the vigilance of individuals'[45] in asserting their rights under such law.

8.3 FREE TRADE AGREEMENTS

The Free Trade Agreements did not specifically provide for judicial involvement in development of the integration sought by these Agreements, though the possibility of establishing arbitration bodies was discussed during negotiations. At the same time, however, they did not preclude such involvement.

8.3.1 Proposed Arbitration Bodies

During the negotiations for the Swedish Free Trade Agreement the Swedish Government indicated willingness to explore all possible arrangements to ensure uniform application of this Agreement. In particular, the introduction of some system of arbitration for settling disputes was envisaged. In a memorandum of 6 September 1971 Swedish willingness was even expressed to accept that any such arbitration body would take account of the case law of the Court of Justice. Apparently, the prospect of judicial pressure from a court in which there was no Swedish judge was preferable to the prospect of the economic pressure which could otherwise be exercised by the Community, particularly pursuant to safeguard clauses.[46] The Community, however, was opposed to such an arrangement because of possible interference with its own decision-making processes. In particular, it was feared that introduction of an arbitration system might result in divergences between decisions of arbitrators and the case law of the Court of Justice.[47] Establishment of a separate arbitration body under each of the Free Trade Agreements concluded with EFTA States would have rendered such divergences all the more likely.

Community thinking in this regard did not prove easy to change. Hence, although inclusion of 'an impartial legal disposition' in the Swiss Free Trade Agreement was discussed in the early 1980s, the Commission apparently considered such an arrangement not to be possible.[48] On the other hand, the

[45] Case 26/62 *NV Algemene Transport- en Expeditie Onderneming van Gend en Loos* v. *Nederlandse Administratie der Belastingen* [1963] ECR 1, 13.

[46] Cf. Commission Reply by Sir Leon Brittan to Written Question E–1148/94 ([1994] OJ C362/57) by Cristiana Muscardini, regarding Community 'pressure' on Poland to relax restrictions on exports of raw and semi-finished hides to the Community.

[47] *Commission Opinion to the Council on Relations of the Enlarged Community with the EFTA Member and Associated Countries which have not Asked to Join the EEC*, Bull. EC, Supp. 3–71, 11 and the Swedish memorandum of 6 Sept. 1971, which is reproduced in Annex 3 to D. Viklund, *Spelet om Frihandelsavtalet* (Stockholm, 1977). Cf., regarding the need to avoid divergent interpretations of Association Agreements, H. G. Schermers, 'Case C–192/89 *S. Z. Sevince* v. *Staatssecretaris van Justitie*' (1991) *CMLRev.* 183–9, at 185.

[48] *Relations Between the Community and EFTA*, 14th Report of the House of Lords Select Committee on the European Communities, HL(1989–90) 55–2, 43. The matter remained 'very delicate'. See P. J. Kuyper, 'The European Communities and Arbitration' in A. H. A. Soons (ed.), *International Arbitration: Past and Prospects* (Dordrecht, 1989), 181–8, at 187.

Community was willing to accept arrangements for arbitration in relation to more specialist agreements,[49] such as the research agreement between Sweden and Euratom of 1976[50] and the fishing agreement between Sweden and the then EEC of 1980.[51]

8.3.2 European Court of Justice

The Court of Justice recognized that operation of provisions of Free Trade Agreements within the Community could not be allowed to vary from Member State to Member State. Hence, the Court claimed the jurisdiction to interpret such provisions, with a view to ensuring their uniform interpretation throughout the Community.[52]

However, the Court interpreted liberalization requirements in these Agreements so narrowly that their provisions had little relevance to the real issues of integration arising between the Parties. Such interpretation may explain why EFTA traders showed less interest in invoking provisions of Free Trade Agreements[53] than EC Treaty provisions in proceedings before the Court.[54]

8.3.3 National Courts

Provisions of a Free Trade Agreement which had the same characteristics as directly effective provisions of the EC Treaty might, given 'the object and purpose of the Agreement and its context', have direct effects before national courts of Member States.[55] These effects were not precluded by any lack of reciprocity as regards the internal legal effects of such Agreements within EFTA States.[56] However, since the Agreements were not interpreted as requiring the same trade liberalization as the EC Treaty, the direct effects of

[49] Though no such arrangements were made in the Civil Aviation Agreement between Norway, Sweden, and the EC ([1992] OJ L200/21).

[50] Art. XIII of the Agreement for co-operation between Euratom and Sweden in the field of controlled thermo-nuclear fusion and plasma physics ([1976] OJ L162/28). See, similarly, the Co-operation Agreement between Euratom and the Swiss Confederation in the field of controlled thermo-nuclear fusion and plasma physics ([1978] OJ L242/2), Art. 17.

[51] Art. 7(2) of the Agreement on fisheries between the Community and the Government of Sweden ([1980] OJ L226/2). The same arrangement was envisaged in the proposed fishing agreement with Finland of 23 Feb. 1979 ([1979] OJ C69/6), but it was not included in the final version of the agreement ([1983] OJ L192/7). Nor was it included in that with Norway ([1980] OJ L226/48).

[52] Case 104/81 *Hauptzollamt Mainz* v. *C. A. Kupferberg & Cie KG* [1982] ECR 3641, 3662.

[53] In Joined Cases 89, 104, 114, 116–117 & 125–129/85 *A. Åhlström Osakeyhtiö* v. *EC Commission* [1988] ECR 5193 the Finnish Free Trade Agreement was invoked as part of a procedural argument.

[54] Case 22/78 *Hugin Kassaregister AB and Hugin Cash Registers Ltd* v. *EC Commission* [1979] ECR 1869 and Case 86/82 *Hasselblad (GB) Ltd* v. *EC Commission* [1984] ECR 883.

[55] Case 104/81 *Hauptzollamt Mainz* v. *C. A. Kupferberg & Cie KG* [1982] ECR 3641, 3665.

[56] *Ibid.*, 3664. The ECJ declined to follow the views of courts in certain EFTA States on questions of the direct effectiveness of provisions of Free Trade Agreements. See also N. Wahl, 'Prise de Position de la Cour' [1991/92] *Juridisk Tidskrift* 554–761, at 557.

provisions in the former Agreements might be of little avail to a party invoking such provisions.[57]

In Sweden the Swedish Free Trade Agreement was regarded as lacking direct effects,[58] and this lack might be thought to provide a straightforward explanation for the failure of Swedish courts to play a significant role in resolving disputes under the Agreement. However, some decisions suggest that such courts might have been willing to take account of developments in Community law.[59] In one decision[60] reference was made to the Directive on product liability,[61] and in another decision[62] reference was made to the 1968 Convention on the Recognition and Enforcement of Judgments in Civil and Commercial Matters (i.e., the Brussels Convention).[63] It cannot be assumed, therefore, that provisions of the Free Trade Agreement would have been entirely disregarded by Swedish courts.[64] At least, it appears to have been open to the Swedish legislature to provide for national courts to take account of its provisions and the relevant case law of the Court of Justice.[65] Therefore, lack of direct effectiveness in itself may not fully explain the apparent disinterest in the Free Trade Agreement shown by parties to proceedings before Swedish courts.

The inadequacy of this explanation seems to be confirmed by the infrequency with which provisions of the Agreement were invoked before national courts of Member States, where some at least of its provisions were directly

[57] Cf. G. Gaja *et al.*, 'Instruments for Legal Integration in the European Community—A Review' in M. Cappelletti *et al.*, *Integration Through Law* (Berlin, 1986), 113–60, at 139, n. 82.

[58] *Kungl. Maj:ts proposition angående avtal med den europeiska ekonomiska gemenskapen, m.m., given Stockholm slott den 3 november 1972* (Government proposal for the adoption of the Free Trade Agreement), prop. 1972:135, 21. See also, e.g., U. Bernitz, *Internationell Marknadsrätt* (Stockholm, 1986), 79 ff. However, H. Lidgard, 'Sverige–EEG och Konkurrensen' [1974] *SvJT* 18–33, considered that the Agreement had become part of Swedish law through publication in *Kungl. Maj:ts kungörelse om avtalet mellan Sverige och Europeiska ekonomiska gemenskapen* (Royal proclamation of the adoption of the Free Trade Agreement), SFS 1972:698. See also the Supreme Administrative Court dec. 2 Apr. 1987, No. 6117–1986 interpreting Prot. 3 to the Agreement.

[59] Cf. the argument that, even before the EEA Agreement, the ECJ and national courts were obliged to seek to promote the homogeneity of the then EES in D. Thürer, 'The Role of Soft Law in the Actual Process of European Integration' in O. Jacot-Guillarmod (ed.), *L'Avenir du libre-échange en Europe: vers un Espace économique européen* (Zürich, 1990), 131–8.

[60] NJA 1989:66.

[61] Dir. 85/374 of 25 July 1985 ([1985] OJ L210/29) on the approximation of the laws, regulations, and administrative provisions of the Member States concerning liability for defective products.

[62] NJA 1989:10.

[63] Convention on jurisdiction and the enforcement of judgments in civil and commercial matters ([1978] OJ L304/36; [1990] OJ C189//2).

[64] Cf. earlier the inconclusive judgment concerning the Free Trade Agreement itself in *Hans Hauenschild Chemische Fabric KG* v. *AB Kemiska Byggnadsprodukter* [1976] 1 CMLR D9. It was argued that Swiss courts might, in suitable cases, be prepared to go further. See M. Baldi, 'Direct Applicability of Free Trade Agreements between the EEC and the EFTA Countries from a Swiss Perspective' [1985] *Revue Susse de Droit International de la Concurrence* 30–8.

[65] See, regarding product liability, prop. 1990/91:197, *om produktskadelag*.

effective. In fact Swedish companies were more inclined to take proceedings before national courts within the Community on the basis of the EC Treaty[66] than on the basis of the Free Trade Agreement. Presumably, it was assumed that the requirements contained in the latter Agreement were too limited often to be of assistance in resolving trade disputes.[67] The result of the assumption may have been that whatever potential the Agreement did have for resolving such disputes[68] remained largely unexplored.

8.4 EUROPE AGREEMENTS

The European Agreements go further than the Free Trade Agreements in providing for judicial involvement in the integration sought thereby.

8.4.1 Arbitration Bodies

Arbitration may be more acceptable as a means of resolving disputes between Parties to Association Agreements[69] than between Parties to Free Trade Agreements.[70] In the case of the Greek Association Agreement,[71] the Community originally suggested that such disputes should be submitted to the Court of Justice, augmented by a Greek judge, but this arrangement was rejected by Greece.[72] The solution adopted was to provide in Article 67 of the Agreement that disputes concerning the interpretation or application of the Agreement should go to arbitration.

The Europe Agreements follow this precedent. Article 105 of the Polish Agreement provides that in the event of its not being possible to settle a dispute between the Parties within the Association Council, either Party may notify the other of the appointment of an arbitrator; the other Party must then

[66] See, in particular, Case 238/87 *Volvo AB* v. *Erik Veng (UK) Ltd* [1988] ECR 6211. In Case 125/88 *H. F. M. Nijman* [1989] ECR 3533 the Free Trade Agreement was invoked in conjunction with the EC Treaty.

[67] Failure to seek to exploit the potential of an agreement can apparently have extreme consequences. At least in the case of the Overseas Countries and Territories, association under Arts 131–6 EC could lapse as a result of the failure of an associated country to use its associated status. See Trabucchi A. G. in Case 147/73 *Carlheinz Lensing Kaffee-Tee-Import KG* v. *Hauptzollamt Berlin-Packhof* [1973] ECR 1543, 1551.

[68] Cf. U. Bernitz, 'The EEC–EFTA Free Trade Agreements with Special Reference to the Position of Sweden and the Other Scandinavian EFTA Countries' (1986) 23 *CMLRev.* 567–90, at 573.

[69] Cf. the arbitration arrangements in the Yaoundé Convention ([1970] JO L282/2), Art. 53.

[70] Cf., in connection with relations between the Community and the USA, B. E. Carter, 'A Code of Conduct for EC–US Relations' in J. Schwarze (ed.), *The External Relations of the European Community, in particular EC–US Relations* (Baden-Baden, 1989), 131 at 135.

[71] [1963] JO 294.

[72] H. Smit and P. Herzog, *The Law of the European Economic Community: A Commentary on the EEC Treaty* (New York, 1976), 6–417.

also appoint an arbitrator within two months. The Association Council is to appoint a third arbitrator. These arbitrators are to decide on the dispute by majority vote. Each Party to the dispute must take the steps required to implement the decision of the arbitrators.

The willingness of the Community to accept such arrangements for arbitration in Association Agreements is comparable with Community attitudes within GATT, which is said to reflect Community concern regarding GATT-inconsistent actions by the United States.[73] More fundamentally, it may reflect recognition of the difficulties of reconciling a 'legal' regime for completion of the internal market with a 'political' regime for liberalization of international trade.[74]

8.4.2 European Court of Justice

The Court of Justice has not yet had the occasion to deliver a ruling concerning any of the Europe Agreements. However, in connection with the Turkish Association Agreement, the Court claimed jurisdiction to give preliminary rulings on the interpretation of an Association Agreement 'in so far as it [was] an act adopted by one of the institutions of the Community'.[75] In contrast to the earlier position of the Court, adopted in relation to the Greek Association Agreement, such jurisdiction was not expressed as being limited by the framework of the Community legal system.[76] Likewise, the Court will deliver such rulings on the interpretation of acts of joint bodies created by such Agreements.[77]

8.4.3 National Courts

Provisions of Association Agreements may be directly effective within the Community in the same circumstances as provisions of Free Trade Agreements, 'regard being had to . . . the purpose and nature of the Agreement'.[78] Equally, decisions adopted by an Association Council under an Association Agreement may be directly effective.[79] To this extent, it seems that provisions

[73] J. H. Jackson, 'EC '92 and Beyond: Comments from a U.S. Perspective' [1991] *Aussenwirtschaft* 341–8, at 347.

[74] Cf. the conclusions drawn from 'the changes which had occurred in the international economy in recent years' by Tesauro A. G. in Case C–327/91 *France* v. *EC Commission* [1994] ECR I–3641, I–3644.

[75] Case C–192/89 *S. Z. Sevince* v. *Staatssecretaris van Justitie* [1990] ECR I–3461, I–3501.

[76] Case 181/73 *R. & V. Haegeman* v. *Belgian State* [1974] ECR 449, 460.

[77] Case C–192/89 *S. Z. Sevince* v. *Staatssecretaris van Justitie* [1990] ECR 3461/3501. See, most recently, Darmon A. G. in Case C–355/93 *Hayriye Eroglu* v. *Land Baden-Württemberg* [1994] ECR I–5113, I–5117. The same reasoning would imply that the Court also had jurisdiction to deliver rulings on the 'validity' of such acts under Art. 177(b) EC.

[78] Case 12/86 *Meryem Demirel* v. *Stadt Schwäbisch Gmünd* [1987] ECR 3719, 3752.

[79] Case C–192/89 *S. Z. Sevince* v. *Staatssecretaris van Justitie* [1990] ECR 3461, 3501–4.

of the Europe Agreements and decisions of Association Councils or Association Committees established thereby may entail rights to be enforced by national courts of Member States.

Moreover, a Joint Declaration regarding Article 63(3) of the Polish Agreement was annexed to the Agreement. According to this Declaration, the Parties may request the Association Council at a later stage, and after the adoption of the implementing rules referred to in Article 63(3), to examine to what extent and under which conditions certain competition rules may be directly applicable, taking into account the progress made in the integration process between the Community and Poland. However, experience of the operation of the Free Trade Agreements raises doubts about the likely real impact of conferring direct applicability on these rules.

8.5 EEA AGREEMENT

The importance of judicial control for integration seems to have been fully recognized in the negotiations for the EEA Agreement. At the same time, however, it became clear during these negotiations that concern for Community autonomy and the sovereignty of EFTA States rendered arrangements for such control problematic.

8.5.1 Proposed EEA Courts

The draft EEA Agreement envisaged the creation of two EEA Courts. Both the composition and the jurisdiction of the proposed courts raised controversial issues.

Composition

There was support, at least in the academic literature, for an EEA Court based on the model provided by the European Court of Human Rights.[80] This Court contains a judge from each member country of the Council of Europe, irrespective of whether or not the country concerned has ratified the European Convention for the Protection of Human Rights and Fundamental Freedoms, and determines whether there has been a breach of the Convention by a Party thereto. On the basis of this model, it was suggested that the existing Court of Justice should be replaced by an EEA Court containing judges from each EEA State.[81]

[80] Editorial in (1989) 26 *CMLRev.* 341–4.

[81] A more radical proposal was that an EEA Tribunal should be established. To underline its independence from the existing ECJ, it should not contain judges drawn from the latter. In addition, an EFTA judge *ad hoc* might be appointed to sit on the bench of the existing ECJ in cases of special EFTA interest. See *Relations Between the Community and EFTA*, n. 48 above, 146–7.

Establishment of an EEA Court along the lines suggested would have meant that Community law would be interpreted and applied by a judicial body which, formally at least, was not required to maintain the same commitment to integration as the existing Court of Justice.[82] Hence, continued integration within the Community might have been endangered.

In the event, a less radical solution was envisaged in the draft EEA Agreement. Article 95(1) of the draft Agreement provided for establishment of an 'independent EEA Court, functionally integrated'[83] with the Court of Justice. There would be twelve judges, five from the Court of Justice and one from each EFTA State.[84] Article 95(2) of the draft provided that, when sitting in plenary session, the EEA Court would be composed of five judges from the Court of Justice and, on the basis of rotation, three of the judges nominated by the EFTA States.[85]

All disputes between Contracting Parties or cases when the EEA Court was seised by the EEA Joint Committee were to be dealt with in plenary session. However, Article 95(3) provided that, at the request of this Court, the EEA Council might allow it to establish Chambers, each consisting of three or five judges. 'An appropriate balance of ECJ and EFTA judges, taking into account the nature of the cases,' was to be laid down in the Statute of the EEA Court.

In addition, there was to be established 'an independent EEA Court of First Instance'.[86] It was to have ensured the legal control of decisions of the EFTA Surveillance Authority (ESA) relating to competition rules applicable to undertakings. Each EFTA State was to nominate one judge to the Court. The Court was to be composed of three of the judges nominated by the EFTA States, on the basis of rotation, and two judges of the existing Court of First Instance.[87]

The integration of these two new courts with the Court of Justice was to have depended not only on the presence of some members of the latter but also on a system 'inspired'[88] by the Lugano Convention.[89] However, a system

[82] This problem was apparently raised during EEA negotiations. See Club de Bruxelles, *EC/EFTA: The Future European Economic Area* (Brussels, 1991), 158. See also the sources cited in B. Brandtner, 'The Drama of the EEA: Comments on Opinions 1/91 and 1/92' in O. Jacot-Guillarmod (ed.), *Accord EEE: Commentaires et réflexions* (Bern, 1992), 300–28, at 304, n. 19.

[83] This formula was clearly a compromise between the desire of EFTA States for an independent common court linked with the existing ECJ and the desire of the Community for a court more tightly bound to the latter. Cf. DN, 13 May 1991.

[84] The EFTA States sought a court with a 'balanced' composition. See HLSG-V-W 20/90, para. 7.

[85] These arrangements followed those envisaged in the EC–EFTA Joint Ministerial Statement of 14 May 1991 (EFTA Bull. 2/1991, 7–9, para. 22). The EC–EFTA Joint Ministerial Statement of 19 Dec. 1990 (EFTA Bull. 1–1991, 22–25, para. 18) had merely referred to 'an EEA judicial mechanism' and in the Oslo Declaration of Mar. 1989 the EFTA Prime Ministers had merely referred to the possibility of establishing 'common mechanisms for the settlement of disputes' (EFTA Bull. 2/1989, 4, para. 14).

[86] Art. 101(1) of the draft EEA Agreement.

[87] *Ibid.*, Art. 101(2).

[88] EC–EFTA Ministerial Statement of 14 May 1991 (EFTA Bull. 2/1991, 7–9), para. 22.

[89] Convention on jurisdiction and the enforcement of judgments in civil and commercial matters, Done at Lugano 16 Sept. 1988 ([1988] OJ L319/9). See sect. 5.3.3 above.

which merely required a court to 'pay due account' to the judgments of other courts[90] might be thought inadequate to ensure that the new courts and the existing Court of Justice would act consistently with each other.[91]

According to the Court of Justice in *Opinion 1/91*,[92] problems of possible case law inconsistency could have been accentuated rather than mitigated by the arrangements in the draft EEA Agreement designed to create organic links between the EEA Court and the Court of Justice.[93] The EEA Court was to ensure the sound operation of rules on free trade and free competition under an international treaty which created obligations only between the Contracting Parties. In contrast, the Court of Justice had to secure observance of a particular legal order and to foster its development with a view to achieving the objectives set out in particular in Articles 2, 7a, and 102a of the EC Treaty[94] and to attaining a European Union among the Member States. Consequently, depending on whether they were sitting on the Court of Justice or on the EEA Court, the judges of the Court of Justice who were members of the EEA Court would have to apply and interpret the same provisions but using different approaches, methods, and concepts in order to take account of the nature of each instrument and of its particular objectives. In those circumstances, it would be very difficult, if not impossible, for those judges, when sitting in the Court of Justice, to tackle questions with completely open minds where they had taken part in determining those questions as members of the EEA Court.[95] The system might even raise doubts about the confidence which individuals were entitled to have in the ability of the Court of Justice to carry out its functions in complete independence.[96]

[90] The initial reaction of the ECJ to the Lugano Convention was 'equivocal'. See J. Minor, 'The Lugano Convention: Some Problems of Interpretation' (1990) 30 *CMLRev.* 507–19, at 518.

[91] Such problems were simply mentioned in passing by the Swedish Ministry of Justice in *Ett Europeiskt Ekonomiskt Samarbetsområde (EES) och den Svenska Grundlagen* (Ds 1990:58), 37. Cf., the view that possible conflicts with the case law of the European Court of Human Rights, if the Community became a Party to the European Convention on Human Rights, would not be a serious problem in the Commission Memorandum of 4 Apr. 1979 (Bull. EC, Supp. 2/79), 15.

[92] Opinion 1/91 (*Draft Agreement between the Community, on the one hand, and the countries of the European Free Trade Association, on the other, relating to the creation of the European Economic Area*) [1991] ECR I–6079, I–6107.

[93] It has been argued, however, that the presence of one *ad hoc* judge would not have affected decision-making of the existing ECJ, because his voice 'would inevitably be submerged by the preconceived consensus of judges bound by their common allegiance to the Community'. See P. Pescatore, 'The Dynamics and Homogeneity of the European Economic System' [1991] *JFT* 295–320, at 319.

[94] Art. 2 defines the task of the Community; Art. 7a provides for completion of the internal market; and Art. 102a envisages economic convergence.

[95] Art. 16 of the Statute of the ECJ, contained in a Prot. annexed to the EC Treaty, prohibits members from taking part in the hearing of a 'case' in the disposal of which they have already participated as members of another court or tribunal.

[96] In the past the view had been taken that an agreement with a third state which did not exclude such a possibility would be incompatible with the EC Treaty. See Opinion 1/76 (*Draft Agreement establishing a European laying-up fund for inland waterway vessels*) [1977] ECR 741, 761–2.

Such problems may have been heightened by a more particular consideration, which was not mentioned by the Court of Justice. Dissenting judgments may not be delivered by its members,[97] and the same principle would presumably have applied to the planned EEA Courts.[98] Hence, individual judges of the Court of Justice might have lacked the means to avoid identification with judgments delivered by the new Courts which might be inappropriate to be followed in the Community legal order.

Jurisdiction

Problems concerning the composition of the planned EEA Courts were closely bound up with jurisdictional issues. Article 96(1) of the draft EEA Agreement provided that the EEA Court would be competent for the settlement of disputes between the Contracting Parties, actions concerning the surveillance procedure regarding the EFTA States, and appeals concerning decisions in the field of competition initiated by the ESA.[99]

As regards disputes between the Contracting Parties, Article 96(2)(a) of the draft Agreement provided that the EEA Court could be seised by the EEA Joint Committee or the Contracting Parties in accordance with Article 117 of the draft. Article 117(1) provided that the EEA Joint Committee or a Contracting Party might bring a matter under dispute which concerned the application and interpretation of the Agreement before the EEA Court. Before doing so, however, a Contracting Party would be required by Article 117(3) first to submit the matter to the EEA Joint Committee. If it was not resolved after two consecutive meetings of the Committee, either the Committee should, unless otherwise decided, or a Contracting Party might, bring the matter before the EEA Court. For the Community it would have been for the Commission to bring the matter before the EEA Court. Article 97 of the draft required the Contracting Parties and the surveillance authorities to take all necessary measures to comply with the resulting judgments of the Court.

This approach to the role of the EEA Court apparently reflected the earlier thinking of the High Level Steering Group.[100] According to a proposal from this Group, conflicts between EEA law and national law should be resolved at the international level. Decisions of the European Court of Human Rights, which can find national law to be incompatible with the European Convention

[97] Art. 27(5) and (6) of the Rules of Procedure of the ECJ ([1982] OJ C39/1).

[98] As regards the EFTA Court, this principle is now embodied in Art. 8 of Prot. 5, on the Statute of the EFTA Court, to the Agreement between the EFTA States on the Establishment of a Surveillance Authority and a Court of Justice ([1994] OJ L344/1).

[99] These arrangements followed those envisaged in para. 22 of the EC–EFTA Joint Ministerial Statement of 14 May 1991 (EFTA Bull. 2/1991, 7–9). Apparently EFTA States had sought a provision equivalent to Art. 164 EC. See O. Jacot-Guillarmod, 'Droit international et droit communautaire dans le futur Traité instituant l'EEE' [1991] *RSDIE* 59–80, at 72.

[100] This was an EC–EFTA body responsible for co-ordinating the activity of the 5 working groups which prepared the ground for formal EEA Agreement negotiations.

on Human Rights and deliver a judgment binding the country concerned to amend its national law,[101] were seen as providing an appropriate model.[102]

The EEA Court would also have had a role to play in the settlement of disputes between Community and EFTA institutions. Article 96(2)(c) of the draft EEA Agreement provided that the Court could be seised by the Commission or the ESA in cases of conflict of competence arising under the competition provisions of Chapter 1 of Part IV of the Agreement.[103]

Finally, the EEA Court was to have 'internal jurisdiction' within EFTA. Article 96(3) of the draft provided that the Court might be seised under the provisions of a separate agreement between the EFTA States establishing an ESA by:

(a) the ESA under the surveillance procedure referred to in Article 116 regarding the fulfilment of the obligations under this Agreement by the EFTA States;
(b) an EFTA State or a natural or legal person in actions against the ESA.

As regards the latter category of actions, Article 102 of the draft envisaged that the EEA Court of First Instance would have jurisdiction in actions brought by a natural or legal person against a decision by the ESA relating to the implementation of the competition rules applicable to undertakings, if that decision was addressed to that person or if it was of direct and individual concern to him. Appeals against such judgments could be made to the EEA Court itself by a natural or legal person[104] in accordance with the same provision.

The further possibility was considered that the EEA Court might have jurisdiction to deliver preliminary rulings[105] at the request of national courts, in accordance with a procedure based on that in Article 177 of the EC Treaty.[106] Indeed, it was originally envisaged that the Court would have 'comprehensive and exclusive competence for the monitoring and proper functioning of the EES-rules'.[107] Apparently, however, there were indications that such an arrangement would have been unacceptable to the existing Court of Justice,[108] and the Commission mandate for EEA negotiations referred to

[101] Art. 53 of the Convention.

[102] Statement by the Foreign Trade Minister to the Swedish Parliament on 5 Oct. 1989 (*Riksdagsprotokoll* 1989/90:4, 12 ff.).

[103] I.e., the provisions containing the rules applicable to undertakings.

[104] Art. 96(2)(b) of the draft.

[105] Or 'reasoned opinions' (HLSG/V/W/20/90, para. 7).

[106] *Sverige–EFTA–EG* (Utrikesdepartementets handelsavdelning, 1990), 134.

[107] According to an unpublished Commission report on the results of the meeting of the EC–EFTA High Level Steering Group of 20 Mar. 1990. However, there was no reference to such competence in the EC–EFTA Joint Declaration of 14 May 1991 (EFTA Bull. 2/1991, 7–9).

[108] E.-U. Petersmann, 'Constitutionalism, Constitutional Law and European Integration' [1991]. *Aussenwirtschaft* 247–80, at 276. O. Jacot-Guillarmod, 'Droit International et Droit Communautaire dans le Futur Traité Instituant l'EEE' [1991] *Aussenwirtschaft* 317–40, at 327, identifies a switch by the Community from a rule-oriented approach to a power-oriented one. The Community attitude may also have been linked with abandonment of the requirement that EEA law be directly effective within EFTA States. See below sect. 8.5.5.

the jurisdiction planned for the new Court in less expansive terms.[109] No reference was made to preliminary rulings, and the draft EEA Agreement itself made no provision for the EEA Court to deliver such rulings.

Although the draft Agreement thus envisaged more limited jurisdiction for the EEA Court than may originally have been planned, the jurisdictional arrangements in the draft were still objectionable to the Court of Justice. According to *Opinion 1/91*,[110] the Agreement would be an act of one of the institutions of the Community within the meaning of Article 177 of the EC Treaty, and so the Court of Justice would have jurisdiction to give preliminary rulings on its interpretation. It would also have jurisdiction to rule on the Agreement in the event that Member States failed to fulfil their obligations thereunder. Where, however, an international agreement provided for its own system of courts, the decisions of courts within that system would be binding on the Community institutions, including the Court of Justice. In itself that would not be incompatible with Community law. However, the Agreement took over an essential part of Community law and sought to secure homogeneous interpretation, though Article 6 did not require the EEA Court to follow interpretations given by the Court of Justice after signature of the Agreement. Therefore, the demands of homogeneity would determine not only the interpretation of the rules of the Agreement itself but also the interpretation of the corresponding rules of Community law. In so far as it thus conditioned the future interpretation of the Community rules on free movement and competition, the machinery of courts provided for in the Agreement was found to conflict with Article 164 of the EC Treaty and, more generally, with the very foundations of the Community.

The objection might be raised to this ruling that different interpretations of the EC Treaty and the EEA Agreement could quite reasonably be maintained to the extent demanded by the differences in their respective objectives. Certainly, the Court of Justice was able to ensure that interpretations of Free Trade Agreements did not interfere with the development of its case law under the EC Treaty. However, difficulties of insulating case law under the EC Treaty from 'external interference' might have been greater in the case of the EEA Agreement than the Free Trade Agreements, given that the former is clearly designed to secure more intensive integration than the latter.

Indeed, the EEA Court could effectively have become a court of appeal from the Court of Justice in relation to EC Treaty requirements embodied in the

[109] According to para. 11 of the draft *Directives de Négociation*, annexed to the Commission Communication concerning a proposed Council decision authorizing the Commission to negotiate an agreement with the EFTA states on the creation of a European Economic Space, the EEA Court would have been responsible for the interpretation of the Agreement and the settlement of disputes between the Parties.

[110] Opinion 1/91 (*Draft Agreement between the Community, on the one hand, and the countries of the European Free Trade Association, on the other, relating to the creation of the European Economic Area*) [1991] ECR I–6079, I–6105.

EEA Agreement.[111] The Court of Justice chose a very particular 'constitutional' example to illustrate this possibility but could have used more general reasoning related, for example, to the law governing the 'four freedoms', i.e., the free movement of goods, persons, services, and capital.[112] The example chosen by the Court centred on Article 2(c) of the draft Agreement, which defined the expression 'Contracting Parties'. As far as the Community and the Member States were concerned, the expression covered the Community and the Member States, the Community, or the Member States depending on the case.[113] The EEA Court might be called upon to make a determination on which variation of the definition should apply in a particular case.[114] In doing so, it would have to rule on the respective competences of the Community and the Member States as regards matters covered by the Agreement.[115] Consequently, the jurisdiction conferred on the EEA Court could adversely affect the allocation of responsibilities defined in the EC Treaty and, hence, the autonomy of the Community legal order, respect for which must be assured by the Court of Justice pursuant to Article 164 of the EC Treaty. The exclusive jurisdiction of the Court of Justice in relation to such matters was confirmed by Article 219 of the EC Treaty and Article 87 of the ECSC Treaty.[116] Therefore, to confer that jurisdiction on the EEA Court would be incompatible with Community law.

Such considerations, combined with arrangements for 'integration' of the EEA Court with the Court of Justice, may have produced fear that the creation of the EEA Court could put a strain on decision making by the Court of Justice, particularly given that members of the latter may not deliver dissenting judgments.[117] In effect, the Court apparently considered that the planned judicial arrangements for reconciling institutional separation with application and development of common rules could jeopardize the performance of its

[111] Art. 120 of the EEA Agreement deals with the relationship between the EEA Agreement and existing agreements between the Community and one or more EFTA States, but it does not refer to the relationship between the EC Treaty and the EEA Agreement.

[112] Such reasoning might have put the Court on firmer ground. The example chosen did not relate to particular problems raised by the EEA Agreement but to problems raised by any 'mixed' Agreement to which the Community and the Member States are Parties.

[113] Inclusion of such a definition was by no means novel. Cf., e.g., the Interpretative Declaration on the definition of the expression 'Contracting Parties', attached to the Turkish Association Agreement ([1964] JO 3687, 3700). Art. 25(2) of the same Agreement also provides that the Association Council may decide to submit a dispute relating to the application or interpretation of this Agreement to the ECJ 'or any other existing court or tribunal'.

[114] The 'mixed' character of the EEA Agreement had already raised controversy, and the Commission had threatened the Council and the Member States with proceedings before the ECJ. Cf. the first footnote to the draft *directives de négociation*.

[115] Such matters had previously been classified as internal Community matters, in which third states had no need to interfere. See Opinion 1/73 (*Draft Convention of the International Atomic Energy Agency on the Physical Protection of Nuclear Materials, Facilities and Transports*) [1978] ECR 2151, 2180.

[116] The implication is that no other court can rule on questions raised by such agreements.

[117] Cf. *Relations Between the Community and EFTA*, n. 48 above.

own functions within the Community. Certainly, the very nature of the relationship between a court and the rules which it interprets and applies is such that heavy demands are placed on judicial arrangements designed to achieve such a reconciliation. In the view of the Court of Justice, the plans for the creation of EEA Courts failed to meet these demands, and so the plans were abandoned.

8.5.2 Arbitration Bodies

In EEA negotiations ideas were aired of arbitration as a means of settling disputes between the Parties[118] and, more particularly, as a means of resolving problems of possibly divergent interpretations as between the Court of Justice and the planned EEA Court, though the latter idea was quickly abandoned.[119] The final version of the EEA Agreement envisages only a limited role for arbitration.

The role allocated to arbitration depends on Article 111(4) of the Agreement, which deals only with disputes concerning the scope or duration of safeguard measures taken in accordance with Article 111(3) or Article 112 and the proportionality of rebalancing measures taken in accordance with Article 114.[120] Disputes concerning the justification for adoption of such measures are apparently not covered. Moreover, the dispute must first be brought before the Joint Committee.

If the Joint Committee fails to resolve the dispute within three months, any Contracting Party may refer it to arbitration under the procedures laid down in Protocol 33, on Arbitration Procedures. The arbitration award shall be binding on the Parties to the dispute. However, Article 111(4) stipulates that no question of interpretation of the provisions of this Agreement referred to in Article 111(3), i.e., those which are 'substantially identical' to corresponding provisions of Community law,[121] may be dealt with by such arbitration.

Thus the Court of Justice apparently retains exclusive jurisdiction to determine the requirements of the former provisions, which presumably include several safeguard clauses, though not Article 112.[122] As the Court itself concluded in *Opinion 1/92*, where pursuant to Article 228 of the EC Treaty the Court found the revised draft of the EEA Agreement to be

[118] E.g., the Swedish Government spoke of arrangements for dispute settlement by a group of legal experts within the Joint Committee, an EC–EFTA panel or a regular court of arbitration. See *Redovisning av det svenska integrationsarbetet våren 1988–mars 1989* (Utrikesdepartementets handelsavdelning 1989), 132.

[119] According to an EFTA proposal of Jan. 1992, while the ECJ would have jurisdiction over competition decisions of the Commission, disputes regarding other EEA law might be settled through binding arbitration involving the Joint Committee. See *European Report*, No. 1739 (29 Jan. 1992).

[120] See sect. 3.5.3 above.

[121] The ECJ referred in this connection simply to 'identical provisions' ([1992] ECR I–2821, I–2844).

[122] See, regarding this provision, sect. 3.5.3 above.

compatible with this Treaty, such arrangements are 'not liable adversely to affect the autonomy of the Community legal order'.[123]

However, this conclusion may not be entirely consistent with the general approach of the Court in *Opinions 1/91* and *1/92*. For example, in ruling on a dispute concerning the scope or duration of a safeguard measure under Article 112, the arbitrators may have to interpret and apply the principle of proportionality. This principle is not only of fundamental importance in the case law of the Court of Justice, but its operation also affects the extent of the powers retained by Member States in fields such as public policy.[124] The possibility cannot be excluded that the interpretation of the arbitrators may diverge from that of the Court of Justice, and homogeneity objectives may imply[125] that the latter would have to take account of that interpretation in interpreting provisions of the EC Treaty.

8.5.3 European Court of Justice

Abandonment of plans for EEA Courts as well as imposition of strict limits to arbitration possibilities, whether or not their imposition effectively secures the objectives of the negotiators of the EEA Agreement, were clearly designed to protect the role of the existing Court of Justice within the Community. As a consequence, however, the danger may arise that the development of the EEA could be jeopardized by the existence of a judicial vacuum in the legal regime governing EC–EFTA relations. From a Community perspective it might have been thought appropriate for the Court of Justice to fill this vacuum,[126] but such a solution would have been far from unproblematic for the EFTA States.

Plenary Jurisdiction

Commission President Delors had originally suggested that EFTA States might be willing 'to transpose the common rules essential to the free movement of goods into their domestic law and, in consequence, accept the supervision of the Court of Justice, which has demonstrated its outstanding competence and impartiality'.[127] The idea of granting generalized supervisory jurisdiction to the Court of Justice[128] does not, however, seem to have been pressed by

[123] [1992] ECR I–2821, I–2844.

[124] See sect. 3.2.1 above.

[125] There is no express provision to this effect. Art. 111(4) of the EEA Agreement simply provides that an arbitration award is binding on parties to the dispute. No reference to arbitral decisions is made in Art. 106, which establishes an EEA information system. See sect. 8.5.6 below.

[126] Art. 4 EC entails that this must be done in accordance with Art. 181 (arbitration clauses) or 182 (special agreements) thereof.

[127] EP Debs. No. 2–373, 76, 17 Jan. 1989.

[128] Such a solution may apparently have been acceptable to Sweden and Austria, but not to Finland or Switzerland. See SvD, 20 Jan. 1992. See also, regarding Finnish attitudes, L. Sevón, 'Legal Issues in the Negotiations on a European Economic Area' [1991] JFT 278–87, 286–7.

Community representatives.[129] As a result, less straightforward arrangements than those advocated by the Commission President were introduced.

According to the arrangements actually introduced, EFTA States accept the relevant case law of the Court of Justice made prior to the signature of the EEA Agreement. This acceptance is required by Article 6 of the EEA Agreement, which reproduces Article 6 of the draft Agreement. It provides that without prejudice to future developments of case law, the provisions of this Agreement, in so far as they are identical in substance to corresponding rules of the EC Treaty, the ECSC Treaty, and acts adopted in application of these two Treaties, shall in their implementation and application be interpreted in conformity with the relevant rulings of the Court of Justice[130] given prior to the date of signature of this Agreement.[131]

However, the Court of Justice considered that Article 6 of the draft Agreement failed to secure homogeneity. It was concerned only with rulings of the Court of Justice given prior to the date of signature of the Agreement. Since the case law would evolve, it would be difficult to distinguish the new case law from the old and hence the past from the future.[132]

For the future Article 104(1) of the draft EEA Agreement was concerned with future developments in the case law. It sought, in full deference to the independence of courts, to ensure as uniform an interpretation of this Agreement as possible. To this end, it addressed the EEA Court, the EEA Court of First Instance, the existing Court of Justice, the existing Court of First Instance and the courts of the EFTA States. Each of these courts should, when applying and interpreting respectively the provisions of this Agreement or provisions of the EC Treaty and the ECSC Treaty, as amended or supplemented, or of the acts adopted in pursuance thereof, which were identical in substance to the provisions of this Agreement, pay due account to the principles laid down by

[129] Though frequent mention was made of the idea of establishing 'an additional chamber' of the ECJ. See, e.g., the Interim Report of the Committee on External Economic Relations on economic and trade relations between the European Community and the EFTA countries, EP Doc. A3–146/90, 7. The Commission also suggested giving jurisdiction to deliver preliminary rulings to the ECJ enlarged with one *ad hoc* judge from the EFTA State concerned (HLSG/V/W 20/90, para. 4).

[130] It was calculated that up to the date of signature 947 rulings relevant to provisions of the Community Treaties substantially reproduced in the EEA Agreement had been delivered. See O. Jacot-Guillarmod, 'Préambule, Objectifs et Principes' in O. Jacot-Guillarmod (ed.), n. 82 above, 49–75, at 55, n. 23.

[131] See, more particularly, Art. 2(1) of Prot. 28, on Intellectual Property, concerning the exhaustion of rights doctrine developed in the case law of the ECJ (such as Case 3/78 *Centrafarm BV* v. *American Home Products Corp.* [1978] ECR 1823), and the adaptation of Art. 2(8) of Dir. 89/665 of 21 Dec. 1989 ([1989] OJ L395–33) on the co-ordination of the laws, regulations, and administrative provisions relating to the application of review procedures to the award of public supply and public works contracts by Annex XVI, Procurement.

[132] Opinion 1/91 (*Draft Agreement between the Community, on the one hand, and the countries of the European Free Trade Association, on the other, relating to the creation of the European Economic Area*) [1991] ECR I–6079, I–6103.

any relevant decisions delivered by the other courts.[133] Hence, future homogeneity was not to be exclusively conditioned on the case law of the existing Court of Justice.[134]

This arrangement was modified in response to *Opinion 1/91*.[135] Article 105(1) of the Agreement now envisages a central role for the Joint Committee in securing homogeneity.[136] In particular, Article 105(2) requires this Committee to keep under constant review the development of the case law of the Court of Justice and the EFTA Court. To this end, judgments of these Courts shall be transmitted to the Committee. If the Committee, within two months after a difference in the case law of the two courts has been brought before it,[137] has not succeeded in preserving the homogeneous interpretation of the Agreement, the procedures laid down in Article 111 may be applied.[138]

Article 111(3) deals with disputes concerning case law regarding provisions of the Agreement which are identical in substance to corresponding rules of the EC Treaty, ECSC Treaty, and acts adopted in application of these two Treaties. If such a dispute has not been settled within three months after it has been brought before the EEA Joint Committee, the Contracting Parties to the dispute may agree to request the Court of Justice to give a ruling (*se prononcer*) on the interpretation of the relevant rules.[139] If such a request is

[133] Art. 1(2) of the Agreement between Norway and Sweden and the EC on Civil Aviation ([1992] OJ L200/21) went further in seeking to secure the position of the ECJ. It provided that the provisions laid down by the regs and dirs specified at any time in the Annex should be interpreted in accordance with the interpretations provided by the ECJ or the Commission applicable to Arts 4 to 6, to the corresponding Arts EC and to those regs and dirs Such interpretations handed down after the signature of the Agreement should be communicated to Norway and Sweden. On request by a Contracting Party the Joint Committee should exchange views pursuant to Art. 13 on the implications of such interpretations for the proper functioning of the Agreement. If the Joint Committee did not take the decisions pursuant to Art. 1(2) within 6 months of the date of referral, the Agreement should cease to be in force.

[134] According to the Commission, the 'ideal solution' would have been for EFTA States to commit themselves to acceptance of future rulings of the Court, but this solution proved 'totally unacceptable' to them. See the Commission observations in Opinion 1/92 (*Draft Agreement between the Community, on the one hand, and the countries of the European Free Trade Association, on the other, relating to the creation of the European Economic Area*) [1992] ECR I–2821, I–2833.

[135] Opinion 1/91 (*Draft Agreement between the Community, on the one hand, and the countries of the European Free Trade Association, on the other, relating to the creation of the European Economic Area*) [1991] ECR I–6079.

[136] The Commission characterizes this role as securing the 'reception' of rulings of the ECJ on the part of EFTA States. See the Commission observations in Opinion 1/92 (*Draft Agreement between the Community, on the one hand, and the countries of the European Free Trade Association, on the other, relating to the creation of the European Economic Area*) [1992] ECR I–2821, I–2833.

[137] The European Parliament argued that a Joint Committee could not work effectively to interpret judgments of the ECJ or resolve differences caused by diverse judicial decisions (*ibid.* I–2837).

[138] Art. 105(3) of the EEA Agreement.

[139] It has apparently been agreed that in such circumstances the Commission will request the Court to deliver an Art. 228 Opinion. See Opinion 1/92 (*Draft Agreement between the Community, on the one hand, and the countries of the European Free Trade Association, on the other, relating to the creation of the European Economic Area*) [1992] ECR I–2821, I–2834.

made, the dispute may effectively be settled by a ruling of the Court. Since the ruling is to be binding, the nature of the function of this Court as conceived in the EC Treaty is not changed.[140] At the same time, since the agreement of EFTA States is necessary for a matter to be referred, such states are protected against compulsory jurisdiction of a Court on which none of their nationals sits. This reconciliation of conflicting demands is achieved, however, at the expense of denial of judicial protection to private persons.

Adverse consequences for such persons may be exaggerated, if the Joint Committee does not reach agreement on a solution within six months of the initiation of this procedure or if, by then, the Contracting Parties to the dispute have not decided to ask for a ruling by the Court of Justice. In such circumstances, a Contracting Party may, in order to remedy possible imbalances, either take a safeguard measure in accordance with Article 112(2)[141] and following the procedure of Article 113 or apply Article 102[142] *mutatis mutandis*. It is unclear precisely what can be suspended under Article 102 in such circumstances,[143] and the mutation envisaged might even be regarded as so affecting that provision as to permit suspension of provisions of the Agreement itself.[144]

The apparent implication is that while importance is attached to maintaining homogeneity of EEA law, priority is accorded to preserving the role of the Court of Justice within the Community legal system. If there is to be a judicial settlement of any dispute arising in relation to its case law, that settlement can only be provided by this Court. If a settlement is provided by the Joint Committee, the case law of the Court is not to be prejudiced. As was stipulated in an Agreed Minute *ad* Article 105 of the EEA Agreement, decisions taken by the Joint Committee under this provision might not affect (*affecte*) this case law.

According to *Opinion 1/92*,[145] the power entailed for the Joint Committee was compatible with the EC Treaty, if the principle embodied in the Agreed Minute was laid down in a form binding on the Contracting Parties. The Court was apparently satisfied that this condition was met, though its reasoning was not clear. The Court simply stated that 'it has been established that the principle set out in the "*procès-verbal agréé ad* Article 105" is binding on

[140] *Ibid.* I–2844.

[141] Such measures must be limited with regard to scope and duration to what is strictly necessary, and priority must be given to measures which will least disturb the functioning of the Agreement.

[142] Art. 102(5) allows for suspension of affected parts of an annex.

[143] An Agreed Minute *ad* Art. 111 simply states that suspension is not in the interest of the good functioning of the Agreement and all efforts should be made to avoid it.

[144] According to A. T. Laredo, 'The EEA Agreement: An Overall View' (1992) 29 *CMLRev.* 1199–213, at 1207–8, it is only part of an Annex to the Agreement which may be suspended.

[145] Opinion 1/92 (*Draft Agreement between the Community, on the one hand, and the countries of the European Free Trade Association, on the other, relating to the creation of the European Economic Area*) [1992] ECR I–2821, I–2842.

the Contracting Parties'. Although this Agreed Minute related only to Article 105, the Court considered that the interpretation according to which this principle also bound the Joint Committee in the context of Article 111[146] was the only interpretation that was consistent with the jurisdiction to interpret the relevant rules conferred on the Court by Article 111(3).[147] Possibly, the Court was influenced by the Commission statement that the principle embodied in the Agreed Minute would be confirmed by a declaration to be entered in the Council minutes prior to conclusion of the Agreement,[148] though the previous case law of the Court suggests that the effect of such declarations is limited.[149]

Such problems may have belatedly occurred to the drafters of the EEA Agreement. Protocol 48 to the Agreement, concerning Articles 105 and 111, now provides that decisions taken by the EEA Joint Committee under Articles 105 and 111 may not affect (*porte atteinte*) the case law of the Court of Justice. By virtue of Article 119, this Protocol is an integral part of the Agreement.

Preliminary Rulings

According to Article 104(2) of the draft EEA Agreement, provisions on the possibility for an EFTA State to allow a court or tribunal to ask the Court of Justice to express itself (*s'exprime*) on the interpretation of an EEA rule were to be laid down in Protocol 34. Article 1 of the draft Protocol provided that when a question of interpretation of provisions of the Agreement, which were identical in substance to provisions of the Community Treaties, as amended or supplemented, or of acts adopted in pursuance thereof, arose in a case pending before a court or tribunal of an EFTA State, the court or tribunal might, if it considered this necessary, ask the Court of Justice to express itself on such a question. This procedure was apparently intended to reconcile the need for uniform interpretation with objections of EFTA States to rule by 'foreign' judges.[150]

More particularly, the procedure was apparently designed to achieve this reconciliation within the framework of an Agreement which failed to secure direct effects for rules embodied therein. If this failure meant that national courts in EFTA States would not be expected to apply such rules themselves but only their version as reproduced in national law, the role of the Court of Justice might need to be different from the role it performs in the preliminary rulings procedure under the EC Treaty. It might be particularly inappropriate

[146] However, Art. 111 is concerned with disputes regarding application of the Agreement generally and Art. 105 exclusively with case law disputes, and it is not immediately clear why a minute relating to the latter should apply to the 'context' of Art. 111.

[147] [1992] ECR I–2821, I–2843.

[148] *Ibid.* I–2833.

[149] See, e.g., Case C–292/89 *Regina* v. *Immigration Appeal Tribunal, ex parte Gustaff Desiderius Antonissen* [1991] ECR I–745, I–778. See also sect. 4.2.2 above.

[150] Club de Bruxelles, *EC/EFTA: The Future European Economic Area* (Brussels, 1991), 159–60.

to impose on EFTA courts of last resort the kind of obligation to make references to the Court of Justice as is entailed by Article 177(3) of the EC Treaty or to imply that any ruling delivered by the latter Court following such a reference might be binding on them, if what they were expected to apply was not formally EEA law.

However, in *Opinion 1/91*[151] the Court of Justice found it objectionable that EFTA States were left free to authorize or not to authorize their courts or tribunals to refer questions to the Court and that such a reference was not made obligatory in the case of courts of last resort in those states. Furthermore, there was no guarantee that the answers given by the Court in such proceedings would be binding on the national courts making the reference. The procedure entailed was fundamentally different from that provided for in Article 177 of the EC Treaty, and it was unacceptable that the answers which the Court gave to the courts or tribunals in the EFTA States would be purely advisory and without any binding effects.[152] Such a situation would change the function of the Court of Justice as it was conceived by the EC Treaty, namely that of a court whose judgments were binding.[153]

While this change may have been intrinsically unacceptable to the Court, its unacceptability was rendered all the greater by expectations about the conclusions likely to be drawn by national courts of Member States. When such courts had to rule on application of the Agreement, they would have to take account of answers given to the courts of EFTA States. The fact that the answers were not binding on the EFTA courts might give rise to uncertainty about their legal value for courts of Member States. The possibility could not be ruled out that the latter would be led to consider that the non-binding effect of interpretations under Protocol 34 to the EEA Agreement extended to judgments under Article 177 of the EC Treaty. To that extent, there would be an adverse impact on legal certainty, which was essential for the proper operation of the procedure under the latter provision. As a result, the autonomy of the Community legal order in pursuing its own particular objectives might be undermined.[154] In other words,

[151] Opinion 1/91 (*Draft Agreement between the Community, on the one hand, and the countries of the European Free Trade Association, on the other, relating to the creation of the European Economic Area*) [1991] ECR I–6079.

[152] *Ibid.* I–6109–10. The objection of the Court to the non-binding character of such rulings was said to reflect a concern that a fundamental trade advantage would accrue to EFTA States (*European Report*, No. 1730, 17 Dec. 1991). However, States whose courts did not treat such rulings as binding might enjoy less credibility on the part of traders and might thus gain less from free trade. Cf. H. Schmieding, *Lending Stability to Europe's Emerging Market Economies* (Kiel Working Paper No. 481, Kiel, 1991).

[153] Cf., regarding the 'opinions' which the Commission may provide to national courts in relation to competition matters, Notice on co-operation between national courts and the Commission in applying Arts 85 and 86 EC ([1993] OJ C39-6), para. 38.

[154] According to H. G. Schermers, n. 20 above, 1006, the 'important thing is that the Court prevented, as much as possible, the legal order of the Community from being confused and deteriorating'.

the planned new procedure was considered incompatible with the insistence of the Court that preliminary rulings under Article 177 of the EC Treaty have binding character.

Protocol 34 to the EEA Agreement,[155] in its final version, seeks to resolve such problems. Article 1 of this Protocol provides that when a question of interpretation of provisions of the Agreement,[156] which are identical in substance to provisions of Community law, arises in a case pending before a court or tribunal of an EFTA State, the court or tribunal may, if it considers this necessary, ask the Court of Justice to 'decide on' such a question. This provision goes beyond Article 177 of the EC Treaty, in that it expressly recognizes the binding character of the rulings concerned. On the other hand, courts of EFTA States are not obliged to use the new procedure, and EFTA States are not even obliged to make it available to them. According to Article 2 of the Protocol, an EFTA State which intends to make use of this Protocol shall notify the Depositary and the Court of Justice to what extent and according to what modalities the Protocol will apply to its courts or tribunals.[157]

Intervention Rights for EFTA States

A Declaration by the Community on the Rights for the EFTA States before the EC Court of Justice, annexed to the EEA Agreement, went beyond questions of the jurisdiction of the Court of Justice under the EEA Agreement.[158] It required the introduction of rights for EFTA States and the ESA to intervene in proceedings before the Court of Justice and, to this end, amendment of Articles 20 and 37 of the Statute of the Court of Justice and the Court of First Instance.[159]

[155] On the possibility for courts and tribunals of EFTA States to request the ECJ to decide on the interpretation of EEA rules corresponding to EC rules.

[156] According to Art. 119, the Agreement includes the Prots and Annexes as well as acts referred to in the latter, as adapted for the purposes of the Agreement.

[157] The Swedish Government did not envisage providing for Swedish courts to request such rulings, because amendment of the Constitution would have been necessary to allow for binding rulings to be requested by such courts. See *EES-Avtalets införlivande m. m.* (Ds 1992:14), 27. Although the view of the Ministry of Justice was that no such amendment was necessary (*Ett Europeiskt Ekonomiskt Samarbetsområde (EES) och den Svenska Grundlagen*, Ds 1990:58; see also U. Bernitz, 'Onödig grundlagsändring' (1990-91) *JT* 727–9), the Government was concerned to leave no doubt in EEA Agreement negotiations as to the ability of Sweden to fulfil EEA obligations (*Propositionen om ändring i regeringsformen med anledning av ett europeiskt ekonomiskt samarbetsområdet*, prop. 1990/91:65, 29).

[158] See also the Declaration by the EC on the Rights of Lawyers of the EFTA States under Community law, concerning rights of lawyers before the ECJ and CFI and legal privilege.

[159] In relation to merger control, the right is granted to EFTA States themselves to bring proceedings before the ECJ. In particular, Art. 6(2) of Prot. 24, on Co-operation in the Field of Control of Concentrations, entitles them to challenge a Commission decision to refer a notified concentration to national authorities of an EFTA State on 'distinct market' grounds. In such cases any EFTA State may 'appeal' to the ECJ, on the same grounds and conditions as a Member State under Art. 173 EC, and in particular request the application of interim measures, for the purpose of applying its national law.

Amendment of Article 37 of the Statute means that the intervention rights of EFTA States are no longer limited to plenary proceedings brought by private persons. Such States, as well as the ESA, are now also entitled to intervene in proceedings between Community institutions, between Member States, or between a Community institution and a Member State, provided that 'one of the fields of application of the [EEA] Agreement is concerned'.[160] In such proceedings broader policy issues may be aired than in proceedings brought by private persons, and so EFTA States may have opportunities, which were previously denied to them, to participate in proceedings leading to judicial resolution of such issues.

Amendment of Article 20 of the Statute means, in turn, that EFTA States, as well as the ESA, are now entitled to make submissions or observations in proceedings before the Court of Justice when a preliminary ruling is being delivered, again provided that 'one of the fields of application of [the EEA] Agreement is concerned'.[161]

The role which EFTA States may now play in proceedings before the Court of Justice potentially constitutes an element of an autocontrol system within the EEA,[162] whereby it may be ensured that in the future development by this Court of Community law relevant to application of the EEA Agreement account is taken of EFTA interests. Prospects for development of such a system may be enhanced by the creation of EFTA Courts and the role which may be played by national courts of EFTA States.

8.5.4 EFTA Courts

Article 108(2) of the EEA Agreement provides for the EFTA States to establish a Court of Justice, to be known as the EFTA Court.[163] A Declaration by the Governments of the EFTA States Concerning a Court of First Instance, annexed to the EEA Agreement, declares that the EFTA States will also establish a court of first instance for cases in the field of competition, should the need arise.

Plenary Jurisdiction

The EFTA Court has jurisdiction with regard to the application of the EEA Agreement, particularly in actions concerning the surveillance procedure

[160] Art. 1.4 of Dec. 94/993 of 22 Dec. 1994 ([1994] OJ L379/1) amending the Prot. on the Statute of the ECJ. [161] *Ibid.*, Art. 1.3.

[162] Cf., regarding control by the ECJ of Commission acts under the 2nd Lomé Convention ([1980] OJ L347/1), Case 118/83 *CMC Cooperativa Muratori e Cementisti* v. *EC Commission* [1985] ECR 2325. Such control is not affected by inclusion in agreements with third states of arrangements for settlement of disputes by arbitration. See Case 267/82 *Développement SA and Clemessy* v. *EC Commission* [1986] ECR 1907, 1918.

[163] Prot. 5 to the Agreement between the EFTA States on the Establishment of a Surveillance Authority and a Court of Justice ([1994] OJ L344/1) contains the Statute of the new Court.

regarding EFTA States; 'appeals' concerning decisions in the field of competition initiated by the ESA;[164] and the settlement of disputes between two or more EFTA States.[165]

This Court is thus intended to uphold the rule of law in relation to EFTA decision-making and to assist in ensuring application of the requirements of EEA law in EFTA States without interfering with the role of the existing Court of Justice within the Community. In other words, the jurisdiction of the EFTA Court is apparently intended to be 'internal' to EFTA. In practice, however, the integration sought by the EEA Agreement might make complete separation of its role from that of the existing Court of Justice difficult to maintain. For example, a challenge could apparently be brought before the EFTA Court against the ESA on the ground that it had unlawfully exercised jurisdiction belonging to the Commission under Article 56 of the Agreement.[166] Such proceedings might require this Court to rule on the question whether trade between Member States was appreciably affected.[167]

It may be an oversimplification to regard such possibilities solely as creating a threat to the homogeneity of EEA law.[168] The Agreement between the EFTA States on the establishment of a Surveillance Authority and a Court of Justice[169] provides for the EFTA Court to take due account of developments in the case law of the Court of Justice.[170] At the same time, the possibility cannot be excluded that a dialogue of a two-way character may develop. Although, as the Court of Justice noted in *Opinion 1/92*,[171] the final version of the EEA Agreement contains no provision requiring it to pay due account to the decisions of other courts, it is unlikely that this Court will entirely disregard rulings of the EFTA Court. The determination of the Court of Justice to interpret international agreements 'objectively, regardless of considerations relating to reciprocity in the implementation of such agreements by other parties', does not apparently preclude reference to interpretations by third states and their courts.[172] In the framework of the EEA Agreement at

[164] I.e., review of the legality of such decisions.

[165] Arts 31, 32, 35, 36, 37, and 39 of the Agreement between the EFTA States on the Establishment of a Surveillance Authority and a Court of Justice. These heads of jurisdiction correspond to those of the ECJ under Arts 169, 173, and 170.

[166] Disputes between the two regarding action to be taken or with regard to the examination of a complaint may be referred to the Joint Committee under Art. 109(5) of the EEA Agreement.

[167] See sect. 4.5.4 above. Again, a Member State might bring proceedings claiming that its competence in relation to merger control had been violated by the ESA contrary to Art. 57(2)(b) of the EEA Agreement. A ruling on such an issue could have implications for relations between the Commission and Member States.

[168] Cf. the argument that judicial relations in the EEA resemble the solution found by the ECJ for co-operation with national courts of Member States in competition cases in H. G. Schermers, n. 20 above, at 994. [169] [1994] OJ L344/1. [170] Art. 3(2) of the Agreement.

[171] Opinion 1/92 (*Draft Agreement between the Community, on the one hand, and the countries of the European Free Trade Association, on the other, relating to the creation of the European Economic Area*) [1992] ECR I–2821, I–2841.

[172] Case 236/83 *University of Hamburg* v. *Hauptzollamt München-West* [1984] ECR 3849, 3865.

least, such reference may be more than simply an expression of judicial policy. Article 3 of the Agreement provides that the Contracting Parties shall take all appropriate measures, whether general or particular, to ensure fulfilment of the obligations arising out of this Agreement and shall abstain from any measure which could jeopardize the attainment of the objectives of this Agreement. This provision might be said to entail an obligation on the Court of Justice to take account of rulings of the EFTA Court.[173]

Advisory Opinions

Article 34 of the Agreement between the EFTA States on the Establishment of a Surveillance Authority and a Court of Justice[174] provides that national courts of EFTA States may request advisory opinions from the EFTA Court.[175] According to the Swedish Government, this procedure is of a different nature[176] from that for preliminary rulings.[177]

However, the practical effectiveness of the advisory opinion procedure, like that of the preliminary ruling procedure, may be largely dependent on attitudes of national courts. Depending on the attitudes of courts in EFTA States, the former procedure could play an important role in the development of EEA law. Indeed, co-operative attitudes on their part might enable advisory opinions to make the same kind of essential contribution to development of trade liberalization requirements in the EEA Agreement as preliminary rulings, such as that delivered in *Cassis de Dijon*,[178] have made to development of trade liberalization requirements in the EC Treaty.

More particularly, provided that there is a 'genuine dispute', the Court of Justice will deliver a preliminary ruling under Article 177 of the EC Treaty which enables a national court of one Member State to determine whether the

[173] Certainly, the ECJ has found implicit in the corresponding provision in the EC Treaty—Art. 5—mutual duties of 'sincere co-operation' imposed on Member States and Community institutions. See, regarding national courts, Case 80/86 *Kolpinghuis Nijmegen BV* [1987] ECR 3969, 3986.

[174] [1994] OJ L344/1. This procedure was to be available to Swedish courts. See *EES-Avtalets införlivande m. m.* (Ds 1992:14).

[175] It is also provided that an EFTA State may in its internal legislation limit the right to request an advisory opinion to courts and tribunals against whose decisions there is no judicial remedy under national law.

[176] *EES-Avtalets införlivande m. m.* (Ds 1992:14), 22. Hence, the Government considered that amendment of the Constitution was unnecessary for the purpose of enabling Swedish courts to make use of the Art. 34 procedure. *Regeringens skrivelse om ändring i regeringsformen med anledning av ett europeiskt ekonomiskt samarbetsområde*, Skr. 1991/92:58.

[177] The view of the Swedish Government was that a preliminary ruling procedure would be the most secure and effective means of ensuring uniform interpretation and application of EEA law. See *Ett Europeiskt Ekonomiskt Samarbetsområde (EES) och den Svenska Grundlagen* (Ds 1990:58), 37 and *Propositionen om ändring i regeringsformen med anledning av ett europeiskt ekonomiskt samarbetsområdet*, prop. 1990/91:65, 18. Finnish views seem to have been similar. See L. Sevón, n. 128 above, 282.

[178] Case 120/78 *Rewe-Zentral* v. *Bundesmonopolverwaltung für Branntwein* [1979] ECR 649.

legal provisions of another Member State are compatible with Community law.[179] If analogous use were to be made of advisory opinions under the EEA Agreement, such opinions could contribute to judicial application of EEA law throughout the EEA.

In other words, unprecedented opportunities are created for judicial realization of the potential of an agreement between the Community and third states for contributing to integration between the parties thereto.

8.5.5 National Courts

National courts of EFTA States have a critical role to play in contributing to the integration sought by the EEA Agreement. A possible arrangement for seeking to exploit their potential might have been suggested by the Canada–United States Free Trade Agreement.[180] This Agreement provided that Contracting Parties might intervene in the proceedings of a domestic court or administrative body where the interpretation of the Agreement was at issue and might submit their own views.[181] Introduction of such an arrangement for the Community or the Member States in relation to proceedings before national courts of EFTA States may have been regarded as incompatible with the desire of the latter States to limit encroachment on their sovereignty. Its introduction for EFTA States in relation to proceedings before national courts of Member States might have been regarded as unnecessary because of the opportunities provided for them in relation to proceedings before the Court of Justice. The implications for sovereignty of the Member States might also have been unacceptable. In this connection, it might be noted that the Commission failed to obtain the right to intervene in national court proceedings in the Member States[182] to secure compliance with the procedural rules governing the award of public supply and works contracts.[183]

While the EEA arrangements that have been made may be thought less intrusive into national judicial proceedings, their potential effects may be far more pervasive. These arrangements envisage incorporation of EEA law within the national legal systems of the EFTA States.

179 Sect 8.2.1 above. 180 [1988] ILM 281. 181 Art. 1808 of this Agreement.

182 Such a right was envisaged in Art. 2 of the original Commission proposal of 1 July 1987 ([1987] OJ C230/6). Art. 3 of the amended Commission proposal of 25 Nov. 1988 ([1989] OJ C15/8) merely required Member States to ensure that the competent administrative and judicial bodies allowed the Commission to ensure respect for the precedence of Community law in the course of the administrative or judicial procedure envisaged in the proposal. This clause was omitted from the version adopted by the Council. Cf. the suggestion of the ECJ in Case C–234/89 *Stergios Delimitis* v. *Henninger Bräu AG* [1991] ECR I–935, I–994 that a national court called upon to apply Art. 85(1) EC might contact the Commission as to its intentions regarding the possibility of an exemption under Art. 85(3) being granted.

183 Dir. 89/665 of 21 Dec. 1989 ([1989] OJ L395–33) on the co-ordination of the laws, regulations and administrative provisions relating to the application of review procedures to the award of public supply and public works contracts.

Incorporation Techniques

The importance of the internal legal effect of EEA rules within EFTA States seems to have been generally recognized during negotiations for the EEA Agreement. According to the draft Commission mandate for the negotiations, it was envisaged that individuals would be able directly to invoke provisions of the Agreement and future EEA acts before national courts of Member States and of EFTA States.[184] Such acts 'would, as appropriate, have direct effect throughout the EEA after their entry into force'[185] and be enforceable before such courts.[186] However, questions concerning appropriate legal techniques for securing such effect as well as the constitutional implications proved controversial.

The Swedish Government accepted the aim of achieving essentially the same effects for EEA law throughout the EEA area. Anywhere within this area there should, according to the Government, be a competent body to deal with complaints.[187] It was originally envisaged, however, that the EEA Agreement and acts referred to in Annexes to this Agreement would come into force when approved by the Swedish Parliament.[188] In other words, they would only have legal force after implementation at the national level (*efter implementering på nationell nivå*).[189] This language implied that the obligations embodied in EEA provisions rather than the terms of such provisions would be given legal effect through their embodiment in Swedish measures.[190]

Such arrangements, however, were apparently regarded by the Community as inadequate for EEA purposes. Hence, Article 7 of the EEA Agreement adopts a rather more radical approach. It provides that acts referred to or contained in the Annexes to this Agreement or in decisions of the EEA Joint Committee shall be binding upon the Contracting Parties and be, or be made, part of their internal legal order[191] as follows:

(a) an act corresponding to an EC regulation shall as such be made part of the internal legal order of the Contracting Parties;

[184] Para. 13 of the draft *Directives de Négociation.*

[185] According to an unpublished Commission report on the results of the meeting of the EC–EFTA High Level Steering Group of 20 Mar. 1990.

[186] Para. 13 of the *Directives de Négociation.*

[187] *Dagens Industri*, 9 May 1990.

[188] See, generally, regarding Swedish dualism, *Internationella överenskommelser och svensk rätt*, SOU 1974:100.

[189] *Redovisning av det svenska integrationsarbetet April 1990* (Utrikesdepartementets handelsavdelning, 1990), 50.

[190] Such an approach would have reflected that apparently envisaged in para. 11 of the Joint Communiqué issued by EFTA Ministers and the Commission after their Geneva meeting in Nov. 1988 (EFTA Bull. 4/1988, 2–3).

[191] The EC–EFTA Joint Ministerial Statement of 19 Dec. 1990 (EFTA Bull. 1/1991, 22–5) had referred to EEA decisions as having 'the character of public international law', which would be 'effectively applicable' at the same time throughout the EEA (para. 17).

(b) an act corresponding to an EC directive shall leave to the authorities of the Contracting Parties the choice of form and method of implementation.[192]

More particularly, paragraph 7 of Protocol 1, on Horizontal Adaptations, states that rights and obligations imposed upon the Member States or their public entities, undertakings, or individuals in relation to each other, shall be understood to be conferred or imposed upon Contracting Parties, the latter also being understood, as the case may be, as their competent authorities, public entities, undertakings, or individuals.[193]

To meet these requirements, the Swedish Government envisaged that the EEA Agreement and future EEA acts should, like the EC–EFTA Conventions on the Single Administrative Document[194] and on the Common Transit Procedure,[195] be incorporated within Swedish law (*inkorpereringsmetoden*).[196] According to this method, the Government might simply enact a domestic measure, such as a regulation (*förordning*), stating that a given EEA act was valid for Sweden (*gälla för Sveriges del*). The terms of the EEA act needed only to be annexed to the regulation and did not have to be reproduced in the regulation itself.[197] By such means it was hoped that the effective application of EEA law in Sweden could be secured without any formal transfer of legislative powers or Constitutional amendment.[198]

Potentially, such arrangements might produce the same results as direct applicability in Community law. However, the view of Swedish Government lawyers that incorporation into Swedish law of instruments such as the above two conventions was equivalent to securing their directly applicability[199]

[192] Similarly, Art. 9(1) of the Agreement on Civil Aviation ([1992] OJ L200/21) required that Norway and Sweden should ensure that Arts 4, 5, and 6 and the provisions of the regs and dirs specified in the Annex were applied in their territories and enforced with the same effect as in the Community. Art. 9(2) required that the Contracting Parties should ensure that the rights which devolved from Arts 4, 5, 6, 7, and the above mentioned regs and dirs might be invoked before the national courts. Cf. Art. 20(1) of the Swedish Free Trade Agreement with the ECSC ([1973] OJ L350/76), which obliged Sweden to take the measures required continually to achieve the same effects as those produced by the implementing decisions taken by the Community in relation to steel prices.

[193] According to the 8th recital in the Preamble to the EEA Agreement, the Contracting Parties are convinced of the important role that individuals will play in the EEA through the exercise of the rights conferred on them by this Agreement and through the judicial defence of these rights.

[194] [1987] OJ L226/1; SFS 1987:1126; SÖ 1988:6.

[195] [1987] OJ L134/1; SFS 1987:1119; SÖ 1988:7.

[196] S. Hecksher, 'EG och de svenska domstolarna' [1991] *SvJT* 221–35, at 227.

[197] *EES-Avtalets införlivande m. m.*, Ds 1992:14.

[198] Indeed, no such transfer was apparently discussed in EEA negotiations. See *Propositionen om andring i regeringsformen med anledning av ett europeiskt ekonomiskt samarbetsområdet*, prop. 1990/91:65, 8.

[199] P. Lindh, 'Institutional Developments and Linkages—A Response' in M. Robinson and J. Findlater (eds.), *Creating a European Economic Space: Legal Aspects of EC–EFTA Relations* (Dublin, 1988), 109–13, at 111.

seems unsustainable. The essence of direct applicability is that individual acts of incorporation by domestic institutions are unnecessary.

Even though the essence of direct applicability may thus not have been reflected in Swedish arrangements, the contradictions involved in the practice of voluntary harmonization[200] were still accentuated. If there was a legal obligation systematically to incorporate acts adopted by EEA institutions into Swedish law, it became difficult to deny that there was a substantial transfer of legislative powers. To the extent that Constitutional compliance is a matter of substance as well as form, it is not clear that the need for Constitutional amendment really was avoided by reliance on the incorporation method.

At the same time, there were some reasons for doubting the capacity of the incorporation method to secure internal effects for EEA law. In practice, Swedish institutions might be less than efficient in incorporating in national law EEA acts with which they disagreed, and delays and inaccuracies could prevent uniform application of the relevant rules.[201] The likelihood of such difficulties arising would have depended, of course, partly on the direction of EEA developments.[202]

More particularly, it is not clear how such a method could have accommodated the direct effectiveness of EEA acts equivalent to Community directives.[203] The latter are not themselves applicable within Member States, and homogeneity demands would apparently have implied no obligation for Sweden to incorporate (as opposed to implementing) their EEA equivalents in national law. However, obligations embodied in directives must be respected by national courts of Member States when they interpret national law and must be enforced by such courts against the State.[204]

The solution envisaged in Protocol 35 to the draft EEA Agreement was to secure for EEA acts corresponding to Directives formally more complete legal effects within EFTA States than they might enjoy within the Community. According to Article 1 of the Protocol, the Contracting Parties took into account that when implementing a part of an act corresponding to a Directive, which was clear, precise and unconditional, Article 7(a) of the Agreement should apply. However, this provision was omitted from the final version of the Protocol.[205]

[200] See sect. 5.3.2 above.

[201] *Relations Between the Community and EFTA*, n. 48 above, 27–8.

[202] In this connection, Art. 102(3) of the EEA Agreement (see sect. 6.5.3 above) might be designed to lessen the risk that such difficulties might arise.

[203] *Ett Europeiskt Ekonomiskt Samarbetsområde (EES) och den Svenska Grundlagen* (Ds 1990:58), 28–30.

[204] See sect. 8.2.2 above.

[205] The Community was apparently reluctant to accept that the distinction between regs and dirs had relevance in the context of 'an international law' agreement of the EEA kind. See O. Jacot-Guillarmod, 'Droit International et Droit Communautaire dans le Futur Traité Instituant l'EEE' [1991] *Aussenwirtschaft* 317–40, at 334.

Given its omission, Sweden considered that acts corresponding to directives need only be 'transformed' into Swedish domestic legislation or other measures.[206] In the event of deficient or defective transformation, however, much might have been left to depend on 'creative interpretation' by Swedish courts.[207]

Supremacy

Fundamental issues arose concerning the relationship between Swedish law incorporating or transforming EEA law and other Swedish law. The Swedish Government envisaged that any existing national law which conflicted with EEA rules would have to be amended and that care would be taken to ensure that conflicting national law was not adopted in the future.[208] In the event that any such conflict did arise, it would be for Swedish courts to apply the established principle that national law should, in the absence of express provision to the contrary, be interpreted as far as possible in a manner consistent with treaty obligations.[209]

However, it was agreed at an EC–EFTA Ministerial Meeting of May 1991 that internal legislative provisions would be introduced by EFTA States, in order to ensure that in cases of conflict EEA rules would prevail over 'other provisions of their internal legal order'.[210] This approach was followed in Protocol 35 to the draft EEA Agreement, on the implementation of EEA rules. The Preamble to the Protocol noted that the Agreement aimed at achieving a homogeneous European Economic Area, based on common rules, without requiring any Contracting Party to transfer legislative powers to any EEA institution. Hence, homogeneity would have to be achieved through national procedures. Accordingly, Article 1 of the Protocol provided that for cases of possible conflicts between implemented EEA rules and other statutory provisions, the Contracting Parties[211] undertook to introduce, if necessary, a statutory provision to the effect that EEA rules should prevail in these cases.[212]

In Sweden it was originally envisaged that this requirement could be met by a statutory provision that national legal provisions conflicting with any

[206] *Europeisk ekonomiska samarbetsområdet*, prop. 1991/92:170, 5.

[207] Cf. the view of Finnish officials that the task of national courts could 'to some extent be facilitated by interpretations and principles in the Government Bill to Parliament for ratification of the EEA Treaty' (L. Sevón, n. 128 above, 281–2). Such a practice might not have been readily reconcilable with the dynamism envisaged for the EEA.

[208] *Ett Europeiskt Ekonomiskt Samarbetsområde (EES) och den Svenska Grundlagen* (Ds 1990:58), 29. It was said that amendment of the Constitution so as to secure supremacy for EEA law in Sweden would be a solution disproportionate to the limited practical problem to be tackled. See *Propositionen om ändring i regeringsformen med anledning av ett europeiskt ekonomiskt samarbetsområdet*, prop. 1990/91:65, 11.

[209] *Ibid.* 227–8.

[210] EC–EFTA Ministerial Statement of 14 May 1991 (EFTA Bull. 2/1991, 7–9), para. 23.

[211] In the final version of Prot. 35 this obligation is imposed only on EFTA States.

[212] It did not deal with rules in the EEA Agreement itself or with the relationship between Community law and EEA law.

national provisions fulfilling EEA obligations might only be applied if a specific stipulation was made to this effect.[213] However, this arrangement was apparently considered inadequate. Hence, Article 5 of the Act on the EEA[214] provided that the application of provisions of this Act and any other national legal provisions fulfilling EEA obligations might not be hindered by any conflicting national legal provision.

Such arrangements are theoretically unnecessary within the Community itself. According to the Court of Justice, the supremacy of Community law is an inherent feature of the Community legal system.[215]

This difference between EEA law and Community law, particularly the implication in Protocol 35 to the draft EEA Agreement that the Contracting Parties were not required to recognize the principles of direct effect and supremacy entailed by its case law,[216] was stressed by the Court of Justice in *Opinion 1/91*.[217] Apparently, the Court doubted whether the kind of integration entailed by the EC Treaty could be secured within the EEA without EFTA acceptance of the full constitutional consequences of such integration.[218]

However, the possibility cannot be ruled out that the EFTA Court will treat the integration sought by the EEA Agreement as implying the creation of a 'new legal order'. Attempts by the Court of Justice judicially to overcome perceived problems in national approaches to Community law[219] may then come to have their counterparts in EEA developments. In other words, the supremacy of EEA law may come to be asserted by the EFTA Court as an inherent feature of the EEA legal system.

8.5.6 Information System

Judicial realization of the potential of the EEA Agreement may be facilitated by the information system established by its Article 106. The system is designed to ensure as uniform an interpretation as possible of the Agreement, in full deference to the independence of courts.[220] It concerns judg-

[213] Art. 5 of the Draft Act on the EEA (*EES-avtalets införlivande*) (Ds 1992:14).

[214] SFS 1992:1317.

[215] See sect. 8.2.2 above.

[216] Hence, the requirements of Art. 6 of the draft Agreement did not extend to essential elements of the case law which were irreconcilable with the characteristics of the Agreement.

[217] Opinion 1/91 (*Draft Agreement between the Community, on the one hand, and the countries of the European Free Trade Association, on the other, relating to the creation of the European Economic Area*) [1991] ECR I–6079, I–6102. See sect. 2.4. above.

[218] According to the Swedish Government, the EEA Agreement is essentially an ordinary international law agreement. There is no question of legislative powers being transferred to an international body. See *EES-Avtalets införlivande m. m.* (Ds 1992:14, 13). See also *Sverige–EFTA–EG 1991* (Utrikesdepartementet, 1992), 189.

[219] See sect. 8.2.2 above.

[220] Whereas Art. 105(1) of the EEA Agreement only requires the EEA Joint Committee to act 'to achieve the objective of the Contracting Parties to arrive at as uniform interpretation as possible of the provisions of the Agreement', the 15th recital in the Preamble states that 'the objective of the Contracting Parties is to arrive at and maintain a uniform interpretation and application of this Agreement'.

ments of the EFTA Court, the Court of Justice and Court of First Instance, and the courts of last resort of the EFTA States. It requires, in particular, transmission to the Registrar of the Court of Justice of judgments delivered by all such courts on the interpretation and application of, on the one hand, the EEA Agreement or, on the other hand, the EC or ECSC Treaty, as amended or supplemented, as well as the acts adopted in pursuance thereof in so far as they concern provisions which are identical in substance to those of this Agreement.

This system is reminiscent of the Lugano Convention,[221] which was regarded as a possible model for judicial co-operation in the EEA.[222] Within its more limited scope of application the Convention might be thought more demanding[223] than the information system established by the EEA Agreement. However, the latter system cannot appropriately be considered in isolation but, rather, as an arrangement facilitating judicial fulfilment of more general obligations in the Agreement regarding homogeneity.

As such, the EEA information system certainly seems more developed than that established by the Civil Aviation Agreement between Norway, Sweden, and the Community.[224] According to the third clause in the Preamble to the latter Agreement, the Parties desired to prevent, in full deference to the independence of the courts, divergent interpretations and to arrive at as uniform an interpretation as possible of the provisions of this Agreement and those provisions of Community legislation which were substantially reproduced in this Agreement. To this end, Article 1(2) merely provided for future interpretations by the Court of Justice or the Commission of EC Treaty provisions corresponding to provisions of the Agreement and of regulations and directives specified in the Annex to be communicated to Norway and Sweden. At the request of a Contracting Party, the Joint Committee was to exchange views pursuant to Article 13 on the implications of such interpretations for the proper functioning of the Agreement. The EEA information system need not have such one-sided operation, and it may assist the EFTA Court and national courts of EFTA States in playing a positive role in the development of EEA law.

8.6 CONCLUSION

Within the EC Treaty framework autocontrol is central to the role of the judiciary, in that national courts control their own national authorities in

[221] Convention on jurisdiction and the enforcement of judgments in civil and commercial matters, Done at Lugano 16 Sept. 1988 ([1988] OJ L319/9).

[222] EFTA Group of Legal Experts, 'Possible Models for Co-operation between the EC and EFTA Countries', EFTA-GLE 4/87, 5–8. See also *Sverige—EFTA—EG 1988* (Utrikesdepartementets handelsavdelning, 1989), 125.

[223] See sect. 8.5.1 above.

[224] [1992] OJ L200/21.

accordance with trade liberalization and other requirements embodied in the Treaty.[225] Thus the progress of Community integration cannot be identified simply with the strengthening of supranational bodies as against national authorities.[226]

Within the frameworks provided by the Free Trade Agreements the judiciary did little to overcome the limits to the trade liberalization requirements embodied in these Agreements, and it is unclear whether the judiciary will overcome the limits to such requirements in the Europe Agreements. In contrast, the kind of trade liberalization and other requirements embodied in the EEA Agreement, combined with the opportunities created for the judiciary to ensure respect for such requirements, may be mutually reinforcing in promoting attainment of the objectives of this Agreement.

It might be objected that problems of legal frameworks for integration between the Community and third states—essentially problems of reconciling institutional separation with application and development of common rules—do not readily lend themselves to a judicial solution. Support for the objection might be sought in the finding of the existing Court of Justice that creation of an EEA Court would be incompatible with the EC Treaty. The result of this finding was abandonment of plans for establishment of the latter Court. Abandonment of these plans might be expected to preserve the institutional autonomy of the Community only at the cost of endangering homogeneity of EEA law.

Certainly, the importance of a third party to enforce agreements is usually stressed as a condition for maintenance of complex exchange[227] and is reflected in the arbitration arrangements in the EEA Agreement. These arrangements might be said to highlight rather than to compensate for a fundamental flaw—the absence of a supreme EEA Court[228]—in the EEA scheme for securing EC–EFTA homogeneity.[229]

On the other hand, the liberalization and other requirements embodied in the EEA Agreement oblige Parties to take account of the interests of other Parties. To the extent that their courts uphold this obligation, the resulting autocontrol may enable the individual trader to become 'a decentralized agent monitoring

[225] Cf. the Commission's perception of the role of national courts in the Notice on cooperation between national courts and the Commission in applying Arts 85 and 86 EC ([1993] OJ C39/6), para. 34.

[226] W. Wallace, *The Transformation of Western Europe* (London, 1990), 78–9. Indeed, it has been argued that, as between Member States, the introduction of a 'two-tier system' of integration neither contravenes the basic principles of Community law nor conflicts with the general concept of integration. See E. Grabitz and B. Langeheime, 'Legal Problems Related to a Proposed "Two-Tier System" of Integration within the European Community' (1981) 18 *CMLRev.* 33–48, at 41.

[227] See, e.g., D. C. North, *Institutions, Institutional Change and Economic Performance* (Cambridge, 1990), 14.

[228] Cf. the view that without an EEA Court having more than 'limited tasks' the EEA Agreement would probably be 'a very traditional public international law treaty' (L. Sevón, n. 128 above, 286).

[229] Cf. N. Wahl, n. 56 above, 559.

compliance'[230] with EEA law, and such law may respond to network expectations fostered by integration processes. To the same extent, problems of cheating and of relative gains, on the resolution of which integration might be said by the 'realist' school of international relations to depend,[231] may be countered. In substance, some limitation of Community action may be implied, but such limitation is an expression of, rather than a threat to, the Community law requirements embodied in the EEA Agreement.[232]

[230] This language is employed in relation to the Art. 177 procedure by J. Weiler, 'The Transformation of Europe' (1991) 100 *Yale Law Journal* 2403–83, at 2421.

[231] J. M. Grieco, *Cooperation among Nations* (London, 1990).

[232] Case 120/78 *Rewe-Zentral AG* v. *Bundesmonopolverwaltung für Branntwein* [1979] ECR 649 established the country of origin principle and had the effect of opening up domestic regulations. Cf. H. Siebert and M. J. Koop, 'Institutional Competition. A Concept for Europe' [1990] *Aussenwirtschaft* 439–62. In the EEA context it is Community decision making which may be opened up in this way.

9

Conclusions

Trade liberalization provisions in the EC Treaty operate as elements in a general scheme to secure conditions of undistorted competition for extension of trading activity beyond the domestic market into the Community market. The liberalization requirements entailed by these provisions do much to secure reduction of trade obstacles. Together with other requirements embodied in the Treaty, they also facilitate harmonization. They do so by providing a legal framework for reconciliation of what might be seen as a conflict of objectives between a law harmonization policy oriented merely towards market integration as such and a legislative policy oriented towards the substantive quality of regulations, or between 'functional' harmonization designed to secure the establishment of the common market and 'substantive policy' harmonization.[1]

The existence of such a framework and the capacity of the judiciary to uphold and develop it have much greater significance for integration than might be suggested by analysis relying on the established doctrinal distinction between 'negative' and 'positive' integration.[2] This distinction tends to treat liberalization and harmonization as separable processes. In practice under the EC Treaty the two processes may interact.[3] When engaged in harmonization, the Community institutions must take account of liberalization requirements[4] as well as other requirements embodied in this Treaty,[5] and judicial control may be available to ensure that they do so.[6]

[1] Cf. J. Falke and C. Joerges, *'Traditional' Harmonization Policy, European Consumer Protection Programmes and the New Approach* (European University Institute Working Paper, Law No. 91/13 Florence, 1991), 5. Cf., regarding 'facilitative' and 'protective' legislation, A. McGee and S. Weatherill, 'The Evolution of the Single Market—Harmonization or Liberalization' (1990) 53 *MLRev*. 578–96.

[2] See, e.g., Falke and Joerges, n. 1 above, 95.

[3] There may be a 'structural set', involving 'the mutual convertibility of rules and resources in one domaine of action into those pertaining to another'. See A. Giddens, 'A Reply to my Critics' in D. Held and J. B. Thompson (eds.), *Social Theory of Modern Societies: Anthony Giddens and His Critics* (Cambridge, 1989), 249–301, at 299.

[4] In formal terms a blurring of the distinction between the respective fields of application of provisions such as Arts 57(1) and 59(1) EC may result. The former provides for the enactment of dirs for the mutual recognition of diplomas, so as to make it easier for persons to take up and pursue activities as self-employed persons. Art. 59(1) prohibits restrictions on freedom to provide services. See W.-H. Roth, 'The European Economic Community's Law on Services: Harmonization' (1988) 25 *CMLRev*. 35–94, at 57.

[5] See, regarding those embodied in Art. 39 EC, Case 249/85 *Alboko Margarinefabrik Maria von der Linde GmbH & Co. KG* v. *Bundesanstalt für Landwirtschaftliche Marktordnung* [1987] ECR 2345, 2360.

Hence, Community decision-making is legally structured, and the uncertainty and transaction costs otherwise involved[7] in decision-making are reduced.[8] In effect, the tendency of informational barriers[9] and 'free-rider' concerns[10] to hinder the adoption of mutually beneficial decisions is countered. As a result, continuous incremental change[11] may be facilitated by the liberalization and other requirements embodied in the EC Treaty.

Agreements with third states may contain liberalization provisions with the same wording as EC Treaty provisions. However, if the former provisions cannot be treated as elements of a scheme to secure conditions of undistorted competition for extension of trading activity beyond the domestic market, they may, as in the case of the Free Trade Agreements, be interpreted individually as entailing less demanding liberalization requirements than their counterparts in the EC Treaty.

The more limited are liberalization requirements in agreements with third states, the more dependent on harmonization is reduction of obstacles to trade between the parties. In particular, resort to the 'new approach' to harmonization, which is rendered feasible within the Community by the mutual recognition of national regulations demanded by the trade liberalization requirements in the EC Treaty,[12] may not be feasible under agreements with third states. The consequence is not simply that harmonization arrangements in such agreements may be overloaded. The overloading may also mean, as practice under the Free Trade Agreements suggests, that the harmonization in which third states may feel the need to participate is of the 'voluntary' kind. Such harmonization is not adapted to taking account of the interests of, and conditions in, such states.

Institutional arrangements in agreements between the Community and third states may be unable to counter such problems. The limitations to the liberalization required by the Free Trade Agreements meant that the joint bodies established under these Agreements sought reciprocity by reference to the

[6] The interpretation of the resulting legislation may also be affected. When the wording of such legislation is open to more than one interpretation, preference must be given to that which renders the provision most consistent with the favoured EC Treaty interpretation. See Case 218/82 *EC Commission* v. *EC Council* [1983] ECR 4063, 4075; Case 205/84 *EC Commission* v. *Germany* [1986] ECR 3755, 3812.

[7] Cf. A. Moravcsik, 'Negotiating the Single European Act' [1991] *International Organization* 19–56, at 27.

[8] As E. B. Haas, *The Uniting of Europe: Political, Social and Economic Forces* 1950–1957 (Stanford, 1968), 523 put it, Member States are 'engaged'.

[9] S. Weber and H. Wiesmith, 'Issue Linkage in the European Community' [1991] *JCMS* 255–67, at 258.

[10] Cf. H. Schmieding, *Lending Stability to Europe's Emerging Market Economies* (Kiel Working Paper No. 481, Kiel, 1991).

[11] See D. C. North, *Institutions, Institutional Change and Economic Performance*, (Cambridge, 1990) 89, regarding the conditions for such change.

[12] Cf. J.-M. Sun and J. Pelkmans, 'Regulatory Competition in the Single Market' [1995] *JCMS* 567.

demands of domestic policies[13] rather than to manage the operation of liberalization requirements.[14] In such circumstances, the weaknesses of institutional arrangements reliant on joint decision-making alone were exaggerated.

The terms of the Europe Agreements give little indication that lessons have been drawn from problems in the operation of the Free Trade Agreements. The former may have the advantage of rendering more permanent the liberalization steps which the Community had previously taken in favour of Central and East European States on a unilateral basis.[15] Their mere conclusion may, rather like the '1992 programme' within the Community, also have psychological effects on traders and even add to the credibility of reform programmes[16] and new institutional systems[17] in such states. However, the economies of the latter may not be well equipped to take full advantage of the limited liberalization likely to be secured by the Agreements.

Harmonization arrangements in the Europe Agreements may be unable to compensate for the limits to the liberalization required by these Agreements.[18] Express provision is made therein for the Central and East European States concerned to engage in 'voluntary' harmonization.[19] Such harmonization may be particularly ill adapted to taking account of structural economic problems as severe as those faced by such states.[20] Thus while possibly improving their legal access to the Community market, it may do less to assist development of their economic capacity to exploit the trading opportunities entailed.[21]

[13] Cf., regarding negotiations for bilateral agreements with Switzerland, the conclusions published by the Council when adopting the *directives de négociation*, on 31 Oct. 1994 (Bull. EU 10–1994, 1.3.17).

[14] Minimum harmonization may counter the demands of regulatory competition and increase the effective scope of individual states to maintain domestic regs. See J.-M. Sun and J. Pelkmans, n. 12 above, 76–7.

[15] Unilateral concessions can apparently be withdrawn unilaterally. See Case 90/77 *Hellmut Stimming KG* v. *EC Commission* [1978] ECR 995, 1009.

[16] See S. Edwards, *On the Sequencing of Structural Reforms* (OECD Working Paper No. 70, Paris, 1989), regarding the crucial importance of the credibility of such programmes.

[17] See, regarding the need to ensure that market actors attach credibility to these new systems, H. Schmieding, op. cit.

[18] Cf. the Opinion of the Economic and Social Committee of 29 Mar. 1990 on the EC's economic relations with the countries of Eastern Europe, CES(90)381, which stressed that Community relations with Central and Eastern European states should not result in Community firms facing unfair competition (para. 2.11) or in slowing integration within the Community (para. 2.1).

[19] A close relationship between reduction of trading obstacles and harmonization may not be simply a matter of political preferences. Cf., regarding the 'dire need for foreign investment and economic reform', C. Brzezinski, 'The EC–Poland Association Agreement: Harmonization of an Aspiring Member State's Company Law' (1993) 34 *Harvard International Law Journal* 105–48, at 121. Rather, the relationship may be an inherent element in integration of mixed economies.

[20] D. Kennedy and D. E. Webb, 'The Limits of 'integration: Eastern Europe and the European Communities' (1993) 30 *CMLRev*. 1095, 1116.

[21] Such problems may have been less apparent when liberalization moves by the Community in relation to trade with Poland took place mostly within the framework of the Phare Programme, which was not concerned with issues of reciprocity. See Reg. 3906/89 of 18 Dec. 1989 ([1989] OJ L375/1) on economic aid to the Republic of Hungary and the People's Polish Republic. See, generally, J. Pelkmans and A. Murphy, 'Catapulted into Leadership: the Community's Trade and Aid Policies vis-à-vis Eastern Europe' [1991] *Revue d'Intégration Européenne* 125–51.

Institutional arrangements in the Europe Agreements, though essentially reliant on joint decision-making, are more developed than those in the Free Trade Agreements, and provision is made in the former for a political dialogue.[22] Nevertheless, despite their intrinsic value,[23] such arrangements cannot easily fill a legal vacuum resulting from the limited character of liberalization requirements. While integration may, to some extent, be viewed as a series of dynamic disequilibria which create the conditions and the pressure for further extension and deepening,[24] its activation may be difficult to disassociate from the operation of sufficiently demanding liberalization requirements.[25] It is the operation of these requirements (and the readiness of traders to invoke them[26]) which creates pressures for regulatory competition and/or harmonization. If the liberalization requirements in the Europe Agreements prove too limited to create such pressures, the institutional arrangements in these Agreements are unlikely to overcome 'the limits of integration'[27] as between the Community and third states.

The EEA Agreement might be thought to offer a more likely basis for overcoming such limits. In contrast to the Free Trade Agreements and the Europe Agreements, the EEA Agreement not only reproduces the terms of many EC Treaty provisions. Through incorporation of the case law of the Court of Justice it also seeks to embrace the trade liberalization and other requirements embodied in these provisions and deriving from the EC Treaty framework. The implication is that EEA law entails application of far-reaching liberalization requirements to EC–EFTA trade, while at the same time recognizing various requirements other than those of trade liberalization. As a result, not only may liberalization be more successful than in the context of relations between the Community and other third states, but also harmonization problems may be lessened.

Neither the Community nor the EFTA States can legally adopt measures restricting the liberalization required by the EEA Agreement without establishing a justification in the other requirements also embodied therein. Rather,

[22] The Czech Republic, Hungary, Poland and Slovakia were already kept informed of decisions taken within the framework of European political co-operation. See the First Report of the House of Lords Select Committee on the European Communities, *Enlargement of the Community*, HL(1992–93) 5, 36.

[23] Cf., regarding 'political before economic membership', *ibid.*, 15. Cf., in the case of Turkey, the Report of the Committee on Foreign Affairs and Security on EC–Turkey relations, EP Doc. A3–0193/92, 11.

[24] L. Tsoukalis, op. cit., 303.

[25] Such considerations explain why, in the case of Community relations with Central and Eastern European states, 'the key element in the strategy to narrow the gap is preparation of the Associated States for integration into the internal market of the Union'. See the Conclusions of the Presidency of the European Council meeting of Dec. 1994 (Bull. EC 12–1994, I.13).

[26] J.-M. Sun and J. Pelkmans, n. 12 above, 73.

[27] D. Kennedy and D. E. Webb, n. 20 above. However, it may be an oversimplification to argue that the 'level of institutional integration contained in the Association Agreements may simultaneously indicate and dictate the portion of the EC's institutional priority which will be given to the Association Countries and their advocates within the EC itself' (*ibid.* 1111–2).

there is an incentive for each EEA State[28] to take account of the interests of others[29] in harmonization efforts to reconcile reduction of trading obstacles with respect for other requirements embodied in the Agreement. To this extent, the EEA Agreement might be thought to remove pressures on EFTA States to join the European Union itself for 'fear of economic discrimination'.[30]

It is true that the institutional arrangements made by the EEA Agreement may, in many respects, entail little more than formalization of previous EC–EFTA practice. However, substantially different arrangements could not easily have been introduced, given the concern, stressed throughout EEA negotiations to protect the decision-making autonomy of the Parties. For the Community the underlying commitment to preservation of supranationalism[31] demanded EFTA exclusion from involvement in Community 'decision-taking'. For their part, the EFTA States presumably sought to avoid fully subjecting themselves under the EEA Agreement to the supranationalism associated with membership of the European Union.[32] Hence, the EEA Agreement, despite the difficult constitutional issues raised and the challenges posed to traditional integration theory, may offer the only realistic model for close integration of third states with the Community.[33]

Resort to this model in other agreements between the Community and third states in Europe might not simply offer an alternative to introducing the institutional reforms,[34] such as allocating a 'reduced role' to smaller Member States,[35] which could be needed to maintain 'efficiency' of decision-making in

[28] A threshold between 'co-operation' and 'integration' may be crossed. Cf. T. Heller and J. Pelkmans, id. op., 322.

[29] To the extent that differences of perception are reduced, conflicts of interest may more readily be resolved by compromise and bargaining to give each party some satisfaction of its respective interest. See S. Strange, 'The Persistence of the Problems in EC–US Relations: Conflicts of Perception' in J. Schwarze (ed.), *The External Relations of the European Community, in Particular EC–US Relations* (Baden-Baden, 1989) 109–8, at 115.

[30] Cf. P. G. Nell, 'EFTA in the 1990s: the Search for a New Identity' [1990] *JCMS* 327–58, at 355.

[31] Commissioner F. H. J. J. Andriessen, 'Europe at the Crossroads', Tenth Annual Paul Henri Spaak Lecture, Harvard, 1990, 7 expressed the issue as being the extent, if any, to which the Community would 'have to share some of its sovereignty and autonomy with EFTA'.

[32] In 1988 the then Secretary-General of EFTA wrote that EFTA would not develop supranational structures and policies (EFTA Bull. 1/1988, 13–15).

[33] It may also be sufficiently flexible to avoid the problems of a 'proliferation of European institutions'. Cf. *Enlargement of the Community*, n. 22 above, 19.

[34] 'The Community as presently constituted . . . cannot encompass enlargement'. See the Report of the Committee on Institutional Affairs on the structure and strategy for the EU with regard to its enlargement and the creation of a Europe-wide order, EP Doc. A3–0189/92, 15.

[35] The idea of reducing their role is predictably controversial. See, e.g., *Europe* No. 5727 (11/12 May 1992). The official position was simply that 'by the end of 1992, specific decisions must in any case be taken on the number of members of the Commission and of the Parliament, in the light, *inter alia*, of the size of the Parliament in an enlarged Community'. See *Europe and the Challenge of Enlargement*, Bull. EC, Supp. 3/92, 20. However, in the case of Cyprus and Malta, they 'are very small states, and the question of their participation in the Community institutions would have to be resolved in an appropriate manner in accession negotiations' (*ibid.* 17–18).

a European Union expanded to include most European states.[36] More fundamentally, the model may have implications for problems of centralization in the existing Union,[37] which are not only serious in themselves but, more particularly, may also affect prospects for integration between the Community and third states generally.[38]

Such problems are partly those inherent in any over-centralization. A highly aggregated level of jurisdiction, as perhaps has been exemplified in the case of the common agricultural policy, may be too easily accessible to strongly organized and potentially rigidifying interests[39] resistant to the realities of integration[40] and potentially harmful to society as a whole.[41] The problems are also particular to Europe, where trade liberalization requirements in the EC Treaty mean that traders may have incentives to 'capture' Community rather than national institutions[42] and where the very redefinition of the European polity produces a legitimacy crisis.[43]

[36] See, e.g., para. 3 of the Resolution of the European Parliament of 30 Nov. 1994 ([1994] OJ C363/16) on the strategy of the EU to prepare for the accession of the countries of Central and Eastern Europe, with a view to the European Council in Essen (9–10 Dec. 1994). Cf. the view that integration within the Community is currently 'sought on a bureaucratic-centralist basis' and that this approach to integration magnifies the difficulties of admitting Central and Eastern European States to Union membership (G. Wettig, 'Security in Europe: A Challenging Task' [1992] *Aussenpolitik* 3–11, at 9–10).

[37] The EEA Agreement 'amounts to extensive legal harmonization and integration for which even existing supranational structures of the game within the Community often are no longer adequate'. See T. Cottier, 'Constitutional Trade Regulation in National and International Law: Structure–Substance Pairings in the EFTA Experience' in M. Hilf and E.-U. Petersmann (eds.), *National Constitutions and International Economic Law* (Deventer, 1993), 409–42, at 430.

[38] Trade relations with third states generally are hindered by the 'imperfect constitutional settings' of the Union (*ibid.* 434).

[39] Cf. K.-H. Ladeur, 'European Community Institutional Reforms: Extra-National Management as an Alternative Model to Federalism' (1990/2) *LIEI* 1–21, at 10, and 14–15. This danger may be exaggerated in a Community where decision-making is too remote for the public to monitor. See V. Curzon Price, 'The Threat of "Fortress Europe" from the Development of Social and Industrial Policies at a European Level' [1991] *Aussenwirtschaft* 119–38, at 137.

[40] Cf. J. Fagerberg, 'The Process of Economic Integration in Europe: Consequences for EFTA Countries and Firms' [1991] *Co-operation and Conflict* 197–215. Resurgence of such interests might validate the argument in S. J. Silvia, 'The Social Charter of the European Community: A Defeat for European Labor' (1991) 44 *Industrial and Labor Relations Review* 626–43, 629 that conditions have only temporarily 'opened the system of relationships, making policy [within the Union] more fluid'.

[41] Changes in the institutional environment created by interest groups are, in general, not optimal for a society, because such groups seek to secure such changes to maximize their own utility rather than social welfare. See H. Dicke and R.J. Langhammer, *The Institutional Framework and External Dimension of the EC Internal Market* (Kiel Working Paper No. 453, Kiel, 1990), 2.

[42] Cf., regarding the reduction, or even the elimination, of incentives to capture the latter, J.-M. Sun and J. Pelkmans, n. 12 above, 71.

[43] J. Weiler, 'The Transformation of Europe' (1991) 100 *Yale Law Journal* 2403–83, at 2473. The Commission recognizes that the crisis may be exacerbated by enlargement but sees the solution in terms of strengthening the role of the European Parliament. See *Europe and the Challenge of Enlargement*, Bull. EC, Supp. 3/92, 15.

The EEA Agreement suggests solutions to such problems, because it implies the possibility that considerable integration may be achievable without the centralization of power demanded by established theories of supranationalism.[44] The Agreement implies, in particular, that the Court of Justice must take account of the judgments of the EFTA Court and that the European Commission must take account of the practice of the EFTA Surveillance Authority. The independence of the Court of Justice and the Commission from national governments is unaffected, but the supreme power which they enjoy under the EC Treaty may be countered.[45] In other words, increased pluralism in Community decision-making is implied.

Tendencies towards increased pluralism may be reinforced by the very nature of the liberalization requirements and other requirements embodied in the Agreement. These requirements oppose policy-induced market segmentation within the EEA and demand that 'internal' policies are 'deparochialised'[46] rather than replaced. It is not so much that 'the Leviathan is tamed',[47] but that it may become involved in pluralist integration.[48] Individual states, like the Community, may play a role within the framework of the EEA Agreement that is biassed against the centralization of power rather than the interventionism associated with the mixed economy.[49]

These implications arise from the EEA Agreement not so much because this Agreement was based on the EC Treaty model of integration modified to meet EEA needs as because it was fashioned, particularly in response to *Opinion 1/91*,[50] to respect the judicially perceived demands of this model. The ironical result of the modification is that the EEA Agreement embodies the real pluralist potential of the EC Treaty model rather than the kind of supranationalist theories—that kind which stresses the importance of centralization of supreme power in the hands of supranational institutions more than the independence of such institutions from national governments—with which it has been imbued in rulings such as *Opinion 1/91*.

44 An integration model adapted to the current integration of network relationships rather than the more traditional kind of supranationalism which aims at integration of states may be embodied in the EEA Agreement. The EC Treaty, though the Community is unavoidably involved in network integration, may appear less well adapted. Cf. the argument in J. Weiler, n. 43 above, 2483 that '[t]oday's Community is impelled forward by the dysfunctioning of its present architecture'.

45 Cf. the concept of 'extranationalism' in K.-H. Ladeur, n. 39 above.

46 Cf. *ibid.*

47 H. Siebert, *The New Economic Landscape in Europe* (Oxford, 1991), 6.

48 Cf. W. Streeck and P. C. Schmitter, 'From National Corporatism to Transnational Pluralism: Organized Interests in the Single European Market' [1991] *Politics and Society* 133–64, at 151.

49 Cf. W. Wallace, *The Transformation of Western Europe* (London, 1990), 65–7.

50 Opinion 1/91 (*Draft Agreement between the Community, on the one hand, and the countries of the European Free Trade Association, on the other, relating to the creation of the European Economic Area*) [1991] ECR I–6079.

To the extent that the implications of the EEA Agreement for integration theories and practice are recognized and developments within the Union are influenced, these developments may render the Union more accommodating of the pluralism in its decision-making necessary for closer integration between the Community and third states generally.[51] In other words, the practice of supranationalism in Community decision-making may become more favourable to such integration.

However, limits to integration between the Community and third states may still derive from limits to Community decision-making itself. The latter limitations reflect the fact that integration apparently has two aspects: the organic and the intergovernmental.[52] The organic aspect depends primarily on the incrementalist practice of the Community institutions. The demands of democratic legitimacy and the reality that resolution of distributional issues requires more than mere 'efficiency' of decision-making may set limits to what can be achieved by these institutions.[53] These limits mean that formal negotiations of a more traditional kind may become necessary for the progress of integration.

Such negotiations, which represent the intergovernmental aspect of integration, entail bargaining by the Member States themselves beyond the scope of operation of the EC Treaty. Participation therein is essentially reserved to the Member States by the Treaty on European Union. This Treaty requires unanimous agreement among Member States to major steps towards more intensive integration[54] or to enlargement.[55] The unanimity requirement creates for Member States an environment favourable to the grant and, rather than abstinence from such integration,[56] the acceptance of side payments. As a result, for example, successive enlargements and moves towards monetary union have been accompanied by major developments in Community regional policy.[57] Bargaining of this kind may be a precondition for incremental

[51] At present, Central and East European countries 'are forced to choose between, on the one hand, the hope (but not the promise) of EC integration and, eventually, membership and, on the other hand, flexibility in developing strategies and policies. Our judgment is that resolving, rather than acquiescing in, this dilemma deserves greater attention from both West and East' (D. Kennedy and D. E. Webb, n. 20 above, 1117).

[52] Cf. W. Wallace, *The Transformation of Western Europe* (London, 1990), 106, regarding the interaction between partial political bargains and the undirected evolution of informal integration.

[53] Cf. the concept of 'integration capsules' in T. Heller and J. Pelkmans, n. 2 above, 346.

[54] See Art. N of the TEU, regarding amendment of the EC treaty.

[55] Art. O of the TEU.

[56] Once an international organization has been established, abstinence can be costly both because an abstaining state forfeits input into further decision-making and because it foregoes whatever benefits result. Hence, instead of abstaining, states may reach agreement at a level of integration above the lowest common denominator. See A. Moravcsik, n. 7 above, 26.

[57] A. Evans, *The Law of EU Regional Policy* (Deventer and Stockholm, 1995).

decision-making in the Council of the Union[58] along 'path dependent' lines.[59]

In a formal sense the position of Member States under the EC Treaty and that of third states under agreements with the Community may be comparable. In both cases limits are set to the evolutionary capacity of obligations previously accepted in the relevant instrument. Once these limits are met, expansion of the obligations requires the express consent of the states to which the expanded obligations are to apply.

In a real sense, however, there is a critical difference between the position of Member States under the EC Treaty and that of third states (particularly those in Europe) under an agreement with the Community, given the impact on such states of developments within the Community. Only a Member State is entitled to prevent other Member States from agreeing among themselves on an objectionable expansion of an obligation in the EC Treaty. As a result, only Member States have opportunities to be fully involved in negotiations which may lead to Community developments having important consequences for relations between the Community and third states.

This situation is unaffected by the EEA Agreement. The latter does not compromise the freedom of Member States to engage in bargaining with each other beyond the scope of the Agreement, and the Court of Justice was apparently concerned in *Opinion 1/91* that judicial arrangements in the draft Agreement should not prevent developments in EEA law from accommodating the consequences of the bargains made between Member States. The revisions of the draft designed to meet these concerns may be seen as ensuring that the Agreement need not prejudice moves by Member States towards monetary and political union.[60]

At the same time, however, the final version of the EEA Agreement may have secured only a marginal role for EFTA States able and willing to participate in such moves. This consideration may, at least partly, explain the dissatisfaction of many EFTA States with this Agreement.[61] Austria and

[58] See, e.g., W. Sandholtz and J. Zysman, '1992: Recasting the European Bargain' [1989/90] *World Politics* 94–128.

[59] Cf. D. C. North, n. 11 above. The particular stage at which such bargaining becomes necessary depends on a range of political factors and thus varies. See, e.g., regarding the influence of President de Gaulle in securing adoption of the common agricultural policy, J. Pinder, 'Positive Integration and Negative Integration: Some Problems of Economic Union in the EEC' [1968] *The World Today* 88–110.

[60] Note, e.g., the concerns expressed in the statement of Commission President Delors to the European Parliament, EP Debs No. 2–373, 76, 17 Jan. 1989. By the same token, it seems that the importance of economic and political homogeneity among Parties to an instrument like the EEA Agreement should not be exaggerated.

[61] According to the Swiss Ambassador to the United Kingdom, negotiations for the EEA Agreement demonstrated that it was not possible to be treated as an equal partner with other European countries without being a member of the Union. See *Enlargement of the Community*, n. 22 above, 15.

Sweden, in particular, seem to have regarded the Agreement as little more than a transitional arrangement pending their accession to the Union itself.

The result of such dissatisfaction—accession of Austria, Finland and Sweden to the Union—may be that the EEA Agreement itself[62] will be unable to offer a framework[63] for closer integration of Central and Eastern European States with the Community.[64] However, the real significance of the EEA construction may be that it poses a challenge to established integration theories and constitutes a model for integration throughout Europe[65] and beyond,[66] which avoids the constraints[67] of the 'broadening or deepening' debate.[68] Establishment of an EEA-type organization,[69] adapted to the special needs of Central and Eastern European states[70]

[62] The Commission apparently remains committed to ensuring the effectiveness of the EEA. See *European Report*, No. 1997 (30 Nov. 1994). See, similarly, regarding the commitment expressed by the EEA Council, Bull. EU 12–1994, 1.3.14.

[63] Art. 128(1) of the EEA Agreement provides that any European state becoming a member of EFTA may apply to become a Party to this Agreement.

[64] Cf. W. Kostrzewa and H. Schmieding, 'EFTA Option for the Reform States of Eastern Europe' [1990] *World Economy* 501–14; E. Ems, *The Role of EFTA in European Economic Integration* (EFTA Occasional Paper No. 40, Geneva, 1992); and M. Jakobson, *Europe in the 1990s: No Stability in Sight* (EFTA Occasional Paper No. 37, Geneva, 1992); S. Peers, 'An Ever Closer Waiting Room? The Case for Eastern European Accession to the European Economic Area' (1995) 32 *CMLRev*. 187–213.

[65] Cf. the idea advocated by the European Parliament of a 'system of confederative co-operation in Europe' involving the Community and 'a number of functionally or regionally oriented confederations' in its Resolution of 20 Jan. 1993 ([1993] OJ C42/124) on the structure and strategy for the EU with regard to its enlargement and the creation of a Europe-wide order, paras. 11–14.

[66] See, regarding the Euro-Mediterranean partnership, the Council Report for the European Council in Essen concerning the future Mediterranean policy (*Agence Europe*, No. 6376, 11 Dec. 1994); regarding the idea of regional integration between Turkey and Central Asian states of the former Soviet Union, *Financial Times*, 9 Mar. 1992; regarding the idea of a 'complementary common market' for Russia and associated states, *Enlargement of the Community*, n. 22 above, 14; regarding the ex-Soviet States generally, *Financial Times*, 4 Apr. 1992; and regarding the Maghreb States, *Financial Times*, 30 Mar. 1992. Cf. A. Bressand, 'Beyond Interdependence: 1992 as a Global Challenge' [1990] *International Affairs* 47–65, at 64, regarding the potential of a reformed GATT or OECD, and J. Pinder, 'The Future of the European Community: A Strategy for Enlargement' [1992] *Government and Opposition* 414–32, regarding the Council of Europe and the Conference on Security and Co-operation in Europe.

[67] The need for a broader perspective than that associated with such debate is stressed by H. Kramer, 'The EC and the Stabilisation of Eastern Europe' [1992] *Aussenpolitik* 12–21, at 15.

[68] 'The experience of successive accessions to the Community disproves the thesis that *l'approfondissement* and *l'élargissement* are incompatible'. See R. Sadurska, 'Reshaping Europe—or "How to Keep Poor Cousins in (their) Home": A Comment on The Transformation of Europe' (1991) 100 *Yale Law Journal* 2501–10, at 2507. For a more circumspect approach see N. Nugent, 'The Deepening and Widening of the European Community: Recent Evolution, Maastricht, and Beyond' [1992] *JCMS* 311–28.

[69] Cf., regarding ideas of an 'Espace économique USA–CE', R. Schwok, *Les Relations entre les Etats-Unis et la Communauté Européenne* (Geneva, 1992), 167–74.

[70] To distinguish simply between Union internalizing of the adjustment problems of such states (through admitting them to membership) and adoption of a 'very active external policy' (*Enlargement of the Community*, n. 22 above, 5) may underestimate the potential flexibility of legal frameworks for integration.

unable[71] or unwilling to participate fully in integration processes[72] and perhaps even providing a dynamic and effective framework for their 'affiliate membership' of the Union,[73] might demonstrate rather than exhaust the potential of this model.[74]

[71] The European Parliament stresses that 'negotiations for accession should be based on the *acquis communautaire* with no opt-outs' (para. 16 of the Resolution of 30 Nov. 1994 ([1994] OJ C363/16) on the strategy of the EU to prepare for the accession of the countries of Central and Eastern Europe, with a view to the European Council in Essen (9–10 Dec. 1994)) and that 'the granting of exemptions, such as those concerning accession to the EMU and the Union's social policy, must not be repeated' (*ibid.* para. 34). See also the Opinion of the Economic and Social Committee of 25 Jan. 1995 ([1995] OJ C102/40) on relations between the EU and Russia, Ukraine and Belarus, para. 3.11.

[72] The Swedish Government, e.g., considers that the EEA Agreement could provide a model for co-operation between these states and the Community. See *Sverige–EFTA–EG 1989* (Utrikesdepartementets handelsavdelning, 1990), 19.

[73] It is only on the basis of such a model that a status of this kind could be introduced under the existing Treaties. Cf. T. M. Lettieri, 'Problemi Relativi all'Adhesione dell'Austria alle Comunità Economiche Europee' [1991] *RDE* 69–87. Recognition of a status for associated states between that of Member States and that of third states is implicit in the case law of the ECJ. See Opinion 1/94 (Competence of the Community to conclude international agreements on services and on the protection of intellectual property) [1994] ECR I-5267, I-5394.

[74] Cf. F. H. J. J. Andriessen, n. 31 above. Note also the argument that development of European integration beyond the Community and avoidance of the division of the world into three trading blocks, i.e., the Community, Japan, and the USA, are closely linked in E. Jahn, 'The Future of Europe, Eastern Europe and Central Europe' in R. J. Hill and J. Zielonka (eds.), *Restructuring Eastern Europe: Towards a New European Order* (Aldershot, 1990), 203–18.

Bibliography

ABRAMS, R. K., *et al.*, *The Impact of the European Community's Internal Market on the EFTA* (Washington, 1990)

ADDISON, J. T. and SIEBERT, W. S., 'The Social Charter of the European Community: Evolution and Controversies' [1991] *Industrial and Labor Relations Review* 597–625

ALLEN, J. J., *The European Common Market and GATT* (London, 1960)

ALTING VAN GEUSAU, F. A. M., 'Problèmes Institutionnels des Communautés Européennes' [1966] *Cahiers de Droit Européen* 227–50

ANDRIESSEN, F. H. J. J., 'Europe at the Crossroads', Tenth Annual Paul-Henri Spaak Lecture, Harvard, 1990

ANTUNES, L. M. P., 'L'Article 90 du Traité CEE: Obligations des Etats Membres et Pouvoirs de la Commission' [1991] *Revue Trimestrielle de Droit Européen* 187–209

AREEDA, P., *Antitrust Analysis* (Boston, 1981)

AYRAL, M., 'Essai de Classification des Groupes et Comités' [1975] *Revue du Marché Commun* 330–42

——— 'The European Economic Space—Characteristics and Outlooks from an EC Point of View', *Skrifter utgivna av institutet för immaterialrätt och marknadsrätt* No. 46, 20–8

BAEL, I. VAN, 'EEC Anti-Dumping Law and Procedure Revisited' [1990] *Journal of World Trade* 5–23

——— 'Public Procurement and the Completion of the Internal Market: Law and Practice' [1989] *Legal Issues of European Integration* 21–48

——— and BELLIS, J.-F., *Anti-Dumping and Other Trade Protection Laws of the EEC* (2nd edn. London, 1990)

BALDI, M., 'Direct Applicability of Free Trade Agreements between the EEC and the EFTA Countries from a Swiss Perspective' [1985] *Swiss Review of International Competition Law* 30–8

BALDWIN, R. E., 'The Case against Infant–Industry Tariff Protection' [1969] *Journal of Political Economy* 295–305

——— 'The Political Economy of Protectionism' in J. N. Bhagwati (ed.), *Import Competition and Response* (Chicago, 1982), 263–86

——— 'Rent–Seeking and Trade Policy: An Industry Approach' [1984] *Weltwirtschaftliches Archiv* 662–76

——— *Trade Policy in a Changing World Economy* (New York, 1988)

BARENTS, R., 'New Developments in Measures Having an Equivalent Effect' [1981] *Common Market Law Review* 271–308

BELLIS, J.-F. 'The Interpretation of the Free Trade Agreements Between the EFTA Countries and the European Community' [1985] *Swiss Review of International Competition Law* 21–30

——— *et al.*, 'Further Changes in the EEC Anti-Dumping Regulation: A Codification of Controversial Methodologies' [1989] *Journal of World Trade Law* 21–34

BELLO, J. H., 'Midterm Report on Binational Dispute Settlement Under the United States–Canada Free-Trade Agreement' [1991] *The International Lawyer* 489–516

BERGQUIST, M., *Sverige och EEC: en statsvetenskaplig studie av fyra åsiktsriktningars syn på svensk marknadspolitik* 1961–1962 (Stockholm, 1970)

BERNARD, N., *Le Comité Economique et Social* (Brussels, 1972)

BERNITZ, U., 'Om Statliga handelsmonopol i EG och enligt frihandelsavtalen' [1973] *Tidsskrift for Rettsvitenskap* 514–37

——— 'Onödig grundlagsändring' (1990/91) *Juridisk Tidskrift* 727–29

——— 'Sveriges EG-anknytning i rättsligt perspektiv' [1989/90] *Juridisk Tidskrift* 47–69

——— 'The EEC–EFTA Free Trade Agreements with Special Reference to the Position of Sweden and the Other Scandinavian EFTA Countries' [1986] *Common Market Law Review* 567–90

——— *Internationell Marknadsrätt* (Stockholm, 1986)

BESELER, H.-F. and WILLIAMS, A. N., *Anti-Dumping and Anti-Subsidy Law: The European Communities* (New York, 1986)

BIEBER, R., *et al.* (eds.), *1992: One European Market* (Baden-Baden, 1988)

BLANKART, F. A., 'Die Bedeutung des Abkommens zwischen den EFTA-Ländern und Spanien im Rahmen der europäischen Integration' [1981] *Aussenwirtschaft* 88–99

BLOMBERG, B., 'EG + EFTA = EES' [1990] *Vår Föda* 263–68

BOGDAN, M., 'Något om EG-reglerna avseende offentlig upphandling' [1991] *Förvaltningsrättslig Tidskrift* 86–96

BOGDANY, A. VON, *The New Democracies in the Eastern Europe and the European Communities* (Working Paper No. 2, Research Centre on the EEC, Gdansk, 1990)

BOLTUCK, R. D., 'An Economic Analysis of Dumping' [1987] *Journal of World Trade Law* 45–54

BONDE, J.-P., 'Får EG:s inre marknad en social dimension?' [1989] *Pockettidningen* 32–6

BORCH, A., *Romatraktatens artikkel 37: Saerlig om bestemmelsens betydning for A/S Vinmonopolet ved et norsk EF-medlemskap* (Oslo, 1991)

BOUDANT, J., *L'Anti-Dumping Communautaire* (Paris, 1991)

BOURGEOIS, J. H. J., 'The EC in the WTO and Advisory Opinion 1/94: An Echternach Procession' [1995] *Common Market Law Review* 763–87

——— 'EEC Control over International Mergers' [1990] *Yearbook of European Law* 103–32

——— 'The EFTA Countries and EC Legal Systems: is Integration Possible? Comment' in J. Jamar and H. Wallace (eds.), *EEC-EFTA: More Than Just Good Friends?* (Bruges, 1988), 299–304

BRANDER, J. A. and SPENCER, B. J., 'Export Subsidies and International Market Share Rivalry' [1985] *Journal of International Economics* 83–100

BRANDTNER, B., 'The Drama of the EEA: Comments on Opinions 1/91 and 1/92' in O. Jacot-Guillarmod (ed.), *Accord EEE: Commentaires et réflexions* (Bern, 1992), 300–28

BREDIMA-SAVOPOULOU, A. and TZOANNOS, J., *The Common Shipping Policy of the EEC* (Amsterdam, 1990)

BRESSAND, A., 'Beyond Interdependence: 1992 as a Global Challenge' [1990] *International Affairs* 47–65

BROCK, G., 'East could get à la carte menu for joining EC', *The Times*, 20 April 1991

BRONCKERS, M., 'Business Strategies for a Unified Market. Comment' in J. Jamar and H. Wallace (eds.), *EEC–EFTA: More Than Just Good Friends?* (Bruges, 1988), 61–7

——— and QUICK, R., 'What Is A Countervailable Subsidy Under EEC Trade Law' [1989] *Journal of World Trade Law* 5–31

BROUWERS, G., 'Free Movement of Foodstuffs and Quality Requirements: Has the Commission Got it Wrong?' [1988] *Common Market Law Review* 237–62

BRUNNER, H. E., 'Die Ursprungsregeln im europäischen Freihandelsraum' [1977] *Aussenwirtschaft* 55–63

BRÖCKNER, J. and ROHWEDER, H. C., *Barriers to International Trade: Methods of Measurement and Empirical Evidence* (CERUM Working Paper 1990:16, Umeå, 1990)

BUESS, T., 'Perspektiven für eine engere Zussammenarbeit zwischen der Europäischen Gemeinschaft und den EFTA-Mitgliedstaaten' [1985] *Aussenwirtschaft* 341–87

BULMER, S., 'The European Council's First Decade: Between Interdependence and Domestic Politics' [1985] *Journal of Common Market Studies* 89–104

CAPELLI, F., 'Les Relations CE/Etats–Unis et la Réalisation du Marché Intérieur' in J. Schwarze (ed.), *The External Relations of the European Community, in Particular EC–US Relations* (Baden-Baden, 1989), 139–43

CARLSSON, I., 'Schweden in Europa' [1988] *Europa-Archiv* 323–30

CARTER, B. E., 'A Code of Conduct for EC–US Relations' in J. Schwarze (ed.), *The External Relations of the European Community, in Particular EC–US Relations* (Baden-Baden, 1989), 131–9

CATALANO, M., 'I Poteri dell'Assemblea Parlamentare Europea' [1971] *Rivista di Diritto Europeo* 31–47

CAVES, R. E., 'Industrial Policy and Trade Policy: The Connections' in H. Kierzkowski (ed.), *Protection and Competition in International Trade* (Oxford, 1987), 68–85

CHALMERS, D., 'Repackaging the Internal Market—The Ramifications of the *Keck* Judgment' [1994] *European Law Review* 385–403

CHURCH, C., 'The Politics of Change: EFTA and the Nordic Countries' Responses to the EC in the Early 1990s' [1990] *Journal of Common Market Studies* 401–30

CLERGERIE, J.-L., 'Le Rejet Européen de la Candidature de la Turquie' [1991] *Revue du Droit Public et de la Science Politique* 1567–91

CLOSE, G., 'External Relations in the Air Transport Sector: Air Transport Policy or the Common Commercial Policy?' [1990] *Common Market Law Review* 107–27

CLUB DE BRUXELLES, *EC/EFTA: The Future European Economic Area* (Brussels, 1991)

COCCIA, C. M., 'Osservazioni sulla Immunità Penale dei Parlamentari Europei' [1985] *Rivista di Diritto Internazionale* 824–35

COOMBES, D., *The Future of the European Parliament* (London, 1979)

CORBETT, R., 'Testing the New Procedures' [1989] *Journal of Common Market Studies* 359–72

CORDEN, W. M., *Trade Policy and Economic Welfare* (Oxford, 1974)

COTTIER, T., 'Constitutional Trade Regulation in National and International Law: Structure–Substance Pairings in the EFTA Experience' in M. Hilf and E.-U. Petersmann (eds.), *National Constitutions and International Economic Law* (Deventer, 1993), 409–42

CRAMÉR, P., 'Funderingar kring permanent neutralitet och integration i västeuropa' in U. Nordlöf-Lagerkranz (ed.), *Svensk neutralitet Europa och EG* (Stockholm, 1990), 27–51

——— and ÖSTLING, L., *Svenskt statsstöd och samhandel med EEC* (Gothenburg, 1986)

CRONEBORG, R., 'Taking Stock of the Dialogue: The View From EFTA' in J. Jamar and H. Wallace (eds.), *EEC–EFTA: More Than Just Good Friends?* (Bruges, 1988), 322–7

CURZON, V., *The Essentials of Economic Integration* (London, 1974)

CURZON PRICE, V., 'EFTA and the European Communities: What Future for 'Greater Europe'?' [1985] *Annuaire européen* 109–38

——— *1992: Europe's Last Chance? From Common Market to Single Market* (Institute of Economic Affairs, London, 1988)

——— 'Industrial Trade Policy in a Period of Rapid Industrial Change' [1986] *Aussenwirtschaft* 201–23

——— 'La Suisse et le Marché Unique de 1992: une Comparaison entre les scénarios 'First best' et 'Least best' ' [1990] *Schweizerische Zeitschrift für Volkswirtschaft und Statistik* 215–29

——— 'The Threat of 'Fortress Europe' from the Development of Social and Industrial Policies at a European Level' [1991] *Aussenwirtschaft* 119–38

DAHLBERG, Å., and JOHANSSON M. (eds), *Att Arbeta i Europa* (Stockholm, 1990)

DANELIUS, H., 'Sveriges avtal med de europeiska gemenskaperna—juridiska aspekter' [1973] *Svensk Juristtidning* 97–114

DAVENPORT, M., *The Charybdis of Antidumping: A New Form of EC Industrial Policy?* (Discussion Paper 22, Royal Institute of International Affairs, London, 1989)

——— 'The Economics of Antidumping and the Uruguay Round' [1990] *Intereconomics* 267–73

DAVIGNON, E., 'The Future of the European Steel Industry' [1980] *Annals of Public and Cooperative Economy* 507–19

DE LANGE, H., 'Taking Stock of the EC–EFTA Dialogue' in J. Jamar and H. Wallace (eds.), *EEC–EFTA More Than Just Good Friends?* (Bruges, 1988), 310–21

DE SCHACHT, F., 'Situation et Perspectives des Relations entre la CEE et l'AELE au Lendemain des Entretiens Franco–Britanniques' [1966] *Revue du Marché Commun* 641–51

DE SOTO, J., *La Communauté Européenne du Charbon et de l'Acier* (Paris, 1967)

DE THOMASIS, G., 'Project d'Union Européenne à la Veille de la Campagne Pour les Deuxième Elections Européennes' [1984] *Revue du Marché Commun* 212–4

DENTON, R., 'The Non-Market Economy Rules of the European Community's Anti-Dumping and Countervailing Duties Legislation' [1987] *International and Comparative Law Quarterly* 198–239

DEWOST, J. L., 'La Présidence dans le Cadre Institutionnel des Communautés Européennes' [1984] *Revue du Marché Commun* 31–4

DICKE, H., and LANGHAMMER, R. J., *The Institutional Framework and External Dimension of the EC Internal Market* (Kiel Working Paper No. 453, Kiel, 1990)

DIDIER, P., 'EEC Anti-Dumping Rules and Practices' [1980] *Common Market Law Review* 349–69

DIXIT, A., 'International Trade Policy for Oligopolistic Industries' [1984] *Economic Journal* 1–16

DOHLMAN, E., *National Welfare and Economic Interdependence: The Case of Sweden's Foreign Trade Policy* (Oxford, 1989)

DUE, O., 'General Introduction to a Discussion on the Principles of Community Law Seen in the EEA Perspective' [1991] *Tidskrift utgiven av Juridiska föreningen i Finland* 288–94

DUFF, A. M., 'The Report of the Three Wise Men' [1981] *Journal of Common Market Studies* 237–54

DUNLOP, J. and KING, R. N., 'Regional Economic Integration and GATT: The Effects of the EEC–EFTA Agreements on International Trade' [1974] *Law and Policy in International Business* 207–35

EDWARDS, G., 'The Relevance of Theory to Group-to-Group Dialogue' in G. Edwards and E. Regelsberger (eds.), *Europe's Global Links* (London, 1990), 201–18

EDWARDS, S., *On the Sequencing of Structural Reforms* (OECD Working Paper No. 70, Paris, 1989)

EEK, H., 'Neutralitet, neutralitetspolitik och EEC' [1971] *Svensk Juristtidning* 1–21

EHLERMANN, C.-D., and CAMPOGRANDE G., 'Rules on Services in the EEC: A model for Negotiating World-Wide Rules?' in E.-U. Petersmann and M. Hilf (eds), *The New GATT Round of Multilateral Trade Negotiations* (Deventer, 1991), 481–98

——— 'The Financing of the Community: The Distinction between Financial Contributions and Own Resources' [1982] *Common Market Law Review* 371–92

EKDAHL, H., *EG 1992—utmaningen för svensk industri* (Stockholm, 1989)

——— *EGs och EFTAs handelspolitik* (Industriförbundet, Arbetsrapport 4, Stockholm, 1988)

EL-AGRAA, A. M., *The Economics of the European Community* (2nd edn., London, 1985)

ELVANDER, N. and GUSTAVSSON, R., *EG—Integration och Suveränitet* (Stockholm, 1989)

ETHIER, W. J., 'Dumping' [1982] *Journal of Political Economy* 487–506

EVANS, A. 'Anti-Dumping Law and Third Countries: A Case Study' in A. Evans and P. Falk (eds), *Integration and Transformation: Polish–Swedish Perspectives* (Umeå, 1992), 219–81

——— 'Article 85(3) Exemption: 'Allowing Consumers a Fair Share of the Resulting Benefit'' in M. Goyens (ed.), *EC Competition Policy and Consumers* (Brussels, 1985), 99–120

——— 'Institutional Arrangements for Integration of Third Countries with the EC' in A. Evans and P. Falk (eds.), *Transformation and Integration: Polish—Swedish Perspectives* (Umeå, 1992), 165–215

——— 'Legal Frameworks for Trade Liberalisation' in A. Evans and P. Falk (eds.), *Transformation and Integration: Polish—Swedish Perspectives* (Umeå, 1992), 25–98

——— 'Nationality Law and European Integration' [1991] *European Law Review* 190–215

——— 'Participation of National Parliaments in the European Community Legislative Process' [1981] *Public Law* 388–98

——— 'Secondary Immigration Control and EEC Law' [1984] *New Law Journal* 965–7

——— 'The Enforcement Procedure in Article 169 EEC: Commission Discretion' [1979] *European Law Review* 442–56

——— *The Law of EU Regional Policy* (Deventer and Stockholm, 1995)

——— and FALK, P. (eds.), *Integration and Transformation: Polish—Swedish Perspectives* (Umeå, 1992)

——— and FALK, P., *Law and Integration: Sweden and the European Community* (Stockholm, 1991)

——— and MARTIN, S., 'Socially Acceptable Distortion of Competition: EC Policy on State Aid' [1991] *European Law Review* 79–111

——— and D'OLIVEIRA, H. U. J., 'Nationality and Citizenship' in A. Cassese *et al.* (eds), *Human Rights and the European Community: Methods of Protection* (Baden-Baden, 1991), 299–350

EWANDER, H. *Avveckling av tekniska handelshinder* (Industriförbundet, Arbetsrapport 12, Stockholm, 1989)

FAGERBERG, J., 'The Process of Economic Integration in Europe: Consequences for EFTA Countries and Firms' [1991] *Co-operation and Conflict* 197–215

FINGER, J. M., 'Subsidies and Countervailing Duties' in P. K. M. Tharakan (ed.), *Policy Implications of Antidumping Measures* (Amsterdam, 1991), 175–89

FISCHER, F., *Die Institutionalisierte Vertretung der Verbande in der europäischen Wirtschaftsgemeinschaft* (Kiel, 1965)

FLAESCH-MOUGIN, C., 'Les Accords Externes de la CEE (1 juillet 1986/31 octobre 1989)' [1990] *Revue Trimestrielle de Droit Européen* 457–518

FLAM, H., *Reverse Dumping* (Institute for International Economic Studies, Stockholm, 1985)

——— and HORN, H., 'Ekonomiska konsekvenser för Sverige av EGs inre marknad' in *Svensk ekonomi och Europaintegration* (Ekonomiska Rådet, Stockholm, 1990)

FOREST, P., 'Il Mecanismo Decisionale Comunitari visto attraverso il Consiglio dei Ministri delle Comunità Europea' [1982] *Diritto Comparato e degli Scambi Internazionale* 755–85

FRAZER, T., 'Competition Policy after 1992: The Next Step' [1990] 53 *Modern Law Review* 609–23

FRIEDRICH, K., 'Die Freihandelsabkommen der Europäischen Gemeinschaften mit den EFTA–Staaten' [1983] *Neue juristische Wochenschrift* 1237–42

GAISFORD, J. D., and MCLACHLAN, D. L., 'Domestic Subsidies and Countervail: The Treacherous Ground of the Level Playing Field' [1990] *Journal of World Trade* 55–77

GAJA, G., *et al.*, 'Instruments for Legal Integration in the European Community—A Review' in M. Cappelletti *et al.*, *Integration Through Law* (Berlin, 1986), 113–60

GANSHOF VAN DER MEERSCH, W. G., *Organisations Européennes: les Institutions* (Brussels, 1963), vol. 2

GASTEYGER, K., *Europa zwischen Spaltung und Einigung 1945–1990* (Bonn, 1990)

GERBET, P., 'La Genèse du Plan Schuman' [1956] *Revue Française de Science Public* 525–53

GIDDENS, A., 'A Reply to my Critics' in D. Held and J. B. Thompson (eds), *Social Theory of Modern Societies: Anthony Giddens and His Critics* (Cambridge, 1989) 249–301

GILSDORF, P., *Assoziierungsabkommen der Europäischen Wirtschaftsgemeinschaft* (Saarbrücken, 1990)

GOLD, M., 'Managing Dumping in a Global Economy' [1988] 21 *George Washington Journal of International Law and Economics* 503–38

GOLDSCHMIDT, E., 'EF og Norden' [1990] *Nordisk Administrativt Tidsskrift* 296–308

GORMLEY, L., *Prohibiting Restrictions on Trade Within the EEC* (Amsterdam, 1985)

GRADIN, A., 'West European Integration: The Swedish View' [1989] *European Affairs* 20–5

GREENWALD, J., 'Negotiating Strategy' in G. C. Hufbauer (ed.), *Europe 1992: An American Perspective* (Washington, 1990), 345–88

GREENWAY, D., *International Trade Policy. From Tariffs to the New Protectionism* (London, 1983)

——— and THAKARAN, P., *Imperfect Competition and International Trade* (Sussex, 1986)

GRIECO, J. M., *Cooperation among Nations* (London, 1990)

GROEBEN, H., VON DER, *et al.*, *Kommentar zum EWG Vertrag* (Baden-Baden, 1983)

GROLIG, O. and BOGAERT, P., 'The Newly-Amended EEC Anti-Dumping Regulation: Black Holes in the Common Market' [1987] *Journal of World Trade Law* 79–87

GRUSZECKI, T. and WINIECKI, J., 'Privatisation in East–Central Europe: A Comparative Perspective' [1991] *Aussenwirtschaft* 67–100

GUGGENHEIM, P., 'Organisations Economiques Supranationales, Indépendance et Neutralité de la Suisse' [1962] *Zeitschrift für Schweizerisches Recht* 221–343

HAALAND, J. I., and NORMAN, V., *EFTA and the World Economy: Comparative Advantage and Trade Policy* (EFTA Occasional Paper No. 19, Geneva, 1987)

HAAS, E. B., *The Uniting of Europe: Political, Social, and Economic Forces 1950–1957* (Stanford, 1968)

HAILBRONNER, K., 'Legal Aspects of the Unification of the Two German States' [1991] *European Journal of International Law* 18–41

HAKOVIRTA, H., 'The Nordic Neutrals in Western European Integration: Current Pressures, Restraints and Options' [1987] *Cooperation and Conflict* 265–73

HALLSTRÖM, P., and QUITZOW, C. M., 'Gemenskapsrättens förbud mot fiskal diskriminering i perspektivet European Economic Space' [1989–90] *Juridisk Tidskrift* 311–22

HAMILTON, C. B. (ed.), *Europa och Sverige* (Stockholm, 1989)

——— *Restrictiveness and International Transmission of the 'New' Protectionism* (Institute for International Economic Studies, Stockholm, 1986)

——— *The New Protectionism and International Economic Integration* (EFTA Occasional Paper No. 21, Geneva, 1987)

HARROPS, J., *The Political Economy of Integration in the European Community* (Aldershot, 1989)

HART, M., 'A North American Free Trade Agreement: The Elements Involved' [1991] *The World Economy* 87–102

HAWK, B., 'The American (Anti-trust) Revolution: Lessons for the EEC?' [1988] *European Competition Law Review* 53–87

HAYDER, R., 'Neue Wege der europäischen Rechtsangleichung?' [1989] *Rabels Zeitschrift für ausländisches und internationales Privatrecht* 622–98

HAYES-RENSHAW, F., LEQUESNE C., and LOPEZ, P. M., 'The Permanent Representatives of the Member States to the European Communities' [1989] *Journal of Common Market Studies* 119–37

HAYMANN, M., 'Joint Ventures and Mergers as a Test-Mark for a European Competition Law Between EEC and EFTA: Switzerland as an Example' [1990] *World Competition* 5–29

HECKSHER, S., 'EG och de svenska domstolarna' [1991] *Svensk Juristtidning* 221–35

HELPMAN, E., and KRUGMAN, P., *Market Structure and Foreign Trade* (Cambridge, Massachusetts, 1985)

HENIG, S., 'The Institutional Structure of the European Community' [1973] *Journal of Common Market Studies* 373–409

——— 'New Institutions for European Integration' [1973] *Journal of Common Market Studies* 129–38

HERIN, J., *Rules of Origin and Differences Between Tariff Levels in EFTA and in the EC* (EFTA Occasional Paper No. 13, Geneva, 1986)

HILF, M., 'Settlement of Disputes in International Economic Organisations: Comparative Analysis and Proposals for Strengthening the GATT Dispute Settlement Procedures' in E.-U. Petersmann and M. Hilf (eds), *The New GATT Round of Multilateral Trade Negotiations* (Deventer, 1991), 285–322

HINDLEY, B., 'The Economics of Dumping and Anti-Dumping Action: Is there a baby in the bathwater?' in P. K. M. Tharakan (ed.), *Policy Implications of Antidumping Measures* (Amsterdam, 1991) 25–43

HINE, R. C., *The Political Economy of European Trade* (Hemel Hempstead, 1985)

HIRDMAN, S., 'Sverige, EG och neutraliteten' [1989] *Tiden* 333–9

HOFFMAN, W. C., 'Germany's New Environmental Liability Act: Strict Liability for Facilities Causing Pollution' [1991] *Netherlands International Law Review* 27–41

HORLICK, G. N., and SHUMAN, S., 'Non-Market Economy Trade and US Anti-Dumping/Countervailing Duty Laws' [1984] *The International Lawyer* 807–40

HORNSBY, S. B., 'Competition Policy in the 80's: More Policy Less Competition?' [1987] *European Law Review* 79–101

HOROVITZ, D., 'Dealing with Dumping in the EEC–EFTA Free Trade Areas' [1989] *European Competition Law Review* 540–56

——— 'EC–Central/East European Relations: New Principles for a New Era' [1990] *Common Market Law Review* 259–84

HUFBAUER, G. C., (ed.), *Europe 1992: An American Perspective* (Washington, 1990)

——— 'An Overview' in G. C. Hufbauer (ed.), *Europe 1992: An American Perspective* (Washington, 1990), 1–64

——— *Procedures for Monitoring and Disciplining Government Aids* (EFTA Occasional Paper No. 30, Geneva, 1989)

——— and SCHOTT, J. J., *Trading for Growth: The Next Round of Trade Negotiations* (Institute for International Economics, Washington, 1985)

HUGHES, G., and HARE, P., 'Competitiveness and Industrial Restructuring in Czechoslovakia, Hungary and Poland' in *European Economy* (Special Edition No. 2, The Path of Reform in Central and Eastern Europe, EC Commission, Brussels, 1991), 83–105

HUMMER, W., and SCHWEITZER, M., 'Möglichkeiten und Grenzen der Dynamisierung der Beziehungen Österreichs zu den Europäischen Gemeinschaften' [1987] *Europa-Archiv* 343–50

HURNI, B. 'EFTA–EC Relations: Aftermath of the Luxembourg Declaration' [1986] *Journal of World Trade Law* 497–506

HURTIG, S., 'The European Common Market' [1958] *International Conciliation* 317–81

HÖSLI, M. 'Decision-making in the EEA and EFTA States' Sovereignty' [1990] *Aussenwirtschaft* 463–94

ISAACS, G., 'La Rénovation des Institutions Financiers des Communautés Européennes Depuis 1970' [1977] *Revue Trimestrielle de Droit Européen* 736–810

JACKSON, J. H., 'EC '92 and Beyond: Comments from a U.S. Perspective' [1991] *Aussenwirtschaft* 341–8

——— and VERMULST, E. A., *Anti-Dumping Law and Practice: A Comparative Study* (New York, 1990)

JACOBS, F. G., 'Anti-Dumping Procedures with regard to Imports from Eastern Europe', in M. Maresceau (ed.), *The Political and Legal Framework of Trade Relations Between the European Community and Eastern Europe* (London, 1989), 291–308

——— 'Isoglucose Resurgent: Two Powers of the European Parliament Upheld by the Court' [1981] 18 *Common Market Law Review* 219–26

JACOT–GULLIARMOD, O. (ed.), *Accord EEE: Commentaires et réflexions* (Bern, 1992)

——— 'Droit International et Droit Communautaire dans le Futur Traité Instituant l'EEE' [1991] *Aussenwirtschaft* 317–40

——— 'How Far Should the Cassis de Dijon Principle Developed in the Case Law of the European Court of Justice Be Introduced into EC–EFTA Relations' in M. Robinson and J. Findlater (eds.), *Creating a European Economic Space: Legal Aspects of EC–EFTA Relations* (Dublin, 1988), 193–206

JACQEMART, C., 'Les Règles d'Origine dans les Accords de Libre Echange Conclus entre la CEE et les Pays de l'AELE' [1974] *Revue du Marché Commun* 182–8

JACQUÉ, J.-P., 'The Draft Treaty Establishing the European Union' [1985] 22 *Common Market Law Review* 19–42

JAHN, E., 'The Future of Europe, Eastern Europe and Central Europe' in R. J. Hill and J. Zielonka (eds), *Restructuring Eastern Europe: Towards a New European Order* (Aldershot, 1990), 203–18

JAMES, S., 'Industrial Policy After 1992: Making the Most of the Internal Market' in D.H. Gowland and S. James (eds), *Economic Policy After 1992* (Aldershot, 1991), 20–45

JOLIET, R., 'Droit des Marques et Libre Circulation des Marchandises: l'Abandon de l'Arrêt Hag I' [1991] *Revue Trimestrielle de Droit Européen* 169–85

JOLLES, P. R., 'Herausforderung des EG-Binnenmarktprogrammes für die schweizerische Wirtschaft und Politik' [1988] *Aussenwirtschaft* 291–8

JONSSON, B., 'Will EFTA be within the Single Market' [1989] *EIU European Trends* 55–63

JÄGER, M., 'Die sogenannte Entwicklungsklauseln in den Abkommen der EWG mit den Rest—EFTA—Staaten, inbesondere der Schweiz' [1972] *Aussenwirtschaft* 323–39

KAMINSKI, B., 'The Framework of Soviet–East-Central European Economic Relations in the 1990s' in R. F. Staar (ed.), *East-Central Europe and the USSR* (New York, 1991), 37–58

KAPTEYN, P. J. G., and VERLOREN VAN THEMAAT, P., *Introduction to the Law of the European Communities* (London, 1973)

KAWECKA-WYRZYKOWSKA, E., *The Poland–EEC Agreement on Trade and Commercial and Economic Cooperation: Its Significance for Poland* (World Economy Research Institute, Warsaw, 1989)

KENNEDY, D., and SPECHT, L., 'Austria and the European Communities' [1989] *Common Market Law Review* 615–41

——— 'Austrian Membership in the European Communities' [1990] *Harvard International Law Journal* 407–61

KENNEDY, D., and WEBB, D. E., 'The Limits of Integration: Eastern Europe and the European Communities' [1993] *Common Market Law Review* 1095–117

KEOHANE, R. O., and HOFFMANN, S., 'Institutional Change in the 1980s' in R. O. Keohane and S. Hoffmann (eds.), *The New European Community* (Boulder, 1991), 1–39

KLEPPE, P., *EFTA–NORDEK–EEC: Analys av de nordiska ländernas integrationsproblem* (Stockholm, 1970)

KOOPMAN, G. and SCHARRER, H.-E., *Scenarios of a Common External Trade Policy for the EC after 1992* (Institut für Wirtschaftsforschung Report No. 84, Hamburg, 1990)

KORAH, V., 'Interpretation and Application of Article 86 of the Treaty of Rome: Abuse of a Dominant Position Within the Common Market' [1978] *Notre Dame Lawyer* 768–98

KOSTRZEWA, W., and SCHMIEDING, H., 'EFTA Option for the Reform States of Eastern Europe' [1990] *World Economy* 501–14

KRAMER, H., 'The EC and the Stabilisation of Eastern Europe' [1992] *Aussenpolitik* 12–21

KRENZLER, H. G., 'The Dialogue between the European Community and the United States of America: Present Form and Future Prospects' in J. Schwarze (ed.), *The External Relations of the European Community, in Particular EC–US Relations* (Baden-Baden, 1989), 91–103

——— 'Die Rolle der Kabinette in der Kommission der Europäischen Gemeinschaften' [1974] *Europa Recht* 75–9

——— 'Zwischen Protektionismus und Liberalismus: Europäischer Binnenmarkt und Drittlandsbeziehungen' [1988] *Europa-Archiv* 241–8

KRUEGER, A. O., 'The Political Economy of the Rent-Seeking Society' [1974] 64 *The American Economic Review* 291–303

KRUGMAN, P., *EFTA and 1992* (EFTA Occasional Paper No. 23, Geneva, 1988)

KRÄMER, L., 'Environmental Protection and Article 30 EEC Treaty' [1993] 30 *Common Market Law Review* 111–43

KULMS, R. 'Competition, Trade Policy and Competition Policy in the EEC: The Example of Antidumping' [1990] *Common Market Law Review* 285–313

KUNGLIGA VETENSKAPSAKADEMIEN, *Sverige och Europa—det vetenskapliga samarbetet* (Documenta No. 48, Stockholm, 1989)

KUZMIK, J. T., 'A Community Export Price Offset' [1988] 25 *Common Market Law Review* 317–31

LADEUR, K.-H., 'European Community Institutional Reforms: Extra-National Management as an Alternative Model to Federalism' [1990/2] *Legal Issues of European Integration* 1–21

LAIRD, S., and YEATS, A., 'Trends in Nontariff Barriers of Developed Countries, 1966–1986' [1990] *Weltwirtschaftliches Archiv* 299–325

LAMBRINIDIS, J. S., *The Structure, Function and Law of a Free Trade Area* (London, 1965)

LANDAU, A., 'L'Espace Economique Européen après Maastricht: Les Défis de la Communauté Européenne' [1992] *Il Politico* 281–96

LAPRAT, G., 'Les Groupes Politiques en le Parlement Européen' [1975] *Revue du Marché Commun* 22–30

LASOK, D., and BRIDGE, J. W., *Law and Institutions of the European Communities* (4th edn., London, 1987)

LAURSEN, F., 'The Community's Policy Towards EFTA: A Regime Formation in the European Economic Space' [1990] *Journal of Common Market Studies* 303–25

LAUWAARS, R. H., 'The European Council' [1977] 14 *Common Market Law Review* 25–44

LAZAR, F., 'Structural/Strategic Dumping: A Comment on Richard Boltuck's 'An Economic Analysis of Dumping'' [1988] *Journal of World Trade Law* 91–3

LE LIEVRE, L. R., and HOUBEN, L. G., 'EC Versus Japan: The Community's Legal Weapons' [1987] *Common Market Law Review* 427–55

LEBORGNE, D., and LIPIETZ, A., 'How to Avoid a Two–Tier Europe' [1990] *Labour and Society* 177–99

LEGRAND-LANE, R., 'Vers une Relance Institutionnelle de la Communauté Européenne' [1985] *Etudes* 293–305

LEMAN, C., 'Patterns of Policy Development: Social Security in the United States and Canada' [1977] *Public Policy* 261–91

LENAERTS, K., 'Regulating the Regulatory Process: 'Delegation of Powers' in the European Community' [1993] *European Law Review* 23–49

LEOPOLD, P. M., 'Community Law-Making: Opinions of the European Parliament' [1982] *Oxford Journal of Legal Studies* 454–9

LIDGARD, H. 'Sverige–EEG och konkurrensen' [1974] *Svensk Juristtidning* 18–33

——— 'Tre års frihandelssamarbete med EEC' [1976] *Svensk Juristtidning* 689–714

LINDBERG, L., and SCHEINGOLD, S. A., *Europe's Would-be Polity* (Englewood Cliffs, New Jersey, 1970)

LINDH, P., 'Institutional Developments and Linkages—A Response' in M. Robinson and J. Findlater (eds.), *Creating a European Economic Space: Legal Aspects of EC–EFTA Relations* (Dublin, 1988) 109–13

LIPSEY, R. G., and LANCASTER, K., 'The General Theory of the Second Best' [1956] *Review of Economic Studies* 11–32

LIPSTEIN, K., 'The Legal Structure of Association Agreements with the EEC' [1974–75] *British Yearbook of International Law* 201–26

LISEIN-NORMAN, M., 'La Dépendance Economique de la Suède à l'Egard de l'Europe Occidentale' [1974] *Revue du Marché Commun* 373–81

LLAVERO, M. V., 'The Possible Direct Effect of the Provisions on Competition in the EEC–EFTA Free Trade Agreements in the Light of the Kupferberg Decision' [1984/2] *Legal Issues of European Integration* 83–101

LOCH, M. T., *Die Assoziierungs und Präferenzpolitik* (Berlin, 1984)

LOUIS, J. V. *et al.*, *Le Droit de la Communauté Economique Européenne* (Brussels, 1980), Vol. 12

LOWE, P., 'The Reform of the Community's Structural Funds' [1988] 25 *Common Market Law Review* 503–21

LUCRON, C. P., 'Vers l'Espace Economique Européen, L'Europe du Deuxième Cercle' [1990] *Revue du Marché Commun* 527–31

LUIF, P., 'Decision Structures and Decision-Making Processes in the European Communities' Relations to the EFTA Countries: A Case Study of Austria' [1983] *Österreichisches Zeitschrift für Aussenpolitik* 139–60

LYSÉN, G., *Introduktion till EG-rätten* (2nd edn., Uppsala, 1989)

——— 'Some Views on Neutrality and Membership of the European Communities: The Case of Sweden' [1992] *Common Market Law Review* 229–55

——— 'Varumärken som konkurrensbegränsande medel—en komparativ betraktelse utifrån frihandelsavtalet mellan Sverige och EEC' [1982] *Svensk Juristtidning* 461–90

MAAG, A., *Das Verbot Wettbewerbsverfälschender Beihilfen im EWG-Vertrag und im Freihandelsabkommen zwischen der Schweiz und der europäischen Wirtschaftsgemeinschaft* (Bern, 1979)

MANCINI, C. F., 'L'Incorporazione del Diritto Comunitario nel Diritto Interno degli Stati Membri delle Comunità Europee' [1988] *Rivista di Diritto Europeo* 87–100

MARCH HUNNINGS, N., 'Enforceability of the EEC–EFTA Free Trade Agreements' [1977] *European Law Review* 163–89

MARESCEAU, M. (ed.), *The Political and Legal Framework of Trade Relations Between the European Community and Eastern Europe* (London, 1989)

MARTIN, A. M., 'Le Comité des Représentants Permanents' [1980] *Cahiers de Droit Européen* 25–53

MATTIONI, A., 'Lo Sviluppo Democratico delle Comunità e il Ruolo del Parlamento Europeo' [1982] *Diritto Comunitario e degli Scambi Internazionali* 431–49

MAYRZEDT, H., 'Beziehungen zwischen EWG und EFTA Kritischer Ruckblick und Ausblick' in P. du Bois and B. Hurni (eds.), *L'AELE d'Hier à Demain* (Geneva, 1987), 139–47

MCGEE, A., and WEATHERILL, S., 'The Evolution of the Single Market—Harmonisation or Liberalisation' [1990] *Modern Law Review* 578–96

MCLAUGHLIN, D., 'The Work and Aims of the Economic and Social Committee of the EEC and Euratom' [1976–77] *Journal of Common Market Studies* 9–28

MEEHAN, D., *An Outline of EEC Anti–dumping Law and Practice* (Working Paper No. 2, Research Centre on the EEC, Gdansk, 1990)

MEIJ, A. W. H., and WINTER, J. A., 'Measures Having an Equivalent Effect to Quantitative Restrictions' [1976] 13 *Common Market Law Review* 79–104

MERCIAI, P., 'Safeguard Measures in GATT' [1985] *Journal of World Trade Law* 41–66

MERLINI, C., *Economic Summits and Western Decision Making* (London, 1984)

MERRITT, G., *Eastern Europe the USSR: The Challenge of Freedom* (London, 1991)

MESSERLIN, P. A., 'The EC Antidumping Regulations; A First Economic Appraisal, 1980–83' [1989] *Weltwirtschaftliches Archiv* 563–87

——— 'Nonborder Measures to Assist Industry' in J. M. Finger and A. Olechowski (eds.), *The Uruguay Round* (Washington, 1987), 127–36

MICHELMANS, H., 'The Community Decision-Making Process' in D. Lasok and P.

Soldatos (eds.), *Les Communautés Européennes en Fonctionnement* (Brussels, 1981), 147–70

MIDDLETON, R., 'Some Non-Tariff Barriers to Trade in EFTA and EEC', *EFTA Bulletin*, 9/1972, 18–19

MILAS, R., 'Les Relations entre la Communauté Européenne et les Pays Nordiques' [1984] *Revue du Marché Commun* 534–43

MILJAN, T., *The Reluctant Europeans* (London, 1977)

MITCHELL, J. D. B., 'The Tindemans Report—Retrospect and Prospect' [1976] 13 *Common Market Law Review* 455–70

MITRANY, D., *A Working Peace System* (Chicago, 1966)

MOLLER, J. O., 'Financing European Integration: The European Communities and the Proposed European Union' in R. Bieber *et al.*, *An Ever Closer Union* (Brussels, 1986), 73–102

MONNET, J., *Mémoires* (Paris, 1976)

MORTELMANS, K., 'Article 30 of the EEC Treaty and Legislation Relating to Market Circumstances: A Time to Consider a New Definition?' [1991] *Common Market Law Review* 115–36

MUNCH, F., 'Prolégomènes à une Théorie Constitutionnelle des Communautés Européennes' [1961] *Rivista di Diritto Europeo* 127–37

MUOSER, T., *Finnlands Neutralität und die Europäische Wirtschaftsintegration* (Baden-Baden, 1986)

MUSGRAVE, R. A., *The Theory of Public Finance* (New York, 1959)

NELL, P. G., 'EFTA in the 1990s: The Search for a New Identity' [1990] *Journal of Common Market Studies* 327–58

——— '1992: la Nouvelle Dimension de la Politique d'Intégration de la Suisse' [1989] *Revue du Marché Commun* 536–45

NELLO, S. S., 'Some Recent Developments in EC–East European Economic Relations' [1990] *Journal of World Trade* 5–24

NENE, C., '1992 et la Clause de l'Article 115: A Quand une Politique Commerciale Commune?' [1988] *Revue du Marché Commun* 578–83

NICHOLL, W., 'Historique de la Composition de la Majorité Qualifiée dans Conseil en Vertu des Traités' [1986] *Revue du Marché Commun* 135–7

——— 'La Procedure de Concertation Entre le Parlement Européen et le Conseil' [1986] *Revue du Marché Commun* 11–15

NICOLAIDES, P. 'How Fair is Fair Trade?' [1986] *Journal of World Trade Law* 148–62

——— 'The Antidumping Policy of the European Communities' [1990] *Intereconomics* 273–9

NORBERG, S., 'European Community Anti-Dumping Laws Their Actual and Potential Application to EFTA Countries: Some Comments from an EFTA Point of View' [1987] *Tidsskrift for Rettsvitenskap* 638–50

——— 'Skapandet av ett Europeiskt Ekonomiskt Samarbetsområde (EES)—rättsliga utmaningar från ett EFTA-perspektiv' [1989] *Svensk Juristtidning* 89–101

——— 'The Free Trade Agreements of the EFTA Countries with the EC—Experiences and Problems' [1988] *Svensk Juristtidning* 77–107

NORMAN, V., 'EFTA and the Internal European Market' [1989] *Economic Policy* 423–65

NORTH, D. C., *Institutions, Institutional Change and Economic Performance* (Cambridge, 1990)

NUTTALL, S., 'The Commission: Protagonists of Inter–regional Cooperation' in G. Edwards and E. Regelsberger (eds.), *Europe's Global Links* (London, 1990), 143–57

O'CLÉIREÁCAIN, S., 'Europe 1992 and Gaps in the EC's Common Commercial Policy' [1990] *Journal of Common Market Studies* 201–17

OHLSSON, L., *Consequences of the EC for Swedish Manufacturing Industry* (Industriförbundet Working Paper No. 7, Stockholm, 1988)

D'OLIVEIRA, H. U. J., 'Is Reverse Discrimination Still Permissible Under the Single European Act?' in *Forty Years on: The Evolution of Postwar Private International Law in Europe* (Amsterdam, 1990), 71–86

OLIVER, P., 'Measures of Equivalent Effect: A Reappraisal' [1982] 19 *Common Market Law Review* 217–44

——— *The Free Movement of Goods in the EEC* (London, 1988)

OLMI, G., 'Les Resources Propres aux Communautés Européennes' [1971] *Cahiers de Droit Européen* 379–427

PATTERSON, E. R., 'Improving GATT Rules for Non–Market Economies' [1981] *Journal of World Trade* 185–205

PEDERSEN, T., 'EC–EFTA Relations: Neighbours in Search of a New Partnership' in G. Edwards and E. Regelsberger (eds.), *Europe's Global Links* (London, 1990), 97–111

PEERS, S., 'An Ever Closer Waiting Room? The Case for Eastern European Accession to the European Economic Area' [1995] 32 *Common Market Law Review* 187–213

PELKMANS, J., 'Europe 1992: Internal and External' in F. Laursen (ed.), *EFTA and the EC: Implications of 1992* (Maastricht, 1990), 5–29

——— and EGAN, M., *Fixing European Standards: Moving Beyond the Green Paper* (CEPS Working Document No. 65, Brussels, 1992)

——— and MURPHY, A., 'Catapulted into Leadership: The Community's Trade and Aid Policies vis-à-vis Eastern Europe' [1991] *Revue d'Intégration Européenne* 125–51

PEREZ, P., 'Concluding Reports: Looking into the Crystal Ball' in J. Jamar and H. Wallace (eds.), *EEC–EFTA: More Than Just Good Friends?* (Bruges, 1988), 367–70

PESCATORE, P., 'The Dynamics and Homogeneity of the European Economic System' [1991] *Tidskrift utgiven av Juridiska föreningen i Finland* 295–320

PETERSMANN, E.-U., 'Constitutionalism, Constitutional Law and European Integration' [1991] *Aussenwirtschaft* 247–80

——— 'Strengthening the Domestic Legal Framework of the GATT Multilateral Trade System: Possibilities and Problems of Making GATT Rules Effective in Domestic Legal Systems' in E.-U. Petersmann and M. Hilf (eds.), *The New GATT Round of Multilateral Trade Negotiations* (Deventer, 1991), 33–113

PETRÉN, G., 'The Nordic Countries and the Common Market' in *Legal Problems of an Enlarged Common Market* (London, 1972), 191–5

PFALLER, A., *et al.* 'The Issue' in A. Pfaller *et al.* (eds), *Can the Welfare State Compete?* (London, 1991), 1–14

PHLIPS, L., *The Economics of Price Discrimination* (Cambridge, 1983)

PIEHL, E., *Strukturen der politischen Architektur Europa* (Berlin, 1991)

PINDER, J., *The European Community and Eastern Europe* (London, 1991)

——— 'Positive Integration and Negative Integration: Some Problems of Economic Union in the EEC' [1968] *The World Today* 88–110

PLESSOW, U., *Neutralität und Assoziation mit der EWG* (Cologne, 1967)

PORRO, G., *L'Integrazione Giuridica nell'Associazione Europea di Libero Scambio* (Milan, 1983)

PRYCE, R., *The Political Future of the European Community* (London, 1973)

PUSLECKI, Z., *Der EG-Binnenmarkt und die Sich Reformienden Staaten Mittel und Osteuropas* (Working Paper No. 4, Research Centre on the EEC, Gdansk, 1991)

PÅLSSON, L., *EG-rätt* (Lund. 1976)

——— 'Luganokonventionen' [1990] *Svensk Juristtidning* 441–70

RABAEUS, B., '1973—a Turning Point for EFTA and for the Trading Arrangements of Western Europe' [1973] *Annuaire européen* 54–66

RACK, R. (ed.), *30 Jahre danach: neue Perspektiven für die Beziehungen der EFTA-Staaten zur Europäischen Gemeinschaft* (Baden-Baden, 1987)

RAGNEMALM, H., 'EG-Paragrafen' [1977] *Förvaltningsrättslig Tidskrift* 167–83

REGELSBERGER, E., 'The Dialogue of the EC/Twelve with Other Regional Groups: A New European Identity in the International System' in G. Edwards and E. Regelsberger (eds.), *Europe's Global Links* (London, 1990), 3–26

REICH, N., 'The 'November Revolution' of the European Court of Justice: Keck, Meng and Audi Revisited' [1994] *Common Market Law Review* 459–92

——— 'Protection of Diffuse Interests in the EEC and the Perspective of 'Progressively Establishing' an Internal Market' [1988] *Journal of Consumer Policy* 395–417

REUTER, P., *International Institutions* (London, 1958)

——— 'Le Plan Schuman' [1952] *Revue des Cours* 523–640

REYMOND, C., 'Institutions, Decision-making Procedure and Settlement of Disputes in the European Economic Area' [1993] 30 *Common Market Law Review* 449–80

RINGSTEDT, N., *Europa och Konsumentpolitiken* (Konsumentverket, Rapport 1989/90:7, Stockholm, 1990)

ROSENTHAL, D. E., 'Competition Policy' in G. C. Hufbauer (ed.), *Europe 1992: An American Perspective* (Washington, 1990), 293–343

ROUAM, C., 'L'Espace Economique Européen: un Horizon Nouveau pour la Politique de Concurrence' [1992] *Revue du Marché Commun* 53–7

RYDING, S.-O., *EGs miljöpolitik* (Industriförbundet, Arbetsrapport 14, Stockholm, 1989)

SACCHETTINI, A., 'La Coopération Européenne dans le Domaine de la Recherche Scientifique et Technique (COST)' [1974] *Revue Trimestrielle de Droit Européen* 445–63

SADURSKA, R., 'Reshaping Europe—or 'How to Keep Poor Cousins in (their) Home': A Comment on The Transformation of Europe' [1991] 100 *Yale Law Journal* 2501–10

SAHM, Y., 'Die Verfassung der Europäischen Gemeinschaft für Kohle und Stahl' [1951] *Europa-Archiv* 3977–85

SANDHOLTZ, W., and ZYSMAN, J., '1992: Recasting the European Bargain' [1989/90] *World Politics* 94–128

SAPIR, A., 'Les aspects extérieurs du grand marché européen' [1989] *Revue d'Economie Politique* 692–719

SCHARPF, F. W., 'The Joint-Decision Trap: Lessons from German Federalism and European Integration' [1988] *Public Administration* 239–78

Schermers, H. G., 'Comment on Weiler's The Transformation of Europe' [1991] 100 *Yale Law Journal* 2525–36

——— *International Institutional Law* (Alphen van Rijn, 1980)

Schmitt, N., 'New International Trade Theories and Europe 1992: Some Results Relevant for EFTA Countries' [1990] *Journal of Common Market Studies* 53–73

Schricke, C., 'La CEE et l'OCDE à l'heure de l'Acte Unique' [1989] *Revue Générale de Droit International Public* 801–30

Schricker, G., 'European Harmonisation of Unfair Competition Law—a Futile Venture?' [1991] *International Review of Industrial Property and Copyright Law* 788–801

Schütte, M. and Hix, J.-P., 'The Application of the EC State Aid Rules to Privatizations: The East German Example' [1995] 32 *Common Market Law Review* 215–48

Schwarze, J. (ed.), *The External Relations of the European Community, in Particular EC–US Relations* (Baden-Baden, 1989)

Schwed, J. J., 'Les Questions Ecrites du Parlement Européen à la Commission' [1970] *Revue du Marché Commun* 365–8

Schwok, R., 'Balancing Burdens and Benefits: EFTA's view. Commentaire' in J. Jamar and H. Wallace (eds.), *EEC–EFTA: More than Just Good Friends?* (Bruges, 1988)

Seeler, H.-J., 'Vertrag zur Gründung der Europäischen Union' [1984] *Europa Recht* 41–53

Senti, R., 'Ein EFTA–EG–Freihandelsvertrag für Dienstleistungen: Vorschlag eines Konzeptes' [1988] *Aussenwirtschaft* 367–84

Sevón, L., 'Legal Issues in the Negotiations on a European Economic Area' [1991] *Tidskrift utgiven av Juridiska föreningen i Finland* 278–87

Shigehara, K., 'External Dimension of Europe 1992: Its Effects on the Relationship between Europe, the United States and Japan' [1991] *Bank of Japan Monetary and Economic Studies* 87–102

Siebert, H., *The New Economic Landscape in Europe* (Oxford, 1991)

——— and Koop, M. J., 'Institutional Competition. A Concept for Europe' [1990] *Aussenwirtschaft* 439–62

Silver, D. B., and Bustin, G. L., 'Settlement of EEC Antidumping Proceedings' [1985] *The International Lawyer* 1273–87

Silvia, S. J., 'The Social Charter of the European Community: A Defeat for European Labor' [1991] *Industrial and Labor Relations Review* 626–43

Simon, D., 'Ordre Public et Libertés Publiques dans les Communautés Européennes' [1976] *Revue du Marché Commun* 201–23

Sjöstedt, G., 'Nordic and World Economic-Political Co-operation: Competition, Adaptation or Participation?' [1987] *Cooperation and Conflict* 209–26

Smit, H., and Herzog, P., *The Law of the European Economic Community* (New York, 1976), Vol. 1

Smith, A., *An Inquiry into the Nature and Causes of the Wealth of Nations* (rev. edn., New York, 1937)

Snape, R. H., 'International Regulation of Subsidies' [1991] *The World Economy* 139–63

Snyder, F., 'Ideologies of Competition in European Community Law' [1999] 52 *Modern Law Review* 149–78

Sola, N. F., 'Relations avec les Pays de l'AELE et de l'Est, Aspects Juridiques' [1990] *Revue du Marché Commun* 208–15

Spinelli, A., 'Riflessioni sul Trattato-Costituzione per l'Unione Europea' [1984] *Annuario di Diritto Comparato e di Studi Legislativi* 27–52

Staar R. F. (ed.), *East-Central Europe and the USSR* (New York, 1991)

Stechow, A. von, 'The Council of Ministers: The Constraint on Action' in G. Edwards and E. Regelsberger (eds.), *Europe's Global Links* (London, 1990), 161–8

Stegmann, K., 'Anti-Dumping Policy and the Consumer' [1985] *Journal of World Trade Law* 466–84

——— 'EC Anti-Dumping Policy: Are Price Undertakings a Legal Substitute for Illegal Price Fixing?' [1990] *Weltwirtschaftliches Archiv* 268–98

Steiner, J. M., *Textbook on European Community Law* (London, 1988)

Stenberg, H., 'Sweden and the Internal Market—Situating Some Problems' [1989] *Legal Issues of European Integration* 89–107

Sterndahlen, C., 'Sveriges utrikeshandel och konkurrenskraft på EG' in Statens Industriverk, *Svensk Industri inför EG'92* (SIND 1989:2, Stockholm, 1989), 63–83

Strange, S., 'The Persistence of the Problems in EC–US Relations: Conflicts of Perception' in J. Schwarze (ed.), *The External Relations of the European Community, in Particular EC–US Relations* (Baden-Baden, 1989), 109–18

Streeck, W., and Schmitter, P. C., 'From National Corporatism to Transnational Pluralism: Organised Interests in the Single European Market' [1991] *Politics and Society* 133–64

Stålvant, C.-E., 'Sverige och europeisk politisk integration' [1988] *Internasjonal Politikk* 39–56

——— 'Sweden: The Swedish Negotiations with the EEC' [1973] *Scandinavian Political Studies* 236–45

——— 'The Different Faces of Neutrality. Comment' in J. Jamar and H. Wallace (eds.), *EEC–EFTA: More Than Just Good Friends?* (Bruges, 1988), 262–8

Sun, J.-M., and Pelkmans, J., 'Regulatory Competition in the Single Market' [1995] *Journal of Common Market Studies* 567–89

Sundberg–Weitman, B., *Discrimination on Grounds of Nationality* (Amsterdam, 1977)

Sveriges Riksbank, *Årsbok 1973* (Stockholm, 1974)

Tangwy, J., 'L'Europe à Douze: la Réforme Institutionnelle ou la Mort' [1985] *Esope* 11–15

Taraszkiewicz, J., 'Polish Exports to the EC: Barriers and Stimuli' in A. Evans and P. Falk (eds.), *Transformation and Integration: Polish and Swedish Perspectives* (Umeå, 1992), 11–23

Teschl, A., 'EFTA–EG och framtiden: ur en EFTA-parlamentarikers synvinkel' *EFTA Bulletin* 3/1985, 1–2

Tjänstemännens Centralorganisation, *Sverige och EG* (Stockholm, 1988)

United Nations Conference on Trade and Development, *Common European Economic Space* (New York, 1991)

Vandoren, P., 'Mise en Oeuvre de la Politique Anti-Dumping de la CEE contre les Importations en Provenance des Pays à Commerce d'Etat' [1988] *Revue du Marché Commun* 198–214

Verloren van Themaat, P., 'The Contribution of the Establishment of the Internal

Market by the Case Law of the Court of Justice of the European Communities' in R. Bieber *et al.* (eds), *1992: One European Market* (Baden-Baden, 1988), 109–20

VERMULST, E., and WAER, P., 'European Community Rules of Origin as Commercial Policy Instruments' [1990] *Journal of World Trade* 55–100

VERRILL, C. O., 'Non-market Economy Dumping: New Directions in Fair Value Analysis' [1988] *George Washington Journal of International Law and Economics* 427–37

VIGNES, D., *Communauté Européenne du Charbon et de l'Acier* (Paris, 1956)

VIKLUND, D., *Spelet om frihandelsavtalet: en kritisk studie i svensk utrikespolitik 1959–1972* (Stockholm, 1977)

——— *Sweden and the European Community* (Stockholm, 1989)

VINER, J., *Dumping: A Problem in International Trade* (Chicago, 1923)

WAELBROECK, J., 'The Logic of EC Commercial and Industrial Policy Making' in A. Jacquemin (ed.), *European Industry: Public Policy and Corporate Strategy* (Oxford, 1984), 99–125

WAELBROECK, M., 'Enforceability of the EEC–EFTA Free Trade Agreements: a Reply' [1978] *European Law Review* 27–31

WAHL, N., 'Prise de Position de la Cour' [1991/92] *Juridisk Tidskrift* 554–61

WAITE, J. L., 'The Swedish Paradox: EEC and Neutrality' [1974] *Journal of Common Market Studies* 319–33

WALLACE, H., *National Governments and the European Communities* (London, 1973)

——— 'Vers un Espace Economique Européen: Chances et Difficultés d'une Negotiation Conclue au Finish' [1991] *Revue du Marché Commun* 694–703

WALLACE, W., *The Transformation of Western Europe* (London, 1990)

WALLENBERG, P., 'Submit the Internal Market to Global Forces' [1988] *European Affairs* 116–9

WEBER, A., 'Schutzklauseln der Freihandeslabkommen EWG–EFTA' in H.-G. Koppensteiner (ed.), *Rechtsfragen der Freihandelsabkommen der Europäischen Wirtschaftsgemeinschaft mit den EFTA-Staaten* (Vienna, 1987), 267–86

WEIDEMANN, R., 'The Anti-Dumping Policy of the European Communities' [1990] *Intereconomics* 28–35

WEILER, J., 'The Transformation of Europe' [1991] 100 *Yale Law Journal* 2403–83

WEINSTOCK, V., 'Les Conseils—Rapport Introduction' in *Semaines de Bruges, 1980* (Bruges, 1981), 53–90

WEISS, F., 'The European Free Trade Association After Twenty-five Years' [1985] *Yearbook of European Law* 287–323

——— 'The Law of Public Procurement in EFTA and the EEC: The Legal Framework and its Implementation' [1987] *Yearbook of European Law* 59–111

WELLENSTEIN, E. P., 'The Free Trade Agreements Between the Enlarged European Communities and the EFTA-Countries' [1973] 10 *Common Market Law Review* 137–49

——— 'The Relations Between the European Communities and Finland' [1983] 20 *Common Market Law Review* 714–24

WESSLAU, H. G., and GUSTAFSSON, L., 'Dumping och subsidier vid export till den Gemensamma Marknaden' [1983] *Svensk Juristtidning* 518–34

WETTER, T., 'Trade Policy Developments in the Steel Sector' [1985] *Journal of World Trade Law* 485–96

WETTIG, G., 'Security in Europe: A Challenging Task' [1992] *Aussenpolitik* 3–11

WHITE, E. L., 'In Search of the Limits to Article 30 of the EEC Treaty' [1989] 26 *Common Market Law Review* 235–80

WIGNY, P., *Communauté Européenne du Charbon et de l'Acier: un Témoignage sur la Communauté des Six* (Luxembourg, 1957)

WIJKMAN, M., *Patterns of Production and Trade in Western Europe: Looking Forward After Thirty Years* (EFTA Occasional Paper No. 32, Geneva, 1990)

WIKLUND, C., 'The Zig-Zag Course of the Nordek Negotiations' [1970] *Scandinavian Political Studies* 307–36

WILCZYNSKI, J., 'Dumping and Central Planning' [1966] *Journal of Political Economy* 250–64

WILLE, E., 'The Conciliation Procedure and the European Parliament's Pursuit of Legislative Power' [1984] *Il Politico* 489–500

WILS, G., 'The Concept of Reciprocity in EEC Law: An Exploration into these Realms' [1991] 28 *Common Market Law Review* 245–74

WILS, W. P. J., 'The Search for the Rule in Article 30 EEC Much Ado About Nothing?' [1993] *European Law Review* 475–92

WINTERS, L. A., 'Reciprocity' in J. M. Finger and A. Olechowski (eds.), *The Uruguay Round* (Washington, 1987), 45–51

WOODLAND, P., 'Le Processus Legislatif dans la Communauté Economique Européenne' [1985] *Revue du Marché Commun* 503–11

WYATT, D., and DASHWOOD, A., *The Substantive Law of the EEC* (2nd edn., London, 1987)

ZELLENTIN, G., 'The Economic and Social Committee' [1962–63] *Journal of Common Market Studies* 22–8

ZIELINSKA-GLEBOCKA, A., *The Economic European Community and Poland: The Development of Trade Relations* (Working Paper No. 4, Research Centre on the EEC, Gdansk, 1991)

ÅSLUND, A., *Systemic Change in Eastern Europe and East-West Trade* (EFTA Occasional Paper No. 31, Geneva, 1990)

ÖHLINGER, Th., 'Rechtsfragen des Freihandelsabkommens zwischen Österreich und der EWG' [1974] *Zeitschrift für ausländisches öffentliches Recht und Völkerrecht* 656–87

Index